Information Systems and Organizational Structure

Information Systems and Organizational Structure

Edited by
Erwin Grochla and Norbert Szyperski

Walter de Gruyter · Berlin · New York 1975

Erwin Grochla,
Professor of Business Administration and Organization Theory, Executive Director of BIFOA, University of Cologne, Cologne, Federal Republic of Germany.

Norbert Szyperski,
Professor of Business Administration and Planning Theory, Director at BIFOA, University of Cologne, Cologne, Federal Republic of Germany.

Library of Congress Cataloging in Publication Data

Information systems and organizational structure.

A selection of papers presented at a conference organized by the Betriebswirtschaftliches Institut für Organisation und Automation an der Universität zu Köln, Aug. 1973.
In English, with German abstracts.
Includes bibliographical references and index.
1. Management information systems-Congresses.
2. Industrial organization-Congresses. 3. Business-Congresses. I. Grochla, Erwin. II. Szyperski, Norbert. III. Cologne. Universität. Betriebswirtschaftliches Institut für Organisation und Automation.

T58.6.15 658.4'03 75-4821
ISBN 3-11-004803-5

 Typesetting: IBM-Composer Studio Feldafing. – Printing: Color-Druck, Berlin. – Binding: Lüderitz & Bauer, Berlin. –
Printed in Germany

ISBN 3 11 004803 5

Preface

In August 1973 the Betriebswirtschaftliches Institut für Organisation und Automation an der Universität zu Köln (BIFOA) organized a symposium on "Organizational Structure and the Structure of Information Systems". This volume contains a selection of the papers presented at the conference, many of them in a revised form which reflects the discussions during the symposium. Before we attempt to summarize the focal topics of these discussions as an introduction to this volume, we should like to give a brief overview of the objectives and the development of the BIFOA[1].

The official start of the research work at the BIFOA was on April 1, 1964. At that time computer-related research concentrated almost exclusively on problems of hardware and software, neglecting the organizational aspects of computer application. This one-sided research orientation provided the main motivation to establish the BIFOA as a center for research on

- the requirements on organizational structure and work flow in business and administrative organizations imposed by the application of computers;
- generalized frameworks and masterplans of computerized information systems, from which individual design schemes could be derived;
- concepts and curricula for the education and training of computer specialists and users.

This program of research on the organizational problems of computer application is closely interrelated with the educational activities of the BIFOA. The educational program encompasses on the one hand workshops and seminars where new findings of organization theory and new concepts of system design are communicated to practitioners. On the other hand, the Department of Economics and Business Administration of the University of Cologne offers an increasing number of courses on organization theory and principles of system design, which are taught by members of the BIFOA staff. This program of courses is organized in close cooperation with the chairs for organization theory (Prof. Dr. Erwin Grochla) and for business planning (Prof. Dr. Norbert Szyperski).

The first "International Symposium" of the BIFOA was held in 1968. This type of research conference was devised to provide a platform for the exchange

1 Grochla, Erwin: Beiträge des BIFOA zur Organisation und Betriebsinformatik in Forschung und Lehre. 10 Jahre Betriebswirtschaftliches Institut für Organisation und Automation an der Universität zu Köln (BIFOA). In: Angewandte Informatik, Vol. 16 1974, No. 4, pp. 140–149.

of research findings and the discussion of a problem area from different scientific perspectives. The participants are invited by the BIFOA so as to achieve a stimulating international mix of scientists and practitioners. The topics that are discussed during a symposium are determined largely by the paper presented by the participants.

Five symposia have been held. The first one in 1968 dealt with the problems of economic selection of computer applications. The papers and discussions of about 30 scientists and practitioners from several European countries provided a comprehensive overview of theoretical concepts and practical approaches to the economic analysis of computer application[2].

In 1970, 61 experts from the USA, Canada, Great Britain, Scandinavia, Austria, Switzerland, France and Germany participated in a symposium on "MIS – A Challenge to Scientific Research". This conference was organized not only to assess the state of the art, but primarily to discuss promising directions of MIS-related research and pitfalls in the design of management information systems[3]. About 50 scientists and practitioners from Australia, Belgium, USA, Great Britain and Germany met in 1972 for the BIFOA symposium on "Model and Computer Based Corporate Planning". This symposium was part of CORPIS, a large scale research and development project in the field of corporate planning. The presentations and discussions during this conference gave an indication of the wide range of problems for which the current theoretical approaches to planning or the practical design efforts can not yet offer adequate solutions[4].

The 1973 symposium on "Man-Computer Interaction in Management Planning and Control" was organized jointly by the European Institute for Advanced Studies in Management, Brussels, and the BIFOA. In this conference, which was attended by 47 participants from eight countries, an attempt was made to present and to integrate the findings of design-oriented research into man-machine decision systems and the practical experience gained from actually building and operating such systems.

---

2 Grochla, Erwin (Ed.): Die Wirtschaftlichkeit automatisierter Datenverarbeitungssysteme. Betriebswirtschaftliche Beiträge zur Organisation und Automation. Schriftenreihe des Betriebswirtschaftlichen Instituts für Organisation und Automation an der Universität zu Köln, Bd. 8, Wiesbaden 1970.

3 Grochla, Erwin and Norbert Szyperski (Eds.): Management-Informationssysteme. Eine Herausforderung an Forschung und Entwicklung. Betriebswirtschaftliche Beiträge zur Organisation und Automation. Schriftenreihe des Betriebswirtschaftlichen Instituts für Organisation und Automation an der Universität zu Köln, Bd. 14, Wiesbaden 1971.

4 Grochla, Erwin and Norbert Szyperski (Eds.): Modell- und computergestützte Unternehmungsplanung. Betriebswirtschaftliche Beiträge zur Organisation und Automation. Schriftenreihe des Betriebswirtschaftlichen Instituts für Organisation und Automation an der Universität zu Köln, Bd. 22, Wiesbaden 1973.

In August 1973, financial support from the German Federal Ministry for Research and Technology made it possible for the BIFOA to invite more than 80 scientists and interested practitioners from 14 countries to the symposium on "Organizational Structure and the Structure of Information Systems". This general topic was chosen to emphasize the relationship between the two aspects of organizations. Each of these organizational variables has been studied extensively. However, there are as yet only few systematic studies of their interdependence. Furthermore, this general topic very appropriately represents the particular research interest of the BIFOA, which is reflected in the words "Automation" and "Organisation" in its name.

In this symposium, the papers presented and discussed in eight different workshops centered around three problem areas:

- Analysis and diagnosis of information systems *(Section I)*;
- Interdependence between different types of organizational structure and the structure of the information systems *(Section II)*;
- Model and computer based tools for the design of information systems *(Section III)*.

The basic premise of *Section I* was that the effectiveness and efficiency of large scale information systems can be kept under control only through formal analysis and diagnosis. A growing number of companies are recognizing the necessity to develop tools for the task of analyzing their information systems. However, the available mathematical theories for the most part do not appear to be an appropriate basis for the description and analysis of complex information systems. Thus it will be necessary to develop new theoretical approaches and more powerful algorithms. The papers by *Adam, Mattessich, Nastansky/Drumm and Langefors* point out some of the problems involved.

Another very important aspect is the intensity of the analysis and diagnosis and the scope of organizational phenomena that are included. Some part of the existing communication network may not coincide with formal organizational channels. As the informal communication may be very important for the organization as a whole, it should be included in the analysis of the information system. This may pose severe problems of measurement and description. If the analysis is not restricted to some type of subsystem but covers all elements of the information system, then the decision processes in which the information is used have to be included in the analysis. With this growth in the scope and complexity of the task of analyzing the information system it may even become economically feasible to establish a special department or group to perform the analysis on a permanent basis.

In *Section II* of the symposium the relationship between the organizational structure and the information system was discussed. The papers of this section represented two groups of conceptual approaches, which could be labelled "management-oriented" (see the papers by *Galbraith, Emery and Kieser/Kubicek*) and "technology-oriented" (papers by *Edström, Stone and Whisler*), respectively. These papers and the discussion in this section confirmed that the interdependence of information system and organizational structure should be investigated from different theoretical perspectives. Presently, it would be premature to consider one or the other type of approach as more fruitful. It is only through a combination of conceptual studies and empirical research that it will be possible to work out a comprehensive set of guidelines for an integrated design of the organizational structure and the information system operating within that framework.

The three workshops of *Section III* dealt with models and computerized tools for the design and control of information systems. Among the central topics were the possibility of adopting models and techniques from the fields of logistics and work scheduling, the standardization of certain elements of information systems, and, primarily, the problems of developing instruments for the computer-aided design of information systems. These instruments correspond to the second stage of a long range research program in the field of computer application, which encompasses the three stages of (1) individual information systems, (2) systems for the computer-aided design of information systems, and (3) information utilities. These three types of computerized information systems are the strategic guideposts of a large-scale research program of the BIFOA, which is funded by the German Federal Government[5]. Information utilities could, of course, provide elements of systems of stages (1) or (2) as well as the analytic tools discussed in *Section I.*

In the presentations and discussions during the symposium some very important problems were dealt with. Attempts to solve these problems could be and actually are based on rather different conceptual foundations. This multiplicity of promising research approaches is reflected in the diversity of the papers presented. In the past the organizational structure and the structure of the information system had been almost identical. The application of computers has transformed the information system and has rendered it structurally different, and to some degree isolated, from the organizational structure.

However, with the growing part that the computer begins to play within the man-machine information system, the identity of organizational structure and

5 This research program on management information systems encompasses a completed pilot study and three projects which are still under way (CORPIS, ISAS, SIMMIS). Each of these interdisciplinary research projects is carried out by cooperating groups of experts from a business company, software specialists, and research workers of the BIFOA staff; cf. "Vorschlag für ein MIS-Forschungsprogramm", vorgelegt vom Betriebswirtschaftlichen Institut für Organisation und Automation an der Universität zu Köln. Forschungsbericht DV 71–01 des Bundesministeriums für Bildung und Wissenschaft, Datenverarbeitung, Leopoldshafen 1971 (BMBW–FB–DV 71–01).

information system will gradually be restored. As a starting point for research into this relationship conceptual models (e.g. *Emery, Galbraith*) are as appropriate as empirical studies of the interaction between the organizational structure and the information system (e.g. *Edström, Kieser/Kubicek*). Research should proceed from both perspectives in an integrated fashion in order to gain better knowledge about feasible design alternatives of information systems within certain organizational contexts, and about the factors affecting their performance.
In the discussions during the BIFOA symposium it became evident not only that the knowledge about the relationships between the information system and the organizational structure is still unsatisfactory, but also that there is a severe gap between the state of scientific knowledge and the utilization of this knowledge in the practice of organizational design. Both, scientists and practitioners called for a closer co-operation.

Due to the limited space in this volume only a selection of English-language papers on the interdependence of information system and organization structure, and on the problems of information system design can be published here. All other papers included in the more than 1,000 pages of conference material will be published in a special volume of the BIFOA-Arbeitsberichte[6]. Thus a comprehensive documentation of the papers presented at the BIFOA symposium is provided.

We want to express our gratitude to all scientists and practitioners who contributed to the symposium through the presentation of papers and through their participation in the discussions. Thanks are due to the members of the Program Committee, especially to Prof. Hurst, Mr. Pott, Prof. Teichroew, and Prof. Whisler, as well as to the members of the BIFOA staff who contributed to the success of this symposium. Special thanks are due to Bernhard Schareck, who was responsible for the organization of the symposium and for the editorial tasks in connection with the publishing of this volume.

Cologne, February 1975

Erwin Grochla
Norbert Szyperski

---

6 Grochla, Erwin and Norbert Szyperski (Eds.): Organisationsstrukturen und Strukturen der Informationssysteme. BIFOA-Arbeitsbericht 74/5, Köln 1974.

Contents

Preface 5
Authors 23
Introduction 29

The design of computer-based information systems – a challenge to organizational research *(Erwin Grochla)* 31

1. Introduction 31
2. Organizationally relevant structural areas in the design of computer-based information systems 33
   2.1 Application concept and user concept as the basis for system design . . . 33
      2.1.1 The application concept as point-of-departure in the design . . . 33
      2.1.2 Adaption in the user system 34
   2.2 Cooperative system design 37
      2.2.1 The project group as agent in system designing 37
      2.2.2 Management's role 38
   2.3 Systematic control of the design process 39
3. The use of EDP equipment in the design of a computer-based information system . 40
   3.1 The necessity of computer application in system design 40
   3.2 Points of departure for a computer-based system design 41
      3.2.1 Profiting from experience 41
      3.2.2 Profiting from research projects 42
   3.3 Possibilities and limits 44
      3.3.1 Present Restrictions 44
      3.3.2 Possible areas of intensified research 45
4. The job of organizational research 45

References 48
German abstract 51

Part 1
Interrelationships between organizational structure and information system 53

The measurement of organization structure and information structure *(Adolf Adam)* 55

1. Introduction 55
2. Three hypotheses 55
3. "Organimetrics" – a new approach to organizational theory 58
   3.1 The term "organimetrics" 58
   3.2 What does classical information theory accomplish? 59
4. Interrelationships between "organimetrics" and information theory 61

References 63
German abstract 63

Discontinuities of computerization – a study of French companies
(Anders Edström and *Louis Naugès)* 65

1. Introduction 65
2. Systems development in the organization 66
3. Variables in the computerization process 68
4. An outline of the study 70
5. Results 71
6. A model of the computerization process 77
7. Conclusions 79

Figures 81
References 93
German abstract 93

Integrated information systems and their effects on organizational
structure *(James C. Emery)* 95

1. Independence versus integration of systems 95
2. Independence through structure 95
   2.1 Decoupling 96
   2.2 Ignoring minor interactions 97
   2.3 Coordination among subsystems 97
3. Trade-off between independence and integration 98
4. Integrated information systems 99
5. Integration of information processing 100
6. Integration of organizational activities 101
7. Distributed systems – the wave of the future 102

German abstract 103

Information processing determinants of organization structure
(Jay R. Galbraith) 105

1. Information processing model 105
2. Mechanistic model 105
   2.1 Coordination by rules or programs 106
   2.2 Hierarchy 106
   2.3 Coordination by targets or goals 106
3. Design strategies 107
   3.1 Creation of slack resources 108
   3.2 Creation of self-contained tasks 108
4. Investment in vertical information systems 110
5. Creation of lateral relationships 111
   5.1 Direct contact 111
   5.2 Liaison roles 111
   5.3 Task forces 111
   5.4 Teams 112
   5.5 Integrating roles 112
   5.6 Managerial linking roles 113
   5.7 Matrix organization 113
6. Choice of strategy 114

References 114
German abstract 115

The change in information flows by a Management Information Centre (MIC) *(Helmut Garbe)* 117

1. The initial situation 117
2. The tasks of a Management Information Centre 118
   2.1 The operation of existing information flows 118
   2.2 The disclosing of existing information flows 118
   2.3 The active influencing of existing information flows 119
3. The consequences of an MIC for the information flows of an information system . 119
   3.1 The changes in information flows through the transfer of operation tasks to the MIC 120
      3.1.1 The transfer of permanent communication processes to the MIC . . 120
      3.1.2 The transfer of stochastic communication processes to the MIC . . 121
   3.2 The changes in information flows through the disclosing of the existing information system 121
      3.2.1 The description of the current information system 122
      3.2.2 The information system documentation 122
      3.2.3 The availability of the documentation to authorized persons . . . 122
   3.3 The changes in information flows through the inclusion of the MIC in the structuring process 123
      3.3.1 Creating a general strategy of the development of a management information system 123
      3.3.2 Influencing initiatives for change 124
      3.3.3 Assessing possibilities for change 125
      3.3.4 Realizing of permitted alterations 126
4. The organizational significance of the MIC 126

References 128
German abstract 129

The impact of computer technology on organizational power structures *(Bo Hedberg, Anders Edström, Wolfgang Müller* and *Bernhard Wilpert)* . . 131

1. Background 131
2. Definition of major concepts 132
   2.1 Computer technology and related concepts 132
   2.2 Power 134
   2.3 Interaction between structure and process 134
3. Conceptual framework 135
   3.1 Approach 135
   3.2 Independent variables 136
   3.3 Intervening variables 139
   3.4 Dependent variable 140
4. Hypotheses 143
5. Research methodology and design 145

References 147
German abstract 148

The impact of new techniques for management control on the information system and organization *(E. Gerald Hurst, Jr.)* 150

1. Introduction 150
2. Management control 150
   2.1 Measurement decisions 152
   2.2 Analysis decisions 152
   2.3 Action decisions 152
3. New techniques 153
   3.1 Planning languages 154
   3.2 Interactive computer systems 154
   3.3 Mathematical programming 155
   3.4 Bayesian statistics 155
   3.5 Control charts 155
   3.6 Mathematical control theory 155
   3.7 Search theory 156
   3.8 Machine-aided medical diagnosis 156
4. Potential impact 156
   4.1 Effect on the information system 156
   4.2 Effect on the organization 157
   4.3 Difficulty of implementation 157
5. Conclusions 158

References 158
German abstract 161

An organizational concept for the design of Management Information Systems *(Alfred Kieser* and *Herbert Kubicek)* 163

1. From computer Taylorism to computer Human Relation 163
2. A model of the interrelationships between context, structural differentiation, coordination mechanisms, and individual behavior 165
3. Coordination in organizations: Empirical results 167
   3.1 Coordination mechanisms 167
   3.2 The influence of context on organization structure 168
      3.2.1 Size of organization 169
      3.2.2 Dynamics of the environment 169
      3.2.3 Technology 170
      3.2.4 Diversification 170
   3.3 The influence of the organization structure on individual behavior . . . 170
4. The coordination potential of MIS 171
   4.1 Decrease of structural differentiation 171
   4.2 Relationships between MIS and the coordination instruments . . . 173
      4.2.1 Coordination by planning 173
      4.2.2 Coordination by hierarchical ad-hoc decisions 173
      4.2.3 Self-Coordination 174
      4.2.4 Coordination by programming 176
5. The implementation of the coordination potential of MIS 177
6. Conclusion 178

References 179
German abstract 183

Economics and information structure in organization design (*Charles H. Kriebel*) . . . 186

1. Introduction . . . 186
2. Information economics and organization design . . . 187
3. Information structure and management systems . . . 190
4. Conclusions . . . 193

References . . . 195
German abstract . . . 196

Comments on the influence of information technology on organizational structure in insurance industry (*Bernhard Schareck* and *Ewald Barten*) . . . 197

0. Introduction . . . 197
1. Components of the organizational structure . . . 198
2. Basic tasks in insurance companies . . . 198
3. The use of EDP equipment in insurance companies of the Federal Republic of Germany . . . 200
   - 3.1 The current situation . . . 200
     - 3.1.1 The hardware installed . . . 200
     - 3.1.2 Typical areas of computer application . . . 200
   - 3.2 Future trends . . . 204
4. The effects of modern information technology on departmentalization and work flow patterns . . . 204
   - 4.1 Changes in the work flow of the collection of premiums and investment . 204
   - 4.2 Different effects on departmentalization . . . 205
   - 4.3 Some conclusions from an empirical survey of the effects of EDP on the organizational structure of insurance companies in the Federal Republic of Germany . . . 207
     - 4.3.1 Reorganization of departments . . . 207
     - 4.3.2 Growth of personnel . . . 210
     - 4.3.3 Variations of the span of control . . . 211
     - 4.3.4 Effects on the number of hierarchical levels . . . 212
     - 4.3.5 Changes in the amount of communication . . . 212
5. Summary and conclusion . . . 213

References . . . 214
German abstract . . . 216

Information systems for organizations of the future (*William H. Starbuck*) . 217

1. Introduction . . . 217
2. From evolutionary information systems . . . 219
3. . . . to self-designing systems . . . 223
   - 3.1 How can systems allow for errors or inadequacies in their designs? . . . 223
   - 3.2 How can a system optimize criteria which are still being discovered? . . 224
   - 3.3 How can a system accomodate and encourage the exercise of intelligence? . 225
4. . . . and to information systems for tomorrow . . . 226

References . . . 227
German abstract . . . 228

Changes in organizational design induced by the introduction of computerized information systems – a longitudinal study in the electricity industry *(Derek Stone)* . . . 230

1. Introduction . . . 230
   1.1 The electricity industry in England and Wales . . . 231
   1.2 The Northwestern Electricity Board (Norweb) . . . 231
2. Organizational changes . . . 232
   2.1 Observed Changes by task . . . 234
3. The provision and sale of electrical energy . . . 234
   3.1 Engineering staff . . . 234
   3.2 Meter reading and billing . . . 234
4. The sale of appliances . . . 236
5. The provision of services on a contractual basis . . . 236
6. Support functions . . . 236
   6.1 Accounting and Administration . . . 236
   6.2 Transportation . . . 237
   6.3 Stock holding and purchasing . . . 237
7. Assessment and conclusions . . . 237

Appendices . . . 239
References . . . 244
German abstract . . . 244

Man, organization and computer – a contingency analysis *(Thomas L. Whisler)* . . . 246

1. Purpose and the thesis of the paper . . . 246
2. The complex organization . . . 247
3. Information processing and decision making activities . . . 249
   3.1 Sensing . . . 249
   3.2 Information processing . . . 250
   3.3 Regulation . . . 250
   3.4 Problem recognition . . . 250
   3.5 Situation diagnosis . . . 250
   3.6 Action selection . . . 250
4. Limitations of the individual as an information processor: Organizations and computers as alternative defenses . . . 251
   4.1 Limitations of the individual . . . 251
   4.2 The organization as a defense . . . 252
   4.3 Computer systems as a defense . . . 254
   4.4 Summary . . . 254
5. Limitations of the individual as a decision maker: organizations and computers as alternative defenses . . . 255
   5.1 Limitations of the individual . . . 255
   5.2 The organization as a defense . . . 256
   5.3 Computer systems as a defense . . . 257
   5.4 Summary . . . 258
6. Situational factors: Uncertainty, repetitiveness and volume . . . 259
   6.1 Uncertainty in decision making . . . 259

6.2 Repetitiveness and volume . . . 260
6.3 Combining the factors . . . 261
7. Discussion . . . 262
References . . . 265
German abstract . . . 266

Part 2
Information system development . . . 269

The Management Information System: The initiation and adoption of an organizational innovation *(Robert Duncan)* . . . 271
1. Introduction . . . 271
2. Characteristics of organizations as they affect the innovation process . . . 271
2.1 Complexity . . . 272
2.2 Formalization . . . 273
2.3 Centralization . . . 275
2.4 Interpersonal relations . . . 277
2.5 Dealing with conflict . . . 277
3. Conclusion . . . 278
References . . . 278
German abstract . . . 279

Information system and organizational concept – analysis of an innovation process from the pragmatic point of view *(Heinz Göhre)* . . . 281
1. Introduction . . . 281
2. Premises . . . 283
3. Analysis of the actual status . . . 286
3.1 The organization science in theory and practice . . . 286
3.2 The role played by information within the organizational system . . . 287
3.3 The organization as an organism . . . 291
4. Problems concerning actual-nominal transition . . . 294
4.1 Type of innovation process . . . 294
4.2 Problem areas involved in the innovation processes . . . 295
5. Objectives for the nominal status . . . 299
5.1 Necessity of the innovation . . . 299
5.2 Public objectives . . . 301
5.3 Organization-related objectives . . . 303
5.4 Structuring the organization according to the "principle of mutual dependence through services" . . . 305
6. Summary . . . 307
References . . . 309
German abstract . . . 309

Control structure and formalized information analysis in an organization *(Börje Langefors)* . . . 311

1. A first stage of design work and the first level of the system design . . . 311
   1.1 System specification . . . 311
   1.2 Steering objects . . . 312
   1.3 System design . . . 312
   1.4 First step of precedence analysis (on the crudest level) . . . 312
   1.5 List of precedents of operational goals (g, r, t) . . . 312
2. Second step of precedence analysis . . . 312
   2.1 List of precedents of forecast possible sales (g, r, t) . . . 313
3. Third step . . . 313
   3.1 List of precedents of earlier sales results (g, r, t') . . . 313
4. Workability diagnosis . . . 315
5. Goals are to be negotiated. This calls for information to all concerned. . . . 317
6. Component analysis – more detailed info-structure . . . 318
   6.1 Components list of operating sales goals (g, r, t) (terminal pro-concept) . . . 319

References . . . 322
German abstract . . . 322

The Four-Flows Model as a tool for designing the information system of an organization *(Jean Louis Le Moigne)* . . . 324

1. Small computer systems with direct access, large mass memories: New fact for management . . . 324
2. A "simple" theory of the Information System of an organization . . . 325
3. The criteria for defining the contents of the data base of the organization . . . 330
4. The four-flows model: Tool for locating generators of primary information and organization of the data base . . . 333
5. The implementation of an information system based on the four-flows model . . . 337
6. Conclusion . . . 339

References . . . 340
German abstract . . . 340

nformation economics and the notion of "Management Information ;ystem" *(Richard Mattessich)* . . . 342

1. Is MIS a mirage? . . . 342
2. The information economic approach to MIS . . . 343
   2.1 Contributions by Butterworth, Demski, Feltham and others . . . 344
   2.2 Summary of the Butterworth-Feltham meta-model . . . 352
3. Simplification versus interpretation . . . 353
4. The testing of the general theory and its interpretations . . . 356

References . . . 360
German abstract . . . 363

A model for the construction of a cost-minimal communication tree
(Ludwig Nastansky and *Hans Jürgen Drumm)* 365

1. Introduction 365
2. The organizational problem 365
3. The decision model 366
   3.1 The construction of the communication network 366
   3.2 The formulation of the optimization problem 367
   3.3 A small example 369
   3.4 The solution of the optimization problem 371

Appendix 372
Example I: Organization of cost-minimal intro-company communication . . . 372
Example II: Cost-minimal network of computer terminals as part of management information system 372
Example III: Organization of cost-minimal introduction of a new product . . 379

References 379
German abstract 380

Automatic interfacing of application software in the GPLAN framework
(Jay F. Nunamaker, Jr., John Pomeranz and *Andrew Whinston)* 382

1. Introduction 382
2. GPLAN framework 382
   2.1 User 384
   2.2 Data Management System and interfacing mechanism 384
   2.3 Problem-oriented query language and analyser 385
   2.4 Models 385
   2.5 Data base 386
   2.6 A working example of the interfacing mechanism 387
      2.6.1 Pre-processing operations 388
      2.6.2 Run-time operations 388
3. Typical GPLAN applications 390
   3.1 GPLAN/SODA (Systems Optimization and Design Algorithm) . . . 390
   3.2 GPLAN/WPC (Water Pollution Control) 392
4. Conclusion 393

References 394
German abstract 395

Computer assisted analysing, controlling and constructing tools
for information systems design *(Vesa Savolainen)* 397

1. Introduction 397
2. The general invariant stage division of systems design 398
3. Tools for analysing a system and controlling system work 399
   3.1 DOC 399
   3.2 DIFOP1 399
   3.3 Measures of systems complexity 402

4. Tools for describing a system 403
4.1 The method of Lundeberg 403
4.2 A stratified system as the frame model of systems description 404
5. Tools for implementation and construction 405
5.1 From precedence analysis to decision tables 405
5.2 The automatic grouping of processes 405
5.3 The computer in the design of physical file organization 406
5.4 A simple reporting language which is well adapted to the user 406
6. Conclusions 407

References 408
German abstract 409

The use of models and associated software in the design of wicked systems *(Arne Sølvberg)* 411

1. Introduction 411
2. Tame and wicked problems 411
3. A DPS for IPS-design 413
3.1 IPS-models 414
4. Full scale experiments 415
4.1 SINTEF's information system (SAPO) 416
4.2 The library system 417
4.3 Experimental conclusions 420
5. Making a DPS for DPS-design 421

References 422
German abstract 422

The information analysis of administrative systems based on statute law – some aspect of the Legol-project *(Ronald K. Stamper)* 424

0. Introduction 424
1. Underlying concepts 424
2. The reason for investigating statute law 426
2.1 Progress so far 427
2.2 Conciseness 427
3. An example of Legol 427
4. Structure of a Legol system definition 430
4.1 Meaningfulness of the system definition 431
4.2 E-semantics 431
4.3 Semantic(s-) types and categories 432
5. Use of Legol in information analysis 434
6. Use of Legol in information design 434
7. Status of the project – April 1973 435

References 435
German abstract 436

An introduction to computer-aided documentation of user requirements for computer-based Information Processing Systems
(Daniel Teichroew, Walter J. Rataj and *Ernest A. Hershey)* 438

1. Introduction and summary 438
2. A model of information processing in organizations 439
   2.1 Organizations 439
   2.2 Information systems 442
   2.3 Information Processing Systems (IPS) 443
   2.4 What is necessary to describe an Information Processing System? . . . 445
3. Building Information Processing Systems 446
   3.1 An overview of the evolution of the system building process 446
   3.2 The phases in the system building process 447
   3.3 Documentation of data in the system building process 449
   3.4 Alternative organization of the system building process 450
4. Present methods for determining information requirements 452
   4.1 Current methods for determining and stating requirements 452
   4.2 Categorization of the requirements determination phase 453
   4.3 Approaches to determining information requirements for the proposed system 454
   4.4 Alternative criteria used to set specifications 455
5. Computer-aided methods for determining information requirements 455
   5.1 Basic philosophy 455
   5.2 Necessary components of a computer-aided method 456
   5.3 Requirements of a Problem Statement Language (PSL) 457
   5.4 Requirements of the Problem Statement Analyzer (PSA) 458
   5.5 Environmental criteria for a computer-aided method 459
6. The costs and benefits of computer-aided methods 459
   6.1 The cost factor 460
   6.2 The benefits of computer-aided methods 461

References 463
German abstract 464

Model management systems *(Hartmut J. Will)* 467

1. Introduction 467
2. Model bank 468
   2.1 Assumptions 468
   2.2 Structures 470
3. Model management 472
   3.1 Objectives 472
   3.2 Functions 473
4. Modelling software 474
   4.1 User functions 476
   4.2 Computer functions 476
   4.3 Model management support 477
5. Conclusions 478

References 481
German abstract 482

Index 485

Authors

Adam, Adolf, Prof. Dr.,
Johann Kepler-Universität, Linz/Austria
(The measurement of organization structure and information structure)

Barten, Ewald, Dr.,
Siemens AG and Universität zu Köln/FRG
(Comments on the influence of information technology on organizational structure in insurance industry)

Drumm, Hans Jürgen, Prof. Dr.,
Universität Regensburg/FRG
(A model for the construction of a cost-minimal communication tree)

Duncan, Robert, Prof., Ph. D.
Northwestern University, Evanston, Ill./USA
(The Management Information System: The initiation and adoption of an organizational innovation)

Edström, Anders, Prof. Dr.,
European Institute of Business Administration INSEAD, Fontainebleau/France and University of Gothenburg/Sweden
(Discontinuities of computerization – a study of French companies)
(The impact of computer technology on organizational power structures)

Emery, James C., Prof., Ph. D.
Wharton School of Finance and Commerce, Philadelphia/USA
(Integrated information systems and their effects on organizational structure)

Galbraith, Jay R., Prof., Ph. D.,
European Institute for Advanced Studies in Management, Brussels/Belgium and Wharton School of Finance and Commerce, Philadelphia/USA
(Information processing determinants of organization structure)

Garbe, Helmut, Dr.,
Betriebswirtschaftliches Institut für Organisation und Automation an der Universität zu Köln (BIFOA), Köln/FRG
(The change in information flows by a Management Information Centre – MIC)

Göhre, Heinz, Dr.,
Messerschmidt-Bölkow-Blohm, Ottobrunn b. München/FRG
(Information system and organizational concept – analysis of an innovation process from the pragmatic point of view)

Grochla, Erwin, Prof. Dr.,
Seminar für Allgemeine Betriebswirtschaftslehre und Organisationslehre der Universität zu Köln and Betriebswirtschaftliches Institut für Organisation und Automation an der Universität zu Köln (BIFOA), Köln/FRG
(The design of computer-based information systems – a challenge to organizational research)

Hedberg, Bo, Prof. Dr.,
International Institute of Management, Berlin (West) and University of Gothenburg/Sweden
(The impact of computer technology on organizational power structures)

Hershey, Ernest A.,
University of Michigan, Ann Arbor/USA
(An introduction to computer-aided documentation of user requirements for computer-based Information Processing Systems)

Hurst, Jr., Ernest G., Prof., Ph. D.,
European Institute for Advanced Studies in Management, Brussels/Belgium, and University of Pennsylvania, Wharton School, Philadelphia/USA
(The impact of new techniques for management control on the information system and organization)

Kieser, Alfred, Prof. Dr.,
Freie Universität Berlin, Institut für Unternehmungsführung, Berlin (West)
(An organizational concept for the design of Management Information Systems)

Kriebel, Charles H., Prof., Ph. D.,
Carnegie-Mellon University, Pittsburgh, Penn./USA
(Economics and information structure in organization design)

Kubicek, Herbert, Dr.,
Seminar für Allgemeine Betriebswirtschaftslehre und Organisationslehre der Universität zu Köln, Köln/FRG

(An organizational concept for the design of Management Information Systems)

Langefors, Börje, Prof. Dr.,
University of Stockholm/Sweden and Netherland Institute for Advanced Study in the Humanities and Social Sciences (N.J.A.S.), Wassenaar/Holland
(Control structure and formalized information analysis in an organization)

Le Moigne, Jean Louis, Prof. Dr.,
Université d'AIX-Marseille/France
(The four-flows model as a tool for designing the information system of an organization)

Mattessich, Richard, Prof. Dr.,
University of British Columbia, Vancouver/Canada
(Information economics and the notion of "Management Information System")

Müller, Wolfgang, Priv.-Doz., Dr.
International Institute of Management, Berlin (West) and University of Hamburg, Hamburg/FRG
(The impact of computer technology on organizational power structures)

Nastansky, Ludwig, Ass.-Prof. Dr.,
Universität des Saarlandes, Saarbrücken/FRG
(A model for the construction of a cost-minimal communication tree)

Naugès, Louis,
European Institute für Advanced Studies in Management, Brussels/Belgium
(Discontinuities of computerization – a study of French companies)

Nunamaker, Jr., Jay F., Prof., Ph. D.,
University of Arizona, Tucson, Arizona,USA
(Automatic interfacing of application software in the GPLAN framework)

Pomeranz, John,
Purdue University, Lafayette, Ind./USA
(Automatic interfacing of application software in the GPLAN framework)

Rataj, Ernest A.,
University of Michigan, Ann Arbor/USA
(An introduction to computer-aided documentation of user requirements for computer-based Information Processing Systems)

Savolainen, Vesa, Ph. Lic.,
University of Tampere/Finland
(Computer assisted analysing, controlling and constructing tools for information systems design)

Schareck, Bernhard, Dipl.-Kfm.,
Betriebswirtschaftliches Institut für Organisation und Automation an der Universität zu Köln (BIFOA), Köln/FRG
(Comments on the influence of information technology on organizational structure in insurance industry)

Sφlvberg, Arne, Prof., Lic.-Techn.,
Computing Centre at the University of Trondheim/Norway
(The use of models and associated software in the design of wicked systems)

Stamper, Ronald Keith,
School of Economics, London/Great Britain
(The information analysis of administrative systems based on statute law – some aspect of the Legol-project)

Starbuck, William H., Prof., Ph. D.,
International Institute of Management, Berlin (West)
(Information systems for organizations of the future)

Stone, Derek,
Graduate School of Business Studies, London/Great Britain
(Changes in organizational design induced by the introduction of computerized information systems – a longitudinal study in the electricity industry)

Teichroew, Daniel, Prof., Ph. D.,
University of Michigan, Ann Arbor/USA
(An introduction to computer-aided documentation of user requirements for computer-based Information Processing Systems)

Whinston, Andrew B., Prof., Ph. D.,
Purdue University, Lafayette, Ind./USA
(Automatic interfacing of application software in the GPLAN framework)

Whisler, Thomas L., Prof., Ph. D.,
University of Chicago/USA
(Man, organization and computer – a contingency analysis)

Will, Hartmut J., Prof., Ph. D.,
University of British Columbia, Vancouver/Canada
(Model management systems)

Wilpert, Bernhard, Dr.,
International Institute of Management, Berlin (West)
(The impact of computer technology on organizational power structures)

Introduction

The design of computer-based information systems – a challenge to organizational research

By *Erwin Grochla*

1. Introduction

We live today in a world in which business is confronted with progressively increasing demands from its environment. These demands manifest themselves for example in:

- more rapid technological change,
- shortening of product life-cycles,
- greater economic concentration,
- greater interdependence of national markets,
- growing competitive pressure.

The rising complexity and dynamics of the environment surrounding these phenomena are in turn closely linked to a greater pressure for economic growth, and thus to a corresponding expansion of business's task volume. These developments are now posing new problems in the mastery of specific tasks, and in the processes that are needed to carry out these tasks, both in business management and in public administration.

We shall now turn to a number of measures that can be taken to solve these problems. It seems to me that the necessary adjustment of organizational structures and of information systems are to be seen in the foreground, with the emphasis on greater flexibility and response.

While in the past a functional staff-line organization was the dominant universal organizational concept (and thus, an organizational monism), today the differentiation of business environmental situations calls for an organizational pluralism. This pluralism is evident in the development and implementation of new organizational forms, such as the divisional organization, the matrix organization, and the team-oriented structures.

The introduction of automatic data processing installations has led to considerable changes in the firm's information systems. The primary change has been the shift from man as the sole information-processing agent to a mechanical system that supports and even in part replaces man. The earlier personnel, and essentially line information system is now being replaced by progressively more complex man-machine information systems whose structures are directly determined by information needs.

These adjustment measures are capable of reducing external complexity, but only at the expense of a greater internal complexity in the relations between the agents, man and the machine. We have given up the dream that the computer is the problem-solver par excellence. Systems Theory has helped us to realize that it is not enough to introduce qualitatively better elements (the agents) into the information process. Rather, the degree of goal achievement essentially depends on the coordination between the elements. And these relations determine the complexity of the system.

The growth in internal complexity is especially evident in:

- a greater structural differentiation and more intensive horizontal communication,
- a closer integration of information processing tasks, and, as a result of this:
- a more efficient interdependence of organizational structure and information systems.

This means that when the computer is introduced as an agent into business information systems, the organizational plan can no longer confine itself to man-man relations, but rather must be extended to include man-machine relations.

In this way, the computer not only helps to solve problems, but at the same time it creates considerable organizational difficulties.

These problems, inherent in new technological possibilities, along with the corresponding organizational questions are the subject of discussion at this symposium. In this context the greatest problem, it seems to me, lies in the coordination of the technical dimensions of a computer-based information system with a spate of organizational and social questions. Technical potential and organizational changes have to be coordinated in the realization of an optimally efficient structure[1]. Thus, the structure of a computer-based information system cannot orient itself simply around the real technical possibilities, but rather it must primarily be seen as the integration of mechanical and personnel system components.

Whether or not business can meet greater environmental demands depends not on a one-sided improvement of information technology, nor on simple changes in organizational structure; rather, it depends entirely on an optimally efficient structure.

The problematic in the required structural strategy does not lie solely in the practical coordination mentioned above; it lies in part in the organization of the structural process itself. Hitherto, this area has been fraught with difficulties.

We have made an effort in this symposium to cover the whole spectrum of relevant structural questions. Three problem areas have been laid out, namely

1. the formal analysis and diagnosis of the information systems themselves,

---

1 E. Grochla: Organisation und Automation. Wiesbaden 1966, p. 87; H. Kubicek: Ein Konzept zur Berücksichtigung organisatorischer und sozialer Aspekte beim Einsatz moderner Informationstechnologien. In: ONLINE, Vol. 11 1973, pp. 606–619.

2. the practical coordination of information system and organization structure,
3. the organization of the structural process.

These divisions are reflected in the various workshops that have been set up.

From an organizational point-of-view problem areas 2 and 3 are especially important. In the following, I should like to go into these areas in more detail, since they involve factors essential to the successful structuring of a computer-based information system. For the immediate future a central task in Organization Research lies in the definition of possible solutions to these problems. My general point of departure – in line with my introductory remarks – bypasses hardware/software questions, and places in the foreground the organizational phenomena relevant to application and use concepts.

2. Organizationally relevant structural areas in the design of computer-based information systems

Success in the structuring of a computer-based information system is essentially determined by four factors:

(1) the quality of the application concept,
(2) the quality of the user concept,
(3) a cooperative system design,
(4) a systematic control of the designing process.

An Organization Research that is practice oriented must begin with these criteria of success.

2.1 Application concept and user concept as the basis for system design

2.1.1 The application concept as point-of-departure in the design

The point-of-departure in the design must comprise, in terms of the approach, indicated above, a detailed analysis of the decisional logic and informational links of the tasks to be mastered within the information system. The results of this study constitute an application concept[2].

Both the information processing tasks assigned to the computer, as well as the information structure that must be established around these tasks are determined by this concept. The information structure can be arrived at through the following:

2 E. Grochla: Die Gestaltung allgemeingültiger Anwendungsmodelle für die automatisierte Informationsverarbeitung in Wirtschaft und Verwaltung. In: Elektronische Datenverarbeitung, Vol. 11 1970, pp. 49–55; E. Grochla: Das Engagement der Unternehmensführung bei der Entwicklung computergestützter Informationssysteme. In: Fortschrittliche Betriebsführung, Vol. 22 1973, p. 68.

- what input-information is necessary to carry out the task that has been defined,
- what is the source of this input-information,
- what output-information is established in the process,
- what tasks is this output-information required for.

The application concept, although required for all system design processes, is especially a prerequisite for the establishment of an integrated information system.

The „Kölner Integrationsmodell" (KIM), developed by the Betriebswirtschaftliches Institut für Organisation und Automation (BIFOA), can be seen as a first step towards a general application concept that, in this preliminary phase, does not yet cover characteristics peculiar to individual industries[3]. The model comprises the most important information processing tasks of an idealized business firm in the industrial sector and consolidates them in an integrated task structure. In this way, a basic framework for the development of integrated business information systems has been established.

At present, the application possibilities of the „Kölner Integrationsmodell" are limited. However, a more detailed model („Hauptmodell") is now being developed for a specific kind of firm (machinery) as a part of the current research project MIDAM. This means a step forward in the expansion of the basic model into a comprehensive model system. The value of a business-specific application concept consists in its ability to provide both the basis for the planning of technical and material factor input, as well as for the organizational adaption of the user system. Thus, the concept being designed constitutes the first step towards the development of machine and program components. Coordinated with the overall complex of technical standards, the second step must involve an adaption of organizational conditions and working patterns in the user system to the task structure. The conceptual foundations for this step, the implementation of the technical-functional system design, can be called the „user concept". These foundations ultimately determine the efficiency of the whole system. The operational potential of automated data processing can only be fully deployed when the users act in line with the procedural rules required by the system. In the case of the user concept, it is the planning of organizational changes in the user system on the one hand, and the determination of the measures of social influence, such as orientation and training on the other hand, that should lead to the immediate acceptance by the user.

2.1.2 Adaption in the user system

In Organizational Research the question of an adequate user concept has often been approached through an analysis of the effects of computer implementation

---

3 E. Grochla: Die Integration der Datenverarbeitung. Durchführung anhand eines integrierten Unternehmungsmodells. In: Bürotechnik und Automation, Vol. 9 1968, pp. 108–120; E. Grochla und Mitarbeiter: Integrierte Gesamtmodelle der Datenverarbeitung. Entwicklung und Anwendung des Kölner Integrationsmodells (KIM). München–Wien 1974.

on both the organization and man. Numerous studies have been written that deal with these problems[4]. However, their conclusiohs have by and large little relevance to design; and tend to be predictions of future developments rather than an aid to organizational design in the development of a specific information system.

The inadequate practical use of so many conclusions can, no doubt, be mainly explained by the fact that the consequences were not conceived and formulated explicitly as the results of conscious design processes, but rather as the result of more or less mechanical relations between the technical characteristics and the organizational and social dimensions of the information system in question.

In contrast to that approach, it seems more meaningful to use the conditions of decision-making, as well as the performance parameters of the agents in the system design as the points of departure in a scientific discussion of adequate user concepts.

An important question in connection with practical organizational changes is raised, for example, by centralization or decentralization possibilities in the implementation of a computer[5]. However, this has been accompanied by a far too global view of the factor relations. In my opinion, a distinction has to be made between an information, and a decision-making centralization or decentralization. While for certain data-processing tasks, central facilities (data processing departments or general-purpose centers) are by and large more meaningful, which specialization we might call a centralization of information, division of responsibility does not necessarily indicate a clear-cut trend in the automation of information processes[6].

---

4 See among others: E. Grochla: Organisation und Automation, op. cit.; A. Kieser: Einflußgrößen der Unternehmungsorganisation. Unveröffentlichte Habilitationsschrift, Köln 1973, pp. 190–217; M.W. Meyer: Automation and Bureaucratic Structure. In: American Journal of Sociology, Vol. 74 1969, pp. 256–264; C.A. Myers (ed.): The Impact of Computers on Management. Cambridge, Mass. 1967; D. Parisi: The Impact of a Change in Information Technology on Management Organization Structure, Decision Making and Interpersonal Relations in a Large Insurance Company. Diss. Northwestern Univ. 1966; R. Stewart: How Computers Affect Management, London 1971; T. Whisler: The Impact of Computers on Organizations, New York 1970.

5 E. Grochla: Zur Diskussion über die Zentralisationswirkung automatisierter Datenverarbeitungsanlagen. In: Zeitschrift für Organisation, Vol. 38 1969, pp. 47 – 53; R. R. Reichenbach, C. A. Tasso: Organizing for Data Processing. AMA Research Study No. 92, New York 1968, p. 23 seqq.

6 Compare the conflicting results of R.S. Adams: The Effects of Information Technology on Management and Organization. Diss., Louisiana State Univ. 1965, pp. 87, 115 seqq.; M.Ch. Lee: Effect of Electronic Data Processing upon the Management Organization of a Large Shoe Manufacturing Company. Diss. Washington Univ. 1963, pp. 149–159. W.E. Reif: The Effect of the Computer upon the Management Structure. Diss. Univ. of Iowa 1966, pp. 108–114; M.A. Silver: An Evaluation of the Impact of an Integrated Data Processing System on the Organization of a Manufacturing Company. Diss. Columbia Univ. 1962, pp. 3, 228.

This lack of unity, also evident in the effects of automated data processing in other organizational magnitudes, can be explained by the fact that the use of the means of information technology represent only one of the many factors of influence on organizational structures; and thus dependence, and the nature of the influence of other factors are essential to an understanding of the whole.

In other words, information technology exercises only a partial influence on the firm's organization, and is certainly never the exclusive influence. Nevertheless, most studies overlook the other factors of influence, such as the size of the firm, the type of business, characteristics of its economic and social environment, among others. This approach leads to a lack of possible explanations in a given situation, as well as to contradictory research results[7].

This means that however interesting and even impressive the results might be that have been achieved in efforts to coordinate technological and organizational conditions, they fall short of what is needed to make practice-related recommendations.

Equally as important as the coordination of the technological and organizational factors is the preparation of the user for the planned information system[8]. An information system will remain ineffective as long as the new user fails to adapt to the computer-based process and to apply the flow of data to his decision-making.

Full acceptance by the user is one of the most important strategic goals in the designing of the system. The preparation of the prospective user and his superiors is really a question of creating a positive attitude towards automatic data proces-

7 P. Sadler: Social Research on Automation. In: SSRC Research Review, London 1968, p. 27; see also the critique of empirical contributions to the research into information technological consequences in: H. Kubicek: Der Zusammenhang zwischen Informationstechnologie und Organisationsstruktur. In: Zeitschrift für Organisation, Vol. 41 1972, pp. 287–296; examples of multicausal organization explanation concepts are to be found in: P.N. Khandwalla: Uncertainty and the "optimal" design of organizations. Working Paper, TIMS XIX. Meeting, Houston, April 1972; A. Kieser: Einflußgrößen der Unternehmungsorganisation, op. cit.; D.S. Pugh, D.J. Hickson, C.R. Hinings, C. Turner: The Context of Organization Structures. In: ASQ, Vol. 14 1969, pp. 91–114; besides this orientation seems necessary at a uniform descriptive concept of organization theory such as the approach of Pugh et. al. published in 1963 and used in a number of empirical studies, see e.g. J. Child: Organization Structure and Strategies of Control: A Replication of the Aston Study. In: ASQ, Vol. 17 1972, pp. 163–177; D.S. Pugh, D.J. Hickson, C. Hinings, K. MacDonald, C. Turner, T. Lupton: A Conceptual Scheme for Organizational Analysis. In: ASQ, Vol. 8 1963, pp. 289–315; D.S. Pugh, D.J. Hickson, C. Hinings, C. Turner: Dimensions of Organization Structures. In: ASQ, Vol. 13 1968, pp. 65–105.

8 The personal problems of the users after introducing the new system and possibilities of reducing the frictions are described in: J.B. Bower and J.B. Sefert: Human Factors in Systems Design. In: Management Services, Vol. 2 1965, No. 6, pp. 39 – 50; E. Hardin: The Reactions of Employees to Office Automation. In: The Monthly Labor Review, Vol. 83 1960, No. 9, pp. 925–932; E. Mumford and O. Banks: The Computer and the Clerk. London 1967, p. 195 seqq.

sing, towards the task-filling processes (motivational preparation), as well as creation of the professional conditions for the use of ADP (functional preparation). The individual steps towards realization of these goals are quite often both motivational and functional, involving especially orientation and training of the future user during the process of system design[9].

The steps needed to overcome the difficulties in the construction of an information system are not inconsiderable, mainly because the final goal cannot be achieved via a simple act of transformation. Rather, each step only constitutes a partial transformation in the desired direction.

The decisive questions in the designing process at the planning stage give way to other questions once the implementation phase has been reached: while the application concept and the organizational changes present largely conceptual problems, personnel training involves mainly problems of motivation and behavior.

2.2 Cooperative system design

In addition to effecting changes in organizational and social patterns, the organization of the designing process can be instrumental in the implementation of the new application concept. The most important strategy at this point consists in a cooperative system design by the area specialists, system specialists and management.

2.2.1 The project group as agent in system designing

Special teams or project groups are usually set up to carry out the system designing process[10]. An especially important aspect in the setting up of these teams is the reliance on area specialists.

---

9 H. Fischer: EDV-Einsatzplanung und Mitarbeiterschulung. In: Zeitschrift für Organisation, Vol. 40 1971, pp. 423–431; U. Jaeggi and H. Wiedemann: Der Angestellte im automatisierten Büro. Stuttgart 1963, p. 211 seqq.; H.C. Mann and L.K. Williams: Observations on the Dynamics of a Change to EDP Equipment. In: ASQ, Vol. 5 1960, No. 2, pp. 217–256; H. Zuberbühler: Elektronische Datenverarbeitung in der Industrie. Ergebnisse einer empirischen Untersuchung. Bern und Stuttgart 1972, pp. 60–63, 137 seqq.

10 For the various concrete forms of organization see S. Blumenthal: Management Information Systems: A Framework for Planning and Development. Englewood Cliffs 1969, p. 106 seqq; R.L. Martino: Project Management and Control. New York 1964; W.G. Ryan and G.A. Steiner: Industrial Project Management. New York 1968; R. Tomlin: Managing the Introduction of Computer System, op. cit., p. 44 seqq; K. Zimmermann: Die Projektgruppe als Organisationsform zur Lösung komplexer Aufgaben. In: Zeitschrift für Organisation, Vol. 39 1970, pp. 45–51; the necessity of cooperation of future users in the project jobs is stressed by G. Mans: Erfolgsfaktoren für MIS-Projekte. In: Zeitschrift für Organisation, Vol. 41 1973, pp. 190–196.

A decisive condition for effective project group work consists in the members being largely or even completely released from their usual responsibilities, thus enabling a close personal effort and a professional approach to the system design.

An adequate realization of this professional approach requires the cooperation of area specialists, data processing and organizational specialists. Their cooperative effort will bring divergent specializations into play and quite often produces motivational effects, meaning that the area specialists will identify themselves with the new information system.

In principle it should be desirable to redefine the division of responsibility within the project group for each individual phase in the designing process, for the knowledge required in each phase is very different[11]. Thus, area specialists should have the decisive function in the definition of the problems to be confronted and in the organizational changes that will have to be effected, while the data processing specialists should have the decisive function in the system development and programming phases.

The specialists in question could be staff members, the superiors of the actual users, or the actual users themselves. It is of course of great practical importance that the participants have an exact knowledge of the procedures and the problems peculiar to their area.

The motivational effects for the actual users, however, will probably be determined more by irrational factors. Their identification with the information system can only be expected if an atmosphere of cooperation and understanding is created during the system designing process. This does not necessarily mean that future users be involved in all phases of the process. It is of greater importance that these users are given the feeling that they have the possibility of being heard during the process, and that they are in a position to influence certain aspects of the system.

2.2.2 Management's role

The second important factor on the cooperation side consists in management's involvement in the system designing process[12]. This involvement will lead espe-

---

11 E. Grochla: Automatisierung der Automatisierung. Möglichkeiten und Grenzen der computer-gestützten Gestaltung von betrieblichen Informationssystemen. In: Zeitschrift für betriebswirtschaftliche Forschung, Vol. 25 1973, pp. 413 – 429; the different requirements of the design process are dealt with by F.C. Mann and L.K. Williams: Observations on the Dynamics of a Change to Electronic Data Processing Equipment, op. cit., p. 231.

12 E. Grochla: Die Gestaltung entscheidungsorientierter Informationssysteme als Aufgabe der Unternehmungsführung. In: Datascope, Vol. 2 1971, No. 5, pp. 1 – 7;
E. Grochla: Das Engagement der Unternehmensführung bei der Entwicklung computergestützter Informationssysteme, op. cit. pp. 65 – 72; E. Grochla: Gestaltung und Überwachung computergestützter Informationssysteme zur Unterstützung des Managements im Entscheidungsprozeß. In: Zeitschrift Interne Revision, Vol. 8 1973, No. 1, p. 3;

cially to improved conditions for the implementation of system proposals, since the ultimate decisions will of course be determined by formal authority. If top management has sanctioned the designing and implementation decisions, then in general there will be considerably less conflict and resistance to the construction of the information system[13].

In this context it must be emphasized that the initiative for the active support we have been speaking about must come from the men at the top. Their readiness to cooperate, in turn, depends on their own attitude towards construction of an information system. This attitude can be encouraged by an orientation and training program for management. However, the necessity of management's cooperation does not necessarily mean that top management be involved; it is more important that the managers of the departments or divisions to be affected by the information system be involved. If, for example, only one department is going to be affected by the system, the participation of the manager of this department should be sufficient. Involvement of top management only seems to be necessary if the system under design is an integrated information system that will affect the whole firm, or if it is an MIS geared to the information needs of the top management. The integration of a partial system into a more comprehensive system requires a strategy that involves the work of the whole firm, and thus it is the representatives of top management who will be in the best position to map out this strategy.

2.3 Systematic control of the design process

The final factor in determining the success of the system is the control during the designing process. System designing projects are usually highly complex affairs, but since they are also limited in time and scope the stages in their development can be watched. In this way, the development can be structured up to a certain point by formalizing and planning measures, making the various stages more transparent and reducing the risk of planning errors. The degree of control necessary always depends upon the characteristics of the proposed system and upon the amount of time and personnel involved in the designing process.

The instruments needed for a systematic process control are especially:

- the laying down of formal rules (guidelines, instructions) and the use of forms to document the work done and its results (checklists, written reports etc.), and
- time and cost figures (networks, budgets).

Formalization, i. e. the written control of relevant facts, can include especially the breakdown of restricted tasks, the division of decision-making authority, commu-

---

McKinsey & Co.: Unlocking the Computer's Profit Potential. In: Computers and Automation, Vol. 18 1969, No. 4, p. 33.

13 E. Grochla: Das Engagement der Unternehmensführung bei der Entwicklung computergestützter Informationssysteme, op. cit. p. 70.

nication flow between the individuals working on the system design (especially on the flow between future users and data-processing personnel), and can also include the required reports[14]. The required process of documentation, represented by the pertinent forms, covers the development of the information system, in particular its task, information-structural, mechanical and program aspects. The completeness, the unity and continuity of this process, which are assured through formal rules or a form-technical structuring of the work-process, in general speed up work and improve control possibilities[15].

The second control complex consists in the time and cost factors[16]. They can be drawn for a specific designing project from comprehensive plans (e. g. stage plans, total budgets for the implementation of system designing projects), and can also be worked out in the form of cost and time estimates, net plans, budgets etc. for individual project phases. Of importance in this context is also the efficiency analysis that have to be made in the various phases of the designing process, which will continually require a review of the relevant factors influencing economic efficiency and a quantification and evaluation of results or of projected conditions.

3. The use of EDP equipment in the design of a computer-based information system

A large number of further problems arise in the development of an information system with the best possible design efficiency, even when the system designing process is centered around the strategies and measures already discussed. This has rightly led to the realization that the computer should be given a role in the designing process, or at least that some of the phases in the process should be automated.

3.1 The necessity of computer application in system design

Even at the design level of the information system it usually becomes clear that the work, from definition of the problems to the first operation of the system, covers too great a period of time, or, to be more specific, the system will have already been

14 An empirical definition of various means of process control is given by R. F. Powers: An Empirical Investigation of Selected Hypotheses Related to the Success of Management Information System Projects. Diss., Univ. of Minnesota 1971.

15 Of considerable importance for the standardizing forms and methods in systems design are e. g. ARDI and BISAD; for ARDI see in: J. Tagg: A System for Systems Design. In: Data Processing, Vol. 11 1962, No. 1, pp. 46 – 52; for BISAD see in: W. Hartmann, H. Matthes, A. Proeme: Management Information Systems Handbook. New York 1969.

16 C. P. Lecht: The Management of Computer Programming Projects, published by the American Management Association, New York 1967, p. 47 seqq.; K.G. Mc Laren and E. L. Buesnell: Network Analysis in Project Management. London 1963.

outdated by unnoticed, but inevitable changes before it can be put into use. In addition, the effort required to manage all of the relevant data is too big. These problems are of course made all the more complex through human limitation, which becomes evident in the discrepancy between the designing tasks on the one hand, and human designing potential on the other.

But also in the application of information systems the lack of system efficiency can make itself felt, or can be caused by the failure to integrate individual restricted tasks, in other words by an inadequate system design. A further difficulty consists in the fact that completed systems are not always open to variation, not least because of inadequate documentation.

A reliable method to close the gap between theoretically possible and actually realized designing efficiency is to be found in the more effective use of computer potential, not only for current information systems, but also for the designing of such systems. If we assume that with an automation of data processing, greater efficiency and/or greater economy in data processing, as well as in real and nominal business operations can be achieved[17], and that the designing of an information system is to be seen also as a special data-processing task, then it becomes clear that this greater efficiency and economy can also be achieved in a computer-based designing process.

3.2 Points of departure for a computer-based system design

3.2.1 Profiting from experience

In certain limited areas of information system design it has become evident that in general practice the necessity of relying on EDPMs is recognized, and that to a certain extent consequences have been drawn from this fact. However, the application of instruments for computer-based system design has largely been restricted to a limited number of large-scale users.

The part of system planning that usually is done without a computer, but for which software assistance is available, is the selection of an ADP system. In addition to measurement and analysis systems for the preparation of evaluations of existing installations, simulation models can be used that make possible a reconstruction of hardware characteristics and software functions. These simulation models can be constructed with the help of general simulation languages; a broader computer support, however, is provided by simulation systems that automatically construct the model, or that at least support this process with an appropriate language[18].

---

17 E. Grochla: Grundlagen der Wirtschaftlichkeit automatisierter Datenverarbeitung. In: Zeitschrift für Organisation, Vol. 34 1970, p. 334.

18 Rainer Bischoff, Arthur Tollert: Simulation als Hilfsmittel der computergestützten Gestaltung von Informationssystemen. BIFOA-Arbeitsbericht 72/8, Köln 1972.

The possibility of delegating specific tasks to the ADPMs is provided especially during system implementation. This is standard practice in the creation of machine codes from the instrumental sequence of a problem-oriented program language. The extent of support that the computer, with the help of so-called higher program languages, provides in the creation of programs depends upon the type of language used. Characteristic for most languages, however, is that the formulated problem solutions must be more or less adapted to the sequential processing nature of the computer.

We now come to the question as to whether the role of the programmer cannot be restricted to a more problematic area, with the ADPM taking over a further, built-in task of program production, namely the codifying. This possibility is offered by the plotting software, available from various ADP producers and software manufacturers, and which are now coming into greater use in West Germany.

They permit processing to be described in plotting table form, and then with the help of a computer to be translated into the appropriate sequence of the programming language.

Standard programming also transfers parts of program production to the computer. The point of departure is a formulation of key words in generator languages, from which a generator then creates a program framework, containing a control for the program and linking the individually designed program components to each other. The same goal, but different levels of realization and application will allow for a combination of decision table technique and standardized programming[19]

3.2.2 Profiting from research projects

While in business a computer-based procedure has been confined to a few limited areas of application (in which the possibilities available have yet to be fully taken advantage of), various research projects have already focused on the question as to how entire task complexes or even the whole process of designing a system could be delegated within a closed system to an ADPM, or how at least these ends could be reached in a computer-based system.

The first work in the area of computer-based system designing was AUTOSATE (Automated Data System Analysis Technique), a method developed by the Rand Corporation between 1962 and 1965 for the analysis of military bases[20].

With AUTOSATE the system designer can capture all of the formalized information flows, irrespective of their individual transmission forms, so that e. g. telephone

---

19 Horst Strunz: Entscheidungstabellentechnik und Normierte Programmierung als Verfahren der computergestützten Programmerstellung. In: Studienkreis Paul Schmitz: Die Wirksamkeit von Programmiersprachen. Wiesbaden 1972, pp. 397 – 417.

20 O. T. Gatto: AUTOSATE. An Automated Data Systems Analysis Technique. Rand-Memorandum RM – 3188 – PR, Santa Monica, Calif., May 1962.

calls, oral messages, letters and telex messages all qualify as input. The original is then translated into a form legible to the machine, with a special program system then being able to produce a series of analyses and evaluating lists[21]

Some of the knowledge necessary for the designing of computer-based information systems that can be won from these lists is:

- evaluation of the level of integration as well as of the level of centralization and decentralization of the information system,
- classification of the information processing stations into origin, control and destination categories,
- spotting and isolation of redundant data files and forms.

The work done on graph theory by Börje Langefors has led to a number of research projects; his Theoretical Analysis of Information Systems[22] is a seminal study on the planning of mathematical procedures in the design of information systems. For example, the Scandinavian projects CADIS[23] and CASCADE[24] were both influenced by Langefors. Both are computer-based documentation and analysis systems that use Langefors terminological and methodological foundations for a logical description of real systems and for a generation of corresponding output complexes.

The most comprehensive attempt to develop a system for the computer-based designing of information systems, project ISDOS (Information System Design and Optimization System), has been underway in the USA since 1967, under the direction of Daniel Teichroew[25]. The object is to develop an integrated program system that can move from a description of the information needs in a so-called problem description language to a largely automatic creation of programs and data files, and that can also suggest the adequate hardware setup.

Even if the concept of an automatic system generator must for the time being remain a rather remote goal, it is nevertheless clear that limited, but promising advances have been made[26].

---

21 A further explanation of the system with the aid of examples can be found in: Richard Schaefer: AUTOSATE – Automated Data Systems Analysis Technique. Darstellung des Verfahrens und Anwendungen in der Praxis. In: Systeme der computergestützten Systemgestaltung. BIFOA-Arbeitsbericht 72/7, Köln 1972, pp. 11 – 90.

22 Börje Langefors: Theoretical Analysis of Information Systems. Lund (Sweden) 1968.

23 J. Bubenko and O. Köllhammar: CADIS-Computer-Aided Design of Information Systems. In: Computer-Aided Information Systems, Analysis and Design, ed. by Janis Bubenko Jr., Börje Langefors, Arne Sølvberg. Lund (Sweden) 1972, pp. 119 – 140.

24 P. Aanstad, G. Skylstad, A. Sølvberg: CASCADE – a Computer-based Documentation System. In: Computer-Aided Information Systems, Analysis and Design, op. cit. pp. 93 – 112.

25 Daniel Teichroew: Methodology for the Design of Information Processing Systems. In: Proceedings of Fourth Australian Computer Conference, part. 2, Adelaide (Australia) 1969, pp. 629 – 634.

3.3 Possibilities and limits

The examples mentioned above show that practice and research are thinking more and more about the necessity of a computer-based designing process. The relevant question at this point is where the limits lie in a computer application to restricted tasks and task-complexes, and where promising possibilities for further development can be expected[27].

3.3.1 Present Restrictions

The restrictions fall into three categories:
1. methodological restrictions,
2. factor restrictions,
3. economic restrictions.

To 1: A comprehensive analysis of the experience that has hitherto been acquired in the development of systems for computer-based system designing shows that the designing of an information system still seems to be a creative, innovative activity which cannot readily be reduced to the automatic level. The main reason for this probably lies in research gaps, especially in shortcomings in empirical-cognitive and practical knowledge of the variables determining an information system. One has of course to expect that considerable difficulties will be involved in the planning of an adequate optimizing procedure. Studies of individual systems have shown that an automated procedure is rather limited in a decision-making situation in which an end-function cannot clearly be defined, or in which secondary conditions either are not recognized or constitute a complex pattern of interdependencies.

These methodological restrictions are qualified, however, by man-machine system generators that include heuristic procedures and suboptimizing models.

To 2: Factor restrictions include the lack of qualified specialists who are in a position to work out systems for system design. Hardware also constitutes a limitation. It must be assumed that the amount of material that would have to be processed in an automated system designing project is enormous, and that the available calculator capacity would be in part inadequate. This applies both to the required storage capacity and computer time as well as to the characteristics of the required peripheral units. However, these considerations only reflect the present state of the art, and are not restrictions of a fundamental nature.

---

26 Some of these developments are demonstrated by Volker Schaedel: ISDOS – Information System Design and Optimization System. Ein System zur automatisierten Gestaltung von Informationssystemen. In: BIFOA-Arbeitsbericht 72/7, op. cit., pp. 291 – 345.

27 This question is extensively discussed by Horst Strunz, Rainer Bischoff, Frank Nick, Volker Schaedel, Richard Schaefer, Arthur Tollert: Möglichkeiten und Grenzen der computergestützten Gestaltung von Informationssystemen. BIFOA-Arbeitsbericht 72/6, Köln 1974.

To 3: An economic analysis of computer-based system designing is problematic, since in the traditional meaning of the phrase, an economic analysis means a juxtaposing of costs and services – which would be premature at this point.

An economic analysis of systems for automated system design can really only be carried out indirectly, via improvements in the firm's decision-making situation, which can lead to a constant improvement in real and nominal business processes. Thus, an isolated and cost-oriented comparison of procedures would be based on one-sided assumptions.

Independent of this, however, a continuing tendency towards sinking equipment costs in relation to the costs for ADP personnel can be assumed, which will in turn stimulate the development of greater automation in system designing.

3.3.2 Possible areas of intensified research

The fact that only a limited number of tasks in system designing can today be carried out with a computer-base, is for the long-run not particularly satisfactory, and thus it is incumbent upon the universities, ADP producers, software manufacturers, as well as the users to work on solutions to these problems.

The removal of these methodological restrictions will inevitably involve long and complicated research projects, and thus can probably best be carried out in the context of the theoretical research done at the universities. At the same time, this research will require a broad empirical base, so that e. g. new methods can continually be tested and checked in the form of pilot projects.

The universities, ADP producers, software manufacturers, and users can all play equal roles in removing the factor restrictions. Some of today's restrictions will certainly be overcome by the technical developments of tomorrow. At the same time an improvement of human resources can only be achieved through an improved and more intensive training of system designers.

And finally, economic restrictions will recede into the background as advances are made in the methodological and factor areas. In addition, we can expect that, as is the case in the operation of information systems, system designing will also be affected by efforts to be more economical – which will mean that automation will become more important in system designing.

4. The job of organizational research

This survey was intended as a summary of the problems which today confront Organization Research. The preliminary systematizing of these questions is an important prerequisite to structured research planning. Even if all of the points that have been made here are aspects of the same basic problem, the distinctions are necessary since they would correspond to the individual research projects; the various aspects themselves are of greatly varying magnitudes and require very different methodological approaches. The main justification for such a summary, however, is to prevent work on individual projects that could not be integrated into the main stream of research.

There is a further point that, it seems to me, is also of fundamental significance, namely the fact that in the past a certain isolation developed both in the defining of the relevant questions as well as in research, and that this isolation had a negative influence on various efforts that were being made.

It seems to me that there is little point to academic research working apart from any contact with the business world, just as there is little point to an individual firm attempting to solve its problems without the aid of research institutions. An efficient research strategy can only be based on a cooperative effort that would combine the experience of the business world with the fruits of research. There are two forms that this cooperation might take:

– The use of classical instruments of empirical social research in cross sectional and longitudinal studies. Here the research concepts should be the product of a dialogue, with academic research evaluating the data provided from the practical experience sphere.

– In addition, there is a special form that seems to me to be especially useful, a new approach called “running research“ or “research by development“. This involves a combined effort by research and practice to develop a computer-based system (running system) at the practical level that satisfies the requirements of a particular business. The resulting systems then serve as models for users who want to develop comparable systems. At the same time, the researchers involved in the project will translate their findings into general terms, thus making a contribution to general development.

Both of these approaches are currently being used by me and my colleagues.

– At my department, questions concerning the user concept and the organization of the designing process are being pursued with the help of cross-section analyses. Thus far a number of explorative studies have been conducted to work out more precise concepts and to create the prerequisites needed for continued fruitful research. The results have contributed greatly to an understanding of the problems with which the practical sphere is confronted, while the measurement instruments we have used have by and large proven reliable. In this way we have established a foundation that will prove adequate to the challenges to Organization Research that we have sketched in this paper.

– The second approach is being used in a broader context at BIFOA. While the emphasis in the projects mentioned above has been clearly on organizational and social aspects, here it is the data-technical aspect that is in the foreground. Five comprehensive projects have been set up to pursue the following questions:

– Project ISAS (to develop an information system for the administrative control of business) involves the design of a business-specific information system with subsystems for sales planning, production planning and profit planning in batch transactions, as well as an interacting subsystem for investment calculation and planning. The subsystems will be integrated with the help of a data bank supervised by an appropriate data bank management system.

– Project CORPIS (to develop an information system for general business planning) involves the design of business-specific models and computer-based general business planning systems. One of the goals is a simulation model that will help to improve medium-range profit, finance and investment planning.

– Project SIMMIS (to develop a simulation model of the planning, control and information system which in turn will serve as a design and implementation instrument for MIS) does not involve the creation of systems to solve the central business problems, but rather it concerns itself with instruments that can be used to develop such systems (generator approach). The resulting instruments, in the form of software packages, are especially intended to evaluate present systems and for the ex-ante control of new system concepts (formal diagnosis). The possibilities of computer-based system designing also fall into this category.

– A fourth project (MIDAM) is concentrating on the further development of BIFOA's basic model into a user concept (KIM). In cooperation with a professional business association, work is being done to develop a trade-specific version of the basic model, and also to produce design and manipulation software for an improved implementation of application models.

– The fifth project (MICOM) is mainly concerned with hardware questions. New technological developments now offer a multitude of possibilities for the combination of very different hardware elements. The project is studying the present forms of computer network systems and their commercial and organizational aspects.

In other words, we are trying to use a methodological pluralism in approaching the many questions that are being raised in the computer-based information system field. Experience thus far has shown that there is no single superior research method in this field. And if any one method were to be given a preeminent position, it would have to be the dialogue between academic research and the practical sphere. Despite many promising developments we are nevertheless still at the beginning, with a multitude of obstacles before us. The more we encourage an exchange of ideas, the more readily we will be able to spot meaningless developments, thus increasing the probability that the long-range goals can be reached. This symposium will, it is hoped, constitute one step forward in the solution of the problems we have discussed here. It is my hope that the opportunities for discussion that are presented by this symposium will be taken advantage of, that joint progress will be made towards a solution of these problems, and that each participant will depart with the feeling that his preparations and contribution have contributed to the success of the symposium.

References

[1] Aanstad, P., G. Skylstad, A. Sølvberg: CASCADE – A Computer-Based Documentation System. In: Computer-Aided Information Systems Analysis and Design, ed. by J. Bubenko et. al., Lund (Sweden) 1972.

[2] Adams, R.S.: The Effects of Information Technology on Management and Organization. Diss. Louisiana State Univ. 1965.

[3] Bischoff, R. and A. Tollert: Simulation als Hilfsmittel der computergestützten Gestaltung von Informationssystemen. BIFOA-Arbeitsbericht 72/8, Köln 1972.

[4] Blumenthal, S.: Management Information Systems: A Framework for Planning and Development. Englewood Cliffs 1969.

[5] Bower, J.B. and J.B. Sefert: Human Factors in Systems Design. In: Management Services, Vol. 2 1965, No. 6, pp. 39–50.

[6] Bubenko, J. jr. and O. Köllhammar: CADIS – Computer-Aided Design of Information Systems. In: Computer-Aided Information Systems, Analysis and Design, ed. by Janis Bubenko, Jr.; Börje Langefors; Arne Sølvberg. Lund (Sweden) 1972.

[7] Child, J.: Organization Structure and Strategies of Control: A Replication of the Aston Study. In: ASQ, Vol. 17 1972, pp. 163–177.

[8] Fischer, H.: EDV-Einsatzplanung und Mitarbeiterschulung. In: Zeitschrift für Organisation, Vol. 40 1971, pp. 423–431.

[9] Gatto, O.T.: AUTOSATE – An Automated DATA Systems Analysis Technique. Rand-Memorandum RM – 3188 – PR, Santa Monica, Calif., May 1962.

[10] Grochla, Erwin: Organisation und Automation. Wiesbaden 1966.

[11] Grochla, Erwin: Die Integration der Datenverarbeitung. Durchführung anhand eines integrierten Unternehmungsmodells. In: Bürotechnik und Automation, Vol. 9 1968, pp. 108–120.

[12] Grochla, Erwin: Zur Diskussion über die Zentralisationswirkung automatisierter Datenverarbeitungsanlagen. In: Zeitschrift für Organisation, Vol. 38 1969, pp. 47–53.

[13] Grochla, Erwin: Grundlagen der Wirtschaftlichkeit automatisierter Datenverarbeitung. In: Zeitschrift für Organisation, Vol. 39 1970, pp. 329–336.

[14] Grochla, Erwin: Die Gestaltung allgemeingültiger Anwendungsmodelle für die automatisierte Informationsverarbeitung in Wirtschaft und Verwaltung. In: elektronische datenverarbeitung, Vol. 11 1970, pp. 49–55.

[15] Grochla, Erwin: Die Gestaltung entscheidungsorientierter Informationssysteme als Aufgabe der Unternehmungsführung. In: Datascope, Vol. 2 1971, No. 5, pp. 1–7.

[16] Grochla, Erwin: Gestaltung und Überwachung computergestützter Informationssysteme zur Unterstützung des Managements im Entscheidungsprozeß. In: Zeitschrift Interne Revision, Vol. 8 1973, No. 1, pp. 1–17.

[17] Grochla, Erwin: Automatisierung der Automatisierung. Möglichkeiten und Grenzen der computergestützten Gestaltung von betrieblichen Informationssystemen. In: Zeitschrift für betriebswirtschaftliche Forschung, Vol. 25 1973, pp. 413–429.

[18] Grochla, Erwin: Das Engagement der Unternehmensführung bei der Entwicklung computergestützter Informationssysteme. In: Fortschrittliche Betriebsführung, Vol. 22 1973, pp. 65–72.

[19] Grochla, Erwin und Mitarbeiter: Integrierte Gesamtmodelle der Datenverarbeitung. Entwicklung und Anwendung des Kölner Integrationsmodells (KIM). München–Wien 1974.

[20] Hardin, E.: The Reactions of Employees to Office Automation. In: The Monthly Labor Review, Vol. 83 1960, No. 9, pp. 925–932.

[21] Hartmann, W., H. Matthes, A. Proeme: Management Information Systems Handbook. New York 1969.

[22] Jaeggi, U. and H. Wiedemann: Der Angestellte im automatisierten Büro. Stuttgart 1963.

[23] Khandwalla, P.N.: Uncertainty and the "optimal" design of organizations. Working paper, TIMS XIX. Meeting, Houston, April 1972.

[24] Kieser, A.: Einflußgrößen der Unternehmungsorganisation. Unveröffentlichte Habilitationsschrift, Köln 1973.

[25] Kubicek, Herbert: Der Zusammenhang zwischen Informationstechnologie und Organisationsstruktur. In: Zeitschrift für Organisation, Vol. 41 1972, pp. 287–296.

[26] Kubicek, Herbert: Ein Konzept zur Berücksichtigung organisatorischer und sozialer Aspekte beim Einsatz moderner Informationstechnologien. In: ONLINE, Vol. 11 1973, pp. 606–619.

[27] Langefors, Börje: Theoretical Analysis of Information Systems. Lund (Sweden) 1968.

[28] Lecht, C.P.: The Management of Computer Programming Projects. Ed. by the AMA – American Management Association, New York 1967.

[29] Lee, M.Ch.: Effect of Electronic Data Processing upon the Management Organization of a Large Shoe Manufacturing Company. Diss. Washington Univ. 1963.

[30] Mann, F.C. and L.K. Williams: Observations on the Dynamics of a Change to EDP Equipment. In: ASQ, Vol. 5 1960, No. 2, pp. 217–256.

[31] Mans, G.: Erfolgsfaktoren für MIS-Projekte. In: Zeitschrift für Organisation, Vol. 42 1973, pp. 190–196.

[32] Martino, R.L.: Project Management and Control. New York 1964.

[33] Mc Kinsey & Co.: Unlocking the Computer's Profit Potential. In: Computers and Automation, Vol. 18 1969, No. 4, pp. 24–33.

[34] McLaren, K.G. and E.L. Buesnell: Network Analysis in Project Management. London 1963.

[35] Meyer, M.W.: Automation and Bureaucratic Structure. In: American Journal of Sociology, Vol. 74 1969, pp. 256–264.

[36] Mumford, E. and O. Banks: The Computer and the Clerk. London 1967.

[37] Myers, C.A. (ed.): The Impact of Computers on Management. Cambridge, Mass. 1967.

[38] Parisi, D.: The Impact of a Change in Information Technology on Management Organization Structure, Decision Making and Interpersonal Relations in a Large Insurance Company. Diss., Northwestern Univ. 1966.

[39] Powers, R.F.: An Empirical Investigation of Selected Hypotheses Related to the Success of Management Information System Projects. Diss., Univ. of Minnesota 1971.

[40] Pugh, D.S., D.J. Hickson, C. Hinings, K. MacDonald, C. Turner, T. Lupton: A Conceptual Scheme for Organizational Analysis. In: ASQ, Vol. 8 1963, pp. 289–315.

[41] Pugh, D.S., D.J. Hickson, C. Hinings, C. Turner: Dimensions of Organization Structures. In: ASQ, Vol. 13 1968, pp.65–105.

[42] Pugh, D.S., D.J. Hickson, C.R. Hinings, C. Turner: The Context of Organization Structures. In: ASQ, Vol. 14 1969, pp. 91–114.

[43] Reichenbach, R.R. and C.A. Tasso: Organizing for Data Processing. AMA Research Study No. 92, New York 1968.

[44] Reif, W.E.: The Effect of the Computer upon the Management Structure. Diss., Univ. of Jowa 1966.

[45] Sadler, P.: Social Research on Automation. In: SSRC Research Review, London 1968.

[46] Schaedel, Volker: ISDOS – Information System Design and Optimization System. Ein System zur automatisierten Gestaltung von Informationssystemen. In: BIFOA-Arbeitsbericht 72/7, Köln 1972, pp. 291–345.

[47] Schaefer, R.: AUTOSATE – Automated Data Systems Analysis Technique. Darstellung des Verfahrens und Anwendungen in der Praxis. In: Systeme der computergestützten Systemgestaltung. BIFOA-Arbeitsbericht 72/7, Köln 1972, pp. 11–90.

[48] Silver, M.A.: An Evaluation of the Impact of an Integrated Data Processing System on the Organization of a Manufacturing Company. Diss. Columbia Univ. 1962.

[49] Steiner, G.A. and W.G. Ryan: Industrial Project Management. New York 1968.

[50] Stewart, R.: How Computers Affect Management. London 1971.

[51] Strunz, Horst: Entscheidungstabellentechnik und Normierte Programmierung als Verfahren der computergestützten Programmerstellung. In: Studienkreis Paul Schmitz: Die Wirksamkeit von Programmiersprachen. Wiesbaden 1972, pp. 397–417.

[52] Strunz, Horst, R. Bischoff, F. Nick, V. Schaedel, R. Schaefer, A. Tollert: Möglichkeiten und Grenzen der computergestützten Gestaltung von Informationssystemen. BIFOA-Arbeitsbericht 72/6, Köln 1974.

[53] Tagg, J.: A System for Systems Design. In: Data Processing, Vol. 11 1969, No. 1, pp. 46–52.

[54] Teichroew, Daniel: Methodology for the Design of Information Processing Systems. In: Proceedings of Fourth Australian Computer Conference, part 2, Adelaide (Australia) 1969, pp. 629–634.

[55] Tomlin, R.: Managing the Introduction of Computer Systems. London 1970.

[56] Whisler, T.: The Impact of Computers on Organizations. New York 1970.

[57] Zimmermann, K.: Die Projektgruppe als Organisationsform zur Lösung komplexer Aufgaben. In: Zeitschrift für Organisation, Vol. 39 1970, pp. 45–51.

[58] Zuberbühler, H.: Elektronische Datenverarbeitung in der Industrie. Ergebnisse einer empirischen Untersuchung. Bern und Stuttgart 1972.

German abstract
Die Gestaltung computer-gestützter Informationssysteme als Herausforderung an die Organisationsforschung

Von *Erwin Grochla*

Die zunehmende Komplexität und Dynamik der Umwelt stellt die Betriebe heute bei der organisatorischen Strukturierung vor erhebliche neue Probleme. Insbesondere erfordert sie die Schaffung leistungsfähiger Informationssysteme, mit deren Hilfe die Betriebe auf Umweltänderungen schnell und zweckmäßig reagieren können. Die Entwicklung der Computertechnik bietet in diesem Zusammenhang vielfältige Möglichkeiten einer verbesserten Informationsverarbeitung. Ihre Anwendung schafft jedoch gleichzeitig neue Probleme. Faßt man Betriebe (und ihre Subsysteme) als komplexe Mensch-Maschine-Systeme auf, so wird deutlich, daß eine effiziente Aufgabenerfüllung nur über eine Abstimmung der technischen Dimensionen des Informationssystems mit der gesamten Organisationsstruktur erreicht werden kann, d.h., es geht um einen optimalen Wirkungszusammenhang beider Komponenten. Von diesem Wirkungszusammenhang und nicht von den einzelnen Komponenten alleine hängt es ab, ob die Betriebe den Umweltanforderungen gerecht werden. In Anbetracht der Komplexität jedes einzelnen Phänomens ist die auf den Wirkungszusammenhang ausgerichtete Gestaltung eines der schwierigsten Probleme der heutigen Organisationsforschung.

Bei der Gestaltung von Informationssystemen sollte nach dieser Betrachtungsweise also nicht allein von den realtechnischen Möglichkeiten ausgegangen werden; angemessener erscheint vielmehr eine auf die Integration der maschinellen und personellen Systemkomponenten gerichtete Perspektive, von der aus das Gestaltungsziel in einer effizienten Abstimmung technologischer und organisatorischer Bedingungen gesehen wird. Den Ausgangspunkt der Gestaltung bilden bei dieser Auffassung nicht bestimmte realtechnische Merkmale, sondern die entscheidungslogischen und informationalen Zusammenhänge der von dem gesamten System zu erfüllenden Aufgaben. Diese Zusammenhänge finden ihren Ausdruck in der Anwendungskonzeption, an der sich die hard- und softwaremäßige Ausgestaltung des Informationssystems orientieren muß. Wenn auch die realtechnischen Elemente bei der Realisierung einer konkreten Anwendungskonzeption eine wichtige Bedeutung besitzen, so hängt die Effizienz des gesamten Systems doch vor allem davon ab, wie gut es gelingt, die Konzeption auch im Benutzersystem durchzusetzen (Benutzerkonzeption). Dabei handelt es sich zum einen um die Planung organisatorischer Veränderungen im Benutzersystem und zum anderen um Maßnahmen der sozialen Beeinflussung (Information, Schulung), durch die die Akzeptanz der Benutzer unmittelbar gefördert werden soll.

Der Durchsetzbarkeit von Anwendungskonzeptionen dient neben diesen inhaltlichen Aspekten auch die Kooperation zwischen Systemspezialisten und zukünftigen Benutzern bei der Systemgestaltung, wie sie z.B. in Projektgruppen ihren Ausdruck findet. Durch eine solche Kooperation werden sowohl unterschiedliche Wissensbereiche vereinigt als auch motivationale Effekte erzielt.

Weitere positive Wirkungen im Hinblick auf die Durchsetzungsmöglichkeiten können von einer aktiven Unterstützung der Systemgestaltung durch das Management erwartet werden; sie gründen sich insbesondere auf die hierarchische Autorität des Management und auf seine daraus resultierenden Funktionen bei der Lösung von Konflikten.

Nicht nur die Qualität der entwickelten Soll-Konzeption und das Ausmaß an Kooperation bestimmen den Erfolg eines Projektes, von entscheidender Bedeutung ist darüber hinaus eine systematische Steuerung des Gestaltungsprozesses durch Instrumente wie Netzpläne, Budgetvorgaben, standardisierende Regelungen und Dokumentation.

Eine weitere, heute vieldiskutierte Möglichkeit zur Erhöhung der Effizienz von Systemgestaltungsprojekten besteht schließlich darin, den Computer selbst in einzelnen Phasen des Gestaltungsprozesses als Aktionsträger einzusetzen und damit mehr oder weniger große Abschnitte des Gestaltungsprozesses zu automatisieren (computer-gestützte Systemgestaltung).

Alle diese Probleme dürften gegenwärtig sowohl in das Bewußtsein der wissenschaftlichen Forschung als auch der betrieblichen Praxis gedrungen sein, ohne daß bisher jedocn in allen Fällen adäquate Lösungsvorschläge erarbeitet worden sind. Sie stellen somit weitgehend noch eine Herausforderung an die Organisationsforschung dar, die die Wissenschaft in enger Zusammenarbeit mit der Organisationspraxis bewältigen muß. Die zusammenfassende Betrachtung der relevanten Problemkreise und die Hinweise auf einige bestehende Forschungsprojekte in diesem Beitrag sollen helfen, diesen Forschungsprozeß zu strukturieren und weiterzuführen.

Part 1

Interrelationships between organizational structure and information system

The measurement of organization structure and information structure

By *Adolf Adam*

1. Introduction

The organization of information structures and the information about organization structures respond to each other in syntactical, semantical and pragmatical ways.
The present paper is intended to detect these responses and to give them a logical foundation.
In order to pursue these aims, the information theory, as developed by Shannon and Wiener, is being adapted to an economical representation by use of the "theorem of the conservation of discriminatory informations" (A. Adam, 1972).
Ashby's "variety", which could be interpreted as the possible number of distinguishable states of a system (potential variety) is replaced by the effective variety, which in addition considers the frequency distribution of the states.
The relation: "effective variety $\leqslant$ potential variety" always holds.
Order relations usually result in a reduction of variety.
The relations between variety and degree of organization can be described by the help of algebras and relatives (relational structures).
Ashby and others used dyadic logarithms for expressing effective variety in order to avoid large numbers and multiplications. However, semantical misinterpretations and incorrect pragmatical actions resulted from this device, which is justified purely in its syntactical aspects. Besides, deficient measurement concepts relating to an "information theory of continuous runs of signals" were brought into scientific literature and used by others with lack of criticism.

2. Three hypotheses

Statement 1: Shannon's measures are information-technological input coefficients, but no entropy measures in the sense Boltzmann used them.
Proof: Given sufficiently long texts of x symbols of an m-valued alphabet and of y symbols of an n-valued alphabet, respectively. The distribution (relative frequencies) of the symbols in the text be

$$p_i \geq 0, \quad \sum_{i=1}^{m} p_i = 1 \qquad \text{and} \qquad q_k \geq 0, \quad \sum_{k=1}^{n} q_k = 1.$$

The text systems T_1 and T_2 are equivalent with respect to the set-up of a certain message supply of discriminatory informations:

$$T_1(x, p_i, i \leq m) \equiv T_2(y, q_k, k \leq n) \quad \text{if}$$

$$x \sum_{i=1}^{m} p_i \log p_i = y \sum_{k=1}^{n} q_k \log q_k$$ holds, which can easily be proved.

For one symbol of the alphabet (1) we need y/x symbols of the alphabet (2) on the average, in order to set up equivalent message supplies.

$$H = y/x = \sum_{i=1}^{m} p_i \log p_i \Big/ \sum_{k=1}^{n} q_k \log q_k \quad \text{therefore}$$

represents an information-technological input coefficient which is dimensionless (set/set).

For the purpose of a reference alphabet Shannon uses a standardized (uniformly distributed) binary alphabet. Thus,

$$\sum_{k=1}^{2} q_k \log q_k = -\log 2 \qquad \text{if} \quad q_1 = q_2 = 1/2 \quad \text{and}$$

$$H_2 = \sum_{i=1}^{m} p_i \log p_i/(-\log 2) = -\sum_{i=1}^{m} p_i \,\mathrm{ld}\, p_i,$$

"ld" signifying the dyadical logarithm (with base 2).

This result for H_2 (Shannon) appears to be identical with the entropy relation. However, it is due to the formalism that the standard alphabet renders a coefficient of base conversion for logarithmic systems and therefore veils the history of the measure under discussion. This fact constitutes the source of misinterpretations!

In trying to justify an analogous semantics, structure fetishists have tried Procrustean methods. We presented this example in a rather broad way, since we must impose some responsibility for erroneous political decisions on similar misconstructions in quantitative sociology and economics.

Statement 2: As a useful measure of effective variety for continuous events we suggest the standard deviation of the complete variety domain divided by the standard deviation of the uncertainty interval:

$$d = \sqrt{\sigma^2 + \epsilon^2} / \epsilon;$$

σ^2 designating the variance of the distribution of the variable and ϵ^2 the variance of the uncertainty interval.
The measure, thus defined, expresses how many effectively distinguishable steps (states) occur in the distribution of the variable if a fixed variance of uncertainty ϵ^2 is given. For the units of measurement we introduced the term "diversions". The classical information-theoretical assumption results in mere standard deviations with different parameters. For a normal distribution, as an example, we would gain:

$$H_2 = \sqrt{2\pi e} \cdot \sigma.$$

We notice that σ generally is a quantity with dimension, which contradicts the considerations stated above.

Statement 3: The system and its organizational potentialities are not only determined by the varieties of the system and its subsystems, but by the values of its state variables, i.e. by its specific scaling properties, as well.

Scales	Variables	Scale preserving transformations
nominal scale	classifying variables	one-one mappings (permutative mappings)
ordinal scale	comparative variables	monotonous mappings (isotonic mappings)
interval scale	metrological variables	affine mappings
ratio scale	metrological variables	dilatations
difference scale	metrological variables	translations
absolute scale	counting variables	identical mapping

The classes of scale preserving transformations determine domains of variability within which the properties of the scale remain unchanged.

3. "Organimetrics" – a new approach to organizational theory

3.1. The term "organimetrics"

We notice that the measure of organization increases monotonously as the structure of variables (and scales) becomes simpler. As mentioned earlier, order relation result in a reduction of variety. Since scale preserving varieties are actually blind varieties which do not change the scale properties, they must be considered as a reduction of variety. In other words, beside "state variety" we have to consider the "variety of manifestation" in order to work out a reasonable information theory and a discipline which we name "organimetrics", which is to be conformable with respect to structure.

We shall define "organimetrics" as a system-theoretic discipline of measurement: Given an empirical relational input-output-system. The mapping relations fall into three relational classes:

1) isomorphisms, the one-one mappings in a system
2) homomorphisms, the many-one mappings and
3) polymorphisms, the one-many mappings in a system.

A further characterization would be:

functions

homomorphisms isomorphisms polymorphisms

correspondencies

Most cybernetic systems and analytical models are concerned exclusively with the functional aspect, although the relational aspect and, above all, the polymorphisms (disturbances, noise, several alternatives of decision, random processes etc.) constitute a major part of social systems.

The "golden rule" of polyadaptive systems, with even morphogenesis and morphostasis, reads:

"As much free scope of variety as possible regarding the necessary degree of organization." Too much emphasis on morphogenetics (inconstancy of systems structures) or on morphostatics (fixation of systems structures) leads towards decay or sterile torpidity of intentional organization units.

We are confronted with the question: "Why do we need a statistical organization theory (organimetrics)?"

We may replace this question by a different one: "To what extent can a relational intentional system be directed by imperfect and incomplete informations or its behavior be prognosticated?"

If in an organization unit organizational deficiencies are so prevailing that directability and predictability seem to be hardly possible any more, it is obvious that any attempts to simulate such an organization unit by use of structural diagnosis and prognosis models is futile and senseless.

3.2. What does classical information theory accomplish?

A practical example (optimal coding) shall explain the transmission and translation of a message: $A_1A_1A_3A_2A_1A_4A_1A_2$ in a channel where loss and disturbance occur, into the message $B_1B_1B_2B_2B_1B_3B_1B_3$ by use of a binary alphabet (with symbols: L, 0):

1) Transmitter	A_1	A_1		A_3	A_2		A_1	A_4		A_1	A_2	
2) Coder	0	0		LL0	L0	*	0	LLL		0	L0	*
3) Channel	0	0		LL0	L00		0	LLL		0	L0L	
4) Decoder	0	0	*	L0	L0	*	0	LL	*	0	L	*
5) Receiver	B_1	B_1		B_2	B_2		B_1	B_3		B_1	B_3	

The above table describes the optimal coding of the transmitter (1., 2.) and receiver (4., 5.), the channel (3.), and in addition the disturbance symbols (asterisks in line 2.) and the loss symbols (asterisks in line 4.).
Hence, we can figure a balance of symbol sets:

Input		Output	
transmission symbols	14	loss symbols	4
disturbance symbols	2	reception symbols	12
channel description	16	channel description	16

The flow of utility symbols (transinformation) can be rendered by the relations:

"transmission symbols minus loss symbols" or

"reception symbols minus disturbance symbols".

In our example 10 symbols were transported unchanged through the channel.
"Disturbance symbols plus loss symbols" results in 6 deficiency symbols; thus we have the relation:
"utility symbols plus deficiency symbols" equals the number of those symbols which are necessary for the description of the channel (or the system).
Using the dyadic logarithm (ld) we may establish the following theorem:
"A set M of distinguishable elements with cardinal number m can be described uniquely (and in a meta-language) by a symbol set

$\sigma(M) = m \cdot \text{ld } m$ over a two-valued alphabet,

Example:

1) object language	a_1	a_2	a_3	a_4	m(M)	= 4
2) meta language	00	0L	L0	LL	(M)	= 8

Thus we gained a basic function for the construction of any symbol set statistics. Let $A = (A_1, A_2, \ldots, A_i, \ldots, A_n)$ be a systematic classification of the general quality A according to the specific qualities A_i, $i = 1, 2, \ldots, n$ with the frequency distribution:

$$m(A_1) \equiv m_i, \quad \sum_{i=1}^{n} m_i = m(M).$$

We take $\sigma(A) = \sum_{i=1}^{n} m_i \operatorname{ld} m_i$. This last term gives

the number of those symbols of the symbol set $\sigma(M)$, which drop out as a consequence of a classification by A, for the elements within the classes are not distinguishable any more.

In order to represent the statistic A in the meta language we need

$\sigma(M) - \sigma(A)$ symbols of the two-valued alphabet.

Aside from this plausible interpretation of classical information theory our concept enables us to adjust an elementary organization algebra to this calculus.

	symbol categories	symbol sets	organization algebra
1.	transmission symbols	$\sigma(M)-\sigma(A)$	$(1-A)$
2.	reception symbols	$\sigma(M)-\sigma(B)$	$(1-B)$
3.	channel description	$\sigma(M)-\sigma(AB)$	$(1-AB) = (1-A)+A(1-B) = (1-B)+B(1-A)$
4.	reduction of symbols by double classification	$\sigma(AB)$	AB
5.	loss symbols	$\sigma(B)-\sigma(AB)$	$(1-A)B$
6.	disturbance symbols	$\sigma(A)-\sigma(AB)$	$A(1-B)$
7.	utility symbols	$\sigma(M)-\sigma(A)-\sigma(B)+\sigma(AB)$	$(1-A)(1-B)$

Clearly, a corresponding calculus can be developed for more general qualities (A, B, C, . . .)

It is easy to see that Shannon's measure

$$H_2 = \sigma/m$$

can be derived from the relation:

"number of symbols of one category per element of the original statistical population".

4. Interrelationships between "organimetrics" and information theory

By transposing the symbol-statistical measures (bit-statistics) into the variety statistics: $d = 2^H$, we arrive at the effective number of states in terms of diversions. "Diversions" stand for the effectively distinguishable states, no matter, what manifestations these states have.

Formally, different variety-statistical measure systems could be proposed. In order not to leave the descriptive and explanatory system of conventional mathematical statistics and to preserve structure conformity with the frequency interpretation of probability theory, the syntactical bridge:

$$\text{bits} = \text{ld (diversions)}$$

should be used in appropriate manner, reversing the relation stated above.
In other words:
We choose the object language (organimetrics) in such a way that we may use Shannon's information theory as meta language and that both languages are syntactically isomorphic to each other.
The "semantical compiler" could be arranged in the following way:

	symbol-set statistics (information theory)	variety statistics (organimetrics)
1.	transmitter symbols	variety of input
2.	reception symbols	variety of output
3.	channel description	system variety
4.	reduction of symbols by double classification	mean number of times, an effective state is occupied
5.	loss symbols	contents in homomorphisms (many-one mappings), organization deficiency of the first kind
6.	disturbance symbols	contents in polymorphisms (one-many mappings), organization deficiency of the second kind
7.	utility symbols	contents in isomorphisms (one-one mappings), measure of degree of organization

An organization algebra that can meaningfully be interpreted in information theory and organimetrics constitutes a subalgebra of a Boolean lattice; we may relate the following formal relations to the semantic compiler listed above:

	information theory		organimetrics
1.	$[\sigma(M)-\sigma(A)]/m$	=	$ld\,[d(A)]$
2.	$[\sigma(M)-\sigma(B)]/m$	=	$ld\,[d(B)]$
3.	$[\sigma(M)-\sigma(AB)]/m$	=	$ld\,[d(AxB)]$
4.	$\sigma(AB)/m$	=	$ld\,[d(\bar{A}\bar{B})] = ld\,[d(\bar{A}x\bar{B})]$
5.	$[\sigma(B)-\sigma(AB)]/m$	=	$ld\,[d(A\bar{B})]$
6.	$[\sigma(A)-\sigma(AB)]/m$	=	$ld\,[d(\bar{A}B)]$
7.	$[\sigma(M)-\sigma(A)-\sigma(B)+\sigma(AB)]/m$	=	$ld\,[d(AB)]$

From the formalism we derive that the (multiplicative) valuation theorems of a Boolean algebra hold:

1. $d(A)d(\bar{A}) = d(M) = m$
2. $d(A)d(B) = d(AxB)d(AB)$

Furthermore, the relational properties of a Boolean lattice:

$$1 \leqslant d(AB) \leqslant d(A), \qquad d(B) \leqslant d(AxB) \leqslant m$$

as well as:

$$d(A\bar{B}\bar{C}) \leqslant d(A\bar{B}),\ d(A\bar{C}) \leqslant d(A) \text{ etc. hold.}$$

The well-known aesthetic measure of the American mathematician G.D. Birkhoff (1933) is defined as

"order/complexity" or in an organimetric way

$$d(AB)/d(AxB) = 1/[d(A\bar{B})d(\bar{A}B)] \leqslant 1$$

We have the value "1" only for exact isomorphism, whereas the minimum of the "degree of organization" will result if system input and system output are statistically independent, which is equivalent to

$$d(AxB) = d(A)d(B) \text{ or } d(AB) = 1$$

The degree of organization can also be interpreted as the reciprocal value of the product of the organization deficiencies of the first and second kind. Thus we recognize the characteristic property of this measure as a "degree of efficiency".

These remarks should answer – at least in its main aspects – the question of the statistical measurability of information and organization structures.

Our concept is simple, clear, fertile (since it connects two disciplines), complete (organization algebra) and free of contradictions.

The variety calculus as presented in this paper enables us to formalize the main theorem of organization theory: "Qualitative and quantitative maximization of potential variety while minimizing effective variety" as minimax theorem. Qualitative maximization refers to the different categories of variables of the respective organizational unit.

It is based on an elementary state statistics and its essential contributions are a structure-preserving reduction of informations or a transition from a statistical state description (of the complex system) to a structure description (statistics of morphisms), respectively.

In the case of linear-relational systems the variety measures can be expressed by compositions of determinants over covariance matrices.

In modern systems and organization theory more attention will have to be placed on relational systems. The restriction on merely functional systems is an undue limitation of the structures of reality.

References

[1] Adam, A.: Informatik – Probleme der Mit- und Umwelt. Opladen 1971.

[2] Adam, A.: Von der Erhaltung der Information. In: Statistica Neerlandica, Vol. 26, 1972, No. 3.

[3] Das Elektronengehirn. Theorie und Praxis der Automation. Zwölf Beiträge führender amerikanischer Wissenschaftler. Sammlung Wissen und Leben 1, Wiesbaden (o.J.).

[4] Grell, Heinrich (ed.): Arbeiten zur Informationstheorie I–V. Berlin ab 1957.

[5] Shannon, Claude E. and Warren Weaver: A Mathematical Theory of Communication. University of Illinois Press. 1949.

[6] Wiener, Norbert: Cybernetics. The Technology Press and John Wiley, 1948.

German abstract
Zur Messung von Organisations- und Informationsstrukturen

Von *Adolf Adam*

Zwischen der Organisation von Informationsstrukturen und der Information über Organisationsstrukturen besteht eine gewisse syntaktische, semantische und pragmatische Entsprechung.

Die Untersuchung von Adam versucht, diese Entsprechungen aufzudecken und zu begründen.

Die Messung von Informations- und Organisationsstrukturen verlange eine integrierte Behandlung der einschlägigen klassifikatorischen (unterschiedsmeßbaren), komparativen (rangmeßbaren) und metrologischen (abstandsmeßbaren bzw. quasiabstandsmeßbaren) Merkmalssysteme und der darauf gründbaren Sachverhaltswelten.

Gegenstand der meßbaren Informations- und Organisationsdeterminanten sind die Strukturgehalte der Systeme:

1. Funktionen (Homomorphismen einschließlich Isomorphismen)
2. Korrespondenzen (Polymorphismen einschließlich Isomorphismen)

Weiterhin werden folgende Maße des Gehaltes an

1. mehr-eindeutigen Zuordnungen zwischen Merkmalskategorien oder „Varietätsverluste" des Systems
2. ein-eindeutigen Zuordnungen zwischen Merkmalskategorien oder die „Organisiertheit" schlechthin und
3. ein-mehrdeutige Zuordnungen zwischen Merkmalskategorien oder die „Blindvarietät" (Schattenvarietät, Schleiervarietät), die durch Störungen, Auswahlmöglichkeiten usw. bedingt sind,

unterschieden.

Zusätzlich wird von dem Maßsystem

1. eine klare Deutungsmöglichkeit der einzelnen Maßgrößen (semantisches Problem) gefordert. Dabei muß hinter dem Maßsystem (Modell) ein strukturgetreues Realsystem (Wirklichkeit) stehen.
2. Das Bilanzaxiom (Erhaltungssätze) im Maßsystem muß erfüllt sein (syntaktisches Problem), um überhaupt ein systematisches Messen zu gewährleisten.

Aus später näher erläuterten Gründen werden folgende Beziehungen festgelegt:

Einsatzvarietät	=	Organisiertheit mal Varietätsverluste.
Ausstoßvarietät	=	Organisiertheit mal Blindvarietät.
Systemvarietät	=	Einsatzvarietät mal Blindvarietät = Ausstoßvarietät mal Varietätsverluste (Verlustvarietät).
Varietätsmängel	=	Varietätsverluste mal Blindvarietät.
Systemvarietät	=	Organisiertheit mal Varietätsmängel (Desorganisiertheit) usw.

Die Bilanzverknüpfungen sind hier multiplikativ (quasiadditiv).

Der Übergang von den Organisationsstrukturen zu den Informationsstrukturen ist durch eine isomorphe Abbildung und über eine „semantische Brücke" möglich. Damit ist auch der Zusammenhang zwischen Organisation und Information klargestellt.

Die Begründung der Maßsysteme geschieht nicht axiomatisch im mathematischen Sinn, sondern pragmatisch (aus der Sache selbst), wobei aber auf eine strikte Konsistenz (Widerspruchsfreiheit) und Abbildungstreue Rücksicht genommen wird. Die Unvollkommenheit und Unvollständigkeit der Basisinformationen gehen als wesentliche Bestandteile in das Beschreibungssystem ein, und diese bestehenden Mängel werden als gravierende Bestandteile der Entscheidungsaussagen herausgestellt.

Die praktische Anwendbarkeit des Maßkonzeptes wird an Beispielen demonstriert.

Discontinuities of computerization – a study of French companies

By *Anders Edström* and *Louis Naugès*

1. Introduction [1]

The development of information technology in general, and computer technology in particular, has presented management of organizations with new possibilities and alternatives in exercising planning, decision-making and control. Since the use of the computer has potentially far reaching impacts on job content, structure and economic performance of an organization, it is important to study what kind of choices organizations have made and are making with respect to computer applications.

Studies of computer use have been pursued along several different lines and can roughly be characterized as descriptive, explanatory and normative. The descriptive studies have dealt with computer applications at a point in time (the state of the art) or the development of computer applications over time (the computerization process) [3]. The explanatory studies have dealt with the relationship between technology or task complexity and computer use [1] and with the relationship between computer use and organizational structure and functioning [8, 9]. The normative studies have concentrated on conditions for high profitability and effectiveness of computer applications [7].

The present study is mainly descriptive in focus, but we conjecture on the basis of the data a model for the explanation of the computerization process. The computerization process, that is, the implementation of new computer applications is studied in its organizational context and attempts are made to relate it to changes in structure, technology and people both within the information systems function and the organization as a whole. The purpose is to get a better insight into the organizational dynamics of computerization. To the best of our knowledge none has previously tried to study how the development of computer applications over time relates to changes in equipment, structure and people which hence is our claim for novelty. Apart from studying the computerization process and its relationship to other organizational changes the purpose has been to compare organizations which entered the development of computer systems relatively early and those which entered later with respect to process characteristics and also to compare manufacturing and non-manufacturing firms.

---

1 Work reported in this paper has been sponsored by the European Institute of Business Administration and Le Delegue à l'Informatique.

2. Systems development in the organization

The development of computer systems is part of the information systems function. Other parts of that function are they mainly performed by the information systems department (ISD). It is in the ISD that the technical expertise for systems development is concentrated and most of the development activity is taking place. In describing this part of the organization we utilize the descriptive scheme proposed by Leavitt (1964) (figure 1). Technology refers in this context to the computer hardware and software available and structure to the formal organization of the ISD. The task is system development and people refer to those persons carrying out this task. The ISD is just a part of the organization which is integrated more or less closely with the main stream of organizational activities.

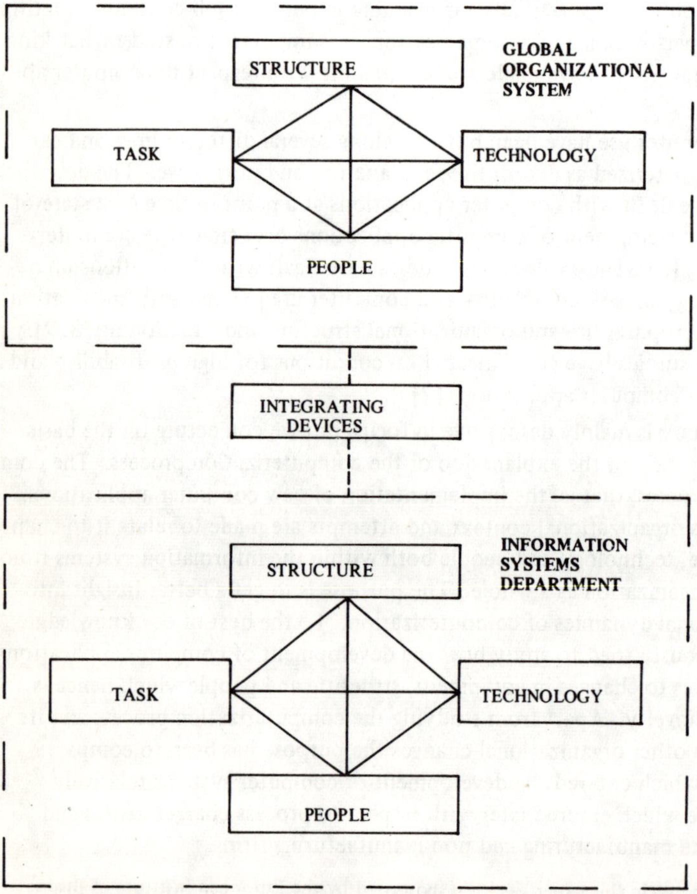

Figure 1. Information systems activities in an overall organizational context

The main stream activities refer to those activities which the power center of the organization, that is top management, attend to. Top management work within the context of a system which we have termed the global organizational system to contrast it with the subsystem which ISD constitutes. The same descriptive scheme is used to describe the global system as was used for the subsystem. Technology refers now to the basic production technology or technologies and task to management of the product/market scope of the organization. The overall structure can be characterized, for instance, by product divisions, area divisions, departments or a mixture of these.

The information system activities are integrated into the main stream of organizational activities in several different ways. First it will be integrated through the formal structure. We call this the organizational location of the ISD. The head of ISD may formally report to the head of accounting, the controller or the president of the company, for instance. Secondly, it may be integrated through the systems and procedures in the organization, for instance, through the long range planning system. It has become more common with a long range plan of information systems development which relates information systems to main stream activities. Thirdly, special integrative devices may be set up for system development. We see the inclusion of organizational analysis within the ISD as one such coordinating device. The existence of various types of committees and information systems coordinating groups will be another example. Finally, of course, the integration of information systems within the organization will rely heavily on people.

In the computerization process there will be a dynamic interaction between structure, task, technology and people within the information systems function. A new department head is appointed who has a different view of what applications should be developed or how activities should be organized. This in turn may effect the need for new equipment. Major changes in the above variables are termed discontinuities. The discontinuities are to be distinguished from the more gradual changes that always occur and which do not mean that the system state is different. Such gradual changes may be smaller changes in equipment like adding faster tapes or a new line printer. It may also be the development of a new application within an area where computerization is already well under way. Parallel to the interaction within the subsystem (ISD) changes will occur within the global system. The extent to which there will be a strong interaction between the global system and the subsystem will depend on how strong the latter is integrated with the main stream activities. This degree of integration will change over time as the computerization process develops.

Empirical research has so far not uncovered any direct impact of computerization on the global system. Research reviewed by Hofer [5], for instance, show that the impact of computer technology has until now been local rather than global.

It may be that the reason for this is that the impact of computerization is more indirect. Computerization offers even top management new possibilities of running the organization but the desirability of these new alternatives are determined by other factors. Computerization is facilitating rather than a direct determinant. The reverse side of the interaction, that is, the influence of the global system on the use of the computer seems to also have been lacking [7].

We would conjecture that this is because top management do not perceive any relevant new possibilities for them through computerization although they can well see the need for its local use.

3. Variables in the computerization process

In analysing the computerization process we have to define the levels of the variables, that is, the discontinuities which is our way of identifying important changes and to get some comparability between firms. Identifying discontinuities is, of course, only a problem if changes don't naturally occur in discontinuous steps. Changes in equipment and in computer applications present the most difficulty.

The changes which have identified as important within the ISD system have been changes in

– Equipment,
– Applications,
– Changes in the organization of the ISD,
– Change of department head for the ISD.

The classification of changes has been done after the data have been collected, but is presented at this point for the sake of a logical flow in the presentation. Regarding equipment we have identified four changes or steps. Since the vast majority of the organizations use IBM equipment, it is easiest to identify the changes in terms of IBM models. The first stage is the introduction of an IBM 1401 or an equivalent machine. The second is a transition to IBM 360 equipment, and the third is an upgrading of model in the 360 series or adding a second machine. The fourth stage is a transition to the 370 series. We have identified these stages by $E_1, \ldots, E_4$. On each level or stage several changes can occur. We may, for instance, have several changes of models within E_3.

Identifying discontinuities in applications is a somewhat more difficult problem. Our somewhat arbitrary classification identifies again four stages $(A_1, \ldots, A_4)$. The first is applications for pure record keeping purposes and for producing certain documents like payslips and invoices. The second class of applications are those concerned with management control information. Examples are comparing budgets against actual results or comparing inventory records against recorder points. Thirdly we come to a class of applications which actually involve programmed decision-making where the computer suggest operational production plans, selects suppliers or order quantities. In the fourth category we include applications that concern the longer range planning in the organization. Examples of such applications are predicting balance sheets and income statements and sales forecasting for the medium and long term. It is clear that it is not easy to clearly distinguish between the different categories.

Changes in the design of the ISD department have been identified as follows ($S_1, \ldots, S_4$). The first structure is an undifferentiated structure where programmers, analysts and operators are hard to distinguish. The second stage is a structure where system development is clearly separated from the actual computer production activities. The third structure is when the system development becomes further differentiated in terms of application groups. Analysts and programmers specialize in, for instance, financial and accounting systems. The fourth structure recognizes the broader impacts of computer systems by including a function line "conception" or organizational analysis which is supposed to make sure that the computer application is well integrated and meets with operational requirements. The last stage is also treated under integrating devices.

The changes in department head has just been identified as a change with no attempt to collect data on the qualifications of the new department head, for instance.

Regarding the integration of the ISD system we have identified three terms for integration. First, organizational location, where we have been able to identify three stages ($O_1, \ldots, O_3$). The first one includes cases where the department head reports to the head of accounting or personnel. In the second case he reports to a director of control or administration or finance with a somewhat broader organizational responsibility. In the last stage the ISD reports directly to top management.

Long range planning of information systems which is the second form of integration has not been divided up into different levels either it exists or doesn't exist. The variable is identified as P.

The final form of integration is really – S_4 – which is the highest level of structure which we have previously identified.

Concerning the global system we have only identified changes in leadership defined as the change of company president, changes in overall organizational structure and changes in ownership. The basic technologies and tasks have not been investigated directly and no data have not been collected for these variables. The reason has been practical constraints which have forced us to concentrate on the variables of most interest to us.

4. An outline of the study

The present study is part of a larger project studying the implementation of information systems in sixteen French companies. The companies have been selected so that they will provide a specific cross section of different information systems to study. The sample may be regarded as a quota sample. As part of our study of the implementation of specific systems we have collected data through personal interviews on the range of applications within the different companies. The instrument for collecting information about applications has been a translation into French of an exhaustive list of applications utilized previously by de Brabander et al. [1]. The instrument consists of a list of 152 different applications which can be found in an industrial organization. The non-industrial companies filled out the relevant parts of the list and were asked to add important applications which were not covered by the list. The applications which are not well covered in non-industrial firms, tend to be operational applications which are often an integral part of the "production" technology rather than of direct relevance to management. A system for processing checks in a bank is an example.

Two interviews were held in two different companies in the original sample as a pilot study before collecting additional data on the computerization process. On the basis of these interviews a questionnaire was designed and sent to the companies in our sample. We have received data from twelve of the companies in time to be included in the present report. The questionnaire was sent to the head of the information systems department.

The questionnaire is an attempt to reconstruct after the fact the main events of the computerization process. The information asked for is such, however, that people tend to be able to remember it without much trouble. Our pilot interviews had shown this to be the case.

A few characteristics of the twelve companies are given below. The size distribution is given in Table 1.

Number of employees	Number of organizations
< 2000	3
2000 < 4000	0
4000 < 6000	7
> 6000	2
	12

Table 1. The size distribution of the firms

The computer experience of the firms are given in Table 2. The starting point is the year an electronic computer was first introduced.

Year of computer introduction	Number of organizations
< 1964	2
1964 – 1966	4
1966 – 1968	4
1968 >	2
	12

Table 2. Computer introduction in the studied firms

The original sample of sixteen companies consists of half manufacturing firms and half non-manufacturing firms. The present subset includes five manufacturing and seven non-manufacturing companies.

The introduction of long range planning of computer applications is shown in Table 3.

Year in which long range planning is introduced	Number of Organizations
< 1968	0
1968 – 1970	1
1970 – 1972	5
1972 >	2
Not yet introduced	4
	12

Table 3. The introduction of long range planning of computer applications

5. Results

The results of the study will be presented in three different parts. First we will look at the present situations. Where are the companies today regarding computerization? Secondly we will look at how they got where they are today. What series of changes have they gone through? Finally, we will address the question of the interaction of ISD with the global system.

A summary picture of the present situation is given in Table 4 and 5. We are here presenting the state of the ISD system and the present state of integration of the

State variable / External variable	Equipment				Structure				Applications				No. of Appl.			Scope of Appl.		
	E_4	E_3	E_2	E_1	S_4	S_3	S_2	S_1	A_4	A_3	A_2	A_1	50	50–20	20	Larg	Med.	Small
Early (6)	3	2	1	–	2	2	2	–	4	2	–	–	1	4	1	1	3	2
Late (6)	4	2	–	–	3	1	2	–	4	2	–	–	1	4	1	1	4	1
Manuf. (5)	3	2	–	–	3	1	1	–	4	1	–	–	2	3	–	2	2	1
Non-manuf. (7)	4	2	1	–	2	2	1	–	4	3	–	–	–	5	2	–	5	2

Table 4. Present state of the ISD system

State variable / External variable	Org. Location			Planning		Integr. Dev.	
	O_3	O_2	O_1	Yes	No	Yes	No
Early (6)	3	3	–	3	3	2	4
Late (6)	3	3	–	6	–	3	3
Manuf. (5)	1	4	–	5	–	3	2
Non-manuf. (7)	5	2	–	4	3	2	5

Table 5. Present state of integration of ISD with the global system

ISD system with the global system. The system states are related to the time of entry into computerization and the nature of the organizational task, manufacturing and non-manufacturing. The early adopters are those companies which started computerization with second generation equipment, that is, IBM 1401 or equivalent. They all introduced a computer in 1965 or earlier. The state variables have all been explained earlier except the scope of applications. The scope of applications is assessed on the basis of how many different organizational functions are depending on computer applications.

If we look at the difference between early and late adopters it is clear that the degree of computerization if anything is larger among the late adopters. If we look at manufacturing versus non-manufacturing we see a stronger relationship than between time for adopting the computer and the state of computerization. It also turns out that the manufacturing firms dominate among the late adopters. Four of five manufacturing companies are late adopters. It thus seems on the basis of our small sample that the nature of the task is the best predictor of the state of computerization. This is consistent with the results of de Brabander et al. [1]. Similar results have also been obtained in organizational studies [4, 2] where they find relationships between task complexity and formalization. It is indicative also that the two firms with the largest number of applications and largest scope are manufacturing firms with production in batches or mixed continuous and batch production. The two manufacturing firms with smallest number of applications have continuous production. This is consistent with a prediction on the basis of task complexity.

We have attempted to get information on how much companies spend on systems development. Regarding budget data the information is very incomplete and the only indicator we have is the number of analysts and programmers which are employed. The average number of analysts are given in Table 6.

	Man.	Non-man.
Early	28	29
Late	20	20

Table 6. The average number of programmer/analysts

It should be emphasized again that we only have one early adopter among the manufacturing firms. The data give a weak but yet indication that the late adopters have achieved their computerization with less investment in systems development. We may speculate that they might have used more of outside expertise in order to achieve computerization faster, but we don't have any data to verify that.

Turning to the state of intergration we find this also reflects the nature of the task. The organizational location of the ISD is quite different in manufacturing and non-manufacturing firms. We find that only in one case does the ISD report directly to the president in the former type of firm while it is the common practice for the latter. The plausible explanation would be that in firms with higher task complexity we would expect a more differentiated structure and because of limits on the span of control it would be less likely that ISD would report directly to the president. Planning and integrating devices are more common in manufacturing firms. A more detailed picture of the integration will be given below.

The data on the computerization process is presented in two ways. First, we will look at the change in particular variables over time, then we give a more aggregate description of the change process. Table 7 presents the results for single variables.

External variables \ State variables	Equipment	Structure of ISD	Organizational location	Change in department head
Early	1.9	3.5	6.0	4.7
Late	2.1	2.4	3.1	2.3
Manuf.	2.0	2.7	4.0	2.3
Non-manuf.	1.9	3.2	4.8	4.5

Table 7. The average time in each state

In Table 7 we have computed the average time in a particular state. Our definition of state is in Table 7 taken to include also changes within levels of the variables. For equipment this means that we have taken all changes of models and additions of new computers as a change in state. From the results of Table 7 we can see that the rate of equipment change is identical across firms. The rate of change in other variables is much greater among late adopters than among early adopters. In our small sample and since the process has been going on for a relatively short time, it is difficult to make reasonable comparisons between the first and second half of the computerization process, for instance.

It seems clear that the faster computerization process will lead to a more rapid organizational adaptation. One may speculate whether the faster process among late adopters have caused a larger strain on the organization. We have no data to support this.

Table 8 gives a more aggregate picture of the computerization process. In the table we have indicated when changes have occured in the different variables. If we compare the early and late adopters it is apparent that the early adopters much more often have integrated their computer activities within the existing organiza-

Year / Company	1961	1962	1963	1964	1965	1966	1967	1968	1969	1970	1971	1972	1973
1								P S_3 O_2	A_1 A_2 A_3 E_3		A_4	E_4	
2								E_2 S_1 A_1 A_4			O_3 S_2	P A_2	E_4 A_3
3							E_2 O_2 S_2 A_1	A_2		O_2	E_3 A_3	O_3	P E_4
4							E_2 O_3 S_2 A_1			S_4 A_4 E_3 A_2		E_4	P
5							E_2 O_2 S_2 A_1		O_2 S_2	P	S_2 A_4	E_3 O_2	S_4
6						E_2 O_2 S_2 A_1				S_3 P	E_3 A_2	O_2 A_3 S_4	
7					E_1 A_1			E_2 O_3 S_2		E_3 P A_2		S_4	E_4
8					E_1 A_1		E_2 S_2 A_2			S_3 P	O_2	E_4	
9				E_1 S_2 A_1 O_3					E_3 A_4	S_2		E_3 S_2	
10				E_1 A_1						E_2 O_3 S_2 A_2		A_4	
11			E_1 O_2 S_2 A_1		E_2 A_3		A_3 A_2			E_3 P		E_4 S_4 A_4	
12	E_1 A_1			E_2 A_2		O_2		S_3 A_4	E_3				

Table 8. An aggregate account of the computerization process

tional structure for developing punched card applications.[2] They have not developed a more advanced structure until they passed to third generation equipment. Another apparent fact is that changes in the different variables tend to go together. Structural changes are often combined with the arrival of new equipment, for instance. Integrating mechanisms like planning tend to develop later in the computerization process.

Planning is an organizational response to increased computerization and not something which is set up beforehand.

We turn finally to an account of the interactions between the ISD system and the global system. The interaction patterns in the firms studied are included as an appendix to the paper. In the account of the interaction we are looking at the changes which occur within the global system, in the integration mechanisms and within the ISD. Evidently it is impossible for us with the present design to say anything about the cause effect relationships. We have to rely on conjectures. It may still give us insights into the dynamics of computerization, however.

Company one may serve as a good starting point since its computerization process is a special case not found among the others. In this company the computerization process is initiated from the global system to serve the needs of top management. A change in ownership leads to the appointment of a new president. The new president requires computerization and a plan is developed to guide the development work as well as an organization to carry it out. The ISD reports to the director of administration and control since the main purpose is to make good management control possible. Essentially within three years a total integrated operational planning and control system is developed. At the end of this a major structural change is undertaken in the global system. It seems apparent and it is also confirmed in interviews that computerization was seen as the tool which would make effective decentralization possible. The process relied heavily on people as integrating devices especially the head of ISD who was as much a manager as a systems specialist in outlook but also formalized planning played a major role. It would have been impossible to mobilize the resources and get the systems accepted without the strong commitment of top management and the effective integration of system development into the global system.

In company one it was realized at the start that the computer could serve as an effective tool for management control. This realization came much later in the other firms' processes of computerization although approximately at the same point in time 1969/70. It seems also to be coupled with a rather general move towards divisionalized decentralized structures. It is indicative that company one was the last to start computerization and that its president was American. It could, hence, rely on already existing evidence of the possibilities of computer applications in practice.

2 All companies in the sample had punched card equipment before introducing a computer.

The realization that computer technology offers the possibility of better management control on the global level and hence facilitates decentralization can be seen in company 5, 6 and 8. In those companies major budget and cost control systems coincide with a move to decentralization or changes in management control policy. It seems to us clear that decentralization is mainly determined by environmental factors especially environmental complexity. Computerization is the tool to achieve control in the decentralized structure. The implementation of systems for global management control is introduced in company 10, 11 and 12 around 1969/70. In company 3 and 4 it follows in 1972. Company 2, 7 and 9 do not show a similar pattern. It seems that by 1969 at least half of the companies had realized the computer's potential role in global management control and also moved to implement systems.

The choice of utilizing the computer in planning, for instance, is taken at a somewhat later stage and generally not until the ISD system is well integrated in the global system, most often through information systems planning. Examples of this can be found for company 1, 4, 5 and 11. It is not until 1971/72 that we can see a more general move towards computer application in planning.

The next potential step that the computer can be used for problem solving is nowhere evident.

The scope of computer applications will generally increase after the effective integration of ISD into the global system. Good examples of this can be found for company 1, 5, 6 and 11. This seems natural since managers of the global system have a broader outlook on the organization.

It is not possible to assess the importance of integration relative to other factors in the computerization process such as differences in task and management commitment. The organizations which appear to have achieved the highest level of integration are company 1, 4, 5, 6, 7 and 11. Among these we find four manufacturing companies. The fifth manufacturing company is the one which is least computerized. Company 7 is implementing an organization wide tele-processing system which would have been difficult to develop without good integrating devices.

Integration of the ISD into the global organizational system can operate through people, organizational structure and formal systems. It seems prudent not to rely on only one of these means, but to use them all. Half of the companies have achieved this level of integration by 1972/73. We would predict that these companies in the future will have an advantage for the effective exploitation of computer technology relative to firms with lower levels of integration.

6. A model of the computerization process

Out of the previous description of computerization emerges a model of the process which is presented in Figure 2. It has been the common pattern to start with loca-

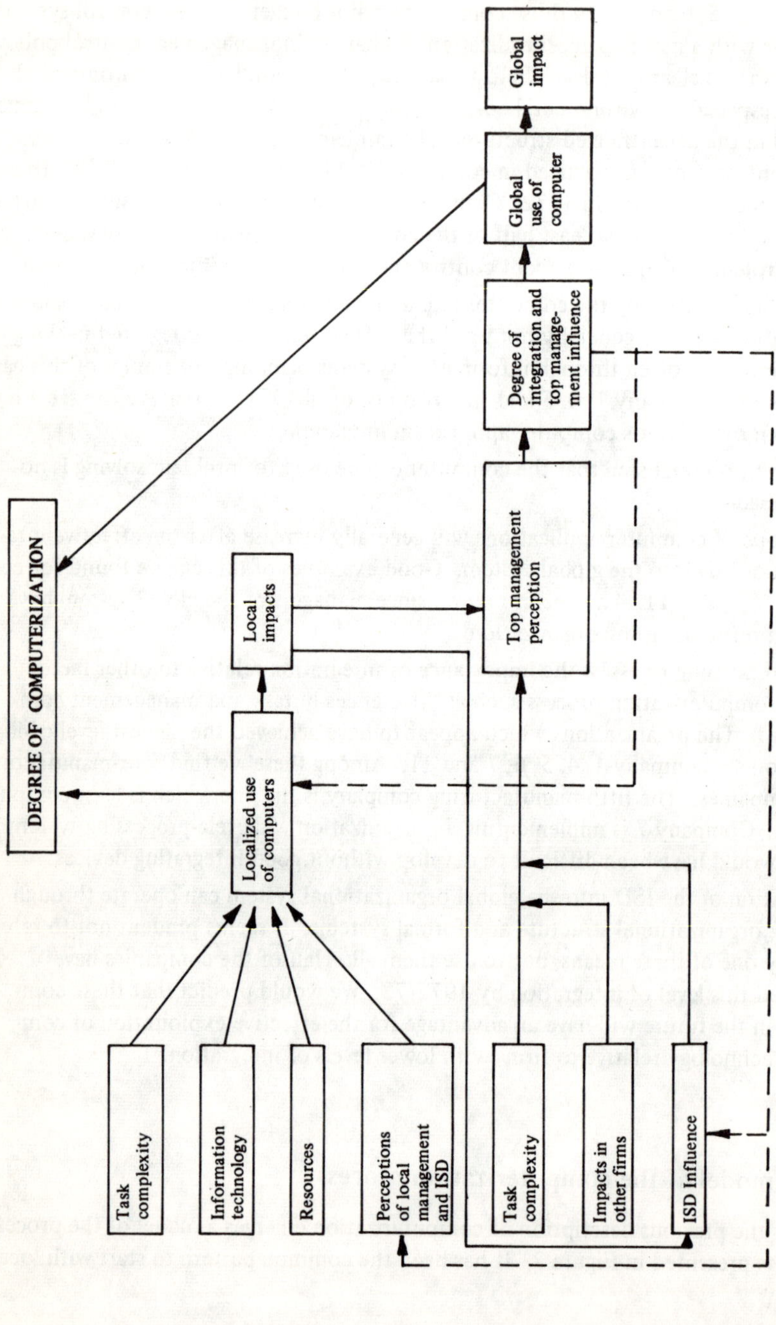

Figure 2. A model of the computerization process

lized use of the computer. Only company one is an exception in our sample. The degree to which the computer is used is determined by task complexity, available technology, available resources internally and the perceptions of the new choices which are possible through computer technology. The localized use of the computer will have local impacts both functional and dysfunctional. The impacts will be visible to managers in the global system. Top management will also be influenced by the characteristics of the organizational task, the impacts of computer applications in other organizations and by ISD influence. Through these forces management perceptions about the possibilities of computer technology will be formed. To the extent that top management finds computerization beneficial it will move to integrate it more closely with the global system and also exert a stronger influence. Computer applications will now appear in a global context like management control and management planning which will lead to global impacts. The increased degree of integration will influence localized use of the computer to fit the global purpose and local management and ISD perceptions. It will also lead to increased possibilities of ISD influence since computerization has become more important.

In our model the perceptions of managers of the choices and alternatives made possible by computer technology plays a key role. The perceptions are based on both internal and external flows of information. Our data show that companies act about the same time in moving towards global management control or planning. This may indicate that there is an efficient flow of information among companies. An interesting question concerns the roles of the computer company representatives and consultants relative to internal sources in spreading information about computer possibilities.

The model also indicates that top management's crucial means for influencing the computerization process are through the design and implementation of appropriate forms for integrating the ISD system with the main stream of organizational activities.

7. Conclusions

In predicting the state of computerization it appears that the nature of the organizational task is a much better predictor of computerization than the time for adopting computer technology. This is consistent with existing results.

The computerization among late adopters led to more changes in organizational structure, organizational location and people than for the early adopters. The effects of time of entry and the nature of the task cannot be separated. A plausible explanation of the results would be that computerization in a differentiated structure leads to more frequent organizational changes both within ISD and in the integration devices, because of the more complex pattern of interdependence in the differentiated structure. The increased complexity in applications and relations between them is mapped into the organization of ISD and its integration with the global system.

It is also apparent that the change in different variables go together. There is a strong interaction between equipment, applications, structure of ISD and people.

It seems likely that there is an interrelationship between structural changes on a global level and computer technology. There is, however, no direct impact of computer technology on the global structure. Computerization facilitates changes which are determined mainly by other factors.

The impact from the global system on the computerization will come after the global implications of computer technology is realized.

We can identify roughly points in time when management has realized the possibilities of computerization for global management control (68/69) and for planning (71/72).

The influence of the global system will be through the establishment of better integration of system development activities. The importance of integration for computerization relative to personal commitment and organizational task cannot be assessed. It seems likely that integration is more effective if several different forms are used. This must again be seen in relation to the organizational task.

We would finally suggest moving to more clinical studies of how the choice of computer applications are made within organizations to get better knowledge of why certain alternatives are chosen rather than others.

Figures

COMPANY 1	1968	1969	1970	1971	1972	1973					
Global	Change in ownership – New President			From Function-al to Divisional Organi-zation							
Integration	IS Planning	Director of Adm. and Control									
System Developm.											
Structure People	Head ISD Project Organiza-tion			Head ISD							
Applica-tions (Task)		Account. Sales Analysis Shipping	Control Inventory Production Sales Purchasing	Integrated Operational Control System	Personnel Production Planning	LT. Planning Control					
Equipm. (Tool)		360/40		360/50	370/155						

COMPANY 2	1968	1969	1970	1971	1972	1973
Global System						
Integration	Director Personnel ↕			Vice President ↕	IS Planning ↕	
System Development		→	→			→
Structure People	Undiffer-entiated			Functional/ Proj. Organisat.		
Applications (Task)	Account-ing		Sales Analysis	Personnel	Control Inventory	Purchasing
Equipm. (Tool)	360/20			360/30		370/135

COMPANY3	1967	1968	1969	1970	1971	1972	1973				
Global System											
Integration	Admin. Director ↕			Top Manager ↕		President ↕					
System Developm.	↕	→	→	↕	→	↕	→				
Structure People	Functional Organization					Functional/ Proj. Organization					
Applications (Task)	Accounting	Financial Control Sales Analysis					Sales Analysis Budget Control Profit Centers				
Equipment (Tool)	360/30				360/40		370/145				

COMPANY 4	1967	1968	1969	1970	1971	1972	1973				
Global System											
Integration	Unclear Respon-sibility	General Adm.		Organiza-tional Analysis Integrated with ISD			IS Planning				
System Developm.		↕	→	↕	→	→	↕				
Structure People		Functional Organiza-tion		Functional/ Proj. Organiza-tion	Head ISD IS Specialist						
Applications (Task)		Sales Analysis Account-ing			Investment LT Planning	Financial Control	LT Planning Control of profit centers				
Equipment (Tool)	360/30			360/40		360/145					

COMPANY 5	1966	1967	1968	1969	1970	1971	1972	1973			
Global System			Recon-structuring Operational Planning and Budgeting				Regional Organiza-tion				
Integration	Director for Developm. and Research			Director of Planning and Budgeting	IS Planning		Director of Finance and Adm.	Organiza-tional Analysis within ISD			
System Developm.											
Structure People		Head ISD	Head ISD	Functional, Proj. Organiza-tion Head ISD		Head ISD					
Applications (Task)		Budget Sales Account-ing Billing	Sales Analysis			LT Planning Personnel Inventory Sales An.	LT Planning	Produc-tion Mainte-nance			
Equipment (Tool)	Service Bureau	IBM 360/30					Univac 1106				

COMPANY 6	1966	1967	1968	1969	1970	1971	1972	1973			
Global System				Decen-tralization product groups							
Integration	Director of Finance				IS Planning		Director of Org. and Control; Org. Analysis within ISD				
System Developm.											
Structure People	Project Organiza-tion				Change in Proj. Organiza-tion		Functional/ Proj. Organiza-tion				
Applications (Task)		Accounting	Inventory Records	Budget Control			Production Personnel Sales				
Equipment (Tool)	360/30					360/40					

COMPANY 7	1965	1966	1967	1968	1969	1970	1971	1972	1973		
Global System						Regroup Services					
Integration				President ↕		IS Planning ↕		Organizational Analysis within ISD ↕			
System Developm.	→	→	→		→		→		→		
Structure People				Crude Functional/ Proj. Org. Head ISD				Change Funct./ Project Organization			
Applications (Task)				Accounting	Personnel	Teleprocessing System					
Equipment (Tool)	1401			360/30		2 x 360/30	360/30 360/40	2 x 360/40	2 x 370/135		

COMPANY8	1965	1966	1967	1968	1969	1970	1971	1972	1973		
Global System						Divisional Structure	New President				
Integration						IS Planning	Director of Finance				
System Developm.											
Structure People						Project/ Functional Organiza- tion					
Applica- tions (Task)	Purchas- ing		Personnel			Major Financial and Accounting Applicat.	Budgeting Inventory				
Equipment (Tool)	1401		360					370			

COMPANY9	1964	1965	1966	1967	1968	1969	1970	1971	1972	1973 .	
Global System											
Integration	President						President Division Manager		President		
System Developm.											
Structure People	Functional Organization		Liaison Personnel in div.				Decentralization of Systems Developm.		Centralization of dev. New Head of ISD		
Applications (Task)	Budgeting	Inventory		Accounting		Financial Control Appl.					
Equipment (Tool)	Gamma 30					360/50	360/65				

COMPANY10	1964	1965	1966	1967	1968	1969	1970	1971	1972	1973	
Global System											
Integration							President Org. Analysis				
System Developm.											
Structure People	Undiff. Structure						Head of ISD	Functional Org.			
Applications (Task)		Inventory					Personnel Sales Analysis Accounting	Cost Control		LT Planning	
Equipment (Tool)	Gamma 10						360/25				

COMPANY 11	1963	1964	1965	1966	1967	1968	1969	1970	1971	1972	1973
Global System										Decentral. by Division	
Integration	Director of Adm.							IS Planning		Integration of Info System and Org. Dev.	
System Developm.											
Structure People	Functional/ Proj. Organiza-tion					Head ISD	Head ISD		Head ISD	Project Org.	Head ISD
Applications (Task)		Payroll	Inventory Records	Production	Production	Accounting	Budget Control			Sales	Pure Plan-ning
Equipment (Tool)	1401		360/30					360/40		2 x 370/135	

COMPANY12	1961	1962	1963	1964	1965	1966	1967	1968	1969	1970	1971	1972	1973
Global System													
Integration	Head of Accounting					Director of Finance and Accounting							
System development													
Structure People	Crude Project Organization							Project/ Functional Org. Head of ISD: Inf. Specialist					
Applications (Task)	Payroll	Personnel Statistics		Accounting					Budgets for fixed and var. Cost: Cash flow				Investment Planning
Equipment (Tool)	1401			2 x 1401		2 x 360/30			360/40		360/50		

References

[1] De Brabander, B., D. Deschoolmeester, R. Leyder and E. Vanlommel: The Effect of Task-Volume and Complexity upon Computer-Use. In: Journal of Business, January 1972.

[2] Child, J.: Predicting and Understanding Organization Structure. In: Administrative Science Quarterly, Vol. 18, 1973, No. 2, 168–185.

[3] Churchill, N., J. Kempster and M. Uretsky: Computerbased Information Systems. NAA Research Study, New York 1969.

[4] Hall, R.: Organizations-Structure and Process. Englewood Cliffs, N.J. 1972.

[5] Hofer, Ch.: Emerging EDP Pattern. In: Harvard Business Review, March–April 1970.

[6] Leavitt, H.: Applied Organization Change in Industry: Structural, Technical and Human Approaches. In: W. Cooper, H. Leavitt and M. Shelly II (eds.): New Perspectives in Organization Research. New York 1964.

[7] McKinsey: Unlocking the Computer's Profit Potential. In: Computers and Automation, April 1969, pp. 24–33.

[8] Stewart, R.: How Computers Affect Management. London 1971.

[9] Whisler, Th.: The Impact of Computers on Organizations. New York 1970.

German abstract
Dynamische Aspekte des Computereinsatzes in der Unternehmung – Ergebnisse einer empirischen Studie

Von *Anders Edström* und *Louis Naugès*

Einsatzzeitpunkt und -intensität des Computers für betriebswirtschaftliche Problemstellungen variieren zwischen vergleichbaren Unternehmungen oft erheblich. Das Aufzeigen der möglichen Ursachen für eine unterschiedliche Intensität der ADV-Anwendungen sowie das Aufdecken des Zusammenhangs zwischen dem Zeitpunkt und der unternehmungsinternen Entwicklung des Computereinsatzes ist das Anliegen dieses Beitrags.

Ausgangspunkt der Untersuchung von Edström und Naugès ist die Definition der Determinanten unterschiedlicher Stufen der ADV-Entwicklung in der Unternehmung. Dabei ist die ADV-Abteilung („information systems department“) das zentrale Untersuchungsobjekt, das durch die verwendete Hard- und Software, die Organisationsstruktur, die Aufgabenstellung und die Aufgabenträger determiniert wird. Außerdem werden die Interdependenzen zwischen signifikanten Veränderungen im ADV-Bereich und Änderungen der gesamten Organisationsstruktur der Unternehmung betrachtet. Die Veränderungen im ADV-Bereich werden durch vier Merkmale erfaßt, die ihrerseits unterschiedliche Werte annehmen können:

- die Hardwareausstattung,
- Art und Umfang der ADV-Anwendungen,
- Änderungen in der Organisationsstruktur der ADV-Abteilung,
- Änderungen in der Leitung der ADV-Abteilung.

Als weitere Variable wird der Integrationsgrad der ADV-Abteilung in der Unternehmung betrachtet, der primär durch die organisatorische Eingliederung der ADV-Abteilung und die Existenz einer langfristigen Planung der ADV-Entwicklungen bestimmt wird.

Die oben dargestellten Determinanten des ADV-Einsatzes wurden von Edström und Naugès im Rahmen einer empirischen Untersuchung in 12 französischen Unternehmungen erhoben. Die Ergebnisse dieser Studie wurden nach drei Gesichtspunkten ausgewertet:

- der augenblickliche Stand des Computereinsatzes,
- die von den Unternehmungen verfolgte ADV-Entwicklungsstrategie,
- das Wirkungsverhältnis zwischen ADV-Bereich und Organisationsstruktur der Unternehmung.

Bei der Charakterisierung des Entwicklungsstandes wird zwischen frühen Anwendern („early adopters") und späten Anwendern („late adopters") unterschieden. Außerdem werden bei der Untersuchung Fabrikations- und Dienstleistungsunternehmungen getrennt erfaßt. Der individuelle ADV-Entwicklungsstand wird mit Hilfe der vorher skizzierten Determinanten bestimmt.

Bei der Erfassung der ADV-Entwicklungsstrategie wird insbesondere die Verweildauer auf einzelnen Entwicklungsstufen beobachtet. Dabei wird wiederum zwischen frühen und späten Anwendern sowie Fabrikations- und Dienstleistungsbetrieben differenziert.

Das Wirkungsverhältnis zwischen ADV-Entwicklung und Organisationsstruktur wird auf der Basis der eingeführten Determinanten unternehmungsindividuell bestimmt. Die Aussagen in diesem Bereich sind allerdings weitgehend auf hypothetischen Vermutungen aufgebaut und mehr als Denkanstöße zu betrachten.

Abschließend entwickeln Edström und Naugès ein Modell, das den Gesamtzusammenhang von ADV-Entwicklung und Organisationsstrukturänderungen erklären soll. Hauptbestimmungsgrößen dieses Modells sind u.a. die Komplexität der Aufgabenabläufe der Unternehmung, der Einfluß der ADV-Abteilung und die aktiven Gestaltungsmaßnahmen der Unternehmungsführung.

Integrated information systems and their effects on organizational structure

By *James C. Emery*

1. Independence versus integration of systems

A system, by definition, is composed of a set of related tasks directed toward a common goal. A system is created as a way of dealing with complexity. A large task, such as managing a business organization, is too complex to handle in a monolithic way; consequently, it is broken down into a hierarchy of subtasks.

The extent to which the components of a system should be integrated is one of the basis issues facing the managers of the system. Integration involves closer coordination, tighter linkages, and greater resource sharing among components. This brings with it certain efficiencies; but it also entails costs, delays, and added complexity. Ideally, we should choose the degree of integration that best balances these opposing effects.

Trade-offs between independence and integration exist in any man-made system. Designers of computer hardware, management information systems, supersonic aircraft, and organizations must all deal with the same basic problem of finding the correct balance between independence and integration.

In order to gain relative simplicity in each of the subsystems -- which, after all, is the reason for fragmenting the system in the first place -- each subunit must be partially isolated from the other subunits. This isolation is achieved in several ways.

2. Independence through structure

The most basic way to isolate the subsystems is through a suitable choice of the system's structure. The intent should be to combine closely related activities within the same subsystem. Conversely, weakly related activities should be placed in hierarchically "distant" subsystems. In this way most communication and coordination can be confined within the boundaries of a subsystem; relatively little coordination needs to be performed across subsystem boundaries. Each subsystem is thus partially isolated from the others.

Subsystems interact with one another through coupling or shared use of common resources. Subsystems are coupled if an output of one serves as an input to the other. Coupled activities interact with one another because a change in the output rate of the supplying activity will affect the input rate of the using activity (and vice versa). Similarly, subsystems sharing a common resource interact with one another because use of the resource by one subsystem reduces the quantity available for the others.

Although it is desirable to combine closely interacting activities into the same subsystem, this can never be done completely. Only a limited number of activities can be combined, for otherwise the subsystem is too complex - i.e., exceeds a desirable "span of control", in terms of conventional organizational theory.

Furthermore, a structure that successfully combines coupled activities may separate activities that share common resources. For example, a project organizational structure for a research laboratory may combine coupled functions (electrical engineering, mechanical engineering, etc.), but at the expense of inefficient sharing of functional resources across project boundaries. A functional organizational structure, on the other hand, may achieve efficient resource sharing, but it may also create problems of coordinating within a project across functional boundaries.

Some interactions thus inevitably exist among subsystems, no matter how well the system is structured. It is therefore necessary to cope with interactions that cross subsystem boundaries while still preserving the relative isolation of each subsystem.

2.1 Decoupling

One of the important means of decreasing the degree of interaction of coupled subsystems is through various forms of decoupling. A common form is the use of a buffer to separate two subsystems. This allows the output rate of the supplying subsystem to differ (in the short run) from the input rate of the using subsystem. For example, a subassembly shop that manufactures component parts almost always feeds into a buffer inventory, from which the assembly department then draws its components. Buffers do not eliminate interactions, for in the long run (depending on the size of the buffer) outputs must balance with inputs. Buffers can, however, substantially reduce the need for close coordination across subsystem boundaries. They therefore can increase the degree of isolation of a subsystem.

Standardization of inputs and outputs -- the interfaces among subsystems -- provides another means of decoupling. If the interfaces remain relatively constant, each subsystem can pursue its activities without detailed knowledge of the inner workings of other subsystems. This ability to treat other subsystems as "black boxes" increases the effective isolation of a subsystem.

Providing each supplying subsystem with some surplus capacity is still another form of decoupling. This allows the subsystem to recover more quickly from a random disturbance, and so the effects of the disturbance are less apt to propagate throughout the system.

The most complete form of decoupling is to eliminate the coupling all together by simply duplicating the supplying activity within the boundaries of each using subsystem. This clearly reduces the system's dependence on other subsystems, and hence increases its isolation.

2.2 Ignoring minor interactions

A large number of interactions that cross subsystem boundaries will persist despite all efforts to isolate subsystems through structure or decoupling. Most of the interactions are relatively minor; they can be ignored without incurring any major penalties. This effectively increases the apparent -- if not the real -- isolation of the subsystem. The marketing vice president, for example, carries on many of his activities without much concern for the detailed effects of his actions on manufacturing and engineering. The manufacturing and engineering vice presidents must similarly ignore the detailed consequences of their actions on marketing. This mutual ignoring of minor interactions is the only feasible way of managing a subsystem.

2.3 Coordination among subsystems

The choice of structure, the use of various forms of decoupling, and ignoring weak interactions are all aimed at increasing the independence of subsystems. The opposite approach is to increase the integration of subsystems by means of greater coordination.

The most stringent form of coordination is achieved through centralized planning. Its purpose is to constrain the separate subsystems so that they jointly achieve the best overall result. For example, the production of all subassembly departments that feed into an assembly section are normally scheduled centrally in order that the plant's manufacturing activities mesh together.

Centralized planning, if it is to be effective, imposes some rather severe information requirements. For one thing, the central planning group must have a "model" of each subunit. The model may be in explicit mathematical form, or it may be relatively informal and intuitive. The key requirement is that the planning group have some basis for predicting the consequences in each subsystem of alternative plans. The planners are thus in a position to select the plan that offers the most favorable overall result.

In addition to having a model of each subunit, the central planning group must also have information concerning the current status of the subunits. In scheduling production, for example, the status information includes the jobs to be scheduled, raw material inventory levels, and the number of employees available for work.

The degree of centralized coordination can vary greatly. At one end of the spectrum, coordination can be loose and infrequent. For example, the corporate production scheduling department may schedule each of several plants in terms of monthly increments for several aggregate product groups. At the other extreme, the coordination can be detailed and frequent -- as in a computer-based process control system. The more detailed and frequent the centralized coordination, the weaker the boundaries that separate coordinated subsystems.

Information requirements grow rapidly as coordination grows stronger. The model of each subunit must consider finer and finer detail. Computational requirements increase as coordination moves toward "real time" planning and control. All of this adds cost and complexity.

A less complete form of coordination is possible. Rather than having their activities directed centrally, subunits can plan their own activities. These independently derived plans can then be disseminated among all interacting subsystems. In some cases a subunit may choose to revise its plan on the basis of the announced intentions of other subunits. Through an iterative process of revisions, the organization might (under certain conditions) converge toward the globally optimum plan.

3. Trade-off between independence and integration

The balance between independence and integration is a fundamental characteristic of a system. Vital trade-offs are involved. The aim should be to implement that degree of integration that minimizes all of the costs affected by the choice.

A high degree of independence among subunits simplifies the task of managing each subunit, but it also has its disadvantages. Buffers can be expensive to maintain. Standardization can impose undesirable rigidities. Surplus resources reduce efficiencies. Duplication of functions reduces resource utilization and economies of scale. Ignoring interactions brings about penalties of suboptimization. All of these means for achieving greater independence thus have a cost.

Integration reduces these costs, but imposes penalties of its own. Coordination involves information processing in the form of data collection, transmission, storage, retrieval, transformation, and display. Systems for performing these processing functions can cost substantial amounts to design, implement, and operate. Delays induced by coordination may also have a cost. More important, perhaps, are the costs of the added complexity and risk involved in managing integrated systems. Not the least of these is the cost of attempting to centralize planning and control, but doing it badly because of insufficient capacity for processing information.

Advances in information technology can alter the optimum trade-off point between independence and integration. As these advances occur, it costs less to perform the information processing associated with coordination. Delays in communications and decision making can also drop significantly. More detailed and realistic decision models, tighter control limits, and more frequent replanning can reduce the penalties caused by poorly conceived centralized plans. If an advance in information technology reduces these costs of coordination (without also causing a corresponding reduction in the costs of independence), the optimum point shifts toward greater coordination and integration.

4. Integrated information systems

The term "integrated information system" has fallen into some disrepute. This is largely due, I believe, to misconceptions about the nature of integration. It is sometimes implied that an integrated system is developed as a unified single system and is thus "completely coordinated and completely consistent".* This is, of course, nonsense. No system is completely coordinated and consistent; it is a matter of degree. An integrated system is simply one in which there exists a relatively high degree of coordination and consistency. When viewed in this way, the concept of integration is a useful one.

Part of the confusion surrounding the issue of integrated information system is caused by the fact that there are really two different systems of concern. One system is the information system itself. The other is the organization it serves. In some discussions of integrated systems the primary focus is on the technical means of processing information. In other cases the focus is on the coordination of organizational activities by means of a (partially) centralized information system. Both aspects are important, but it is useful to draw a distinction between them as a way of gaining a clearer insight into the nature of integrated systems.

* John Dearden: MIS is a Mirage. Harvard Business Review, Jan-Feb 1972, p. 92.

5. Integration of information processing

An integrated information system processes information in a less fragmented way than a system having a relatively low degree of integration. The couplings among subsystems is closely coordinated and a high degree of resource sharing takes place.

These characteristics are manifested in several ways. In an integrated system, data of a given type enter at a single point and are then made available in machine-readable form to all other subsystems that require them. Sales data, for example, might enter the system through the order processing subsystem; they are then available for the forecasting, inventory control, and market analysis subsystems.

An integrated system tends to have a relatively consolidated data base. For example, all data pertaining to a given employee may be consolidated into a single personnel record, rather than existing in a series of fragmented files. The consolidated record is accessed by all programs that need personnel data (payroll, personnel selection, analysis of employee benefits, etc.).

Procedures also tend to be consolidated in an integrated system. A single program, for example, may process both the financial and physical aspects of inventory control, rather than splitting the tasks into separate programs (one probably under the control of the accounting department, the other under control of the logistics department).

An integrated information system tends to have a relatively high degree of resources sharing. The central processor, data base, communication network, generalized systems software, and application packages may all be shared among the organization's processing subsystems.

Integration of this sort offers a number of advantages. It reduces duplication, provides greater consistency throughout the system, and increases resource utilization. It comes at the price, however, of greater complexity and risk. As always, designers of the system should attempt to strike a suitable balance between integration and independence.

Advances in information technology favor a higher degree of integration. The development of powerful computer operating systems, generalized data base management systems, very large computers, and high performance auxiliary storage devices -- all lead toward more integration in a well-designed system that exploits available technology. We have certainly witnessed a clear trend toward such systems, although a great deal remains to be done.

6. Integration of organizational activities

The organization itself should be viewed as a system. Its integration is brought about by means of an information system that aids in the coordination of organizational activities.

Integration of this sort has been achieved in a number of different organizations. Manufacturing firms have been moving toward more integrated logistics systems, with centralized production scheduling and distribution, shared manufacturing facilities, and specialized plants that serve the entire organization. Transportation organizations -- the railroads, airlines, trucking, ocean-freight, and pipeline firms -- have clearly been moving toward more centralized management of operations. Banking, insurance, and other financial organizations have undergone similar changes. Virtually all types of organizations that have substantial coupling among subunits or sharing of common resources have moved toward greater integration.

Integration achieved through centralized planning requires a global data base and formal planning procedures. For example, a scheduling and distribution system for a firm having multiple plants and warehouses would require a data base containing costs and capacities at each location, a matrix of transportation costs, and similar data. It would require a linear programming model or some other formalized decision model to handle the large number of variables and complex relationships that exist in a nationwide logistics system.

The technical, economic, and operational feasibility of integrated planning depends heavily on the state of information technology. The maintenance of a centralized data base relies on advanced communications and data base management software. Sophisticated decision models depend on developments in operations research and the availability of large-scale computers that can economically provide vast computational capacity. Without the supporting technology, centralization is at best expensive and at worst imposes an unworkable, bureaucratic superstructure over the subunits whose activities are supposedly being coordinated.

It is useful, I think, to point out the relationship between integration of the information system and integration of the organization. The information system of an organization can be strongly integrated even though organizational activities are decentralized and uncoordinated. A loose conglomerate of autonomous divisions might, for example, share a common computer system. Each division treats the common computer as an information utility that provides a variety of hardware and software services. Decisions as to how the services are to be applied, and how the division plans and controls its activities, could be delegated completely to division management.

For reasons that have already been discussed, it is probably necessary to have a relatively high degree of integration of the information system before an organization should move toward an integration of organizational activities. Coordination requires the exchange of information among subunits -- one of the important marks of an integrated information system. Thus we can say that an integrated information system is a necessary, but not sufficient, condition for integration of the organization.

7. Distributed systems - the wave of the future

As we have seen, integration is justified to the extent that subsystems interact with one another through coupling or shared use of resources. If the subunits interact only weakly, there is little advantage, and much disadvantage, in a high degree of centralization.

The current interest in distributed computer systems recognizes the value of hybrid systems that contain elements of both centralization and decentralization. In a distributed system, local needs are served by a modest-sized minicomputer. Payroll calculations and detailed control of the production process, for example, might be handled by the local computer. Substantial economies can often be achieved by eliminating the need to transmit strictly local data to a central location. Furthermore, reduced complexity and economies of specialization can come from tailoring the minicomputer to the special needs of local plants.

In addition to meeting local computational needs, the minicomputer can also serve as a remote terminal to a central computer (or possibly one of several computers offering specialized services not available locally). The central computer can provide large-scale, generalized services that cannot be economically supported at each decentralized location. It can also handle coordination across locations. For this purpose it would generally need summarized data about each location. These data can be provided through the decentralized minicomputers which aggregate detailed local data to transform them into the summarized form needed by the central coordinating group.

A distributed system of this sort offers the advantages of both centralization and decentralization. Computing needs that can best be handled locally (because the trade-offs favor simplicity and economies of specialization) can be satisfied by the decentralized minicomputer. Computing needs that can best be handled by a large-scale computer (because the trade-offs favor generality and economies of scale) can be satisfied by a central computer serving all decentralized locations.

A distributed system offers similar advantages in dealing with organizational activities. Strictly local matters can be handled on a decentralized basis (often with the aid of the local minicomputer, but possibly also assisted by the central computer serving strictly as a source of large-scale computing power). Activities that interact relatively strongly with activities at other locations can be handled on a centralized basis. Thus we might find, for example, that marketing activities are handled largely on a decentralized basis, while logistics are handled on a centralized basis. There is nothing incompatible or inconsistent about this hybrid approach. On the contrary, it captures the advantages, and avoids many of the disadvantages, of both centralization and decentralization. I expect to be seeing many organizations moving strongly in this direction.

German abstract
Integration in Informationssystemen und ihre Auswirkung auf die Organisationsstruktur

Von *James C. Emery*

Ein System kann als Komplex von Aufgaben betrachtet werden, die untereinander abhängig und auf die Erreichung eines Zieles ausgerichtet sind. In diesem Sinne dient ein System dazu, durch geeignete Bildung von Subsystemen (-aufgaben) die Komplexität des Gesamtzieles auf eine geeignete Größenordnung zu reduzieren. Die Art der Subsystembildung, das Ausmaß ihrer Integration (Unabhängigkeit) und die Instrumente zu ihrer Koordination sind wesentliche Gestaltungsvariablen für den Manager.

Die Unabhängigkeit der Subsysteme läßt sich durch verschiedene Gestaltungsmaßnahmen beeinflussen:

(1) geeignete Wahl der systeminternen Struktur (Subsystemabgrenzung). Weitgehende Unabhängigkeit der Subsysteme läßt sich mittels Strukturfestlegung dadurch erreichen, daß Elemente mit enger Abhängigkeit jeweils in einem Subsystem zusammengefaßt werden; zwischen den Elementen unterschiedlicher Subsysteme sollen dagegen weniger intensive Abhängigkeiten bestehen. Die Abhängigkeiten zwischen den Systemelementen können auf Input-Output-Beziehungen oder auf der gemeinsamen Nutzung von bestimmten Ressourcen basieren. Sofern diese Beziehungen sich überlagern, entsteht für die Subsystemabgrenzung ein unlösbares Dilemma, da nur jeweils eine Abhängigkeit bei der Strukturfestlegung berücksichtigt werden kann.

(2) Entkopplung abhängiger Subsysteme. Als ergänzende Maßnahme zur Subsystemabgrenzung kann die Entkopplung in einem gewissen Spielraum die Abhängigkeit zwischen Elementen und Subsystemen aufheben. Typische Maßnahmen zur Entkopplung sind die Einrichtung von Zwischenlägern, die Normierung der Schnittstellen zwischen den Subsystemen und die Duplizierung gemeinsam genutzter Funktionen.

(3) Vernachlässigung wenig bedeutsamer Abhängigkeiten. Strukturbildung und Entkopplung können eine Fülle von Abhängigkeiten zwischen den Subsystemen nicht beseitigen. Eine wichtige komplexitätsreduzierende Maßnahme besteht darin, die weniger bedeutsamen dieser Abhängigkeiten bei der Planung der Aktivitäten der einzelnen Subsysteme einfach zu ignorieren.

Komplementär zur Aufhebung der Abhängigkeiten innerhalb des Systems durch die oben genannten Maßnahmen ist ihre bewußte Berücksichtigung durch Integration und Koordination der Subsysteme. Als Koordinationsmechanismen stehen unterschiedliche Formen der Planung im Vordergrund. Ein Extrem wäre dabei eine sehr häufige, verbindliche zentrale Planung; als Gegenpol könnte beispielsweise eine gelegentliche Kommunikation der dezentral erarbeiteten Pläne der einzelnen Subsysteme mit der Möglichkeit einer freiwilligen iterativen Anpassung sein.

Die richtige Entscheidung zwischen Unabhängigkeit und Integration hängt vor allem von den individuell damit verbundenen Kosten ab. Weitgehende Unabhängigkeit vereinfacht die Steuerung der einzelnen Subsysteme, damit entstehen jedoch die Kosten für die Dopplung bestimmter Funktionen, schlechtere Nutzung von Ressourcen und sonstige Folgen lokaler Suboptimierung. Hohe Integration vermeidet diese Kosten, führt jedoch zu Koordinationskosten für umfassende Informations- und Planungssysteme und vergrößert die Komplexität und das Überlebensrisiko des Gesamtsystems.

Die Überlegungen gelten sowohl für computergestützte Informationssysteme in Organisationen als auch für deren Planungs- und Steuerungssysteme. Bei den computergestützten Informationssystemen führt der technische Fortschritt in verschiedener Hinsicht zu verstärkter Integration. Weitgehend unabhängig von der Integration auf dieser Ebene ermöglicht die moderne Computertechnik in Verbindung mit Fortschritten im Bereich der Planungstechnologie und des Operations Research differenzierte Lösungen des Problems der Entscheidungszentralisierung in den Planungs- und Steuerungssystemen der Organisationen. Diese Lösungen werden weniger von Dogmen pro oder kontra Zentralisierung bestimmt sein, sondern den Abhängigkeiten zwischen den Systemelementen und Subsystemen Rechnung tragen und sich an den Koordinationsnotwendigkeiten und dem Effizienzpotential der Integration orientieren.

Information processing determinants of organization structure

By *Jay R. Galbraith*

1. Information processing model

The basic proposition is that the greater the uncertainty of the task, the greater the amount of information that has to be processed between decision makers during the execution of the task. If the task is well understood prior to performing it, much of the activity can be preplanned. If it is not understood, then during the actual task execution more knowledge is acquired which leads to changes in resource allocations, schedules, and priorities. All these changes require information processing during task performance. Therefore the greater the task uncertainty, the greater the amount of information that must be processed among decision makers during task execution in order to achieve a given level of performance. The basic effect of uncertainty is to limit the ability of the organization to preplan or to make decisions about activities in advance of their execution. Therefore it is hypothesized that the observed variations in organizational forms are variations in the strategies of organizations to 1) increase their ability to preplan, 2) increase their flexibility to adapt to their inability to preplan, or, 3) to decrease the level of performance required for continued viability. Which strategy is chosen depends on the relative costs of the strategies. The function of the framework is to identify these strategies and their costs.

2. Mechanistic model

The framework is best developed by keeping in mind a hypothetical organization. Assume it is large and employs a number of specialist groups and resources in providing the output. After the task has been divided into specialist subtasks, the problem is to integrate the subtasks around the completion of the global task. This is the problem of organization design. The behaviors that occur in one subtask cannot be judged as good or bad per se. The behaviors are more effective or ineffective depending upon the behaviors of the other subtask performers. There is a design problem because the executors of the behaviors cannot communicate with all the roles with whom they are interdependent. Therefore the design problem is create mechanisms that permit coordinated action across large numbers of interdependent roles. Each of these mechanisms, however, has a limited range over which it is effective at handling the information requirements necessary to coordinate the interdependent roles. As the amount of uncertainty increases, and therefore information processing increases, the organization must adopt integrating mechanisms which increase its information processing capabilities.

2.1 Coordination by rules or programs

For routine predictable tasks March and Simon have identified the use of rules or programs to coordinate behavior between interdependent subtasks [7, Chap. 6]. To the extent that job related situations can be predicted in advance, and behaviors specified for these situations, programs allow an interdependent set of activities to be performed without the need for inter-unit communication. Each role occupant simply executes the behavior which is appropriate for the task related situation with which he is faced.

2.2 Hierarchy

As the organization faces greater uncertainty its participants face situations for which they have no rules. At this point the hierarchy is employed on an exception basis. The recurring job situations are programmed with rules while infrequent situations are referred to that level in the hierarchy where a global perspective exists for all affected subunits. However, the hierarchy also has a limited range. As uncertainty increases the number of exceptions increases until the hierarchy becomes overloaded.

2.3 Coordination by targets or goals

As the uncertainty of the organization's task increases, coordination increasingly takes place by specifying outputs, goals or targets [7, p. 145]. Instead of specifying specific behaviors to be enacted, the organization undertakes processes to set goals to be achieved and the employees select the behaviors which lead to goal accomplishment. Planning reduces the amount of information processing in the hierarchy by increasing the amount of discretion exercised at lower levels. Like the use of rules, planning achieves integrated action and also eliminates the need for continuous communication among interdependent subunits as long as task performance stays within the planned task specifications, budget limits and within targeted completion dates. If it does not, the hierarchy is again employed on an exception basis.

The ability of an organization to coordinate interdependent tasks depends on its ability to compute meaningful subgoals to guide subunit action. When uncertainty increases because of introducing new products, entering new markets, or employing new technologies these subgoals are incorrect. The result is more exceptions, more information processing, and an overloaded hierarchy.

3. Design strategies

The ability of an organization to successfully utilize coordination by goal setting, hierarchy, and rules depends on the combination of the frequency of exceptions and the capacity of the hierarchy to handle them. As the task uncertainty increases the organization must again take organization design action. It can proceed in either of two general ways. First, it can act in two ways to reduce the amount of information that is processed. And second, the organization can act in two ways to increase its capacity to handle more information. The two methods for reducing the need for information and the two methods for increasing processing capacity are shown schematically in Figure 1. The effect of all these actions is to reduce the number of exceptional cases referred upward into the organization through hierarchical channels. The assumption is that the critical limiting factor of an organizational form is its ability to handle the non-routine, consequential events that cannot be anticipated and planned for in advance. The non-programmed events place the greatest communication load on the organization.

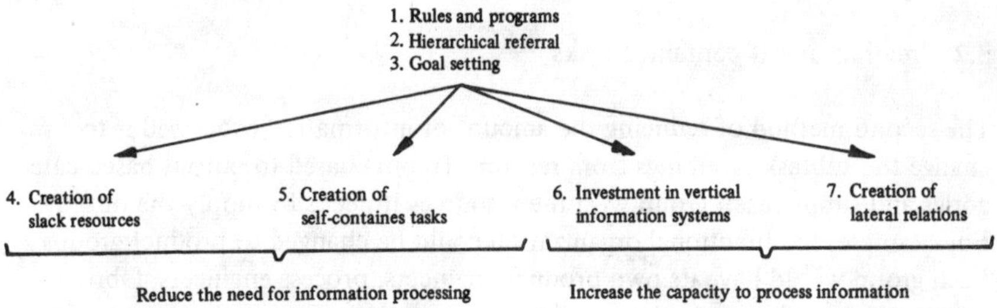

Figure 1. Organization design strategies

3.1 Creation of slack resources

As the number exceptions begin to overload the hierarchy, one response is to increase the planning targets so that fewer exceptions occur. For example, completion dates can be extended until the number of exceptions that occur are within the existing information processing capacity of the organization. This has been the practice in solving job shop scheduling problems [7]. Job shops quote delivery times that are long enough to keep the scheduling problem within the computational and information processing limits of the organization. Since every job shop has the same problem standard lead times evolve in the industry. Similarly budget targets could be raised, buffer inventories employed, etc. The greater the uncertainty, the greater the magnitude of the inventory lead time or budget needed to reduce an overload.

All of these examples have a similar effect. They represent the use of slack resources to reduce the amount of interdependence between subunits [7; 1]. This keeps the required amount of information within the capacity of the organization to process it. Information processing is reduced because an exception is less likely to occur and reduced interdependence means that fewer factors need to be considered simultaneously when an exception does occur.

The strategy of using slack resources has its costs. Relaxing budget targets has the obvious cost of requiring more budget. Increasing the time to completion date has the effect of delaying the customer. Inventories require the investment of capital funds which could be used elsewhere. Reduction of design optimization induces the performance of the article being designed. Whether slack resources are used to reduce information or not depends on the relative costs of the other alternatives.

The design choices are among which factors to change (lead time, overtime, machine utilization, etc.) to create the slack and by what amount should the factor be changed. Many operations research models are useful in choosing factors and amounts. The time-cost trade off problem in project networks is a good example.

3.2 Creation of self-contained tasks

The second method of reducing the amount of information processed is to change the subtask groupings from resource (input) based to output based categories and supply each group with the resources it needs to supply the output. For example, the functional organization could be changed to product groups. Each group would have its own product engineers, process engineers, fabricating and assembly operations, and marketing activities. In other situations, groups can be created around product lines, geographical areas, projects, client groups, markets, etc., each of which would contain the input resources necessary for creation of the output.

The strategy of self-containment shifts the basis of the authority structure from one based input, resource, skill or occupational categories to one based on output or geographical categories. The shift reduces the amount of information processing through several mechanisms. First, it reduces the amount of output diversity faced by a single collection of resources. For example, a professional organization with multiple skill specialities providing service to three different client groups, must schedule the use of these specialties across three demands for their services and determine priorities when conflicts occur. But, if the organization changed to three groups, one for each client category, each with its own full compliment of specialties, the schedule conflicts across client groups disappears and there is no need to process information to determine priorities.

The second source of information reduction occurs through a reduced division of labor. The functional or resource specialized structure pools the demand for skills across all output categories. In the example above each client generates approximately one-third of the demand for each skill. Since the division of labor is limited by the extent of the market, the division of labor must decrease as the demand decreases. In the professional organization, each client group may have generated a need for one-third of a computer programmer. The functional organization would have hired one programmer and shared him across the groups. In the self-contained structure there is insufficient demand in each group for a programmer so the professionals must do their own programming. Specialization is reduced but there is no problem of scheduling the programmer's time across the three possible uses for it.

The cost of the self-containment strategy is the loss of resource specialization. In the example, the organization foregoes the benefit of a specialist in computer programming. If there is physical equipment there is a loss of economies of scale. The professional organization would require three machines in the self-contained form but only one, large, time-shared machine in the functional form. But those resources which have large economies of scale or for which specialization is necessary may remain centralized. Thus it is the degree of self-containment that is the variable. The greater the degree of uncertainty, other things equal, the greater the degree of self-containment.

The design choices are the basis for the self-contained structure and the number of resources to be contained in the groups. No groups are completely self-contained or they would not be part of the same organization. But one product divisionalized firm may have 8 of 15 functions in the division while another may have 12 of 15 in the divisions. Usually accounting, finance, and legal services are centralized and shared. Those functions which have economies of scale, require specialization or are necessary for control remain centralized and not part of the self-contained group.

The first two strategies reduced the amount of information by lowering performance standards and creating small autonomous groups to provide the output. Information is reduced because an exception is less likely to occur and fewer factors need to be considered when an exception does occur. The next two strategies accept the performance standards and division of labor as given and adapt the organization so as to process the new information which is created during task performance.

4. Investment in vertical information systems

The organization can invest in mechanisms which allow it to process information acquired during task performance without overloading the hierarchical communication channels. The investment occurs according to the following logic. After the organization has created its plan or set of targets for inventories, labor utilization, budgets and schedules, unanticipated events occur which generate exceptions requiring adjustments to the original plan. At some point when the number of exceptions becomes substantial it is preferable to generate a new plan rather than make incremental changes with each exception. The issue is then how frequently should plans be revised - yearly, quarterly, or monthly? The greater the frequency of replanning the greater the resources, such as clerks, computer time, input-output devices, etc., required to process information about relevant factors.

The cost of information processing resources can be minimized if the language is formalized. Formalization of a decision-making language simply means that more information is transmitted with the same number of symbols. It is assumed that information processing resources are consumed in proportion to the number of symbols transmitted. The accounting system is an example of a formalized language.

Providing more information, more often, may simply overload the decision maker. Investment may be required to increase the capacity of the decision maker by employing computers, various man-machine combinations, assistants-to, etc. The cost of this strategy is the cost of the information processing resources consumed in transmitting and processing the data.

The design variables of this strategy are the decision frequency, the degree of formalization of language, and the type of decision mechanism which will make the choice. This strategy is usually operationalized by creating redundant information channels which transmit data from the point of origination upward in the hierarchy where the point of decision rests. If data is formalized and quantifiable this strategy is effective. If the relevant data are qualitative and ambiguous, then it may prove easier to bring the decisions down to where the information exists.

5. Creation of lateral relationships

The last strategy is to selectively employ joint decision processes which cut across lines of authority. This strategy moves the level of decision making down in the organization to where the information exists but does so without reorganizing around self-contained groups. There are several types of lateral decision processes. Some processes are usually referred to as the informal organization. However, these informal processes do not always arise spontaneously out of the needs of the task. This is particularly true in multi-national organizations in which participants are separated by physical barriers, language differences, and cultural differences. Under these circumstances lateral processes need to be designed. The lateral processes evolve as follows with increase in uncertainty.

5.1 Direct contact

Direct contact between managers who share a problem. If a problem arises on the shop floor, the foreman can simply call the design engineer and they can jointly agree upon a solution. From an information processing view the joint decision prevents an upward referral and unloads the hierarchy.

5.2 Liaison roles

Liaison roles when the volume of contacts between any two departments grows, it becomes economical to set up a specialized role to handle this communication. Liaison men are typical examples of specialized roles designed to facilitate communication between two interdependent departments and to bypass the long lines of communication involved in upward referral. Liaison roles arise at lower and middle levels of management.

5.3 Task forces

Task forces, direct contact and liaison roles, like the integration mechanisms before them, have a limited range of usefulness. They work when two managers or functions are involved. When problems arise involving seven or eight departments, the decision making capacity of direct contacts is exceeded. Then these problems must be referred upward. For uncertain, interdependent tasks such situations arise frequently. Task forces are a form of horizontal contact which is designed for problems of multiple departments.

The task force is made up of representatives from each of the affected departments. Some are full-time members others may bc part-time. The task force is a temporary group. It exists only as long as the problem remains. When a solution is reached each participant returns to his normal tasks.

To the extent that they are successful, task forces remove problems from higher levels of the hierarchy. The decisions are made at lower levels in the organization. In order to guarantee integration, a group problem solving approach is taken. Each affected subunit contributes a member and therefore provides the information necessary to judge the impact on all units.

5.4 Teams

The next extension is to incorporate the group decision process into the permanent decision processes. That is as certain decisions consistently arise, the task forces become permanent. These groups are labeled teams. There are many design issues concerned in team decision making such as at what level do they operate, who participates, etc. [4, Chap. 6 and 7]. One design decision is particularly critical. This is the choice of leadership. Sometimes a problem exists largely in one department so that the department manager is the leader. Sometimes the leadership passes from one manager to another. As a new product moves to the market place, the leader of the new product team is first the technical manager followed by the production and then the marketing manager. The result is that if the team cannot reach a consensus decision and the leader decides, the goals of the leader are consistent with the goals of the organization for the decision in question. But quite often obvious leaders cannot be found. Another mechanism must be introduced.

5.5 Integrating roles

The leadership issue is solved by creating a new role -- an integrating role [5, Chap. 3]. These roles carry the labels of product managers, program managers, project managers, unit managers (hospitals), materials managers, etc. After the role is created, the design problem is to create enough power in the role to influence the decision process. These roles have power even when no one reports directly to them. They have some power because they report to the general manager. But if they are selected so as to be unbiased with respect to the groups they integrate and to have technical competence, they have expert power. They collect information and equalize power differences due to preferential access to knowledge and information. The power equalization increases trust and the quality of the joint decision process. But power equalization occurs only if the integrating role is staffed with someone who can exercise expert power in the form persuasion and informal influences rather than exert the power of rank or authority.

5.6 Managerial linking roles

As tasks become more uncertain it is more difficult to exercise expert power. The role must get more power of the formal authority type in order to be effective at coordinating the joint decisions which occur at lower levels of the organization. This position power changes the nature of the role which for lack of a better name is labeled a managerial-linking role. It is not like the integrating role because it possesses formal position power but is different from line managerial roles in that participants do not report to the linking manager. The power is added by the following successive changes:

a) The integrator receives approval power of budgets formulated in the departments to be integrated.
b) The planning and budgeting process starts with the integrator making his initiation in budgeting legitimate.
c) Linking manager receives the budget for the area of responsibility and buys resources from the specialist groups.

These mechanisms permit the manager to exercise influence even though no one works directly for him. The role is concerned with integration but exercises power through the formal power of the position. If this power is insufficient to integrate the subtasks and creation of self-contained groups is not feasible there is one last step.

5.7 Matrix organization

The last step is create the dual authority relationship and the matrix organization [3]. At some point in the organization some roles have two superiors. The design issue is to select the locus of these roles. The purpose is to create a balance of power between the managerial linking roles and normal line organization roles.

6. Choice of strategy

Each of the four strategies has been briefly presented. The organization can follow one or some combination of several if it chooses. It will choose that strategy which has the least cost in its environmental context. (For an example, see [2]). However, what may be lost in all of the explanations is that the four strategies are hypothesized to be an exhaustive set of alternatives. That is, if the organization is faced with greater uncertainty, due to technological change, higher performance standards due to increased competition, or has diversified its product line to reduce dependence, the amount of information processing is increased. The organization must adopt at least one of the four strategies when faced with greater uncertainty. If it does not consciously choose one of the four, then the first, reduced performance standards, will happen automatically. The task information requirements and the capacity of the organization to process information are always matched. If the organization does not consciously match them, reduced performance through budget overruns, schedule overruns will occur in order to bring about equality. Thus the organization should be planned and designed simultaneously with the planning of the strategy and resource allocations. But if the strategy involves introducing new products, entering new markets, etc., then some provision for increased information must be made. Not to decide is to decide, and it is to decide upon slack resources as the strategy to remove hierarchical overload.

There is probably a fifth strategy which is not articulated here. Instead of changing the organization in response to task uncertainty, the organization can operate on its environment to reduce uncertainty. The organization through strategic decisions long term contracts, coalitions, etc., can control its environment. But these manoevers have costs also. They should be compared with costs of the four design strategies presented above.

References

[1] Cyert, Richard and James March: The Behavioral Theory of the Firm. Englewood Cliffs, N.J. 1963.

[2] Galbraith, Jay R.: Environmental and Technological Determinents of Organization Design: A Case Study. In: Lawrence and Lorsch (eds.): Studies in Organization Design. Homewood 1970.

[3] Galbraith, Jay R.: Designing Matrix Organizations. In: Business Horizons, Feb. 1971, pp. 29–40.

[4] Galbraith, Jay R.: Organization Design. Reading, Mass. 1973.

[5] Lawrence, Paul and Jay Lorsch: Organization and Environment. Harvard Business School, Boston, Mass. 1967.

[6] Lorsch, Jay and Paul Lawrence: "Environmental Factors and Organization Integration". Paper read at the Annual Meeting of the American Sociological Association. Boston, Mass. August 1968.

[7] March, James and Herbert Simon: Organizations. New York, N.Y. 1958.

[8] Pounds, William: The Scheduling Environment. In: Muth and Thompson (eds.): Industrial Scheduling. Englewood Cliffs, N.J. 1963.

[9] Simon, Herbert: Models of Man. New York, N.Y. 1957.

German abstract
Aspekte der Informationsverarbeitung bei der organisatorischen Gestaltung

Von *Jay R. Galbraith*

Ausgehend von der These Herbert Simons, daß die Möglichkeit zur Strukturierung organisatorischer Systeme durch das kognitive Leistungspotential des Menschen beschränkt werde, werden in diesem Beitrag die Ursachen für die Begrenzung aufgezeigt und analysiert. In den Vordergrund der Betrachtung wird der Einfluß der Unsicherheit der Aufgabenstellung auf die Vorgehensweise bei der organisatorischen Gestaltung gestellt. Hinsichtlich verschiedener Unsicherheitsgrade werden alternative Gestaltungsstrategien entwickelt und diskutiert. Ergebnis der Überlegungen ist ein Gestaltungsrahmen, der einen Ansatz zur Integration unterschiedlicher organisatorischer Gestaltungselemente bietet.

Managemententscheidungen sind nicht unbedingt isolierte individuelle Problemlösungsprozesse, die nur einen einzelnen Manager alleine betreffen. Oft handelt es sich um Entscheidungen über die Strukturierung der Aufgabenerfüllung, d.h. die von anderen zu erfüllenden Teilaufgaben werden in einer ganz bestimmten Weise aufeinander abgestimmt. Somit handelt es sich bei Managemententscheidungen zu einem großen Teil um Koordinationsentscheidungen.

Nach der Erläuterung mehrerer Koordinationsmechanismen (Regeln, Programme, Hierarchie, Ziele) diskutiert Galbraith vier Gestaltungsstrategien, die einzeln oder in Kombination angewendet werden können. Steigt z.B. die Aufgabenunsicherheit und somit die Nachfrage nach Informationen an, muß die Organisation handeln – dies kann auf zweifache Weise geschehen:

(1) Der Umfang der zu verarbeitenden Informationen kann reduziert werden.

(2) Die Fähigkeit, Informationen zu verarbeiten, kann vergrößert und verstärkt werden.

Für beide Alternativen werden jeweils zwei Wege aufgezeigt, ein Schaubild verdeutlicht den Zusammenhang.

Eine fünfte Strategie wird nur angedeutet – dabei wird nicht die Organisationsstruktur geändert, sondern statt dessen kann die Organisation versuchen, ihre Umwelt (den organisatorischen Kontext) zu beeinflussen und beispielsweise durch langfristige Kontrakte, Koalitionsbildung etc. den Unsicherheitsgrad zu reduzieren. Die Auswahl dieser Strategien hängt von deren relativen Kosten ab, und Galbraith weist darauf hin, daß bei einer Entscheidung für die zuletzt genannte Strategie ebenfalls Kosten entstehen, die den Kosten für die anderen vier Gestaltungsstrategien jeweils gegenübergestellt werden müssen.

The change in information flows by a Management Information Centre (MIC)

By *Helmut Garbe*

1. The initial situation

The structure of information flows in information systems in business organizations is generally the product of more or less systematic processes of organizational structuring. In the past the human agents concerned were easily able to comprehend this structure in its entirety and those concerned with the organizational processes of restructuring also had relatively good opportunities of acquiring the necessary insights at short notice if necessary. Coordination problems in these systems were comparatively easy to solve because the decentralization of the authority to structure meant that the organizational subsystems to be coordinated were very small. The persons concerned were sufficiently flexible to deal with the small number of interdepartmental tasks and the information flows that resulted from them. There is a comparable situation when electronic data processing (EDP) is employed to fulfil individual tasks. The structural changes in information flows within the organizational areas which may be thus brought about are adjusted on a decentralized basis, while human agents continue to be employed for those information flows resulting from interdepartmental tasks.
With the design of complex computerized systems the individual tasks of the various organizational subareas of the organization have to be coordinated with each other and with regard to numerous tasks that concern more than one particular area. The related structural changes in information flows mean that the greater the changes or the longer the EDP is employed the less the human sender (the supplier of data to the EDP) can know about the context where the information is used. A similar situation arises with the recipients of the information. For them the context whence the information originates becomes obscured and they are either not prepared to apply without reservation the information transmitted to them or they are not in a position to maintain the reservations that the matter requires. This development is particularly stimulated by the setting up of data banks in business enterprises, especially since with the data banks i.e. the relationships between sender and recipient which had previously been clearly recognizable are split up into two processes independent of each other in time, i.e. that of storing information and that of retrieving it.

The more the intelligibility of information flows is endangered or impaired, the more necessary it becomes to counter this development with organizational measures. It is above all important to restore the intelligibility reduced by the use of EDP, to coordinate the elements of the information system and constantly to bring them into line with current requirements.

2. The tasks of a Management Information Centre

One of the possible approaches to the solution of the problems mentioned above is to establish a special organizational unit, a Management Information Centre (MIC). Depending on the underlying concept, the MIC would have to carry out one or more of the following basic tasks:

- the operation of existing information flows,
- the disclosing of available information flows,
- the active influencing of existing information flows.

2.1 The operation of existing information flows

The setting up of an MIC can have as its aim the insertion of a primarily operative organizational unit into the handling of all information flows between human agents and the EDP, or between the EDP and the people who use it. In this role the MIC acts as a reception point for all information flows that have a human sender and EDP as recipient or it acts as a distribution point for all information flows with EDP as sender and a human recipient.

In this role the MIC is not responsible for information flows between two persons or between two computer systems or within one system. In addition the following three questions are not defined with the task:

1. whether the MIC carries out the process of collection and distribution passively within the framework of defined structures,
2. whether the MIC works actively within available structures,
3. whether the MIC can alter the structures and processes of the existing information flows.

2.2 The disclosing of existing information flows

The task of an MIC can also be to reveal the existing information flows in an enterprise. This assignment contains three organizational areas. Firstly, the current situation of the existing information flows has to be described and documented. In addition, the changes in information flows have to be noted and the existing documentation modified correspondingly. Finally, the MIC acting on requests from other people in the enterprise, has first of all to check their authority and subsequently to put at their disposal the required amount of documentation.

This assignment for an MIC assumes that not only that part of the information system already carried out by EDP is documented but also the human areas, comprising all periodically recurrent information flows or those contingent on events. There is no limitation of the task to those information flows on an operative, dispositive or strategic level.

2.3 The active influencing of existing information flows

When an MIC is assigned the task of actively influencing the existing information system, there are two subtasks involved: the identification of information flows in need of change and the carrying out of the changes. The identifying of possible changes assumes on the one hand an appropriate familiarity with the current situation. On the other hand, guide-lines are necessary which can be used to evaluate the need for changes. In addition to this task of identifying areas of potential improvement, the MIC has to accept and consider suggestions for redesign from other organizational units. The actual carrying out of the changes includes essentially all measures to change the structure of process of an existing information flow or to set up an additional information flow.

If such a task of active influencing is assigned to an MIC, the first job is to determine in which form the MIC receives the necessary data. Furthermore, the guide-lines for changes have to be established and finally the interdependencies have to be fixed between the MIC and the organizational units responsible up till then (and in the future) for the design of the organization.

3. The consequences of an MIC for the information flows of an information system

Establishing an MIC will have a number of different consequences for the information flows of an information system, depending on which of the basic tasks outlined above or which combination of them is assigned to the MIC.

3.1 The changes in information flows through the transfer of operation tasks to the MIC

If the MIC is given the task of handling the information flows, i.e. if it is to take an active part in the communication between sender (EDP or person) and recipient (EDP or person), then the two cases of the permanent or periodic information flows and the stochastic information flows must be contrasted with each other for an analysis of the changes.

3.1.1 The transfer of permanent communication processes to the MIC

If an MIC is included in permanent communication processes, only those information flows are affected which previously existed between the individual specialist departments and the EDP. In these cases the MIC is given collection and distribution tasks which had previously been the job of other organizational units, e.g. the receiver point of the computer centre. As a result of the involvement of the MIC there is either a shift of the given information flows or - as should be very much expected - the information flows have to go through one extra processing stage. This situation comes about when the MIC has a collector and distributor function but the transfer to and from the computer centre continues to be carried out through the corresponding department in the computer centre. In neither case are there any further structural consequences for the information flows.

The involvement of the MIC in the permanent communication processes can, apart from the transfer of collection and distribution duties, also be primarily aimed at a centralization of information flows. This could be the case where a summarizing of the information flows to the EDP is necessary (the integration of several capturing processes) or where there is a condensing of the information flows that proceed from the EDP to various users (printed output, centrally controlled enquiry media, central reporting, documentation office). The related changes in the information structure are, however, not typical of the establishment of an MIC but are solely determined by the concept underlying the condensing.

Apart from structural changes, the establishment of an MIC can cause changes in the processes of information flows, possible in such a way that the content of the information flows is changed or quantitative or temporal changes result. However, a closer analysis of these process changes shows that - apart from possible delays where there is an additional processing station - they are not caused by the assignment of a reacting collector and distributor function to the MIC.

If the duties of an MIC are broadened to include the tasks of checking the completeness, accuracy and meaningfulness of information flows, it becomes particularly clear that the transfer of permanent operating tasks to the MIC is primarily a problem of terminology i.e. the naming of those agents entrusted previously or in the future with these reacting collector and distributor tasks.

3.1.2 The transfer of stochastic communication processes to the MIC

Apart from periodic or permanent information flows the information system of an enterprise contains numerous aperiodic or unique information flows caused by events. These stochastic information flows are first caused by an event in the form either of a state in the EDP or of an enquiry from a person addressed to the system. Organizational difficulties are caused by enquiries since here - according to the situation - sometimes considerable effort is needed to translate the enquiry. The greater the demands made by the programming language or the higher the position of the enquirer in the hierarchy, the sooner it becomes necessary to call in a special unit to operate the necessary process of interaction with the EDP. If an MIC is established in these cases the resulting changes in the structure and content of information flows correspond to the changes in the case of permanent operating duties.

If the enquiry to the EDP is precisely formulated or if the event takes the form of a state in the data base, then - according to the situation - either exclusively emission and delivery processes are required or additional processing and preparation processes. These stochastic processes, however, are only affected by the establishment of an MIC insofar as the results need interpreting and the MIC undertakes this task. It can be concluded from these observations that the transfer of communication processes to an MIC as a result of stochastic information flows will not (or in the case of the interpretation of enquiry and result only marginally) change the structure and operation of information flows any more than to the extent described for permanent processes.

3.2 The changes in information flows through the disclosing of the existing information system

The disclosing of structural and procedural aspects of the existing information system is a very important basic task of the MIC. As conceived in this interpretation of the duties of an MIC it is an additional service function within the organization created to cope with the complexity of the computerized information system. One of the goals of this service function would be to improve the ability and readiness to offer and to supply additional information on the basis of the existing information system. There will be varying consequences for the information flows as a whole, corresponding to the subtasks of a disclosing of the information system.

3.2.1 The description of the current information system

The first step in the description of the information system is to measure and assess a number of qualitative or quantitative aspects. In order to generate these data, special information flows have to be set up. These may either be established for a single occasion or may be activated recurrently in connection with changes in the basic information system which is being described. These information flows differ markedly from the basic information flows which they describe; this difference has to be taken into consideration in a discussion of changes in information flows caused by the establishment of an MIC.

3.2.2 The information system documentation

Once the most important current aspects of the information system have been determined it is necessary to compile the whole of the system-descriptive features in one unified data base, to make an evaluation of them possible according to various characteristics and if necessary to bring them up to date. No direct change in existing information flows will come about as a result of this subtask of the disclosing of the information system, as long as the MIC carries out the information system documentation manually. On the other hand, if the system documentation is stored in EDP then there is first a corresponding information flow between MIC and EDP (or the computer centre). From the point of view of the computer centre this information flow is of the same character as the information flows from various specialist departments to the EDP. From the point of view of the MIC, however, it is of an entirely different character from the other infoımation flows between EDP and MIC, since with the latter the MIC functions only as collector and distributor but not as user. Essentially, however, the only conclusion that can be drawn from this distinction is to supervise the MIC.

3.2.3 The availability of the documentation to authorized persons

A feature of the third and very important subtask in disclosing the information system for those authorized is that authorized persons in the enterprise can obtain insights into certain selected parts of the data base. As a result this secondary task produces additional information flows between the authorized user and the MIC and these are, on the one hand of a primarily enquiry-character and on the other of a primarily system-descriptive character. These information flows are directed predominantly at assisting the expression of needs by the user and the statement of offers on the basis of the current situation. They have no direct effects beyond this on the structure and course of all available information flows.

3.3 The changes in information flows through the inclusion of the MIC in the structuring process

Every information system has to be continually adapted to the changing configurations within and without the enterprise. Amongst other things, this includes the identifying of opportunities for alterations or the need for alterations and activities for actually carrying out the alterations necessary. Seen in this light, an MIC stresses the importance of a task already being carried out before the establishing of an MIC. In this interpretation of the tasks of an MIC attention must be paid on the one hand to the extremely close dependencies in content between the basic tasks of an MIC, and, on the other, to the close interdependencies between the tasks of an MIC and certain aspects of the task of organization.

3.3.1 Creating a general strategy of the development of a management information system

In the past the development of many information systems was marked by short-term considerations in order to take account of such things as information bottle-necks, technical development in the hardware area etc. In contrast, the establishment of an MIC is often related to the enterprise's policy of supplementing short-term aims by evolving or developing further a general long-term strategy for shaping the information system. This long-term strategy can serve as a guide-line for all future changes in the information system. The primary interest here is not in the question who is authorized to work out the general strategy (MIC, computer centre, organization department, top management). The criteria which determine the general strategy which has to be worked out and which sets the targets and also the consequences for the existing information flows are all of much greater importance.

As a result of a general strategy based upon the user's attitude towards information, a knowledge of the supply available increases the ability and readiness of users to express their requirements. Correspondingly, there is a sharp increase in information flows directed at disclosing the information system and this indirectly leads to a subsequently high rate of change in the current system. In contrast to this, a strategy which primarily aims at simplifying the data used in the enterprise (fields, sets, files) or at creating an overall plan of the information supply results in a low rate of change and a decrease in the number of existing information flows.

3.3.2 Influencing initiatives for change

Practical experience shows that existing information systems are only subject to change when this is initiated by persons or equipment. A distinction must be made between two cases. The initiative for change can first proceed from the individual who acts as sender, supplying other individuals or EDP with information, or it can proceed from the recipient. In this situation the initiative of the sender or user is generally directly related to his own information flows or to his own tasks. Thus, it can come about that while the structure of the information flows remains unchanged, additional information is required, supplementary information flows are needed or stored information is more frequently requested. Leaving aside other factors such as people's false conceptions of their own tasks, misplaced prestige thinking or inadequate regard for economy, this means that the user's initiative articulated that structure of information flows or those process features which from the user's point of view are most relevant to the current system.

Thus it has become clear that there can be a positive correlation between the creative determining of needs and the corresponding initiative for change.

The greater the user-orientated initiative, the more differentiated the information structure will probably become. The reason for this is, amongst other things, the tendency of the user only to take the initiative when extensions of the information system are desired.

The initiative for change, however, can also proceed from a person who is an element in the information system but does not act as a user or sender. Such cases of initiatives independent of users can come about when certain transmitting or processing points or other departments (organization department, computer centre, MIC) indicate the need or opportunity for change. These initiatives are concerned with changing aspects of the processes of existing information flows, removing demonstrably superfluous information flows or summarizing several information flows together. Thus the primary tendency of such user-independent initiatives is to make improvements in the structure or processes of the existing information system. In other words, the changes help to reduce the demands made on existing capacities.

In both cases a striking feature of the initiatives is the self-interest of the initiators and consequently this can lead to conflicts between those concerned.

The establishment of an MIC neutralizes this effect produced by the initiative. There is no longer a direct confrontation between the specialist interests of the users and the operating interests of the computer centre. The MIC can act as a balancing agent or in its turn - from the point of view of the information system as a whole - can itself take the initiative. These initiatives could be directed against the "hoarding" of information by certain persons or be aimed at a user-orientated expansion of supply based on the outlines of information needs.

3.3.3 Assessing possibilities for change

In the past the initiatives for a change in an existing information system often led to a solution being worked out for the particular situation to be changed and this solution then remained the basis for the restructuring. To the extent that the volume of initiatives for change rises, it becomes increasingly necessary to assess the content of these initiatives and to manage their realization or modification. A distinction must be made here between two separate cases. In the first place the initiative can point to a change which is regarded as an alternative to the existing situation. In contrast, two proposed solutions diverging in content may both present themselves as possible alternatives, i.e. both are suited to achieving a necessary change or improvement.

The necessary assessment of opportunities or necessities for change in these cases can first of all be carried out by the MIC on the basis of the existing documentation of the existing information system. According to the situation, the alternatives that will then be preferred are those that lead to simplifying the structure or the operation of information flows or those alternatives with consequences that can be combined particularly well with the existing information flows. If a general strategy on the development of the information system obtains, then the MIC will have to align the alternatives supplementarily or primarily with the details of the long-term aims set. In this case the effects on the structure of the information flows will directly correlate with the aims set.

The initiatives for change, however, can also be judged on the basis of user interests. In this case the user would be encouraged - using extracts of the existing information system made available to him and giving the cost functions or calculation structures - to consider his assessment of the uses of an alternative. In the long-term this would benefit the articulation of user-dependent utility functions. This development can have consequences at very many levels of the structure and content of the information flows but these consequences will not correlate primarily with the establishment of the MIC but with the disclosing of the documentation and its use.

Finally, other factors have to be considered in the assessment of initiatives for change - such as questions of organizational expediency, admissibility legally or within the enterprise, or consistency with the policy of the enterprise.

3.3.4 Realizing of permitted alterations

Two distinct situations can be contrasted with the realizing of any alternative selected; firstly the carrying out of the alteration in the actual information system and secondly the entering of this in the documentation.

First of all, during the carrying out of the alteration many situations can arise in which the MIC, by virtue of its knowledge of the actual information system, is able to effect the realization without involving other units. This would be the case with the creation of an additional information flow (an addition to the recipients of reports), with user-induced changes in the frequency and form of information flows, or with additions to or reductions in their content. Consequently, greater flexibility towards alterations is a feature of these situations since after a corresponding expression of need to the MIC the necessary changes in need can be directly dealt with. This welcome flexibility can only be produced through an organizational unit which has tasks outlined for the MIC.

In contrast, changes in the structure and content of information flows cannot be realized in this form when the structure of a defined processing task has to be changed and the concept for the new solution has first of all to be worked out. Neither are they possible when additional information processing tasks have to be included in the information system. These cases require the involvement of other units, particularly the specialist departments involved and the organization department. Since the MIC is included in this structuring process, there arises simultaneously with the setting up of an MIC the need for corresponding communication processes of a co-structuring nature to be provided for or established. On the other hand, in these cases the changes in the structure and content of information flows caused by the establishing of an MIC will not exceed the extent already discussed.

If changes in the state of the information system have been completed or if they are imminent, then the corresponding system-descriptive features have to be captured and included in the documentation. The consequent information flows to the EDP or MIC have already been discussed under the disclosing of the information system as the task of the MIC.

4. The organizational significance of the MIC

As can be concluded from its actual tasks in individual cases the MIC, as an additional unit, can become to varying degrees an instrument for influencing the existing information system. If the MIC is exclusively employed to operate information flows already documented, hardly any positive results will accrue from what would primarily be a change in terminology in the description of certain tasks. Assigning the task of disclosing the existing information flows to the MIC will admittedly have extremely meaningful results but will not mean any direct improvements in the information system, only indirect improvements acting in conjunction with other measures. Many benefits will be derived from involving the MIC in the processes of the permanent further development of the information system, particularly in conjunction with a development strategy and an emphasis on initiatives for change. Yet it is only a combination of the tasks of an MIC which can supply benefits which justify support for the setting up of an MIC.

The establishing of an MIC and the relation of the assignments discussed will - apart from the effects on the system of information flows - make the following four communication paths necessary:

- The communication processes between the specialist departments and the MIC serve - apart from the active or reacting operation of existing information flows - to influence the user in the way he seeks and uses information. This encourages more precise formulation of the need for information and/or information supply and leads in the long run to a rationalization of the information system. It will also bring about greater understanding on the part of the user for the formalities and an improvement in the tasks fulfilled by the users.

- The communication processes between the computer centre and the MIC are firstly directed at the operating of existing information flows and, if necessary, the bringing up to date and use of the documentation. In addition, the computer centre is sent directives, suggestions and requests about realizable alterations in the information system. In this way the computer centre is relieved of the cooperation with users and enabled to meet more efficiently the information need caused by events.

- The communication processes between the organization department and the MIC have as their goal assistance with organizational structuring processes. This is achieved by making available all the required integral features of the system by assessing organizational alternatives and by passing on (interpreting) or formulating initiatives from inside or outside.

- The communication processes between the business management and the MIC are aimed - apart from merely operating existing information flows to the management - firstly at interpreting or expressing the general strategy for the development of the management information system. In addition, they are necessary in order to show or to bring up to date the framework of the MIC's activities and to allow supervision to be maintained over all the activities of the MIC.

It can be deduced from these communication processes in their entirety that the stronger the organizational position of the MIC is, the greater will be the direct and more especially the indirect effects its activities will have on the structure and content of information flows. The exemplary effect of the establishing of this unit must be safeguarded by an adequate hierarchical solution. Only a central MIC, acting independently and occupying an influential place in the hierarchy can fulfill the demands connected with the desire to develop and use active management information systems.

References

[1] Brommer, R.: Das Informationsverhalten bei der Nutzung eines Informationszentrums. In: Struktur und Steuerung der Unternehmung bei automatisierter Datenverarbeitung. 6. BIFOA-Fachtagung, 12.–13. April 1972, Köln, part 2, ed. by Erwin Grochla and Norbert Szyperski. Köln 1973.

[2] Garbe, Helmut: Die Steuerung von Informationsbedarf und Informationsangebot – Instrumente und Konsequenzen. In: Struktur und Steuerung der Unternehmung bei automatisierter Datenverarbeitung. 6. BIFOA-Fachtagung, 12.–13. April 1972, Köln, part 2, ed. by Erwin Grochla and Norbert Szyperski. Köln 1973.

[3] Garbe, Helmut: Aufgaben der Systemdiagnose zur Beurteilung bestehender Informationssysteme. In: Angewandte Informatik, Vol. 16 1974, No. 4, pp. 159–164.

[4] Grochla, Erwin, Helmut Garbe and Reinhard Gillner: Gestaltungskriterien für den Aufbau von Datenbanken. Opladen 1973.

[5] Hum, G.: Neue Denkansätze für die Organisationsplanung zentraler Funktionseinheiten der Information und Kommunikation. In: ZfD, Zeitschrift für Datenverarbeitung, Vol. 10 1972, No. 7 October, pp. 550–553.

[6] Innerhofer-Innhof, Harald: Das Management Informationszentrum als Bindeglied zwischen Computer und Manager. In: Struktur und Steuerung der Unternehmung bei automatisierter Datenverarbeitung. 6. BIFOA-Fachtagung, 12.–13. April 1972, Köln, part 2, ed. by Erwin Grochla and Norbert Szyperski. Köln 1973.

[7] Koreimann, Dieter S.: Aufgaben und Organisation einer betrieblichen Informationsstelle. In: BFuP, Betriebswirtschaftliche Forschung und Praxis, Vol. 15 1963, p. 160.

[8] Meltzer, M.F.: The Information Center. Managements's Hidden Asset. American Management Association 1967.

[9] Roller, Peter: Organisatorische Aspekte des Informations-Management als Aufgabe in Organisationsforschung und -praxis. In: Struktur und Steuerung der Unternehmung bei automatisierter Datenverarbeitung. 6. BIFOA-Fachtagung, 12.–13. April 1972, Köln, part 2, ed. by Erwin Grochla and Norbert Szyperski. Köln 1973.

[10] Weigand, K.H.: Informations-Operator (Infop) – Skizze eines neuen Berufsbildes. In: Struktur und Steuerung der Unternehmung bei automatisierter Datenverarbeitung. 6. BIFOA-Fachtagung, 12.–13. April 1972, Köln, part 2, ed. by Erwin Grochla and Norbert Szyperski. Köln 1973.

[11] Will, H.J.: Datenbank-Systeme. In: ZfB, Zeitschrift für Betriebswirtschaftslehre, Vol. 41 1971, No. 12, p. 815–844.

German abstract
Die Veränderung der Informationsflüsse durch ein Management-Informationszentrum

Von *Helmut Garbe*

Solange betriebliche Informationssysteme primär Personen als Aktionsträger enthalten, ist die Struktur der Informationssysteme hinsichtlich der Sender-Empfänger-Relation aller Informationsflüsse mit ihren qualitativen, quantitativen und temporären Aspekten relativ gut überschaubar. Diese Situation ändert sich durch den Einsatz der ADVA zur Erfüllung einfacher oder komplexer Einzelaufgaben nur wenig. Mit der Gestaltung komplexer Anwendungssysteme, insbesondere in Fällen einer (bzw. mehrerer) Datenbank(en) werden jedoch Informationsflüsse erforderlich, bei denen der jeweils personelle Sender (bzw. Empfänger) immer weniger Kenntnis über den Verwendungskontext (bzw. Entstehungskontext) der Information besitzt. Ursachen hierfür sind u.a. die Vernachlässigung wichtiger Aspekte der Sender- bzw. Empfängerrelationen bei ADVA und die durch Speichermedien ausgelöste Aufspaltung der Sender-Empfänger-Relation in Einspeichern und Abrufen des Speicherinhalts.

Zur Sicherstellung dieses aus organisatorischen Gründen notwendigen Wissens über das bestehende Informationssystem (bzw. zu dessen Wiederherstellung) ist eine organisatorische Gliederungseinheit erforderlich, das Management-Informationszentrum (MIZ). Die Hauptaufgaben dieser Einheit liegen in

- der Abwicklung bestehender Informationsflüsse[1] zwischen den personellen Sendern (bzw. Empfängern) und der ADVA,
- der Offenlegung bestehender Informationsflüsse für alle berechtigt interessierten Personen und
- der Vorbereitung und Durchführung von Veränderungen des Informationssystems.

Ein derartiges Management-Informationszentrum kann auf der Basis seiner Teilaufgaben analysiert werden. Dabei ist festzustellen, ob und welche Konsequenzen sich hinsichtlich der Struktur des Informationssystems ergeben können.

1. Aus der Aufgabenstellung der Abwicklung bestehender Informationsflüsse zwischen der ADVA (als Sender und Empfänger) und den personellen Benutzern resultiert eine Verlängerung dieser Informationsflüsse um eine Aktionsstufe. Daraus ergeben sich keine weiteren Konsequenzen auf die Struktur des Informationssystems und keine inhaltlichen Veränderungen der Informationsflüsse.

---

1 Diese Auffassung ist nicht unbestritten, ist doch ein Teil des Kommunikationsverkehrs aus verschiedenen Gründen kaum mit dem Konzept einer derartigen Abwicklungsstelle vereinbar.

2. Die Offenlegung der Struktur des bestehenden Informationssystems mit allen strukturellen und prozessualen Aspekten als rein administratives Eruieren, Dokumentieren und Aktualisieren der Sachverhalte induziert keine Veränderungen der Informationsstruktur.
3. Bei der Vorbereitung und Durchführung von Veränderungen des Informationssystems lassen sich mehrere, in den Konsequenzen unterschiedliche Fälle gegenüberstellen. Einmal können die Veränderungen bestehende Informationsflüsse strukturell oder prozessual so beeinflussen, daß der personelle Benutzer (als Sender und/oder als Empfänger) nicht davon betroffen wird (benutzerneutrale Veränderungen). Zum anderen können Informationsflüsse verändert werden, weil die Sender ihr Informationsangebot und/oder die Empfänger ihren Informationsbedarf strukturell bzw. prozessual abwandeln (benutzerbedingte Veränderungen).

Zielsetzung dieses Beitrages ist nun zunächst, die verschiedenen Aktivitätstypen eines MIZ zu diskutieren. Darauf aufbauend sollen die Möglichkeiten erarbeitet werden, um durch organisatorische Richtlinien für die Aktivitäten eines MIZ erwünschte (unerwünschte) Wirkungen auf das vorhandene Informationssystem zu initiieren bzw. zu verstärken (zu behindern bzw. auszuschließen). Lassen sich derartige Möglichkeiten nachweisen und werden sie in späteren Untersuchungen in der Praxis bestätigt, dann bildet das MIZ den Mittelpunkt für die Gestaltung zukünftiger bzw. für die Umgestaltung bestehender Informationssysteme.

The impact of computer technology on organizational power structures

By *Bo Hedberg, Anders Edström, Wolfgang Müller* and *Bernhard Wilpert*

1. Background

The development of computer technology has aroused intense speculation about its potential impact on jobs, managers and organizational structures. The diversity of opinions among organization theorists regarding the likely effects of computer technology is well known. In addition, different empirical studies seem to show conflicting results. Whisler [19], for example, shows in his study of insurance companies that computerization leads to an increased centralization of control. Klatzky [10], however, finds in a study of a government organization that the implementation of computer systems leads to increased decentralization of decision-making and hence control. At present, we do not have a theory to resolve such contradictions, which may depend on differences in concepts, measurements, organizational tasks or environmental conditions. Much more empirical research in different organizational contexts is needed to resolve such paradoxes.

The implementation of computer technology has multiple effects. It therefore seems prudent to confine a study of computer impacts to one or a few areas that appear to be of critical importance. The exercise of power or control in organizations undoubtedly qualifies as an important area for such studies.

It is increasingly clear that power or control in organizations is emerging as a central issue in modern organization theory. One reason is that certain environmental changes, such as changes in the labor market and in manpower qualifications, give greater weight to the increased societal emphasis on power equalization and democratization in industry and public administration. Effects of environmental forces on organizational structure and behavior are thus once more placed into the center of theorizing, this time with a perspective on the implications for distributing organizational power. – A changing self-concept of the work force accompanies this general trend towards democratization. It is marked by efforts to improve the quality of working life with the ultimate objective to increase opportunities for better self-fulfillment. Therefore, satisfaction and the differential degrees of alienation as a consequence of different organizational governance structures remain an important challenge for organization theory and research. – And finally, the relationships of structure and technology have always been a central set of issues for organization theory. Computer technology and organizational structure constitute a special case of this general class of issues. It is in connection with the demands for power equalization that this case acquires a new and exciting quality. – It follows that the concept of organizational power, tightly linked up with the problems of organizational governance, epitomizes a large variety of theoretically and practically very important problems.

Organizations seem to need a certain amount of centralization of control: that is, some individuals will always have more control than others. Von Bertalanffy [2], for instance, argues that this is a universal principle of systems. An interesting question is then, of course, to what degree power or control can and will be decentralized under different technological and environmental conditions. It is the purpose of our present research to throw some light on this question. More specifically, however, we intend to study how the introduction of computer systems will affect the distribution of power among organizational members engaged in a common task. Such changes in power will be manifested in the decision-making process, particularly in the resolution of conflict. We feel that research in this area has both great social relevance and considerable theoretical interest. The purpose of the present paper is to present a conceptual framework for the study of impacts of computer technology on organizational power structures and to discuss its operationalization and use in empirical research.

2. Definition of major concepts

2.1 Computer technology and related concepts

Basic to any discussion of computer technology and its impacts is the concept of an information processing system (IPS). An IPS is a system for collecting, storing, processing and distributing information in order to facilitate or perform a decision-making or operative task [13, 14]. In principle, an IPS can be either a machine or a human being. We will be interested particularly in IPS which decision-makers use to support decision-making, which means according to the definition of IPS as support to their own IPS. Thus, computer technology has allowed organizations to develop information processing systems with new characteristics.

Computer technology we have taken to mean the concepts by which hardware and software elements are combined to achieve certain objectives. Computer technology is realized or implemented in a workable computer system. The process of developing a computer system is called system development.

System development can in turn be divided into three phases.

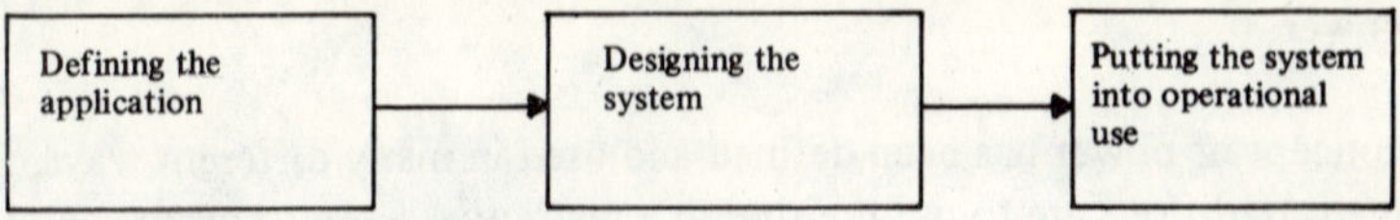

Fig. 1. The system development process

Defining the application refers to the initiation of the project and the determination of the goals, scope and information support of the system. The scope refers to the organizational functions and tasks which are effected by the system. Information support indicates what support the manager gets from the system.

If we break down the managerial decision-making process into the three common phases – intelligence, design and choice [16] – we find that a computerized system can give support in any one of these phases.

In the intelligence phase, the manager receives reports about the states of the world and his own performance which may indicate to him that an action is needed. In exception reports the triggering of new actions is particularly emphasized. We will call the information about the state of the world data support. In the design phase, in which the search for and development of alternatives for action occurs, it can be beneficial to use various kinds of decision models. A simulation model, for instance, allows one to test different assumptions about external factors and also the impacts of different decision alternatives. In the choice phase, in which the action to take is selected, information support can be through a normative model, which directly indicates to the decision-maker the best alternative according to a specific criterion. We will distinguish between data support and models as the two main categories of information support.

The initial phase of the system development process is usually carried out in a feasibility study in which the major characteristics of the new system are determined. During this phase organization members can potentially influence the outcome with respect to the future structure and performance of the IPS [7]. The design of the system constitutes the more detailed system analysis, i. e. programming, procedures design etc. The effect of influence on this phase will vary by system. If the information support includes models, influence will be quite important in shaping the output. Otherwise influence on this phase may result just in minor modifications of the system. Still, participation in the design phase will provide a more detailed knowledge about its functioning.

Putting the system into operational use refers to the conversion from a previous system to the new system. Influence during the last phase is mostly related to timing, speed of conversion, parallel operation etc. Its impact is largely limited to operational procedures.

2.2 Power

The concept of power has been defined and used in many different ways. The two main traditions are to use it either in a restrictive sense to mean coercion [18], or in a broad sense meaning the capacity to influence the behavior of others [5]. We will use power in the more restrictive sense to mean the ability against opposition to get one's way in an organization [1], either directly through one's own actions or indirectly through others. By preferring the narrower definition of power we want to forego a study of power phenomena in all possible situations: the decision implies that for our purposes power be studied only in the context of conflictual decisions. In that sense we use "power in conflict situations" as a selection criterion for decisions to be studied. The actual measures of power, however may very well cover also the broader definitions. In fact, it seems desirable to also investigate the inter-relationship of various power measures within specific conflict situations.

We find it interesting to observe conflict situation in at least two respects. First, situations in which the potential for conflict is large, such a resource allocation processes (e. g. budgeting R & D), and which are of great organizational significance in the generation of change. Secondly, situations in which computer systems will change the organization's reaction to conflict from one of bargaining to one of analytical problem-solving [11]. This result would depend on the possibility to reduce perceptual and goal differences through, for instance, the introduction of an overall planning model.

Power will always be related to a specific decision-making situation and the corresponding decision-making process. We can look at power in relation to the outcome of the process, to the process itself or to the definition of the decision-making situation. In the first case, the power of a decision-maker becomes evident if the outcome of the joint decision-making task corresponds to his own preferences. In the second, his power, as observed directly or perceived by others, will be apparent in his influence on the decision-making process itself. Finally, power can be exerted in the formulation of the problem itself, as we see summed up in the old saying, "I don't care who chooses the optimization criterion as long as I can choose the constraints".

2.3 Interaction between structure and process

By the structure of an organization we mean its stable characteristics; for instance, its particular set of social units and the relationships between these units. Within the structure we can observe processes as an ongoing flow of activities. There is a constant interaction between process and structure. The structure can be seen as a mold or a set of constraints for the processes [6]. Processes in turn may lead

to conflicts which may be resolved by a revision of the structure. Some structural characteristics, such as authority relationships, are formalized and explicit. But other of the informal structure can only be studied through the observation of processes or by interviewing involved members of the organization.
In our case, we see system development as a process of planned organizational change which will modify the existing structure. According to the considerations above, this process is going on within a structure and is hence partly determined by it. We thus have a situation of an interactive relationship between process and structure.

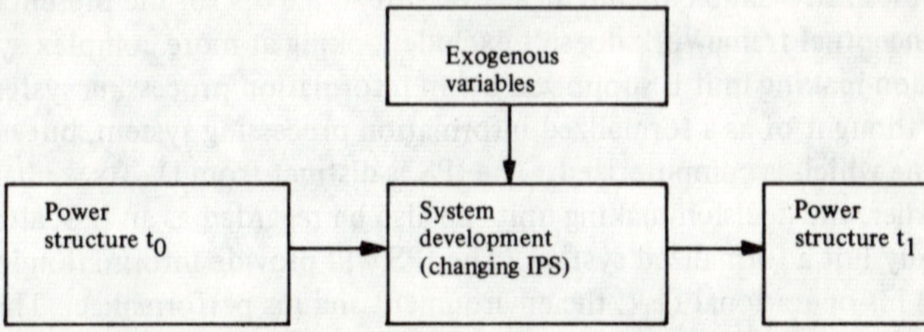

Fig. 2. Interaction between system development and power structure

The above chart implies that to understand the power structure at t_1 we need to understand how power was exercised over system development. Very often the influence over system development will come from sources other than the particular subsystem which it will affect primarily. Thus influence over system development will be a major determinant of the power distribution at t_1. We therefore need to see how influence over system development is exercised.

3. Conceptual framework

3.1 Approach

This research proposal adopts a contingency theoretical approach to the study of power and influence in organizations as it was developed by Hickson et al. [9] and Heller [8]. Phenomena of power and influence are here considered as functions of important configurations of actors (individuals or collectives such as organizational units), situational (institutional) constraints or opportunities, and environmental context [20]. In this contingency theoretical framework technology – in our case: the implementation of a new computerized IPS – is assumed to be one of the major factors in influencing the outcome variable: intra-organizational power distribution.

We look upon the organization as a decision-making system. In general, we will not study the total organization, but rather a subsystem performing specific decision-making and operational tasks. Operational tasks are defined as organizational activities – such as sales and production – for which a decision making unit is responsible. Decision-making tasks, on the other hand, are the decisions relevant to those activities as for example, the determination of a sales budget.

In order to see how power is determined by other structural characteristics, we will have to briefly describe the task and the components of the system (Figure 3a). The decision-making units (D_i) can represent individuals or larger social units. We have hypothesized a simple hierarchical structure as a basis for the presentation, but the conceptual framework doesn't exclude looking at more complex systems. Each decision-making unit is supported by an information processing system (IPS_i). The IPS is thought of as a formalized information processing system, but not necessarily one which is computerized. The IPS is distinct from D. As we have indicated earlier, the decision-making unit can also be regarded as an IPS, although it is generally not a formalized system. The IPS will provide information input to D about his operational task, the environment and his performance. The set of all IPS's form the information system (IS). The IS can be more or less centralized (Figure 3b). In Figure 3b, a central IPS exists which serves all D_i's, but each unit has a more limited IPS as well. Only in a theoretical case is all information processing centralized to one system.

The total decision-making task is solved by all decision-making units jointly. Each D_i is responsible for a specific subtask. As an example, we may take the allocation of resources for the marketing of different products. In this case, D_1 will represent the marketing manager while D_2 and D_3 are brand managers. Each brand manager is responsible for planning his product or product group, while the global task is the allocation of resources to the different product groups.

In the decision-making process the different D_i's will have to arrive at a common solution. In the face of opposition each D_i will attempt to influence the common outcome so that it conforms to his own preferences. His capability to do this depends on the nature of the operational and decision-making task, how easily the D_i himself can be replaced or substituted for, and on how efficient is his control of the information system. How these variables interact in determining his power will be spelled out in more detail below.

3.2 Independent variables

Table 1 lists the various variables to be considered as related to the introduction of a computer system. The information system can be organized along either centralized or decentralized lines. Here we are taking the end points of a continuum

VARIABLES	DATA COLLECTION AND INFORMATION SOURCES
INDEPENDANT VARIABLES	Interviews will be complementes by
Information System (IS)	
1. Centralization / Decentralization	Design documents
2. Authority 3. Accessability	Organizational manuals and system documentation
Information Support (ISUP)	
4. Data – Scope – Degree of detail – Currency – Availability – Accuracy	Outputs from IS and system documentation
5. Model – Relevance – Comprehensiveness – Availability	Outputs and system documentation
Development of the Information System	
6. Influence on different phases of the development process	Questionnaire Process documentation
7. Participation in different phases of the development process	Questionnaire Process documentation
Characteristics of D_i	
8. Goals 9. Information processing capability (age, education)	
INTERVENING VARIABLES	
10. Control of information system 11. Nature of decision-making process 12. Uncertainty in decision-making task 13. Ability to cope with uncertainty 14. Substitutability	– Direct observation
15. Relation of operational subtask to total task (centrality of tasks)	Existing performance statistics
DEPENDENT VARIABLE	
16. Power	Direct observation (AOG) Questionnaire (IPS, CG)

Table 1. Classes of variables in the framework

in which intermediate states are common. The end points have been illustrated in Figure 3a and 3b. The degree of centralization of the information system can be assessed through studies of design documents and interviews.

The authority over the information system is established in its responsibilities for maintaining and changing the system of IPS_i's. Such authority is mostly the consequence of decisions taken at higher management levels. The accessability of the information system refers to how freely D_i's can have access to common or other's

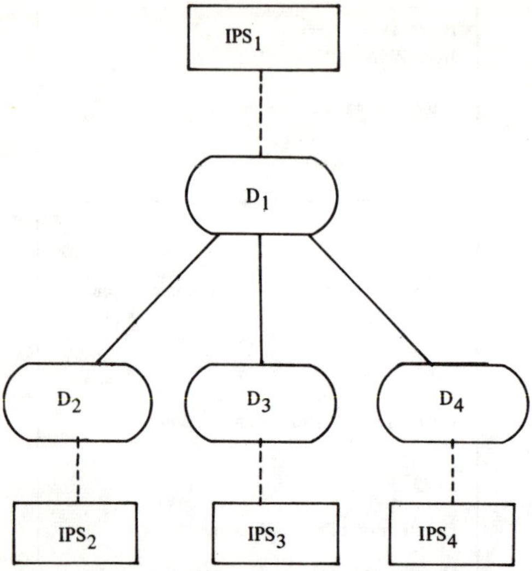

Fig. 3a. A management subsystem with a decentralized information system

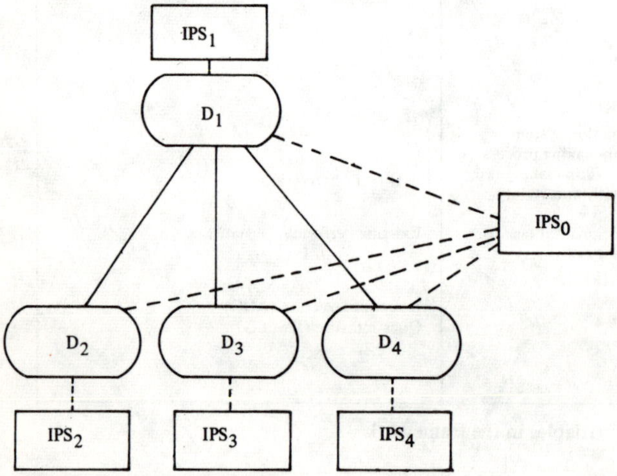

Fig. 3b. A management subsystem with a centralized information system

IPS's. Since authority is not always documented, interviews would be needed here as well. Design documents and interviews will be the main sources of information for assessing accessability to the information system.

We divide information support into data support and models. In order to be able to distinguish changes in ISUP following the implementation of a computer system, we need to identify its different attributes. In our consideration of data support we distinguish between

- Scope,
- Degree of Detail,
- Currency,
- Availability,
- Accuracy.

The scope of data support refers to the part of the organization and its environment which is covered by information support. Degree of detail is self-explanatory, while currency refers to the time lag between the occurance of an event or state and the time until information about it is available. Availability refers to the length of time it takes to access information within the system. Accuracy again needs no explanation.

Model support is characterized by its relevance, comprehensiveness and availability. Relevance refers to the relation between the model and the problem at hand. Comprehensiveness refers to the completeness of the model's incorporation of the relevant variables, which is particularly crucial when the model contains the important objectives. These first two characteristics are partly overlapping. We use availability here to have the same meaning as in relation to data support. Information support characteristics will have to be assessed through studies of output from the information system and through interviews.

Another set of independent variables which we will consider includes the influence and participation of D_i's during the phases of the establishment of the new system. Their influence and participation can lead them to acquire a certain amount of expertise regarding the information system. Influence and participation can be measured through questionnaires.

Finally, we also include among the independent variables such characteristics of D_i's as goals and information processing capability [13]. We will not assess the information processing capability directly. Instead, we will use surrogate variables such as age and education.

3.3 Intervening variables

The power resulting from the control of information flows has not been widely studied. A study by Pettigrew [15] indicates, however, that a manager's desire to control information is an important factor in the decision to acquire a computer. How the information system is being controlled will show in the degree to which a D_i monopolizes certain information or expertise in interpreting its output. This can also be seen in any changes made in the system. These factors in the control of the information system can be studied through direct observation and interviews.

The effect of the D_i's control of the information system will vary, depending on whether the actual decision-making process is an analytic or a bargaining process [11]. An analytic process is characterized by the search for information on available alternatives and the consequences attached to those alternatives. The bargaining process will be characterized by threats, falsification of position etc. The nature of the process is difficult to determine without direct observation.

In the tradition of Hickson et al. [9], we identify the following factors as power contingencies for a particular D_i: the uncertainty of the decision-making task; his ability to cope with uncertainty; his substitutability and the centrality of the task.

The uncertainty of the task refers to the uncertainty of the information inputs. We may have an incomplete, inprecise or not up-to-date view of the real world as well as inadequate information about performance and cause/effect relationships. The ability to cope with uncertainty is difficult to disentangle from task uncertainty. It refers to the decision-maker's ability to absorb uncertainty and hence provide others with an input which they can act upon as if it were certain. The importance of uncertainty absorption is shown among others by Crozier [4]. The main information source will here be interviews.

Substitutability refers to the notion of available alternatives. It is easier to replace the decision-maker with another person if the task is routine and involves little uncertainty absorption. The more scarce the alternatives, the more dependent the system will be on the particular D_i, which increases his power. Substitutability can be assessed by considering the time it takes to train a person for the particular subtask.

Centrality is the degree to which the decision-making unit is interlinked into the system or rather, the relation between the subtask and the total task. The part can have an immediate and pervasive impact on the whole. In our simple hierarchical system the idea of centrality takes on a simplified form. Since all the decision-making unit have a direct impact on the total task, the severity of the impact will be the important characteristic. The severity of a subtask can be estimated by looking at the sales volume or profit of the different product groups, for example once again, in the case of the allocation of a marketing budget.

Changes in the design of the information system will have an impact on the intervening variables and they in turn will determine the power of a decision-making unit (cf. figure 6).

3.4 Dependent variable

For our dependent variable we propose to work with three different specifications of power. The first refers to the influence over the outcome of the task. As Abell proposes [1], we intend to measure the effects of interunit power through the differences that can be observed in critical phases of the decision-making process in terms of

IPO = initial preferred outcome of a unit,

MPO = modified preferred outcome of a unit after a phase of bargaining, with other units towards the final result (collective outcome),

CO = collective outcome, the final decision.

The measure of the power in terms of the outcome is the gradient from the unit's aspirations (A) in terms of its IPO's to the final decision outcome (O). The steeper the Aspiration-Outcome-Gradient (AOG), the smaller is the power of a unit in the decision-making process.

Secondly, we will measure power as relative to participation in the decision-making process. We propose to study the decision-making behavior of two interlocking levels of management (pairs of superiors – subordinates) as perceived by the two dyadic partners. We will measure the degree of perceived influence and power sharing with Heller's [8] Influence-Power-Sharing-Continuum (IPC) which basically distinguishes five prominent styles or modes of decision behavior.

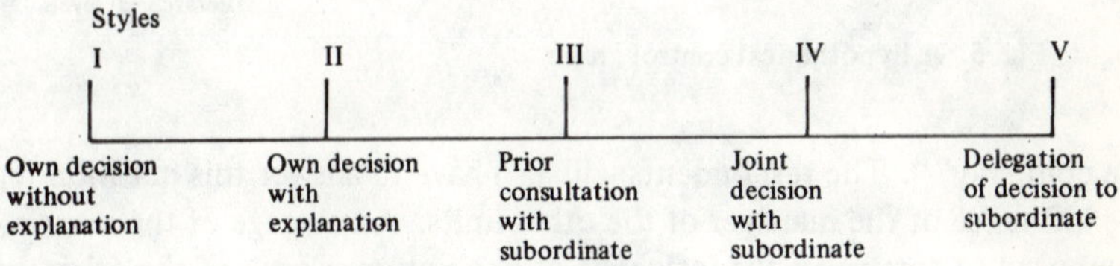

Fig. 4. Influence-Power-Sharing-Continuum (IPC)

By treating the IPS as a cumulative percentage scale, a weighted Decision Centralization Score (DCS) can be obtained for each member of a dyad. This score indicates the degree to which a superior allows his subordinate to participate in decisions in terms of information participation (Styles I-III) or in terms of the degree to which a superior incorporates the subordinate's view in the outcome of decisions (Style IV-V). The higher the DCS, the lower we assume the degree of participation between two levels of management in intra-unit decision-making to be.

Finally, power as perceived interpersonal influence has been studied extensively by Tannenbaum and others [17]. Power is measured on what is called a Control Graph (CG). Members of an organizational unit are asked to indicate on a five-point scale the amount of influence which their unit and other units – identified by hierarchical levels – exert upon each level of hierarchy. Figure 5 shows a hypothetical control graph.

Members of each unit are asked such questions as, "In general, how much say or influence does the manager of your unit have on what the following units do in

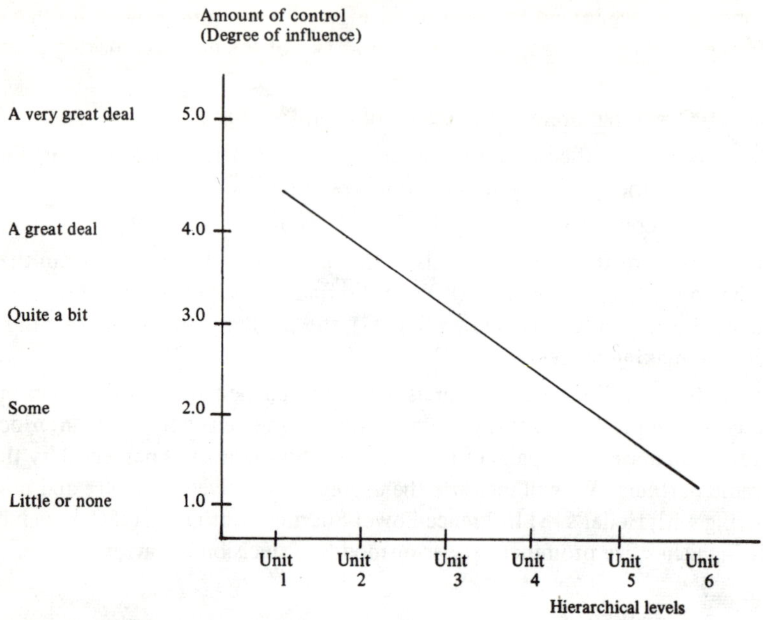

Fig. 5. A hypothetical control graph

the company?". The respondents will also have to answer this question regarding the influence of the manager of the other units. An average of the responses is computed to determine the influence of one unit over each of the other units, each at a different level. We thus have as many means as there are levels in the hierarchy for each unit. The average of these averages will represent the unit's power.

The three different power measures which we propose to employ in the context of contentious decision situations are geared towards three distinct manifestations of organizational power:

(1) Structural Power of bargaining parties (organizational units or alliances) as measured by the outcome of decisions against their original ambitions: the Aspiration-Outcome-Gradient.

(2) Inter-level power within organizational units, measured in terms of different degrees of hierarchical control over information that is relevant for the decision: the Influence-Power-Sharing-Continuum.

(3) Inter-level power across organizational units: the Control Graph.

These three measurements complement each other and it will be very informative to observe their differential sensitivity to the introduction of a computerized IPS.

An overview of all independent, intervening, and dependent variables in their assumed interrelationships is given in Figure 6.

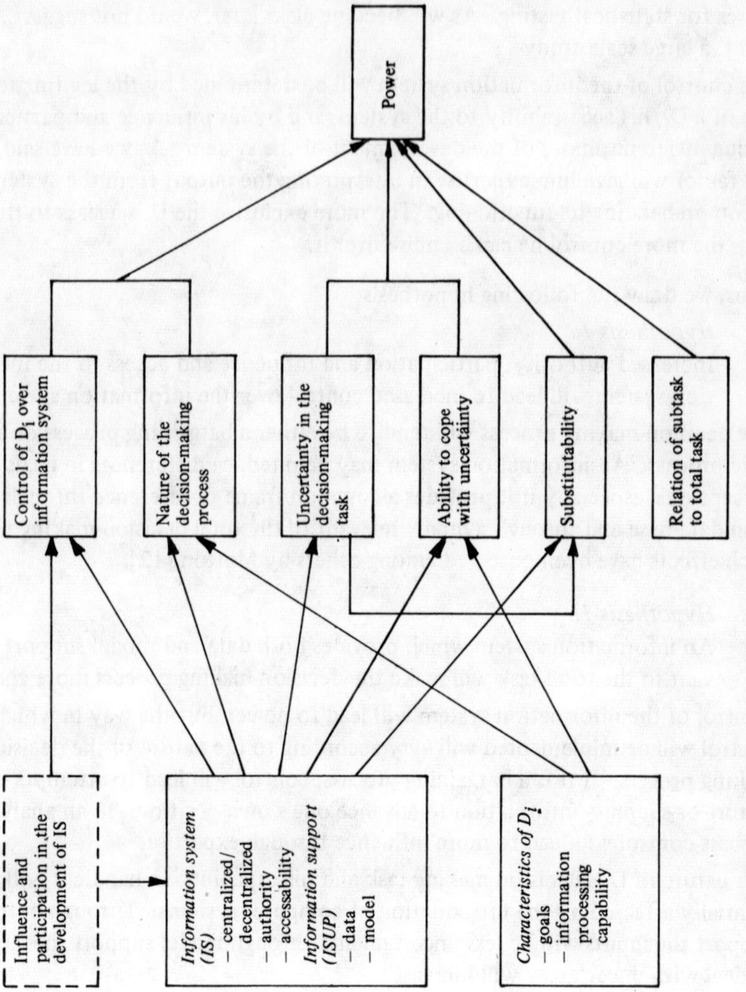

Fig. 6. Relationships between variables in the framework

4. Hypotheses

Having established our conceptual framework, we are now in a position to generate a number of hypotheses which we hope to corroborate in empirical research. The hypotheses should be regarded as guidelines for observation rather than hypotheses for statistical testing. As will become clear later, we do not suggest, at this point, a large scale study.

The control of the information system will be determined by the legitimate authority of a D_i, his accessability to the system, and by his influence and participation during different phases of the development of the system. As we have said, this last factor will give him expertise in interpreting the output from the system and in comprehending its functioning. The more exclusive the D_i's access to the system, the more control he can exercise over it.

Thus, we draw the following hypothesis:

Hypothesis 1a

Increased authority, participation and influence and access to the information system will lead to increased control over the information system.

The decision-making process will tend to be either a bargaining process or an analytic process. An information system may help reduce differences in goals and perceptions, especially if it provides a common frame of reference through a common data base and through a model relevant to the total decision-making tasks. Such effects have been observed among others by Morton [12].

Hypothesis 1b

An information system which provides both data and model support relevant to the total task will make the decision-making process more analytic.

Control of the information system will lead to power, but the way in which the control will be implemented will vary according to the nature of the decision-making process. If it is a bargaining process, control will lead to attempts to distort or suppress information to advance one's own position. In an analytic process control will lead to more influence through expertise.

The nature of D_i's decision-making task and his capability to handle it will be substantially affected by the introduction of computer systems. Through better data support the inputs will be less uncertain and through model support the capability to deal with uncertainty will increase.

Hypothesis 2

Substantial improvements in data support and model support will lead to less task uncertainty and a greater capability to cope with remaining uncertainty.

Such improvements can be in any one of the areas of information support which we have previously identified. Even though computer systems may lead to a better capability to cope with uncertainty, they may also lead to a higher degree of substitutability of managerial personnel. The more that coping with uncertainty relies on explicit models which are accessible and easy to use, the more transferable is the ability of the decision making unit. This is emphasized in hypothesis 3.

Hypothesis 3

Increased ability to cope with uncertainty which depends on the use of explicit and generally accessible information support will lead to increased substitutability of decision makers.

We would assume that the centrality of the task will be affected only in the long run and not immediately by the implementation of computer technology. In studies of computer impacts we need to separate its effect from the effect of the computer system. In our simple hierarchical structure we may investigate the following hypothesis:

Hypothesis 4

Greater relative importance of the operational subtask of D_i will lead to increased power.

The impact of computer technology will be through the intervening variables. The intervening variables in turn will have an impact on power.

Hypothesis 5

Increased control of the information system, increased ability to cope with uncertainty, less substitutability and larger relative task importance lead to increased power.

The above hypotheses are contingent upon each other and point to areas of investigation. The purpose of the present research is to refine and elaborate them on the basis of empirical observations. We regard our present work as a step in a continuing process of hypothesis generation and empirical investigation.

5. Research methodology and design

Any researcher is faced with a trade-off between the number of situations which could be studied and the depth in which one can study each case. By studying a larger number of situations, we could make useful comparisons across tasks and organizations. But, since the emphasis within a given area of research is bound to change over time, and since knowledge of the subject is limited and it is uncertain which variables are really the important ones, it makes sense to start with a limited number of situations studied in more depth. As knowledge accumulates it will be possible to be more selective in collecting data and to explore to what extent results from a limited number of case studies can be generalized to other contexts. It is our assessment that the impact of computer technology on management is an area in which we have seen much speculation but very little empirical research. We therefore favor a case study approach.

In choosing the context for our empirical research, we prefer decision-making situations which generally tend to show

- existence of conflict
- task uncertainty.

Clearly task uncertainty generally moves with conflict, but not necessarily. We have chosen cases with high task uncertainty because of the potentially higher impact of the computer system in such situations. In well-structured situations the computer has been more readily applied, but these are also examples of lesser managerial significance. If we want to study "purer" management situations we will have to find cases characterized by high task uncertainty.

Empirical situations which may show the above characteristics are:

- Allocation of resources for marketing of different products,
- Allocation of resources to investment projects including R & D projects,
- Aggregate scheduling decisions.

The impacts which we will study will emanate from a particular computer system and not from computerization in general.

Having chosen our context, we are placed in other difficulties. Ideally, we would like to do a before/after study; that is, a study of the managerial system before a computer system is introduced and after it has been implemented. However, this would be very difficult to do. First, it requires advance knowledge that a computer system is going to be introduced. Secondly, since the impacts of computer technology really start as soon as the system development project is initiated and since most systems of any size take one-and-one-half to three years to develop, a study of this type would be a long run effort indeed. In practice we are therefore forced to accept situations in which the computer system, if not already implemented, is close to implementation. We will thus have to reconstruct the change process after the fact. This reconstruction has to be done through careful interviews and through studies of whatever documentation exists. Experience has shown that this is possible [3]. The problem of reconstructing processes really recurs in each phase of our study. For example in our study of power distribution in the managerial system, should we rely on people's perception of power or should we try to directly observe it? This is particularly crucial when we are looking at power in relation to the outcome. People have a natural tendency to rationalize and legitimize after the fact. Hence, questions on the initial preferred outcomes (IPO) will most certainly not give a true picture of the situation, although certain corrections can be made by measuring the social perception of other units. The study of power and participation will certainly be more revealing if we can directly observe it in the management process. The difficulties here reflect the fact that the decision situations we are interested in occur with low frequency. One may have to wait close to a year to observe the complete cycle of the budgeting process. Since we want to undertake several case studies, this may again lead us to a long-run project. The problems inherent in longitudinal studies of processes are substantial and practical constraints will often force one to take a less than ideal route. If the before/after study seems infeasible, are there any other possible methods by which we could achieve at least quasi-control? It may be very difficult to find comparable situations – that is, a second and similar situation into which a computer system has not been introduced. There may be different divisions or departments within the same company which are comparable except for the introduction of a computer system. But it seems to us that one should not be too optimistic about finding such an ideal case. Only with extreme luck could such a situation be found. It seems that we are forced to make conjectures about the impact of computer technology on the basis of studies after the change has occured.

References

[1] Abell, P.: Organizations as Bargaining Systems: Measuring Intra-Organizational Power. (Unpublished paper).

[2] Bertalanffy, L.v.: An Outline of General System Theory. In: Britisch Journal for the Philosophy of Science, I, No. 2/1950, pp. 150–151.

[3] Brinkmann-Herz, D.: Entscheidungsprozesse in den Aufsichtsräten der Montanindustrie. Berlin 1972.

[4] Crozier, M.: The Bureaucratic Phenomenon. London 1964.

[5] Dahl, R.: The Concept of Power. In: Behavioral Science 2/1957, pp. 201–215.

[6] Edström, A.: Limits to the Design of MIS. In: INSEAD Research Paper, No. 74/1972.

[7] Edström, A.: Conceptualization of the Design Problem for MIS. In: Journal of Management Studies, June 1973.

[8] Heller, F.: Managerial Decision-Making. London 1971.

[9] Hickson, D., C. Hinings, C. Lee, R. Schneck and J. Pennings: A Strategic Contingencies Theory of Intra-Organizational Power. In: Administrative Science Quarterly, 16/1971, pp. 216–229.

[10] Klatzky, S.: Automation, Size and the Locus of Decision-Making: The Cascade Effect. In: Journal of Business, 43/1970, pp. 141–151.

[11] March, J. and H. Simon: Organizations. New York 1958.

[12] Morton, M.S.: Management Decision Systems: Computer Based Support for Decision-Making. Division of Research, Harvard Business School. Boston, Mass. 1971.

[13] Müller, W.: An Information Processing Approach to Organizations. Preprint Series. International Institute of Management. Berlin 1973.

[14] Müller, W.: Ansätze für eine Theorie der Informationsverarbeitung in der Unternehmung. Wiesbaden 1974.

[15] Pettigrew, A.: 1972, Information Control as a Power Resource. In: Sociology, 6/1972, pp. 187–204.

[16] Simon, H.: The New Science of Management Decision. New York 1960.

[17] Tannenbaum, A.: Control in Organizations. New York 1968.
[18] Weber, M.: The Theory of Social and Economic Organization. Glencoe, Ill. 1947.
[19] Whisler, Th.: The Impact of Computers on Organizations. New York 1970.
[20] Wilpert, B. and F. Heller: Power-Sharing at Senior Management Levels. In: Omega, Vol. 1, No. 4/1973.

German abstract
Der Einfluß der Computertechnologie auf organisatorische Machtstrukturen

Von *Bo Hedberg, Anders Edström, Wolfgang Müller* und *Bernhard Wilpert*

Der Einsatz von Computersystemen ist begleitet von einer Unzahl von Spekulationen über die Auswirkung solcher Systeme auf die Personal-, Aufgaben- und Organisationsstrukturen. Empirische Untersuchungen haben in der Vergangenheit oft recht unterschiedliche Ergebnisse über diese Wirkungsverhältnisse geliefert. Wissend um die Vielfältigkeit der organisatorisch relevanten Effekte des Einsatzes von Computersystemen, beschäftigt sich der Beitrag von Hedberg et al. auf einen ganz spezifischen Aspekt, nämlich die Beeinflussung der organisatorischen Machtstrukturen durch den Computer. Es wird ein Wirkungsmodell entwickelt, das den Zusammenhang zwischen Computereinsatz (unabhängige Variable) und Änderungen in der Machtstruktur (abhängige Variable) durch die Einführung zwischengeschalteter Variabler herstellt.

Als eine Gruppe unabhängiger Variabler des Modells werden die Organisation des Informationssystems (= System zur Sammlung, Speicherung, Verarbeitung und Verteilung von Informationen zur Unterstützung operativer und dispositiv-strategischer Aufgaben) und die spezifische Form der Unterstützung durch Informationen definiert. Dabei wird die Organisation des Informationssystems (IS) durch

– den Grad der Zentralisierung oder Dezentralisierung,
– die Autorität für Änderungen des IS und
– die individuelle Zugriffsmöglichkeit von Aufgabenträgern (Di) auf das IS

bestimmt. Die Art der Informationsunterstützung ist durch Daten- oder Modellunterstützung charakterisiert. Deskriptoren der Datenunterstützung sind dabei Umfang, Detaillierungsgrad, Schnelligkeit und Genauigkeit. Die Modellunterstützung wird durch die Abbildungsgenauigkeit und die Schnelligkeit des Modelloutput beschrieben.

Ein weiterer Satz unabhängiger Variabler betrifft den Einfluß und die Beteiligung von Aufgabenträgern (D_i) am Systementwicklungsprozeß sowie die relevanten Merkmale von Aufgabenträgern.

Zwischen der Gruppe der unabhängigen Variablen und der abhängigen Variablen (Macht) werden eine Anzahl zwischengeschalteter Variabler definiert, die einerseits die abhängige Variable direkt beeinflussen, andererseits von den unabhängigen Variablen direkt beeinflußt werden. Im einzelnen werden folgende zwischengeschaltete Variable genannt:

– Freiheitsspielraum bei der Interpretation von Informationen durch die Aufgabenträger,
– Charakter des Entscheidungsprozesses,
– Unsicherheitsgrad der in den Entscheidungsprozeß eingehenden Informationen,
– Unsicherheitsabsorptionsfähigkeit von Aufgabenträgern,
– Substitutionsgrad von Aufgabenträgern,
– Verhältnis der einzelnen Aufgaben von D_i zur Gesamtaufgabe der Unternehmung.

Nach der Skizzierung des Modells werden verschiedene Meßansätze zur Erfassung einer Machtveränderung beschrieben.

Auf der Basis des Wirkungsmodells werden abschließend folgende Hypothesen formuliert:

– Eine Erhöhung der Beteiligung, des Einflusses und der exklusiven Zugriffsmöglichkeit auf das Informationssystem führt zu einer erhöhten Kontrolle über das Informationssystem.
– Ein zentralisiertes Informationssystem, das Daten- und Modellunterstützung bietet, führt zu einer Formalisierung der Entscheidungsprozesse.
– Verbesserungen bei der Daten- und Modellunterstützung führen zu geringerer Aufgabenunsicherheit und erhöhen die Unsicherheitsabsorptionsfähigkeit.
– Eine erhöhte Unsicherheitsabsorptionsfähigkeit aufgrund entsprechender Unterstützung durch das IS führt zu erhöhter Substituierbarkeit der Aufgabenträger.
– Eine Erhöhung der relativen Bedeutung einzelner Aufgaben (von D_i) führt zu erhöhter organisatorischer Macht (von D_i).
– Eine erhöhte Kontrollmöglichkeit des IS, eine erhöhte Unsicherheitsabsorptionsfähigkeit, eine geringere Substituierbarkeit und eine erhöhte Bedeutung einer Teilaufgabe hinsichtlich der Gesamtaufgabe führen zu erhöhter organisatorischer Macht.

Über diese Hypothesen, die noch empirisch abgesichert werden müssen, können die einzelnen Variablen miteinander verknüpft werden und somit Aussagen über die Veränderung der Machtstruktur durch den Einsatz der Computertechnologie gemacht werden.

The impact of new techniques for management control on the information system and organization

By *E. Gerald Hurst, jr.*

1. Introduction

Even though control comprises a very large part of the typical manager's job, consuming a good deal of his time and other resources, studies in the area of management control appear to have taken a back seat to those in planning during recent years. To be sure, the areas of planning and control are inextricably linked, and many authors of works on planning acknowledge this fact. But those publications which use the terms planning and control as if they were one word tend to spend the bulk of their time discussing planning. Control is summarized simply as what one does when things don't go according to plan. To be sure, if there were no plans there would be nothing to control, so any exercise of control must be preceded by a hopefully well laid plan. But the best laid plans can indeed go "aglay", and in all but the most trivial cases the determination of what has gone wrong, and the design and implementation of corrections, is a difficult job.
To aid in this job, recent advances in a variety of fields appear to have applicability to the study and exercise of management control. These new techniques and technologies arise in a variety of contexts, and range from new ways of viewing the organization through new mathematical techniques all the way to new devices. In this paper, some of these advances are listed and assessed in terms of their potential impacts on management control. To provide a basis for this discussion, some of the meanings of control in the management context are explored, and the definition accepted for the purposes of this paper is elaborated.

2. Management control

It is helpful to examine the several uses of the term control in an enterprise. Perhaps the most commonly understood use of the term concerns the utilization of accounting-related data to give the owners and managers a stewardship report on the enterprise, and to assign causes for either poor or exemplary performance. Most managers would give a related definition if asked to describe the control function in their firms. Indeed, this set of activities is usually supervised by a person known as controller.

A second somewhat different use of the term control in the enterprise would be preceded by the words production, operation or process. The context here is usually the day-to-day operation of the area producing the primary product or service of the firm. Control in this case consists of the detailed determination of the performance of the process, from which decisions about its operations are made. For example, a decision might be made about whether to continue producing output or to stop and repair the process, based on a statistical examination of the output. An even narrower use of the term is in quality control. Here, the decision is made about whether to accept or reject items which have been produced based on an examination of their quality.

Definitions delineating the various facets of management activity have been proposed by Anthony. In that work, he proposes a framework which consists of three different levels of managerial activity. The three distinct areas are strategic planning, management control and operational control. Strategic planning deals with the overall objectives of the organization, as might be expected. Management control is "the process by which managers assure that resources are obtained and used effectively and efficiently in the accomplishment of the organization's objectives".

Operational control, by contrast, is "the process of assuring that specific tasks are carried out effectively and efficiently". In management control, heavy importance is placed on interpersonal interaction, operation within the context of the policies and objectives developed in strategic planning, and the setting of performance standards for operational control. Operational control is mainly concerned with performing the low-level tasks which have been specifically delineated in the management control activity.

Anthony's definitions seem to correspond closely to Ansoff's categories of strategic, administrative and operational decision making, which is to say that they are associated with the different levels within the organization. We prefer to center our definition on a manager, whatever his position within the enterprise. We include in our definition of management control the relevant decision tasks which do not depend on the context of his responsibility. Our working definition for management control will be the set of measurement, analysis and action decisions used to manage in a timely fashion the continuing operation of a process.

Because of the generality of level, the concept of process is more broadly defined here than is the usual case. A process is not limited to such product producers as a chemical plant or an assembly line. Rather, we include all means by which some set of given and at least partially controllable inputs is converted into a desirable set of outputs; in short, we mean any entity which is being managed by the decision maker. So the normal production line is included, but so is the process of converting salesmen's time into sales, as well as the process of converting medical test results into useful information for doctors. We include any dynamic operation which is subject to control, whether small in scope or large, whether at an aggregate or detail level, whether in private enterprise or public domain.

We classify the possible decisions of management control into the three broad categories of measurement, analysis and "action".

2.1 Measurement decisions

This major category includes all the decisions which must be made on the content as well as the frequency with which data are collected. These decisions are clearly not made independently of each other, given the costs of such data collection. Another aspect of measurement is the storage decision, including at least the medium in which storage of the data should take place, the form of the storage, and the length of time data should be stored before being destroyed. Classification of the data is also included in the set of measurement decisions.

2.2 Analysis decisions

This area of decision making has only recently been regarded with any importance at all in the management control process. Analysis was formerly a loose and definitely unprogrammed item in the decision-making cycle. Included in the analysis decision are choice of the model of the process including its uncertainty, the transformation and extrapolation of the data. Both of these are present in the analysis of any type of decision. More unique to the management control decision are the choice of criteria for control and the choice of method for comparison between actual and forecasted results. The generation of alternative actions could also be included in the analysis decision, in spite of the fact that it bridges the gap to the third major category.

2.3 Action decisions

The possible forms of action are the least easy of the three types of management control decision to classify. This is due to the fact that within the broad scope of management control considered here, a large variety of actions are possible. One possible scheme would partition the available sorts of actions into the controllable variables relating to the existing process; the operating goal; the overall process structure; the process contents; and the total process design. These general categories could include a wide variety of different actions depending on the process being considered.

Many definitions do not include all three of these types of decision. For example the standard controllership of the firm largely concerns only the set of measurements which are made. For others only action decisions are appropriately included in control. And some will include in the possible actions for control only those actions which were anticipated as possibilities when planning was originally done. This is analogous to the trajectory correction problem in missile control. That is, control actions are only those which can return the trajectory to that which was originally planned; choosing a new trajectory must be preceded by replanning, and as such is not included in control. The decision about what analysis to perform has generally not been explicitly considered in any definition of management control.

The key feature which separates the control problem from the other decisions the manager faces is the idea of continuing operation. This feature implies several things about the nature of control decisions which distinguish them from planning decisions. The first of these is that the same set of decisions is normally considered repeatedly as new data come in. This is not to say that the decisions are necessarily programmable, but merely that their form or type appears the same structurally. Taken with the human component, it is probably also true that, whatever the time period, the set of decisions is considered at discrete intervals in time. This means that there will be a definite cycling of the measurement, analysis, and action decisions which are considered. The intervals of time may not be regular, and control may be triggered by events rather than the regular passage of time. However, there will be some finite interval, however short, between each set of similar decisions.

In summary, our definition of management control centers on the decision tasks of a manager that are associated with the continuing management of his area of responsibility without regard to its type or level within the enterprise. Because it is broader in scope than many previously stated definitions, both in terms of its level of applicability within the organization as well as the decision areas it encompasses, one would expect that many recent developments might have potential value. Some of the more promising possibilities are considered in the next section.

3. New techniques

Most of the techniques summarized in this section will tend to be related to the analysis decision area of management control, rather than to either the measurement or action areas. For the most part this is a reflection of the author's bias toward and interest in analysis techniques. He confesses to looking at the management control world through "analysis-coloured" glasses. But it seems also to point to the decision area which has been most lacking in the management control process. As was mentioned earlier, analysis of such problems has tended to be informal. Their complexity has precluded any formal attack. The techniques summarized here have tended to enlarge the problems they have approached in their fields of origin, and it is partially this enlargement of problem scope which makes them offer promise to the management control job. It is probably also true that new developments will offer less help in the other two decision areas, especially for the action decision. The generation and choice of actions is the most creative part of the management control job, and as such will be less responsive to technological advances. Indeed, the main feature which distinguishes operations control from management control seems to be the ability to delineate and therefore program the possible actions in operations control.

3.1 Planning languages

Many of the recent advances in planning to which we alluded in the introduction have an indirect impact on the exercise of control; if the content and forms of plans change, the related control necessary will likely change as well. One of the most promising new planning tools is the planning language. Several dozen proprietory computer systems are now on the market for aiding the manager in preparing his plans. These consist of a modelling language in which the manager can construct a specially-tailored model of his enterprise, a convenient means for inserting data, and a series of analysis and report generating options for the examination of alternative strategies. The availability of a formal planning model specifically geared to the firm as well as the means for analyzing it suggest that the plan can easily be controlled by inserting actual operations data when they are received, then making a series of comparisons with the predicted results in a manner analogous to standard variance analysis.

3.2 Interactive computer systems

The contributions of the computer to management started immediately the computer became available, although as is well known it has tended to be most effective on low-level repetitive problems in which turnaround time is not critical. The addition of the capability for a man to interact directly with the computer has begun to impact on uses in higher level management problems. In addition to processing complex models and large amounts of data quickly, the manager can obtain the timely answers to questions necessary to exercise control. He should also soon be able, with the machine's aid, to search for causes of variation not foreseen in the original planning.

3.3 Mathematical programming

Recent work in modeling accounting systems using mathematical programming has added an application of this technique in measurement and analysis for management control to its long list of successful applications. Mathematical programming provides an overall look at the accounting system, and permits the measurement of the effect of individual element changes on the overall results of the enterprise, as well as the opportunity to optimize flows through the system.

3.4 Bayesian statistics

Even if a formal prior-posterior analysis using Bayes' Rule is not performed, this old branch of statistics which has seen so much recent development offers aid in several ways to management control. Of course, there is the fact that new information can be explicitly added as received to compute a new probablistic state of information about a measure of interest. The resultant probability distribution (which is available at all times) can be used to find expected costs in the process. This leads to an extension of variance analysis and management by exception which explicitly combines the uncertainty and costs of being off target. The recent work on the value of information is also based for the most part on the results of Bayesian statistics. It allows measurement decisions to be explicitly considered in terms of the costs and uncertainty in the process.

3.5 Control charts

Developments in process control charts which stem from related advances in Bayesian statistics promise to move this technique from the narrow area of production process control to broader uses in management control. Interestingly enough, the control chart was first suggested in 1915 as charting technique for management by exception. Statistical theory was added in the 1930's to bring it into the province of process control. Explicit updating of the dynamic measures of performance, along with explicit considerations of costs, point to a broadening of the applicability of this technique.

3.6 Mathematical control theory

The set of techniques which is included under this title were developed in response to needs in engineering, particularly in defense-related and process control engineering. Recent contributions have also appeared in economics. It is in some ways a difficult tool to use in management control vis a vis the other management areas, as is discussed later. However, explicit consideration of input variables, output variables, controllable variables, their costs, and the model relating them in a dynamic setting promises to have impact in management control problems. In some cases the tools for optimization which are part of the body of techniques will be directly applicable.

3.7 Search theory

Theoretical developments prompted by the military problem of searching for and distinguishing enemy forces using radar or sonar could be useful in the hunt for sources of variation among the extensive data received by a manager. Approaches to this problem bring experience with thresholds which trigger a response, analogous to the procedures of management by exception. The developments have also considered the problems of dealing with ill-defined and non-commensurate costs of various actions, which has direct relevance in management control.

3.8 Machine-aided medical diagnosis

A somewhat related development which seems also to have contributions to make to management control is machine-aided medical diagnosis. It has been approached as a data processing problem, a Bayesian inference problem, and recently as a problem in epistomology. Formal approaches to medical diagnosis bring practical experience in maintaining qualitative and quantitative history files, experience with an adaptive interactive search procedure, well-developed heuristics for isolating causes, and even tools for analyzing sets of interrelated factors or syndromes. These techniques are only just being used for actual medical analysis, and are still somewhat far from use in management control problems, but the similarity of the structure of the analysis seems very promising.

4. Potential impact

Having seen a sample of the new developments which other disciplines can bring to management control, we close with some brief speculations on the effect these are likely to have on the information system and organization.

4.1 Effect on the information system

Although the different techniques will vary in their impact on the information system, it seems clear that the introduction of an analysis step will not greatly influence the information system directly. Of more critical importance is the effect the information system (or more properly the informatics system) will have on the utilization of each of the techniques. Some of the computation intensive tools appear absolutely dependent on being implemented before being used at all. Others could conceivably be used outside of any formal informatic implementation. But analysis for management control, emphasizing as it does the frequent and timely use of actual data in supporting control decisions, seems to require more than ever the implementation on some real-time basis of any technique which hopes to be used effectively. Emery and others have pointed out the necessity for management science models to be included in formal information systems. Other papers presented at this symposium suggest some effects of this implementation, as well as the means for accomplishing it. We will simply underline its importance for management control.

4.2 Effect on the organization

Because of the previously noted emphasis on analysis techniques, and because of the view that management control is essentially manager-centered, the impacts of the techniques summarized here will perhaps be most profound on the individual manager, who will be able more quickly to analyse larger problems containing more uncertainty. This will tend to expand the territory he can affect, which would continue, if there were no other forces at work, the already observed trend towards recentralization. As a corollary, it also seems likely to thin the staff ranks somewhat. Such analysis tasks as were once performed by a large staff could now be done by the manager himself, perhaps with the aid of one or a few expert analysts between him and the management information system. Actions would continue to be taken as before, but action implementation is normally the job of line rather than staff subordinates. Being able to manage "a piece of the business" which is both larger in extent as well as better understood across the functions would seem, if taken by itself, to lead to a much more hierarchial organization structure. Obviously, other change-producing factors will also intervene, and the effect of these other factors could swamp the expanded analysis ability. But the direction in which improved techniques in management control will push the organization seems clear.

4.3 Difficulty of implementation

While implementation of many of these developments in the management control area will arrive little by little, Anthony's observation that this middle ground will be the last to yield seems appropriate. In his terms, strategic planning and operational control problems have both been more susceptible to formal models than the problems in management control. What seems to be typical is that the problem is being approached from both sides. As an example, consider the use of mathematical control theory in management. On the one hand, economic theorists have been using mathematical control theory to consider different strategies for the economy. This has naturally led to consideration of the theory of the firm, which is strategic analysis for an individual enterprise. As the models for the theory of the firm become progressively more complex and realistic, they can be used to provide guidance in the management control problem. From the other side, control theory was developed in part for use in the process control area. The necessary data for optimal process control, as well as information about the resultant decisions which are made, become the raw data on which a more aggregate management control analysis can be based. The management control problem in the center gets help from both sides.

5. Conclusions

A variety of new developments in other fields seem to have relevance to management control in a broad sense of the term. Many of those seem particularly appropriate to aid in analysis for management control. In appears necessary to implement these techniques in the formal information system of the enterprise in order to have them used, particularly when the frequency and timeliness implicit in the management control problem are considered. Successful implementation will be a force toward recentralization of the organization, although other factors may overcome this effect.

References

[1] Ackoff, R.L.: The Concept of Corporate Planning. New York 1970.

[2] Anthony, R.N.: Management Accounting. 4th ed., Homewood, Illinois 1970.

[3] Anthony, R.N.: Planning and Control Systems: A Framework for Analysis. Harvard University Press 1965.

[4] Bather, J.A.: "Control Charts and the Minimization of Costs". In: Journal Royal Statistical Society B, Vol. 21, No. 1 1963, pp. 49–80.

[5] Barnard, G.A.: "Control Charts and Stochastic Processes". In: Journal Royal Statistical Society B, Vol. 17, No. 2 1959, pp. 239–272.

[6] Beer, S.: Decision and Control New York 1966.

[7] Beer, S.: "On Viable Governors". In: Discovery, Vol. 23, No. 10 1962.

[8] Bellman, R.: Introduction to the Mathematical Theory of Control Processes (2 volumes). New York 1967/1971.

[9] Bellman, R.: "Equipment Replacement Policy". In: Journal of SIAM. September 1955.

[10] Bensoussan, A., E.G. Hurst, Jr., and B. Naslund: Management Applications of Modern Control Theory. Amsterdam 1974.

[11] Benton, W.K.: Use of the Computer in Planning. Reading, Mass. 1971.

[12] Bittel, L.R.: Management by Exception. New York 1964.

[13] Bonini, C.P., R.K. Jaedicke, and H.M. Wagner (eds.): Management Controls: New Directions in Basic Research. New York 1964.

[14] Butterworth, J.S.: "Accounting Systems and Management Decision". Unpublished Ph. D. dissertation. University of California at Berkeley 1967.

[15] Chapple, E. and L. Sayles: The Measure of Management. London 1961.

[16] Comiskey, E.E.: "Cost Control by Regression Analysis". In: Accounting Review, Vol. 41, No. 2/April 1966, pp. 235–238.

[17] Anthony, R.N., J. Dearden, and R. Vancil: Management Control Systems. Homewood, Illinois 1965.

[18] Dearden, J.: Cost and Budget Analysis. Englewood Cliffs, New Jersey 1962.

[19] Deming, R.L.: Characteristics of an Effective Management Control System in an Industrial Organization. Harvard University Press 1968.

[20] Dopuch, N. and J. Birnberg: Cost Accounting: Accounting Data for Management's Decisions. New York 1969.

[21] Dorfman, R.: "An Economic Interpretation of Optimal Control Theory". In: American Economic Review, December 1969.

[22] Eilon, S.: Management Control. London 1971.

[23] Eilon, S.: "Problems in Studying Management Control". In: International Journal of Production Research, Vol. 1, No. 1 1962.

[24] Emery, J.C.: Organization Planning and Control Systems. London 1969.

[25] Fetter, R.B.: The Quality Control System. Homewood, Illinois 1967.

[26] Goetz, B.E.: Management Planning and Control. New York 1949.

[27] Hedberg, B.: On Man-Computer Interaction in Organizational Decision Making. Gothenburg 1970.

[28] Hodge, B. and R.N. Hodgson: Management and the Computer in Information and Control Systems. New York 1969.

[29] Horngren, C.: Cost Accounting: A Managerial Emphasis 3rd ed. Englewood Cliffs, New Jersey 1972.

[30] Hurst, Jr., E.G.: "Choosing a Planning Language". European Institute for Advanced Studies in Management, Working Paper No. 72–32. Brussels 1972.

[31] Ijiri, Y.: The Foundations of Accounting Measurement. Englewood Cliffs, New Jersey 1967.

[32] Ijiri, Y.: Management Goals and Accounting for Control. Amsterdam 1965.

[33] Intriligator, M.D.: Mathematical Optimization and Economic Theory. Englewood Cliffs, New Jersey 1971.

[34] Jaedicke, R., Y. Ijiri, and O. Nielsen (eds.): Research in Accounting Measurement. American Accounting Association 1966.

[35] Kriebel, C.H., R.L. Van Horn, and J.T. Heames (eds.): Management Information and Control Systems. New York 1969.

[36] Lowe, E.: "On the Idea of a Management Control System: Integrating Accounting and Management Control". In: The Journal of Management Studies, Vol. 8, No. 1 1971.

[37] Malcolm, D.G. and A.J. Rowe (eds.): Management Control Systems. New York 1960.

[38] McKeever, J.M. and B. Kruse: Management Reporting Systems. New York 1971.

[39] Morton, M.S.: Management Decision Systems: Computer Based Support for Decision Making. Division of Research, Graduate School of Business, Harvard University 1971.

[40] Bensoussan, A. and B. Naslund: "The Maximum Principle and Financial Decisions under Risk". European Institute for Advanced Studies in Management, Working Paper No. 72–2. Brussels 1972.

[41] Prince, T.R.: Information Systems for Planning and Control. Homewood, Illinois 1971.

[42] Prince, T.R.: Information Systems for Management Planning and Control. Homewood, Illinois 1971.

[43] Pontryagin, L.S., V.G. Boltyanskii, R.V. Gamgreldidze, and E.F. Mischenko: The Mathematical Theory of Optimal Processes. New York 1962.

[44] Raiffa, H. and R. Schlaifer: Decision Analysis. Reading, Mass. 1968.

[45] Malcolm, D.G. and A.J. Rowe: "An Approach to Computer-Based Management Control Systems". In: California Management Review, Vol. 3, No. 3 1961, pp. 4–15.

[46] Sethi, S. and G.L. Thompson: "Applications of Mathematical Control Theory to Finance". In: Journal of Financial and Quantitative Analysis. December 1970.

[47] Simon, H.A.: The New Science of Management Decision. New York-Evanston-London 1960.

[48] Stedry, A.: Budget Control and Cost Behavior. Englewood Cliffs, New Jersey 1960.

[49] Stokes, P.M.: "A Total Systems Approach to Management Control". American Management Association. New York 1968.

[50] Summers, J.K. and E. Bennett: "AESOP – A Final Report: A Prototype On-Line Interactive Information Control System". In: D.E. Walker (ed.): Information Systems Science and Technology. Washington, D.C. 1967.

[51] Ijiri, Y. and G.L. Thompson: "Applications of Mathematical Control Theory to Accounting and Budgeting: The Continuous Wheat Trading Model". In: The Accounting Review, Vol. 45 1970, pp. 246–258.

[52] Taylor, H.M.: "Sequential Control of a Gaussian Process". In: Technometrics, Vol. 9, No. 1 February 1967, pp. 29–41.

[53] Tilemann, T.: „Planungssprachen – Abgrenzung und Analyse ihrer Einsatzmöglichkeiten in entscheidungs-orientierten Informations-Systemen". BIFOA-Arbeitsbericht 72/14.

[54] Tocher, K.D.: "Control". In: Operational Research Quarterly, Vol. 21, No. 2 June 1970, pp. 159–180.

[55] Zannetos, Z.S.: "Toward Intelligent Management Information Systems". In: Industrial Management Review, Vol. 9, No. 3 Spring 1968.

[56] Zannetos, Z.S.: "Toward a Functional Accounting System: Accounting Variance and Statistical Variance Analysis". In: Industrial Management Review, Vol. 7, No. 2 Spring 1966.

[57] Zannetos, Z.S.: "Some Thoughts on Internal Control Systems of the Firm". In: The Accounting Review, Vol. 39, No. 4 October 1964.

[58] Zannetos, Z.S.: "Standard Costs as a First Step to Probablistic Control: A Theoretical Justification, an Extension and Implications". In: The Accounting Review, Vol. 39, No. 2 April 1964.

German abstract

Die Auswirkungen neuer Techniken des Management-Control auf Informationssystem und Organisationsstruktur

Von *E. Gerald Hurst jr.*

Probleme der Kontrollaufgaben des Management haben gegenüber anderen Managementaufgaben – wie beispielsweise der Planung – in der Vergangenheit wenig Beachtung gefunden, obwohl gerade Kontrollfunktionen einen beachtlichen Teil der Management-Ressourcen binden. Gegenstand der Untersuchung von Hurst bilden die neueren Entwicklungen von Management-Control-Techniken, deren Auswirkungen auf die Effizienz der Management-Kontrollen sowie die Vorteile und Einflüsse solcher Techniken beim praktischen Einsatz im Informationssystem der Unternehmung.

Der Begriff Management-Control umfaßt solche Managementtechniken, die sicherstellen, daß benötigte Ressourcen unter Beachtung der jeweiligen Formal- und Sachziele effizient beschafft und verwendet werden. Derartige Managementtechniken unterstützen die Meß-, Analyse- und Durchsetzungsprozesse zur Überwachung und Steuerung der betrieblichen Vollzugshandlungen. Die Mehrzahl dieser Techniken dient vorwiegend der Analyse von Aufgabenerfüllungsprozessen, der Überwachung der betrieblichen Realität mit Hilfe vorgegebener Planwerte und der quantitativen Erfassung von Zielabweichungen.

Eine Auswahl neuerer Entwicklungen des Management-Control sei im folgenden kurz aufgezählt:

- Planungssprachen,
- interaktive Computersysteme,
- mathematische Programmierung,
- Bayessche Statistik,
- Kontrolldiagramme,
- Suchtheorie,
- computergestützte medizinische Diagnostik.

Eingesetzt als Management-Control-Techniken haben diese zum Teil aus anderen Fachbereichen entlehnten Methoden die verschiedensten Auswirkungen auf das betriebliche Informationssystem und die Organisationsstruktur einer Unternehmung. Trotz der Unterschiedlichkeit der Interdependenzen sind die unmittelbaren Auswirkungen einer Einführung der o.a. Analysetechniken auf das Informationssystem einer Unternehmung gering. Bedeutsamer ist hier die Frage, ob das bestehende Informationssystem die nötige Anpassungsfähigkeit zur reibungslosen Implementierung eines Management-Control-Systems besitzt. Insbesondere die rechenintensiven Control-Systeme benötigen einen vergleichsweise hohen Implementierungsaufwand, weil ihr Einsatz eine bestimmte Hardware-Software-Konfiguration voraussetzt, während andere Systeme ohne formale Implementierungsschwierigkeiten benutzt werden können. Trotz des erhöhten Aufwands fordert Hurst, die Implementierung von Management-Control-Systemen von vornherein als Real-Time-System vorzunehmen, da diese Systeme zur Unterstützung von Managemententscheidungen auf aktuelle Informationen über das Betriebsgebaren angewiesen sind.

Daneben gehen direkte Wirkungsbeziehungen vom Management-Control-System auf das Entscheidungsverhalten der Manager aus, die nun in die Lage versetzt werden, größere Probleme als bisher schneller und mit größerer Entscheidungssicherheit zu lösen. Dadurch kann der Aufgabenbereich des einzelnen Aktionsträgers um weitere Handlungsprogramme angereichert werden mit dem Ergebnis einer übergreifenden Rezentralisierung der betrieblichen Führungs- und Entscheidungsaufgaben. Mithin bestehen also starke Interdependenzen zwischen Kontrollsystem und Organisationsstruktur einer Unternehmung. Insbesondere die Kontrollaufgaben der Stäbe können an das Maschinensystem delegiert werden, was zu einer horizontalen Straffung des hierarchischen Stellengefüges führen kann, wenn nicht andere Faktoren diese Wirkungen kompensieren sollten.

An organizational concept for the design of Management Information Systems

By *Alfred Kieser* and *Herbert Kubicek*

1. From computer Taylorism to computer Human Relation

One of the main functions of Management Information Systems (MIS) is the support of managers in ill-defined decision-making.[1] A major problem in MIS design is, therefore, to utilize the potential contained in modern computer development for ill-defined decision-making. The realization of this aim is normally seen in integrated information storage and retrieval systems in which managers can solve their problems in direct interaction with the computer.

The criteria commonly applied to an MIS design defined in this way are quick access to as much relevant and up-to-date data as possible with the help of convenient and fast retrieval procedures [2; 20; 30; 49; 61].

Criteria of this kind are based on functional considerations: The technical potential of computers can be utilized effectively when the computer functions, which amplify some human functions and replace others at higher speed, are directly linked to specific human abilities (problem identification, association etc.) by means of an interactive man-machine-system [22; 29]. By seeing man and computer as competing means for the fulfillment of functions, and by discussing their relative advantages, the impression is created that MIS design can be conceptualized for all organizations in the same way on the basis of technical criteria. From this point of view, the major MIS design problem of a specific organization consists in deciding on the basis of a cost-benefit analysis as to which functions should be assigned to computers and which to men [9].

In such a conceptual framework of MIS design the utilization of the computer potential centers around the questions as to which data volume, which reaction time, what degree of flexibility etc. are adequate for the specific problems of the organization in question. Human jobs are visualized in the abstract from properties of organization members and, therefore, are not qualitatively distinct from computer jobs.

Recently some authors have pointed to the need of considering individual behavior of the users as a determinant of MIS design [33]. Empirical investigations which

---

1 The authors are indebted to Michael Wollnik for his helpful comments on an earlier draft.

have shown that the demand for information is considerably below the information supplied by MIS [18; 59; 72], and some critical thoughts on the "new rationality" it creates, have led to take the acceptance of MIS by its users as the key variable determining efficiency.

A high degree of user convenience of the system which can be reached by easy access, easy to handle user programming languages etc. is seen as instrumental for this acceptance [31; 33]. To take proper account of this aspect in MIS design, participation of users in the design process [42; 43; 51; 62] and a deeper investigation in the psychological implications of MIS applications is needed [33; 44; 45].

The mere functional and technical view of MIS has been compared with the Taylorism approach [44]. Like Taylorism, which intended to optimize the efficiency of work processes by precisely defining procedures to optimize human capacity and endurance, an MIS design strategy orientated toward capacity expansion and the comparative advantages of the computer may lead to dysfunctional behavior. This approach has, therefore, to be seen as one-sided and insufficient. The same objection can, however, be made against an approach which sees user behavior as the major variable. Though it is stressed that "a renaissance of emotional human relations ideas" is not intended [71], a certain affinity cannot be ruled out entirely.

The laboratory experiments on MIS user behavior resemble those which were conducted during the human relations movement and which, until now, could not prove their relevance for organizational design. The critical point of these approaches is that interaction between men, or between man and machine takes place in an organizational vacuum.

In organization theory it took some time, starting from Taylorism and other classical management theories and taking the detour via the human relations movement until concepts were developed which aspire an appropriate balance between variables of work requirements, individual and group behavior and organization structure [11; 37; 39; 57]. Such a detour is avoidable in the construction of concepts for MIS design. In this paper, individual behavior and organization structure are stressed as factors influencing MIS design. The general insight for the concept to be developed is contained in the following quotation on man-machine-systems in general:

> "We need to know precisely what the system is supposed to do, the environment in which it will operate, the inputs it will receive, the operations it will perform on these inputs, and the outputs it is supposed to produce. We also need to know in detail all of the constraints – engineering, environmental, economic and social – under which it must be constructed and operated" [9].

This paper takes special account of the targets of the system and of the environmental or contextual constraints under which it has to operate.

> "Considerations on design cannot restrict themselves to the ends of the system; they have to take into account, at the same time, the given restrictions. Therefore, at the beginning of his work the system designer has to pose the questions: Which restrictions have to be accepted? Which ones can be changed?" [66]

The design strategy proposed in this paper rests on the assumption that managerial decision-making is very rarely an individual process which affects only a single manager. In general, managerial decision-making processes are aimed at the coordination of activities. This means that ends and conditions are to be considered within the general coordination context. The utilization of the computer potential as a goal of MIS design should, therefore, be oriented toward the coordination needs of the organization [24] and should aim at the improvement of conventional coordination instruments. From this point of view the computer potential is first of all to be seen as a coordination potential. The neglect of this aspect could very well be one reason for the "unlocked profit potential" often referred to [17; 42; 43].

Coordination needs are reflected in the organization structure of which coordination instruments are a part. The first step in MIS design should, therefore, be to utilize the computer potential for an improvement of the existing coordination instruments. When, as a result of this process, the system ends and inputs have been determined, the implementation of the system should take place in a context of acceptance by the users. This acceptance is of great importance for the efficiency of any system. It is, however, only a necessary but not the sole condition. A conceptual scheme for MIS design should take into consideration organization structure as well as individual behavior.

2. A model of the interrelationships between context, structural differentiation, coordination mechanisms and individual behavior

The discussion in this paper follows a model which is based on the following interrelationships:

(1) Empirical research has shown that the coordination needs of an organization are determined by such factors as size of the organization (volume of operations), dynamics of the environment, complexity of technology etc. These factors constitute the organizational context.

(2) The context determines the coordination needs indirectly and directly: On the one hand, context determines organizational differentiation, i. e. the number of organizational subunits such as departments or jobs and on the other hand it determines the task structure of these subunits. The specific coordination needs of an organization result from the degree of structural differentiation and from the task structures of the different organizational subunits.

(3) With regard to these coordination needs different coordination mechanisms are implemented in different extents to ensure successful interactions with the specific context.

(4) The introduction of MIS creates possibilities to improve these coordination mechanisms and, within certain limits, to change the extent to which they are used. The implementation of MIS does not effect a levelling so that all organizations with MIS tend to have the same coordination system, but rather allows for a more differentiated combination of the coordination mechanisms with the chance of better reaction to the specific coordination needs (coordination potential of MIS).

(5) The coordination potential of MIS may have feed-back effects on the structural differentiation of organizations. These effects also do not induce a levelling of coordination systems.

(6) The coordination potential of MIS can only be realized if the coordination needs induced by the context and by structural differentiation are taken into consideration along with the different coordination mechanisms while formulating the system concept. MIS and conventional coordination instruments must be understood in terms of their mutual dependence, and be designed with regard to the specific coordination needs they have to fulfil.

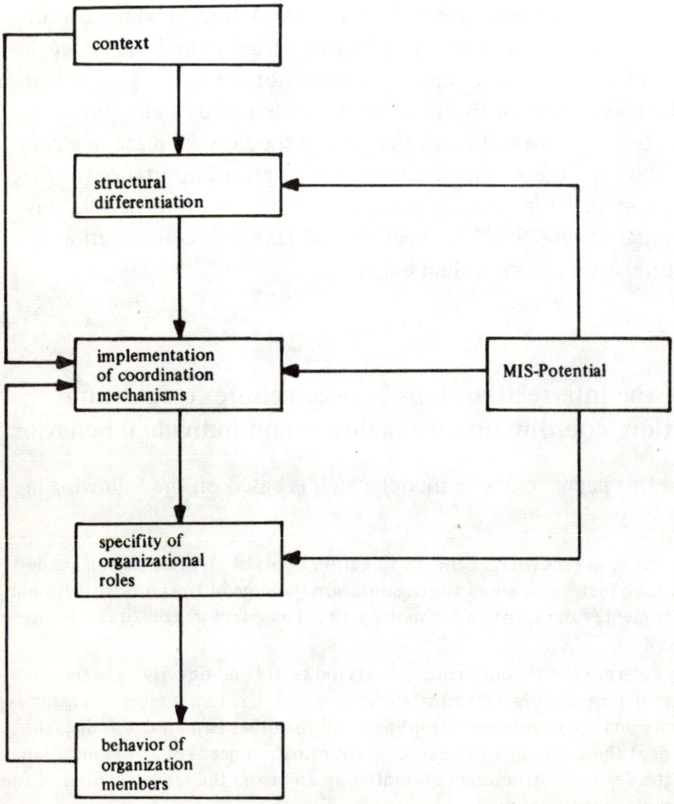

Fig. 1. A model of the interrelations between organizational context, coordination mechanisms, and behavior of organization members

(7) Effects of MIS on individual behavior must be analysed by taking the total coordination system as a frame of reference. The organizational role of the individual is formed by the conventional coordination mechanisms and by the MIS. The organizational role determines to what extent individual needs, e. g. social needs, needs for self-actualization etc. can be realized. The acceptance of MIS by the individual can only be assessed if it is seen as part of the problem of the acceptance of the total organizational role.

These general relationships are shown in Fig. 1 and will be discussed in some detail in this paper. The purpose of this model is to serve as a frame of reference for further empirical research and for practical MIS design.

3. Coordination in organizations: Empirical results

The empirical results which will be presented in this chapter do not concern the influence of MIS on coordination and organization structure. Studies of this kind, so far, have been very crude and can be critisized from a methodological point of view [46]. Instead, empirical studies on the general relationships between context and coordination system or organization structure are reported. These general relationships serve as a basis for the discussion of how MIS can change the coordination system in a given context.

3.1 Coordination mechanisms

On the basis of empirical results the following types of coordination mechanisms can be distinguished:

(1) Self-Coordination by non-hierarchical communication
The interdependent organizational units coordinate themselves; the solutions are not based on decision rules or programs and cannot be predicted with a high degree of precision. This type of coordination is implemented by teams, committee meetings etc.

(2) Coordination by hierarchical decision making
The organizational units in need of coordination have their activities defined by a unit at a higher level. These coordination decisions are not made on the basis of decision rules and are thus also difficult to predict. This type of coordination can be measured empirically by the amount of hierarchical (i. e. vertical) communication.

(3) Coordination by planning
Activities which require coordination between units are scheduled in advance with the help of routines or algorithms. In particular, these plans

contain precise goals for the units in need of coordination. If the problem situation and the planning procedures are known, the outcome of this type of coordination is easily predictable. In empirical studies the measurement of this type of coordination should extend to the scope and intensity of planning activities.

(4) Coordination by programs

The organizational units apply decision rules which secure coordination with other units. These decision rules are written down in the form of job descriptions and rules and regulations handbooks, or they only exist in the form of habits. The extent to which this coordination type is applied can be measured empirically with an analysis of the above-mentioned documents or by interviews with the organization members. Activities which are an outcome of this coordination are highly predictable.

3.2 The influence of context on organization structure

Structural differentiation and coordination mechanisms can be regarded as variables which constitute the organization structure. In this chapter the relationships between context and organization structure are investigated along the lines suggested by the model of Fig. 1 The organizational context is formed by factors which determine complexity and uncertainty of the organization's task. The most important contextual variables are:

- size of the organization,
- dynamics of the environment,
- technology,
- product diversification.

The larger the organization, the more complex its technology, the more dynamic its environment, and the more diversified its products are, the more complex its overall task can be expected to be. The organization reacts to contextual complexity with structural differentiation, i. e. by establishing special subunits [37]: The organization isolates within the overall problem certain subproblems and assigns these subproblems to special subunits. For example the production department can concentrate on problems connected with production, and needs only to deal with that part of the organization's environment which is relevant to production problems. The complexity induced by high diversification can be reduced by setting up special product departments within the sales function or by a divisionalized structure. Since, from the view-point of the decision-maker, task complexity means uncertainty, we also speak of uncertainty reduction through structuring the organization [37; 52].

Structural differentiation decreases external complexity but increases internal complexity: The output of the specialized subunits must be coordinated. The higher the organizational differentiation, the higher the overall coordination needs [48]. These coordination needs are dealt with by different coordination mechanisms. It can be assumed that the coordination system is determined by the context as well as by the form the structural differentiation takes. That is, the organization's context influences its coordination system directly, and indirectly, as shown in Fig. 1.

The following paragraphs discuss the influences of each contextual variable in some detail.

3.2.1 Size of organization

Size of Organization, usually measured in total number of employees, increases structural differentiation. The larger the organization, the more specialized subunits and jobs it is likely to have [6; 12; 39]. Structural differentiation increases organizational complexity. Since coordination by centralized decision-making in a large organization tends to overload the hierarchy, the organization is forced to decentralize decisions with increasing size [6; 10]. However, decentralization of decisions increases the risk that the decisions made at lower echelons are badly coordinated with the general policy of the organization. This risk is reduced by increasing the amount of coordination by programs and plans.

3.2.2 Dynamics of the environment

A dynamic environment influences the coordination needs directly and indirectly. It increases the number of specialized subunits – e. g. it forces the introduction of such subunits as sales forecasting or R & D – as well as structural difference between these subunits. Both tendencies increase organizational complexity, and thus coordination needs [48].

This increase in coordination needs is very difficult to master with hierarchical decision-making alone. It is now of interest, which other coordination mechanisms are predominantly applied for coping with a dynamic environment. Contrary to the stereotype that organizations in a dynamic environment are distinguished by an organic structure [7], recent empirical studies have shown that coordination by programming increases over all with the turbulence of the environment [1].

It can be assumed that especially in a turbulent environment the organization is forced to program as many activities as possible to keep the internal variance low.

By rigid control of the routinizeable processes the organization sets capacity free for unstructured decision making.

Empirical investigations have also shown that the origin of environmental turbulence is important in predicting the type of coordination stressed. Turbulence caused by competitive activity is correlated with self-coordination, i. e. team work and non-hierarchical communication, while turbulence caused by technological change is correlated with the use of formal planning systems [37; 39].

3.2.3 Technology

Integration of workflow activities reduces the need for coordinating production activities. More recent empirical studies demonstrated that workflow technology has only a weak influence on the overall organization structure [13; 35; 39]. This finding contradicts earlier findings [32; 73; 75]. Khandwalla showed, however, that in successful organizations workflow integration correlates with vertical specialization, i. e. specialization of activities which precede or follow production activities. This specialization is induced by the organization's striving to secure sales of a high volume output which leads to the introduction of such specialized functions as sales forecasting, advertising etc. [38].

3.2.4 Diversification

The organization can react to complexity induced by a high degree of diversification by divisionalizing its structure or by intensifying coordination efforts within a functional structure. Evidence from empirical studies is not as affirmative as is this speculative proposition. Divisionalization correlates with the use of formal planning systems [37; 40]. However, when the degree of divisionalization is controlled in statistical analysis, a rather strong partial correlation between diversification and self-coordination in form of teams and programming appears [40].

3.3 The influence of the organization structure on individual behavior

Coordination mechanisms aim finally to induce a certain individual behavior by structuring and defining action fields or roles [23; 24]. Seen under this aspect, coordination mechanisms can be interpreted as expectations of the organization as addressed to the individual members. One of the most interesting questions is to what degree the individual accepts the coordination mechanisms and, in so doing, responds positively to the expectations. Poor acceptance of the coordination system may necessitate a revision of the coordination structure which is indicated in the model by a feedback loop between behavior and implementation of the coordination mechanisms.

Empirical analysis of individual behavior as a function of applied coordination mechanisms is still in a preliminary stage. Empirical results available from one British and one German study may be interpreted as follows [11]: if coordination relies heavily on hierarchical decision making (centralized organization structure) management will perceive a strong routinization of work processes, will show little tendency to behave nonconformingly and will experience little conflict. If decisions are decentralized and programming and planning intensified, managers perceive a deroutinization of their work and expect more nonconforming behavior from their colleagues. While in the British study, anticipated nonconforming behavior corresponded with actual behavior, in the German study nonconforming behavior correlated negatively with programming and planning. Seen from a normative point of view the following comments can be made on the results: the comparison between the UK and Germany indicates that it cannot be taken for granted that indirect coordination by programming and planning will in all instances lead to behavior in accordance with role expectations. The study in the UK reveals the possibility that a narrow role definition by programming and planning increases actual nonconforming behavior and conflict. An explanation for this effect could be that decentralization of decisions increases the need for selfactualization but – limiting freedom of action considerably by programs and plans – hinders its fulfilment. Extending self-coordination seems a better strategy to satisfy the growing need of managers for selfactualization [4].

4. The coordination potential of MIS

After a general discussion of the influences of context and individual behavior on the coordination system, we will now discuss in which way MIS can change these relationships. On the basis of our model (Fig. 1) the following aspects will be discussed in particular:

(1) MIS offers a potential to decrease structural differen tiation;

(2) MIS can be used to improve coordination mechanisms (complementary relationship between MIS and conventional coordination system) and it can be used for the partial substitution of one coordination mechanism by another (substitutive relationships).

4.1 Decrease of structural differenciation

The enormous storage- and computing capacities of modern information technology allow the integration of interdependent tasks into a single task, and, thus, an integration of organizational units which were only loosely linked before the implementation of MIS [27; 69]. This means a reduction of structural differentiation to the extent that capacity limitations are its cause:

> "As organizations deal with their external environments they become segmented into units, each of which has as its major task the problem of dealing with a part of the conditions outside the firm. This is the result of the fact that any one group of managers has a limited span of surveillance" [48].

Emery pictures changes in structural differentiation induced by the computer potential as follows:

> "Information technology affects organizational structure by permitting an increase in the scope of activities falling within a given subunit. As the organization gains enhanced ability to manipulate information, the permitted size of a "manageable" task expands. Global objectives therefore need not be fragmented as finely as before, and the number of organizational subunits can be correspondingly reduced . . . Activities that formerly involved strong interactions among different units may now be included within a single comprehensive unit. Such consolidation obviously reduces the interactions among subunits and permits the coupling of previously decoupled activities" [21].

Examples of such a coupling of activities can be found quite often within the production or logistic functions [64] but are also reported from other functional areas [63; 69; 70].

Only those structural differentiations which are caused by capacity limitations can be reduced by MIS. However, subunits are also formed because organizations try to realize advantages of specialization in the process of uncertainty reduction:

> "To be able to realize divisions of work in problem solving, subsystems are identified within a larger system. This leads to a reduction of complexity within the system. At the same time the system's capabilities for change and adaption are increased since disturbances from the environment can be directed for problem solving to partially independent systems" [74].

With increasing complexity and increasing rate of change of the environment, activities of problem identification, perception of opportunities, bargaining with external units etc. become more and more important. Specialization of these activities leads to structural differentiation which cannot be reduced by MIS. Whisler points to another aspect which is also a consequence of an increasing complex and dynamic environment. He argues that changes in a highly integrated MIS are more expensive than changes in smaller systems in which activities are only loosely linked and changes in one part do not involve fundamental changes in the whole MIS structure [70].

Summarizing, it can be assumed that the broad subunits outline will not be affected significantly as a consequence of MIS [65]. However, within these general subunits (functions, divisions etc.) a reduction of structural differentiation can be expected.

4.2 Relationships between MIS and the coordination instruments

The coordination needs of the organization as derived in the first part of this paper form a frame of orientation for MIS design. The conceptual scheme for MIS design developed in this paper stresses the need for a simultaneous planning of MIS and conventional coordination mechanisms taking into consideration their mutual effects. The evaluation of conventional coordination instruments distinguishes this concept from an approach by Galbraith [24], who establishes a direct relationship between different coordination needs and types of MIS.
In the following we will discuss the relationships between MIS and coordination mechanisms separately for each mechanism.

4.2.1 Coordination by planning

With respect to coordination by planning the MIS potential can be utilized for a quality improvement of this mechanism. This improvement can be brought about by taking into consideration a larger number of interdependencies in the planning process and/or by increasing the actuality of plans [29].
If the planning process does not take account of all the relevant interdependencies between organizational subunits the plans will not correspond exactly to the real situation. Under these circumstances the organizational units are likely to see the plans as unjustified limitations to their activities and their willingness to accept the plans will tend to be low. This is also valid for planning based on data which are imprecise or not up-to-date. These dimensions of formal planning can be improved by an appropriate design of MIS.

> "An increased data handling capability permits high-level planners to develop and manipulate much more detailed and comprehensive formalized models than can be handled by conventional planning techniques . . . detailed plans can be made more realistic and consistent. Comprehensive models submerge relatively unimportant information from the view of the high-level planner. As a result, he is less likely to impose infeasible constraints on lower-level planners" [21].

Of special importance under this aspect are man-machine-communication systems [41]. However, it must be stressed that the call for up-to-date information is not identical with a call for real-time information systems [55]; the timeliness of information is to be seen relative to the time-span of the problems [15].

4.2.2 Coordination by hierarchical ad-hoc decisions

MIS can improve coordination by hierarchical decision making by improving the information basis on which managers make their coordination decisions. As has been indicated above, with increasing size of the organization this coordination instrument loses impetus. MISs can change this relationship if they are designed to increase the manager's capacity for coordinating decisions. With MIS support the manager can scan more alternatives before he makes his choice and, thereby, improve the quality of his decisions [26].

The utilization of MIS for hierarchical ad-hoc decisions can also lead to a replacement of orders which must be accepted by the subordinates without proper insight into the necessities which lead to these orders. With the help of MIS, decisions made in the hierarchy can be transmitted by setting parameters (restrictions) in the information base of the lower echelons. This transmission increases the transparancy between hierarchical levels by making explicit the necessities and consequences of hierarchical decisions. Personal interaction between hierarchical levels is partially substituted by communication with a common data base [64]. Authority based on personality characteristics and formal status thus becomes less important. A new form of rationality is introduced into hierarchical relationships [3] which, for the subordinate, can mean a decrease in personal dependence on the supervisor. The executives, however, are forced to reveal their norms and practices on which their decisions are based:

> " . . . one greatly reduces the probability that managers can order others simply because they have power. This may be threatening to executives who have, up till now, been free to make the organization 'move' even if they had incomplete or invalid information . . . One of the marks of a successful executive has been that he was able to marshal human and financial resources to make his decision come true even if others felt that the decision could not be accomplished. As MIS become more sophisticated there will be less need for ambiguity and self-fulfilling prophecies . . ." [3].

The realization of these improvements in coordination by hierarchical ad-hoc decisions are to a large extent dependent on the readiness of the managers to accept a substitution of formal authority by functional authority [36]. Resistance to this kind of change could be the real cause of the often deplored prejudices of management toward MIS.

4.2.3 Self-coordination

MIS can also be utilized to improve self-coordination between managers. Though in organizations with dynamic and uncertain tasks this coordination instrument is more efficient than hierarchical decision-making, its application is often opposed by top management. The reason may be the risk involved in the decentralized self-coordination, namely the risk that self-coordination on lower levels contradicts top management decisions. MIS which are especially designed for self-coordination can decrease this risk considerably in several respects. An example of such an MIS which relies heavily on self-coordination is described by Morton [55].

In general the risk mentioned above is decreased by a higher reliability of the activities carried through on lower levels and the possibilities of implementing indirect controls.

> "In as much as automation consequently increases the reliability of operations . . . it encourages decentralization of responsibilities by reducing its risk for top management" [6].

The higher reliability of the activities of lower levels is brought about by a better data base which is accessible from all levels [8; 26]:

> "If the decision maker has access to information only about his immediate location, his data base is called local. On the other hand, if the decision maker has access to information concerning the state of affairs in all departments, his data base is global. The scope of the data base available to the decision mechanism affects the ability to make decisions which are consistent with decisions made in other parts of the organization" [24].

The higher levels will consider activities of lower levels more reliable [64], since all levels share a common data base and mutual coordination becomes less dependent on personality factors of the managers involved. When discussion is based on a common data base conflicts are more likely to be resolved in a way which is in accordance with the organization's goals [55].

The implementation of an MIS can also lead to a better insight into the problems of other units with which coordination is necessary [65]. An MIS can, therefore, contribute towards the replacement of win-lose struggles between departments by problem solving behavior [5].

> "In order to capture the wholeness of the problem, the technology must deal not only with the behavior of each department, but also with the interrelationships among the departments . . . To succeed means that the departments which have been locked into win-lose conflicts will have to learn to cooperate with each other" [3].

Argyris doubts, however, that MIS can induce a transition from individual or unit centered thinking to a cooperative one. Contrary to his assumption, empirical investigations have shown that interest in the activities of neighbor departments increases with the expansion of accessible data [36; 47; 64; 65].

On the basis of an MIS which applies terminals with on-line access, it is possible to reach a high standard of self-coordination between departments while keeping the frequency and duration of personal meetings low. Systems which do not allow for direct computer access increase the average time spent in meetings considerably [56] while systems which apply terminals will have drastically reduced it [55]. The reason for these effects must be found in the usual function of committees, meetings etc.

> "Improved information flow will minimize the need to use committees as an information pooling device in addition, it will act to make unnecessary the formation of committees to function as information transmitters" [64].

The possibilities to improve self-coordination with MIS are apt to diminish considerably the risk top management sees involved with this coordination instrument. In addition, the system offers a chance to install indirect controls which function like indirect organization controls to secure consistency of decentralized decisions with organizational goals (see section 3.2.1). The standardization of decision making processes enforced by MIS sets a frame for self-coordination. Consequently, self-coordination on the basis of MIS must be discussed in connection with standardization and programming. The effects of MIS on these coordination instruments will now be dealt with.

4.2.4 Coordination by programming

With respect to the coordination instruments discussed so far MIS could be utilized for an improvement or extension, while in the case of coordination by standardization or programming a substitutive effect can be observed. The programming inherent in modern technologies – in information technologies as well as in production technologies – renders organizational programming in form of job descriptions, organization handbooks etc. superfluous to some extent. Technical programs of this kind are often more strongly adhered to than organizational programs, which is obvious in the cases of the assembly line and input activities for accounting information systems. Blau and Schoenherr have shown this substitutive effect of MIS in their empirical study:

> "Automation standardizes operations, not only directly by mechanizing some tasks but also indirectly by imposing restraints on others that are performed by employees in as much as their performance must conform to the computer set-up. The design of the computer installation serves as an impersonal mechanism of control, which makes operations partly self-regulating and less dependent on supervisory intervention" [6].

While for the coordination instruments discussed so far the coordination potential of MIS was utilized for the intelligence or choice phase of the decision process, standardization refers to the implementation of decisions. Determining who can have access to what data and what techniques are available for the manipulation of these data means a precise definition of the user's roles. Thus with the help of MIS the managers on higher levels can structure the tasks of their subordinate levels more effectively and at the same time less visibly than in applying job descriptions, organizing handbooks etc.

> "These decisions suffice to give top management the power to determine what the organization does and in which direction it is moving, even though everybody within the organization is virtually free to exercise full discretion in his own sphere" [6].

Organizational programs become, therefore, to some extent superfluous in units which are highly structured by MIS applications. Only for units which do not directly interact with the MIS, even if they are highly dependent on MIS activities, can the degree of organizational programming not be reduced. In general, however, it can be expected that the degree of organizational standardization is reduced by the substitution of organizational programming with programming inherent in the information technology [47].

The extent to which a precise definition of individual roles by MIS activities is reasonable depends on the total coordination needs of the organization and on the degree of acceptance by its users. The call for MIS which does not impose any restrictions on the users [45] seems, therefore, too indifferentiated, since such a system does not take account of the specific coordination needs and of the coordination instruments. Taking the acceptance by users into consideration can, however, mean a modification of the system concept which was originally only oriented toward the coordination needs and coordination instruments.

So far, only the general possibilities of utilizing the coordination potential of computers have been discussed. In the last section some problems of implementing this potential will be dealt with.

5. The implementation of the coordination potential of MIS

The problem of implementing the coordination potential of MIS extends to a technical and a behavioral dimension. The technical dimension consists in determining the data base, the retrieval and manipulation techniques which correspond to the specific coordination needs of the organization. The behavioral dimension concerns the requirement that the users have to accept the system and make use of its potential constitutes the behavioral dimension.

A pessimistic view of the latter problem is expressed by Argyris who claims that the coordination potential of MIS cannot be realized because management does not accept the systems:

> "The position is that as MIS become more sophisticated they will tend to create the conditions described above. However . . . man need not be reactive and submissive to a system. Indeed, it will be our argument that if the MIS were used effectively, they could actually free the manager rather than restrict him. Our pessimistic prediction is that man will not tend to use MIS effectively because of the norms of the existing world and the way he has programmed himself to be more incompetent than competent in dealing with people" [3].

This prediction rests on the assumption that the "new rationality" created by MIS leads to feelings of inferiority among management and causes the following dilemma:

> "If he follows the new rationality he will succeed as a manager and fail as a human being. He is damned if he refuses to obey, and he damns himself if he does obey" [3].

To date, the hypothesis that the implementation of an MIS in most cases leads to resistance could not be proven empirically. Some points can in fact be brought forward which reduce its plausibility: the hypothesis presumes a manager whose chances rest on improvisation, increases of personal power and an information policy governed by personal goals [3]. As a general proposition this assumption is as unrealistic as the assumption of classical management theory that the organization members are always behaving functionally. A more realistic view of this problem must take into account that large MIS, in general, comprise a number of hierarchical levels in the organization which can display distinct reactions [14].

In addition, users' reactions are also dependent on the implementation strategy:

> "A fair amount of research has pointed up the fact that resistance to change is a reaction primarily to certain methods of instituting change rather than an inherent human characteristic" [25].

Finally it has to be stressed that the effects of MIS on individual behavior can be interpreted as gradual changes of prevailing organizational conditions [24; 26; 47]. Conventional organization measures as well as MIS aim at a structuring of individual behavior with regard to the organization's goals. The effect of MIS on individual behavior can, therefore, only be investigated in combination with the prevailing or changed organization structure:

> "The studies of the effect of automation on human relations are not to be criticized because of their inconsistent findings: that is almost inevitable. They are to be criticized, instead, because they study the wrong thing. There is an implicit assumption in human relations research on automation that has never been substantiated. The assumption is roughly this: the impact of automation on the worker is direct, it is not mediated by formal organizational structure . . . This assumption is rejected here. The effects of automation on human relations should be assessed only after taking into account the changes in organizational process which automation itself engenders" [54].

On the basis of this, a strong stand against an ambitious MIS can only be justified when the effects of conventional coordination mechanisms on individual behavior are also judged negatively and when the increase in efficiency of conventional coordination instruments by MIS is seen as amplification of negative effects. And Argyris does in fact take this stand. But since, from the perspective of the individual, dysfunctional behavior is predominantly effected by hierarchical ad-hoc decisions while other instruments, preeminently self-coordination, are valued positively – even by Argyris [4] – such a position seems impossible to defend.

6. Conclusion

This paper has tried to indicate that MIS do not lead to a uniform coordination strategy for all organizations [24]. Rather the manifold relationships between MIS and coordination instruments justify the assumption that a coordination system which can rely on an MIS must also be designed to correspond to the coordination needs created by the organization's context. However, MIS allows a certain emphasis of those coordination instruments which are more readily accepted by the users.

The discussion of MIS effects on the coordination system and individual behavior was speculative in part. An empirical investigation of these effects requires a reorientation in social science research on information technologies. Laboratory experiments, man-computer simulation studies [33], which deal with a simplified organizational environment and case studies, which deal with a single real situation cannot do justice to such a research interest [47].

The appropriate research techniques are field studies in which the relationships between different applications of MIS and the coordination instruments, as well as the effects on individual behavior are investigated. Before the field work can take place, however, intensive conceptional work must be done, since the problem is multi-causal and variables of different levels of aggregation will have to be studied (organizational context, structural differentiation, coordination mechanisms in different units, individual roles and attitudes on different hierarchical levels). For computer application on the operational level, a conceptual scheme which takes into consideration these requirements has been developed and tested in an empirical explorative study [47]. For the empirical study of MIS, the ideas developed in this paper should serve as a first step toward the formulation of a conceptual scheme.

As long as empirical results are not yet available practitioners will need a frame of orientation which points to the important technical, organizational, and behavioral problems of MIS design and produces some clues for their solution. As such a frame of orientation, the concept developed in this paper might also be introduced into the discussion.

References

[1] Aiken, Michael and Jerald Hage: The Organic Organization and Innovation. In: Sociology 5/1971, pp. 63–81.

[2] Amstutz, Arnold E.: Market-Oriented Management Systems: The Current Status. In: Journal of Marketing Research 6/1969, pp. 481–496.

[3] Argyris, Chris: Management Information Systems: The Callenge to Rationality and Emotionality. In: Management Science 17/1971, pp. B 275–B 292.

[4] Argyris, Chris: The Applicability of Organizational Sociology. Cambridge, Mass. 1972.

[5] Blake, R.R., H.A. Shepard and J.S. Mouton: Managing Intergroup Conflict in Industry. Houston 1964.

[6] Blau, Peter M. and Richard A. Schoenherr: The Structure of Organizations. New York 1971.

[7] Burns, Tom and G.M. Stalker: The Management of Innovation. London 1961.

[8] Carroll, Donald C.: On the Structure of Operational Control Systems. In: Operations Research and the Design of Management Information Systems. Ed. by John F. Pierce, Jr. New York 1967, pp. 391–415.

[9] Chapanis, Alphonse: On the Allocation of Functions between Men and Machines. In: Occupational Psychology, 39/1965, pp. 1–11.

[10] Child, John: Organization Structure and Strategies of Control: A Replication of the Aston Study. In: Administrative Science Quarterly 17/1972, pp. 163–177.

[11] Child, John: Strategies of Control and Organizational Behavior. In: Administrative Science Quarterly 18/1973, pp. 1–17.

[12] Child, John: Predicting and Understanding Organization Structure. In: Administrative Science Quarterly 18/1973, pp. 168–185.

[13] Child, John and Roger Mansfield: Technology, Size and Organization Structure. In: Sociology 6/1972, pp. 369–393.

[14] Coleman, Raymond, J. and M.J. Riley: The Organizational Impact of MUS. In: Journal of Systems Management 1972, pp. 13–19.

[15] Dearden, John: ‚Time-Span' in Management Control. In: Financial Executive 56/1968, No. 8, pp. 23–30.

[16] Dickson, G.W. and John K. Simmons: The Behavioral Side of MIS. Some Aspects of the "People Problem". In: Business Horizons No. 4/1970, pp. 59–71.

[17] Diebold, John: Bad Decisions on Computer Use. In: Harvard Business Revies 67/1969, No. 1, pp. 14 ff.

[18] Dunlop, R.A.: Some Empirical Observations on the Man-Machine Interface Question. In: Management Information Systems: Progress and Perspectives. Ed. by J.T. Heames, C.H. Kriebel and R.L. Van Horn. Englewood Cliffs 1970.

[19] Elm, Winfried A.: Das Management-Informationssystem als Mittel der Unternehmensführung. Berlin, New York 1972.

[20] Emery, James C.: Organizational Planning and Control Systems. Theory and Technology. New York 1969.

[21] Emery, James C.: The Impact of Information Technology on Organization. In: The Impact of Information Technology on Management Operations. Ed. by William C. House. Princeton, New York, Philadelphia, London 1971, pp. 153–165.

[22] Fitts, Paul M.: Functions of Man in Complex Systems. In: Aerospace-Engineering 21/1962, No. 1, pp. 34–39.

[23] Frese, Erich: Organisation und Koordination. In: Zeitschrift für Organisation 41/1972, pp. 404 ff.

[24] Galbraith, Jay R.: Achieving Integration Through Information Systems. In: Academy of Management Proceedings 12/1968, pp. 111–120.

[25] McGregor, Douglas: The Scanlon Plan Through a Psychologist's Eyes. In: Technology, Industry, and Man. Ed. by C.A. Walker. New York 1968, pp. 124 ff.

[26] Grochla, Erwin: Automation und Organisation. Die technische Entwicklung und ihre betriebswirtschaftlich-organisatorischen Konsequenzen. Wiesbaden 1966.

[27] Grochla, Erwin: Die Integration der Datenverarbeitung. Durchführung anhand eines integrierten Unternehmungsmodells. In: Bürotechnik und Automation 9/1968, pp. 3–14.

[28] Grochla, Erwin: Die Bedeutung der automatisierten Datenverarbeitung für die Unternehmungsführung. In: IBM-Nachrichten 18/1968, pp. 84–90.

[29] Grochla, Erwin: Auswirkungen der automatisierten Datenverarbeitung auf die Unternehmungsplanung. In: Zeitschrift für betriebswirtschaftliche Forschung, 23/1971, pp. 719–732.

[30] Grochla, Erwin: Unternehmungsorganisation. Neue Ansätze und Konzeptionen. Reinbek 1972.

[31] Grochla, Erwin: Das Engagement der Unternehmungsführung bei der Entwicklung computer-gestützter Informationssysteme. In: Fortschrittliche Betriebsführung 22/1973, pp. 65–72.

[32] Harvey, Edward: Technology and Structure of Organizations. In: American Sociological Review 33/1968, pp. 247–259.

[33] Hedberg, Bo: On Man-Computer Interaction in Organizational Decision-Making. A Behavioral Approach. Göteborg 1970.

[34] Hickson, D.J.: A Convergence in Organization Theory. In: Administrative Science Quarterly 11/1966, pp. 224–237.

[35] Hickson, D.J., D.S. Pugh and D.C. Pheysey: Operations Technology and Organization Structure: An Empirical Reappraisal. In: Administrative Science Quarterly 14/1969, pp. 378–397.

[36] Jaeggi, Urs and Herbert Wiedemann: Der Angestellte im automatisierten Büro. Stuttgart 1963.

[37] Khandwalla, Pradip N.: Uncertainty and the "Optimal" Design of Organizations. Working Paper, pres. at TIMS XIX-th Meeting. Houston, Texas 1972.

[38] Khandwalla, Pradip N.: Mass Output Orientation of Operations Technology and "Optimal" Organizational Structure. Working Paper, Faculty of Management, McGill University. Montreal, Canada.

[39] Kieser, Alfred: Einflußgrößen der Unternehmungsorganisation. Der Stand der empirischen Forschung und Ergebnisse einer eigenen Erhebung. Kölner Habilitationsschrift 1973.

[40] Kieser, Alfred: Beziehungen zwischen Organisationsstruktur und Verhalten der Organisationsmitglieder. Unveröffentlichtes Manuskript. Köln 1973.

[41] Kieser, Heinz-Peter: Mensch-Maschine-Kommunikation in Organisationen. Verhaltenswissenschaftliche Aspekte interaktiver Problemlösungsprozesse. Diss. Mannheim 1973.

[42] McKinsey & Co.: Der optimale Einsatz elektronischer Datenverarbeitungsanlagen. In: Zeitschrift für Betriebswirtschaft 34/1964, pp. 37–50.

[43] McKinsey & Co.: Unlocking the Computer's Profit Potential. In: Computers and Automation 18/1969, No. 4, pp. 24–33.

[44] Kirsch, Werner: Auf dem Weg zu einem neuen Taylorismus? In: IBM-Nachrichten 23/1973, pp. 561–566.

[45] Kirsch, Werner and Heinz-Peter Kieser: Verhaltenswissenschaftliche und empirische Forschungsprobleme bei der Entwicklung von MIS. Working Paper. Universität Mannheim.

[46] Kubicek, Herbert: The Study of the Impact of Computerized Information Systems on Management Processes and Organization Structure, Paper presented at the conference "Alternative Organizations: The Impact of Computers and Automation on Management, Structure, and Work Design (ALTORG)", held by the University of Gothenburg

and the International Institute of Management, Berlin, July 21–29, 1974, in Hindas, Sweden.

[47] Kubicek, Herbert: Informationstechnologie und organisatorische Regelungen. Berlin 1975.

[48] Lawrence, Paul R. and Jay W. Lorsch: Organization and Environment. Managing Differentiation and Integration. Homewood, Illinois 1969.

[49] Lutz, T. and H. Klimesch: Die Datenbank im Informationssystem. München, Wien 1971.

[50] Mann, Floyd C. and Lawrence K. Williams: Organizational Impact of White Collar Automation. In: Industrial Relations Research Association. Proceedings of the Eleventh Annual Meeting, Chicago, December 28–29, 1958.

[51] Mans, Günter: Erfolgsfaktoren für MIS-Projekte. Analyse drei getrennter Umfragen. In: Zeitschrift für Organisation 42/1973, pp. 190–196.

[52] March, James G. and Herbert A. Simon: Organizations. New York 1958.

[53] Mertens, Peter and Heinz Kress: Mensch-Maschine-Kommunikation als Hilfe bei Entscheidungsvorbereitung und Planung. In: Zeitschrift für betriebswirtschaftliche Forschung 22/1970, pp. 1–21.

[54] Meyer, Marshall W.: Automation and Bureaucratic Structure. In: American Journal of Sociology 74/1969, pp. 256–264.

[55] Morton, Michael S. Scott: Management Decision Systems. Computer-Based Support for Decision Making. Boston 1971.

[56] Parisi, Dominic G.: The Impact of a Change in Information Technology on Management Organization Structure, Decision Making, and Interpersonal Relations in a Large Insurance Company. Diss. Northwestern University, USA 1966.

[57] Porter, Lyman W. and Edward E. Lawler III: Properties of Organization Structure in Relation to Job Attitudes and Job Behavior. In: Psychological Bulletin 64/1965, pp. 23–51.

[58] Pugh, D.S., D.J. Hickson, C.R. Hinings and C. Turner: The Context of Organization Structures. In: Administrative Science Quarterly 14/1969, pp. 91–114.

[59] Sackman, Harold: Experimental Analysis of Human Behavior in Time-Sharing and Batch-Processing Information Systems. In: Management Information Systems: Progress and Perspectives. Ed. by J.T. Heames, C.H. Kriebel and R.L. Van Horn. Englewood Cliffs 1970.

[60] Sadler, Philip: Social Research on Automation. Social Science Research Council. London 1968.

[61] Schoderbek, Peter P.: Management Systems. New York, London, Sydney 1967.

[62] Schoderbek, Peter P. and James D. Babcock: At Last – Management More Active in EDP. Trends in Involvement and Application. In: Business Horizons 1969, pp. 53–58.

[63] Siegmann, Jack and Bernard Karsh: Some Organizational Correlates of White Collar Automation. In: Sociological Inquiry 32/1972, pp. 108–116.

[64] Silver, Milton A.: An Evaluation of the Impact of an Integrated Data Processing System on the Organization of a Manufacturing Company. Diss., Columbia University 1962.

[65] Stewart, Rosemary: How Computers Affect Management. London 1971.

[66] Szyperski, Norbert: Vorgehensweise bei der Gestaltung computer-gestützter Entscheidungssysteme. In: Computer-gestützte Entscheidungssysteme in Unternehmungen. Ed. by Erwin Grochla. Wiesbaden 1971, pp. 37–64.

[67] Szyperski, Norbert: Wirtschaftliche Aspekte des Einsatzes von Time-Sharing-Systemen in Problemlösungsprozessen. In: Datascope 3/1972, No. 9, 2–13.

[68] Thompson, Victor A.: Bureaucracy and Innovation. Alabama 1969.

[69] Vergin, Roger C.: Computer-Induced Organizational Changes. In: The Impacts of Information Technology on Management Operations. Ed. by William C. House. Princeton, New York, Philadelphia, London 1971, pp. 178–189.

[70] Whisler, Thomas L.: The Impact of Computers on Organizations. New York, Washington, London 1970.

[71] Witte, Eberhard: Das Informationsverhalten in Informationssystemen. Die These von der unvollkommenen Informationsnachfrage. In: Management-Informationssysteme. Ed. by Erwin Grochla and Norbert Szyperski. Wiesbaden 1971, pp. 831–842.

[72] Witte, Eberhard: Das Informationsverhalten in Entscheidungsprozessen. Tübingen 1972.

[73] Woodward, Joan: Industrial Organization: Theory and Practice. Oxford 1965.

[74] Zangemeister, Christof: Werturteil und formalisierte Planungsprozesse. 1. Teil: Urteilskraft und Erfahrung als Elemente systematischer Problemlösung in modell- und computergestützten Planungssystemen. In: Zeitschrift für Organisation 42/1973, pp. 217–224.

[75] Zwerman, William L.: New Perspectives on Organization Theory. An Empirical Consideration of the Marxian and Classical Analysis. Westport, Conn. 1970.

German abstract
Ein organisatorisches Konzept für die Gestaltung von Management-Informationssystemen

Von *Alfred Kieser* und *Herbert Kubicek*

In den bisher vorliegenden Ansätzen zur Gestaltung von Management-Informationssystemen (MIS) stehen Fragen der Technostruktur (Hardware, Software, Implementierung spezifischer Anwendungen usw.) im Vordergrund. Verschiedene Autoren (Argyris, Witte, Kirsch) zeigen nun unter Hinweis auf empirische Ergebnisse auf, daß bei der Gestaltung von MIS eine einseitige Ausrichtung auf technostrukturelle Aspekte, die psychologische Zusammenhänge ausklammert, zu dysfunktionalem Verhalten bei den Benutzern führen kann.

In diesem Zusammenhang wird das Vorgehen bei der Gestaltung von MIS verglichen mit dem Vorgehen des Taylorismus, bei dem die Gestaltung betrieblicher Arbeitsprozesse als rein technisches Problem gesehen wurde. Die Kritik am Taylorismus führte als Reaktion zu der Human-Relations-Bewegung, die den Arbeitsprozeß vornehmlich unter sozialen und psychologischen Aspekten analysierte und gestaltete. Diese Sicht war ebenfalls einseitig; insbesondere wurden in ihr die aufgabenlogischen und organisatorisch-strukturellen Aspekte vernachlässigt.

Bei aller berechtigten Kritik am „Computer-Taylorismus“ wäre es verfehlt, nun eine Computer-Human-Relations-Bewegung einzuleiten. Es ist das zentrale Anliegen dieses Papers darzulegen, daß neben Aspekten des Benutzerverhaltens vor allen Dingen auch Aspekte des Koordinationszusammenhangs in die MIS-Gestaltung eingehen müssen.

Der Argumentation dieses Papers liegt ein Modell zugrunde, das von folgenden Zusammenhängen ausgeht:

(1) In empirischen Untersuchungen hat sich gezeigt, daß die spezifischen Koordinationszusammenhänge einer Unternehmung von solchen Faktoren wie Größe der Unternehmung (Volumen der Operationen), Dynamik der Umwelt, Komplexität der Fertigung und Diversifikation des Angebots (Zahl der Produktarten) abhängen. Die Gesamtheit dieser Faktoren wird in Anlehnung an Pugh u.a. (1969) als organisatorischer Kontext bezeichnet.

(2) Der Kontext beeinflußt die Koordinationsanforderungen indirekt und direkt. Er determiniert zum einen die organisatorische Differenzierung, d.h. die Bildung von organisatorischen Teileinheiten (Abteilungen, Stellen) und zum anderen auch die Aufgabeninhalte dieser Teileinheiten. Die spezifischen Koordinationserfordernisse ergeben sich nun aus dem Aufgabeninhalt der zu koordinierenden organisatorischen Teileinheiten.

(3) In Abhängigkeit von diesen Koordinationsanforderungen werden in verschiedenen Unternehmungen unterschiedliche Koordinationsmechanismen in unterschiedlichem Ausmaß eingesetzt, die eine erfolgreiche Interaktion mit der jeweiligen Kontextsituation sicherstellen sollen.

(4) Der Einsatz von MIS bietet Möglichkeiten, diese Koordinationsmechanismen zum Teil qualitativ zu verbessern und zum Teil den Umfang ihres Einsatzes in Grenzen zu verändern. Er bewirkt keine Nivellierung in der Weise, daß als Folge alle Unternehmungen mit MIS auf einheitliche Koordinationsformen hin tendieren, sondern ermöglicht im Gegenteil differenzierte Kombinationen der unterschiedlichen Koordinationsinstrumente mit den Chancen einer vergleichsweise besseren Reaktion auf die Koordinationserfordernisse (Koordinationspotential von MIS).

(5) Das Koordinationspotential von MIS kann Rückwirkungen auf die strukturelle Differenzierung der Organisation, d.h. auf die Abteilungs- und Stellenbildung haben, aber auch dieser Einfluß wirkt kaum vereinheitlichend auf das Koordinationssystem.

(6) Das Koordinationspotential von MIS kann jedoch nur realisiert werden, wenn bei der Systemkonzeption zum einen den Koordinationsanforderungen durch den Kontext und die strukturelle Differenzierung und zum anderen den in Frage kommenden Koordinationsinstrumenten derart Rechnung getragen wird, daß MIS und konventionelle Koordinationsinstrumente so abgestimmt werden, daß sie in ihrer Kombination den jeweiligen Koordinationsbedarf gemeinsam befriedigen.

(7) Auswirkungen von MIS auf das individuelle Verhalten müssen dementsprechend im Rahmen des gesamten Koordinationszusammenhanges analysiert werden. Alle Koordinationsinstrumente und das MIS zusammen bilden im Sinne von Erwartungen an die Aufgabenträger deren organisatorische „Rollen“ (Stellen) und determinieren dabei, inwieweit persönliche Bedürfnisse, z.B. nach sozialer Anerkennung, Selbstverwirklichung usw. aktualisiert werden können. Die Akzeptanz des MIS durch das Individuum kann daher nur im Zusammenhang mit seiner Akzeptanz der gesamten Rollendeterminanten beurteilt und beeinflußt werden.

Diese generellen Zusammenhänge sind in Abb. 1 wiedergegeben und werden in diesem Paper näher erläutert.

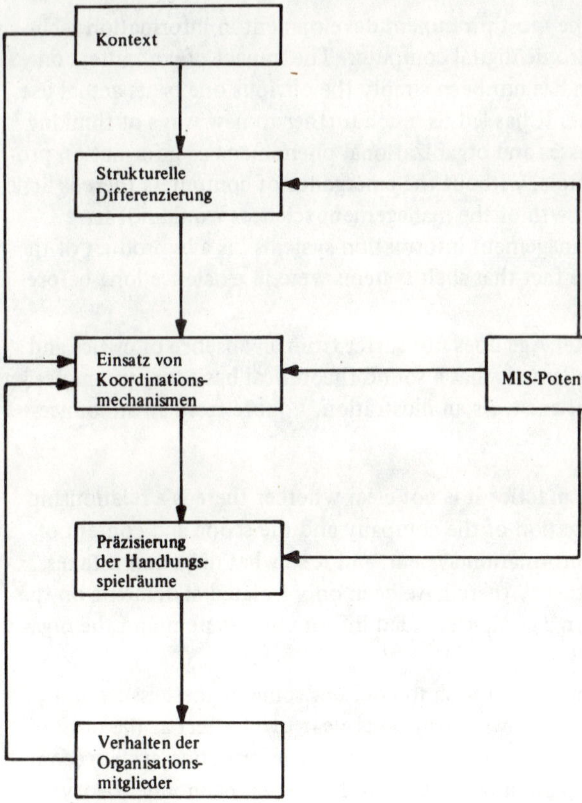

Abb. 1. Ein Modell des Zusammenhanges zwischen organisatorischem Kontext, Koordinationsmechanismen und Verhalten der Organisationsmitglieder

Das vorstehende Modell soll zum einen empirischen Forschungsansätzen als konzeptioneller Rahmen und zum anderen der praktischen Gestaltung von MIS als Orientierungshilfe dienen.

Economics and information structure in organization design

By *Charles H. Kriebel*

1. Introduction

For over a decade now, the most prominent development in information technology has been the electronic digital computer. The impact of computers on management organization has not been simply the obvious one or its actual use as a data processing device. It has led us much further to new ways of thinking about management processes and organizational phenomena as information processing systems. For example, without the emergence of computers there is little doubt that the parallel growth of the management sciences would not have occurred. The phrase "management information systems" is a byproduct of the Computer Age despite the fact that such systems were in existence long before contemporary computers.

Nevertheless, the Computer Age does not suffer from an absence of critics and one continues to hear the lament that a sound theoretical basis for system design and development does not exist. As an illustration, I quote from an announcement on this symposium:

> "Today in economic practice it is not clear whether there is a relationship between the organization of the company and the scope and content of a computer-aided information system, and if so what direction it takes. Even in economic theory there have been only isolated statements on the relationship between a computer-aided information system and the organization structure."

In the limited space of this essay I wish to consider some of these issues and their implications. So that my own position is clear I will assert at the outset that the organization design and the structure of the information system (computer-aided and otherwise) are interdependent. Moreover, economic theory has modeled this interdependence and normative conclusions have been derived. Furthermore I believe these conclusions contain pragmatic corollaries for the practitioner which focus the direction and can serve to guide the design and development of real-world management systems.

Having asserted my position I now will seek to make a case for it.

2. Information economics and organization design

Economic theory is concerned with the efficient utilization of scare resources. To economists a decision is efficient (or optimal) if, among available alternatives, it requires no more (or least) resources for the same outcome level of well-being. Decision problems have been studied under assumed conditions of certain knowledge of the environment (Nature) and when environmental information is uncertain. The economic approach to decision making prescribes how an individual who is faced with a problem of choice under uncertainty should proceed in choosing a course of action that is consistent with his personal basic judgments and preferences. The prescriptions of decision theory concern the efficient choice of information sources (instruments) and terminal actions; the logical process has been designated "information economics."

Efficient choice problems have also been studied in the context of the joint actions of several persons. For example, in the theory of games [15] the problem is to find which (if any) arrangements (or joint decision strategies) exist that would be supported by each player's perceived self-interest, because no change that he might be able to enforce is available to improve his well-being. If such arrangements could be achieved they would be continued, that is, be viable. This problem of viable arrangements in game theory might be called the design of efficient organizations.

Now as a general matter, the meaning of efficient organization is not unambiguous. For a one-person organization the criterion of efficiency is reasonably well-defined in that decision theory dictates that efficient decisions are those choices of information instruments and actions which are consistent with the individual's own personal preferences and judgments. That is, the strategy is "best" and his behavior is rational in a personal rather than a universal sense. The theory does not pretend to provide a description of actual behavior; neither does it constitute a positive theory of an omniscient, all-wise "economic man" who always exhibits perfectly consistent behavior under all eventualities. As a description of actual behavior, one man's rationality may be another man's folly and still be consistent with individual preferences and judgments. Further, to maintain consistency as prescribed by the theory the individual must constantly monitor his subjective inputs and their implications for his actions in a systematic way; the behavior is assumed neither instinctive nor reflexive.

In extending this theory to the many-person decision problem of an organization several complications arise [13, chapter 10]:

1. Individuals in the organization may differ with respect to their action alternatives, their information instruments, and their preferences.

2. The multi-person aspect raises the possibility of uncertainty (communication) about other member's decisions as well as about the states of the external environment.
3. Potential differences in the individual preferences (goals) of members lead to a problem of defining efficiency (optimality) both for the organization as a whole and for its members individually.

For example, alternative concepts of "efficient organization" could include viability as defined above, or equilibrium (partial equilibrium) or Pareto optimality[1]. Similarly, the preferences of individual members could be in conflict with the goals of the organization, i.e., the membership as a group. The state of this theory in economics today is such that there does not exist a generally accepted criterion of multi-person decision efficiency (optimality) and no generally accepted procedure to characterize (resolve) mutual uncertainty about individual behavior in organizations. But this is perhaps more of a commentary on the constitution of "general acceptance" among economists and the complexity of the formalization (and resolution) of group preferences, than anything else.

That is, under given assumptions partial theories of the multi-person decision problem exist which provide explicit conclusions and prescriptive guidelines that are consistent with our economic intuition in an organizational context. By analogy in this regard, the economic theory of the firm [5] is a partial theory of real world production processes, but this does not preclude the pragmatic relevance of many of the conclusions it provides, such as "output selling price ⩾ marginal cost", "equate the marginal products of input factor prices", and so on. As a comparable illustration, the single-person decision theory model provides the simple but useful concept of the value of information, namely, that cost which would equate the maximum net expected utility (payoff) from the decision for the given information to the maximum net expected utility (payoff) from the decision with no (additional) information. The highly pragmatic corollary to this is that information has value only in so far as it can enhance decisions; and, therefore, information should be evaluated within the context of decision processes[2].

In considering the composition of a general model of organizations three categories of variables come to mind for inclusion: informational, economic (or decision related), and behavioral (encompassing preferences). The realization of

---

1 A group decision can be said to be in equilibrium if no one of some specified sub-group of individuals has both the desire and the ability to change the (group) decision by means of a change in their own joint choice of strategies. A so-called Pareto optimal decision exists if for any outcomes e,e' in E, the outcome space, outcome e is not worse than another outcome e' for any member of the group (organization), it is not worse than e' for the group itself.

2 While the guideline does not require elaboration it may be instructive to consult its paraphrasing as discussed in the often cited-and-reprinted article by Ackoff [1] under the heading "A Suggested Procedure for Designing an MIS".

a particular model and the corresponding theory will be a function of the particular variables defined in each category and the postulated relationships among these variables. Over the past several years one of the most promising economic theories of organization in my opinion which has pursued a middle ground approach to the problem is the economic theory of teams developed by Jacob Marschak and Roy Radner [13]. The middle ground of team theory studies the case where the informational and decision variable domains are quite general, but the behavioral variable domain has been parameterized such that all team members are rational in the decision theory sense and have common interests and beliefs. Thus conflict between individual and organizational goals is excluded, and the efficiency (or optimality) criterion is easily defined as in the case of a single decision maker.

More specifically, team theory considers the problem: determine the optimal organizational form (η^*, a^*), an ordered pair of the vectors information structure $(\eta = \eta_1, \ldots, \eta_i, \ldots, \eta_k)$ and team decision rule $(a = a_1, \ldots, a_j, \ldots, a_n)$, which maximizes the expected utility (payoff) of the team $\omega(\eta,a)$, given the team utility function $\omega(\cdot\,,\cdot)$ on H x A for all $\eta \epsilon H$ and $a \epsilon A$. The information structure as a vector of information functions (instruments) η_i specifies for each member i "who know what?" and mathematically is a mapping from the state space X to an information space Y, viz., η:X→Y. The team decision rule is the vector of decision rules a_j for each member of the team and is a mapping from the information space Y to the space of terminal acts, A, i.e., a:Y→A, or $a_j(\eta(x)) = a_j(y) = a_j$ for $x \epsilon X$ and $y \epsilon Y$. As a pre-Computer Age illustration, airline ticket agents were authorized to sell reservations on future flights with only limited information on reservations booked by other agents; one can study the best decision rules to be used by these agents taking into account the joint probability distribution of demand at the various offices, the profit and losses associated with over and under sales of reservations on flights, etc.; cf. [3][3].

Now the logical-mathematical construct of team theory is clearly a partial characterization of the general problem of organization design, even though the theory has attained some maturity. Nevertheless, the formalism illuminates the interdependency between organization and information structures in a useful way, since one can directly assess the economic consequences of the interaction[4]. For example, in most cases the optimal decision rules for individual team members change as the information structure is changed and the potential net gain in organizational efficiency resulting from the modifications can be computed. One can further assess the impact of suboptimizing solutions by computing the opti-

3 Space limitations here do not permit an extended discussion of the team theory model. A comprehensive analysis of the model in a variety of forms is presented in a highly readable manner in the Marschak and Radner book [13].

4 For example, see Part 2 in [13]; and also [9].

mal decision rules assuming the information structure is a given constraint. There is also analysis to suggest that a key behavioral assumption (and limitation) of the basic model, namely, no conflict in goals, can be relaxed with relatively little alternation of the analytical framework. That ist, in [11] we have shown that in a decentralized organization with potential goal conflict the introduction of a transfer price for the cost of capital and a profit sharing compensation plan for managers of the decentralized divisions will induce rational managers to behave as "team members" thus resolving the individual and organizational goal conflicts; see also [7]. Here again it is readily apparent that "information" and organization structure are interdependent; in fact the particular information structure becomes the determinant of the efficiency and viability of the organization structure; see also [12].

At this point in the discussion the non-economist practitioner might be pondering the practical implications of my remarks – especially perhaps those of you with a strong computer systems orientation. The team theory concept of information structure is a mathematical one, usually represented by a multivariate and conditional probability distribution. Whereas the notion of programmed decision rules has become relatively familiar given the development of operations research and the management sciences, on the surface at least, information structure may appear somewhat abstract from the real world of management systems. With this forethought, I will proceed to introduce a compatible and complimentary paradigm for "information structure" which I have found useful for clarifying much of the confusion that often surrounds discussions about "management information systems"; cf. [10].

3. Information structure and management systems

The conceptual framework I have in mind is really quite simple, although additional detail can be incorporated readily. The basic building block of interest is an information structure, defined here as the logical conjunction of a "model of the user" and a "data support structure"; that is,

<information structure> : := <model uf user> <data support structure>.

The model of the user constitutes the output interface of the structure as conceived by the design. It consists of the perceived characterization of end use (or application) of the information structure given a reference population of users. That is, the "model" is fundamentally the representation of the user implemented at the user interface based on the designer's perception of potential use of the structure. For example, the "model" of the user of a public library is generally characterized as fact, reference, or document retrieval; more often than not, the specific needs of individual users (student, research scientist, or housewife, etc.) are not distinguished in the global model.

The data support structure includes the data organization or data partitions (such as, data definition and structure, format and controls, etc.), the bank or store of source data, and the processing operators or programs for data transformation. The conjunctive link between the user model and the data support structure is the language facilities of the information structure; the principal (but obviously not the only) intersection for language occurs on the implemented user representation and the set of data transformations.

Within this framework if we index a particular information structure with the subscript k, an information system is defined as the union (or set-theoretic summation) of all k information structures; that is,

$$\langle \text{information system} \rangle ::= \bigcup_{k \in K} \langle \text{information structure} \rangle_k$$

where K is the appropriate reference index set.

Now even at this elementary level of detail the framework suggests some obvious – but often overlooked – characteristics of any information system[5].

One immediate point is that an information system is the collection of all information structures in an organization. Some of the structures may intersect, e.g., employ the same or overlapping data support structures; other structures may not. Different information structures will serve different users and address different information needs. This diversity of organizational users suggests that different levels of communication, i.e., user languages, are essential in the design of an information system.

For example, in a recent discussion of Generalized Data Base Management Systems (GDBMS), four distinct levels of language for user communication were proposed depending upon whether the reference information was "predefinable" or "unpredefinable", [14]. At the highest or first level of use is the data base administrator or data base manager (see [4] for an extended description), responsible for revision (or redefinition) and design of the data base. The second level of user is the applications programmer, employing a host language class (i.e., Procedure-Oriented Language embedded) of GDBMS with responsibility for writing programs which operate on the data base. The third level of user is the "specifier user" employing a nonprocedural, user-oriented language (e.g., an own Data Management Language or a "forms controlled language") to satisfy unpredefinable information requests, interrogations or updates of the data base. Finally, at the lowest level is the "parametric user" (such as a bank teller or an airline clerk) whose interaction is restricted to predefinable information and who communicates with the data base through predefined structures. While the focus of this particular dis-

---

5 For example, consider the position recently argued by Dearden [6] and the rebuttal by Hanold [8].

cussion deals with data base system designs, the distinction is appropriate for non-data-base designs as well.

Every information structure includes a "model of the user", whether explicitly or implicitly identified by the design. Perhaps a more important consideration at this point, then, is the user model component of information structure for management systems. Since Barnard [2] addressed the subject, most of the management and organizational literature has highlighted decision making as the primary function that distinguishes managerial activity from other behaviors; indeed, other management behavior – such as planning and control – is often defined in terms of decision activity. Thus "management decision process" becomes the user model reference of information structure for management systems; and we might define a "management information system" (MIS) in these terms, viz.

$$\langle \text{MIS} \rangle ::= \bigcup_{k \epsilon K} \langle \text{management decision model} \rangle \langle \text{data support structure} \rangle$$

as before, but where the index set K refers to a particular organization.

Now consider the simple model of a rational decision process shown in Figure 1.

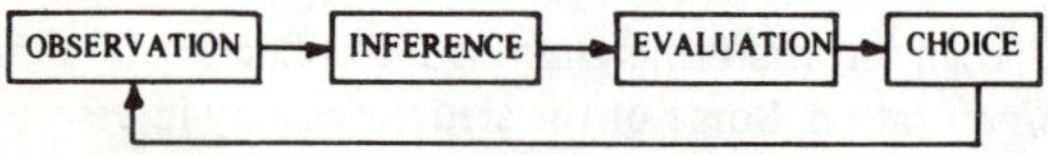

Fig. 1. A simple normative model of management decision activities

Although more elegant models are available for present purposes we can limit the details of our model to four basic stages of activity: observation, inference, evaluation, and choice – where the last stage feeds back to the first in a cycle upon implementation of the action and a commitment of resources. Appending this simple paradigm to the previous framework suggests four potential levels (or stages) of development (maturity) for a management information strcuture depending upon the number of activities which have been formalized and programmed as part of the "user model" representation.

That is, referring to Figure 1 we can dichotomize the sub-stages of activity between the manager and a formalized management information structure where the latter may be computer-based. At the lowest level of development only the activity "observation" has been formalized and programmed as part of the user representation; the subsequent activities from inference to choice in the decision process are performed by the manager. Elsewhere [10] I have referred to such elementary information structures as databanks, examples of which would include transactions processing applications as well as (in my view) most routine accounting systems today. At the most mature level, all activities from observation to choice and the ability to initiate action, commit resources and monitor results have been programmed as part of the structure. This fourth level structure, automated decision, essentially places the manager outside the system since he has fully delegated his authority – although he could revoke this delegation at some future time. The simplest form of the automated decision structure is the "standard operating procedure" in organizations; a more complex example would be a computerized process controll system in a petroleum refinery or some of the contemporary factory inventory control systems. Between the extremes, and defined similarly, are selective-inference and action recommendation structures, respectively. Examples of the former type would include most "scorecard" systems in use as well as interactive management science models designed to respond to management interrogation by "What if . . ." questions. The most familiar example of the third level structure is the advisory staff group or committee, in which line management has delegated authority for a certain area of responsibility (such as corporate planning) but retains final control for decision through review and certification.

I don't think it's necessary to belabor this framwork further, since the concepts relevant to the issue should be obvious at this point and the particular details and terminology are arbitrary. From a descriptive viewpoint many levels of decisions exist in an organization and correspondingly there are many information structures of various type and form involving people as well as EDP. As noted earlier, an economic model of efficient organizations identifies decision and information as the essential structural dimensions of design. I've suggested here that information structure may encompass an entire decision process – and in that sense automate or fully program the activity – or it may serve simply as a data store based on a more elementary representation of the decision process at the user interface. This ist not to imply a normative commentary on any one type of information structure; it merely is recognition of the fact that more sophisticated information structures require more comprehensive models of the user which necessarily entails a deeper understanding (description) of the process supported by the structure. Therefore, it should not be surprising to us to find that at the executive management level in most organizations today the information structures in support of executive decision processes are relatively crude and people intensive, given our understanding of these processes vis-a-vis those at lower levels in the organization. A management information system in this view is the collection of all information structures in the organization; the management organization or system then is the higher aggregation which augments the MIS by the organization's decision process activities.

4. Conclusions

In concluding my case I offer some prescriptive and pragmatic guidelines for system design which I think logically follow from the preceding perspective. As a practical matter systems are not designed at some given point in time against a fixed set of performance criteria; the component information structures evolve over time in response to changing problems and requirements and the successive redefining of criteria. The decision problem of the organizer or the system designer is to provide an equitable tradeoff in the consequences of: (1) "solving the wrong problem" and (2) "solving the right problem too late". Now given a dynamic and constantly changing world, it seems at best a naive strategy in my view that attempts to design a "complete" MIS against some "master plan" for the organization as a whole[6]. In recognizing that an MIS is a collection of information structures in support of different decision processes (problems), it should become apparent that global design strategies are neither necessary nor desirable in most cases. That is, the large scale total system design is often proposed on a technological economies-of-scale argument – particularly with respect to computer hardware costs. To achieve these perceived economies in the "data support" component of information structure across several structures typically requires that the "user model" component be compromised. The result in too many unfortunate cases is myopic economies (if any) wherein "systematic solutions" are provided for "nonexistent problems". In my opinion, the so-called "vertical integration" design strategy in systems suffers from many of these same shortcomings. Even remote recognition of user needs by the "user model" becomes lost at an early stage in the development cycle.

A more enlightened approach to design is to explicitly recognize the modularity of the system at the outset and exploit this structural characteristic in the development process. That is, design modular information structures which focus on specific decision processes and problems – recognizing economic dependencies and/or economies as they may occur. (I think it is far better to localize efforts which solve a specific decision problem than to attempt to generalize efforts in the interests of EDP economy which result in "half-hearted" solutions to many decision problems.) In the development of modular information structures an important consideration for the designer is the specification and definition of the system interface to ensure compatibility of operations across structures as well as at the point of use.

As a final guideline on design in this context, I would caution against the prescription of an "ideal system" versus the reality of some target objective tied to an identified user need. That is, the "ideal" is usually elusive and often serves only to confuse the effort. The only absolute requirement is to improve what currently exists. As a practical matter given limited resources, this only becomes feasible with an incremental approach – structure by structure, user by user.

6 One might pause here to recall the "total systems approach" to MIS popularized in the early 1960's; consider also in this regard more recent proponents of the "corporate data base" approach.

By recognizing the individual user, the manager, as the focal point of the effort we should increase the likelihood that the systems developed will be "solving the right problems at the right time". At least this is the basic argument of my case and maybe in the final analysis the only one that is necessary.

References

[1] Ackoff, R.L.: "Management Misinformation Systems". In: Management Science, December 1967, pp. 147–156.

[2] Barnard, C.: Functions of the Executive. 1938.

[3] Beckmann, M.: "Decision and Team Problems in Airline Reservations". In: Econometrica, Vol. 26/1958, pp. 134–145.

[4] Canning, R.: "The 'Data Administrator' Function". In: EDP Analyzer. 1972.

[5] Cohen, K.J. and R.M. Cyert: Theory of the Firm: Resource Allocation in a Market Economy. 1965.

[6] Dearden, J.: "MIS is a Mirage". In: Harvard Business Review, January–February 1972, pp. 90–99.

[7] Groves, T.L.: "Towards a Theory of Incentives in a Team". Workshop Series 7010, Social Systems Research Institute, University of Wisconsin 1970.

[8] Hanold, T.: "An Executive View of MIS". In: Datamation, November 1972, pp. 65–71.

[9] Kriebel, C.H.: "Information Processing and Programmed Decision Systems". In: Management Science, November 1969, pp. 149–164.

[10] Kriebel, C.H.: "MIS Technology – A View of the Future". In: Spring Joint Computer Conference Proceedings, Volume 40 (AFIPS, 1972), pp. 1173–1180.

[11] Kriebel, C.H. and L.B. Lave: "Conflict Resolution in Economic Organizations". In: Behavioral Science, May 1969, pp. 183–196.

[12] Kriebel, C.H. and M. Lovell: "Quadratic Teams and Economic Organization". In: Econometrica, Juli 1971, p. 257.

[13] Marschak, J. and R. Radner: Economic Theory of Teams. Yale University Press 1972.

[14] Olle, T.W.: "MIS: Data Bases". In: Datamation, November 1970, pp. 47–50.

[15] von Neumann, J. and O. Morgenstern: Theory of Games and Economic Behavior. Princeton University Press 1943; 3d ed., 1953.

German abstract
Wirtschaftlichkeitsüberlegungen und informationelle Aspekte bei der Systemgestaltung

Von *Charles H. Kriebel*

Der Beitrag betrachtet den Zusammenhang zwischen organisatorischer Gestaltung und der Struktur des Informationssystems einerseits unter Wirtschaftlichkeitsaspekten und zum anderen im Zusammenhang mit der Anwendung computergestützter Management-Informationssysteme. Dabei werden beide Gesichtspunkte durch die Interpretation der Informationsstruktur als beschreibendes Element des Entscheidungsprozesses verknüpft. Dem liegt die Aussage zugrunde, daß zwischen der Gestaltung von Organisationsstrukturen und der Struktur des Informationssystems wechselseitige Abhängigkeiten bestehen.

Ergebnis der Überlegungen sind einige pragmatische Aussagen und Vorschläge für die Systemgestaltung. Da es in der Praxis nicht üblich ist, daß komplexe Management-Informationssysteme zu einem festgesetzten Zeitpunkt in exakt spezifizierter Form gestaltet werden, sondern im allgemeinen modulare Teilbereiche zeitlich aufeinanderfolgend zum Einsatz kommen, entwickelt sich die Struktur des Informationssystems in Abhängigkeit von den sich im Zeitablauf ständig verändernden Problemstellungen und Zielen. Für den Systemgestalter stellen sich damit die beiden Alternativen, das falsche Problem zur rechten Zeit oder das echte Problem zu spät zu lösen. Berücksichtigt man schließlich noch, daß Management-Informationssysteme eine Sammlung von Informationsstrukturen zur Unterstützung unterschiedlicher Entscheidungsprozesse beinhalten, so kann daraus gefolgert werden, daß globale Gestaltungsstrategien – wie beispielsweise der „total systems approach" – in einer Vielzahl von Anwendungsfällen weder nützlich noch wünschenswert sind.

Kriebel empfiehlt deshalb den Schwerpunkt der Überlegungen bei der Gestaltung von Management-Informationssystemen auf die ursprünglich vorhandene Modularität der Informationsstrukturen eines Management-Informationssystems zu legen und die dabei erkennbaren strukturellen Eigenschaften für die weitere Systementwicklung zu nutzen. Dies impliziert die Forderung nach einer Gestaltung modularer Informationsstrukturen, die auf bestimmte Entscheidungsprozesse und Entscheidungsprobleme fixiert sind, unter Beachtung der Schnittstellen zwischen den einzelnen Problembereichen und der Wirtschaftlichkeit des Systems in seiner Gesamtheit.

Ausgehend von diesem Gestaltungsansatz unterstreicht Kriebel besonders die Berücksichtigung des individuellen Benutzerverhaltens bei der ökonomischen Gestaltung von Management-Informationssystemen.

Comments on the influence of information technology on organizational structure in insurance industry

By *Bernhard Schareck* and *Ewald Barten*

0. Introduction

It is only with difficulty that one can compare insurance companies with companies of other industries. Many fundamental differences are due to the fact that in the insurance industry the particular "production activity" occurs later in time than the sales activity [9]. Furthermore, insurance companies are paper processing organizations. Therefore, they are subject to a number of influences and developmental trends which are peculiar to this industry.

Insurance companies were among the pioneers in the application of data processing machinery [26]. They have experienced far-reaching changes as a result of the rapid progress in computer technology. However, there is a growing concern in German insurance companies that in spite of these changes there is a widening gap between the current organizational state of affairs and the organizational structure that would allow an effective and efficient use of modern information technology. Management begins to feel that in order to close this gap the strategy of occasional removal of bottlenecks has to be replaced by a thorough reorganization involving primarily the shift from rigid hierarchical structures to more flexible ones [28; 3, p. 132 ff.]. This paper attempts to describe some of the important effects of computer application on the organizational structure of insurance companies [21; 22] and speculates on the development in the near future.

In the USA several studies have been conducted dealing with the effects of computer application on organization structure in insurance companies [29; 36; 38]. Their results and the conclusions drawn by the various authors do not, however, be apply entirely to the situation in the Federal Republic of Germany. The few relevant German studies [11; 34] and most of the American studies share a number of methodological weaknesses (cf. the comparative evaluations of organizational field studies by Kieser [20] and Kubicek [21, p. 290]). These methodological shortcomings of the available empirical studies are one of the main motivations for the present article. It should be interpreted mainly as an attempt to bring the interdependence of organization structure and available information technology to the attention of both practitioners in insurance companies and researchers in the field of insurance management. As far as it reflects the current status of the knowledge on the subject, this article points to the need for a joint effort by practitioners and researchers to study this problem starting from a comprehensive terminological and theoretical basis.

1. Components of the organizational structure

The structure of an organization may be described as a configuration of all organizational units (Stellen), the organizational units being defined as the sum of all tasks (functions) which constitute the scope of duties of individuals [1, pp. 1577 – 1582].

Thus, the organizational structure of the company represents a system of division of labour and cooperation, i. e. it determines who does what, and to what extent one individual has to interact with other colleagues in carrying out his responsibilities in order to help achieve the objectives of the company [37, pp. 23 – 24]. Through the process of organizing, on the one hand the departmental structure of a company comes into existence. It can be conceived as being comprised of organizational units (Stellen) which, when grouped together, form interdependent working groups and departments etc. On the other hand, certain work patterns and procedures (work flow) are established for repetitive tasks. In addition to this network of work flow relationships, the configuration of organizational units and departments are interconnected by a complex communications network which serves primarily as a coordinating mechanism [3, p. 13].

If one wishes to study the influence of the computer on the organizational structure in a systematic and comprehensive fashion, it is a prerequisite that operational definitions of the interesting characteristics of the organizational structure be developed. These definitions should be formulated on the basis of standardized terminology to describe organizational structures [20; 21; 22]. Given the present developmental stage of organization theory, such a terminology is not available nor is its formulation within the scope of this paper. Therefore, this paper has to rely on more or less vague organizational terms in discussing the potential or actual effects of the application of computers on the organization structure. As a basis for this discussion, first a brief description of the task structure and the application of EDP in German insurance companies will be given.

2. Basic tasks in insurance companies

The set of interrelated tasks of a business organization can be subdivided into the formal categories of planning, realisation and control. Planning and control both in the producing industries and in the service industries can be characterized as "operations with objects of the ideal sphere", i. e. as information processing activities [15, p. 67].

It is in the "realisation" phase that insurance companies mainly differ from business organizations in the producing industries.

For whereas the realisation process of the latter deals with objects of both the spheres of realities and ideals, the activities of an insurance company involve only non-material objects, namely information necessary for granting insurance [9, p. 7]. The realisation process of insurance companies comprises collecting, transforming, storing and providing data, i. e. procedures which are connected with the processing of data [32, p. 9 ff.]. The outstanding importance of information processing activities in the workflow of insurance companies makes their organization structure especially sensitive to changes in the information processing technology employed. This will become obvious from the list of basic tasks of insurance companies provided below. It is easy to see that the way in which these tasks are carried out must be affected by the introduction of EDP. In insurance companies there are two broad classes of tasks, the so called "basic tasks" and the "special tasks" [25, pp. 7 – 13; 5, p. 196 ff.].

Basic stages of operation:

- Initial stage involving:–
  - examining the proposal forms,
  - preparing the policy,
  - issuing the insurance policy.
- Follow-up operations:–
  - correspondence,
  - policy amendments,
  - collecting the renewal premiums,
  - reminding procedure,
  - claim/maturity,
  - policy cancellation.

Special operations:–

- e. g. handling personnel records,
  - planning agents' activities,
  - investment.

The comments made in the next chapter reveal that EDP is presently predominantly used in the field of basic stages of operation.

3. The use of EDP equipment in insurance companies of the Federal Republic of Germany

3.1 The current situation

3.1.1 The hardware installed

By 1971 a total number of 205 EDP machines had been installed (75 in Life assurance companies, 33 in Health insurance companies, 95 in Fire and Accident insurance companies and 2 in reinsurance companies) compared to 186 in 1968, and a tendency towards larger computers was becoming evident (see table 1). Whereas in 1968 a total number of 195 insurance companies reported the use of EDP machinery for their data processing and administrative work, the number increased to 249 companies in 1971 [24, I, p. 8,9].

Range of Core Storage Capacity (from . . . to below . . .)	No. of Insurance Companies		Installed			
			EDPM		Core Storage Capacity	
	1968	1971	1968	1971	1968	1971
1 – 32 K	86	61	92	67	1459 K	1 200 K
31 – 128 K	33	48	47	59	2568 K	3 559 K
128 K and larger	14	28	47	79	4149 K	13 000 K
Total	133	137	156	205	8176 K	17 759 K

Table 1. EDP Machinery installed in 1968/1971 [24, p. 12]

3.1.2 Typical areas of computer application

Several studies of the application of EDP in insurance companies unanimously conclude that the computer is still used predominantly for mass data processing in connection with the basic stages of operation. In connection with special operations the use of the computer is still on a very small scale [13; 7, pp. 47 – 49; 23; 24; 31, pp. 39 – 45].

Currently, the companies use approximately 90% of the EDP capacity available for routine work such as preparing portfolio statistics, analysis of the portfolio

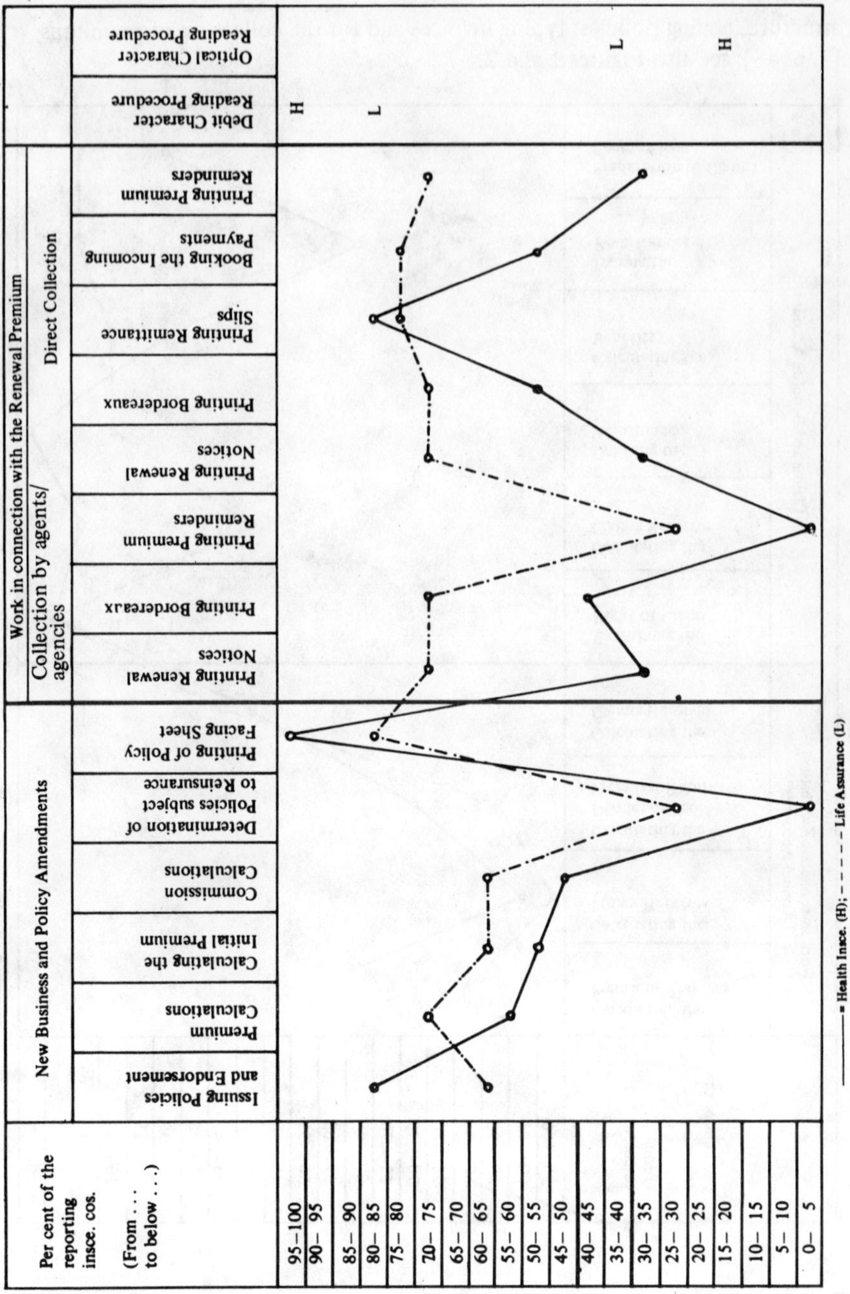

Figure 1. EDP used in Life and Health Insurance Companies in 1971 [24, II, p. 8]
(The lines in figures 1–3 should not be interpreted as indications of developmental trends.)

structure, issuing policies, typing invoices and for the collection of premiums [7, p. 48]; see also Figures 1 and 2.

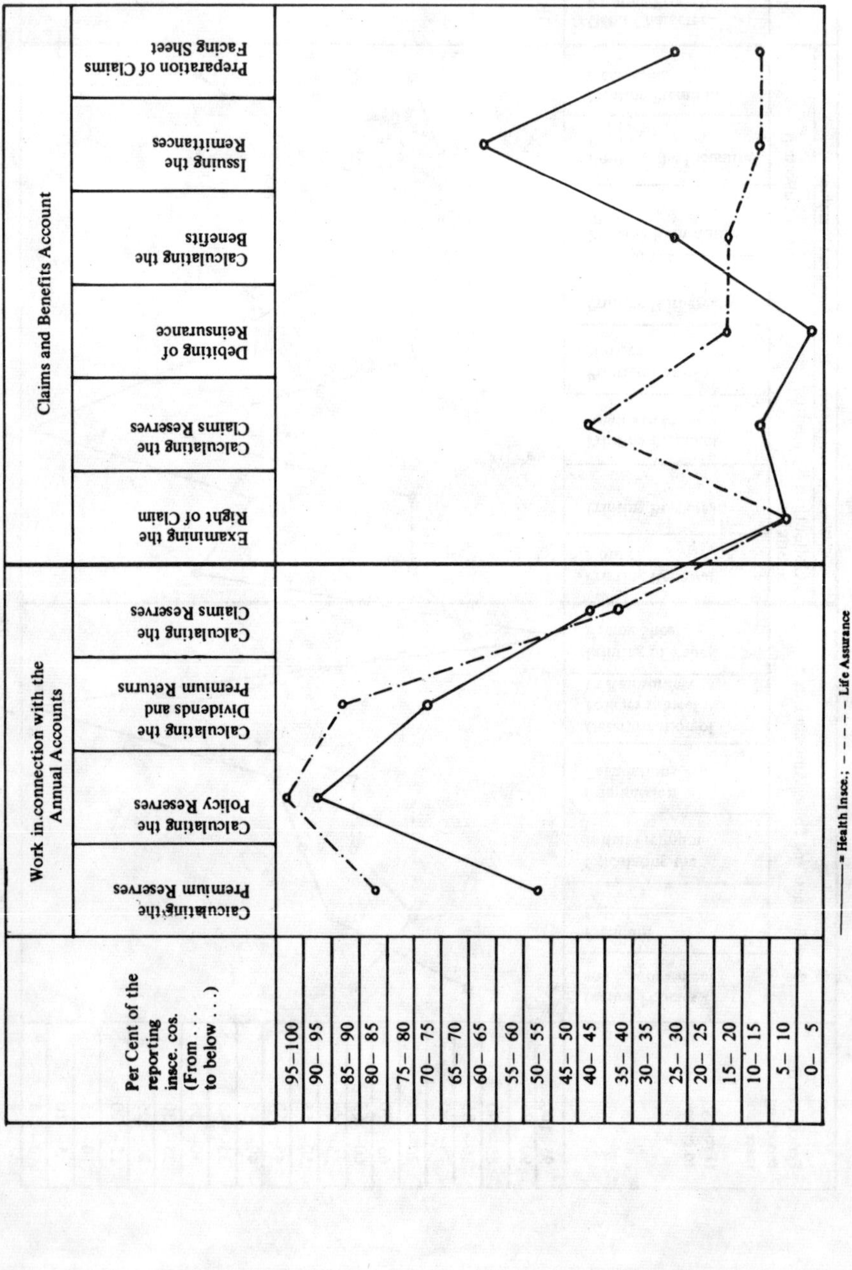

Figure 2. EDP used in Life and Health Insurance Companies in 1971 [24, II, p. 10]

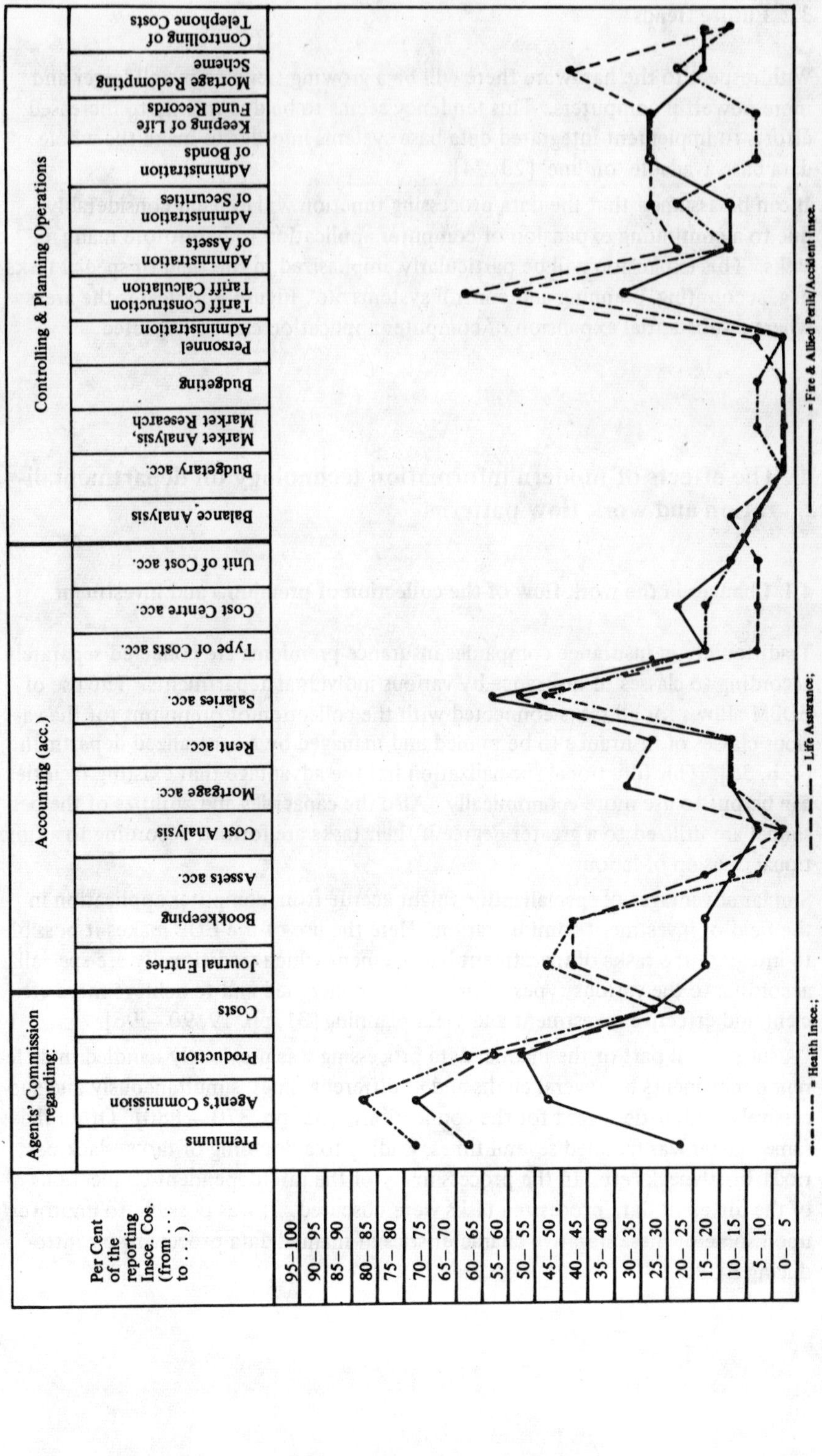

Figure 3. Use of EDP in Life Assurance, Health, Fire & Allied Perils and Accident Insurance Companies in 1971 [24, III, p. 8]

3.2 Future trends

With respect to the hardware there will be a growing trend to install larger and more powerful computers. This tendency seems to be due mainly to increased efforts to implement integrated data base systems in order to make the whole data base available 'on line' [23; 24].

It can be assumed that the data processing function will expand considerably, due to a continuing expansion of computer application to heretofore manual tasks. This expansion will be particularly emphasized in the field of special tasks, e. g. accounting, planning and control systems etc. Figure 3 indicates the areas where a substantial expansion of computer application can be expected.

4. The effects of modern information technology on departmentalization and work flow patterns

4.1 Changes in the work flow of the collection of premiums and investment

Traditionally in insurance companies insurance premiums are collected separately according to classes of insurance by various individual departments. The use of EDPM allows for all tasks connected with the collection of premiums for the various classes of insurance to be pooled and managed by a centralized department [4, p. 35]. This functional specialization has the advantage that existing facilities can be put to use more economically. Also the capacities and abilities of the personnel are utilized to a greater degree if their tasks are formed according to a functional division of labour.

Similar advantages of specialization might accrue from computer application in the field of investment administration. Here the use of the EDP makes it possible to integrate the tasks of investment management which traditionally are specialized according to the various types of investment concerned and to achieve more efficient and effective investment and yield planning [31, pp. 19, 90 – 96].

"A substantial part of the manual data processing was previously handled in different departments by several clerks and at different times, simultaneously and successively with little regard for the connections" [33, pp. 870 – 880]. Often the same matter was handled several times, leading to a doubling of tasks, slack periods, bottlenecks etc. In the process many of the interdependent connections of the different data processing tasks were obscured. It was possible to improve upon some of these negative characteristics of manual data processing by introducing EDP.

4.2 Different effects on departmentalization

The key to an efficient attainment of the company's objectives lies in the "correct" division of tasks and in their integration to work groups and departments. In many insurance companies the particular organizational form chosen is largely a result of tradition and personal interests of top management. Considerations of effectiveness and efficiency still have very little influence on the determination of the organization structure. Figure 4 shows the typical line and staff functions of an insurance company.

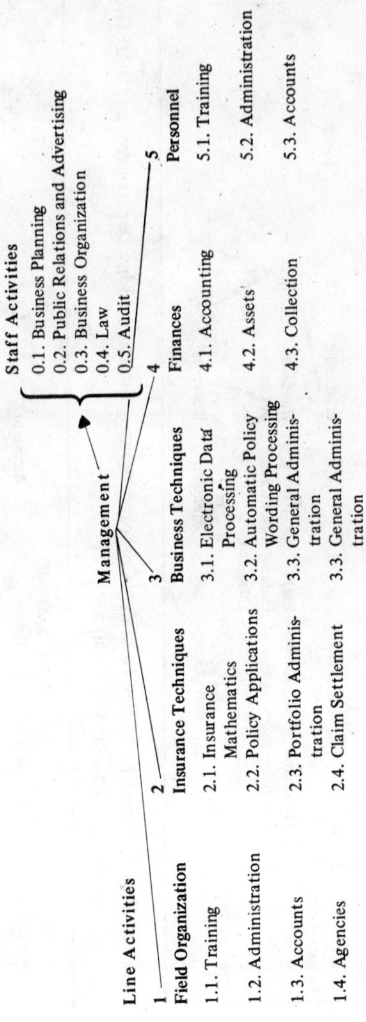

Figure 4. Line and Staff Functions in Insurance Companies [39, p. 1439]

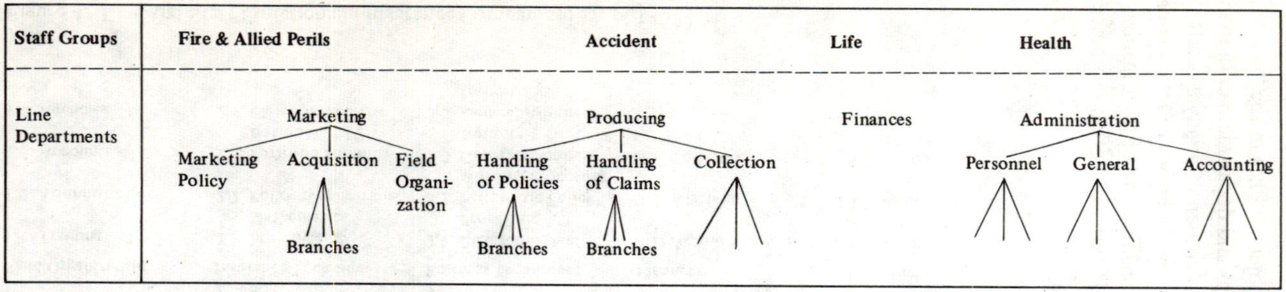

Figure 5. Organization Chart of an Insurance Company showing Functional Line Departments and Staff Groups for Specific Branches of Insurance [12]

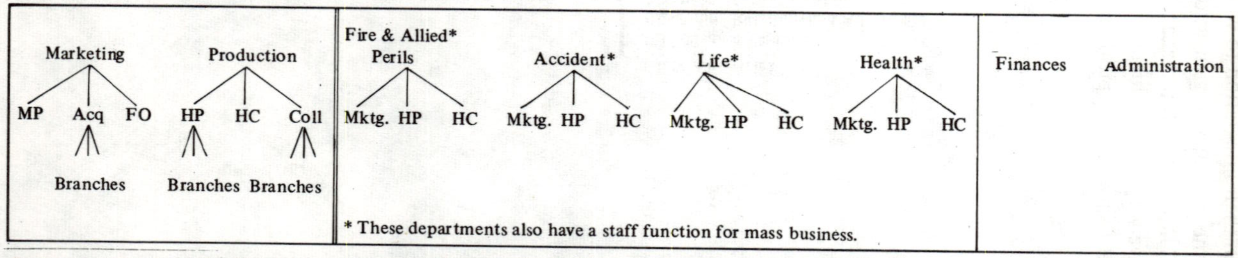

Figure 6. Organization Chart of an Insurance Company with Separate Departments for Mass Business and Individual Business [12]

The growing integration [6, p. 36] renders a coordination of formerly separate functions feasible; accordingly, there is a growing tendency towards functional centralization in German insurance companies.

It would appear that a total of four functional sections are adequate:

- marketing,
- production,
- finance,
- administration.

For the management and clerical activities departments are formed which are responsible for certain functions within the organization. Tasks which are specific to one division can be handled by staff groups who have advisory functions and who prepare information required for decision making.

It seems that the divisional organization which insurance companies still prefer is gradually being replaced by a functional centralization. This tendency will lead to a type of organization structure in which some divisional departments act as advisory staff groups as far as mass business is concerned and as responsible operational units as far as the individual business is concerned (see figure 6).

4.3 Some conclusions from an empirical survey of the effects of EDP on the organizational structure of insurance companies in the Federal Republic of Germany

Outlined below are some conclusions from a survey carried out by SCHÜTZ [34, pp. 27 – 42], who applied the methodology of WHISLER's [38] study to the situation in Germany and examined the relevance of WHISLER's results to the situation of the insurance industry in Germany. Although the SCHÜTZ study surveyed only a relatively small number of insurance companies, the findings give a valid impression of the overall situation. All data used below is taken from this survey.

4.3.1 Reorganization of departments

WHISLER predicts radical changes [38; pp. 47, 57] in the structure of departments, groups etc. within the company. SCHÜTZ examines whether this assertion is true of the situation in Germany.

a) Departments formed following the introduction of EDP

According to both WHISLER and SCHÜTZ, the most substantial changes are to be found in the formation of new departments and groups. As can be seen from the following table, the majority of new departments or groups were formed in the field of electronic data processing. These departments (programming, data acquisition etc.) are created to support data processing. The ensuing changes in the organizational procedures as well as in the formal and informal relationship between the departments can be regarded as direct effects of the introduction of EDP [35, p. 225].

Newly formed departments or groups	No. of insurance companies
yes	12
no	–
function of new departments	**No. of new departments**
Electronic data processing	23
Accounting; Organization & Methods; Internal Control	4
Service functions	4
Total of newly formed departments and groups	31

Table 2. Newly formed departments/groups [34, p. 27]

b) Departments and groups replaced since the introduction of EDP

In accordance with the results of the WHISLER study SCHÜTZ found that in some insurance companies a number of departments or groups had been replaced. The high number of replaced departments or groups confirms the opinion that the computer is taking over more and more data processing and information analysis tasks [16, p. 48].

c) Reorganization of departments and groups which existed prior to the introduction of EDP

Contrary to WHISLER's findings changes of this kind were small in number in German insurance companies.

d) Relocation and centralization of previously decentralized tasks

Replacement of departments or groups	No. of insurance companies
yes	9 (75%)
no	3 (25%)
	12 (100%)
Total of departments or groups replaced	16
... because the tasks were transferred to EDP in full	6 (out of 9 insce. cos.)
... because only part of the tasks was transferred	6 (out of 9 insce. cos.)

Table 3. Replacement of departments/groups [34, p. 28]

Reorganization of departments and groups	No. of insurance companies
yes	5 (40%)
no	7 (60%)
	12 (100%)
Electronic data processing	–
Accounting; Organization & Methods; Internal Control	1
Service functions	11
Total of reorganizations	12

Table 4. Reorganization of departments/groups [34, p. 29]

Because of the specific regional structure of their marketing activities insurance companies often follow a policy of "centralized decentralization" [30, p. 105]. Out of six companies with tasks centralization surveyed five reported that special units within the branch offices handling the collection of premiums had been replaced by a central department.

The results of the SCHÜTZ study reported above indicate that the changes were not as wide-ranging and substantial as the findings of WHISLER's survey would suggest. Moreover, the question arises whether these changes can be attributed exclusively to the introduction to EDP or whether they have been influenced by other factors.

4.3.2 Growth of personnel

A reduction in personnel is considered to be one of the major reasons for the introduction of EDP or for EDP being applied to a specific set of tasks [20, p. 191; 27, p. 178]. If any such replacement of personnel actually does come about, office-workers and first-line supervisors (lower management) are likely to be affected most strongly and most immediately.

The figures in table 5 show that as a consequence of introducing EDP the number of employees on the lower levels decreased substantially (release effect). Also the first-line supervisors were affected considerably. However, only minor changes were reported with respect to the middle and upper management levels.

Hierarchical levels	Companies in which the number of personnel in the affected departments:		
	increased	decreased	remained unchanged
clerks (office workers)	11 (92%)	–	1 (8%)
lower management	5 (42%)	1 (8%)	6 (50%)
middle management	1 (8%)	1 (8%)	10 (84%)
upper management	–	–	12 (100%)

Table 5. Changes in the number of personnel [34, p. 32]

The results for the office workers confirm the assumption that it is mainly on this level that man is being substituted by the computer [8, pp. 99–109; 9, p. 22]. The decline in the number of lower managers can be explained in two complementary ways: Firstly, the transfer of complex planning and decision making tasks to EDPM can lead to a reduction of personnel working in this field and, secondly, the need for managerial positions diminishes due to the smaller number of subordinates (cf. KIESER [20, p. 191]). This second aspect is emphasized also by MÜLLER-LUTZ:

> "A substantial portion of the work previously carried out by employees of the lower salary levels is performed by EDP. The effect of this is a reduction of the supervisory personnel on the lower as well as on the middle management levels; the reason for this reduction – amongst others – is that the work is better organized, less susceptible to errors and can be controlled more effectively" [27, p. 180].

The above figures do not show the overall developmental trend of the number of personnel. On the one hand they cannot represent any "addition effect" of the introduction of EDP, i. e. an increase in the number of personnel due to the hiring of EDP experts. This "addition effect" and also a large expansion of the volume of business could compensate the "release effect" of the introduction of EDP, as far as the total number of personnel is concerned.

4.3.3 Variations of the span of control

Any changes in the span of control are closely connected to changes in the personnel structure. The findings of the SCHÜTZ survey show a tendency towards a reduction of the span of control, particularly on the lower management levels [34, p. 35].

No. of insurance companies	Span of control in the affected departments:		
	decreased	increased	remained unchanged
hierarchical levels:			
lower management	4 (40%)	1 (10%)	5 (50%)
middle management	2 (20%)	–	8 (80%)
upper management	–	–	10 (100%)

Table 6. Changes in the span of control [34, p. 35]

The following table gives a comparison of the changes of the span of control on the lower management levels with the decline in the number of personnel:

Hierarchical levels	Reduction of the number of personnel	Reduction of the span of control
clerks	11 (92%)	–
lower management levels	5 (42%)	4 (40%)
middle management levels	1 (8%)	2 (20%)

Table 7. "Release effect" and the reduction in the lower managerial positions [34, p. 36]

This comparison shows that the relatively insignificant downward trend of span of control in spite of the substantial "release effect" may probably be attributed to a proportional reduction in the lower managerial positions.

4.3.4 Effects on the number of hierarchical levels

Whereas WHISLER foresees a reduction of the number of management levels [38, p. 47 and 55 ff.], the findings of SCHÜTZ do not show any decrease in the number of hierarchical levels.

None of the insurance companies surveyed reported a reduction of management level although there was a substantial "release effect" on the lower levels, which was not compensated as a result of substantial growth. Three of the insurance companies surveyed by SCHÜTZ reported that the number of levels had even increased.

As the contradictory findings of various American studies [29, p. 120; 2, pp. 69, 80 and 93] show, it is very difficult to ascertain any direct effects of the introduction of EDP on the hierarchical structure of the organization.

4.3.5 Changes in the amount of communication

The changes in the tasks of interdependent organizational units as a consequence of the use of the computer make changes in the structure of communication very likely.

Following the approach of WHISLER's study SCHÜTZ examined the changes in the amount of time spent in

- communication with superiors
- communication with colleagues of the same rank
- communication with subordinates

by members of the various organizational levels. SCHÜTZ found that on the clerical and lower management levels no changes in the amount of horizontal or vertical communication occurred.

The middle and higher management levels showed a slight increase in the amount of horizontal and vertical communication. Presumably the introduction of the computer is not the sole factor which caused this trend in the communication relations.

There can be no doubt that the existing organization form and the style of management are intervening variables affecting the communication relationships [18, p. 80 ff.]. GILMAN, for example, assumes that an increase in the amount of vertical communication is likely to occur as the superiors can make use of more intensive contact with their subordinates as a result of the introduction of EDP [14, p. 35 ff.]. On the other hand, a strictly hierarchically orientated organization can resort to the computer with the aim of reducing communication relations. Furthermore it must be taken into consideration that the present efforts to introduce modern organization concepts (e. g. team-oriented organizational structures) also lead to an increase in the amount of interpersonal communication [14, p. 214 ff.].

Summarizing the findings of the survey conducted by SCHÜTZ it can be concluded that the effects of the introduction of EDP in German insurance companies are not nearly as farreaching as could be expected from the results of WHISLER's study. One possible explanation for this difference is that American insurance companies use EDPM to a far greater extent than German insurance companies do. The greater scope and intensity of computer application leads to much more substantial and thus visible changes in the organization.

5. Summary and conclusion

The findings of this descriptive study of the influence of the application of information technology on the organizational structure can be summarized in four theses:

(a) The potential of EDP promotes a high degree of integration of the work flow and may lead to a reduction of low level clerical personnel.

(b) In connection with the introduction of EDP there is a tendency to replace skilled insurance experts by semi-skilled office workers [10, p. 17]. This trend might eventually reduce the importance of tasks which consist mainly of programmed decision making.

(c) The question of whether modern information technology favours certain types of organizational structure cannot be answered conclusively. There appears to be a development in the direction of a modified functional centralization. This type of organizational structure will probably lead to increased efficiency as long as the advantages of functional specialization are not overcompensated by increased coordination requirements.

(d) There is a hard-felt need for guidelines and rules for the effective and efficient organization of insurance companies. These guidelines could facilitate the mutual adaptation of the organizational structure and the structure of information systems. They would have to be based on prognoses of the effects of changes in one of the two organizational variables on the other. These prognoses would require comprehensive empirical research on the interdependence of these variables, which should be carried out from the basis of an integrated theoretical and terminological framework.

References

[1] Acker, Heinrich B.: Stelle. In: Handwörterbuch der Organisation, ed. by E. Grochla, Stuttgart 1969, S. 1577–1582.

[2] Adams, S.: The Effects of Information Technology on Management and Organization. Diss. Louisiana State University 1965.

[3] Baier, Helmut: Die Stab-Linie-Problematik. Eine organisatorische Systemanalyse insbesondere von Versicherungsbetrieben. Karlsruhe 1973.

[4] Bau, Ulrich: Alternative Organisationskonzepte für die Unternehmensleitung und ihre Eignung für Versicherungsunternehmen. Diplomarbeit, Köln, WS 1972/73, p. 35.

[5] Behlert, Karl: Vom Organisieren. 2. Auflage, Stuttgart 1959, pp. 196 ff.

[6] Buss, D., G. Mans, J. Marock and H. Rölle: Stand und Entwicklungstendenzen von Management-Informationssystemen in der BRD. BIFOA-Arbeitsbericht 1971/3, ed. by E. Grochla and N. Szyperski, Köln 1971.

[7] Die elektronische Datenverarbeitung in der Lebensversicherung. In: Die deutsche Lebensversicherung. Jahrbuch 1971, ed. by Pressestelle des Verbandes der Lebensversicherungsunternehmen e.V., Bonn 1971, pp. 47–49.

[8] Delehanty, George E.: Office Automation and the Occupation Structure. A Case-Study of Five Insurance Companies. In: Industrial Management Reviews, Vol. 7 1966, No. 2, pp. 99–109.

[9] Farny, Dieter: Produktions- und Kostentheorie der Versicherung. Veröffentlichungen des deutschen Vereins für Versicherungswissenschaft, Heft 72, Karlsruhe 1965, pp. 10–32.

[10] Farny, Dieter: Konzentration und Kooperation in der Versicherungswirtschaft in betriebswirtschaftlicher Sicht. In: Versicherungswirtschaft, Vol. 28 1973, No. 1, p. 17.

[11] Farny, Dieter: Der Einfluß der EDV auf die Organisationsstruktur des VU. Unpublished paper, October 1972.

[12] Farny, Dieter: Die künftige Organisation des VU im Innen- und Außendienst. Unpublished paper. November 1971.

[13] Gesamtverband der Versicherungswirtschaft: Elektronische Datenverarbeitungsanlagen und EDV-Anwendungen in Versicherungsunternehmen. Köln October 1971.

[14] Gilman, Glen: The Computer Revisited. In: Business Horizons, Vol. 9 1966, pp. 77–89.

[15] Grochla, Erwin: Automation und Organisation. Wiesbaden 1966, p. 67.

[16] Grochla, Erwin: Zur Diskussion über die Zentralisationswirkung automatischer Datenverarbeitungsanlagen. In: Zeitschrift für Organisation, Vol. 38 1969, pp. 47–53.

[17] Grochla, Erwin: Das Büro als Zentrum der Informationsverarbeitung im strukturellen Wandel. In: Das Büro als Zentrum der Informationsverarbeitung, ed. by E. Grochla, Wiesbaden 1971.

[18] Grochla, Erwin: Unternehmungsorganisation. Neue Ansätze und Konzeptionen. Reinbek b. Hamburg 1972.

[19] Hofer, Charles W.: Emerging EDP-pattern. In: Harvard Business Review, March-April 1970, pp. 16–31, 169–171.

[20] Kieser, Alfred: Einflußgrößen der Unternehmungsorganisation – Der Stand der empirischen Forschung und Ergebnisse einer eigenen Erhebung. Habilitationsschrift, Köln 1973, pp. 11–26.

[21] Kubicek, Herbert: Der Zusammenhang zwischen Informationstechnologie und Organisationsstruktur. In: Zeitschrift für Organisation, Vol. 41 1972, No. 6, p. 287.

[22] Kubicek, Herbert: Ein gedanklicher Bezugsrahmen zur Ermittlung und Erklärung der organisatorischen Auswirkungen moderner Informationstechnologien. Working paper. Seminar für allgemeine Betriebswirtschaftslehre und Organisationslehre an der Universität zu Köln, January 1973, pp. 1–6.

[23] Langsch, Lothar: Automatische Datenverarbeitung in der Versicherungswirtschaft (part III). In: der versicherungsbetrieb, Vol. 3 1973, No. 3/4, p. 8.

[24] Langsch, Lothar: EDV-Systeme in Versicherungsunternehmen, part I–III. In: der versicherungsbetrieb, Vol. 2 1972, pp. 8–14; Vol. 3 1973, No. 1/2, pp. 8–13; No. 3/4, pp. 8–12.

[25] Müller-Lutz, H.L.: Grundbegriffe der Versicherungsbetriebslehre. Bd. 1 Organisationswesen. 3rd revised edition, Karlsruhe 1966, pp. 7–13 (Basic principles of Insurance Management, New York 1966, pp. 26–31).

[26] Müller-Lutz, H.L.: Chancen in der Assekuranz. In: Der Volkswirt, Vol. 20 1966, No. 47, p. 2268.

[27] Müller-Lutz, H.L.: Automation der Büroarbeiten. Die elektronische Datenverarbeitung im Büro unter besonderer Berücksichtigung des Versicherungsbetriebes. Leitfaden der Versicherung, Bd. 5. Karlsruhe 1968.

[28] Müller-Lutz, H.L.: Strukturuntersuchungen in Versicherungsunternehmungen. In: Zeitschrift für Versicherungswesen, Vol. 22 1971, No. 4, pp. 109 ff.

[29] Parisi, Dominic G.: The Impact of a Change in Information Technology on Management Organisation Structure, Decision Making, and Interpersonal Relations in a large Insurance Company. Diss. Northwestern University, USA, 1966.

[30] Patzschke, Claus: Betriebswirtschaftliche Aspekte des Einsatzes elektronischer Datenverarbeitungsanlagen im Versicherungsbetrieb. Unveröffentlichte Diplom-Arbeit. Universität zu Köln 1968.

[31] Schareck, Bernhard: Automatisierte Vermögensverwaltung im Versicherungsbetrieb. BIFOA-Arbeitsbericht 74/1, ed. by E. Grochla and N. Szyperski, Köln 1974.

[32] Scherff, Jürgen: Die Entwicklung eines Teilmodells der Kraftverkehrsversicherung auf der Grundlage des Kölner Integrationsmodells. Diplomarbeit Köln, WS 1971/72, pp. 9–12.

[33] Schneller, Herbert: Anwendungsformen der Datenverarbeitung bei Versicherungsbetrieben in Gegenwart und Zukunft. In: Versicherungswirtschaft, Vol. 25 1970, pp. 870–880.

[34] Schütz, G.: Der Einfluß des Computers auf die Unternehmungsorganisation. Eine Replikation und Erweiterung der gleichnamigen Studie von Thomas L. Whisler. Unveröffentlichte Diplom-Arbeit. Universität zu Köln, Köln March 1974.

[35] Stewart, Rosemary: How Computers Affect Management. London-Basingstoke 1971.

[36] Stymne, Bengt: EDP and Organizational Structure: A Case-Study of an Insurance Company. In: The Swedish Journal of Economics, Vol. 48 1966, No. 2, pp. 89–116.

[37] Ulrich, H.: Die Organisation der Planung. In: Grundprobleme der Unternehmungsplanung, ed. by F. Trechsel; H. Ulrich; F. Kneschaurek. Betriebswirtschaftliche Mitteilungen, No. 41, Bern 1968.

[38] Whisler, Thomas L.: The Impact of Computers on Organizations. New York-Washington-London 1970.

[39] Wrieske, Udo-Achim: Die Aufbauorganisation eines VU. In: Versicherungswirtschaft, Vol. 29 1970, No. 22, p. 1439.

German abstract

Gedanken zum Einfluß der Informationstechnologie auf die Organisationsstruktur des Versicherungsbetriebes

Von *Bernhard Schareck* und *Ewald Barten*

Für die Versicherungsbetriebe, die zu den Pionieren des Einsatzes von Datenverarbeitungsanlagen zählen, hat die rasante Entwicklung auf den Gebieten der Hardware und Software sowie der Anwendungssysteme besonders tiefgreifende Auswirkungen gezeigt. Gleichzeitig wird jedoch befürchtet, daß die deutschen Versicherungsunternehmungen einen immer größer werdenden organisatorischen Nachholbedarf hätten. Statt fallweiser Beseitigung von Engpässen wird eine tiefgreifende Neuordnung der Organisationsstruktur, insbesondere die Ablösung starrer, hierarchisch orientierter Strukturen durch flexible Formen gefordert. Vor diesem Hintergrund werden einige Auswirkungen der Informationstechnologie auf die Organisationsstruktur der Versicherungsunternehmung unter Hinweis auf mögliche zukünftige Trends beschrieben.

Nach dem Überblick über den Einsatz automatisierter Datenverarbeitungsanlagen in den deutschen Versicherungsgesellschaften wird generell auf Auswirkungen moderner Informationstechnologien auf Aufbau- und Ablaufstruktur eingegangen.

Es folgt die Darstellung einiger Ergebnisse einer empirischen Untersuchung zu den Auswirkungen auf

- die Gliederung der Fachbereiche,
- den Personalbestand,
- die Leitungsspanne,
- die Zahl der hierarchischen Ebenen und
- die Kommunikationsbeziehungen.

Zum Abschluß werden folgende Thesen formuliert:

1. Die Möglichkeiten der automatisierten Datenverarbeitung begünstigen im Bereich der Ablauforganisation eine hohe Integration, im Bereich der Aufbauorganisation eine Verringerung der Instanzen.
2. Als Folge der zunehmenden Substitution des Menschen durch die Maschine kann ein Trend vom „Versicherungsfacharbeiter" zum angelernten Arbeiter beobachtet werden. Dieser Trend könnte zu einer verminderten Bedeutung dispositionsbedürftiger Teilaufgaben führen.
3. Die Frage, ob Informationstechnologien bestimmte Organisationskonzepte begünstigen, kann nicht eindeutig beantwortet werden. Die Entwicklung scheint in die Richtung einer modifizierten Funktionsgliederung zu gehen. Von diesem Organisationskonzept ist eine höhere Wirtschaftlichkeit der Leitungs- und Realisationsprozesse zu erwarten. Die damit tendenziell verbundene Entscheidungszentralisation kann jedoch mit dem Nachteil eines übermäßig hohen Koordinationsaufwandes behaftet sein.
4. Eine verstärkte empirische Erforschung der Zusammenhänge ist notwendig, um Gestaltungsregeln und -anweisungen für den Organisator zu entwickeln.

Information systems for organizations of the future

By *William H. Starbuck*

1. Introduction

Some years ago, a team of my colleagues was hired to design a production scheduling system. They soon concluded that no existing computational procedures could adequately respond to this particular challenge. So they created new procedures which not only fitted the specific problem but also attracted attention for their mathematical properties alone. Then the team spent several months developing computer software that implemented the new methods efficiently and at low computation cost, and several more months installing the software in the clients' organization - training personnel, adjusting parameters, adding useful options, and the like.

Although the whole project took more than a year and a half, everyone was pleased with the result. The research team had demonstrated how mathematical elegance could be combined with practical relevance; they had published several, well received articles; and if rumors were correct, they had earned a considerable sum of money on the basis of a profit-sharing contract. Perhaps most importantly, the team believed their solution was intellectually far ahead of anything operations research had developed to that time. The clients had also made a great deal of money, of course. They expected to make more, and they too took pride in the sophistication of their production scheduling system. In fact, to operate the new system, the clients hired production engineers who possessed sufficient mathematical and computer background to understand it.

About a year after the scheduling system had been completed and the research team had departed, the team went back to the clients' installation to find out how things were going. After spending several hours with the people who were operating the system, the team members were so enraged they could barely contain themselves. "My God", the team's leader rumbled, "they're trying to improve our system!"

One moral of this story is that experts tend to be egotistical . . . especially outside experts who are hired as consultants. A second moral is that clients have ideas and want to try them out, just like their consultants do.

Please do not misunderstand. I am not advocating that experts should lack egotism, or even that they should be less egotistical than they are. Egotism plays a variety of useful roles in all of the knowledge-selling professions. Consider, for example, how the research team's egotism facilitated the project described above. Pride in their capabilities stimulated the team to undertake a difficult practical problem and helped them convince the clients that the team would be able to achieve the project's goals. The team's self-confidence was a prerequisite for rejecting an inappropriate application of existing techniques and for reporting the newly developed procedures in professional journals. Personal identification with their product kept the team working on small details and refinements until the software package was maximally useful and until the clients were fully satisfied. And the team's conviction that their software represented outstanding accomplishment, made the clients more ready to adapt their organization and procedures to the new scheduling system, and induced the clients to hire personnel who could comprehend the system's rationale.

However, the research team's professional pride also generated dysfunctions. It led them to view their clients as passive, uncreative recipients of a finished product, and it led them to view their product as an achievement of pristine perfection that should remain inviolate from meddling by its insensitive users. In fact, the team was deeply shocked when they discovered their clients had dared attempt improvements.

With these attitudes, the clients did not fully agree. Indeed, the clients had been reluctant to use and to depend upon a scheduling system which they did not understand, and they had finally convinced themselves that they understood it thoroughly. They also saw the system as an evolving solution which had to be readjusted to changing order mixes and changing processing equipment. They thought they saw deficiencies in the system, or at least opportunities to improve it. Certainly, they felt strong needs to participate actively in the shaping of their organization's present and future.

One overall implication is that the research team's egotism was misdirected. They took pride in what they themselves could do without their clients' participation, in the properties of the software package they had written, in the mathematical theorems they had proven. These are evanescent achievements at best. Just how evanescent became apparent soon after the above scenario ended. For other research teams in other cities had been working on alternative scheduling methods, and one of these alternatives became the focus of world-wide theoretical and practical effort. Although I have no first-hand information, it would be astonishing if their clients retained the team's scheduling system longer than four or five years.

What the research team should have been trying to design was not a scheduling system, but a system that could design scheduling systems: a combination of software and people in the clients' organizations who could continually invent, revise, adapt, generate, and modify scheduling systems. The team should have defined their role as similar to that of a teacher who is measured by the quality of his own solutions, and they should have invested their egos in their ability to play such a metagame. A metagame solution can last longer than four or five years even in a rapidly changing environment.

2. From evolutionary information systems . . .

The central design challenge is to allow for solutions to an endlessly and rapidly evolving set of problems, taking into account changes in one's own comprehension of the problems as well as changes in the problems themselves. This challenge is hardly unique to production scheduling systems, of course. It arises systematically in politics and law, in medical practice, in education, in social work, in human relations training, in market research, in operations research, and so forth.

I was first forced to recognize the challenge by a proposed project to design an information system for the German Federal Health Bureau. The project was never actually begun, because senior administrators in the Health Bureau were unconvinced that the benefits from an information system would be worth its operating cost. However, I learned quite a lot from the preliminary conceptual discussions alone.

Until June 1971, the Health Bureau was authorized to appraise only the safety of newly developed drugs. Had there been such a thing as a totally inert drug, the Bureau would have had to approve it for sale. One result was that a very high proportion of the available drugs, over 50 % were considered to be comparatively ineffective preparations of no obvious medical value. Then the Federal Minister of Health announced new regulations stating that preparations must either be composed of substances of known effectiveness or be tested for effectiveness. The Bureau's pharmacologists began considering what it meant to say a substance's effectiveness is known, what kinds of statements should be made about effectiveness, and how effectiveness should be evaluated.

Wolfgang Müller, a colleague at IIM, and I were just then seeking an opportunity to make a socially useful contribution to medical-care, and our search brought us into contact with the Health Bureau and its evaluation problem.

If the Bureau were to take its mandate seriously and make thorough and conscientious evaluations (issues for which the right policies were far from apparent), information lay at the heart of the obstacles. First, there are a very large number of drugs to monitor. Roughly 60,000 preparations are now on sale in Germany; an unknown, but large, number of other preparations which are being used in other countries are probably worth monitoring in the expectation that they may be proposed for the German market; and both numbers have been increasing rapidly. Second, drugs are not easily classified and cataloged. Even single chemical compounds are related to one another in complicated ways, reflecting their complex molecular structures, and their relations in terms of medical effects are much more intricate. Most drugs are mixtures of many compounds and many do not have a well-defined, primary ingredient. Third, effectiveness is not a binary scale. A preparation's effectiveness is contingent upon the disease being treated; a highly effective preparation may produce serious side-effects, including risk of death; a preparation rating as very effective on some absolute scale may be much less effective than the best preparation available. Fourth, the main initial source of information about a drug is the application prepared by the firm seeking to market it. The applications quite naturally emphasize the drugs' advantages and deemphasize their disadvantages, and these biases might be expected to increase when the Health Bureau starts assessing effectiveness. Further, although it would be unfair to say the applications are often deceptive, pharmaceutical firms have been known to submit deceptive applications, and the Health Bureau must be constantly alert to the possibility of deception. Fifth, the possible sources of information about a drug are multitudinous: medical and pharmaceutical journals, clinical reports, applications submitted in other countries, tests performed by licensing bureaus in other countries, rumor and word-of-mouth. And the mapping of these reports onto the set of drugs is fuzzy whenever it is not obscure, because mixtures of ingredients and manufacturing techniques vary slightly from country to country and from manufacturer to manufacturer. At least in some cases, these ostensibly small and unimportant variations have later been recognized as significant. Finally and most importantly, what is known at any one time about a drug is usually less important than what is about to be discovered. Steady progress in the ability to formulate and answer questions is generated by steady progress in analytic and measurement technology, in production techniques, in clinical trials, in the correlation of information from multiple sources, and so forth. Many effects only appear after long use or when drugs are used in combination, possibly when one of today's drugs is combined with a drug that will be invented tomorrow. So there is an extremely high rate of knowledge obsolescence, partly due to deficiencies in today's knowledge and partly due to the spawning of new needs for knowledge.

The Health Bureau's staff had concluded that the first step in drug evaluation was assembling as much relevant information as possible, that this required some sort of information storage and retrieval system, and that it would be very difficult to classify incoming information in such fashion that it could be retrieved whenever it was relevant. As a matter of fact, when they considered the sheer mass of information that ought to be analyzed, the heterogeneous formats in which it arrived, and the high educational levels required to comprehend and classify it, the Bureau's staff did not see how a significant proportion of the relevant information could be brought to bear on a given evaluation. Wolfgang and I had to agree with them. Although in principle every document could be coded with many descriptors, much time and skill would be required to assign descriptors to a single document; and since the descriptors generally did not form logical hierarchies, elaborate and complex search programs would be required to avoid selecting a high proportion of irrelevant documents while simultaneously overlooking a high proportion of the relevant documents.

However, we found most discouraging the rate of change in naturally occurring descriptors. We estimated that an effective storage and retrieval system based on today's terminology would take about five years to complete, by which time it would be inappropriate for nearly half of the documents then being classified. A replacement system, put into development immediately, would be available ten years from now, when the first system would be nearly useless. Thus a sequence of successive information systems would oscillate between, say, 10 % and 60 % effective as shown in Figure 1. The Health Bureau's personnel would be probably make little use of systems with such low performances.

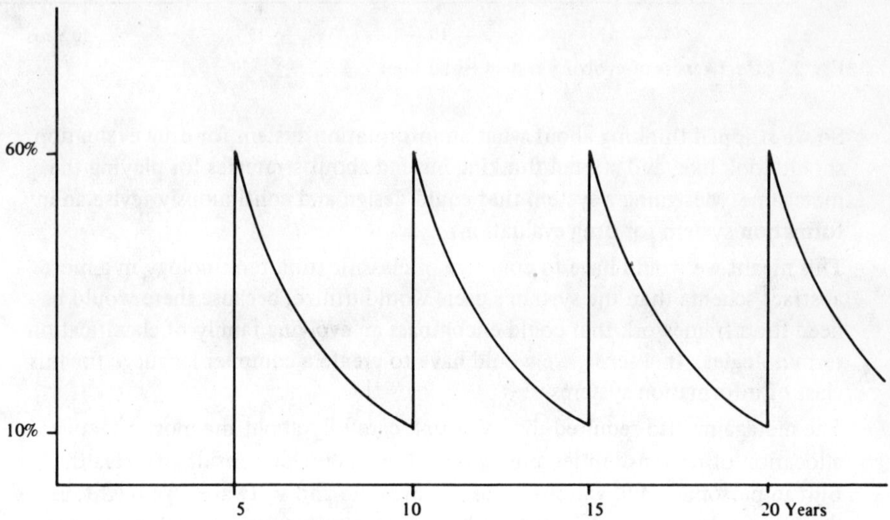

Fig. 1. Effectiveness of discrete successors

Then it occurred to us that a sequence of discrete successors only had tradition to recommend it. An information system could evolve almost continuously, and an evolving system should degrade very slowly. An evolving system should even improve in effectiveness after it first came into operation, as it accomodated itself to its designers' mistakes. An evolving system which began at 60 % effectiveness could achieve an average effectiveness above 60 %, and it should be useful for much longer than five years. Its effectiveness pattern should look something like the solid line in Figure 2.

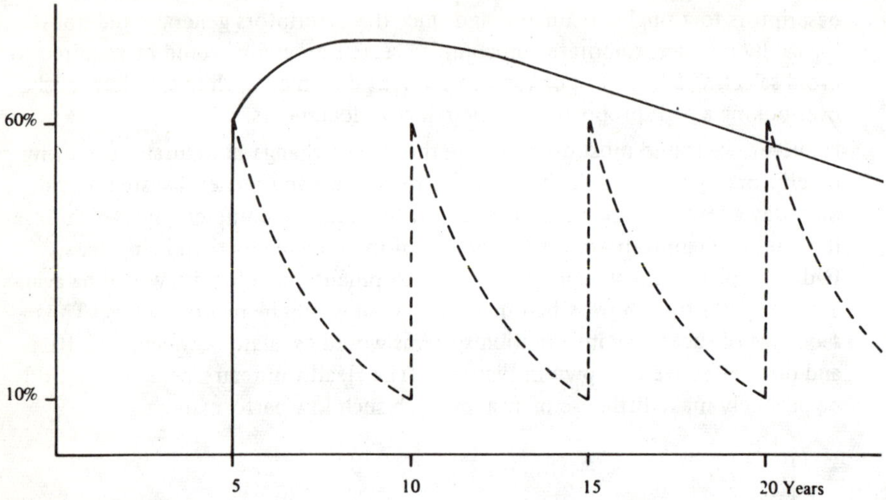

Fig. 2. Effectiveness of evolving system (solid line)

So we stopped thinking about what an information system for drug evaluation should look like, and started thinking instead about strategies for playing the metagame: designing a system that could design and continuously revise an information system for drug evaluation.

This meant we would have to conceive of classification terminology in a more abstract schema than the system's users would utilize, because there would be need for a framework that could encompass an evolving family of classification terminologies. In a sense, we would have to create a compiler language for this class of information systems.

The metagame also required that we think carefully about the most effective allocation of responsibilities among ourselves as outside consultants, Health Bureau personnel, and various kinds of hardware and software. We ought, as the project developed, to transfer whatever expertise we possessed to the information system itself, and if possible, the information system ought to be capable of insights beyond our own. Assigning too much responsibility to hardware and software would limit the system's ability to adapt to unanticipated events, but assigning too much responsibility to people would render the system liable to staff turnover and human fallibilities. Since there would be a tendency for the hardware-software subsystem to acquire more and more responsibility over time, it might be necessary to build in diagnostic counter-balances such as periodic assessments of the degrees of misclassification and distortion.

Finally, because the Health Bureau's personnel would be responsible for the system's long-run survival, success, and acceptance, and because they understood the central substantive issues better than we consultants did, they should be full partners in the system's creation. They should understand all aspects of its composition and rationale, and should control its content. We consultants should avoid becoming personally identified with specific concepts, methods, and techniques ... except perhaps with specific techniques which were needed to start the system into operation but which ought to be replaced soon thereafter. By taking responsibility for these start-up components ourselves, we would make it easier for the Bureau's staff to discard them.

I wish it were possible to reveal how well Wolfgang and I played this metagame, how well we controlled our egos, and what intriguing new ideas the project demanded. But the reality is that the project only survived a few initial discussions and we only begán to glimpse in the most tentative way what success in the metagame would require.

3. ... to self-designing systems ...

However, I have become increasingly convinced that the metagame is the most important game, not only for information systems design, but for all sorts of design projects for social systems. The last few years have brought numerous attempts at social engineering ... and nearly as many failures. Since a high proportion of these failures appear to me to be attributable to faulty design strategies, I have been trying to analyze how the metagame should be played. Three issues seem to be especially crucial.

3.1 How can systems allow for errors or inadequacies in their designs?

Although response to unanticipated events ought to be an important, explicit design criterion, it is rarely incorporated in a system's design. For example, how many production scheduling systems try to allow for machine breakdowns, the arrival of new orders, or errors in estimated cost functions? One basic strategy for anticipating the unanticipated is to carry out sensitivity analyses, and then, if probabilities can be assigned to possible errors or future events, to choose a strategy possessing high expected value and satisfying constraints about the worst disaster which might be experienced. Of course, sensitivity analyses are expensive, but the cost of analysis can be taken into account by imbedding the basic optimization problem in a higher level problem that includes the cost of search [10].

The unanticipated events most difficult to provide for are mistakes by the system's designers. Design weaknesses challenge the designers' objectivity – after all, if the designers really thought they were making a mistake, they would not make it. And design faults are frequently problems that cannot be represented by probability distributions. Probabilities are primarily useful in cases where the designers are aware they have considered two or more possibilities and have made a choice. But probabilities cannot be assigned to events one has not conceived of, and it seems plausible that conceptual failures are likely to cause more severe errors than are caused by explicitly formulated choices.

The basic strategies for coping with design errors and inadequacies are redundancy and diversification. For example, a team of third parties could be engaged to diagnose the conceptual faults in a design; two or more design teams could prepare competing alternatives and then the alternatives could be pursued simultaneously as a portfolio; or provisions could be made for future feedback and performance appraisals in domains where logic says none should be necessary. However, resource constraints always limit the amount of feasible redundancy, few systems can afford the redundancy level of a space ship, and even space ship designers must decide what kinds of redundancy are most important. So two major dilemmas are how many resources to dedicate to controlling design weaknesses and how to allocate the available resources among alternatives which have no probabilities associated with them. The absence of well-defined probability distributions makes it impractical to treat this as an optimization problem in the metagame.

3.2 How can a system optimize criteria which are still being discovered?

One category of design weakness that deserves special consideration is ignorance of the criteria for system effectiveness. Such ignorance is always present to some degree, and it is a dominating characteristic of many design problems. For instance, when should the Health Bureau risk major confrontations with the pharmaceutical industry or the medical association in order to serve the interests of a possibly ungrateful public? Or how much evidence about long-run effects should be required before a drug is made available to everyone whom it appears to help?

One reason effectiveness criteria are ill-defined is that people often do not know how much they will like a possible future state until they have experienced it. Another reason is that criteria are set by organizational and societal governance structures which are themselves unclear: no one knows who should decide. And still another reason is that the ultimate criteria are set by amorphous social aggregates, such as the "public" or a Parliament, that express their reactions better than they express their preferences. It ought to be possible to approach such discovery problems systematically by applying search techniques [4; 7; 9].

However, one of the most important reasons effectiveness criteria are ill-defined is that they shift. Social norms change endlessly, as do the power structures which dictate whose preferences should be considered. The effectiveness of most policies depends on how long they have been in effect: infrequent policy changes allow efficiency to rise through learning, but also allow complacency and slack resources to accumulate. Of course, shifting criteria are more difficult to optimize than stable ones are, especially when the shifts are not monotonic.

Shifting criteria also confront designers with ethical issues. Changing criteria are normally changeable criteria. They respond to the behavior of the system they are evaluating, and so they respond to the system's designers. Designers can accelerate, retard, or divert the rates of change by making the system itself more or less liable to change. Designers' general propensity is probably to over-estimate the natural stability of criteria that are being optimized simply because stable criteria are more easily optimized. But this exaggerates the stability of the designed systems and becomes a self-fulfilling prophecy. One consequence is that social systems tend to preserve the status quo. Another consequence is that social planners find themselves supporting social philosophies with which they may not agree. At what point should the demands of the design process or the designers' personal preferences start to dominate their clients' needs and preferences?

3.3 How can a system accomodate and encourage the exercise of intelligence?

One inference to be drawn from the preceding discussion is that designers should strive for restrained designs which attach no more certainty to assumptions than is essential. Restrained designs also provide opportunities for human components in designed systems to display initiative and to supplement or modify the designers' contributions.

Indeed, explicit decisions about what problems should not be solved are at least as important as explicit decisions about what problems should be. Undertaking a costly, large-scale project to invent a rational solution to a problem will always elicit commitments to the invented solution that are independent of the solution's quality, generality, or stability; and investments of time and effort, power struggles to get a project authorized, or social relations among a project's staff can be emotionally stronger determinants than any intrinsic properties of the project's outputs. If the project's output is distinctly suboptimal, or is a temporarily high-quality local optimum, mounting a large-scale project binds the system to low performance. Furthermore, analytic projects are usually carried out by professional specialists who endorse criteria of excellence having more to do with how analyses are conducted than with what the analyses produce. Unless such analysts are judiciously constrained they will design rational methods of pursuing unwise goals. Far better that systems should non-rationally pursue wise goals.

Probably the most important mechanism for preserving the search for wisdom – a mechanism that is the foundation of many political systems – is intrasystem conflict. Conflict provides sources of strategic diversification, stimulates reexaminations of implicit or traditional premises, and validates nonconformist perceptions and values. It keeps systems adaptively flexible and prevents maladaptive stresses from aggregating [1; 5]. So one design challenge is to build sufficient conflict into a system by making areas of responsibility vague and overlapping and by setting up inconsistent subgoals and information flows. And a corollary design challenge is to incorporate information channels and joint decision-making processes that facilitate low-stress conflict resolution. Excessive levels of conflict or conflicts which cannot be resolved are, of course, debilitating and corrosive.

Designers must also recognize that conflict feeds upon uncertainty and ambiguity, whereas models and decision aids are ordinarily uncertainty absorbers. Herbert Simon [12] argues that information systems should incorporate analytic and synthetic models that reduce the number of stimuli to which human decision makers must attend. Perhaps so; but if so, the models provided to different decision makers should be slightly inconsistent, and the kinds of uncertainty the models absorb should be subject to careful deliberation. The opportunity to absorb uncertainty should not imply the desirability of absorbing it.

4. . . . and to information systems for tomorrow

There are two strategies for designing information systems for organizations of the future. The first starts with forecasts of what tomorrow's organizations will look like and what stresses they will face. For example, more and more firms are operating simultaneously in several countries, trading opportunities in one country off against those in another, creating international regulatory problems, and challenging the autonomy of national governments [8; 15]. Interest groups are advocating and legislatures are requiring representation on governing boards for workers and consumers in addition to owners and financiers, implying increased dependence on intra-organizational decision making in lieu of market processes [3; 16]. Increasing acceptance of cooperative interorganizational networks is putting emphasis on organizations' ability to predict consequences of their acts and, at the same time, is making the causal chains more complex and obscure [2; 6; 13; 14]. Rising standards of living are reducing the importance of industrial organizations and raising the importance of service, distribution, and governmental organizations, and therefore increasing the importance of information processing and the amounts of information to be processed [2; 11].

Then one designs information systems that will meet the needs of tomorrow's organizations, or at least adduces basic principles to guide information system design [12].

Although several questions might be posed concerning the realism and effectiveness of this first design strategy, the central issue it raises is an ethical one deriving from designers' ability to make self-fulfilling prophecies. Designers who plan for a world in which there are, for instance, many cooperative relations among organizations will design information systems that help organizations cope with cooperative relations. If the designs are effective, organizations will find cooperation easier to handle, and they will be encouraged to form cooperative relations. The designers will have, of course, achieved their purposes: they will have designed information systems that match tomorrow's organizations. But the same degree of goal achievement might well have been attained by designing information systems that impeded interorganizational cooperation. The designers' most important contribution seems to be throwing their influence behind one direction of social change instead of another, and they only avoid shaping the future when they design ineptly.

If information system designers are going to facilitate particular kinds of social change, they certainly ought to acknowledge the value premises underlying their social policies, and they should choose their social policies overtly after comparing alternative futures. But it is far from clear that designers ought to control social change, or even that they want to do so. Not only is there something to be said for letting organizations' members participate in the design of tomorrow's organizations, but there is something to be said for incremental design strategies that rely heavily on feedback from today's experiments.

The second way to design information systems for organizations of the future is to play the metagame.

References

[1] Assael, Henry: "Constructive role of interorganizational conflict". In: Administrative Science Quarterly 14 1969, pp. 573–582.

[2] Bell, Daniel: The coming of post-industrial society. Scranton, Pa. 1973.

[3] Blumberg, Paul: Industrial democracy. New York 1969.

[4] Box, George E. and Norman R. Draper: Evolutionary operation. New York 1968.

[5] Coser, Lewis A.: The functions of social conflict. Riverside, N.J. 1956.

[6] Emery, Fred E. and Eric L. Trist: "The causal texture of organizational environments". In: Human Relations 18 1965, pp. 21–32.

[7] Murphy, Roy E.: Adaptive processes in economic systems. New York 1965.

[8] Paquet, Gilles (ed.): The multinational firm and the nation-state. Don Mills, Ontario 1972.

[9] Plant, John B.: Some iterative solutions in optimal control. Cambridge, Mass. 1968.

[10] Reiter, Stanley and Gordon R. Sherman: "Discrete optimizing". In: Society for Industrial and Applied Mathematics Journal 13 1965, pp. 864–889.

[11] Simon, Herbert A.: "Designing organizations for an information-rich world". In: Martin Greenberger (ed.): Computers, communications, and the public interest. Baltimore, Md. 1971, pp. 37–52.

[12] Simon, Herbert A.: "Applying information technology to organizational design". In: Public Administration Review 33 1973, pp. 268–278.

[13] Terreberry, Shirley: "The evolution of organizational environments". In: Administrative Science Quarterly 12 1968, pp. 590–613.

[14] Touraine, Alain: The post industrial society. New York 1971.

[15] Vernon, Raymond: Sovereignty at bay. Scranton, Pa. 1971.

[16] Whisler, Thomas L.: Information technology and organizational change. Belmont, Calif. 1970.

German abstract
Informationssysteme für Organisationen der Zukunft

Von *William H. Starbuck*

Starbuck berichtet von seinen Erfahrungen als Organisationsberater und stellt einige Kriterien heraus, die dazu führten, daß Systembenutzer auch gute Konzepte und Systemrealisationen nicht akzeptierten und innerlich ablehnten. Er führt diese Tatsache auf psychisch bedingte Verhaltensweisen zurück und stellt Überlegungen an, wie Informationssysteme unter Hinzuziehung des Benutzers in effizienter und beide Seiten (d.h. Systemgestalter und Benutzer) befriedigender Weise gestaltet werden können. Die zentrale Aufgabe des Systemgestalters sollte darin bestehen, Lösungen zu erarbeiten, die sowohl Änderungen im Problemverständnis als auch der Probleme selbst berücksichtigen.

Starbuck berichtet dann von einer Entwicklungsstudie für das Bundesgesundheitsamt. Das Projekt – ein Arzneimittel-Auswertungs- und Beurteilungssystem – wurde aus finanziellen Erwägungen nicht durchgeführt, in der Konzipierungsphase konnten jedoch einige wichtige Erfahrungen gesammelt werden, die Starbuck in seinem

Beitrag wiedergibt. Um die Größenordnung dieses Informationssystems etwas zu charakterisieren, seien nachstehend einige Zahlen genannt:

Es waren ca. 60 000 medizinische Präparate zu erfassen, und man ging davon aus, daß eine ähnlich hohe Anzahl ausländischer Präparate ebenfalls erfaßt werden sollte – beide Größen waren zudem von einer starken Zuwachsrate gekennzeichnet. Schon nach den ersten Überlegungen wurde klar, daß bei konventionellem Vorgehen für die Erfassung etwa fünf Jahre benötigt wurden, wobei zu erwarten war, daß dann ca. 50% der dokumentierten Informationen nicht mehr brauchbar sein würden. Aus diesen und anderen näher dargelegten Gründen kam man zu der Auffassung, ein System zu schaffen, das von vornherein nicht darauf ausgerichtet war, alle Informationen in den oben erwähnten Größenordnungen zu erfassen, sondern ein „wachsendes" System zu entwerfen (Generatoransatz). Dies bedeutete die Entwicklung einer neuen klassifikatorischen Terminologie mit einem ungewöhnlich hohen Abstraktionsgrad.

Starbuck nennt drei entscheidende Voraussetzungen solcher Systeme:

(1) Kompensation von systemimmanenten Fehlern oder Fehleinschätzungen. Eine solche Kompensation soll durch gewollte Redundanz und Diversifikation ermöglicht werden, da hierdurch die Generierung alternativer Lösungen gefördert werde. Dabei ist allerdings zu berücksichtigen, daß diese Generierung alternativer Lösungen von verschiedenen Beschränkungen abhängt und das Fehlen gut definierter Häufigkeitsverteilungen über unvorhergesehene Ereignisse eine Problemoptimierung noch nicht ermöglicht.

(2) Optimierung „unbekannter" Zielkriterien. Die Zielkriterien von Systemen variieren unter anderem durch soziale und politische Einflüsse. Daraus resultieren wechselnde Effektivitätskriterien, die zu erfüllen sind. Der Gestalter von Informationssystemen muß sich bewußt sein, wie weit er bei der Strukturierung eigene Vorstellungen oder Zielvorstellungen der Anwender berücksichtigt.

(3) Erweiterung bzw. Anpassung der Intelligenz. Eine Erweiterung der Intelligenz soll u.a. dadurch erreicht werden, daß ganz bewußt latentes Konfliktpotential durch vage abgegrenzte und sich überlappende Verantwortungsbereiche oder durch unkoordinierte Subziele und Informationsflüsse erzeugt wird. Dadurch soll die Generierung non-konformistischer Lösungsvorschläge erreicht werden.

Der Erläuterung dieser drei Voraussetzungen schließt sich ein Ausblick auf die Gestaltung zukünftiger Informationssysteme an. Zwei Strategien werden angedeutet, wobei Starbuck die von ihm am Beispiel des erwähnten Arzneimittel-Informationssystems skizzierte Methode als eine mögliche Gestaltungsstrategie, auch für Informationssysteme zukünftiger Organisationen, bezeichnet.

Changes in organizational design induced by the introduction of computerized information systems – a longitudinal study in the electricity industry

By *Derek Stone*

1. Introduction

This paper describes the organizational changes that have taken place in the North Western Electricity Board (Norweb) since 1967. It is based on two short surveys of the organizational structure and related information systems, one carried out in 1967 at the Board's invitation and one in 1973 at the writer's request.

In 1967 the Board was planning the transfer of routine data processing from its IBM 1401 computers, located at six area offices, to an ICL 4–70 computer located at Headquarters. The writer was asked to "survey the management information used at Headquarters and to prepare a report so that future developments to the information system could be considered". The finding in the report [3], that is most relevant for this paper was that the Board had not fully realised how the 4–70 computer, if used for management purposes, would change its organizational structure. It was pointed out that staff at Board Headquarters would be able to make many of the policy decisions that were then being made at outlying areas, and that day-to-day control of some operations could be centralized. As a result, the responsibilities of Area Managers would be reduced and the Board's internal geographical boundaries could be altered to give economies of scale.

There was understandable concern at Headquarters about the upheaval that such reorganization would bring and it was decided that only the information processing changes and recommended management information changes would be pursued; the organizational hierarchy would be left as it was.

The writer was of the opinion that such a policy would not prove to be feasible. As Leavitt [2], has said, alterations in information technology will impinge on the task, the people and the organizational structure, whether allowed for or not. The 1973 survey gives us the opportunity of seeing to what extent this was true for Norweb. Staff at Headquarters, at Area level and below were interviewed in both surveys; in 1967 to assess the existing information system and to recommend changes, and in 1973 to examine the present system. It should be pointed out that the writer had no contact with this organization between the two surveys; the changes that have occurred were generated internally following the

1967 report. Fortunately, the Board adopts a committee approach to change and it has thus been possible to identify the factors that influenced them to recommend the changes that have occurred.

This paper is organized as follows:–

The electricity industry in England and Wales,
The North Western Electricity Board,
Organizational changes,
Observed changes by task,
Assessment and conclusions.

1.1 The electricity industry in England and Wales

The electricity supply industry in England and Wales is divided into generation and distribution sectors, both responsible to the Secretary of State for Trade and Industry. The Central Electricity Generating Board has a duty to maintain and develop an efficient, coordinated and economical system of supply and to provide bulk supplies to the distribution sector.

There are twelve autonomous Area Boards that are responsible for distribution. Each has power to sell, hire, repair or install fittings as well as to supply and sell electricity. Together they cover some 60,000 sq. miles and serve over 18 million consumers as detailed in the following table:–

1970–71	**Numbers of consumers**	**Units sold x 10^6**
Domestic	16,481,100	66,134
Commercial	1,368,500	28,954
Farms	254,400	2,907
Public lighting	5,300	1,462
	18,109,300	99,457

The Minister is advised on policy by the Electricity Council which consists of a full time Chairman, two Deputy Chairmen and three other members together with the Chairman and two designated members of the Generating Board and the Chairmen of the twelve Area Boards (the distribution sector). The Council meets monthly and thus there is opportunity for matters affecting the internal running of the industry to be raised and discussed between the Boards if necessary.

1.2 The North Western Electricity Board (Norweb)

The North Western Electricity Board covers an area of nearly 5,000 sq. miles and stretches from the Lake District in the North – a predominantly rural area – to the Manchester area in the South – a concentrated urban area. It serves nearly two million consumers, classified as follows:–

1970–71	Numbers of consumers	Units sold x 10^6
Domestic	1,680,400	6,383
Commercial	127,700	2,820
Farms	23,400	266
Industrial	20,000	7,835
Public lighting	300	157
	1,851,800	17,461

It is divided into six areas, each with several districts, and has showrooms and depots within area classifications.

The geographical division and organizational structure for 1967 and 1973 are given in Appendix 1.

The Board's objectives can be divided into two broad categories:–

(1) to distribute and sell electrical energy

(2) to carry on trading activities – principally the sale of appliances and the provision of services on a contractual basis.

To achieve these aims the Board has two main functional areas:–

(a) Engineering; responsible for the maintenance and development of the system.

(b) Commercial; responsible for selling activities, and carrying out contract work.

These are supported by Administrative and Accounting functions.

The line/staff relationships in 1967 and 1973 are shown in Appendix 2.

There is a functional link between Chief Officers at Headquarters and their counterparts at Area and (where applicable) at District. Day-to-day control is exercised by line management, however.

2. Organizational changes

It had been expected that centralization of information processing together with the ability of the computer to take certain decisions automatically would result in:–

(a) the lessening of importance of Area Managers;

(b) the amalgamation of Districts into newly defined regions;

(c) the increased control of Headquarters staff over policy decision making and day-to-day activities.

Examination of the existing structure reveals that:–

(1) Although information processing is centralized, Areas have retained the same decision making powers as before. Their accountability for decisions has been increased by the improvement in the information available at Headquarters.

(2) The removal of information processing has released some time at Area offices. The Area Manager now spends more time on management activities and as a result, costs have been reduced whilst maintaining or improving services to customers. (This conclusion was reached by interviewing the staff – customers have not been approached for their views.) The posts of Area Accountant and Area Secretary have been combined and renamed Administrative Officer.

(3) Centralization of billing processing has led to decentralization of customer services to District level and to the creation of a new post 'District Customer Service Manager' with the responsibility of all customer contacts. Ability to handle queries promptly has encouraged the installation of telephones in showrooms for the use (free) of customers, and written correspondence has been cut down.

(4) Some Districts have been amalgamated to give economies of scale. The major changes that were expected, however, have not taken place. In particular, contract work is still scheduled on a District basis (except for large contract work which is dealt with by specialist teams based on Areas). Engineers do use the computer for technical computation purposes on a batch processing basis but not interactively nor to schedule work.

(5) Stores are still Area responsibilities but a central warehouse is being built and central control of stores is planned. This will include ordering, using a computer program.

(6) The speed with which work could be transferred to the ICL 4–70 was not as high as had been expected; (there has been about a year's time lag). Hence further developments need to be watched to see what further changes take place. Appendix 3 indicates the work done to date and the future work that is planned.

To sum up: The administrative work level at Districts and at Areas has been reduced and continues to be reduced. The time released has led to a change in emphasis in Area responsibilities towards better management of the operational tasks for which they were responsible in 1967 and before. Day-to-day work scheduling is still at District level and, due to the increased ability to liaise with customers, the service given appears to have improved.

The ability to interrogate the computer from District level has, in effect, given each District its own set of records. Hence it has enabled decentralization of decisions on such matters as customer credit-worthiness and the settling of queries.

2.1 Observed changes by task

In this section the major tasks carried out by the Board are briefly described and the changes that have occurred (if any) in the way they are carried out or controlled are indicated. These tasks centre round the provision of electricity and the trading activities, plus such support activities as purchasing and accounting. An initial scan of the subheadings to get an overview of the section before examining each in detail is to be recommended.

3. The provision and sale of electrical energy

3.1 Engineering staff

There are two main categories of engineering staff; Mains Engineers who are responsible for the maintenance and extension of the network and for dealing with emergencies, and Contracting Engineers who are responsible for the installation of appliances and any other contract work that has been obtained by the Commercial section. Contract engineering is responsible to the Commercial function for day-to-day operations although there is a strong functional link with Area and District Engineers who influence the standards of work. The organization of the Mains engineering function is influenced predominantly by geography. Policy decisions are made at Board and Area levels but day-to-day work scheduling is carried out within Districts. It was observed that the time allocated to regular maintenance work is treated as a slack resource so that the variable demands of emergency work can be met while employing a stable work force. There has been no significant alteration in this system between 1967 and 1973.

3.2 Meter reading and billing

In 1967 meter readers kept bulky handwritten record books and, where the meter was of a prepayment type, were responsible for calculating the cost of the electricity used and giving the housewife a rebate from the cash taken from the meter. The books were sent to Area where quarterly accounts were prepared and sent out. Problems with the system included:–

(1) Time-lags between meter reading and bill preparation.

(2) Rebate calculations which slowed up the meter readers.

(3) Customer queries which were often difficult to deal with because record books were not always in one place; customer accounts were not easily accessible in an up-to-date form.

(4) Hire-purchase clearances which took several days at least to obtain.

(5) Preparation of deferred credit sales books was so slow that purchasers were in arrears right from the start.

(6) The sending of 'cut-off' notices to customers for non-payment after they had made a late payment or queried the total, which resulted in bad customer relations.

By 1973 the following changes had taken place:–

(a) The time-lag between meter reading and bill despatch has been very much reduced.

(b) Meter reading is carried out more quickly because no rebates are calculated by the meter reader – the computer sends rebate cheques annually. (This has led to one unexpected problem – over many years the housewife has come to look upon her prepayment meter rebate as a form of saving and many of them objected when this was suddenly removed by the Board – a rebate cheque is not the same because the husband gets it!)

(c) Terminals have been installed in all Districts and all account details can be instantly assessed. District Customer Telephone Enquiry Bureaus have been set up – with telephones in all showrooms – and queries are answered immediately in most cases. There is thus decentralization of decision making with respect to queries, from Area to District level.

(d) Hire purchase clearance is simple via the terminal.

(e) Deferred Credit Sale books are prepared by the computer and distributed promptly.

(f) District Officers can instruct the computer, via the terminal not to send 'cut-off' notices, thereby greatly reducing the customer dissatisfaction problem.

The way in which these changes were introduced was as follows:–

A Committee was set up to consider administration and consumer service below Area level "having regard to changes arising from the introduction of the central computer" and various other experiments that the Board had been conducting. The report that was produced took advantage of the information improvements and recommended organizational changes. In effect, the new information facilities relaxed constraints and allowed organizational changes to be made that would not otherwise have been possible. For example, the new post of Customer Service Manager would not have been workable under the old information processing procedures because his staff could not have handled the queries side of their job – particularly now that Districts are being combined to include 150,000 customers.

4. The sale of appliances

This is a relatively homogenous task which can be planned and controlled from a central point. In fact, control was centralized at Area Headquarters in 1967 before the advent of new information systems. There appear to be three ways in which information handling improvements have influenced this function:–

(1) The telephone link with District Enquiry Bureaus has resulted in more freedom from customer queries. Customers can still pay bills and raise queries at showrooms, but the phone link has improved the service they get and saves salesmen's time.

(2) Hire purchase credit ratings can be obtained quickly – via the telephone to District and terminal link with Headquarters. Hire purchase repayment books are now prepared by the 4–70 and despatched to customers before the first payment is due. This has reduced the number of bad debts.

(3) New appliances are installed more quickly now that customer's requirements are routed through the District Customer Service Manager.

5. The provision of services on a contractual basis

Contracts are a Commercial responsibility. Small contract work is the responsibility of the District Customer Service Manager who has a Contract Engineer reporting to him. Almost all of his work is within his District boundary.
Large contract work is carried out by Contract Engineers who are responsible to the Area Commercial Officer. District boundaries are ignored when scheduling work for these specialist teams. The Board is considering centralizing all contract work at Area level.

6. Support functions

Internally the Board requires several support functions, the principal ones being:–

6.1 Accounting and Administration

The 4–70 has led to centralization of staff in the accounting function and Area staffs have been reduced. The strictness of the routines has also led to closer control in the organization. Structural changes have followed: as already described, some posts at Area have been combined, and a new post has been created at District level.

The 4–70 is under the control of the Chief Accountant but this has not led to its restriction to routine accounting work. It had been predicted that a Management Services Officer, responsible to the Deputy Chairman, would be in charge of the computer. This has not come about, and does not appear to be necessary at the present time because the cooperative attitude of the Chief Accountant encourages other departments to use the computing facilities.

6.2 Transportation

Transport for both labour and appliance deliveries is still scheduled manually at Districts. There is considerable uncertainty involved in the scheduling task, partly due to the need to switch men between tasks and partly because customers may not be home when appliances are delivered. Work is scheduled for about three days in advance and the District Customer Service Manager informs the Area Commercial Officer if he needs more vehicles or if he has a surplus. It is Area responsibility to coordinate these demands between Districts.

6.3 Stock holding and purchasing

The Board is building a central stores and is introducing a computer program to forecast demand and order stocks. Such centralization will reduce staffs at Areas, who at present order and hold their own stocks.

Decision making and responsibility will be transferred from Areas to the Central Purchasing Manager. Districts and showrooms will be able to interrogate stores files via terminals and visual display units. Delivery schedules will still be planned at Districts, because of the need to coordinate the engineering and consumer service aspects of the task.

7. Assessment and conclusions

Jay Galbraith [1] has suggested that organizational design is influenced by three major variables:–

(1) Uncertainty,
(2) The number of elements involved,
(3) The interconnectedness of these elements.

His paper analysed the subject from the point of view of an organization whose task becomes progressively more complex and he suggested that alternative ways of handling this complexity are to improve the information system or to restructure the organization to reduce the need to process information. In Norweb we have the same set of factors but the alteration that took place was in the information system and not in the task. Instead of information processing following the hierarchy with successive condensation at each management level, it is now processed centrally, with direct input from all management levels. Headquarters has more information on Area and District activities than ever before and new communication channels have been opened. The Board has taken advantage of these improvements to gradually change the way it carries out its tasks. This has involved alterations to its management structure but these have followed a series of rather uncoordinated committee reports rather than stemming from an overall plan. On the other hand, this approach seems to be working well since the introduction of change is not being accompanied by the resistances and morale problems that have occurred in similar situations elsewhere.

Following Galbraith, one would expect that the information system changes would allow Norweb to cope with greater levels of uncertainty, more elements and a greater degree of inter-connectedness between elements. To achieve these increases, one would expect to find increased control of day-to-day operations from the centre and fewer and larger geographical divisions within the Board. Such changes are in fact taking place, but at a slower rate than the writer had expected. This appears to be due to delays in the development of the information system and because further changes would involve the Area level of management. In addition, the Board has the philosophy of introducing change slowly to avoid personnel problems. It has deliberately chosen to allow change to evolve through its committee structure. The process has not worked itself out by any means and the writer intends to report on further developments as they occur.

Appendices

NORWEB – Geographical Structure 1967

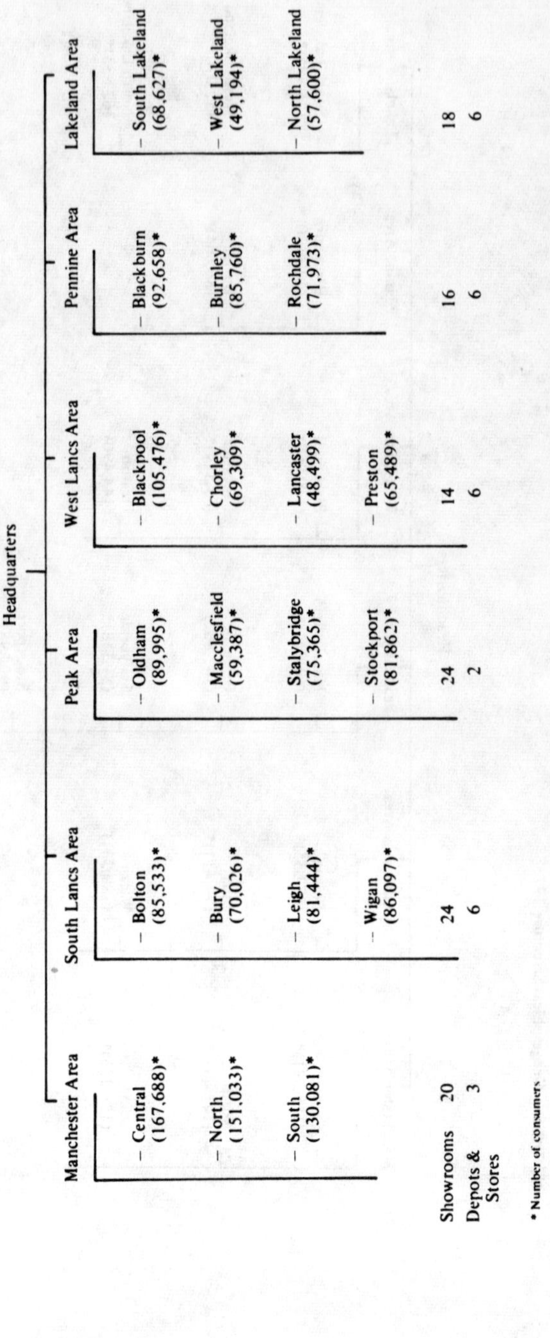

NORWEB – Geographical Structure 1973

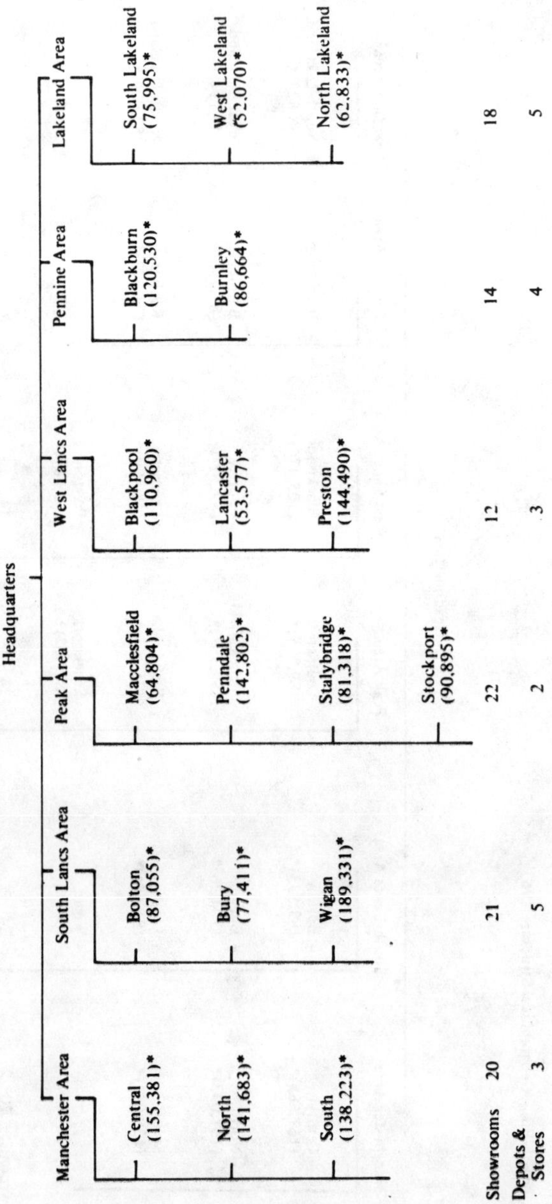

* Number of consumers

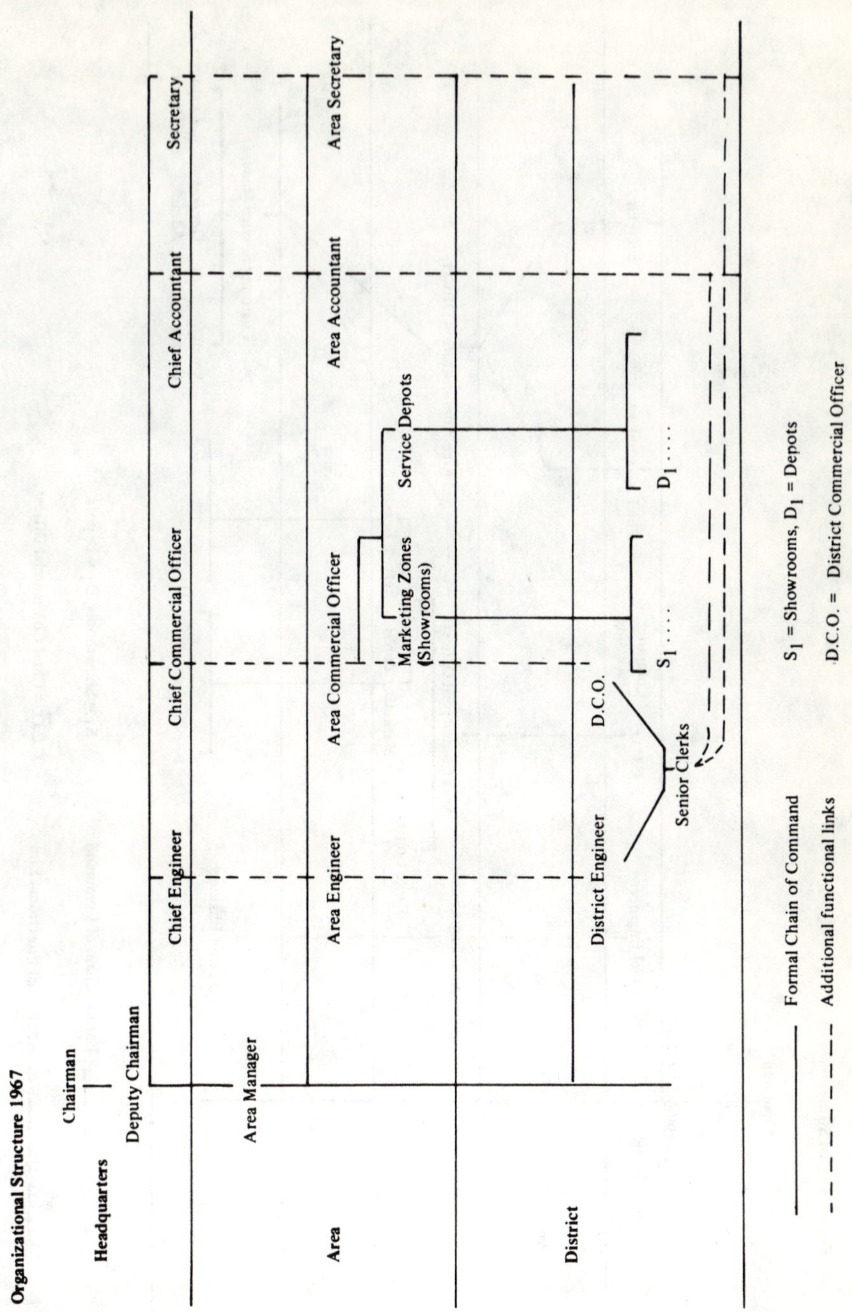
Organizational Structure 1967
Headquarters
Chairman
Deputy Chairman
Chief Engineer
Chief Commercial Officer
Chief Accountant
Secretary
Area
Area Manager
Area Engineer
Area Commercial Officer
Marketing Zones (Showrooms)
Service Depots
Area Accountant
Area Secretary
District
District Engineer
D.C.O.
Senior Clerks
S1 ....
D1 ....
Formal Chain of Command
Additional functional links
S1 = Showrooms, D1 = Depots
D.C.O. = District Commercial Officer

Organizational Structure 1973

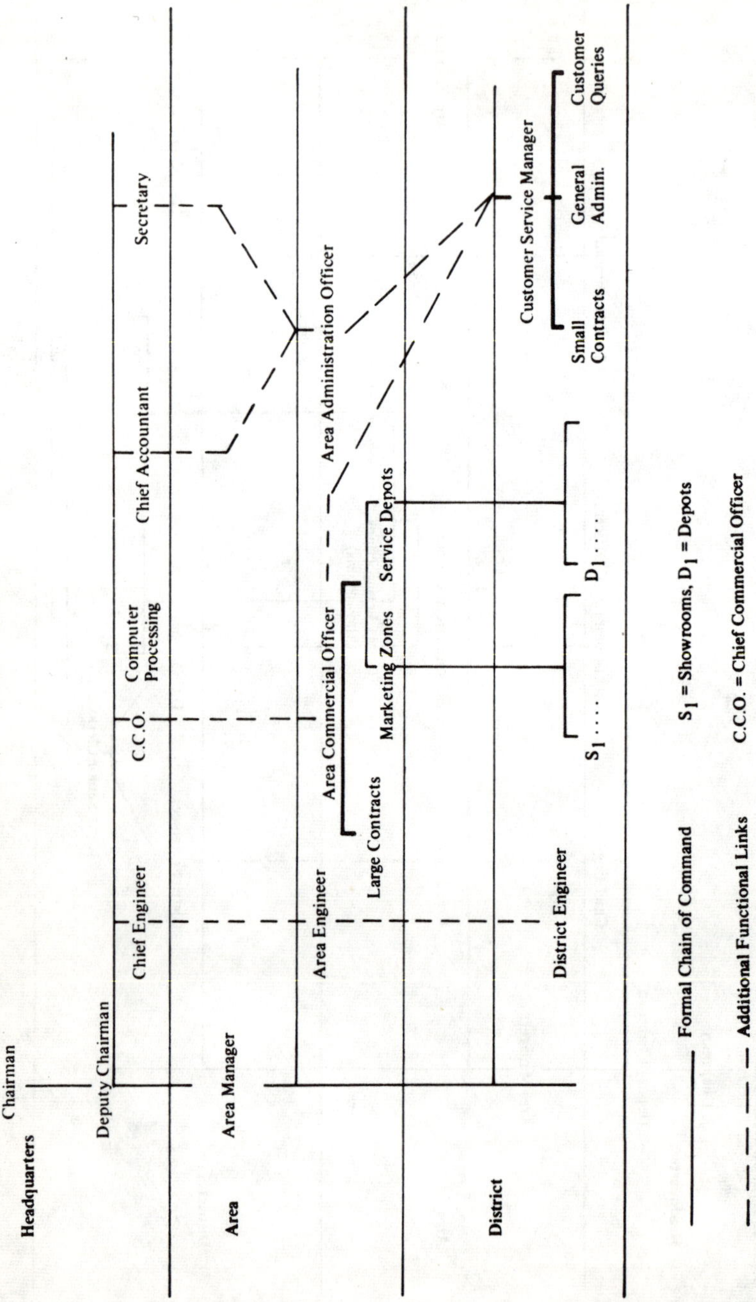

History of NORWEB computing and future plans

1962 – 1963	Installation of IBM 1401 computers at Area Headquarters.
1967	IBM 360/30's installed at Board Headquarters and at the West Lancs Area Headquarters.
1968	Transfer of accounting work from Areas to Headquarters commenced.
	First 1401 released from an Area.
	ICL 4/50 installed at Headquarters.
	ICL 4/70 installed at Headquarters.
	Second ICL 4/70 accepted by Norweb.
1969	ICL 4/50 removed.
	First application put on to 4/70.
1970	Quarterly billing conversion commenced.
	First Terminal enquiry system introduced.
	Last IBM 1401 released from Areas.
	Second ICL 4/70 installed at Headquarters.
1971	IBM 360/25 controlling 1287 Document Reader installed at Headquarters.
	IBM 360/30 released from West Lancs Area.
	Quarterly billing conversion completed.
	Release of IBM 360/30 from Headquarters.
1972	Transfer of residual 1401 applications to the ICL 4/70.
	Release of last IBM 360/30 from Headquarters.

The computer now deals with:—

Customer Accounting,

Payroll,

Stores and Costing,

Commercial Statistics,

Terminal Enquiries,

Productivity Reporting.

Engineering and Commercial Applications:

Demand Forecasting,

Heat Loss Calculators,

Transformer Loading Analysis,

Engineering Calculations.

Projects planned for the future include:–

– Personnel Records Suite,
– New Stores Suite,
– Transport Maintenance Records,
– Direct Data Input via Video Terminals and Associated Kayboards
– Microfile Processing,
– File Management Studies – to yield an integrated Data Base if possible.

References

[1] Galbraith, Jay R.: Organization Design: An Information Processing View. Reading, Mass. 1973.

[2] Handbook of Organization, J.G. March (ed.), Chapter 27

[3] Report No. 1 (unpublished) for Norweb prepared in May 1967.

German abstract
Informationssysteme und Änderungen in der Organisation – Eine Studie über den North Western Electricity Board (NORWEB)

Von *Derek Stone*

Stone beschreibt die organisatorischen Änderungen der im Titel genannten Unternehmung seit 1967. Dabei stützt er sich auf zwei Untersuchungen über die Organisationsstruktur und die entsprechenden Informationssysteme aus den Jahren 1967 und 1973.

Die Situation beider Jahre wird verglichen und die Faktoren, die die beobachteten Veränderungen in Aufbau- und Ablauforganisation induzierten, werden untersucht und kommentiert.

In der zweiten Untersuchung im Jahre 1973 konnte nachgewiesen werden, daß einige, jedoch nicht alle der zunächst erwarteten Änderungen wirklich eingetreten waren.

1. Die Abteilungsleiter hatten ihre Kompetenzen und Entscheidungsfreiheit behalten, aber die Verlagerung der Routinearbeiten erlaubte ihnen mehr Zeit für die Ausübung ihrer täglichen Kontrollfunktionen bei gleichzeitig spürbarer Kostensenkung zu verwenden.
2. Die Zentralisation der Verarbeitung hatte zu einer Kombination zweier Managementstellen auf der Bereichsebene und einer neuen Stelle auf der Distriktebene geführt.
3. Die Möglichkeit der direkten Kommunikation der Systembenutzer durch den Einsatz von Terminals führte zu einer Dezentralisierung der Entscheidungen über Ratenzahlungen und der Verantwortung für die Bearbeitung von Kundenanfragen.
4. Man hatte erwartet, daß die geographisch orientiert arbeitenden Zweigstellen der Gesellschaft zu größeren Einheiten heranwachsen würden. Diese Erwartung konnte im Ansatz bestätigt werden.
5. Konstruktionsarbeiten werden noch dezentral geplant, von der Möglichkeit einer computergestützten Ablaufplanung wurde noch kein Gebrauch gemacht.

Diese Ergebnisse stützen die Thesen von Galbraith bezüglich des Informationssystems und der damit zusammenhängenden Gestaltung der Organisationsstruktur, da in diesem Falle die Informationstechnik und nicht die grundsätzliche Aufgabenstellung geändert wurde. Ebenfalls unterstreichen die Ergebnisse die Vermutung Leavitts, daß Veränderungen der Informationstechnologie Auswirkungen auf andere Teile einer Organisation haben. Dies wird gerade in dieser Studie bestätigt, da das Top-Management beschlossen hatte, die organisatorische Grundstruktur nicht zu verändern.

Man, organization and computer – a contingency analysis

By *Thomas L. Whisler*

1. Purpose and the thesis of the paper

In this paper an attempt is made to map a set of decision situations that could exist in organizations and in which the computer is, or could be, used. The mapping is developed in such a way that the fashion in which the computer is used and its consequent organizational effects can be expected to vary among these situations. In other words, this is a contingency analysis.

The motivation for the exercise is a belief that the literature about computers and organizations, covering the last twenty years, has treated the concepts of computer, organization, and man in a rather slipshod fashion. One consequence has been that we have research "findings" that appear to be unrelated, contradictory, and only occasionally corroborative.

A proper contingency analysis should help sort out this literature and, perhaps, guide future research. A first, and highly speculative, effort is presented here, in the hope that it will be criticized and improved.

The logic of the analysis can be set out quickly: man, the individual, has limitations and imperfections as a rational information processor and decision maker The organization can be viewed as a defense against these limitations, a means of partially overcoming them. The organization, of course, is of ancient origin. The computer, recently arrived, can also be viewed as a potential defense against the limitations of the individual. "Defense" in the case of either the organization or the computer may take the form of substituting for the individual in task performance or complementing him on a comparative advantage basis. Thus, individual man as well as organization – both already in place – are confronted by the computer which may replace or complement either, or both, in varying degrees, in information processing or decision making tasks:

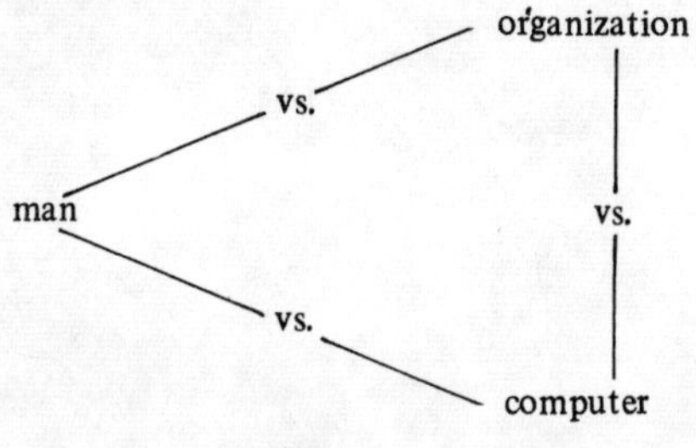

To estimate the potential organizational effects, both structural and performance of the computer (the purpose of the paper) certain factors present in every decision must also be considered. These factors, having both technical and economic implications, are singled out: (a) the degree of uncertainty in the decision, (b) the repetitiveness of the decision and, (c) the volume of information that must be processed. These three factors, dichotomized, yield a 2 x 2 x 2 table categorizing decision situations. Man, organization, and computer can be compared in each of the resultant eight situations. To the extent that decisions of a certain type (of these eight) are specialized to certain organizations or to certain parts of an organization, differentiated organizational effects can be predicted. (The reader can see the end result of this effort in Fig. 3).

In the paper, information processing and decision making are conceptually separated. Operationally, in the organizational context, they must always coexist – that is one implies the other, for information processing has little function apart from decision making, and decision making without information processing is meaningless. Nevertheless, it is usually true that the two tasks are specialized internally within the organization, as will be discussed below.

2. The complex organization

A variety of organizations exist in the modern world, but the largest subset, and the ones considered in this paper, are complex formal organizations. "Formal" means that the organizations are deliberately designed or redesigned, are goal oriented, and are rational (seek to perform efficiently). "Complex" means that the organizations show internal differentiation -- some of their parts or components differ from others (this differentiation is significant in a contingency analysis).

The internal differentiation includes both task and structure differences, the two being interrelated. In simple terms, any time an existing task is differentiated into two subtasks, inevitably new structural components are created. Conventionally, components are thought of either as individual jobs or as departments (groups of jobs), and these components are usually interconnected in such a way that the familiar "tree" chart becomes a useful graphical representation of structure.

Of the great variety of tasks performed by the formal organizations of the world, at least two are common to all organizations. These are the broad tasks of information processing and decision making, tasks which are subdivided and specialized in all but the smallest organizations. These two tasks are performed at all levels of the organization, although there is usually some vertical specialization, so that decision making is more likely to be done at the top and information processing at the lower levels.

Complex organizations are systems in which the components can be either human or non-human. In modern organizations, as new techniques have appeared, there has been a steady intrusion of non-human resources. Popular belief seems to be that the non-human is always substituted for the human resource, even though economists have long recognized that "machines" can be labor using as well as labor saving. For example, in terms of basic physical tasks, it is not hard to find machines that can lift weights that no combination of human beings could lift. But when time and reliability constraints are placed upon task accomplishment, quite frequently the machine becomes complementary to man rather than a substitute. A man and an abacus, for example, can perform certain complex arithmetic operations more quickly and reliably than any man or combination of men can. This is an example of man-machine symbiosis that arises in part because of the difficulty of further partitioning the computational problem. In another example the use of vertical files in offices, it is difficult to decide if the "machine" complements or substitutes for man. Here it is possible to imagine that all of the data in the files could be held in the heads of a mass of individuals, so that it may be simply a matter of economics that we find files existing. In that sense, the machine has substituted for man.

The last two examples above were deliberately chosen to illustrate precomputer machines used in information processing tasks. There are numerous other information processing aids, of course, such as slide rules, logarithm tables, Gantt charts, etc. When we get around to considering computer impacts, the analysis involves similar consideration of augmentation versus substitution. Much of past controversy about computer effects reflects differing beliefs on this matter.

If we were to look at the typical complex organization prior to the arrival of the computer, we might expect to find components in which both information processing and decision making are done by the same individual, or by the same groups. In the case of a business organization, the first situation might be illustrated by the presence of a corporate counsel, a corporate planner, or a corporate economic analyst. The second situation is probably more common and is illustrated by any of the conventional departments such as marketing or production. (These statements that tasks are accomplished by a man or by groups of men, ignore the existence and use of non-computer kinds of machines and machine-like aids. The analytic problem is complex enough as it is. Let us hope that no serious error is introduced by pretending that these other things don't exist).

In large complex organizations, where the opportunities for task specialization exist, we find that there are components which specialize in one or the other of the tasks of information processing and decision making. Again these specialized units might be either individuals or groups. In the business organization individuals such as telephone operators or assistants-to-presidents would illustrate those who specialize in information processing while almost any of the high level officers in the organization are presumably specializing in decision making. It is doubtful if anyone completely specializes in one or the other, but we will assume that they do for analytic purposes. There may be also groups that specialize in information processing such as any records section. Groups may also specialize in decision making as is the case with any standing committee -- for example, the capital allocation committee.

The "man-man" components (groups) that appear in larger organizations are often devices for overcoming the limitations of "man" (individual) components. The bounded rationality of a man in processing information or in making decisions has long been dealt with by the creation of man-man units to extend memory, to broaden the range of alternatives considered, etc. In looking ahead to an analysis in which we speculate that computer-based systems are devices for overcoming limitations of man as an individual as well as men in groups, we should recognize that there is always the possibility that an alternative to computer use is some organizational arrangement. This implies that when the computer first appears it may in fact substitute for groups that in turn have already substituted for individuals.

3. Information processing and decision making activities[1]

Briggs citing the contribution of others, has suggested that all systems (including organizations) have at least these five common functions: sensing, coding, information processing (including transmission, translation, and transformation), regulation (or control), and maintenance [1].

3.1 Sensing

Sensing is the selection of relevant information from the environment, the condition of relevancy requiring that some filtering process be used. Coding is the conversion of the received information into some internally appropriate language.

---

1 In this section two papers are cited as source references. The analytic schemes, they provide, are useful for the present paper, but they are not to be regarded as authoritative, nor are they necessarily superior to other slightly different analyses. Both do, however, review the work of others.

3.2 Information processing

Information processing as Briggs defines it, includes three different activities. One is transmission, a simple moving of information, coded or otherweise, from one place to another. Translation changes the form of the information but not the content. (It seems obvious that coding and translation are synonymous). Finally, transformation changes both the form and content of information and, according to Briggs, consists of applying a weighting function to input information to generate "new" information.

3.3 Regulation

Regulation is an overt action changing the production process where necessary to assure attainment of a goal or target. Finally, maintenance is the servicing and upkeep of the total system.

A paper by Vaughan and Mavor [8], again drawing on the works of others, lists the subtasks in decision making as: problem recognition, situation diagnosis, and action selection. Action selection includes: formulation of action alternatives and of criteria for evaluating them, assignment of differential weights to these criteria, and assessment of alternatives against criteria.

3.4 Problem recognition

Problem recognition according to Vaughan and Mavor, involves a monitoring of an ongoing action or set of actions "on as set of descriptive dimensions, comparing the values of the set against acceptable limits, and determining that the action is still appropriate to the situation".

3.5 Situation diagnosis

Situation diagnosis "is primarily a task area requiring a cycling of inductive inference processes that build diagnostic categories from items of data and their interactions, and deductive processes for testing a given diagnostic category against available data".

3.6 Action selection

Action selection again, is a complex task, involving these four subtasks: formulation of alternative action possibilities, formulation of appropriate criteria for assessing the alternatives, assignment of differential weights or priorities for the criteria, and finally assessment of alternatives against the criteria.

If we map the Briggs' scheme into that of Vaughan and Mavor, we note that there is substantial conceptual overlap, and at the same time, disparity in terminology. Thus, Briggs has a broad category called "information processing", within which one activity is called "transformation." This transformation as he defines it covers a large part of that decision making category that Vaughan and Mavor call "action selection". The problem of distinguishing decision making from information processing remains. In the popular literature of management, decision making seems to be rather narrowly defined as simply choosing one action in preference to others. Such a definition ignores immediately preceding choices such as what information to collect, what elements of the situation are critical, what alternatives to consider, etc. Information processing seems also to have a restricted conventional definition, being largely the collation, storage, and transmission of data. Large parts of the two maps we have just reviewed are not included in these "popular" definitions.

Since the overlap problem mentioned seems to start at that point in the Briggs analysis where he introduces the concept of transformation, we will arbitrarily transfer that activity to the area of decision making. This is particularly convenient because Vaughan and Mavor compare the relative competence of man and computer in what they call decision making activities, and their definition of the latter includes "transformation".

Thus, we wind up defining and bounding information processing in such a way that it includes sensing, transmission (plus storage and retrieval) and translation (or coding). Decision making is defined to include the major tasks of problem recognition, situation diagnosis, and action selection.

4. Limitations of the individual as an information processor: organizations and computers as alternative defenses

4.1 Limitations of the individual

The individual human being can perform all the information processing tasks, but has distinct limitations in the performance of them, limitations which may evoke the use of multiperson systems or computer systems as defenses. Concentration on limitations of the individual in no way denies the possibility that he has unique superiorities in some respects. And, in any analysis of possible substitution, both pluses and minuses must be kept account of. Nevertheless, the individual was here first, and the intrusion of organizations and computer systems into erstwhile individual activity must be regarded as prima facie evidence of certain limitations of the individual.

Consider first the sensing activity. The individual can monitor only a limited number of events [5]. As a sensor, therefore, he can look at only limited parts of the environment at any one time, and only for limited periods of time.

As a sensor, whether for his own purposes or for organizational purposes, the individual uses a filtering process to screen out "noise" and extract information from events going on about him. We know from common experience that he makes mistakes, that he occasionally fails to discriminate between noise and information, accepting the former and rejecting the latter. That is, he misses cues on the one hand, and senses things "that aren't there" on the other. This occurs despite training. A famous example is the rejection by the radar operator of the radar's findings of hostile aircraft at Pearl Harbor.

We need to recognize, on the other hand, the individual's unique superiority in terms of "wide band reception," that is, his ability to "read" information that is presented in many forms. We also credit the individual with the unique ability of "creative pattern perception," that is, seeing configurations of events as information without having been previously "programed" to see these configurations. If he really has the ability, it implies that there has been a higher order of programing into the individual of personal or organizational goals which may override his more focused filtering of environmental events in recognition of information.

With respect to information transmission, the limitations of the individual have been documented in the literature of psychology [2]. Systematic errors of various kinds are quite common where the individual is simply expected to duplicate information that he has received. He averages information, fills in what he perceives to be gaps, fails to send information that is unpleasant to himself or to the recipient, etc. The frailty of man's memory has been documented for ages, making him a very limited and erratic storage and retrieval device. In addition to his propensity for systematic and nonsystematic error, the individual simply has very limited capacity to transmit or to store information.

Again, however we must recognize the attribution to the individual of a unique quality of creativity, that is, the spontaneous retrieval of information from memory that was "never put there". New configurations are called forth by the individual by some process that we don't pretend to understand. These configurations are new or creative in the sense that we don't believe that we could have predicted their emergence on the basis of what information was known to have gone into the individual's memory.

In the translation activity, the individual exhibits the same sort of limitations as he shows in information transmissions. Creativity in translation is unacceptable, or, more accurately, a form of error. This is true since translation is defined as a change of form and not of content.

4.2 The organization as a defense

In defense against the limitations of the individual in information processing, the organization conventionally uses two different strategies: multiplication of effort and specialization of task. The first may be described as having a number of individuals doing the same thing in an effort to collapse the time required, while the second is having different individuals doing different things simultaneously in the effort both to collapse time and to gain certain efficiencies [4]. Thus the organization might assign individuals to separate information processing tasks such as sensing, transmitting, etc., or alternatively, assign a number of individuals to do all of these tasks in some sequential or simultaneous fashion.

Multiperson systems, or organizations, attempt to overcome the limitations of the individual as a sensor by using multiple sensors. Individual unreliability can be overcome in part by redundancy where we assign several people to monitor the same events. Clearly, the problem of resolving discrepencies remains. Third party adjudication is a common scheme, one which obviously involves evaluation of the credibility of the sensor as well as the information provided by the sensor.

Organizations also use multiple sensors to deal with the limited attention span of the individual, and in this case use a diverse task assignment in order to cope with the great range of environmental events that must be monitored.

Other organizational devices include error checking through the analysis of sequential dependencies -- testing the logical consistency of the information reported by sensors. Organizations can also use informed outsiders, thus buying additional sensory equipment as a guard against error.

The organization uses groups of individuals to overcome the limitations of the individual with respect to transmitting information and to storing and retrieving it. Again, specialization is the key strategy and in this case collation of information becomes the residual problem. Although specialization of effort deals with the capacity problem, it does nothing to overcome the problem of systematic error, and if anything it increases the probability of error. We have empirical studies to verify the compounding of error in transmission chains made up of individuals [2]. The general impression one gets from these studies is that these errors are not compensating, but rather are additive.

The comments made about transmission apply also to translation. Thus we could summarize by saying that the organization as a defense against individual limitations in information processing scores its best results strictly in terms of enlarging capacity. Error reduction is possible through the use of redundancy, but it is costly to do this and is entirely dependent upon the efficacy of the schemes for resolving discrepancies and (in the case of transmission and of translation) in collating information. On balance, one has to conclude that the error problem remains very large.

4.3 Computer systems as a defense

With regards to sensing, we recognize that computers, as such, do not sense environmental events directly. Some sort of instrumentation and telecommunications equipment must be employed if the limitations of the human individual are to be overcome. It seems to be true that, in fact, both direct sensing instruments and telecommunications equipment can be more effectively exploited by the presence of a computer because of the high capacity of the computer to absorb information and because it can be used around the clock. Thus again, the basic gain is in terms of capacity. There is, however, potential gain also in terms of the freedom from non-systematic error and from much of the systematic error exhibited by individuals in sensing. Obviously, this latter gain in reliability is best accomplished where instrument sensing is possible such as in the monitoring of physical processes. However, it is also possible to build validity checking programs into computers to guard against sensor error similar to those sometimes built into organizations (see previous section).
In the case of transmission and translation, once again the presence of a computer permits exploitation of telecommunications devices and thus provides a major defense against human error in performance of these activities. Further, computers directly provide immensely greater capacity than the individual has in storage and retrieval of information. The substitution potential of computer for man is great.

4.4 Summary

A. Limitations of the individual in information processing:
   1. Capacity,
   2. Systematic and unsystematic error in sensing, transmitting, translating, storing, and retrieving.

B. Organizational defense:
   1. Deals chiefly with capacity problems through specialization and replication of effort.
   2. Use of redundant channels and error checking programs to reduce error.

C. Computer defense:
   1. High capacity,
   2. High reliability.

5. Limitations of the individual as a decision maker: organizations and computers as alternative defenses

5.1 Limitations of the individual

The comments in this section rely heavily on Vaughan and Mavor. The general picture of the individual that they present (basing their ideas on research of a number of people) is that of a "satisficer" rather than an optimizer. Their thesis is that man-computer cooperation can move decision making closer to a rational optimum.

For example, man is said to be overly conservative or perhaps complacent in the function of problem recognition. He is all too likely to fail to recognize the need to change the plan upon which current action is based. Only a small amount of empirical evidence exists to support this contention, the evidence all coming from decisions on military problems. Little theoretical explanation is provided for this conservatism. Probably, most of us can recall anecdotal evidence of the failure of men to recognize the need for change in time to make an effective adaptation, so that the characterization has some intuitive appeal. If conservatism in problem recognition is a significant systematic error in men, it implies that when the individual adopts a plan of action he tends not to make a conscious note of the kinds of evidence that later would make it important for him to reconsider his plan.

The picture drawn of the individual involved in situation diagnosis is even more discouraging. Man does poorly as a diagnostician where complexity exists, where a variety of cues are presented that require testing of various possible configural relations. He can cope with simple relationships of a one-on-one nature, but does a poor job of combining. In particular, experimental evidence seems to indicate that man almost always thinks in terms that can be modeled as linear relationships, whereas non-linear interactions are, in fact, frequent.

Finally, it is alleged that man prefers to avoid uncertainty. In situation diagnosis this means that he tends to ignore ambiguous or partial data in favor of concrete data, or imputes more diagnosticity to uncertain data than they contain. Forced to use less than concrete data, he settles for the first interpretation that makes sense to him, rather than exploring alternative diagnoses.

In the action-selection phase of decision making, the individual has difficulty generating alternatives, according to Vaughan and Mavor. Man is apt to settle for two or three alternatives where, in retrospect, it is clear that many more were available. It seems quite reasonable that this sort of behaviour reflects time constraints, in part, but on the other hand, such constraints are part of organizational life. Beyond the constraints imposed by deadlines, there are clearly limits on the inventiveness of any individual. "I wish I had thought of it at the time" is a common enough expression.

Allegedly, the individual suffers from a similar problem in the formulation of criteria of evaluation (for selecting action). Man tends to generate only a few of those criteria that might be generally accepted as relevant, and exhibits a tendency to reverse the proper order of things by generating criteria that fit an action he has already selected. (It is conceded by these same authors, however, that the individual is quite effective in weighting criteria). Finally, the individual has difficulty testing alternatives against multiple criteria, with decision quality deteriorating as the number of criteria increase, and with a tendency to defend against complexity by overemphasis upon a single criterion.

5.2 The organization as a defense

Since the organization by definition is a group of people, it seems reasonable that the odds are that someone in the group will recognize the existence of a problem where any individual would not. Unfortunately, the problem arena grows just as surely as the number of individuals grow and because of the universal resort to specializing human efforts in organizations the odds may, in fact, not be raised very much. If we assume that the conservatism of the individual in recognizing a problem is in part at least a function of his reluctance to expend effort "unnecessarily," it is not obvious why several specialists should be any less apathetic than one in this regard. If conservatism results from the general failure of human beings to aggregate data properly when new information is received, it is again difficult to see why several imperfect information processors are an improvement over one where specialization exists[2].

Since there seems to be no automatic safety in numbers, some specific strategies must be devised by organizations to improve problem recognition. One strategy is to provide a regular and recurring review procedure, applied to different problem areas, bringing individuals other than the one primarily responsible for that area into an examination of the state of things. Various sorts of review committees are common in corporations and in other kinds of organizations. The success of this sort of thing would seem to depend upon the review group being staffed with a judicious mixture of those familiar with the area being reviewed and those who are far enough away from it to ask the right kind of naive questions.

Other organizational strategies involve the formulation of procedures for establishing acceptable ranges of performance and other situational data, as

2 There is some evidence that, in the absence of specialization, averaging individual perceptions produces a "more correct" perception than that of any individual. See [3, p. 43].

well as procedures for signaling the appearance of data lying outside this range. Reward and punishment systems that take into account effectiveness (or lack of) in problem recognition can be used also, but they suffer from the weakness of being ex post facto.

The group again becomes an organizational defense in the area of situational diagnosis. Where complex decision problems recur, the groups are permanently constituted. Examples might be the Board of Directors, the Safety Committee, etc. For what appear to be one-shot problems, the common technique is to use "a task force". In either case, if these groups contain diverse skills and knowledge they may perform better than individuals in decomposing analytic problems and resynthesizing them.

A newer scheme in setting up an organizational defense is to specialize the activity of situation diagnosis. The organization provides a staff skill, available to others in the organization, the skill of the decision theorist. Such people (for example, Bayesian analysts) can be discovered at present in operations research groups in certain organizations.

In action selection the common use of groups to generate action alternatives and to enumerate criteria for evaluating them indicates a widespread faith in the superiority of groups over the individual in producing better decisions. However, the mechanism for taking the very last step -- final choice of action -- is critically important. A variety of psychological experiments indicate that making the final choice in the presence of others may not result in the best possible decision.

5.3 Computer systems as a defense

The subject of this section is the one to which the entire article by Vaughan and Mavor was ultimately addressed. After reviewing various empirical findings, their article concludes with a section entitled, "general guides to design of men-computer systems for application to decision making". Below, we largely paraphrase what they say.

To overcome human reluctance to recognize a problem, the computer might be programed at the time that a plan is established in such fashion that tolerance ranges in the values of major situation variables are created. Subsequent data inflow is then examined by the computer and appropriate signals sent to the individual when tolerance ranges are exceeded. On the face of it this appears to be a most simple-minded idea. One suspects that its effectiveness would entirely depend upon the care with which the plan was modeled in the first place, and in particular, the extent to which some sort of sensitivity analysis was applied to the variables for which data are available. A skeptic might wonder if the individual wouldn't ignore the computer's warning as easily as he ignores other sorts of information unless, perhaps, the computer presented the evidence of "out of control" terms of the probable deviation of end results from the target, so that cost consequences are clear. (The Critical Path Method, however, is a step in this direction).

In the area of situation diagnosis, Vaughan and Mavor argue that, first of all, the computer can provide diagnostic categories that the individual might not think of by "trying out" the possibility of various relationships among items of information. Second, they would expect that the "tirelessness" of the computer might easily overcome man's propensity for settling for the first interpretation that makes sense to him. In comment on these ideas, one wonders how feasible it is to develop programs that are general enough to cover a variety of decision problems. In addition, one wonders how costly such program development might be. Clearly, one would need a force of decision theorists and computer experts so that it isn't just the "computer", but a computer plus an organization that one needs to improve this aspect of individual decision making.

Finally in the arena of action selection, Vaughan and Mavor suggest use of the computer to generate action alternatives, and to do so on a conversational basis. This would clearly require specification of goals, of guidelines, constraints on the solution, and of the set of resources available to the decision maker[3]. They also propose the use of the computer to suggest additional evaluation criteria, leaving to the individual the function of weighting these criteria. Vaughan and Mavor see men-machine interaction as reiterative – a cycling process. The objective of such a scheme, obviously, is to overcome the individual's limited capacity to generate alternative actions and decision criteria.

5.4 Summary

A. Limitations of the individual in decision making:

1. Conservatism in problem recognition,
2. Weak analytically in combining information to make diagnoses,
3. Tends to avoid uncertainty in making diagnoses,
4. Generates too few alternatives for action,
5. Generates too few criteria for evaluating action,
6. Weak analytically in testing alternative against multiple criteria.

3 The "corporate model" is built in this fashion. Growing out of the use of the budget as a basic planning tool, it may within the next decade or two be developed to the point where it can function conversationally.

B. Organizational defense:
   1. Use of groups to deal with individual limitations, probably in the following order of effectiveness:
      a) Generating alternatives in criteria for evaluation,
      b) Problem Recognition,
      c) Situation Diagnosis.

C. Computer defense:
   1. Largely speculative, the computer is proposed as partner in all aspects of decision making except weighting of criteria and final selection of action. Possible order of effectiveness:
      a) Problem Recognition,
      b) Situation Diagnosis ("playing with the data"),
      c) Evaluating alternatives against multiple criteria.

6. Situational factors: Uncertainty, repetitiveness and volume

The preceding sections of this paper constitute a comparative analysis of task performance on the part of the individual, the organization, and computer systems. Even if one accepts the analysis as valid, it does not provide answers to these questions: Under what decision conditions will the computer be most (least) intensively used? Under what conditions will it be used in decision making? In information processing? Under what conditions will it substitute for, or complement individual or group effort?

To answer such questions, certain important situational factors must be considered. Three factors that, intuitively, would seem to condition computer intervention are the degree of uncertainty present in the decision situation, the repetitiveness of the decision (the frequency with which it recurs), and the volume of information that must be processed in order to make a decision.

6.1 Uncertainty in decision making

James D. Thompson presents a typology of decision making that distinguishes two kinds of uncertainty surrounding a decision (see fig. 1) [6]. The first relates to preferences about possible outcomes, the second to beliefs about "causation". Varying degrees of uncertainty can exist on both these matters, but for convenience only the extremes are shown in the figure. Equally well, we can read "high uncertainty" or "low uncertainty" for these extremes.

Thompson associates four different kinds of decision strategies with the four conditions of uncertainty. His argument is developed in an interesting fashion,

		Preferences about possible outcomes	
		certain	**uncertain**
Beliefs about causation	**certain**	**computation**	**compromise**
	uncertain	**judgment**	**inspiration**

Fig. 1. Decision strategies for different conditions of uncertainty (from James D. Thompson, op. cit.)

but for present purposes we need not elaborate it. The important point relates to the existence of two dimensions of uncertainty.

Although Thompson does not say so, it would seem logical that decisions about outcome preferences have to be resolved prior to establishing decision strategies on achieving those outcomes. The means for resolution are totally social, involving negotiations, etc. By the time the computer enters the picture preference ordering has been accomplished. Thus we have left the strategies of computation and judgment. We use the first if we are certain about what we want and certain about how to get it. Such low uncertainty does not necessarily make decisions trivial, for they may be quite complex and involve intricate analysis. Where high uncertainty about causation exists, one uses judgment, although as Thompson points out, if the decision recurs frequenty, probability estimates may be used. Thus, we systematize the use of judgment in decision making under uncertainty where the decisions are repetitive.

6.2 Repetitiveness and volume

Repetitiveness may alter the decision making qualitatively as was just suggested, but it probably also alters the economics of computer use. That is, if it appears that computers can be used in some fashion either to augment the individual decision maker or to replace him, the cost of doing so becomes the main issue. It seems reasonable that highly repetitive decisions are the ones most likely to justify the use of computers economically. This statement in no way implies that the performance gain from computer use comes only through cost savings. Particularly in decision making under uncertainty one might expect to see performance enhanced through complementation of the decision maker or the decision making group. But the heavy one-shot costs of analysis and programing probably make repetitiveness a key determinant of computer use.

In information processing tasks it seems obvious that computer use is most likely to be justifiable economically where a high volume of information must be processed. However, the relationship between volume of information and computer intervention is a little more complex than that. Quite often the volume of information sought is itself a matter of decision, having to do with cost of gathering and processing information. We often make do with less information because it "costs too much" to get more. The computer can substantially shift the information cost curve. Sometimes the lowered cost of information leads to foolishness, such as processing of great batches of data which have little value -- but they are cheap.

6.3 Combining the factors

Assuming these three factors to be independent, we can combine them in the table as shown in fig. 2 to specify eight different conditions under which the organization might consider the use of computers. The outcome of such consideration might well differ among these conditions, the outcome having to do with the degree and the nature of computer intervention.

Decision conditions

		high repetitiveness causation certain	causation uncertain	**low repetitiveness** causation certain	causation uncertain
Information processing load	high volume	I	II	V	VI
	low volume	III	IV	VII	VIII

Fig. 2. Eight theoretical conditions under which decision-making and information processing tasks are accomplished

We can make some general predictions:

1. Computer use in organizations will be most common in the upper left conditions (I,II), and least common (or non-existent) in the lower right conditions (VII,VIII). The intensity of use in any given organization should, likewise, be greatest in the upper left and least in the lower right.

2. Decision making applications will be most common in conditions I, II, III, and IV. Information processing applications will be most common in conditions I, II, V, and VI. (Where causation is uncertain, the volume of information "required" is itself uncertain and a matter of judgment).

3. Substitution (computer for individuals or groups of individuals) effects will be strongest in conditions I, II, and V (a combination of high volume with high certainty and/or high repetitiveness). Complementation effects will be strongest in conditions II and IV (a combination of high uncertainty and high repetitiveness).

7. Discussion

Figure 3 represents an attempt to make more specific predictions about the nature of computer intervention and the organizational consequences under each of the eight conditions. Column A lists the situations mapped in figure 2. In column B an attempt is made to cite examples of the situations (invention failed in three cases).
Presumed limitations of the individual specific to each situation are shown in column B. In D and E are posited the organizational defenses and computer defenses that might be devised to cope with individual limitations. The last three columns focus on the computer, considering first its role as substitute for, or complement to, the individual and the organization (F), effects on organizational structure (G), and effects on organizational performance (H). Several observations can be made from figure 3:

1. The effects of computer systems on organization structure (a subject which has been given extensive treatment in the past) are likely to be major ones only in one of the eight decision situations. Thus, only in that part of any organization where the type I decision is predominant will significant structural change occur. This part is typically the "technical core" of the organization [7, pp. 11-12].

2. The organizational impact of computers on performance is likely to be more pervasive than impact on structure for two reasons: (a) type I decisions are apt to be localized as noted; (b) performance effects might be expected in six of the eight decision situations, structural effects in five.

3. The "computer defenses", as described in column E, imply substantial variation in the computer/tele-communication systems appropriate to different decision conditions. The variation occurs on several dimensions: hardware configuration (in general terms), types of programs, and interaction mode. (The descriptions are hap-hazard and unsatisfactory. Needed is a comprehensive typology of computer/tele-communication systems which can be applied to this analysis).

A Situation	B Examples	C Individual Limitations	D Org. Defenses	E Computer Defenses	F Computer Sub/Comp.	G Org. Struct. Effects	H Org. Perform. Effects
HR, HV: I (c)	Logistics planning for mass production, transport	Span of time, knowledge, energy	Cadres, job specialization, sampling	Cybernetic system w/large files & T.C.* equipt	Org. & ind. substitute in all I.P.* and D.M.* tasks except sensing and some translating	Reduced nos. people Centralization of D.M.* Fewer levels change in dept. principle (permanent)	Improved reliability and speed, reduced cost in I.P.* and D.M.*
HR, HV: II (u)	Logistics planning for job shops, Portfolio Mgt., Student Admissions, pricing and bidding decisions on rec. items	As in I, plus possible naivete in combining information in diagnosis and eval. of action alternatives	As in I, plus multiple judges, probability models, committees	Large files & T.C.* equipt, transformation programs, visual display, simulation (conversational system)	Org. & ind. substitute in I.P.* tasks (except sensing, translating); org. and ind. comp. in diag/eval.	Reduced nos. clerks (permanent)	Improved reliability, speed, reduced cost in I.P.*; better decisions
HR, LV: III (c)	Physical Process Control	As in I	As in I, with lower need	Unnecessary (or uneconomic) unless reliability critical	As in I	As in I, but magnitude is small	As in I, except that reliability probably predominant
HR, LV: IV (u)	?	As in I	Committees, probability models, multiple judges	Simulation programs, other transformation progs. (conversational)	Org. and ind. comp. in diagnosis evaluation	None	Better decisions
LR, HV: V (c)	Logistics planning for unit production, engineering design	As in I	Temporary project team	Batch processing of data through std. transformation programs	Modest substitution (temporary) clerks	Reduction in no. of clerks (transitory)	Improved speed reliability
LR, HV: VI (u)	Pricing and bidding decisions on large occasional projects	As in II	Temporary project team, including multiple judges	Std. transformation programs if relevant. Ro. T.C.* equipment	As in V	As in V	As in V
LR, LV: VII (c)	?	None likely	None necessary	None necessary	–	–	–
LR, LV: VIII (u)	?	Possible naivete in combining information in diagnosis and in eval. of act. altern.	Multiple judges	None necessary (I.P.*) or feasible (D.M.*)	–	–	–

*T.C. = tele-communications
D.M. = decision-making
I.P. = information processing

Fig. 3. The effects of computer intervention in eight decision situations

The controversy in the literature, mentioned earlier, about computer impact (or lack of) on organizations and individuals probably arises from the fact that the disputants are using different decision situations as models or as research sitea. The general perception of computer effects upon individuals in organizations seems to be that it is negative and threatening in character; the controversy concerns how bad it really is. There has been an emphasis in the literature upon substitution effects, actual and potentials, which probably reflects an initial tendency, historically, to concentrate computer use in situations where substitution for human effort is an obvious outcome. Applications of this kind probably were emphasized because uncertainty about measurement of cost savings was perceived to be lower than uncertainty about measurement of possible performance gains. Where the computer system could be designed to complement man and augment his performance, the potential net gains might appear to be high but are discounted heavily because of uncertainty. Nevertheless, such applications have been made, here and there, and have simply not fit the "doom" model of computer consequences.

To analyze the probable effect of computer applications upon specific individuals and specific jobs, we would have to start with the sort of job analysis which would tell us the degree to which individual tasks are specialized either to information processing or to decision making and, secondly, would give us information about the volume, repetitiveness, and uncertainty characteristics of these jobs.

I will not attempt this task here, except to give a few casual examples to illustrate the point. We might expect:

1. That where the individual is one of several performing similar tasks, he is vulnerable to computer substitution, except,
2. That those working at the periphery of the organization and at information absorption points internally (sensors and coders) will encounter substantial task reorganization when computers are introduced but will not be vulnerable to substitution.
3. That those whose jobs involve type II and IV conditions (typical of staff departments) will eventually experience job content changes that require learning to converse with the computer in making decisions.
4. That, given the usual vertical specialization of tasks in organizations, top executives characteristically will specialize in decision making in type VI and VIII situations. Consequently their jobs are likely to change very little as a consequence of computer introduction.

Any attempt to move away from the preceding sort of "micro" forecasting (logical in a contingency analysis) to a "macro" forecast of computer impacts requires some evidence, or some beliefs, about the historical trail of computers through organizations. It is my belief (expressed earlier) that applications in type I and type II situations have been predominant in the past. It is in these situations where substitution effects predominate.

Thus, I would speculate that organizational "disturbances" resulting from computer intervention will diminish in the future, as managers move on to those applications where complementation predominates. We must also expect new type I and II situations continually to emerge in organizations as managers pursue their efforts to reduce uncertainty in the "technical core" [7, pp. 148-150]. But since these situations will be new, no computer-associated disturbances will result.

As attention continues to shift from substitution (largely in information processing tasks) to complementation (largely in decision-making tasks) appropriate training for managers in both the near and distant future will emphasize understanding of cognitive aspects of individual decision-making, collective decision-making processes, and conversational interaction with the computer in decision-making.

References

[1] Briggs, George E.: Engineering Systems Approaches to Organization. In: W.W. Cooper, H.J. Leavitt, M.W. Shelly II (eds.): New Perspectives in Organization Research. New York 1964, pp. 479–492.

[2] Campbell, D.T.: Systematic Error on the Part of Human Links in Communication Systems. In: Information and Control, Vol. 1 (1958), pp. 334–369.

[3] Davis, James H.: Group Performance. Reading, Mass. 1969.

[4] Knight, F.H.: The Economic Organization. New York 1951.

[5] Miller, G.A.: The Magical Number Seven, Plus or Minus Two: Some Limits on Our Capacity for Processing Information. In: Psychological Review, Vol. 63 (1956), pp. 81–97.

[6] Thompson, James D.: Decision Making, The Firms and the Market. In: W.W. Cooper, H.J. Leavitt, M.M. Shelly II (eds.): New Perspectives in Organization Research. New York 1964, pp. 334–348.

[7] Thompson, James D.: Organizations in Action. New York 1967.

[8] Vaughan, Jr., W.S. and Anne Schumacher Mavor: Behavioral Caracteristics of Men in Performance of Some Decision-Making Task Components. In: Ergonomics, Vol. 15/3 (1972), pp. 267–277.

German abstract
Manager, Organisationsstruktur und Computereinsatz – Eine Kontingenzanalyse

Von *Thomas L. Whisler*

Die Kapazität des Managers als Informationsgenerator ist eng begrenzt. In dem vorliegenden Beitrag werden deshalb Organisationsstruktur und Computereinsatz als Möglichkeiten einer Kapazitätsausweitung des Informationsverarbeitungspotentials betrachtet. Beide Faktoren konkurrieren dabei untereinander hinsichtlich ihrer Substitutions- und Ergänzungsfunktion für den menschlichen Informationsgenerator. Es werden nun die Auswirkungen verschiedener Kombinationen dieser Faktoren in Hinblick auf spezielle Typen von Entscheidungsaufgaben in der Unternehmung analysiert.

In einem Abschnitt über vorhandene Beiträge in der Literatur zur Informationsverarbeitung und dem Prozeß der Entscheidungsfindung wird auf einen Vorschlag von Briggs hingewiesen, der ein Informationssystem in die Stufen Erfassung, Codierung, Informationsverarbeitung (mit Transmission, Translation und Transformation), Steuerung (oder Kontrolle) und Erhaltung unterteilt.

Dieser Gliederung wird die Aufteilung des Entscheidungsfindungsprozesses von Vaughan und Mavor gegenübergestellt, die die Stufen Problemerkennung, Systemdiagnose und Auswahl aus den erarbeiteten Alternativen vorsieht.

Anschließend werden die Grenzen des menschlichen Individuums bei der Informationsverarbeitung aufgezeigt und diesen Organisationsstruktur und Computereinsatz als mögliche Alternativen gegenübergestellt.

Die Grenzen des einzelnen Individuums liegen vor allen in seiner begrenzten Kapazität und der Unvermeidbarkeit von systematischen und unsystematischen Fehlern bei der Erfassung, Übermittlung, Speicherung und Wiedererlangung von Informationen.

Demgegenüber befaßt sich die Organisation mit der Lösung von Kapazitätsproblemen durch die Spezialisierung in verschiedene Aufgabenbereiche. Um das Auftreten von Fehlern zu vermeiden, werden dabei redundante Übertragungskanäle und Programme zur Fehlersuche benutzt.

Der Vorteil des Computereinsatzes liegt vor allem in seiner großen Kapazität und der hohen Zuverlässigkeit.

Wie bei der Informationsverarbeitung sind dem menschlichen Individuum auch bei der Entscheidungsfindung Grenzen gesetzt. Hierzu gehören die geringe Neigung zu neuen Überlegungen beim Erkennen von Problemen, die geringe Fähigkeit, bei der Erstellung von Diagnosen Informationen zu kombinieren und die Tendenz, bei Diagnosen Unsicherheiten zu vermeiden. Weiter werden zu wenig Handlungsalternativen geschaffen, zu wenige Kriterien für die Festlegung der

Aktionen erzeugt, und es mangelt an der Fähigkeit, Alternativen bei einer Vielzahl von Kriterien richtig abzuwägen.

Demgegenüber ermöglicht die Organisation in ihrer Gruppenstruktur die Überwindung individueller Leistungsgrenzen, wobei folgende Effektivitätsstufen festzustellen sind:

a) die Entwicklung von Alternativen für die Auswertung,
b) die Problemerkennung,
c) die Situationsdiagnose.

Der Einsatz des Computers kommt in nahezu allen Stufen des Entscheidungsprozesses in Frage, außer bei der Gewichtung von Kriterien und bei der endgültigen Auswahl des Vorgehens. Bezüglich der Effektivität ist folgende Reihenfolge möglich:

a) die Problemerkennung,
b) die Situationsdiagnose (Durchspielen der Daten) und
c) die Auswertung der Alternativen unter verschiedenen Gesichtspunkten.

Um die Frage beantworten zu können, unter welchen Bedingungen eine gegenseitige Ergänzung von Individuum, Organisation und Computer möglich und sinnvoll ist, werden einige spezifische Faktoren untersucht, die in jeder Entscheidungssituation auftreten:

1. der Unsicherheitsgrad der Entscheidung,
2. die Wiederholungshäufigkeit der Entscheidung,
3. das zu verarbeitende Informationsvolumen.

Bei der Kombination dieser Faktoren ergeben sich acht Bedingungen, unter denen Entscheidungen und Informationsverarbeitungsaufgaben ausgeführt werden können. Dies wird mit Hilfe eines Schaubildes verdeutlicht.

Part 2

Information system development

The Management Information System: The initiation and adoption of an organizational innovation

By *Robert Duncan*

1. Introduction

This paper views a Management Information System (MIS) as an organizational innovation. The paper will thus focus on the processes of the initiation and implementation of the MIS as an organizational innovation into the ongoing activities of the organization by modifications in organizational structure [15].

Stages of the Innovation Process. The introduction of a MIS into an organization is considered an innovation in that it is often perceived to be new by the unit that is adopting it. The innovation process is defined here as having two phases: Initiation and Implementation. The Initiation Phase consists of three subphases.

(1) Knowledge-Awareness subphase where the organization becomes aware of: a) either the need to innovate – the organization realizes that its information gathering capabilities are not what they should be and thus seeks to use a MIS to improve this situation; b) the organization becomes aware of some new innovation like a MIS and once aware of this new system, feels that they could improve their information processing capabilities – they develop a need.

(2) Attitude Formation subphase where organizational members begin to form positive or negative attitudes toward the innovation.

(3) Decision subphase where the information concerning the innovation is evaluated and a decision is made to actually procede or not in implementing the innovation.

The Implementation Phase consists of two subphases.

(1) Initial Implementation subphase where the organization may initially utilize the MIS on a trial basis to determine if it is practical before setting up a more formal MIS group as Dearden [4, p. 98] suggests.

(2) Continued-Sustained Implementation subphase where the innovation is formalized as a permanent function in the organization [2; 17].

2. Characteristics of organizations as they affect the innovation process

Various organizational theorists [3; 6; 11] have indicated that there is no one best way of structuring the organization for all tasks. Rather, the above research supports the view that the structure of an organization is comprised of a variety of dimensions which may vary from one situation to the next. We will now specifically discuss five organizational characteristics as they affect the innovation process. The five characteristics are: Complexity, formalization, centralization, interpersonal relations, capacity for dealing with conflict.

2.1 Complexity

The degree of complexity of the organization can have various effects on the innovation process. Complexity is defined here in terms of the number of occupational specialties in the organization and their professionalism [9, p. 33] and a very differentiated task structure [16, p. 200]. In a highly complex organization either its output or its technology (the process by which the output is produced) may not be highly specified. Thus, as Wilson [16, p. 201] indicates, each individual will have some latitude to tailor his task to fit his needs. Given the diverse nature in which individual tasks may be defined it becomes very difficult for close supervision to occur. The supervisor may simply not be aware of the specific way each member has tailored his job. The result is that the individual has more of an opportunity to discover areas for innovation.

A high number of occupational specialties with professionalism will result in organizational personnel placing high value on specific knowledge and information to utilize on their job. This diversity in occupational backgrounds can then bring a variety of sources of information to bear which can facilitate awareness or knowledge of innovations at the initiation stage. These varied sources of information simply increase the opportunity for different types of information to be made available to the organization in the development of the MIS. For example, Dearden [4] emphasizes the complexities of designing the MIS by indicating that a variety of individuals with understanding of the different information needs of the organization are required. These diverse individuals are required to make sure the information system reflects the complexity of the information needs of the organization.

However, this diversity or complexity creates a problem for the organization. Wilson [16, pp. 200 – 204] has indicated that high diversity in the organization will lead to organizational members conceiving and proposing more innovations but not adopting these innovations. Wilson's argument is that the high diversity (complexity) makes it difficult for any one source of authority to try and force some consensus toward agreement as to which of the many proposals should be implemented. Thus, there appears to be a basic conflict between the process for the initiation of the innovation and implementation. This organizational dilemma is clearly exhibited in Sapolsky's [13] study of innovation in department stores. The diversity in the reward structure in terms of increased professionalization on the part of retail controllers led to proposals to separate buying and selling functions, the use of computers in merchandising, and the use of sophisticated decision making techniques such as PERT and operations research in merchandise problems. However, the diversity in department store structural arrangements, decentralized decision making authority and the existence of a large number of equally situated subunits frustrated the implementation of these proposed innovations.

From the above discussion it then appears that the complexity of the organization can have both positive and potentially negative effects on various stages of the innovation process. At the initiation stage, highly diverse organizations are apparently able to bring a variety of bases of information and knowledge to bear that can increase the awareness and knowledge of the MIS and the need to implement it in an organization. However, at the implementation stage, high complexity, because of potential conflicts, makes it more difficult for the organization to actually implement the MIS innovation.

The strategy implications for the practitioner concerning the complexity dilemma are several. First, the diversity of an organization or subgroup of an organization might be increased in order to increase the number of innovations proposed during the initiation stage. For example a MIS project group might be composed of several engineers, production managers, and marketing managers to develop a new MIS. The heterogeneous background of this group with its diverse sources of information could generate a lot of new ideas for the system and its components. To facilitate the actual implementation of the MIS innovation, team building activities could be provided to the highly complex group. Team building would help them develop their interpersonal skills and trust so they could deal openly with conflicts and disagreements they would experience in trying to agree on the specific aspects of the MIS to be implemented [7, pp. 112 – 121]. Another alternative would be for the initiation and design of the MIS to take place in a highly complex-diverse MIS project group. Once the proposals for the new MIS were developed, the less diverse more homogeneous functional groups, i. e. marketing, production etc., would work on the design for implementing the system into their respective areas.

2.2 Formalization

By formalization we mean the emphasis that is placed within the organization on following specific rules and procedures in performing one's job. The assumption is that strict emphasis on rigid rules and procedures may prohibit organizational decision makers from seeking new sources of information. Thus, there is simply less opportunity for them to become more aware of the need for a new MIS or the technology required for it.

In considering the relationship between formalization and innovation it is again necessary to consider the particular stage of the innovation process. For example, Shepard [14, p. 474] has indicated that low formalization might be most appropriate at the initiation phase while a higher degree of formalization may be more appropriate during the implementation phase. During the initiation stage, the organization needs to be as flexible and as open as possible to new sources of information and alternative courses of action in designing the MIS. Many rules and procedures might just become constraints under which the organization might have to operate. This seems to be the case Hage and Aiken's [8, p. 511] study of welfare organizations makes in finding a negative relationship [r = –.47] between job codification and program change.

During the implementation stage, however, Shepard [14, p. 474] indicates that a singleness of purpose is required. In order to bring the innovation into practice, Neal and Radnor's [12] study of the successful implementation of operation research-management science activities in large industrial organizations indicated that specific formalized procedures had been developed to facilitate implementation. These procedures covered such factors as formal project selection, long range planning, scheduling, and regular progress reports [12]. The formalization procedures seemed to have reduced the problems of implementing OR/MS activities. Apparently, these formalized procedures, provide both information and specific techniques which facilitate organizational personnel's ability to utilize the innovation. The lack of these more formalized procedures at the implementation stage is likely to lead to both role conflict and role ambiguity. Role ambiguity could result in that without more formal procedures the individual is likely to be unclear concerning how the innovation is to be implemented and how this new innovation is going to affect how he performs his job. Role conflict could also occur, because the lack of specific procedures concerning how the innovation is going to be implemented may lead to conflict with existing rules and procedures.

For example, a new, more centralized MIS might be introduced into an organization. Previously, information channels may have been decentralized and informal, and the information system was fairly unstructured. The new information system is thus a significant change from the old one. To be successfully implemented, it would be necessary that quite specific procedures be communicated to personnel, so that they know that they are now expected to effectively utilize the more centralized communication system. They are thus made aware that the role expectations their superiors have for them concerning the information system have changed, and that the older informal decentralized system is no longer sanctioned.

Once again the practitioner is faced with a dilemma – low formalization seems to facilitate the initiation stage of innovation while higher formalization seems to facilitate the implementation of innovations. In attempting to reduce this dilemma the organization might use different degrees of formalization at the initiation and implementation stages of a MIS innovation. For example, a broad set of operating guidelines might be established for a group that reduces formalization during the initiation phase of the innovation process which as indicated above would potentially stimulate innovation proposals. However, once the proposals were generated the group could then focus on specifying operating rules and procedures as to how the innovation would actually be implemented. This more formalization of the innovation process at the implementation stage would tend to reduce the ambiguity and potential conflict that individuals would experience as they implemented the innovation. They would potentially have a better understanding as to how to use the innovation and how its implementation fit into existing procedures in the organization.

2.3 Centralization

The centralization dimension is conceptualized here in terms of locus of the authority and decision making in the organization. The greater the hierarchy of authority (higher in the organization where the decision takes place) and less the participation in decision making that exists in the organization, the greater the centralization. During the initiation stage of the innovation process there is likely to be a good deal of uncertainty experienced by organizational members [10, 5]. The result is that the information needs for the organization are likely to be high.

A strict emphasis on hierarchy of authority is likely to cause decision unit members to adhere to specified channels of communication and to selectively feed back only positive information regarding their job. They would thus be neglecting any negative feedback which might actually help the organization better identify both the need and technology for a MIS innovation. Also, Shepard [13, p. 471] has pointed out that the ideas for innovation are often generated at some distance from the power center in the organization, so they have to be communicated up the hierarchy. The more bureaucratized the authority structure, the more channels of communication the innovation has to travel through. This then increases the probability that the proposal may get screened out, because it violates the status quo in the organization.

Greater participation in decision making may bring new insights to bear and new sources of information to the innovation process. One can conclude from Dearden [4], Zani [18] and Zannetos [19] that, due to the complexity of designing an overall MIS for the entire organization, a variety of individuals from the user functional areas must make inputs. These inputs are needed to determine what decisions are to be made, what are the important factors in decision making, how and when the decisions should be made, and what information is useful [18, p. 98].

Although the available research is less clear on this, we might suggest once again that the effects of centralization might vary depending upon the stage of the innovation process the organization is in. It is clear that less hierarchy of authority and more participation in decision making can increase the information available to the organization and thus increase knowledge – awareness at the initiation stage. However, as Shepard [14] has indicated when the organization gets to the implementation stage, a more specific line of authority and responsibility is required to reduce the role conflict or ambiguity that might accompany implementation of the MIS innovation. Also, Sapolsky's [13] study of innovation in department stores found that decentralized authority and decision making structures frustrated attempts at implementation because it was difficult for the organization to gather enough influence over participants.

Once again, it appears, the strategy for reducing the innovation dilemma is to utilize different degrees of centralization during the different stages of the innovation process. During initiation, more autonomy could be given to participants in order to facilitate the awareness of the need and technology for the development of a MIS innovation. Then during the implementation stage, the decision process could become more coordinated and centralized as the MIS is implemented.

Above we have specified that there are different configurations of organizational structure that facilitate the innovation processes in its different stages. Specifically it was emphasized that with regard to stimulating the initiation of innovations, a higher degree of complexity, lower formalization and lower centralization facilitate the gathering and processing of information which is crucial to the initiation stage. It was also emphasized that with respect to the implementation phase, a higher level of formalization, centralization and lower level of complexity was likely to reduce role conflict and ambiguity which could impair implementation. This conclusion thus implies that the organization has to shift its structure as it moves through the various stages of innovation.

Below we will discuss two organizational variables – effective interpersonal relationships and conflict resolution capabilities – that appear to be mediators in the organization's ability to differentiate its degree of complexity, formalization and centralization between the two stages of the innovation process. Table 1 provides a summary of these organizational characteristics as they affect innovation.

Initiation Phase	Mediators	Implementation Phase
Higher Complexity	High Capability for Effective Interpersonal Relations	Lower Complexity
Lower Formalization	High Capability for Dealing with Conflict	Higher Formalization
Lower Centralization		Higher Centralization

Table 1. Structural variables and mediating factors affecting the initiation and implementation of innovations

2.4 Interpersonal relations

It may be that an orientation to dealing with interpersonal issues may be important in the innovation process. In MIS innovation situations, organizational participants are faced with uncertainty and strategies for dealing with these situations usually have not been covered by preestablished rules and procedures. Here greater reliance must be placed on the informal network of relationships. For example, Conrath (1968) has studied informal groups in R & D organizations and has pointed out that these informal groups provide important sources of information to the formal hierarchy.

Argyris has also pointed out that the MIS can have some unanticipated negative effects on managers. For example, the new system might reduce their space of free movement by making explicit all behaviors, policies and practices that might have previously been operating covertly.

[1, p. B–277] Also, many of the more important goals and activities for the individual will be defined by the system. The individual will experience less control over his environment and thus, according to Argyris [1, p. B–278] will experience psychological failure.

Argyris [1] indicates that it is important that MIS professionals be aware of their own interpersonal behavior and behave in such a way as to help line executives express their feelings about the new MIS system. The view here is to face up to these strong feelings that line executives might have so the sources of resistance can be reduced. The point is that the initiation and implementation of innovations can be more effectively carried out if emotional problems are not suppressed but dealt with.

2.5 Dealing with conflict

The ability to deal with conflict is also an important mediating variable. For example, during the initiation phase of a MIS innovation there are going to be conflicts concerning the planning and design of the information system. There will also be conflicts about the processes by which the innovation is going to be implemented by the organization. Thus legitimizing conflict as a likely occurrence during the innovation process and as something that should be confronted can facilitate innovation. Confrontation involves placing the relevant facts before the parties involved and then discussing the disputed issues until some agreement is found [11].

Confronting the conflict has the potential for reducing the basis of disagreement and facilitating the opportunity for consensus to occur on what types of innovation proposals will be brought forth and what proposals will be selected for implementation.

3. Conclusion

This paper has viewed the Management Information System as an organizational innovation and has focused on the process of initiation and implementation of this innovation. It has been pointed out that there are different ways for organizing for the innovation process during the above two phases. Thus from the practitioner's perspective there is no one best way to organize for innovation. At the initiation phase of a MIS innovation a higher degree of complexity, lower formalization and lower centralization will facilitate the gathering and processing of information that is required during the planning and design of a MIS. At the implementation stage, a higher level of formalization, centralization and lower level of complexity is likely to reduce the ambiguity that might impair the utilization of the MIS innovation. Also, the organization needs to be able to deal with interpersonal issues and organizational conflicts as they arise during the innovation process.

References

[1] Argyris, Chris: Management Information Systems: The Challenge to Rationality and Emotionality. In: Management Science 17, No. 6/1971, pp. B-275–B-292.

[2] Becker, Selwyn and Thomas Whisler: The Innovative Organization: A Selective View of Current Theory and Research. In: The Journal of Business 40, No. 4/1967, pp. 462–469.

[3] Burns, Tom and G. Stalker: The Management of Innovation. London 1961.

[4] Dearden, John: MIS Is a Mirage. In: Harvard Business Review 50, No. 1/1972, pp. 90–100.

[5] Duncan, Robert: Characteristics of Organizational Environments and Perceived Environmental Uncertainty. In: Administrative Science Quarterly 17 No. 3/1972, pp. 313–327.

[6] Duncan, Robert: Multiple Decision Making Structures in Adapting to Environmental Uncertainty: The Impact on Organizational Effectiveness. In: Human Relations 26 No. 3/1973.

[7] French, Wendell and Cecil Bell: Organization Development: Behavioral Science Interventions for Organizational Improvement. Englewood Cliffs 1973.

[8] Hage, Jerald and Michael Aiken: Program Change and Organizational Properties: A Comparative Analysis. In: American Journal of Sociology 1967.

[9] Hage, Jerald and Michael Aiken: Social Change in Complex Organizations. New York 1970.

[10] Knight, Kenneth: A Descriptive Model of the Intra-Firm Innovation Process. In: The Journal of Business 40 No. 4/1967, pp. 478–496.

[11] Lawrence, Paul and Jay Lorsch: Organization and Environment Boston: Division of Research, Graduate School of Business, Harvard University 1967.

[12] Radner, Michael and Rodney Neal: The Progress of Management Science Activities in Large U.S. Industrial Corporations. In: Operations Research 21 No. 2/1973.

[13] Sapolsky, Harvey: Organizational Structure and Innovation. In: The Journal of Business 40, No. 4/1967, pp. 497–511.

[14] Shepard, Herbert: Innovation-Resisting and Innovation Producing Organizations. In: The Journal of Business 40, No. 4/1967, pp. 470–477.

[15] Whisler, Thomas: Information Technology and Organizational Change. Belmont, California 1970.

[16] Wilson, James Q.: Innovation in Organization: Notes Toward a Theory. In: Thompson, James (ed.): Approaches to Organizational Design. Pittsburgh 1966, pp. 193–218.

[17] Zaltman, Gerald, Robert Duncan and Jonny Holbek: Organizations and Innovations. New York 1973.

[18] Zani, William: Blueprint for MIS. In: Harvard Business Review 48, No. 6/1970, pp. 95–101.

[19] Zannetos, Zenon: Toward Intelligent Management Information Systems. In: Industrial Management Review 1968.

German abstract
Probleme bei der Initiierung und Implementierung von Management-Informationssystemen

Von *Robert Duncan*

In dieser Arbeit werden Management-Informationssysteme (MIS) als eine organisatorische Innovation betrachtet. Dabei konzentriert sich die Untersuchung auf die Prozesse der Initiierung und Implementierung des MIS in den Handlungsablauf der Organisation durch Modifizierungen der Organisationsstruktur.

Der Innovationsprozeß wird durch die beiden Phasen der Initiierung und Implementierung definiert. Dabei besteht die Initiierungsphase aus drei Teilphasen:

1. Kenntnisnahme und Bewußtwerdung,
2. Stellungnahme und Gestaltung,
3. Entscheidung.

Die Implementierungsphase gliedert sich in

1. Anfangsimplementierung,
2. Anschluß- und Dauerimplementierung.

Es werden nun die strukturellen Merkmale der Unternehmensorganisation diskutiert, die sich auf den Innovationsprozeß auswirken und ihn begünstigen oder erschweren. Diese Merkmale sind: Systemkomplexität, Formalisierungsgrad, Zentralisierungsgrad, personelle Beziehungen und die Fähigkeit, sich mit Konflikten auseinanderzusetzen.

Als Lösungsansatz wird ein Modell präsentiert, das anzeigt, daß verschiedene Konfigurationen in der Organisationsstruktur existieren, die den Innovationsprozeß auf verschiedenen Stufen erleichtern.

Bei der Untersuchung stellt sich heraus, daß in der Initiierungsphase der Innovation eines Management-Informationssystems ein höherer Komplexitätsgrad, ein niedrigerer Formalisierungsgrad und eine geringere Zentralisierung die Sammlung und Verarbeitung der Informationen, die auf der Stufe der Initiierung erforderlich sind, erleichtern.

In der Implementierungsphase eignen sich ein höherer Stand der Formalisierung und Zentralisierung und ein niedrigerer Komplexitätsgrad zur Reduzierung solcher Probleme, die die Implementierung eines Management-Informationssystems beeinträchtigen könnten. Weiterhin muß die Organisation im Stande sein, sich mit personellen Fragen und organisatorischen Konflikten zu befassen, sobald diese während des Innovationsprozesses auftauchen.

Damit präsentiert dieser Beitrag ein Konzept für den Prozeß der Initiierung und Implementierung von Management-Informationssystemen. Dabei liefert das vorgestellte Modell dem Manager Hinweise auf praktische Maßnahmen zur Verringerung organisatorischer Widerstände bei der Einführung von MIS.

Information system and organizational concept – analysis of an innovation process from the pragmatic point of view

By *Heinz Göhre*

1. Introduction

The initial situation in the sixties seemed clear. A new technical invention in the form of the computer had become available. The latter's ability to store and process data in bulk promised economic use not only in the field of scientific/technical computations but also in the organizational sector.
According to the classical innovation theory [1],

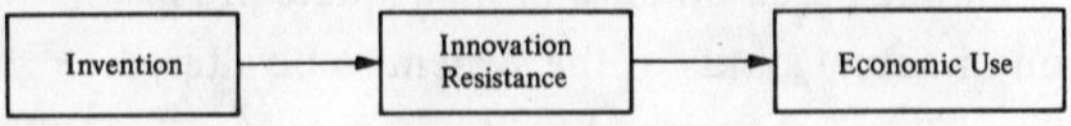

Fig. 1. Classical definition of innovation

some resistance was indeed expected up to the economic break-through of automatic data processing in this sector, too. However, this resistance appeared surmountable.
Unexpectedly enough, the type and extent of the difficulties which arose were much greater than anticipated. They led in some striking cases to the failure of such projects undertaken with great enthusiasm and considerable expenditure. The consequences were disillusionment, perplexity and frustration, which even today have not been fully overcome.
The development described becomes more comprehensible on considering innovation - in the sense of the modern innovation theory [2, 3] - as the "change of system statuses".

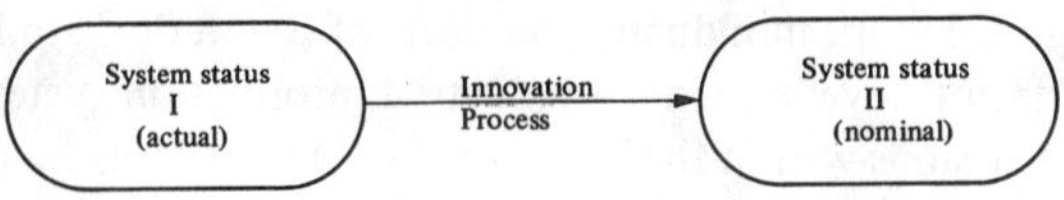

Fig. 2. Innovation as status change

The aim is to change the status of the system "organization" (corporation, authority, other institution) together with the development and introduction of computer-aided information systems. Each organization is - in this case - to be considered as a subsystem of the major social and ecological system.

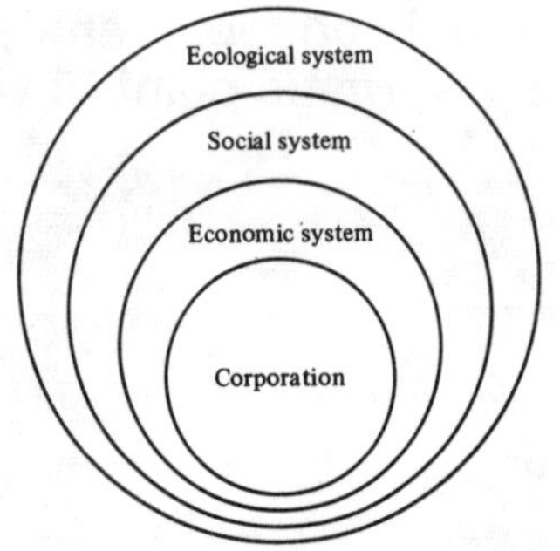

Fig. 3. The corporation as partial system of major system

Any change to a subsystem is inevitably linked with a change to the major systems (and vice-versa).

Unexpected difficulties which occur in the course of an innovation process can in this sense be attributed principally to the following causes:

- Evaluation and planning based on false or inadequate premises.
- Faulty evaluation of actual status of the system to be altered.
- Faulty evaluation of the problems to be overcome in the course of the innovation process (actual → nominal transition of system).
- False objectives for the envisaged nominal system statuses.
- False actions on establishing, planning and implementing the innovation process (methods, procedures, organization, personnel assignment).

The possible causes of failure with regard to the innovation process "Development of Information Systems and their Introduction into Existing Organizations" are analysed according to the above aspects and in the light of previous pragmatic experience.

The consequences to be derived from this problem/system analysis for the organizational concept and for shaping the innovation process are discussed.

The considerations presented here for discussion are based on ten years of constantly reflected empirical work in industry, on years of theoretical studies and practical experience in the development of industrial information systems as well as on intensive discussions within the scope of the "Arbeitskreis Informationssysteme (AKI)" (Working Group for Information Systems) and with colleagues, in particular with Dr. Bernhard Ludwig and Kurt Hübner.

2. Premises

Each human activity is based on certain assumptions – as premises – concerning reality, even if these are largely unconscious and not reflected upon in greater detail. They are the result of one's educational process, specialist training and horizon of experience as well as of the intellectual trends of the era in question.

It appears necessary to examine first of all the premises underlying the development of information systems. Examining the origin of the stimuli leading to this development is helpful.

The existence of the computer as a potential technical aid in rationalising organizational work sequences represented the stimulus to develop information systems in the main branch of development. The initiative was taken by mathematicians, natural scientists and EDP engineers who naturally concentrated on the development of the corresponding hard- and software.

The new discipline Operations Research (termed in German sometimes directly as "corporation research") tended in the same direction. Here again, mainly mathematicians, natural scientists and engineers attempted to attain "scientific management" by means of mathematical optimization methods as well as by developing corporation models, in contrast to the previously predominantly empirical operational management methods.

As far as a subsidiary branch is concerned, stimuli came from the documentation side with the aim of employing the computer to cope with the ever increasing flood of technico-scientific information in the form of literature.

Further stimuli came in more recent times from the systems theory side, this theory teaching that organizations shall be considered as complex systems consisting of various types of elements having information as the connecting element. Cybernetics contributed the theory of organization as a complex system of control loops coupled together, their control requiring nominal information (in the form of planning or given data) as well as actual information (to check and adjust the control loops). Finally, the decision theory attempts to represent organizations as an entity from the point of view of continuous decisions made between alternative actions requiring the appropriate information.

Up to now economic science has reacted in the main passively in attempting to integrate all these impulses, emanating primarily from other disciplines, in its system.

The highly relevant behavioural and social sciences have remained largely neglected. Their contribution has to date been restricted to more or less detailed comments pointing out the need to take behavioural and social science aspects into account.

In conclusion, it should be remembered that the main impulses in the information system sector initially came almost exclusively from mathematicians, natural scientists and EDP engineers. It is also striking that the problem area, which can be summarised in the slogan "organization and information", is considered by the various disciplines primarily from a one-sided, specialist point of view. A comprehensive, interdisciplinary theory of organization really deserving of its name is as yet lacking. The basis for a comprehensive and interdisciplinary science of information is likewise lacking.

Considering the historical perspective shows how the premises developed which are always encountered in literature as well as with those participating in the development of information systems (and - even more markedly - with the decision-making committees). Let us now discuss these premises as follows:

a) Premises concerning the type of problem:

(1) We are dealing - in the scientific sense - with a rational problem which can be solved using methods developed by science and technology.
(2) "Information" is a technico-scientific problem.
(3) Information is primarily a problem of quantitative, mathematisable data.
(4) Information is a problem of data retrieval.
(5) Information is a problem of communications engineering and data processing.
(6) Information is a saleable product.

b) Premises concerning organization:

(7) Organizations shall be considered as static systems which are complete in themselves.
(8) It is possible to define a Standard Organization.
(9) The existing organizational structure and organizational sequences shall be considered in the main as given: however, they can be rationalised with the aid of the computer and the development of information systems.
(10) The organization shall be considered as "machinery to generate products and/or services".
(11) Real organizations can be represented and optimised by means of mathematical models.
(12) Organizations can be interpreted as "machinery to generate decisions".
(13) The information system of an organization shall be considered as a subelement of the organizational system; this can be broken down into subinformation systems which can be regarded independently of one another.
(14) The information system is a subelement of the decision-making system; this again is a subelement of the organizational system.

(15) The information system of an organization is largely independent of the information system of the organization's environment - improvement can therefore be restricted to the internal organizational information system.
(16) Information - as a production factor - shall be considered as equal in status to the factors work and capital.
(17) Improvements made in one organizational sector result automatically in an improvement of the overall organizational system.

c) Premises concerning human beings within the organization:
(18) Man - in the scientific sense - is a rational being, behaves rationally and utilises information in a rational manner.
(19) Man is only of interest within our organizations from the functional point of view or as a production factor, respectively.
(20) Man is of significance within information systems only as a recipient or supplier of information.
(21) Psychological and sociological behaviour patterns of individuals and groups are conspicuous within the organization as a nuisance factor which must be eliminated.
(22) Procedures elaborated by specialists are accepted at once - within the organizational sector, too - as long as they are better and more economical than previous ones.

d) Premises concerning objective and procedure:
(23) The correctly furnished computer and the correct DP programme are all that is necessary in order to cope with the relevant problems.
(24) The objective comprises increasing, improving and correct "selling" of the supply of information.
(25) "Information" and "data" are two different expressions for the same thing.
(26) The focal point of the objective is the development of optimization or simulation models, respectively.
(27) The successful introduction of an information system signifies that the objective has been met, since such systems further operate "automatically".
(28) It is possible to set up isolated sub-information systems, since only weak interaction is the case between these sub-systems.
(29) The largely empirically grown, partly informal existing information system of organizations is so ineffective that it can be replaced easily and economically by rationally established information systems.
(30) Redundant information increases technical expenditure and shall therefore be avoided.
(31) The costs accruing due to information systems are limited primarily to the programming expenditure and the computing costs.

(32) The experts need only be given enough power within the organization in order to improve the latter.

A striking tendency with these premises is the restriction to the purely technical aspect, the mechanistic view of the organization and consideration of the human element within the organization as a "nuisance factor". This inevitably leads to underestimating the overall problems - with all the consequences resulting for target planning, for the employment of funds and for selection of the personnel involved. The fact is often neglected that "improving the information system" must primarily aim at "improving the information behaviour" in the sense of making better use of the information.

The above collection of standard premises makes no claim to completeness or correctness. It is intended to stimulate an urgently needed critical analysis. Such an analysis should consider particularly the applicability of the specific premises, which may be quite valid in certain subsectors but might be misleading in the case of undiscriminating generalizations.

It would be a profitable task for science to establish a catalogue of valid premises and their respective area of application in close cooperation with the empirical side. This catalogue would enable objective assessment of the flood of relevant publications as well as of all larger projects envisaged.

3. Analysis of the actual status

3.1 The organization science in theory and practice

Let us remind ourselves once again that to date an organizational theory deserving of its name dealing with the phenomenon "organization" in its entirety from an interdisciplinary point of view is lacking. Despite a profusion of rudiments concerning this theme [4, 5, 6] taken from pragmatic economic science, the theory of decision, the theory of behaviour and from information engineering, we are still far removed from a consistent theory of organization which can be applied for practical purposes.

The same applies as far as a general, comprehensive science of information is concerned. Here, too, rudiments from the cognition theory, linguistics, science of communication, information and data processing abound, but no consistent, applicable theory exists.

The subject "Informatik" introduced in recent years in German universities cannot fill this gap, dealing as it does primarily with the mathematical/technical aspect of information. Establishing a first branch for "Economic Informatics" at Cologne University does not - encouraging as it is - eliminate the deficiency, either, since it relates to one certain aspect only, namely that of business administration.

This signifies, however, that at present no well-founded scientific basis is at our disposal to describe the actual status (or arbitrary nominal statuses, either) of real organizational systems and their information system. Perhaps relative agreement can be reached on considering organizations as open dynamic cybernetic systems closely involved with their environment.

In practice, economics and administration are still dominated by mechanistic model conceptions as to organization. These consider the organizational system as static and largely isolated. Topical discussion concentrates on the optimum assignment of objectives and means within largely authoritarian, hierarchical organizational structures. From time to time attention is paid to the organizational sequences. Systematic thinking in organizational processes is still only met within exceptional cases.

3.2 The role played by information within the organizational system

Differing and in part contradictory opinions exist as to the role played by information within our organizations - and thus as to the nature of the information system of the organizations. Defining the term "information" already represents a source of discord. The following definition is beginning to gain acceptance among experts dealing concretely with the objective of developing and introducing information systems (Fig. 4).

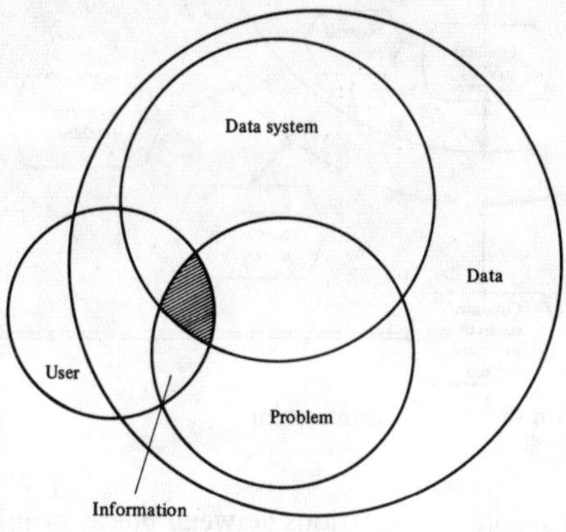

Fig. 4. Definition of the term "information"

- Information comprises the relevant data and data combinations which are relevant for a problem and a user.
- Data are sets of symbols provided with interpretation specifications to represent factual situations.

Seen in this light, "information" is a term on the pragmatic level and "data" on a semantic one. It is important to realise that data only become information on confrontation with a problem and with a user dealing with this problem. In this sense today's "information systems" are usually merely "data processing systems" since they neglect the decisive conversion process of data to information.

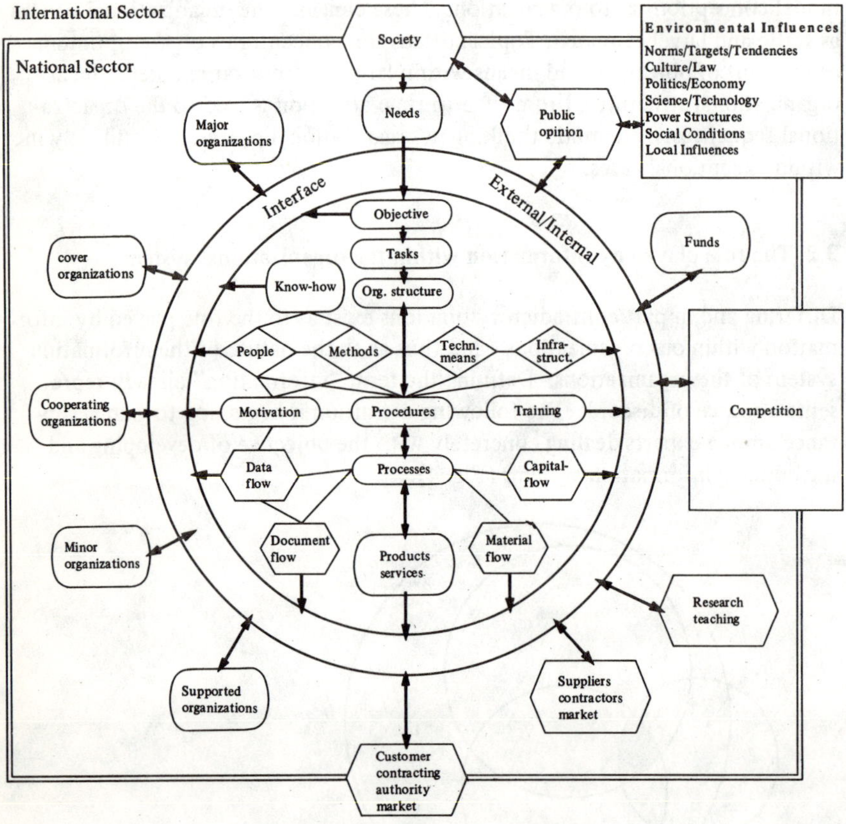

Fig. 5. Information relationships within the organization system

Fig. 5 attempts to indicate the manifold interrelations between pieces of information within the system formed by an organization and its environment. The point of departure for this representation was the situation of a corporation. This can, however, be applied as it stands to an authority or any other institution.

The close interlinkage of the organization with its environment is striking. This forces one to consider the organization as an open system which - in a dynamically changing environment - cannot withdraw from external influences but is compelled to adapt flexibly to the external impulses to change.

A social organization is in the long run only viable as long as it is capable of contributing to meet a need felt by the society of which it is a member. The function of meeting needs leads to the task or objective of the organization which justifies the latter's title to existence. The work breakdown of the objective according to the available resources (personnel, methods, technical means, infrastructure) is the primary determinant of the organizational structure. The resulting tasks initiate a variety of work processes whose sequences comply with certain procedures. The final result of all this effort represents the products and services meeting the social need.

In order to accomplish its objectives, the organization requires the appropriate specialist know-how as well as adequate motivation on the part of those participating in the work processes.

Certain capital, material, documentation and data flows are linked with the work processes which require guidance. It would extend beyond the scope of this paper to discuss the specific data and information required to employ the resources and to guide the flows.

These reflections show that "information" becomes effective within the organization from a variety of aspects. These are primarily:

- The aspect concerning the self-comprehension and self-representation of the organization internally and externally (position of the organization within and with respect to the major systems as well as with respect to its members; external/internal interaction; objective, public relations, employee and management motivation);
- the constitutive aspect (objective, legal form, work breakdown, organizational structure, procedures);
- the behavioural aspect (code of behaviour, management and cooperation forms, settlement of conflicts, rules, procedures);
- the motivating aspect (tasks, style of management, group behaviour, promotion system, recognition/punishment, salary determination, social conditions, procedures);
- the communication aspect (cooperation, exchange of information, mutual understanding);
- the knowledge aspect (specialist know-how, methods, procedures, problem/system consciousness, process knowledge and procedures);
- the control aspect (tasks, planning, control, deployment of resources, flow control, needs/meeting needs, feedback).

One aspect which still plays a large part in our organizations should not be neglected, namely the dominance aspect (knowledge is power; availability of information determines influence, prestige and social status).

In many sectors of economy and administration competition between products or services, respectively, has shifted increasingly to subsidiary services of an informational nature. This information aspect could, generalizing a military expression, be termed

the logistic aspect (product description; application, maintenance, repair instructions, spare parts service).

The above should serve to indicate the manifold aspects of the information system of an organization and their close interrelationship as well as to clarify how many starting points exist for measures to improve organizational information systems, in the first instance without needing the computer for specific cases. Only a relatively small portion of the data required is of a quantitative or formalisable nature. The larger, altogether more important portion consists of texts, figures or graphic representations. The latter usually require interpretation or problem- and user-oriented conditioning.

The task of top management is primarily the strategic identification and definition of an objective as well as its conversion to internal tasks. This requires primarily external data from politics, the economy and jurisdiction as well as data concerning the market and competition. The same applies to know-how at specialist level (Fig. 6).

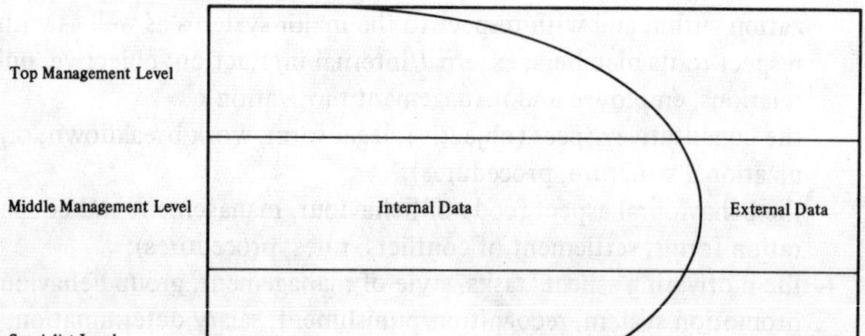

Fig. 6. Internal/external data needs

The great dependence of the organization on external data signifies that the information system of an organization extends beyond the latter's boundaries (Fig. 7). This means that certain documentation and information services of the organization's environment necessarily represent a component part of the information system of the organization.

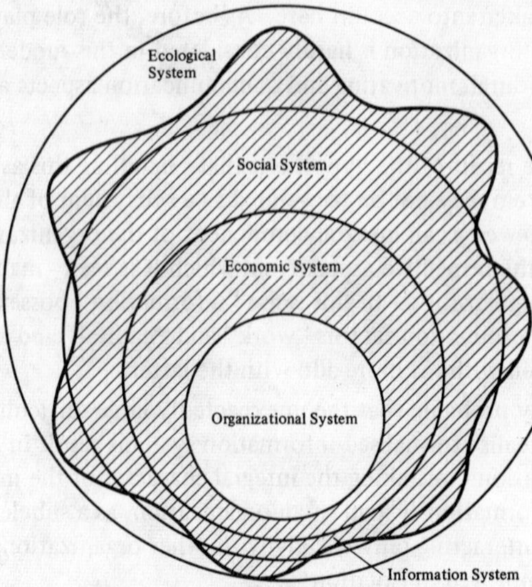

Fig. 7. Organizational system and pertinent information system

3.3 The organization as an organism

Realistic assessment of the actual status (and of possible nominal statuses) of a system is only feasible on the basis of a systems model which corresponds to the actual situation. It shall therefore be investigated as to how far customary notions as to the system "organization" (including its information system) portray the reality satisfactorily.

A more or less unreflected mechanistic model, which considers the organization analogously to a machine whose elements (unfortunately!) consist in part of human beings, represents the basis of organizational practice. Man here is reduced to the function of a cog in the wheel. Information appears mainly as an "information flow" between the parts of the machine (analogously to the electrical current in wiring), and is thus considered primarily from the control aspect. The knowledge aspect is considered - in a functional sense - too. The organization is seen essentially as a closed, static system. This model hardly does justice to reality. Its application easily leads to faulty judgments, false objectives and measures.

A first expansion of the model must lead to consideration of the system as an open one linked closely with its environment. It possesses the dynamic properties of a cybernetic system and is obliged to adapt continuously to environmental changes. The aspect of the self-comprehension of the organization and the constitutive aspect are taken into account here. As before, the role played by human beings within the organization is hardly considered in this model, either, and hence the behavioural, motivating and communication aspects are neglected.

A further step forward is the result of the hypothesis that - handling this as an entity - the information system may not be considered as a subsystem of the organization, but must be viewed as an integral component of the organization which - in accordance with the respective aspect from which it is seen - manifests itself diversely in the organization. In this sense "information" possesses a different quality from the production factors "work" and "capital" and may for this reason not be equated without more ado with the latter.

The assumption seems highly probable that the unexpectedly large difficulties met with on attempting to realise formalised information systems result in particular due to the postulation - mistaking the integral character of the information system - that the information system of an organization, as a subelement of the organization system interacting only weakly with other organizational parts, can be handled and improved in isolation.

Even an organizational model expanded in this way does not offer a well-founded basis for future innovations in this sector, since it still does not take into account the role played by human beings within the organization, especially within the latter's information system, to a sufficient extent. If one accepts the definition that data only become information in confrontation with a person and his problems, it necessarily follows that man with his psychological and group sociology behaviour patterns must be considered as a direct component of the above-defined information system.

In addition, the fact must be taken into account that a real organization - as an independently acting, autonomous system - is more than the sum of its parts. In this sense the question as to the nature of the organizations corresponds to the biological question as to the nature of the organisms. In this connection it should be pointed out that biology, starting from this question, gave the actual impulse in developing a "general systems theory" and not technology [2].

Justice will probably only be done to the real nature of the organizations when they are viewed as biological systems, as a sort of "organism of a higher order" coming into being as the symbiosis of a larger number of humans with technical aids and certain methods (man/machine/method system).

The above reflections appear in the first instance as extremely theoretical and hardly significant for practical purposes, especially since the hypothesis concerning the "organization as an organism" first of all makes a statement only with respect to the type of system organization and does not yet provide a model applicable in practice. This can be countered by the assertion that false hypotheses inevitably result in posing false questions and thus lead astray. However, with the aid of a working hypothesis doing justice to reality it will be possible to classify the wealth of already available experience correctly and to gain new understanding concerning relevant questions (which in the light of previous experience already contain the answers to a considerable extent) in a purposive and systematic manner.

The basic thesis of the systems theory is also of relevance here, namely that knowledge of the type of a system enables transposing already won understanding and experience - initially in the form of additional working hypotheses - to other systems of the same type and of subjecting these to systematic examination.

In the following an attempt is made to gain indications as to organizational principles in nature which may perhaps be applied to organisms of a higher order - such as our organizations - by discussing the homologies and heterologies between highly-developed biological organisms (such as man) on the one hand and organizations on the other.

It is for example of interest in connection with the constitutive aspect of the information system that the structure of biological organisms is largely fixed by information anchored in the genes, whereas the former must and can be organized consciously in the case of organizations. The latter here need on the one hand an additional organ, gaining on the other hand the ability to adapt - in principle unrestrictedly - to the requirements of their environment and thus something resembling potential immortality. Surprisingly enough, only a few organizations have recognised this task and its inherent possibilities and have created the corresponding institutionalised organ (for instance in the form of "organization development" assigned to organization management).

In the same way, most of the essential processes in biological systems are largely automatised by information stored in the genes in the form of a complicated system of control loops coupled with one another and withdrawn from conscious guidance. Only possible disturbances in the course of these processes are indicated by a complex signal (e.g. pain). This results in relieving the consciously controlled functions required for dealing with the environment. Applying this to our organizations, the requirement can be derived that as many internal processes as possible - here to be organized consciously - be automated by self-regulating mechanisms to such an extent that organization management can devote itself fully to asserting the organization in its environment.

Biological organisms can only survive in the long run when they fill a meaningful niche within the system of their environment on the one hand and are in a position on the other hand to adapt to changes in this environmental system as well as recognise dangers threatening them from their environment in good time. Appropriate sense organs and a highly developed internal information system processing these data and triggering suitable impulses serve this purpose of winning environmental data. Our organizations require corresponding institutionalised "sense organs" which should be created and organized consciously. It is astonishing in this connection, too, how many organizations believe that they can cope with this task on a long-term basis aided merely by rudimentally developed, informal systems.

It is also interesting to observe that, in contrast to our organizations, the dominance aspect plays no role within biological organisms - unless morbid degeneracy is the case, signifying in most cases the death of the organism. This is achieved by an organizational principle which I should like to term "principle of mutual dependence by services". According to this principle the human body, for instance, is structured in such a way that none of its organs can expand or even become independent at the expense of other organs, since its existence depends on the existence of all other organs and on balanced interplay between the same. Applying this structurization principle to our organizations could contribute to forestalling the general tendency of individual organizational sectors toward cancerous growth at the expense of others or even of becoming independent within the organization, and to demolishing the barriers linked with the dominance aspect within the information system.

Considering organizations as organisms, as living biological systems, leads to a more realistic understanding of the necessity of implementing basic changes to the organization only cautiously and step-wise. Such biological processes necessitate a certain period of time until the ground is ready for sowing, until the seed of change has come up and the "plant" is fully developed. Those responsible for organizational innovation processes should therefore not be urged to show revolutionary, system-changing elan, but rather "gardener virtues" stamped with the knowledge of the "natural" germination, growth and ripening periods. The attempt to bring about rapid organizational changes by neglecting these laws is certainly one of the causes leading to the failure of such intentions.

4. Problems concerning actual-nominal transition

4.1 Type of innovation process

According to the definition in section 1 (Fig. 2), "Innovation Process" signifies the process whereby a certain system is converted from a given initial status I (Actual) to a new, changed system status II (Nominal). A distinction must be made here between two different types of innovation process.

In the first case - as, for instance, with most larger technical development plans - the initial system status as well as the envisaged system status are relatively familiar. Virgin territory is only reached as far as certain detail questions are concerned. The risk entailed thereby, however, can be restricted to a considerable extent by purposive experimental preliminary investigations (example: development of a combat aircraft; essential new detail: variable geometry wings). The term "Project" has come into use for this type of innovation process.

Innovation processes of the second type are quite different. Here even the actual status of the system concerned is unclear. Nominal statuses which should be attained are correspondingly difficult to define and even more difficult to assess. This means, however, that we are still in the middle of the frist preliminary phase during the course of which the groundwork for later projects must be laid. Thus the primary target of such intentions can only be to obtain sufficient knowledge as to the relevant system, as to its behaviour as well as to potential desirable changes to the system status. That is, these are "Experiments", "research through experimental changes to system statuses". Their aim concerns knowledge, not the achievement of certain new system statuses. Should the latter, however, be defined as the aim, they serve as a means to the end, and not as an end in itself.

It is appropriate in the case of "Projects" to deal with these according to the phase concept and the rules of technical project management. "Experiments" on the other hand, demand developing a suitable management concept for iterative learning processes.

In view of the prevailing uncertainty regarding the premises as well as inadequate knowledge of the system "organization", innovations with respect to larger changes to the information system of the organization are at present to be considered essentially as innovation processes of the second type, i.e., as experiments. Much disappointment could have been avoided had the initiators of such plans been conscious right from the beginning of these facts and had they made this clear to their contracting authorities, too, instead of "selling" these projects with unattainable objectives.

4.2 Problem areas involved in the innovation processes

One of the greatest problems involved in innovation processes is problem consciousness itself. The initiators of such plans as well as the committees responsible for the decision to tackle and finance them are often unaware of the multiplicity of the problems incurred. In this way processes continue to be set in motion in line with the proverb: "Fools rush in where angels fear to tread" without those participating knowing what they have actually let themselves in for.

Certain problem areas which play a more or less important role, depending on the type of innovation, initial situation and actual marginal condition, exist with all innovation processes (Fig. 8). These are discussed briefly in the following in connection with our question.

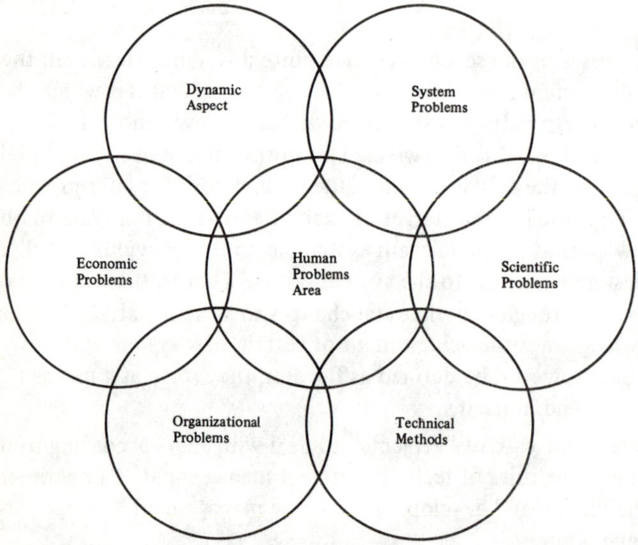

Fig. 8. Problem areas involved in innovation processes

(1) System problems

Innovations, that is, greater changes to the status of a system, can only hold out a prospect of success provided that the relevant system itself, its properties and its interactions with other systems are sufficiently well known, that those participating and involved are agreed as to the new system status to be achieved mutually, and that the requisite specialist skills and resources are available. Should this not be the case, at best only systematic experiments can be undertaken - aimed at better understanding of the system. As the above remarks indicate, as far as the "development and introduction of information systems" are concerned, we are in the main still in this experimental stage.

(2) Scientific foundations

An intention becomes all the more problematic and risky, the less it is based in the relevant field of knowledge on proven theoretical foundations. In our case these foundations are only provided in sufficient measure for practical application in the technico-scientific area. Useful, well-founded practical foundations are largely lacking in systems theory, in the theory of organization, science of information, industrial management, national economy as well as in the behavioural and social sciences, despite a complex wealth of individual results. This means, however: The innovation "development and introduction of information systems" entails an advance into largely unknown virgin territory - accompanied by the corresponding problems and risks.

(3) Technical/methodic problem sector

The prerequisities in the relevant hardware sector (EDP, microfilm technology) are "in principle" provided (the details are the devil here!). Much would still need improvement in the software area, but appropriate solutions are already becoming evident. Although - and since - this sector of technology is undergoing a stormy development period, it is apparent, that a certain conclusion will probably be reached within the next decade entailing a disintegration of the current technical barriers to establishing first-generation large-scale, complex information systems.

(4) Organizational problems

A radical change of consciousness must first of all take root. As long as the fact that "information" represents the integral factor of each organization transforming a conglomeration of personnel, technical and financial resources into a living, acting organism is not fully recognised and the appropriate conclusions drawn, no essential progress can be expected.

The development of effective methods for the management of iterative learning processes and the implementation of exemplary experiments appear of particular importance. The Economics Institute for Organization and Automation at Cologne University (BIFOA) is demonstrating the pattern to be followed in its work carried out in conjunction with well-known corporating and software companies under contract to the German Federal Ministry of Research and Technology.

As far as private and public organizations are concerned, it seems necessary to convert the current implicit handling of information, scattered as it is over the entire organization, to explicit information management considered as a major sector and to find suitable structural organizational solutions.

The greatest problems will be incurred thereby on transition from the current organizational structures and flows to the requisite new structures and flows (to be considered as processes). These problems result from the marginal condition that operations within the organization concerned may not be impaired to any considerable degree by the conversion process.

A further organizational problem extending beyond the scope of the individual organization comprises the development and expansion of the necessary supra-company or public documentation and information systems as well as their interplay with the information systems of the specific organizations.

(5) Economic problems

The economic aspect can be considered at present as the decisive factor limiting future development. The "cost factor information" will only be assessed in the proper light once the importance of the "integral factor information" for the efficiency of our organization is fully recognised and the economy of appropriate measures demonstrated.

It is disadvantageous that the information costs can be collated quantitatively, but that the information benefit - due to its largely qualitative nature - can hardly be estimated. The benefit can currently be assessed in most cases only negatively in line with the motto: "What does not implementing the envisaged action cost?". Add to this that the costs of present, largely implicitly run information handling, estimated by some authors as amounting to over 50 % of the overall costs incurred by an industrial concern - see, for instance, [8, 9] - are as yet presented explicitly in no cost system.

For economic reasons, financing better information management (including appropriate information systems) will have to be effected, at least at the beginning, through rationalizing the existing, primarily informal information system of the organization. The prerequisite here is explicit collection of the costs of the existing information system, hence enabling checking and comparison. This, however, seems hardly feasible unless all information activities are combined to form an organizational entirety.

(6) Dynamic aspect

We now come across a fundamental problem which can perhaps be formulated as follows: "System-changing projects (i.e., innovation processes which attempt to bring about a clearly defined new system status) must be feasible within a period of time which is brief compared to the time within which essential changes to the system and to the system's environment take place".

This problem is already illustrated in technical projects where, for instance, newly developed aircraft (with development periods of at least 5 years) are obsolete compared to the actual state of the art when the customer receives the first machine. This problem is far weightier with respect to innovations in the organizational sector since these - due to the slow rate of fundamental alterations in patterns of behaviour - generally extend over decades.

In the present case we are dealing with such a long-term innovation process which will stretch over at least one decade and which, furthermore, has hardly developed beyond the experimental stage. The change process is occuring within an environment which itself is subjected to extraordinarily rapid alteration, in particular in the areas which are of relevance for the above process. This applies to the objectives and the structure of the respective organization and environment as well as to the state of scientific understanding, information processing technology and the other marginal conditions. Thus the danger arises of having to break off projects at an advanced stage because the original prerequisites are no longer valid, or of putting up with the fact that, due to continuous changes, the projects will never reach a successful conclusion.

This danger can only be counteracted by establishing priorities which take the overall problems into reasonable account (according to the motto: "The slowest ship determines the rate of the convoy"), by far more modest objectives (initially in the form of clearly-defined experiments) and by proceeding systematically and step-wise along the path of a controlled iterative learning process.

(7) Human problem area

Man himself with his psychological and sociological patterns of behaviour probably represents the actual factor determining the rate at which this innovation process can be implemented. The requisite changes to consciousness, motivation and to the behaviour patterns of those concerned represent, according to universal experience, a slow process with a half-life value of many years.

Attempting to accelerate this partial process can easily lead to "a frontal wave" of additional resistance which, once having come into being, can be eliminated only under great exertion.

Intensive enlightenment and training should prepare the ground initially in order to enable a uniform approach to mature based on concordant understanding of the problem. Faulty motivation should be reduced and inevitably conflicting interests settled.

The use of power to accelerate this process is possible to a limited extent only. This can in no way replace the acceptance - absolutely vital in view of the complexity and susceptibility of such organizational systems - on the part of those involved and their willing, active cooperation.

5. Objectives for the nominal status

5.1 Necessity of the innovation

(1) Line of development

In view of the problems described, in many organizations those responsible for it are justified in asking whether it is really necessary to undertake something concrete here and now, or whether it would not be better to leave further development to the "pioneers" and to wait and see how things proceed. In addition some software companies (and manufacturers) give the impression that selling the appropriate finished software and hardware is sufficient to eliminate all problems.

In answer to this question it must be borne in mind that two development trends are currently overlapping in this sector.

Employing data processing machines in the first instance held out a prospect of rationalizing the organizational sector, too. The experience gained in recent years, however, has shown that it is in fact not all that easy to realize this potential. On the contrary, many organizations have come to realize in the meantime that their administrative apparatus has now - subsequent to the introduction of EDP - become more ponderous and more expensive than ever.

In consequence of this disappointment the pendulum is currently swinging to the other extreme, bringing with it the danger of "killing the goose with the golden egg". Some organizations, within the Federal Republic of Germany as well, have apparently gone so far as to abolish their computers - in line with the motto: "It's better manual".

A far more radical and fundamental development has become apparent over the previous decades parallel to the above line of development, linked with the discovery that "information" must be considered as one of Nature's basic parameters - and thus of human society. Its significance can only be indicated approximately within the scope of this treatise with the key words "entropy, molecular biology, cybernetics, systems thinking, communication and motivation". This situation resembles that prior to the discovery of electricity or radioactivity. The effects of these physical parameters were indeed in existence and apparent, but could not yet be recognized as such.

It is this second development which must be encountered within our organizations, too. One cannot shirk the recognition that this previously misjudged, fundamental factor is effective and must be taken into account in addition to those which are already familiar. The question can only read: "How should we act in view of this new situation? ".

Unfortunately developments up to now have taken the wrong path. Had the new findings concerning the importance of information for our organizations already been accepted prior to invention of the computer, such a tool to cope with the problems incurred would be demanded vociferously today. Alas, instead of this the "tool EDP" has almost become an end in itself and must therefore be subordinated again laboriously to its intended purpose.

(2) False objectives

In the light of the current state of knowledge the most commonly encountered objectives: "Economic use through employing the computer in the organizational sector, too" - or, even more narrowly: "How can we operate our ("unfortunately" existing) computer more economically? " are in principle incorrect, since they tackle the problem, misunderstanding its real nature, from the wrong angle.

The current widespread tendency of centralizing EDP activities in order to increase their economy in independent computer divisions or even of transferring these to subsidiary companies called into being to this end illustrates the consequences due to false postulations. EDP is banished from the organization, although the goal can only be "integrating data processing within the organization".

(3) Problem definition

It is my conviction in view of the above-described situation that the general problem definition for each type of organization can only read as follows:

"How can I improve the information system of my organization?".

The first consequence of this is that in future the factor "information" may no longer be left to chance but should be paid at least the same attention as the factors "work" and "capital" today. We must obviously learn to consider information handling as one of the fundamental tasks of every organization. This must be implemented systematically within the framework of an information management system yet to be developed. To this end we require institutionalized organs which handle this on a full-time basis within the organization. All information aspects should be duly considered in this connection. These problems are incurred independently of EDP, although the latter certainly represents a valuable tool, often an indispensable one, in coping with the above.

The above-named problem definition applies not only to the individual organization and to the dealings between the organizations, but also to the major, social sector. However, many of the requisite central documentation and information systems will for economic reasons not even be set up on a national, but only on a European or indeed world-wide basis.

5.2 Public objectives

A profusion of concrete tasks can be derived from the above general problem definition, on the one hand in the supra-company, public sector, and on the other within the specific organization. It should be a matter of course for the individual organizations to become far more actively involved in the general tasks in their own interest, as far as cooperation with one another as well as with the public and research sectors are concerned.

Improving the scientific foundations is of prime urgency. We particularly need a comprehensive, interdisciplinary science of information and an equally comprehensive, interdisciplinary theory of organization. It would be most interesting to examine how far the hypothesis of the organization as an organism is capable of supplying useful concepts.

The parallel development and dissemination of a minimum degree of general knowledge in these fields should be stressed, too. Adequate communication in this sector is currently almost impossible, due to the lack of a general consensus as far as the fundamentals themselves are concerned. Add to this the difficulty of having to develop a uniform problem consciousness, generally acceptable evaluation criteria and joint goals, despite the lack of a common basis of understanding and knowledge with regard to the essentials. In no other area does such Babylonian confusion reign as in that of information and EDP.

The previously neglected theme of management training (for management activities in industry as well as in public administration) is again becoming topical in the Federal Republic of Germany in this context, too.

Standardised definition and coding systems represent a priority task in all relevant areas. Whoever has cooperated in laying down number codes as the prerequisite for applying EDP in certain fields knows how differently terms are used even within the same organization and what immense expenditure is needed to achieve uniform use of the language. He can also estimate the damage to the economy resulting from thousands of organizations continuously incurring such expenditure because of the lack of binding supra-company definition and coding systems. This task falls within the public domain, the costs of which, from the national economic point of view, would be profitable a hundred times over. Furthermore, this could make a valuable contribution to breaking down the communication barriers between individuals as well as between organizations. At the same time the prerequisites for minimum compatibility between the information systems would be attained, the lack of which prejudices the chance of separately developed systems combining to form an efficient national economic communication network.

A further priority task is establishing a network of supra-company, general documentation and information systems. Even merging the individual organizations according to their line of activity does not enable them to set up and operate such systems of their own accord. The personnel and financial expenditure required is so great that the question of tackling this task at least on a European, if not world-wide, level must be given earnest thought.

Implementing exemplary pilot projects with the close cooperation of those on the research and on the practical side sponsored by public funds would be most significant. In this way the learning process could be urged ahead systematically on a broad front in these areas.

In conclusion, let me point out the unreasonableness of continually enlargening the supply of data without undertaking parallel exertions to improve the efficiency of the utilization of such data, that is, their conversion to real information. This is obviously the bottle-neck which must be overcome. Unfortunately, this aspect has to date been paid too little attention on the research as well as the practical side.

5.3 Organization-related objectives

A priority task within the respective organizations is to create the prerequisites for a homogeneous understanding of the problem and - on this basis - to set up a binding objectives and tasks catalogue. This is initially up to top management. The first step should be for this echelon to tackle the following question within the framework of a working seminar lasting several days: "Are we, as an organization, sufficiently well equipped to deal with the problems and tasks which will face us over the next decade? ". The topic "Organization and Information" should be paid particular attention in this context.

Subsequent efforts would do well to take the form of broad schooling for all employees concerning the basic knowledge required for the topic of communication on the one hand, and on the other of examining the real situation of the relevant organization and its particular environment within the scope of detailed problems and systems analyses. These two tasks should - as a first step toward improving the organizational structure - be transferred to a department to be called into being for the purpose of "Organization Development" and directly responsible to the organization management. The next step shall comprise this department drawing up suggestions for the further development of the organizational structure on the basis of continuous systematic investigations in order to ensure - as far as possible in an anticipatory fashion - constant adaptation on the part of the organization to the changing conditions of its environment. Emphasis should be laid in the course of this work on permanent discussion between this team and organization management, since otherwise the inevitable information gap due to learning processes (Fig. 9) would become too great.

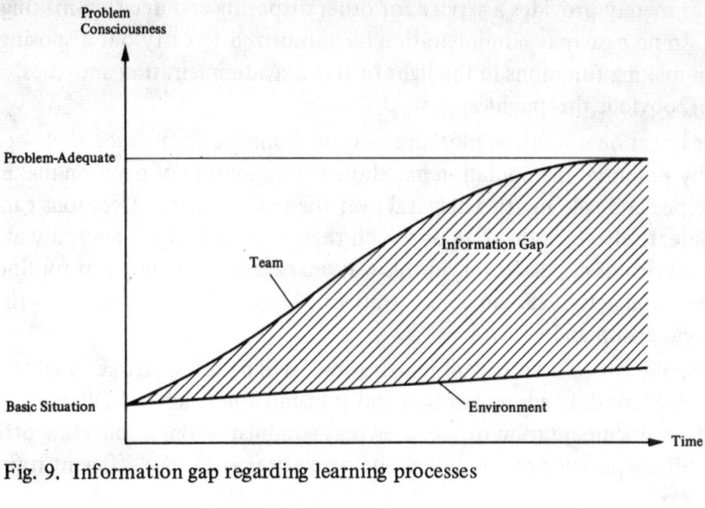

Fig. 9. Information gap regarding learning processes

In the long run, Organization Development should bear the central responsibility for the aspect concerning the self-comprehension and the self-representation of the organization as well as for the constitutive, behavioural and motivating aspect of information.

Further, centralizing all departments currently dealing with information handling and distributed over the organization in one organizational unit appears necessary. "Information handling" signifies all the activities involved in collecting or acquiring, conditioning, storing, processing, evaluating and distributing data. This includes practically all administration activities which on the one hand always comprise data administration and on the other disposing on the basis of such data. A distinction should be made in this sense, for instance, between personnel administration and personnel management, between materials administration and materials disposition, between accountancy and financial budgeting.

Separating data administration and disposition is necessary for two reasons: on the one hand the prerequisites for radical measures to improve the efficiency as well as to rationalize administration (by exploiting the potential inherent in EDP and other technical aids) are only created through centralizing all data administration activities within the organization. On the other hand as far as the dominance aspect is concerned, the "availability of data" concentrated in this way at one point must be separated from "disposing or decision-making based on such data", in order to prevent the equilibrium of the overall organization from becoming disturbed due to such an agglomeration of potential power within the latter.

Let us once again clarify this viewpoint: Concentrating all data administration activities in one "modern administration" is only justified on condition that the latter merely provides a service for other disposing and decision-making bodies. In no case may administration be authorized to carry out disposing or decision-making functions in the light of its data administration activities, however, obvious this might appear.

This organizational solution moreover - again from the dominance angle - prevents any potential manipulation based on a combination of decision-making competence and sole right to disposal over the relevant data. Decisions can be made objectively since the data on which they are founded are neutrally at everyone's disposal. Moreover, in this way management, relieved of routine administration activities, can concentrate on the actual tasks of target definition, leadership and control.

Naturally the above-defined "administration" will be given charge of all technical devices for data administration and transmission (such as EDP, microfilm office, documentation office, drawings administration, duplicating office, tracing office, printing office, telephone, telewriter etc.). An efficient training

department is also required for systematic promotion of the learning process as well as for the absolutely essential training prior to and accompanying projects. This department should be responsible for disseminating the rapidly developing external know-how in this sector within the organization, too.
Thus "administration" has competence as far as the communication, knowledge, control, guidance and logistic aspect of the organizational information system is concerned. In this way all angles of the information system are covered institutionally and concentrated meaningfully in conjunction with the above-defined "organization development".
Much could still be said regarding the concept of such "central (data) administration", the tasks to be assigned to such an organ as well as the criteria for the inner structure of this organizational unit and the internal organization of the work flows. However, such a discussion would extend far beyond the scope of this treatise. Let us therefore now consider merely one possible structure as an example of such an administrative concept (Fig. 10).

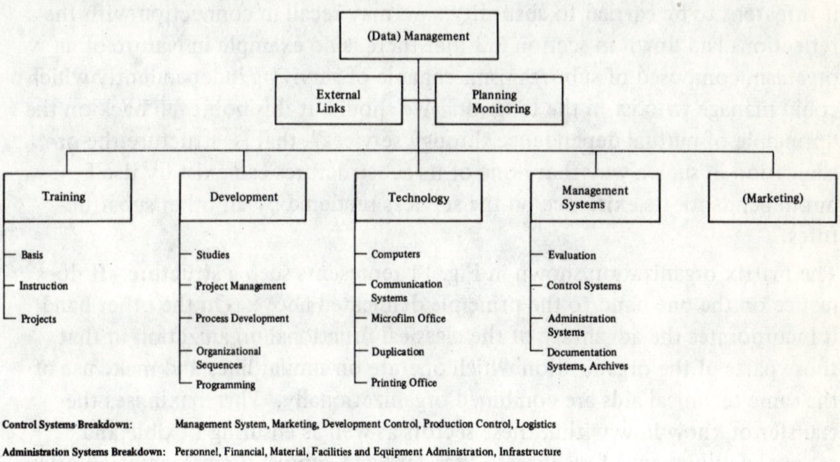

Fig. 10. Breakdown of a modern administration system

5.4 Structuring the organization according to the "principle of mutual dependence through services"

Many lamentations are voiced in most of our organizations with regard to the tendency of "principalities", "kingdoms" or even "empires" forming within the organization. This is particularly striking in divisionalised corporations, the individual divisions tending to consider themselves as "companies within the company" and as such of becoming independent.

It is certainly correct to delegate the responsibility in large corporations as far as possible over lower échelons. It is also correct to concentrate the responsibility for specific products or product groups - in contrast to the traditionally functional organization - in institutionalized departments created to this end which are uprated with respect to the other functions.

Is it really necessary, however, for "companies within the company" to be established by breaking down the corporation into divisions according to product groups, said divisions being furnished with all the attributes of an autonomous company, such as its own staffs, its own development, production and marketing departments and, above all, its own independent administration? Can it be a source of surprise if such elements of a corporation, equipped as they are to lead a self-sufficient existence, develop a strong tendency to becoming independent? Can one seriously expect such complete organisms not to lead their own lives and not attempt to evade unification endeavours at a higher level and other restraints as far as is humanly possible?

It appears - once again - that a principle is exaggerated to such an extent that it threatens to be carried to absurdity. We may recall in connection with the reflections laid down in section 3.3 that there is no example in Nature of an organism composed of suborganisms capable of surviving independently which could manage to exist in the long run. We should at this point fall back on the "principle of mutual dependence through services", that is, structure the organization in such a way that none of its substructures can exist by itself but depends for its existence on the services rendered by all other substructures.

The matrix organization shown in Fig. 11 represents such a structure. It does justice on the one hand to the principle delineated above. On the other hand, it incorporates the advantage of the classical functional organization in that those parts of the organization which operate on similar lines and make use of the same technical aids are combined organizationally. This maximises the transfer of know-how within these sectors as well as ensuring flexible and rational deployment of resources. Standardized company representation oriented according to product groups is assured with regard to the environment, and firm project and product management result within the company. Finally, the "administration" creates the homogeneous "nervous system" of the organization which was found lacking in the considerations set forth in section 3.3.

The argument is often brought forward against such organizational forms that on the one hand the specialist sectors (development, production, logistics) are not motivated adequately with regard to the projects or products, respectively, and that on the other hand there is a danger of insufficient capacity loading within specialist sectors. This argument can be countered by proposing that individual programme management negotiate long-term "lease contracts" with

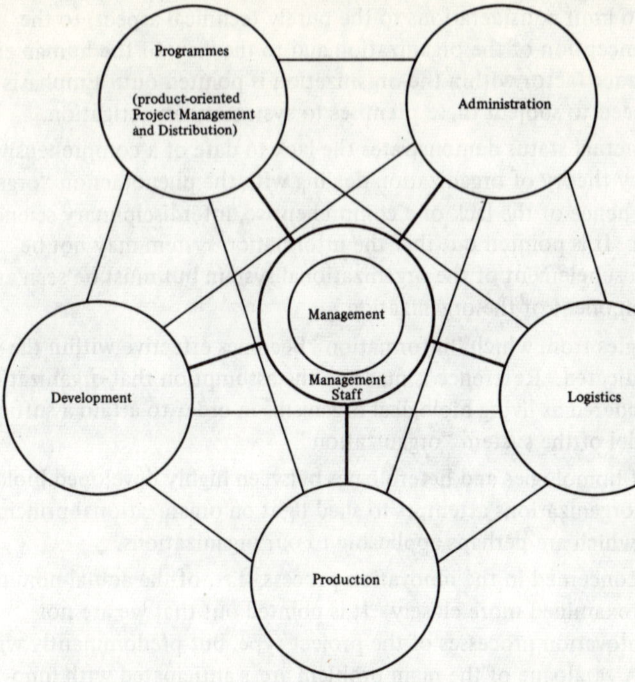

Fig. 11. Organization based on the principle of mutual dependence through service

the specialist sectors for the resources they require. These contracts may only be amended successively in accordance with the possibilities for expanding or reducing capacities. At the same time the specialist sectors could be subdivided flexibly according to product groups in line with these lease contracts.

6. Summary

The possible causes underlying the difficulties incurred or anticipated on developing information systems and their incorporation in existing organizations are examined, and possible conclusions drawn from this analysis are discussed on the basis of the modern conception of the innovation process as the process of transition from a certain initial system status to an envisaged, better system status.

It must in the first instance be borne in mind that the essential impulses in this sector have up to now come almost exclusively from mathematicians, natural scientists and EDP engineers. A compilation of the usual premises forming the largely unconscious basis of the relevant literature is presented and the tendency to limit considerations to the purely technical aspect, to the mechanistic conception of the organization and to the view of the human element as a nuisance factor within the organization is pointed out. Emphasis is laid on the need to subject these premises to systematic investigation.

Analysing the actual status demonstrates the lack to date of a comprehensive, interdisciplinary theory of organization dealing with the phenomenon "organization"; and hence of the lack of a comprehensive, interdisciplinary science of information. It is pointed out that the information system may not be considered as a subelement of the organizational system but must be seen as an integral component of the organization.

The various angles from which "information" becomes effective within the organization are indicated. Reference is made to the assumption that organizations should be considered as living biological organisms in order to attain a sufficiently realistic model of the system "organization".

A discussion of homologies and heterologies between highly developed biological organisms and organizations attempts to shed light on organizational principles within Nature which are perhaps applicable to our organizations.

The problems concerned in the innovation process - i.e., of the actual-nominal transition - are examined more closely. It is pointed out that we are not dealing with innovation processes of the project type, but predominantly with experiments. A catalogue of the main problem areas anticipated with innovation processes provides an aid in illustrating the complex problems facing us here specifically.

Potential objectives for the nominal status of our organizations are presented for discussion. It is pointed out that two overlapping lines of development exist which can be characterized as "use of the computer in the organizational sector" and "information as a basic parameter in Nature".

The question is broached of how far the individual organization is compelled to implement such innovations and whether one should not recommend those concerned to wait and see what course developments will take. Reference is made to the false objectives common today concentrating too much on EDP as well as on the consequences thereof. The fundamental problem is defined as the question: "How can I improve the information system of my organization? ".

Emphasis is laid on the need for systematic operation of an "Information Management System" (also without EDP) and the creation of appropriate institutionalized organs within the organization. It is suggested that the central responsibility for the aspect of the self-comprehension and the self-representation of the organization as well as of the constitutive, behavioural and motivating aspect of information be borne by "Organization Development" to be called into being for this purpose and directly subordinate to the organization management.

It is suggested at the same time that all departments dealing with information handling be combined to form one "Central (Data) Administration". A distinction must be made here between data administration and disposition. This organ shall bear responsibility for the communication, knowledge, control, guidance and logistic aspect of the information system. A potential breakdown of such a modern administration system is discussed.

In conclusion, structuring the organization - in contrast to the divisionalised organizational structure - according to the "principle of mutual dependence through services" is proposed.

References

[1] Bleicher, Knut: Organisation als System. Wiesbaden 1972.

[2] Fuchs, Herbert: Systemtheorie und Organisation. Wiesbaden 1973.

[3] Göhre, Heinz: Innovationen in der Wirtschaftspraxis – Ein Erfahrungsbericht aus der Sicht eines Unternehmens der Luft- und Raumfahrt-Industrie. NRW-Fortschrittsberichte, Heft 146/1973.

[4] Grochla, Erwin: Erkenntnisstand und Entwicklungstendenzen der Organisationstheorie. In: Zeitschrift für Betriebswirtschaft, Vol. 39 1969, pp. 1–22.

[5] Grochla, Erwin: Unternehmungsorganisation – Neue Ansätze und Konzeptionen. Reinbek b. Hamburg 1972.

[6] Kieser, Alfred: Management von Innovationen. In: Innovation in der Wirtschaft. Ifo-Institut für Wirtschaftsforschung. München 1970.

[7] Kieser, Alfred: Voraussetzungen erfolgreicher Innovationen – Ergebnisse empirischer Untersuchungen. NRW-Fortschrittsberichte, Heft 146/1973.

[8] McDonough, A.M.: Information Economics and Management Systems. New York 1963.

[9] Wild, Jürgen: Die Fünf-Milliarden-Verschwendung. In: Wirtschaftswoche. Vol. 27 1973, No. 5, pp. 55–57.

German abstract
Informationssystem und Organisationskonzept – Analyse eines Innovationsprozesses aus der Sicht der Praxis

Von *Heinz Göhre*

Die Ausgangssituation in den sechziger Jahren schien klar. Mit dem Computer stand eine neue technische Erfindung zur Verfügung. Seine Fähigkeit zur Speicherung und Verarbeitung großer Datenmengen versprach einen wirtschaftlichen Nutzen nicht nur auf dem Gebiet wissenschaftlich/technischer Berechnungen, sondern auch im organisatorischen Bereich.

Nach der klassischen Innovationstheorie war zwar mit einigen Widerständen bis zum wirtschaftlichen Durchbruch der automatischen Datenverarbeitung auch auf diesem Gebiet zu rechnen. Diese Widerstände schienen jedoch überwindbar zu sein.

Überraschenderweise waren die auftretenden Schwierigkeiten nach Art und Umfang sehr viel größer als erwartet. In einigen Fällen führten sie zum Fehlschlag der mit großem Elan und erheblichem Aufwand in Angriff genommenen Projekte. Ernüchterung, Mutlosigkeit und Frustration waren die bis heute nicht völlig überwundenen Folgen.

Die geschilderte Entwicklung wird verständlicher, wenn Innovation als „Veränderung von Systemzuständen" betrachtet wird.

Im vorliegenden Fall wird mit der Entwicklung und Einführung computergestützter Informationssysteme die Veränderung des Zustandes des Systems „Organisation" (Wirtschaftsunternehmen, Behörde, sonstige Institution) angestrebt. Dabei ist jede Organisation als Teilsystem des übergeordneten gesellschaftlichen und ökologischen Systems zu betrachten.

Mit der Veränderung eines Teilsystems ist zwangsläufig eine Veränderung der übergeordneten Systeme verbunden (und umgekehrt).

Bei einem Innovationsprozeß auftretende unerwartete Schwierigkeiten lassen sich in diesem Sinne prinzipiell auf folgende Ursachen zurückführen:

– Falsche oder unzureichende, der Beurteilung und Planung zugrunde gelegte Prämissen,
– Falsche Beurteilung des Istzustands des zu verändernden Systems,
– Falsche Beurteilung der beim Innovationsprozeß zu bewältigenden Problematik,
– Falsche Zielsetzung für die angestrebten Sollzustände des Systems,
– Falsche Vorgehensweise bei Grundlegung, Gestaltung und Durchführung des Innovationsprozesses (Methoden, Verfahren, Organisation, Personaleinsatz).

Anhand der vorliegenden praktischen Erfahrungen werden die möglichen Fehlerursachen für den Innovationsprozeß „Entwicklung von Informationssystemen und ihre Einführung in bestehenden Organisationen" unter den oben aufgeführten Gesichtspunkten analysiert.

Die aus dieser Problem-/System-Analyse abzuleitenden Konsequenzen für das Organisationskonzept und für die Gestaltung des Innovationsprozesses werden zur Diskussion gestellt.

Control structure and formalized information analysis in an organization

By *Börje Langefors*

1. A first stage of design work and the first level of the system design

The early phase of analysis/design of an information system has to be very crude in order to cover the whole subsystem, plus enough environment, in a short enough time. However, crude in our methods does not mean vague, it means leaving aside details to be specified later, but being precise in that which is stated. This means that in the crude stage strategic decisions for the project are made. And the crude subsystem structure is checked for workability before further design work. The continued work goes on systematically from the crude design. In this stage the information analysis defines crude information kinds which we refer to as pro-concepts. Succedent design work eventually defines exactly the content of all pro-concepts by specifying all elementary info kinds or e-concepts. A very crude pro-concept may just name a class of properties, e. g. "sales info" or a class of objects, e. g. "customers" but often a class of objects plus a suggestion of properties form together the descriptive name of a pro-concept. Thus in this study we start by specifying a pro-concept by stating that the class of objects it is concerned with is "product group (g), region (r), time period (t)" and the property class is "operational sales goals". We see now that already the specification of this pro-concept raises important decisions to be made by corporate management. Thus management may have told us to design a system for generating sales goals and now we have to respond by asking what classifications are to be used to define the objects to be controlled. According to our pro-concept suggestion above an object for control in this system would be identified by (product group, region, time) = (g, r, t), for any permissible value of g, r and t. Note that this specification of object classifications, already, specifies precisely what aggregated information we shall need to provide in the system, regardless of what kinds of properties of these objects that we will specify later. Note also that by specifying the object classification as stated one, already, defines an important organizational structuring and an info structuring as well. We assume that as a starting point we are given the task of studying or designing a (sub)system as specified.

1.1 System specification

An information system that will generate proposals for corporate goals for Sales and Marketing, suitable for goal steering of these operations. (With "corporate goals" we mean goals to be used by corporate management to coordinate the major parts of the enterprise.)

1.2 Steering objects

Objects for goal steering: product groups per regions, twice a year.

1.3 System design

Use information precedence analysis to aid in drafting a candidate subsystem structure (or a number of alternative subsystem structures).
Remark: Info precedence analysis is a method that takes advantage of the fact that it is possible to find potential info precedents of any specified crude information kind (pro-concept) without the need for analysis and specification of the information processing involved. The results are not unique and need not to be. But, of course, a unique choice has to be made.

1.4 First step of precedence analysis (on the crudest level)

Terminal pro-concept (crude system output info)

* Operational sales goals (g, r, t) for product group (g), region (r) and time period (t) – where "t" will be set at each execution.

1.5 List of precedents of operational goals (g, r, t)

* Forecasts possible sales (g, r, t);
* Other forecasts, e. g. production (g, r, t); (initial)
* Other corporate operational goals, e. g. production (g, r, t); (initial)
* Other corporate plans of relevance here; (initial)

  Note

  "(initial)" is used to indicate that the info in question is provided from outside the present subsystem.

2. Second step of precedence analysis

Having obtained a list of pro-concepts which are potential precedents of the system output we can now take the second step by finding, in turn, lists of precedents for all these pro-concepts. We note that all of them except one have been tagged "(initial)". Thus the pro-concept "Forecast possible sales (g, r, t)" is the only one for which we have to determine further precedents, in a second step.

2.1 List of precedents of forecast possible sales (g, r, t)

* Earlier sales results (g, r, t');
* Market states (g, r, t'); (initial)
* Economical development (t'); (initial)
* Forecasting models
  (t' = set of earlier time periods relative to "actual time".
  t' is determined by the forecast model used.)

3. Third step

3.1 List of precedents of earlier sales results (g, r, t')

* Earlier individual sales results (per article, per place, date) (initial);
* Definitions of product groups and regions (initial)

Now the analysis of the first, crudest, level is complete (as far as the path chosen for illustration is concerned). Thus "Earlier individual sales' results" are data to be collected or retrieved from the data base and input to the present system. The results so far are shown in Fig. 1.

In Fig. 1 is used a graphical "description language" which is seen to be equivalent to the description by lists which is another "description language". Both these languages have the important advantage, at this stage of analysis/design that they contain no "implementation oriented" elements and thus are intelligible to users without expert knowledge of computers. This is also important for the reason that it would be highly unsuitable to suggest implementation deoisions at this stage. Of the two description languages the lists are more flexible but users ask for the graphs. Graphs are troublesome to change which makes it important to have computer assistance, so that the computers can re-draw graphs. A third, useful, "description language" is the use of system matrices. Note that it is not the question of which language to use. Each has its advantages so all three ought to be available for use in distinct situations. Their logical equivalence makes it easy to change between them. Note that by taking advantage of the fact that the computing processes need no separate symbols in the descriptions we greatly simplify the documents which enhances the possibility for overview and thus magnify our capacity for system design.

Note that already at this level (Fig. 1) has a number of key decisions been brought up, to be tackled by corp. management early enough to enable a careful decision-making. For instance:

* Which of the indicated precedents of "Forecast possible sales" (or possible less expensive substitutes) are to be used or, rather, at what cost should they still be used?

- * Are there other information kinds that are relevant?
- * Which product groups are to be defined?
- * Which object classification is to be used (what regions, what time periods)?
- * How is “corporate plans“ to influence the sales goals?
- *** Is the system as drafted a workable system with respect to the system specification?

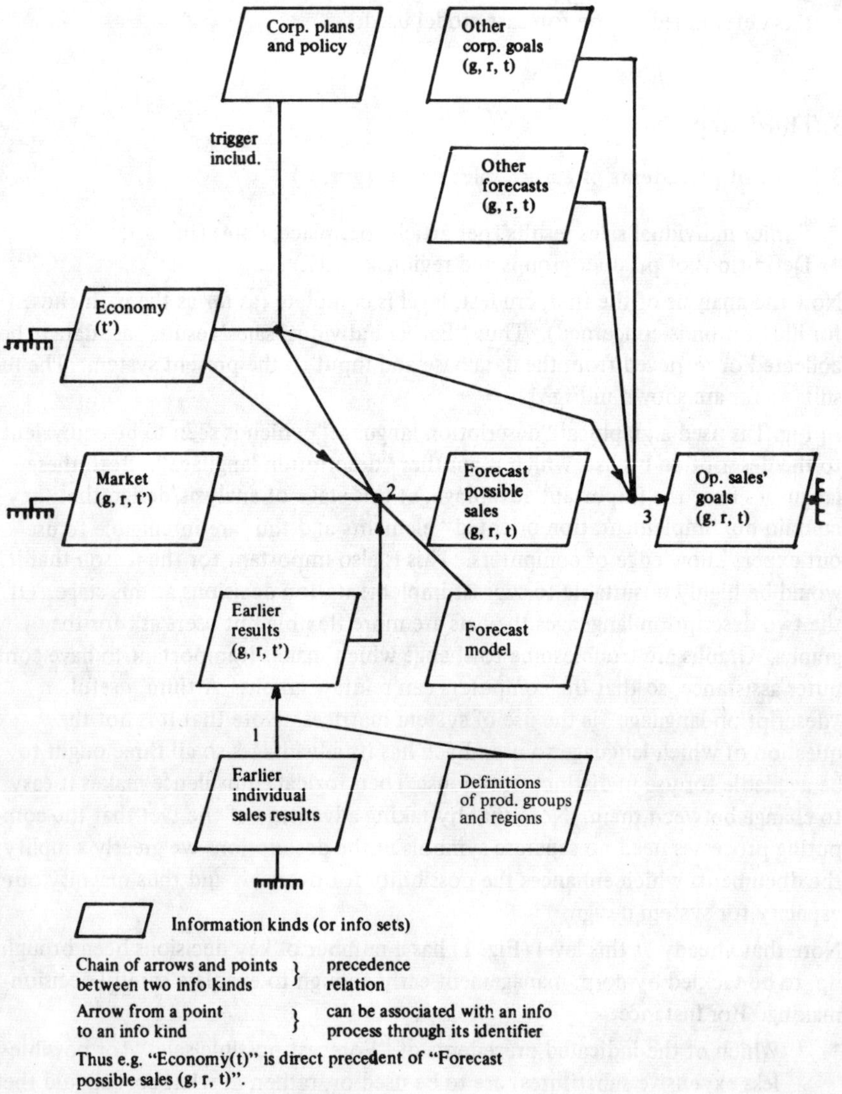

Fig. 1. Graphical “description language”

If these questions are not handled properly before further design work is done, and with proper management involvement, failure is to be expected. We have obtained here an analytic illustration of why so many systems have been failures, as it is typical of common work not to handle these problems properly.

4. Workability diagnosis

By using the information precedence analysis method we have constructed the subsystem structure in a way which proceeds systematically and at the same time gives a systematic workability "guarantee" from a technical point-of-view. However to check workability of a goal proposal system we should also check against available knowledge about how to use goals for steering. We shall see that by doing so we find that the system as specified so far is not workable.

First, however, we shall make some observations regarding the info need that we have specified.

In Fig. 1 "Forecast possible sales (g, r, t)" and "Earlier sales results (g, r, t')" appear as local to the present system. However, characteristic of information system design, contrary to traditional EDP routine design, is to consider information of general utility as "belonging" to the whole system. "General utility" is about equivalent, at this stage, to "generally meaningful information" (within the total object system, e. g. the company). Both of the pro-concepts mentioned are of this kind and, thus, are to be available to the whole system. That they are shown as internal to this system indicates that this system would have to be responsible for their production and storing in the system. One must then, however, check whether they are already required or produced by other subsystems. This can be done by inspection of the total precedence matrix (Thais). But if this matrix is not (yet) available one still has to see whether they should rather be produced by some other subsystems. We may conclude that we had better enter a separate subsystem which computes the aggregate info "Earlier sales' results (g, r, t')" and store it in the info system (the data base if you like). In this way we are able to trigger this production independently of the production of "Operational sales goals" to satisfy other, possible needs. On the other hand it is easy to see that the info "Earlier sales' results" is indeed needed elsewhere as it is needed already in the goal steering system itself, of which the present system is a subsystem. Thus it is fundamental to goal steering to establish results info to compare with set goals. By our systems analysis approach we thus were able to avoid the duplicated (and possibly multiple) production of the info "Earlier sales' results". As this aggregation will be a fairly large retrieval and processing operation this was an important advantage obtained from systematic analysis. In the common, less stringent way of system design, this advantage is likely to have been missed and, in fact, this kind of mistakes is common.

What we have said about "Earlier sales' result" may also be true for "Forecast possible sales (g, r, t)". We leave this subject however.

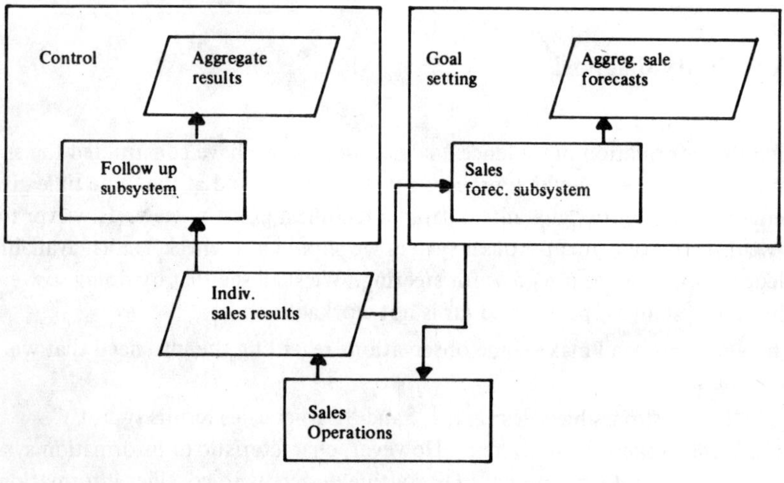

Fig. 2a. Expected results of traditional design, where workability diagnosis is ignored.

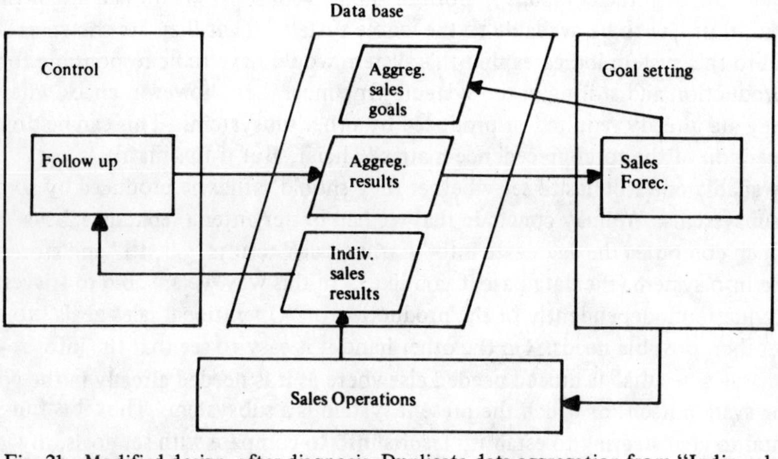

Fig. 2b. Modified design, after diagnosis. Duplicate data aggregation from "Indiv. sales results" is avoided.

5. Goals are to be negotiated. This calls for information to all concerned.

An important factor in checking our design (subsystem structure) for workability is whether it satisfies known conditions for suitable goal structuring. In turning to this problem we note that goals are not only logical means for rational coordination and action. They are also means for motivating people. The logical function of the goals fails if the psychological/social function is not handled satisfactorily. Thus the latter function is necessary for workability. It is known from theory and praxis of goal steering (or "management by objectives") that only if those who are to fulfil the goals have accepted them as theirs will the goals have their intended effects. We see that our design did not consider this point. Before corporate management can decide on the goals to set for the "Sales-function" they will have to negotiate them with the management of "Sales". "Sales" will then need to see what the goals would mean for the different units within "Sales". We assumed that corporate management decided to set sales goals for product groups/regions/semiannually and assume now that, in their turn, sales management wants to set goals instead for product groups/districts/monthly (i. e. (g, d, t")) where "districts" are parts of "regions". But again, these goals need be negotiated (this time, with individual salesmen). Thus goals should also be generated for product groups/salesmen/weeks or (g, s, t"').

We have found, as a result of our workability check, that the goal generating system should generate and distribute goal information as shown in Fig. 3. If there are e. g. 10 districts per region and 10 time periods t" per time period t and if there are 10 salesmen per district and five time periods t"' per period t" we find that there are 100 times more objects in the set (g, d, t") than in (g, r, t) and there are 50 times more objects in (g, s, t"') than in (g, d, t") so that there are about 5000 more objects to treat by our system than first drafted, just because of the need to support negotiation of the goals. Further, the negotiation procedure will also require an iteration of the whole goal generation procedure, one or several times. Of course it is important to detect such a requirement for drastic change in system design as early as we did thanks to the workability review. This is the more so as the corresponding changes occur in the precedent pro-concept: "Earlier demands". As these are obtained through aggregation, a lot of data processing work is saved by computing first "Earlier demands (g, s, t"')" and then, through aggregation of these, compute "Earlier demands (g, d, t")" and, then through further aggregation "Earlier demands (g, r, t)".

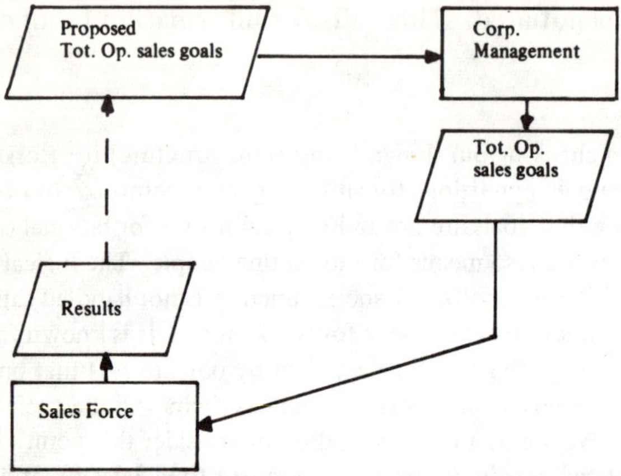

Fig. 3a. Goal system structure from traditional design, where workability diagnosis is ignored.

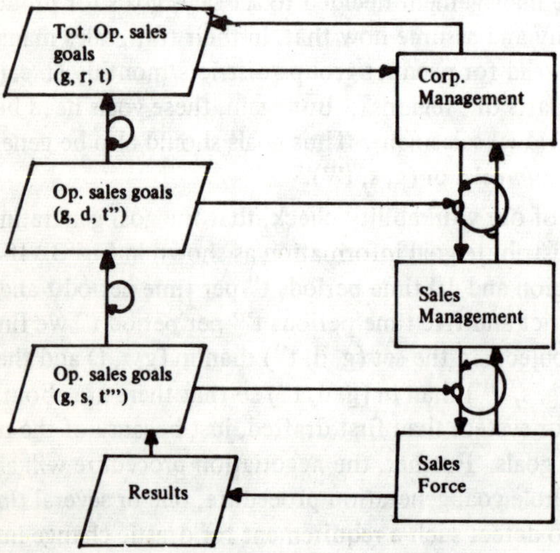

Fig. 3b. Goal system structure after workability diagnosis.

6. Component analysis – more detailed info structure

After the first and crudest level info structure has been completed and carefully reviewed for workability by the intended system user (corporate management in this case) then (and only then) it is time to specify more details. Thus we take the necessary steps to transfer to the next, finer, level. The first step in this transfer also involves the user (corporate management). It consists of specifying more details of what information components are to constitute the terminal information (pro-concept) which was earlier only indicated by the property kind "Operating sales goals" and by the indication of the object classification "(g, r, t)". Thus we now specify what component goals the user wants to have in the system. To simplify we assume the following, short list[1]:

6.1 Components list of Operating sales goals (g, r, t) (terminal pro-concept)

* Amount sold (g, r, t),
* Profit contribution (r, t),
* Market share (g, r, t),
* Company image (r, t).

Having taken part in this first step towards the second level, as well as in the work on the first level, the user might now want to be able to delegate to the systemeers (= systems analysts and designers) to continue the work of completing the second level, guided by the first level specification plus the list of terminal components (as well as working through further levels).

In the present example (and usually) the user management will have to be partially involved also in the further work on the second level as well as in its workability checking. Thus once the components of the terminal pro-concept "Operational sales goals" have been defined we repeat the precedents analysis, applying it now to all the terminal components (bottom block in Fig. 4).

Thereby the subsystem associated with the arrow "3" in Fig. 1 becomes the subsystem block "3" in Fig. 4[2] containing the arrows 31 – 34. We see, for instance, that the new terminal component pro-concept "Profit contribution" requires the new information precedent "Profit contribution/item" and it is probably necessary to have the user management involved in its further specification. In Fig. 4 we see that the first step of precedence analysis on level 2 introduced 3 new info kinds (Profit contribution/item, Forec. market, Market). Further analysis now requires precedence analysis from these three new pro-concepts. It also requires component analysis of the earlier precedents (Forec. poss. sales, Corp. plans, other Corp. goals) followed by precedence analysis from these ten components.

---

1 A somewhat more extensive list with comments was presented by the author in the BIFOA conference 1970: see [2].

2 Fig's 4 and 5 are drawn in a way similar to a proposal by [3] with the main modification being that we attach the subsystem identifiers to the lines between a point and an info block, rather than to the point (according to a suggestion by Ola Langefors). This allows a more concise graph. For instance 31 and 32 of Fig. 4 start at the same point and could therefore not be identified at the point. In this way the precedents of an info block are the precedents of all its precedent points.

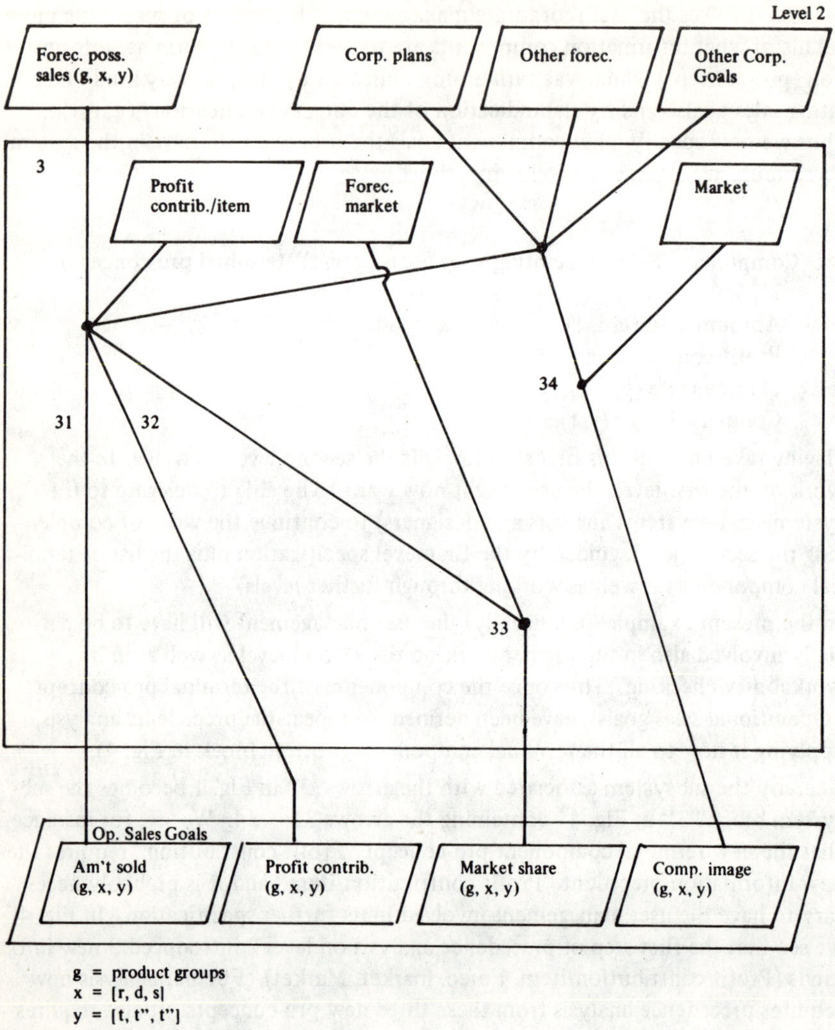

Fig. 4. Precedents Analysis – all terminal components

We illustrate this further analysis only from "Forecast poss. sales". The component analysis of "Forecast poss. sales" merely leads to replacing it with "Forecast possible amount sold (g, x, y)". This is to say we are already down to an elementary information kind here, an e-concept, which cannot be broken down further. It follows that the precedents ought to be identical to those found already in level 1, Fig. 1. Those, however, are now, in this level (level 2), to be broken down into components. In Fig. 5 we have done this component analysis which leads an expansion of the precedence bundle No. 2 (in Fig. 1), which is now the bundle of "Forecast possible amount sold (g, x, y)". It is shown in Fig. 5 that for e. g. "Market" the two components "Branch sales" and "Market coverage" are defined. For "Earlier sales' results (g, r, t)" we introduced an additional pro-concept, rather than splitting it into components. Thus a new pro-concept "Earlier" was obtained which contains "Earlier demand" and "Earlier sales' results" as components. Further the precedence bundle "2" thus expanded is now split into a set of smaller bundles 21 – 24 which are all described in Fig. 5 as belonging to the subsystem 2.

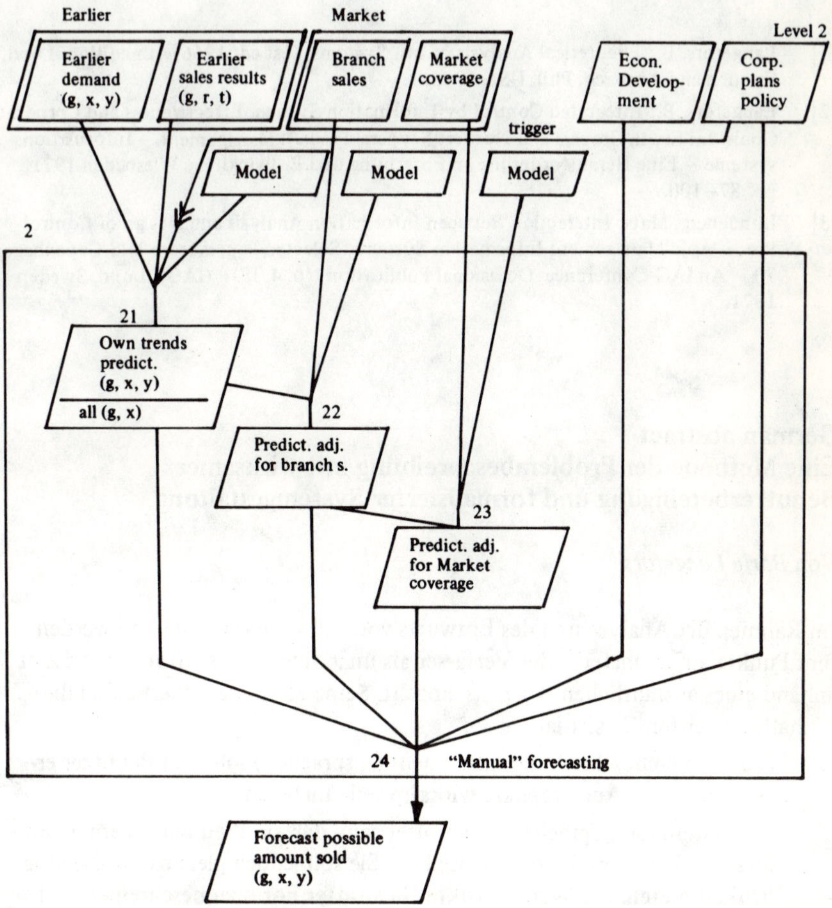

Fig. 5. Specification of the e-process 21

The new bundle (or subsystem) 21 is now an elementary bundle in the sense that all its terminal concepts and its two data precedents are all e-concepts. Thus the next design step may be to specify the e-process for 21 and those of the data involved that are not already specified.

It should be obvious that in some parts of the system our analysis has already led us down to simple subsystems for which the implementation (including mathematical modelling and computer programming) is quite straight-forward. This is the case, for instance, with the subsystem 21 (Fig. 5).

References

[1] Langefors, B.: Theoretical Analysis of Inf. Systems. (1st ed. 1966) 4th edition. Lund, Sweden and Aurbach, Phil. USA 1973.

[2] Langefors, B.: Integrated Control by Information System. Effectiveness and Corporate Goals. In: Erwin Grochla and Norbert Szyperski (eds.): Management – Informationssysteme – Eine Herausforderung an Forschung und Entwicklung. Wiesbaden 1971, pp. 87–100.

[3] Lundeberg, Mats: Interaction Between Information Analysis and Design of Control Processes in Management Information Systems. Selected Papers from MIS Copenhagen 70 – An IAG-Conference, Occasional Publication No. 4, IFIP (IAG), Lund, Sweden 1971.

German abstract
Eine Methode der Problembeschreibung mit wirksamer Benutzerbeteiligung und formalisierter Systemgestaltung

Von *Börje Langefors*

Im Rahmen der Analyse und des Entwurfs von Informationssystemen werden fünf Punkte aufgeführt, die der Verfasser als unabdingbar ansieht und auf die er anhand eines ausführlichen Beispiels eingeht. Seine Methode sichert dabei die Einhaltung der fünf Essentials:

(1) Ein Problembeschreibungsinstrument (-„sprache“) soll dem Benutzer erlauben, an der Analysephase wirksam teilzunehmen.

Dabei muß die „Sprache“ so gestaltet sein, daß sie allen Benutzern erlaubt, ihre Probleme mit ihr zu beschreiben. Sie soll jedoch gleichzeitig die Möglichkeit bieten, die Systemstruktur in straffer Form zu beschreiben und zu analysieren (Graphen, Listen, Matrizen). Die Analysearbeit muß dabei in Phasen eingeteilt werden und die Systemstruktur bis hin zur Programmstruktur in Stufen (levels) und Moduln.

(2) Die richtige Strukturierung und die Realitätsnähe der Beschreibung und sich ergebender Entwürfe müssen durch eine hierarchisch modulare Vorgehensweise, die schließlich in der strukturierten (normierten) Programmierung endet, gesichert werden.

Dabei wird die Systembeschreibung in der ersten Phase sehr grob sein. Die Art der Beschreibung ermöglicht jedoch schon inhaltliche Prüfungen (workability) und dies sogar in der Weise, daß dieser Gestaltungslevel gleichzeitig Rahmen – und damit Kontrolle – der nächsten Level ist. Auf diese Weise sind sehr frühzeitig Wünsche des Management integrierbar, die sich schließlich bis zur Programmebene auswirken können.

(3) Sinnvolle inhaltliche Prüfungen und Fehlerbeseitigungen müssen schon in den ersten Phasen der Gestaltungsarbeit durchgeführt werden können.

Damit ergibt sich über Punkt (2) hinaus gleichzeitig die Möglichkeit, schon auf der ersten Stufe sinnvolle Konsistenzprüfungen durchzuführen. Fehler auf der ersten Stufe werden also nicht in tiefer gegliederte Stufen übernommen, ein Sachverhalt der bei den gängigen Systemanalysemethoden keineswegs vermeidbar ist.

(4) Die Art der Analyse muß einen dauernden Abgleich zwischen der Informationssystemstruktur und der Organisationsstruktur ermöglichen.

Diese Methode erlaubt das durch ihre formalisierte Arbeitsweise und durch ihre formalisierten Prüfungen, die auch gegen die Entscheidungsstruktur und damit Organisationsstruktur der Unternehmung durchführbar sind: eine Harmonisierung von Informationsstruktur und Organisationsstruktur findet statt.

(5) Die Vollständigkeit der Analyse – und Entwurfsmethodologie muß gesichert sein; es muß also gewährleistet sein, daß durch diese Methode die wirklichen Bedürfnisse der Unternehmung bei der Implementierung zur Geltung kommen.

Wenn Langefors auch nicht den Schwerpunkt auf diesen Punkt legt, so ist durch die Beteiligung des Benutzers von Anfang an gewährleistet, daß sich die Benutzerspezifikationen in Anforderungen an Dateien, Datenbänke und Verarbeitungsprozeduren usw. niederschlagen, die dann eine problemadäquate Grundlage für die Programmierung darstellen.

The FOUR-FLOWS MODEL as a tool for designing the information system of an organization

By *Jean Louis Le Moigne*

1. Small computer systems with direct access, large mass memories: New fact for management

The image of informatics in an organization has been until now an image of complexity; for many people, the installation of a computer has had the result of rendering intelligible for them something which was previously (for them) simple or at least comprehensible. An apparently minor technological innovation, the development of small information systems with direct access, large mass memories at a small cost, is going to solidly transform this image, making us discover once again, that according to the words of H.A. Simon [9, p.2], "a new wonder arises at how complexity was woven out of simplicity".

It is a known fact that a medium sized organization (let us say less than five hundred people) can have at its disposal today, for the sum of $ 100,000, equipment comprising for example: a central processing unit with 16 or 32 k bytes of core, a direct access mass memory unit of 10 to 50 million bytes, a tape cassette or a paper tape reader, a card reader, medium speed printer and 5 to 10 teletype or visual display terminals permitting in particular the gathering of data-on-line (see Fig. 1). This configuration allows the utilization of the classical language compilers (COBOL, FORTRAN, Conversational BASIC for example) and permits the storage of important files and a library of commonly used programmes. The exploitation of this system requires little by way of personnel and turns out to be relatively simple. Most managers and employees of the organization easily get used to manipulate the terminals, and the new image of informatics which takes shape becomes as a result rather profoundly transformed: "not only is it not expensive, and will become less and less so, they tell us, but it is no longer complicated (at least for the user)".

This new image is still spreading slowly, as slowly but as surely as the growing perception of the utility of small systems for the management of organizations. Numerous indeed are those information system specialists who are trying to put the brakes on this spread: experts in complexities, perceived or real, it is not in their best interests to encourage a transformation which reveals certain underlying simplicities, proving the uselessness of their intervention between the members and the information of the organization.

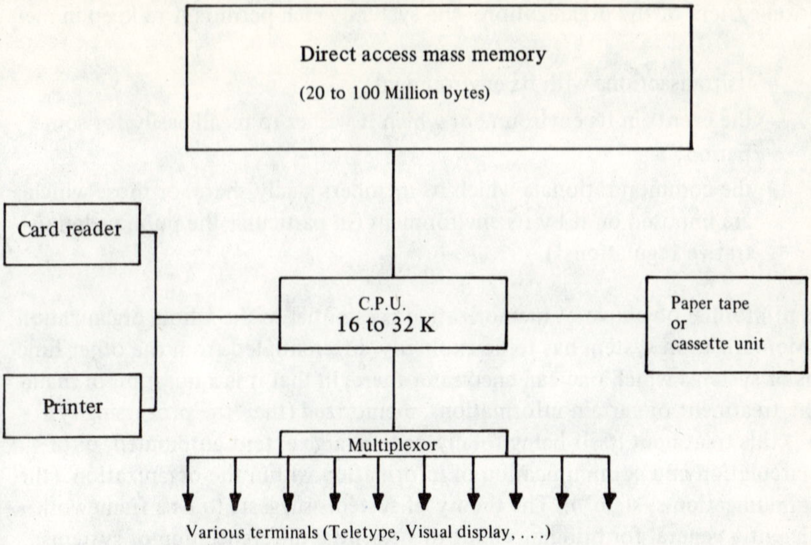

Fig. 1. Computer configuration satisfying the needs of an average organization (cost less than $ 120.000)

This resistance finds support in another image, complementary without doubt to the preceding. Even if they agree that COMPUTER systems become simpler for the user, managers asked themselves about the INFORMATION system of the organization; and the articles which they read on automation of the design process, on sophisticated data processing packages, on the distinctions between organic and functional analysis, on the wide varieties of management information systems, convince them of this new and growing complexity: that of the information system or at least that of the analysis and design of the system. The "comptrollers" who propose to christen these information systems as CONTROL systems do not contribute one supposes, to clarify the debate.

2. A "simple" theory of the information system of an organization

It nevertheless seems possible today to propose a framework which is simple, general, and practical, for first defining and then designing the information system of an organization. To ease the burden of the presentation by avoiding nuances which necessitate the discussion of particular cases, we will consider here only an average relatively classical organization, the type most frequently encountered. The information system can in effect be considered as the memorization system of the organization: the system which permits it to keep in memory:

- its transactions with its environment;
- the events in its environment which it wishes to recall easily for some period;
- the common rationale which its members gladly share, or those which are imposed on it by its environment (in particular the public administrative regulations!).

This primordial objective of memorization is essential to the whole organization: the Memorization system has to be explicitly differentiated from the other functions or systems which one can encounter there; in that it is a question of mainly the treatment of certain informations, memorized (the "the processing system") this treatment itself being totally or to a large extent automated, or of the circulation and communication of information within the organization (the "communication system"). The theory of systems suggests to us a framework sufficiently general for bringing about this essential differentiation of systems, which some people still believe useful to present as the unique central nervous system of the human organism generalized to the level of the organization. (We adopt here the distinction between the terms organism and organization suggested by Boulding (1956) or Ackoff [2]). The myth of a unique organizational control system defined by a simplistic extrapolation of the nervous system of an organism has, it seems to us, been pushed long enough. Today we can constrast it with the general framework of a set of autonomous systems, having their own objectives, their own boundaries, and their own functions. These systems are:

1. An information system, having the mission of collecting, storing, and retrieving information (representation of facts or reasoning) with the aid of supports commonly called "data and program banks".
2. Systems aiming to produce information for a quasi-legal usage, often called "automated administrative systems", which fetch from the information system the raw material on which they are fed. (Those systems are often called "E.D.P. systems" in many business organizations!)
3. Decision systems, common to the entire organization. These include the planning – programming and budgeting (surveillance) system, often called the control system, and others, much more "personalized", conceived and installed at the pleasure of each manager. These systems also draw a very large part of their input from the information system.
4. A communication system, finally, usually called an organizational flowchart, or organization structure. It defines a certain number of procedures for the communication of information between the decision systems; that is to say,

between the managers of the organization, all also connected to the same information system.

Fig. 2 succinctly summarizes this analysis. It minimizes the totalitarian integrator role sometimes conferred on the information system. But it is not in fact the memory which coordinates. This mission is without doubt less noble than that of the integrated system, but it is better defined and by the same token more realistic.

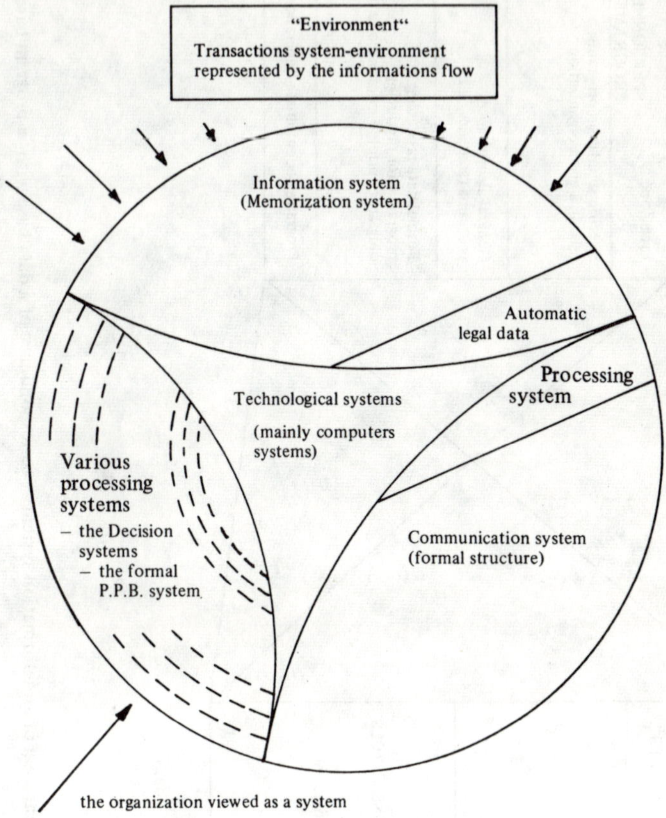

Fig. 2. Representation of information, decision, automatic processing and communication systems within the organization

This differentiation between the systems of memorization, processing and communication of the information within the organization turns out to be simple and at the same time operational. It leads most notably to the distinction between the task of the manager, who seeks to create new decision rationales from that of the computer specialist, who has the mission of storing and permitting access to those previously developed rationales which can usefully be stored.

Likewise, it underlines the necessity for a memorization of information which interests the organization without imposing immediately the biases or personal filters of the manager, who first recalls such or such fact (and we all know that this first rememberance is often if not always the financial or accounting figure requested by the powerful "comptroller"!).

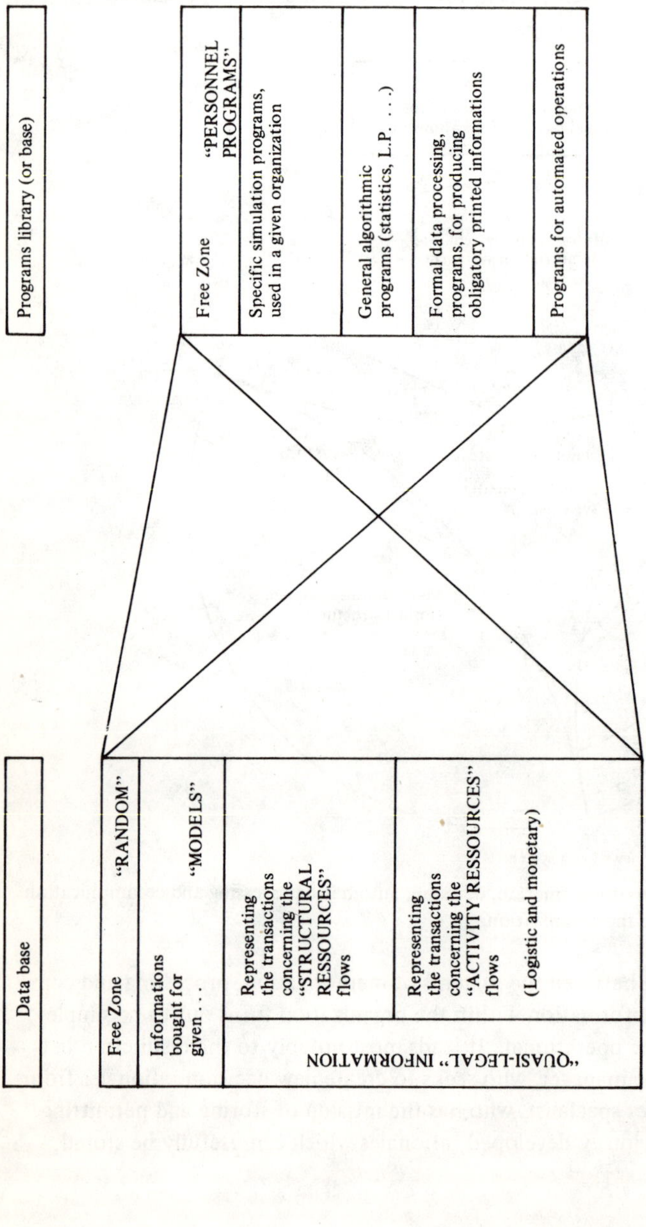

Fig. 3. Pictorial representation of an information system – correspondence of a data base with a program base

This differentiation leads to a new image of the information system, summarized in Fig. 3.: the permanent correspondence between a data bank - representation of the relationship between the organization and its environment - (see [6, p.44]) and a program – bank a reservoir of programmed models with the managers want to keep in memory and to which they wish easy access.

The differentiation likewise permits one to demonstrate one of the specific characteristics of decision systems, a characteristic which both the experts in operational research and the sellers of time sharing seem to neglect quite often. Whether it is a question of budget, of plan, of operational control, or of the analysis which a manager makes prior to taking a decision, the rationale he uses is not "self-contained", as contrasted with the rationale of a researcher in a scientific laboratory or an engineering firm. We reproduce here the interesting illustration of this difference proposed by J.C. Emery (see Fig. 4). In management,

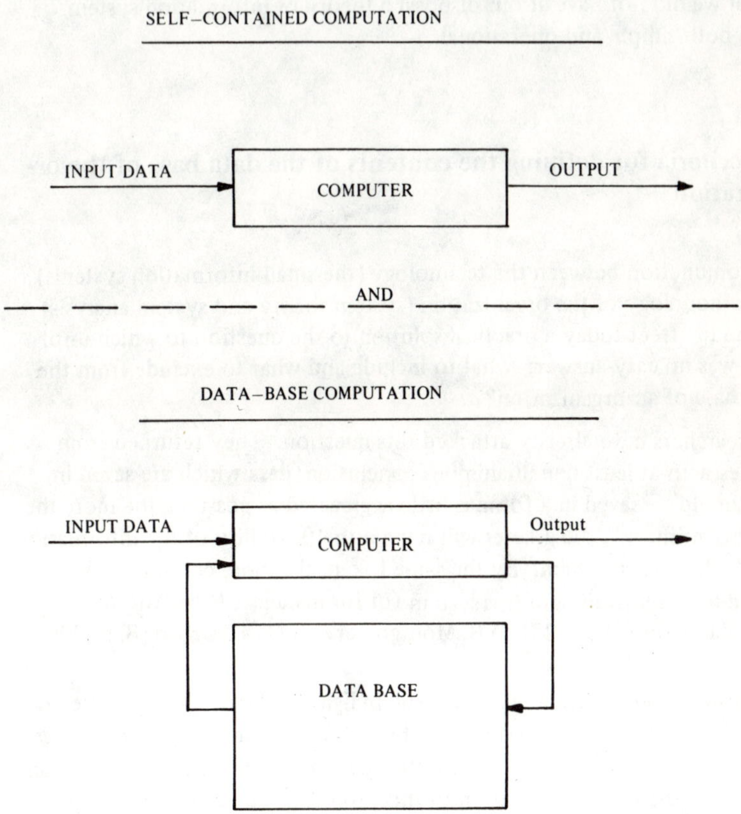

Fig. 4. Self-contained computation and data base computation (taken from J.C. Emery – [4, p. 493])

the reasoning behind a decision takes roots not only in current facts or ideas (self-contained computation) but also and above all in numerous other facts which are stored in the data bank, (artificial memory of the organization). The rationale for the decision is built on this data bank ("data base computation").

The theory of information systems (systems of organizational memorization) with which we are thus left has, it seems, the merit of simplicity. If some decision rationales and administrative regulations complex to automate, not all of them are. And this possible complexity will probably affect only some of the decision systems (planning, automation of administration, etc.) but it will not concern the information system as such. Moreover, this conceptual simplicity leaves a fundamental question in the shadows: what are the criteria which are at the disposal of the organization for defining the contents of the data bank which constitute the essential element of its information system? It is probably because this question has not until now received a satisfactory economic response that we did not have at our disposal a theory of information system which was both simple and operational.

3. The criteria for defining the contents of the data base of the organization

A happy conjunction between the technology (the small information systems) and the methodology of the organization (system theory and system analysis) permits one to effect today a practical solution to the question to which until now there was no easy answer: what to include and what to exclude from the data bank base of an organization?

Several researchers have already attacked this question. They returned from their studies with at least one unanimous conclusion; data which are saved in memory, should be saved in a form as little aggregated as possible; the more the data remain "primary", the greater will remain the flexibility of the information systems which maintain them. By the same token, the more certain will be the survival and the effectiveness of this system (of for instance: R.N. Antony [3, p. 119], Z.S. Zannetos [10, p. 22], D.B. Montgomery and G.L. Urban [8, p. 209], J.C. Emery [6, p. 49]).

This conclusion would seem a bit unrealistic in light of the cost of mass memory until the last few years. However, J.C. Emery noticed the change in progress when he said: "The ability to store primitive data and aggregate them on an ad-hoc basis offers the only real solution to this problem. To be sure, the technical requirements for such a system are quite demanding, but they are by no means beyond present capabilities. It is becoming increasingly feasible to store, retrieve, and manipulate vast quantities of detailed data. These advances strongly militate in favor of maintaining a much more detailed data base than formerly feasible".

The technological evolution of the small systems with direct access large mass memory that we emphasize in section 1, confirms, four years later, the tendency which Emery noticed. Whoever has experience in a medium-sized organization will agree that the necessary memory capacity will be between 20 and 200 million bytes, that is to say, in the range of capacity normally and economically supported by small computer systems. We favor here the information which managers are likely to require directly and unexpectedly. It is quite evident that the usual mass memory devices (magnetic disks, cassettes, tapes, paper tapes, punched cards, ...) permit us to carry the capacity of the memory to infinity but impose constraints on the speed of access. In general these constraints are acceptable when it is possible to program in advance the desired period of access to the "old rememberances". If the technology permits one to enlarge the capacity of the artificial memory of the organization, a thousand times, memory directly and economically accessible, the methodology engendered by the systems analysis permits one to define a selection screen which separates that information which the organization must - or wants to - keep in memory from the unceasing flood of information which circulates in the world. The theory of open systems in fact teaches the essential role of the "input variables" and "output variables" in the understanding and behavioral orientation of a given system. The transactions between the system and its environment are even the instrument of a knowledge of a system. One observes that the system always tries to keep in memory, with priority, its own experiences in its relations with the "rest of the world". These are exceedingly important for a system, and the theory confirms the reasons which justify an effort toward favoured memorizations of these transactions. This is the result of its permanent adaptations which are necessitated by an often changing environment and by multiple objectives. This privileged role of the transactions at the boundary (not at all numerous with regard to the innumerable other inter-relationships which muddle the internal system and its environment) are going to prove extremely significant for the analyst who seeks to define - or to select - the information which the organization must collect with high priority in its data base.

If in fact we accept the today familiar representation of the organization as an open system, we can in general very easily localize these transactions of the "system-organization" with its environment. We even notice that in a fashion remarkably general, nearly all organizations seek to establish a representation of each of these transactions and to record this representation on a physical device (paper, magnetic device, ...). This permits us to define a family of information types: those which represent the transactions system - environment. We say "represent"; in fact, without exception, the transaction concerns an object independent of the information which represents it (it concerns material goods, services, monetary values, personnel, equipment). This family of information is original to different aspects for the organization which emits it each time it interacts with its environment.

The information is really "primary"; that is to say, it does not result from a combination of other information. Most typical is a customer order: information is born at the moment it arrives in an organization.

It is all specific to the organization. From the flood of information which circles the planet, this information would not exist if the organization at whose boundaries it has been generated did not exist. (Thus a country ceases to exist - at least in the eyes of an economist - when the customs agents stop representing by statistical information the input-output transactions which characterize its foreign trade!).

On the other hand, it is generated in a generally very small number of locations. We know that an organization is a partially open system. A location where a transaction can physically arise, such transactions characterizing the input and output of the system which come from and goes to its environment are, in most cases, easy to list: the back door of the factory, the lobby for the offices, the mail room, etc. In these places, or nearby, or in those places which are easily related to the telecommunication network, it is possible to gather information, which is to say: to establish a formal representation of the transaction which is produced there. It is for this reason that we propose to christen these places the "generators of information-transactions" (or primary information).

They have finally a characteristic which is going to prove decisive for the global economies of the information systems: the gathering of these information - transactions on a physical device (at least paper) is imposed by legal or quasi-legal considerations defined by the environment. (The environment also wishes to know the activity of the organization-system, and it knows that it is sufficient to be interested in the transactions at the boundaries). One can scarcely sell without an invoice, and without a delivery notice; one can scarcely deliver anything without an order slip; one can scarcely make an employee work without a payroll voucher ... there are as many representations (by information) as there are system-environment transactions. These informations, in a very large number of cases, must not only be gathered (recorded) but they must also be memorized. Copies of invoices must be saved for at least five years in France, for example. (Everyone knows the importance which the institution has placed for a long time on its journal in the accounting system as an exclusively monetary representation of all the transactions of the organization system with its environment, each entry being presumed to represent a transaction).

The concept of information - representation of the transactions of the system with its environment and the related concept of the generators of primary information, constitute the criteria for selecting the informations which we sought for creating the data bank of the organization (the living image of a continuing relationship). This criterion is going to prove valuable for guiding the task of the analyst charged with the design of the corresponding information system. It remains to illustrate succinctly the procedures of implementation: the technique of analysis for locating the generators of primary information.

4. The four-flows model: Tool for locating generators of primary information and organization of the data base

Research on the "generators of information transactions", of which production must be first channelled into the data bank, is going to be greatly facilitated by a framework whose permanence has astonished all the researchers who have considered it. It describes major types of relatively homogeneous flows which traverse the organization system issuing from and returning to its environment: flows of resources, in the broad sense of the term, which the organization removes from its environment, manages, and transforms before returning them there.

It was J.W. Forrester [7], who, it seems to us, was the first to identify these flows. At the end of quite different analyses, Blumenthal [5] and Ackoff [1] arrive also at the same conclusions: conclusions whose simplicity astonishes and reassures! Each member element of these flows, traversing and then being transformed by the system-organization, causes a transaction when it crosses the boundary of the system, either at input or output. These are the transactions which could and which should be represented by "primary informations" (in the sense defined in Section 3). The theory of systems brings here also a general framework for presenting these four flows, by the distinction which it makes between the activity (or performance) variables and the structural variables of B. Gross, 1966. The first of these circulate in general at great speed (leading to the large frequency of emission of the resultant transaction information); the second by way of contrast have a low speed. Essentially, the "logistic flows" (raw material, finished products, services) and the monetary flows will be the variables characterizing the activity, or the performance of the organization system; the "personnel flows" and the "flows of asset elements" (included are the intangible assets such as the client files and product files, for example) characterize usually the structure of the organization. The measurement of the frequency of emission of each of the "information generators" will clearly permit the several reclassifications which the diversity of organizations will cause in the generality of this model. This measurement is in general among the simplest to make. It is sufficient to request the clerk in charge of the management of printing to determine the speed of each type of printed goods in his charge. Many of them have in fact been designed for gathering transaction data; (invoices, order slips, employment folders, deposit slips, etc.).

We will not give a detailed discussion here of the specific contents of each of these flows. Interesting when it is done on a concrete example, this discussion rapidly becomes boring when presented in general terms.

Figure 5 presents this model in the classical form of systems analysis, and Figure 6 points out the generation of the information associated with the transactions initiated by the elements of the diverse flows into and out of the boundaries of the system-organization. Each transaction is represented by a piece of information which is immediately collected by a new flow, artificial and independent of the precedents. Forrester has perfectly identified this flow of transaction (while differentiating a little arbitarily, it seems to us, one particular flow, that of "orders"; in other words, that flow representing the transactions for the exit of finished goods, exits relevant to the logistic flow in the models which we have picked[1].

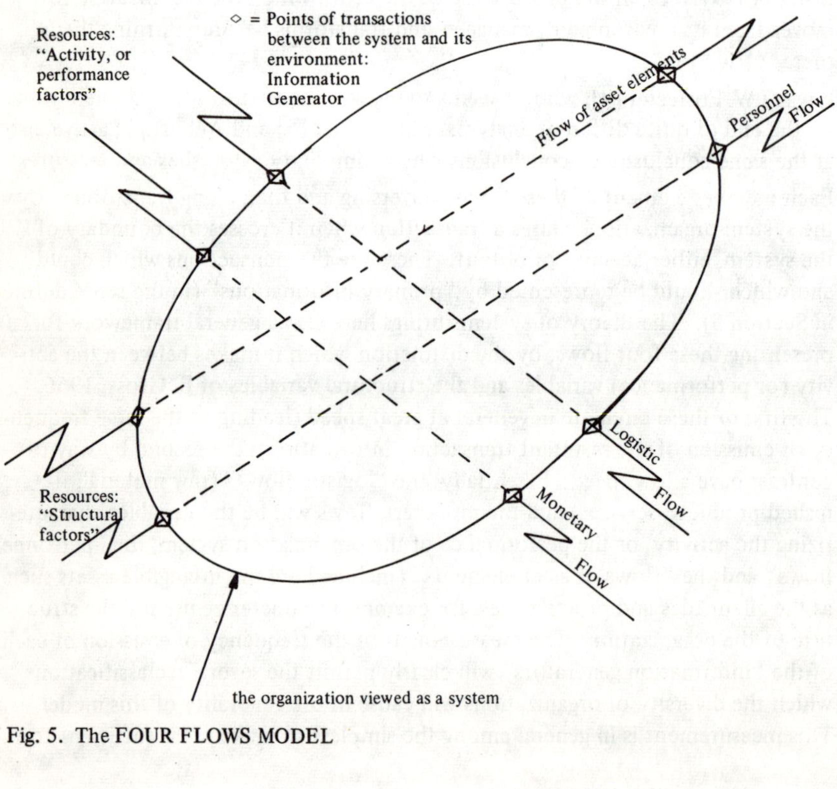

Fig. 5. The FOUR FLOWS MODEL

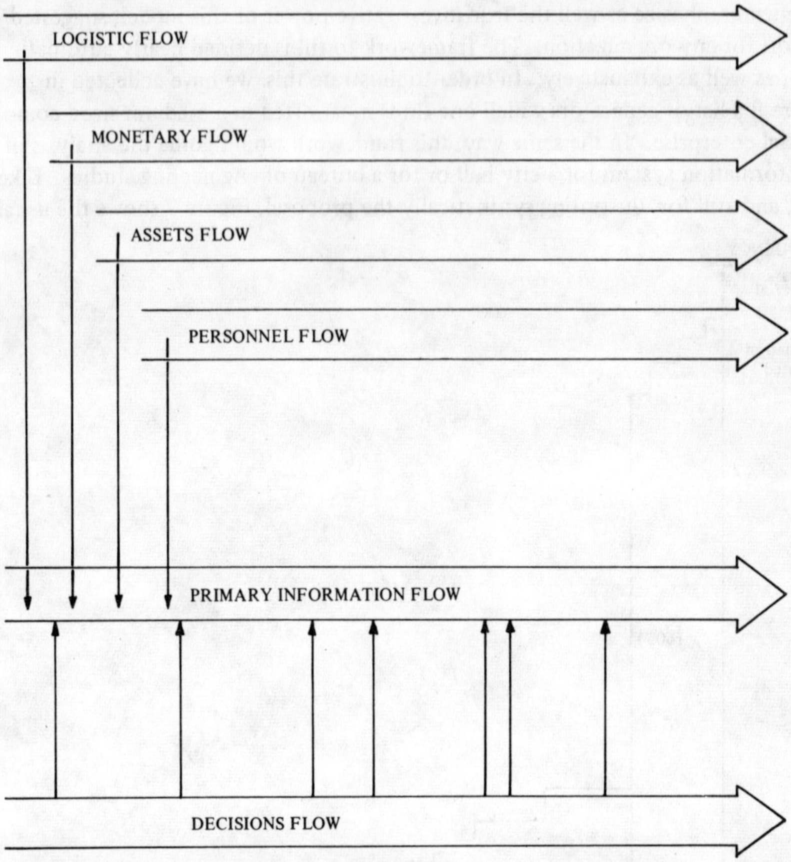

Fig. 6. The primary information flow based on the four resources flows

---

1 The identification of the monetary flow permits the explanation of the long term confusion between the accounting system and the information system. By its very nature, in fact, the monetary flow can only become a part of the measure where it has previously been represented by an information flow (all expressed in the same monetary unit of measure). A certain number of these representations are themselves images of transactions affecting one of the three other physical flows. It was tempting to reduce their representation to a single representation in homogeneous monetary units. This was even more so because the accounting model of the monetary flow permitted, at least apparently, a formal control of the "totality" of this representation. Differentiation between the monetary and accounting flow is relatively recent and is not yet widely accepted. This explains, we believe, a large portion of the difficulties which the analysts of information systems encounter when they are moved to alter the actual if not legal monopoly of accounting in the systemic representation of the organization.

We must emphasize as well the true investigative power of this model, suggested a priori for any organization. The framework to fill is defined nearly automatically, as well as exhaustively. In order to illustrate this, we have collected in Figure 8 a list of generators which one finds most often in a medium sized commercial enterprise. In the same way, this framework would guide the analysis of an information system for a city hall or for a bureau of engineering studies. Likewise, and still for illustrating synthetically the proposal, Figure 7 shows the usual-

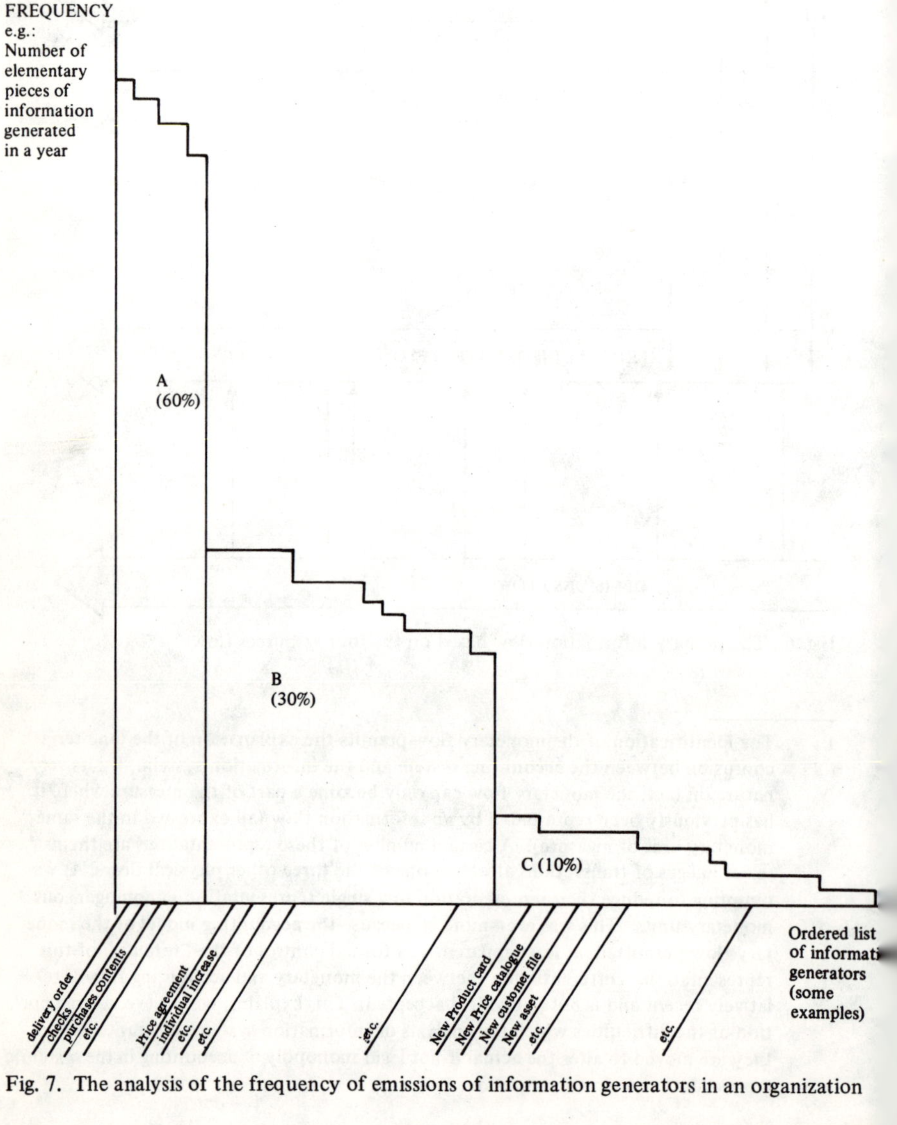

Fig. 7. The analysis of the frequency of emissions of information generators in an organization

ly observed division of the generators of information as a function of their frequency of emission, in the same enterprise type being used as a reference. We verify without surprise that this frequency division obeys the ABC rule of inventory.

5. The implementation of an information system based on the four-flows model

The flow chart defining the principal data banks of an information system permits us to overturn diametrically the concept on which many ambitious and well studied projects have failed. This is the concept according to which it is the final information - that information which the managers or the accountants of the organization are presumed to need - which determines in nature, in frequency, and in precision the basic data to record. Paradoxically, without doubt, we conclude the reverse; the basic data to record with the highest priority are those which characterize the experience of relationships of the organization with its environment. This is not only because this recording is nearly obligatory (which permits the cost of this recording to be carried by the obligation itself), but also because it is to these experiences that the managers of the organization will make their first appeal in order to understand and to orient their own systems.
The paradox is only apparent or rather it is only defined, in conjunction with a preconceived idea which has already had a long life: that is to say, with a hypothesis that an information system must be established on a base of information which the managers legally need in order to make decisions (of, for instance, W.M. Zani, 1970 - p. 98). It seems to us that R.N. Anthony had already sensed the ambiguous character of this process, as witness the quotation which is reproduced in Figure 8.

It of course remains that this general rule for the construction of data banks can be adapted to very diverse situations. We propose a global typology of the data bank in Figure 9: to the information-transactions (or "quasi-legal") information, in that its gathering is nearly vital for the organization), we can add several specific files which are in general less voluminous because of their costs. These files are those which the organization purchases in its environment because it wants to have at its disposal, over and above its own records, the memory of certain events. These events purchased and stored periodically and listed very selectively. They characterize some section of the environment and when combined with the implementation of some models which seems representative, lead to the name "information for models". Let us anticipate finally the case of that information which will interest the organization for a time, without its being

FLOW OF RESOURCES CHARACTERIZING THE ACTIVITY	LOGISTIC FLOW	MONETARY FLOW
IN PROCESS AND HISTORIC	– order file – inventory file (in volume) – supply in order file – shipment file – planning file	– file of "bank deposits" – file of "invoice copies (debts)" – customer account files
	– chronological order file (often represented by the invoice file)	– general accounting files (a file by account or group of accounts: the "entries")

FLOW OF RESOURCES CHARACTERIZING THE STRUCTURE	FLOW OF ASSET ELEMENTS	PERSONNEL FLOW
INTANGIBLE ASSETS	– customer file – product file – supplier file	– personnel file – payroll file – specific files (social work, training . . .)
TANGIBLE ASSETS	– descriptive equipment file – (data book)	

Fig. 8. The data files of an average organization classified as a function of the "POSITION" of the generators of primary information (four-flows-model)

able to predict yet the duration of this interest, (from which comes the name "random" information). – Fig. 9 ignores a fourth type of informations stored in the data base, previously mentioned: the representation of the decision previously made in the organization (previous budget etc. ...).

Our intention was to propose a scheme to the analyst charged with the design of the information system of an organization. The limitations on this communication do not permit us to consider all of the complementary aspects necessary in practice for implementation. In particular, we ignore deliberately the considerations relative to the creation of the program bank and to the program model, or to the memorization of a specific flow which we have not mentioned to this point, that of the information representing the decisions taken by the orga-

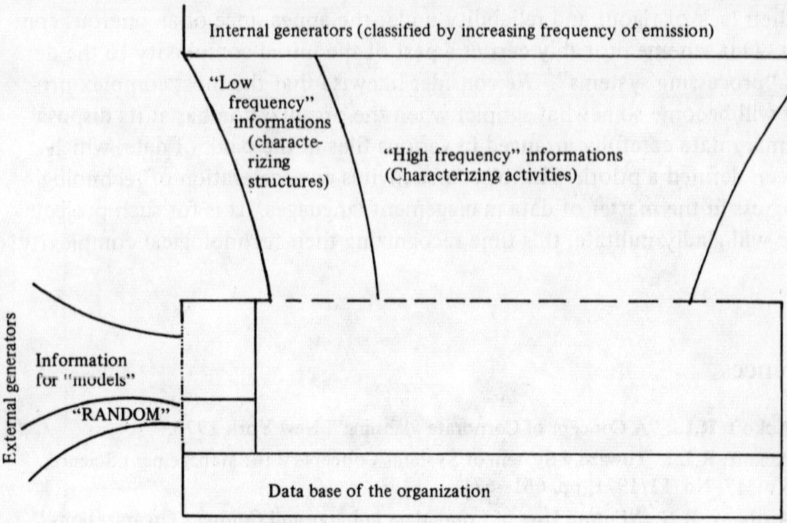

Informations generated	
Outside	Inside
– "for models" – "RANDOM"	– "High Frequency" (activity) – "Low Frequency" (structure)

Fig. 9. Typology of information circulating in the organization

nization. We have had the occasion to consider these aspects elsewhere (Le Moigne 1973).

6. Conclusion

Our intent, in essence, is to restore simplicity or, if you prefer, to probe deeply enough the "complex" for recovering the "simple" of which it is woven. The analysis and design of information systems - systems for memorization in an organization appear to us today to be able to be presented as a simple task, and this remark causes us to denounce certain plans or certain total packages which mask their lack of rigour and reliability under the appearance of an onerous complexity. Our scheme probably carries a part of the initial complexity to the design of "processing systems". We consider likewise that the most complex processing will become somewhat simpler when the organization has at its disposal the primary data carefully arranged in various files in the bank of data, which have been defined a priori. This of course invites an acceleration of technological progress in the matter of data management languages. It is for such projects that we will gladly militate, this time recognizing their technological complexity!

References

[1] Ackoff, R.L.: "A Concept of Corporate Planning". New York 1970.

[2] Ackoff, R.L.: "Toward a System of Systems Concepts". In: Management Science, Vol. 17, No. 11/1971, pp. 661–671.

[3] Anthony, R.N.: "Future Uses of Computers in Large and Complex Organizations". In: Computer and Management – The Leatherbee Lectures – 1967". Boston – Harvard University Graduate School of Business Administration, pp. 106–121.

[4] Aronofsky, J.S.: "Progress in Operations Research: Relationship between operation research and the computer", Vol. 111, New York 1969.

[5] Blumenthal, S.C.: "Management Information Systems – A Framework for Planning and Development". Englewood Cliffs, N.J. 1969.

[6] Emery, J.C.: "Organizational Planning and Control System: Theory and Technology". New York 1969.

[7] Forrester, J.W.: "Industrial Dynamics". Cambridge, Mass. and New York 1961.

[8] Montgomery, D.B. and G.L. Urban: "Marketing Decision-Information Systems: An Emerging View". In: Journals of Marketing Research, Vol. 7, May, 1970, pp. 226–234.

[9] Simon, H.A.: "The Sciences of the Artificial". Cambridge, Mass. 1969.

[10] Zannetos, Z.S.: "Management Information Systems and the Management Process: New Direction". Cambridge, Mass, Sloan Working Paper No. 243–267/1967, p. 20.

German abstract
Das Vier-Kanal-Modell: Instrument zur Gestaltung betrieblicher Informationssysteme

Von *Jean Louis Le Moigne*

Die stürmische technische Entwicklung auf dem Gebiet der automatischen Datenverarbeitung (z.B. Mini-Computer, große Direktzugriffsspeicher) macht im Bereich komplexer Anwendungssysteme (MIS) grundlegend neue Konzeptionen möglich und erforderlich. Der Computer wird mehr und mehr zum „Gedächtnis" der Unternehmung. Für den Benutzer stellt diese Veränderung eine Vereinfachung der Beziehungen zwischen Manager und Computersystem dar.

Le Moigne schlägt in seiner Konzeption eine Trennung der drei funktionalen Subsysteme Informationsspeicherung, Informationsverarbeitung und Kommunikation vor. Ein Vier-Kanal-Input/Output-Modell stellt die Grundlage für die inhaltliche Gestaltung und Organisation des Informationsspeichersystems (Datenbanksystems) dar. Es werden vier Informationsströme unterschieden:

a) zwei verrichtungsorientierte Ströme (logische und monetäre Informationen) und

b) zwei strukturorientierte Flüsse (Informationen über Personal und Vermögenselemente unter Einschluß der Kunden- und Produktzusammensetzung).

Jeder der acht „Übertragungspunkte" (Input und Output der vier Kanäle) bildet einen der acht „Primärinformationsgeneratoren" einer Organisation. Diese lassen sich leicht ermitteln und hinsichtlich ihrer Übertragungsrate (Gestaltungsanforderungen an die Datenbank) bewerten.

Weiterhin stellt Le Moigne kurz dar, wie ein Informationssystem mit Hilfe des von ihm entwickelten Modells implementiert werden kann. Dabei wird deutlich, daß abweichend von vielen anderen Ansätzen für eine effiziente Systemgestaltung nicht von den Endinformationen ausgegangen wird, um die für den Benutzer relevanten Informationen zu bestimmen. Mit Hilfe des vorgestellten Modells läßt sich in bestimmtem Umfang eine „Vereinfachung" oder Reduktion komplexer Zusammenhänge durchführen.

Information economics and the notion of "Management Information System"

By *Richard Mattessich**

1. Is MIS a mirage?

The expression "Management Information System" (or its customary abbreviation "MIS") has recently become a pervading term, exercising in its wake a good deal of magic over the minds of accountants, businessmen, economists, management scientists and even laymen. However, in our critical age the spell of magic wears off rapidly, and the result is reaction if not disappointment. Such a reaction is well manifested in an article by Professor John Dearden of Harvard University: "MIS is a mirage" (Harvard Business Review, Vol. 50, No. 1, Jan.-Febr. 1972). This article seems to have found a wide response, and by now has become, if not renowned, at least notorious. Although my paper must not be regarded as a rejoinder to Professor Dearden, I am much concerned about the present confusion prevailing over this very important, but now castigated, concept. On the one hand I agree with a great many statements in Dearden's article: I certainly do not deny that the concept of MIS, so far at least, is "embedded in a mishmash of fuzzy thinking and incomprehensible jargon", and I would not suggest that Dearden has set up a straw issue. Yet I do believe that Dearden, in his perceptive observation of the general abuse of the expression „management information system", has gone too far and poured the baby out with the bath water. The major reason for this is to be found in his own misuse of that term, namely in identifying MIS with what is generally designated as the fully integrated MIS. If this sweeping identification would not run counter to what is usually meant by "MIS" in the current business literature, I would have much less hesitation in agreeing with him that MIS conceals "a completely unworkable concept". Before abolishing a well-established notion one should try to give meaning in a more rigorous fashion. Of course Dearden is fully aware of the prevailing terminological confusion and its pitfalls. Indeed, the explicit definitions of MIS encountered in practice and theory contribute nothing to guide Dearden away from the precipice into which he throws this scapegoat of a term. Thus the blame might not have to be laid on him but on those supplying him and all

* The author wishes to acknowledge gratefully financial assistance for this research project from the Canada Council and the University of British Columbia.

of us with inoperable definitions of MIS.[1] The practice of coining vague, descriptive definitions of areas or systems constitutes, in my humble opinion, a great curse of our discipline. Such definitions may satisfy the whim of a moment, making us believe they delineate the category to be defined. But they neither draw sharp boundaries nor do they convey much knowledge about the essence of the definiendum. Yet if descriptive definitions merely lull us into a comfortable dream, what alternative do we have? It is this alternative, and not so much Dearden's paper, I should like to talk about.

With progressive use of the term MIS it becomes obvious to an increasing number of experts that the content of this expression cannot be derived philologically. That is to say: not every information-procuring device within the managerial orbit should be addressed as a MIS or as part thereof. To give this term direction and stability we might have to restrict it to a formalizable process of repetitive nature and of somewhat permanent structure. Thus the task of this paper is to explore whether recent extensions of information economics can help us in giving meaning to the notion of MIS, and whether it is possible to test this notion in connection with its various interpretations.

2. The information economic approach to MIS

During the last two decades or so economists like Jacob Marschak,[2] Roy Radner[3] and others[4] have devoted a good deal of brain power to interpret information as

1 Dearden cites Walter Kennon's definition offered in "MIS Universe" Data Management, September 1970: "A management information system is an organized method of providing past, present and projection information relating to internal operations and external intelligence. It supports the planning, control and operational information in the proper time-frame to assist the decision-maker".

2 Jacob Marschak: "Towards an Economic Theory of Organization and Information". In: Decision Processes, ed. by R. M. Thrall, C. H. Coombs and R. L. Davis, New York 1954, chapt. 14.
idem: "Remarks on the Economics of Information". In: Contributions to Scientific Research in Management, Los Angeles 1959.
idem: Problems in Information Economics". In: Management Controls: New Directions in Basic Research, ed. by C. P. Bonini, R. K. Jaedicke and H. M. Wagner, New York 1964, pp. 38–74.
idem: "Economics of Information Systems". In: Journal of American Statistical Association, March 1971.
Jacob Marschak and Roy Radner: Economic Theory of Teams, New Haven 1972.

3 Roy Radner: "The Evaluation of Information in Organizations". In: Proceedings of the 4th Berkeley Symposium on Mathematical Statistics, Vol. 1, Berkeley 1961, pp. 491–530.

4 George J. Stigler: "The Economics of Information". In: Journal of Political Economy, Vol. 69, 1961, pp. 213–225; C. B. McGuire and R. Radner (eds.): Decision and Organization, New York 1972.

a commodity. This commodity, although having a value and obeying the laws of economics, has certain peculiarities of its own. The most striking of which lies in the fact that the power and benefit of information is the ability to change the belief of a person, or more precisely, to change the degree of belief in a specific expectation which a certain person may harbour. But what is the use of such a change in belief? Can actually a value be attributed to it? Scholars more than any other group of people realize that knowledge or information per se can be immensely gratifying and generate utility in a person. But economists are not so much concerned with information as a purpose in itself than with information as a means to an end. Thus it is not so much the economic theory of consumption than that of production which is applied in information economics. Of course to conclude that the value of a bit of information arises out of the added benefit which one obtains by acting on the basis of this information instead of acting without it, is too simplistic an inference – at least in situations where this information is valid only for the long run. Again economists focus their interest on these probabilistic events and the overall expected value of such information. Thus information economics evolves out of economic decision theory almost as naturally as a butterfly grows out of the pupa's cocoon. But the advent of information economics does not seem to be the final stage in this evolutionary cycle.

Most recently some accountants – in the attempt to impose a more rigorous frame upon the loosely knit structure of traditional accounting theory – have taken up the basic notions of information economics and are trying to forge a practically useful tool. These scholarly endeavours are hoped to lead ultimately to a general theory of management information systems giving thereby the term MIS a more definite and less controversial meaning. Hence, these efforts deserve our attention and if necessary a constructive critique.

2.1 Contributions by Butterworth, Demski, Feltham and others

Information economics regards information as a resource having a value, a cost and related features.[5] It also is concerned with the improvement of a priori probabilities by means of additional information, converting the former into a posteriori probabilities (Bayesian approach). Thus the jump from decision theory to information economics is a small one. Indeed, the question "how much is this (additional) information worth?" already looms in many decision theoretical issues, even without further elaboration. The information model resembles its parent in many features, and the major differences lie in the probability concept assigned, as well as in the expansion necessary for transgressing from the "value of an information" to the "value of an information system". This transfer becomes obvious when considering that information economics is not only interested in

5 Cf. Henry Theil: Economics and Information Theory, Chicago 1967.

the value of a specific information signal, but in the value of an entire information system. By stripping the decision model and the information model to their very bones we can easily recognize those similarities and differences (see Table 1).

Primitive Decision Model		**Primitive Information Model**[6]	
$E_a = \sum_{e=1}^{m} u_{ae} \cdot p_e$		$E_{ai} = \sum_{e=1}^{n} u_{ae} \cdot p_{ei}$	
$V_D = \max_a E_a$		$V_i = \max_a E_{ai}$	
u_{ae}	utility of action a if event e occurs	$V_S = \sum_{i=1}^{r} V_i \cdot p_i$	
p_e	prior probability that event e will occur	u_{ae}	utility of action a if event e occurs
E_a	expected value of action a	p_{ei}	conditional probability that event e occurs provided information i is received (in system S)
V_D	value of best decision D		
For both models:		E_{ai}	expected value of action a at receiving information i
a =	1, . . . , m	V_i	value of best action upon receiving information i
e =	1, . . . , n	p_i	(prior) probability that information i is received (in system S)
i =	1, . . . , r	V_S	value of pertinent information system S
$\max_a$ =	maximize over the range of all actions a = 1, . . . , m		

Table 1. Structural Comparison

In Table 1 the first two equations on either side represent a decision model, with the difference that the probability assignment of the information-decision model is expressed under the condition that a specific information signal is received. The resulting sum-total of all utilities and probabilities in both cases yield expected values of all possible actions from which the maximal (expected) value has to be chosen. The information model then goes a step further by assigning (prior) probabilities (with respect to the occurrence of each possible information signal) to the value of the various informations possible. This sum-total yields a new (ex-

6 For a similar but more elaborate presentation of the information economics model see: James C. Emery: Organizational Planning and Control Systems, New York 1969, pp. 66–107.

pected) value, namely the value of a specific information system V_S. The full-fledged information models (not shown in Table 1) then may determine the optimal information system among alternatives, calculating value differentials ($\Delta V_{S'} = V_{S'} - V_S$) between two systems S and S′ or two versions (original or improved respectively) of one and the same system. Of course, this is a description of the information model in less than a nutshell – a fact that becomes obvious by considering the various aspects and complexities that have been dealt with so far, and the many more problems still unresolved.

It cannot be the task of this paper to expose all those details, but I should like to offer a concise evolutionary survey of what has been undertaken along these lines during the past five years.[7] Two major pioneering efforts in elaborating and analyzing the information model from the management and accounting point of view were undertaken in two doctoral dissertations in Berkeley, both completed in the year 1967. One by John Butterworth under the title "Accounting Systems and Management Decision: An Analysis of the Role of Information in the Management Decision Process", the other by G. A. Feltham in his doctoral dissertation "A Theoretical Framework for Evaluating Changes in Accounting Information for Managerial Decisions" (U. C. Berkeley, 1967) which formed the basis for his book Information Evaluation[8] published in the spring of 1973. The work of both authors is rigorously mathematical but more converging towards each other than overlapping. However, for the last couple of years these two scholars have been collaborating closely in teaching jointly two graduate seminars on information economics at UBC as well as writing a relevant paper on "Mathem. Decision Models in Managerial Accounting."[9]

---

7 This, at the same time, gives me an opportunity to report to you on the research presently going on at the Accounting and Management Information Systems Division of the University of British Columbia – of course we have no monopoly on this kind of research. Especially Stanford University has been heavily engaged in a similar project, but not in a competitive, rather in a co-operative way with UBC. In this connection UCLA and T. J. Mock's dissertation on "The Evaluation of Alternative Information Structures" (Berkeley, 1969) and his paper "Concepts of Information Value and Accounting" in The Accounting Review, October 1971, pp. 765–78 should also be mentioned.

Research closely related to "information theory", but not following the lines of information economics à la J. Marschak and R. Radner, has been carried out by Henry Theil, Economics and Information Theory, Chicago 1967) and by Baruch Lev, Accounting and Information Theory (American Accounting Association 1969).

8 Vol. 5 of the Studies in Accounting Research, American Accounting Association, 1973. A first survey of results growing out of Feltham's thesis can be found in his "The Value of Information", Accounting Review, Vol. 43, No. 4, October 1968, pp. 684–696.

9 Working Paper of the Faculty of Commerce and Business Administration – UBC Vancouver, November 1972.

In his dissertation Butterworth tries, among other things, to connect information economics with the network and matrix approach. By doing so he focuses his attention more on the accounting aspects and particularly on the information system structure as represented by the chart of accounts. Such a classificatory structure is mathematically best represented by a system of partitions (i. e. a hierarchy of equivalence classes[10]) to which Butterworth successfully applies the notions of "fineness" and "courseness" suggested by Radner and Marschak. Thus for Butterworth the information system seems to be above all a chart of accounts, and the problem he faces is the determination of the comparative value of alternative account structures. He points out that his major concern is to reveal the structural interdependence of the information and decision function, and the integration of both. But this statement ought not to make the reader believe that Butterworth matches a broad range of information purposes with the corresponding information structures. He rather restricts himself to the distinction between the planning problem (determination of the optimal set of activities), the reporting problem (measurement of the activities), and the controlling problem (analyzing the discrepancies between the planned and the actually measured balances). The concern with the control aspect later found an echo in Information Analysis where Demski devotes Chapter 6 to the development of this issue. Although Butterworth's dissertation contains a restatement of the Marschak-Radner model in a dynamic form (made necessary by the sequential nature of accounting information), it does not contain any multi-period models.

Feltham, in his Information Evaluation, envisages the interdependence of the information and action (decision) system as depicted in Figure 1[11]. In contrast to Butterworth he takes multi-period models into consideration and distinguishes clearly between the information evaluator (e. g. the accountant) and the decision maker (e. g. the manager). This distinction becomes not only important in cases where these two functions are fulfilled by different persons, but draws attention to the fact that the accountant's decision to choose a specific information system is distinct from but related to the manager's operational decisions of investing, producing, marketing etc. It demonstrates that the information evaluator must specify the relevant action alternatives, events, conditional returns and probabilities, and thus predict the relationship between the information and the decision maker's choice.[12] Feltham, in contrast to Butterworth, is little concerned with

---

10 Cf. Accounting and Analytical Methods (1964), pp. 33 and 452ff.

11 Taken from p. 22 of Feltham's dissertation (reprinted with permission of the author). See also Figure 2.1, p. 11 of Information Evaluation.

12 This is well and concisely put forth in "The Use of Models in Information Evaluation" under the joint authorship of G. A. Feltham and J. S. Demski (The Accounting Review, Oct. 1970, pp. 623–640). This article won the award of the American Institute of Certified Public Accountants as being one of the notable contributions to accounting literature during the calendar year 1970.

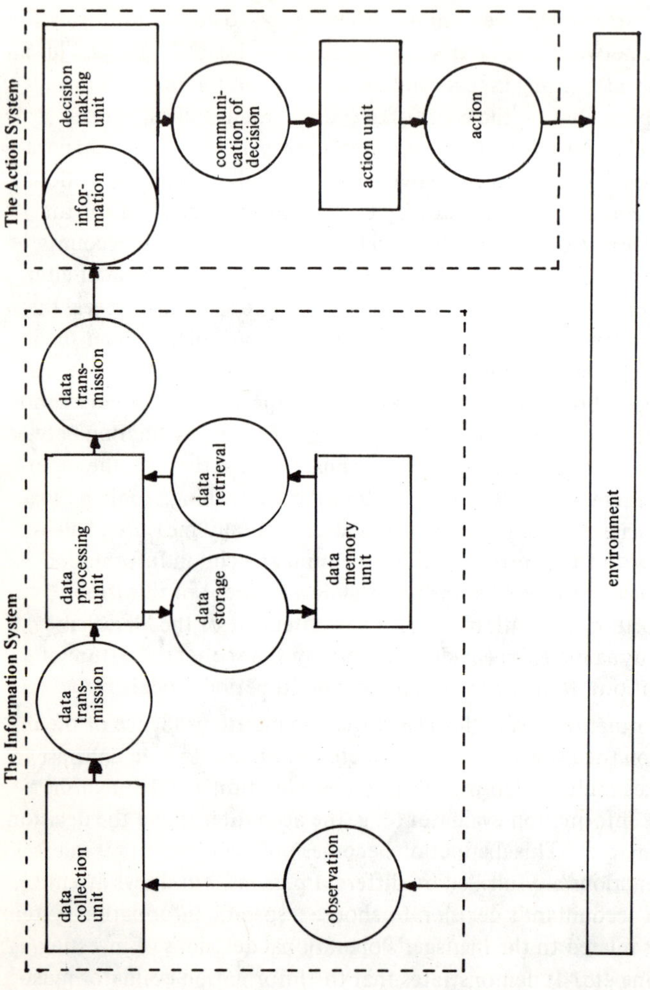

Fig. 1. Interdependence of the information and action (decision) system

the specific accounting aspects of the MIS, instead he gives special attention to the conceptual clarification of many other information economic issues, (e. g. criteria for information decisions, changes in payoff partitions, changes in probability distributions, timeliness, accuracy and system errors). I consider Chapter 5 one of the most important ones of his book. It deals with model simplifications and starts from the idea that

> "the information evaluation model developed in the preceding chapter is designed to be the best representation of the decision situation that the information evaluator

> could develop. However, any such model would be too costly to develop and solve and, thus, simplifications must be made in the model when it is applied. Of course, any simplifications may reduce the quality of the decisions made . . .
> This chapter describes a number of the simplifications that are made in decision models and describes how these simplifications might be evaluated".[13]

Such an approach might permit a search for that management information system which is optimal, quasi-optimal or satisfactory for a specific purpose or context. But in fairness to Butterworth, it has to be pointed out that this issue, although present, was not yet as fully developed in Feltham's original dissertation as it is in his book. The latter may have benefited from an article which Feltham authored jointly with Butterworth. This article develops a meta-model for MIS, and thus deserves special consideration later on.

But first let us pay some attention to Feltham's cooperation with Demski, Horngren and Jaedicke in the forthcoming book on A Conceptual Approach to Cost Determination.[14] This innocent title hardly betrays the influence which information economics and Feltham's pertinent research exercised upon the conceptual clarification of cost issues in general. This research study was carried out at Stanford University (from 1968 – 72) under the generous financial sponsorship of the American Institute of Certified Public Accountants.

In contrast to traditional cost studies the Stanford study focuses on the choice of alternative cost accounting structures. Since these are information systems, the relationship to information economics is obvious, but so is the relationship to alternative systems of cost concepts. In my interpretation this study envisages every conceptual scheme about cost as a mere convention, but supposes that depending on the costing purpose one convention might be "better" or "more efficient" than the others. Thus beside the task of finding a specific model optimal or quasi-optimal for a specific purpose, the question of the general conceptual cost framework suitable for an entire category of problems arises. Therefore this study concentrates less on how costs are used, than on the task of specialization and the cost accountant's information choice problem. Here we clearly encounter two decision makers and two decisions, since the decision process of the accountant (in choosing a specific cost scheme) is differentiated from but related to the manager's decision process of maximizing profit or satisficing related criteria. Hence the previously formulated distinction between "information evaluator" and "decision maker" becomes prominent also in this study, but under a slightly different terminology. The latter seems to be an improvement since Feltham's and Demski's "information evaluator" may not only evaluate information and information systems, but is likely also to make decisions about the information system to be used. Of course in such a choice situation the cost-benefit relationship of the informa-

13 Information Evaluation, p. 52.

14 (Stanford: 1972, mimeographed; to be published in 1973).

tion system, or in this case, of the costing system, plays a vital role. And the study gives explicit consideration to measurement cost as well as to the recognition of uncertainties; both of these aspects have hitherto been too much neglected in cost accounting.[15]

Since time does not permit to discuss this Conceptual Approach to Cost Determination in any detail, I may restrict myself to mention shortly one more feature which I consider especially noteworthy. This is the utilization of an axiomatic or semi-axiomatic approach with theorems and rigorous mathematical proofs. Use is made of it not only in Chapter 2 (which concentrates on rational choice and thus may be expected to present well-known axioms of choice) but also in Chapter 3 which deals with "Cost Assessment as a Problem of Optimal Information Choice" as well as in Chapter 5, discussing "Cost Functions in a Product Decision Context", and partly in some other chapters. Thus we are dealing with a most rigorous conceptual analysis upon which future cost accounting may draw for a long time to come.

A further accounting work in the area of applied, or, better said, extended information economics is Joel S. Demski's book on Information Analysis.[16] As mentioned in its preface, it is designed as a supplementary text for management ac-

---

15 From this point of view the Stanford study as well as other studies here discussed constitute an extension of some thoughts I expressed already in 1964 in Accounting and Analytical Methods. The prime purpose of this book was to point out that "modern accounting can no longer be satisfied to ascertain that certain legal or semi-legal rules have been obeyed, its major task ought to be concerned with the question whether an optimal or satisfactory set of hypotheses was chosen for a specific objective within a well-defined context" (p. 251). I also referred to cost accounting by asserting that there "a wide range of estimation procedures are available" and that "depending upon the relation of the benefit of this hypothesis for the management of the firm to the cost of producing this hypothesis and operating with it" (p. 236) a more or a less sophisticated costing hypothesis would have to be accepted. In later publications I repeatedly stressed similar ideas: see R. Mattessich: "The Impact of Electronic Data Processing and Management Science upon Accounting Theory". In: Modern Accounting Theory, ed. by M. Backer, Englewood Cliffs 1966, p. 516; idem: "Neue erkenntnistheoretische Probleme der Betriebswirtschaftslehre". In: Betriebswirtschaftliche Forschung in internationaler Sicht, ed. by H. Kloidt, Berlin 1969, pp. 28–29; idem: "Systemsimulation und neue Aufgaben des betrieblichen Rechnungswesens". In: Der Computer im Dienste der Unternehmungsführung, ed. by. W. Busse von Colbe und R. Mattessich, Gütersloh 1968, pp. 175, 188–190; idem: Die wissenschaftlichen Grundlagen des Rechnungswesens, Düsseldorf 1970, pp. 22, 78, 243, 260, 266; idem: "Some Thoughts on the Epistemology of Accounting". In: Proceedings of Second International Conference 1967 on Accounting Education, London 1970, pp. 50–51; idem: "Methodological Preconditions and Problems of a General Theory of Accounting". In: The American Accounting Review, July 1972, pp. 470, 478–487.

16 Reading, Mass. 1972.

counting courses. It is the first book of this kind, and offers an excellent survey of this area, emphasizing the previously mentioned distinction between the complete or ideal information model and some possible simplifications (e. g. as to action element specification, state specification, probability function, utility assessment, restrictions on decision variables). It also contains practical illustrations and applications of the abstract model such as "capital acquisition models", "control models" and the "analysis of information systems" for evaluation purposes. Here too the distinction between the information evaluator and the decision maker is utilized and the important problem of those information evaluators unable to predict with certainty their managers' decision models is discussed.

Before closing this latter-day historical survey, I should like to draw your attention to several more recent contributions by Butterworth, partly in cooperation with other co-authors. His paper "The Accounting System as an Information Function"[17] is a reflection of major results gained in his dissertation; it thus deals with the relation of information economics to double-entry information systems and their aggregation issues, and offers guidelines for selecting the proper accounting systems. The two papers "Bounds on the Value of the Information in Uncertain Decision Problems"[18] by W. T. Ziemba and J. Butterworth, and "On the Comparative Value of Information Systems"[19] by J. E. Butterworth deal both with the computational task of finding bounding methods and approximations for ordering the value of alternative information systems. The second of these two points concentrates more on the accounting aspects and discusses with precision such important concepts as "informativeness" and "finesse". While a third paper "Mathem. Decision Models in Managerial Accounting"[20] by J. E. Butterworth and G. A. Feltham provides a meta-model for information systems and searches for simplifications of the meta-model for different purposes. Since I consider this last paper of special interest let me present to you the entire meta-model with short references to the envisaged simplifications.

In contrast to the Feltham-Demski distinction between information evaluator and decision maker, here the distinction between subordinate and manager (who might not fully control the actions of the subordinate) is emphasized at first.

---

17 Journal of Accounting Research, Vol. 10, No. 1, Spring 1972, pp. 1–27.

18 Presented by invitation at the NATO Advanced Study Institute on Mathematical Programming, in Figueira da Foz, Portugal, June 1972.

19 Journal of Accounting Research (forthcoming).

20 First draft of Working Paper No. 204 of the Faculty of Commerce and Business Administration – University of British Columbia, November 1972.

2.2 Summary of the Butterworth-Feltham meta-model

Variables:[21]

Set	**Vector**	**Explanation**
$A_t = \{ a_t \}$	$a = (a_1, \ldots, a_T)$	of *actions* (of managers and subordinates)
$D_t = \{ d_t \}$	$d = (d_1, \ldots, d_T)$	of *decisions*
$H_t = \{ \eta_t \}$	$\eta = (\eta_1, \ldots, \eta_T)$	of *information systems*
$S_t = \{ s_t \}$	$s = (s_1, \ldots, s_T)$	of *system states* (based on relevant preceding events)
$u_t = \{ u_t \}$	$u = (u_1, \ldots, u_T)$	of *uncontrollable events* (affecting outcomes or information signals)
$y_t = \{ y_t \}$	$y = (y_1, \ldots, y_T)$	of signals
$x_t = \{ x_t \}$	$x = (x_1, \ldots, x_T)$	of *outcome variables* (relevant to manager's behavior)
	$\bar{d}_t = (d_1, \ldots, d_{t-1})$	of *decision history*
	$\bar{y} = (y_1, \ldots, y_{t-1})$	of *signal history*
	$r = r_1 + \ldots + r_T$	payoff over period

Basic Relationships (*reflecting manager's perceptions)

$a_t = \alpha_t (s_t, u_t, d_t, \eta_t) \ldots$	action function*
$d_t = f_t (\bar{d}_t, \bar{y}_t) \ldots$	decision function*
$r_t = \omega_t (x_t) \ldots$	payoff (utility) function
$s_{t+1} = F_t(s_t, u_t, a_t, \eta_t) \ldots$	system state function*
$x_t = \rho_t (s_t, u_t, a_t, \eta_t) \ldots$	outcome function
$y_t = g_t (s_t, u_t, a_t, \eta_t) \ldots$	information function
$p(s_1, u_1, \ldots, u_t) \ldots$	joint probability distribution over initial state and uncontrollable events

$$EV^*(\eta) = \max_{d_1 \in D_1} \Big\{ \sum_{y_1} \sum_{x_1} [\omega_1 (x_1) + V_2 (d_1, y_1 \mid \eta)]\, p(x_1, y_1 \mid d_1, \eta) \Big\} \ldots$$

.... manager's expected value of information system η for periods 1 through T

$$V_t(\bar{d}_t, \bar{y}_t \mid \eta) = \max_{d_t \in D_t} \Big\{ \sum_{y_t} \sum_{x_t} [\omega_t (x_t) + V_{t+1}((\bar{d}_t, d_t), (\bar{y}_t, y_t) \mid \eta)]\, p(x_t, y_t (\bar{d}_t, d_t) \bar{y}_t, \eta) \Big\} \; t = 2, \ldots, T$$

... maximum expected pay-off for periods t through T, given that the decision and signal histories at the start of period t are $(\bar{d}_t, \bar{y}_t)$, and information system η is being used.

$V_{T+1}(\bar{d}_{T+1}, \bar{y}_{T+1} \mid \eta) \equiv 0$

$p(x_t, y_t, \bar{d}_{t+1}, \bar{y}_t, \eta) \ldots$ this joint probability distribution (over the outcome in period t and the signal received during that period, for a certain decision and signal history, given information system η) is derived from previous relationships.

3. Simplification versus interpretation

Due to many computational and other complexities the solution of this system of equations is practically infeasible. But the value of this meta-model lies not merely in providing an impressive conceptual scheme, it may also be used as a basis from which simplified and thus computationally feasible models can be derived. Therefore the bulk of the Butterworth-Feltham paper deals with simplifications already encountered in the literature, identifying their limiting conditions and bringing them, so to say, upon the common denominator of the meta-model. Categorizing these simplifications according to model components, the two authors discuss in some detail planning models,[22] control models, general conceptual models,[23] ex post valuation models, deviation investigation models,[24] and information timing

21 The subscripts t-l, t, t+l etc. are indices of successive time periods, while T refers to the last time period contemplated.

22 See L. R. Amey: The Efficiency of Business Enterprise, London 1969; C. S. Colantoni, R. P. Manes and A. Whinston: "Programming, Profit Rates and Pricing Decisions". In: Accounting Review, Vol. 44, No. 3, July 1969; J. S. Demski: "An Accounting System Structured on a Linear Programming Model". In: Accounting Review, Vol. 42, No. 4, October 1967; R. S. Kaplan and G. L. Thomson: "Overhead Allocation via Mathematical Programming Models". In: Accounting Review, Vol. 46, No. 2, April 1971.

23 See J. S. Demski: "Decision Performance Control". In: Accounting Review, Vol. 45, No. 1, January 1970, and idem: "Optimal Performance Measurement". In: Journal of Accounting Research (forthcoming).

24 See Mohamed Onsi: "Quantitative Models for Accounting Control". In: Accounting Review, Vol. 42, No. 2, April 1967; F. S. Luh: "Controlled Cost: An Operational Concept and Statistical Approach to Standard Costing". In: Accounting Review, Vol. 43, No. 1, January 1968; T. R. Dyckman: "The Investigation of Cost Variances", Journal of Accounting Research, Vol. 7, No. 2, Autumn 1969; T. Ozan and T. R. Dyckman: "A Normative Model for Investigation Decisions Involving Multioriginal Cost Variances". In: Journal of Accounting Research, Vol. 9, No. 1, Spring 1971; N. J. Gonedes: "Accounting for Managerial Control: An Application of Chance-Constrained Programming". In: Journal of Accounting Research, Vol. 8, No. 1, Spring 1970; J. S. Demski: "Information Improvement Bounds". In: Journal of Accounting Research, Vol. 10, No. 1, Spring 1972.

models.[25] Of course, various models previously presented by Butterworth and Feltham represent in themselves simplifications of the meta-model. Therefore the last section of the Butterworth-Feltham paper is devoted to an examination of the features which were suppressed in those models.[26]

Out of this paper by Butterworth and Feltham arises an issue which has not yet received attention but which I consider important from a methodological as well as practical point of view. Succinctly, it can be put in the following question: May this meta-model be regarded as a "general theory" and its simplifications as "interpretations" in the philosophic sense of the word? If this question can be answered in the affirmative, then we might be a good step closer to the task of giving a more precise meaning to the notion of MIS. The task of giving meaning is the subject of semantics,[27] and only a "semantical definition"[28] (in contrast to a descriptive or nominal one) can lead us to a meaningful concept of MIS. Thus we require a general theory of MIS, the axioms of which become the necessary and sufficient conditions of the pertinent semantic definition. Of course, this may not give us a meaning of MIS which is acceptable to everyone. But if this definition comprises, through further interpretation, most of the models that systematically and periodically supply information to management then the resistance against such a concept should be less difficult to break.

Now several questions have to be answered: (a) Does the Butterworth-Feltham meta-model supply us with the necessary and sufficient conditions required by a

---

25 N. J. Gonedes: "Optimal Timing of Control Messages for a Two-State Markov Process". In: Journal of Accounting Research, Vol. 9, No. 2, Autumn 1971.

26 Concluding the survey-part of this paper, I should like to point out two things: (1) that the contributions here discussed cannot be fully appreciated without the mathematical subtleties worked out in detail and with considerable precision in these publications, and (2) that I had to omit from my discussions other papers that deal with information evaluation in accounting and management, without however supplying the pertinent models: e. g. R. H. Crandall: "Information Economics and Its Implications for the Further Development of Accounting Theory". In: Accounting Review, Vol. 44, No. 3, July 1969; and Jürgen Wild: "Zur Problematik der Nutzenbewertung von Informationen". In: Zeitschrift für Betriebswirtschaft, Vol. 41, No. 5. The book Das Informationsverhalten in Entscheidungsprozessen, edited by E. Witte, Tübingen 1972, was not available to me before finishing this paper.

27 "A syntactical system L becomes a semantical system when rules are given in its metalanguage M which determine a necessary and sufficient truth condition for every sentence of the system. These rules, often embodied in a recursive definition, lead to a definition of truth." Donald Kalish: The Encyclopedia of Philosophy, Vol. 7, pp. 350–351.

28 Two variations of a meta-theory with semantical definitions of (double-classificational) accounting or accounting system were offered in R. Mattessich: Accounting and Analytical Methods, (p. 19–20) and idem: Die wissenschaftlichen Grundlagen des Rechnungswesens, (p. 34). References to further interpretations were made in these books through reference to specific hypotheses (see pp. 41–45 and 232–291, or pp. 49–105 respectively).

semantical definition of MIS? (b) Can the simplifications envisaged by these two authors satisfy the requirements of further interpretation? [29] (c) If questions 1 and 2 have to be negated is it possible to modify the meta-model and its simplifications such as to accommodate them to the scientific-philosophic requirements? and finally "Which tests are available to support the acceptability of the general theory as well as its interpretations? "

A semantically correct presentation of the Butterworth-Feltham meta-model would have to represent the seven sets and nine vectors as well as the payoff summation as seventeen existential propositions, and their elements as primitive notions, of the over-all system. The functions listed under "Basic Relationships" would have to be formulated as ten bounded universal propositions expressing behavioral and technical relations as well as a joint probability distribution. The second, derived probability function would properly be called a theorem.

Through this reformulation, i. e. by way of the existential and universal quantifiers, each equation of the Butterworth-Feltham model can be converted into a proposition amenable to the assignment of truth values – even without further interpretation. However, interpretation will be needed for two tasks (i) for the design of models for specific purposes and (ii) for the empirical testing of the meta-model.

So far so good, but the answer to the next question, whether the simplifications mentioned in the Butterworth-Feltham paper constitute proper interpretations of the meta-model, must be given in the negative. Every model or interpretation of a general and not fully interpreted theory must fulfill all the necessary and sufficient conditions of this theory. But each simplification listed, deliberately suppresses one or the other, usually even several, of these conditions. Thus this meta-model with simplifications does not seem to fulfill the requirements of a general theory with interpretations. Yet, there might be a way out of this dilemma.

If each "suppression" could be formulated as a borderline case of the pertinent condition,[30] or alternatively if all those simplifications could be eliminated which do not permit such a formulation (hence denying to those models the title MIS), then the situation might be saved, and the hope of conceptual clarification of MIS through this extension of information economics does not need to be abandoned. Not only for the sake of giving meaning to MIS, but also for the sake of

---

29 I deliberately use the term "further interpretation" because interpretation is a matter of degree, and the first step towards interpretation is found already in the semantical definition of the field itself. J. N. Phillips: "Degrees of Interpretation". In: Philosophy of Science, Vol. 39, No. 3, September 1972, distinguishes three major "degrees" of interpretation which he subdivides into no less than fifteen steps or "minor" degrees.

30 So for instance could the suppresssion of one or all probability distributions be reformulated as an assumption of a distribution with a value of 1 at a single point.

designing a scientifically acceptable framework, I hope that these two authors will give thought to that particular aspect. But assuming this hurdle can be overcome, let us at last direct our attention to the problem of testing.

4. The testing of the general theory and its interpretations

The theory envisaged in the Butterworth-Feltham paper is obviously not a pure or cognitive but an instrumental theory. Therefore the testing procedure cannot be geared toward the question whether the theory reflects reality at a sufficient degree of reliability. What ought to be tested is (1) whether each of its models serves its purpose (including the consideration of context) sufficiently well, and (2) whether the general theory (meta-model) is consistent with all its interpretations. The second point is more complex than it seems at a first glance. To my mind an instrumental theory[31] cannot be satisfied by definitely accepting a meta-model based on theoretical reflections only. The meta-model can serve only as a starting point for preliminary interpretations. If these interpretations serve their purposes properly only if further structural adjustments, affecting the meta-model, are made, then the latter too must be adjusted. Thus we require a recursive but non-circular procedure of testing empirically the interpretations and through them the general theory. I suggest that such a recursive testing procedure would have to be applied to the Butterworth-Feltham meta-model, and should like to close this paper by discussing in principle the individual steps of such a procedure.

A specific MIS, or MI-Model as we might call it in conformity with methodological practice, is tested by determining whether it is, for a well-defined purpose, the most "satisfactory" system under the circumstances. The basic routine of such a test is presented in Figure 1. The set of all basic assumptions or conditions (axioms) is designated by B_i, and it is assumed that m alternative basic sets are feasible (i = 1, . . . , m). Each set B_i is furthermore assumed to contain a set of n specific and complementary hypotheses H_{jk} (j = 1, . . . , n; k = 1, . . . , x). For each of these n hypotheses we assume the existence of x alternatives; we might speak for the sake of convenience of x alternative sets, but these sets must not be confused with the sets arising out of various combinations of complementary hypotheses; these combinations are reflected by different subscripts j and k, thus yielding a possible number of (2!/j!k!) alternatives. Figure 2 assumes that each hypothesis is tested individually (together with its basic set B_i) – see:

---

31 For details about instrumental theories I should like to refer the reader to my forthcoming book on Instrumental Reasoning and Decision Systems (1974).

$S_i = B_i + H_{jk}$. (But under certain circumstances it might be more practical to test from the outset a whole set of complementary hypotheses as an entity.) If this hypothesis (together with basis B_i) fulfills its purpose, it is considered acceptable and the next complementary hypothesis (increase j by l) can be tested. When all complementary hypotheses of one set are found acceptable individually for the purpose under consideration, then the pertinent combination is tested in its entirety (see loop at the extreme right of Figure 2); if satisfactory, the testing process for that particular model can be stopped; if not satisfactory, the next alternative combination has to be tested.

However, it is more likely that previous to this event, one or the other hypothesis (in combination with basis B_i) turns out to be non-satisfactory. Then the reason for this failure must be determined. If it lies in the specific hypothesis (see Figure 2: "Is failure due to H_{jk}? – Yes"), then that hypothesis has to be exchanged for a more appropriate one (increase k by l). If, however, the failure is not due to the specific hypothesis (see Figure 2: "Is failure due to H_{jk}? – No") but due to the set of basic conditions, then this provisional set B_i has to be substituted by set B_{i+l} and so on, until a satisfactory basis is discovered. In this way the semantical definition and general theory is subjected to verification or refutation every time a specific MI-Model undergoes the required test. In this way all deficiencies (preventing the fulfillment of a preconceived sufficiency criterion) of the basic assumptions could be amended in time. But since this may require considerable patience, it is advisable to eliminate in advance those weaknesses of the basis which can be determined upon "theoretical" reflection.[32]

Although the suggested testing procedure is recursive, it is by no means circular because the general system is not merely tested by checking whether the specific system fulfills all the originally stipulated conditions of the meta-model, but by ascertaining that the ultimate purpose of every specific system is fulfilled, and by a willingness to change the meta-model if necessary. This should demonstrate that a semantical definition, even if preliminary, might be superior to those traditional definitions which at a closer look do not go far beyond saying that a management information system is a system that provides information to management.

However, there exists a major objection against our argument. It is undeniable that the fulfillment of the purpose of a management information system is very

32 At this point one might reflect upon possible weaknesses of the Butterworth-Feltham meta-model: Is the empirical basis on which this theory rests broad enough? Are the availability assumptions with regard to certain probability distributions and utility functions justified? Do the authors make implicit assumptions which ought to be made explicit? Here T. J. Mock's dissertation and paper "Concepts of Information Value", Accounting Review, Vol. 42, No. 4, October 1967 might become relevant. He not only presents one of the first empirical studies in this area but also points out that the concept of information value used in information economics is one-sided and ought to be complemented or broadened.

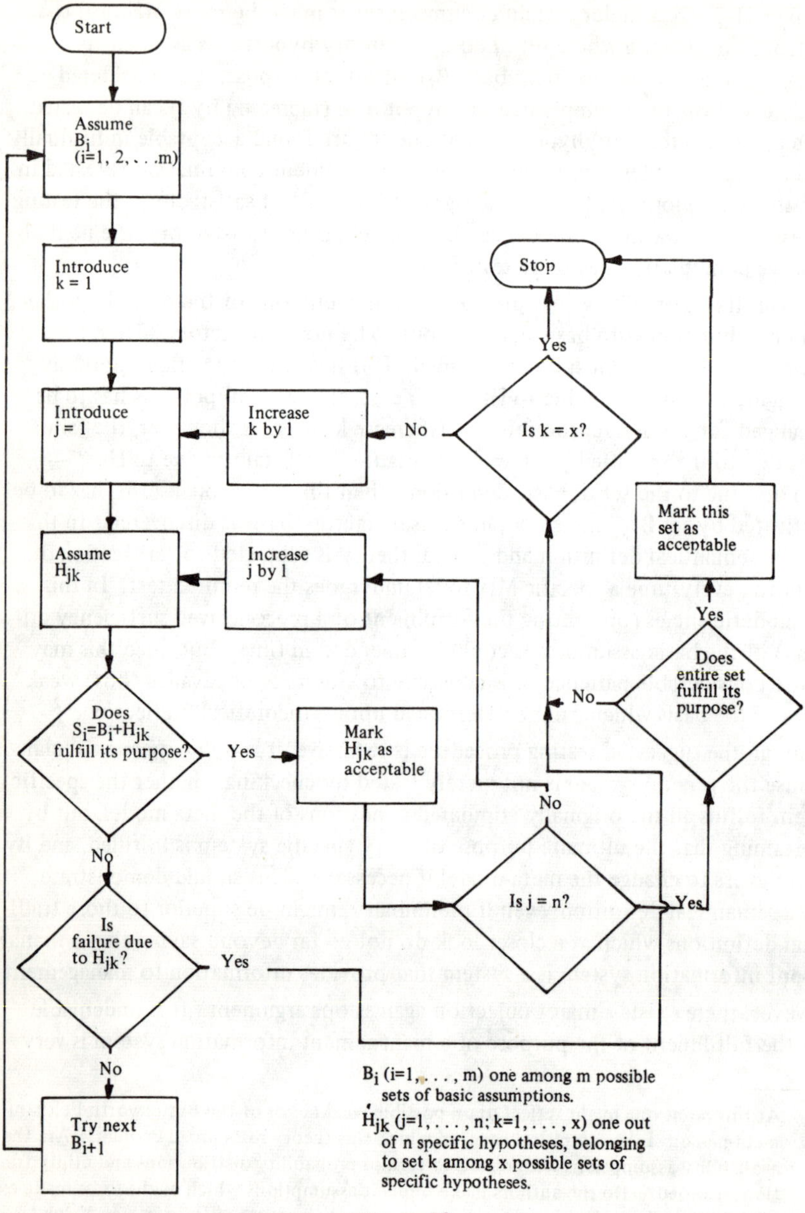

Fig. 2. Testing of general and specific systems[33]

---

[33] Assistance from my colleague Professor A. Dexter in improving this flow-chart is gratefully acknowledged by the author.

difficult and occasionally impossible to test. The performance of an MIS is indeed very different from the performance of a mechanical device, like an engine, motor-coach etc. The latter are amenable to many measures for ranking their comparative performances, whereas the former are not readily accessible to such measures. Recent experiments in this direction have not yielded completely satisfactory results, and there is little hope that the means developed by information theory (Shannon and Weaver etc.) will serve as measures for the degree of task-achievement of a management information system. Some counter-arguments can be advanced in opposition to the above-mentioned objection:

(1) The cost involved in the design and operation of a specific MIS necessitates at least a vague vision (a) of the absolute net benefit this system generates for the entity, and (b) of the relative net benefit in comparison with alternative systems. Where such vision or estimate does not exist, the system has no raison d'être. It should either be abolished or the control mechanism of the super-entity embracing the MIS should be improved.

(2) The very fact that considerable funds are wasted because of neglecting the measurement of the task-fulfillment of the MIS, speaks for the urgency of creating a sound and well-grounded theory that makes this kind of measurement possible. Such a theory cannot be developed on the basis of a descriptive definition of MIS. The suggestive power of such a definition might be psychologically satisfying to some laymen, practitioners and theorists, but it will remain without operational content or benefit.

(3) The computerization of the MIS tends in direction of both increasing sophistication and higher cost. This enforces better control over the MIS and more urgent concern for attaining measures of reliability and efficiency of this system. Whereas a manually or mechanically operated accounting system may get along

---

The following presumptions underly the flow chart presented above:

(1) At least one of the n sets of basic assumptions (B_i, i = 1, . . . , n) is acceptable for all specific interpretations (i. e. fulfills their purposes).

(2) If there are several sets of basic assumptions acceptable for all specific interpretations the choice between these sets has to be based on additional criteria that lie beyond the system here presented.

(3) In each specific interpretation (i. e. in each set k of hypotheses H_{jk}, k = 1, . . . , x) only some but not all of the n possible hypotheses will be used. The various sets of (specific) hypotheses are distinguished only by different combinations of hypotheses chosen from the set of possible hypotheses (i. e. this set is assumed to be exhaustive).

(4) The question "Does $S_i=B_i+H_{jk}$ fulfill its purpose? " implies that it is possible to test each hypothesis individually, i. e. in connection with the set of basic assumptions B_j but independent of the rest of (specific) hypotheses H_{lk}, $l = 1, \ldots, n$ except $l \neq j$.

(5) The question "Does entire set fulfill its purpose? " also implies that the set contains all hypotheses required for a specific purposes. If several sets of hypotheses H_{jk} fulfill the same purpose, we presumed that this purpose can be divided into sub-purposes so that for each sub-purpose only one set of (specific) hypotheses is acceptable. In the case of such unanticipated subdivisions further rounds of testing will be required.

with fairly vague efficiency estimates, a computerized MIS will be in greater need of more reliable measurements of task-achievement.

(4) The difficulty encountered with efficiency measurements of MIS lies not merely in the nature of this task but in the fact that traditional accounting did not give sufficient thought to this problem and thus did not create any theory capable of coping with it.

Yet, in spite of many genuine and difficult problems, we harbour no doubts that most of them will be solved in one way or another by accountants, management information experts or others. There is no cause to be pessimistic on account of these difficulties; on the contrary, they merely prove that accounting research is not an empty or trivial task. For a time many persons seemed to have succumbed to the fallacy that our discipline, apart from historical descriptions, has fulfilled its purpose, and no longer is challenged by meaningful theoretical problems. Nothing could be farther from the truth. As this article may have demonstrated, the actual academic task of the accountant – that of scientifically designing and testing management information systems – has hardly begun, and a vast, fertile plain has opened in front of his mental vision. Will he face the challenge or will he leave it to others to plough this field of his?

References

[1] Amey, L.R.: The Efficiency of Business Enterprise. London 1969.

[2] Butterworth, J.E.: The Accounting System as an Information Function. Journal of Accounting Research, Vol. 10, No. 1, Spring 1972, pp. 1–27.

[3] Butterworth, J.E.: On the Comparative Value of Information Systems. Journal of Accounting Research (forthcoming).

[4] Butterworth, J.E. and G.A. Feltham: Mathematical Decision Models in Managerial Accounting. First draft of Working Paper No. 204 of the Faculty of Commerce and Business Administration – University of British Columbia, November 1972.

[5] Butterworth, J.E.: Accounting Systems and Management Decision: An Analysis of the Role of Information in the Management Decision Process. Berkeley 1967.

[6] Colantoni, C.S.; R.P. Manes and A. Whinston: Programming, Profit Rates and Pricing Decisions. Accounting Review, Vol. 44, No. 3, July 1969.

[7] Crandall, R.H.: Information Economics and Its Implications for the Further Development of Accounting Theory. Accounting Review, Vol. 44, No. 3, July 1969.

[8] Dearden, J.: MIS is a Mirage. Harvard Business Review, Vol. 50, No. 1, Jan.–Febr. 1972.

[9] Demski, J.S.: An Accounting System Structured on a Linear Programming Model. Accounting Review, Vol. 42, No. 4, October 1967.

[10] Demski, J.S.: Decision Performance Control. Accounting Review, Vol. 45, No. 1, January 1970.

[11] Demski, J.S.: Information Improvement Bounds. Journal of Accounting Research, Vol. 10, No. 1, Spring 1972.

[12] Demski, J.S.: Information Analysis. Reading, Mass. 1972.

[13] Demski, J.S.: Optimal Performance Measurement. Journal of Accounting Research (forthcoming).

[14] Dyckman, T.R.: The Investigation of Cost Variances. Journal of Accounting Research, Vol. 7, No. 2, Autumn 1969.

[15] Emery, J.C.: Organizational Planning and Control Systems. New York 1969.

[16] Feltham, G.A.: The Value of Information. Accounting Review, Vol. 43, No. 4, October 1968 pp. 684–696.

[17] Feltham, G.A.: Information Evaluation. Vol. 5 of the Studies in Accounting Research, American Accounting Association, 1973.

[18] Feltham, G.A. and J.S. Demski: The Use of Models in Information Evaluation. Accounting Review, Oct. 1970, pp. 623–640.

[19] Feltham, G.A.; J.S. Demski; L. Horngren and R.K. Jaedicke: A Conceptual Approach to Cost Determination. Stanford 1972, mineographed; to be published in 1973.

[20] Gonedes, N.J.: Accounting for Managerial Control: An Application of Chance-Contrained Programming. Journal of Accounting Research, Vol. 8, No. 1, Spring 1970.

[21] Gonedes, N.J.: Optimal Timing of Control Messages for a Two-State Markov Process. Journal of Accounting Research, Vol. 9, No. 2, Autumn 1971.

[22] Kalish, D.: The Encyclopedia of Philosophy, Vol. 7.

[23] Kaplan, R.S. and G.L. Thomson: Overhead Allocation via Mathematical Programming Models. Accounting Review, Vol. 46, No. 2, April 1971.

[24] Kennon, W.: MIS Universe. Data Management, Sept. 1970.

[25] Lev, Baruch: Accounting and Information Theory. American Accounting Association, 1969.

[26] Luh, F.S.: Controlled Cost: An Operational Concept and Statistical Approach to Standard Costing. Accounting Review, Vol. 43, No. 1, January 1968.

[27] Marschak, J.: Towards an Economic Theory of Organization and Information, Chpt. 14 of Decision Processes, ed. by R.M. Thrall, C.H. Coombs and R.L. Davis, New York 1954.

[28] Marschak, J.: Remarks on the Economics of Information. In: Contributions to Scientific Research in Management, Los Angeles 1959.

[29] Marschak, J.: Problems in Information Economics. In: Management Controls: New Directions in Basic Research, ed. by C.P. Bonini, R.K. Jaedicke and H.M. Wagner, New York 1964, pp. 38–74.

[30] Marschak, J.: Economics of Information Systems. Journal of American Statistical Association, March. 1971.

[31] Marschak, J. and Roy Radner: Economic Theory of Teams. New Haven 1972.

[32] Mattessich, R.: Accounting and Analytical Methods. Homewood, Ill. (1964).

[33] Mattessich, R.: The Impact of Electronic Data Processing and Management Science upon Accounting Theory. In: Modern Accounting Theory, ed. by M. Backer, Englewood Cliffs 1966.

[34] Mattessich, R.: Neue erkenntnistheoretische Probleme der Betriebswirtschaftslehre. In: Betriebswirtschaftliche Forschung in internationaler Sicht, ed. by H. Kloidt, Berlin 1969, pp. 28–29.

[35] Mattessich, R.: Systemsimulation und neue Aufgaben des betrieblichen Rechnungswesens. In: Der Computer im Dienste der Unternehmungsführung, ed. by W. Busse von Colbe und R. Mattessich, Gütersloh 1968.

[36] Mattessich, R.: Die wissenschaftlichen Grundlagen des Rechnungswesens. Düsseldorf 1970.

[37] Mattessich, R.: Some Thoughts on the Epistemology of Accounting. In: Proceedings of Second International Conference 1967 on Accounting Education. London 1970.

[38] Mattessich, R.: Methodological Preconditions and Problems of a General Theory of Accounting. The American Accounting Review, July 1972, pp. 470, 478–487.

[39] Mattessich, R.: Instrumental Reasoning and Decision Systems. Reader, 1974.

[40] McGuire, C.B. and R. Radner (eds.): Decision and Organization. New York 1972.

[41] Mock, T.J.: Concepts of Information Value. Accounting Review, Vol. 42, No. 4, October 1967.

[42] Mock, T.J.: The Evaluation of Alternative Information Structures. Berkeley 1969.

[43] Mock, T.J.: Concepts of Information Value and Accounting. Accounting Review, Oct. 1971, pp. 765–778.

[44] Onsi, Mohamed: Quantitative Models for Accounting Control. Accounting Review, Vol. 42, No. 2, April 1967.

[45] Ozan, T. and T.R. Dyckman: A Normative Model for Investigation Decisions Involving Multioriginal Cost Variances. Journal of Accounting Research, Vol. 9, No. 1, Spring 1971.

[46] Phillips, J.N.: Degrees of Interpretation. Philosophy of Science, Vol. 39, No. 3, Sept. 1972.

[47] Radner, R.: The Evaluation of Information in Organizations. In: Proceedings of the 4th Berkeley Symposium on Mathematical Statistics. Vol. 1, Berkeley 1961, pp. 491–530.

[48] Stigler, G.J.: The Economics of Information. Journal of Political Economy, Vol. 69, 1961, pp. 213–225.

[49] Theil, H.: Economics and Information Theory. Chicago 1967.

[50] Wild, J.: Zur Problematik der Nutzenbewertung von Informationen. Zeitschrift für Betriebswirtschaft, Vol. 41, No. 5, 1971, pp. 315–334.

[51] Witte, E. (ed.): Das Informationsverhalten in Entscheidungsprozessen. Tübingen 1972.

[52] Ziemba, W.T. and J.E. Butterworth: Bounds on the Value of the Information. In: Uncertain Decision Problems, Figueira da Foz, Portugal, June 1972.

German abstract
Informationsökonomik und der Begriff des „Management-Informationssystems"

Von *Richard Mattessich*

Der Artikel beginnt mit Bezugnahme auf Professor Deardens Ansicht, daß der Ausdruck „Management Information System" (MIS) einer Illusion ohne Inhalt gleichkommt. Der Autor stimmt dieser Ansicht nicht bei, gibt aber zu, daß die Bezeichnung in jüngster Zeit Verwirrung, vielleicht sogar Mißbrauch zur Folge hatte. Er nimmt Stellung gegen jene Definitionen des Begriffs MIS, die dafür keine klaren Bedingungen stellen und auf diese Weise scharfe Abgrenzung vermeiden. Die vorliegende Arbeit versucht daher im Wege der Informationsökonomik den Begriff MIS zu klären bzw. ihm einen klaren Inhalt zu geben.

Die von J. Marschak, R. Radner und anderen entwickelte Informationsökonomik (ein Grenzgebiet der Volkswirtschaftslehre und der statistischen Entscheidungstheorie) betrachtet Information als Ware, die den Glaubens- oder Vertrauensgrad einer Person in eine bestimmte Art von Ereignissen im Durchschnitt günstig zu verändern vermag, somit Wert besitzt bzw. wirtschaftlichen Gesetzmäßigkeiten unterstellt ist. Das Grundproblem der Informationsökonomik und ihrer Erweiterung durch Fachleute des betrieblichen Rechnungswesens (Butterworth, Demski, Feltham, Horngren, Jaedicke, Mattessich, u.a.m.) liegt im Testen des MIS, im Messen seines Wertes und letztlich in der Auswahl des besten unter allen verfügbaren Alternativsystemen. Schließlich wird in diesem zweiten Abschnitt an einem stark vereinfachten Fall die enge Verwandtschaft zwischen dem statistischen Entscheidungsmodell und dessen Erweiterung, dem informationsökonomischen Modell, dargestellt.

Der dritte Abschnitt geht dann auf die Beiträge der Rechnungsfachleute (vor allem jene der ehemaligen Schüler und gegenwärtigen Kollegen Mattessichs, der Professoren Butterworth und Feltham der Universität von Britisch Kolumbien) ein. Auf die Beziehungen dieser UBC-Studien, sowie der Stanford-Studien von Demski, Horngren, Jaedicke etc., zu Mattessichs Accounting and Analytical Methods (1964) und späteren Arbeiten wird in Fußnote 15 kurz eingegangen.

Der vierte Abschnitt zeigt, wie der vom Autor (1964) vorgeschlagene und verwirklichte Gedanke des rechnungsmäßigen Metamodells von Butterworth und Feltham auf die Informationsökonomik angewandt wurde, und wie dadurch der theoretische Wert eines Informationssystems mathematisch ermittelt werden kann.

Der vierte Abschnitt bespricht, welche Vereinfachungsmöglichkeiten des obigen Modells gegeben sind und wie die in der Rechnungsliteratur des letzten Jahrzehnts dargebotenen Modelle unter diesen Vereinfachungstypen kategorisiert werden können. Auch wird der Unterschied zwischen Modellkonstruktion als Interpretation und Modellkonstruktion als Vereinfachung analysiert. Schließlich wird die Frage erörtert, ob die Axiome des Metamodells von Butterworth und Feltham als notwendige und ausreichende Bedingungen einer rigorosen semantischen Definition des MIS akzeptiert werden können. Diese Methode mag uns keine Definition bieten, die nach jedermanns Geschmack ist, wenn aber diese semantische Definition so umfassend ist, daß sie durch ihre weite Interpretationsmöglichkeiten die meisten Rechnungs-Informationsmodelle umfaßt, dann wäre der Widerstand gegen diese Definition leichter zu brechen.

Im letzten Abschnitt wird schließlich aufgezeigt, daß die allgemeine MIS Theorie (d.h. das Metamodell) nicht allein, sondern nur zusammen mit ihren Interpretationen (spezifischen Modellen) getestet werden kann. Anhand eines Computer-Flußdiagramms wird besprochen, wie im Prinzip ein solches Testverfahren rekursiv, aber unter Vermeidung von Zirkularität, ablaufen könnte. Auf die damit verbundenen Schwierigkeiten und ihre eventuelle Überwindung wird zu allerletzt eingegangen.

A model for the construction of a cost-minimal communication tree

By *Ludwig Nastansky* and *Hans Jürgen Drumm*

1. Introduction

For several years there have been increasing efforts to solve organizational problems by mathematical decision models. One can roughly distinguish three basic fields of research in solving organizational problems by means of quantitative methods. The first problem area includes personnel assignment problems which can be formulated and partly solved by procedures of mixed integer programming [1; 5; 4]. The second problem area contains problems of work flow planning and project management; usually they can be solved by network analysis techniques [3, pp. 58–80]. The third area has to do with the structure of communication systems and control of communication processes; these problems can be formulated by means of flow models and combinatorial algorithms; optimal solutions can be found under special conditions [9, pp. 140–161].

In this paper we consider the last problem area mentioned, yet we present a model of a very general type. This model is also appropriate for the solution of different problems, which do not belong to those of the communication system type [7]. Here our model will be used for the solution of what are called "structure-problems" in organizations. The model is based on graph theoretical methods; the basic structure of the optimizing problem belongs to a set of combinatorial procedures (cf. [2, chapt. II]).

First we develop the general organizational problem. Then the model will be formulated, followed by a small example and a summary of the solution procedure. In the appendix we shall demonstrate the efficiency of the model by help of three different exemplary decision situations. The first example deals with the diffusion of information on several decision-, staff- and executing units or stations. The second example deals with the construction of a management information system using a specific number of terminals. The third example demonstrates, how a new product can be optimally introduced through several different distribution channels.

2. The organizational problem

Usually the units or stations of an organization are linked by a set of communication paths. If a specific information has to be transmitted to one or several stations, the source of information can use a direct or an indirect – if not even several – communication path. The choice of a certain path depends on several items as for example the cost of communication, the term of communication or the capacity of the communication means. Moreover it can be necessary to include certain stations into a communication path, if official channels must be used, or if the information has to reach some stations in any case. Usually cost can be attributed to every communication path. It can therefore be sensible to choose the communication paths such that total cost of communication will be minimized. So the point is to select one or several cost-minimal communication paths out of a set of feasible communication paths. The following constraints must be satisfied:

(a) A certain number of stations must belong to the optimal path since they have to be informed about the communication process.

(b) Some communication paths cannot be used if a minimum speed of communication cannot be reached, or if the information cannot be transmitted within a feasible intervall of time.

(c) Some communication paths cannot be used, if they don't have a certain minimum-capacity.

If all communication paths, not satisfying constraints (b) and (c), are eliminated, our organizational problem can be formulated by means of the graph theory and solved by the algorithm subsequentyl described.

3. The decision model

3.1 The construction of the communication network

In the model we have a source of information S. The set S may consist of one or more different stations. Information has to be transmitted to recipients of information. All these receiving stations are defined as set T. It makes no difference whether the stations of set T only receive information from S or whether they also forward received information to subsequent stations. In the latter case, the stations act as recipients of information as well as relay stations for informations. Beside the sets S and T we have the set B of pure relay stations. These stations receive informations only to transmit them. They can be used for the transmission of information, but they do not have to be.

Information has to be transmitted from the source of information to the recipients of information. We suppose any pair i, j [$i \neq j; i, j \in T \cup R$] of relay stations to be in an unequivocal hierarchical order. This means: if there is any path of communication between station i and station j there is only one feasible direction for the flow of information over all possible paths between station i and station j. Thus, we exclude the possibility of a station to be located either before or after another station at the end of the decision process. We define all stations of the sets S, T, and R to be the nodes of a graph G. The set of all nodes of G is $N = S \cup T \cup R$. We assign an arc (i, j) to any possible case of information transmission from a station $i \in N$ to a station $j \in N$ $[i \neq j]$. The totality of these possible elementary ways of information transmission is defined as the arc set A of G. The cost c_{ij} of elementary communication from i to j are given for each arc (i, j) $\in A$ by the function C. The quantities determining the c_{ij} depend on the specific situation for which the model is to apply. If the problem is to construct a new communication network we have to consider cost which are fixed cost in the sense of short-term periodical planning. If we want to solve the problem of using an existing communication network in a cost-minimal way, c_{ij} will consist of variable cost components. As a consequence of this cost interpretation, the c_{ij} will be non-negative and naturally greater than zero.

The result of these definitions is the directed costdigraph G = (N, A, C). G has no (directed) cycles. This follows from the assumption of unequivocal hierarchy. Thus, a node indexing is possible such that for each arc $(i, j) \in A$ we have $i < j$. This is often advantageous for the purpose of simplifying bookkeeping in algorithms. From now on G will be called communication network.

3.2 The formulation of the optimization problem

The graph G represents all possible, technically feasible ways of information transmission for the underlying problem, and it contains the cost of elementary information transmission. The problem is now to extract a cost-minimal communication tree out of the communication network; i.e. we have exactly one path of communication from the source of information to each recipient of information.

Frequently this kind of a combinatorial decision model can be formulated as a linear (0,1)-programming problem. For this purpose, we assign a variable x_{ij} to each arc $(i, j) \in A$. $x_{ij} = 1$ says that we use the elementary way of communication transmission from station i to station j in the communication network, $x_{ij} = 0$ means that we do not use this elementary way.

P_j denotes the set of all direct predecessor nodes of station $j \in N$. S_j is the set of all direct successor nodes of station $j \in N$. The cardinality $|S_j|$ is the number of all direct successors of j.

The objective function of the linear (0,1)-programming problem is:

$$(1\!-\!1) \qquad \sum_{(i,j) \in A} c_{ij} \; x_{ij} \qquad \text{Min!}$$

The constraints are:

$$(1\text{–}2)\qquad \sum_{i \in P_j} x_{ij} = 1 \qquad [j \in T]$$

$$(1\text{–}3)\qquad |S_j| \sum_{i \in P_j} x_{ij} \geqslant \sum_{k \in S_j} x_{jk} \qquad [j \in R]$$

$$(1\text{–}4)\qquad x_{ij} \in \{0,1\} \qquad [(i,j) \in A]$$

Constraint (1–2) guarantees that each station j of the set T receives informations by means of a communication path from the source S. Constraint (1–3) asserts that there is no path of communication transmission leading out of a node j when there is no path leading to j. Moreover, this constraint allows, that all ways of information transmission leading out of node j (there are $|S_j|$ such ways) can be used if there is only one path leading to j. Constraint (1–3) is not necessary for stations $j \in T$ because constraint (1–2) guarantees for these stations in any case that a communication path is leading to them.

The objective function (1–1) together with the constraints (1–2) through (1–4) assert that the optimal solution of the linear (0,1)-programming problem defines a communication tree from the source of information to all recipients of information. The leaves of the tree are all recipients of information which only receive and do not forward information. It is possible to have a kind of degeneracy not resulting in a (0,1)-solution defining a tree because we allowed arcs with zero cost. In this case, we only have to remove some of the arcs with zero cost from the directed graph defined by the (0,1)-solution until the graph turns into a tree. This is a simple bookkeeping procedure but no optimization problem. As far as formulation and interpretation are concerned our problem of constructing a cost-minimal communication tree is quite similar to the ordinary problems of finding a cost-minimal flow in networks. The basic difference between the two problems is that in our problem we distinguish only the cases "information flow yes" (associated variable equal to one) and "information flow no" (associated variable equal to zero) for each elementary way of information transmission.

Once we have the case "information flow yes" for one elementary way of information transmission to a relay station we can forward the informations from this relay station so subsequent stations without any influence on the quantity of the information flow to this relay station. As a consequence, the cost of information transmission to a station do not depend on whether or not information is forwarded from this station. The flow conservation property of the ordinary network flow model, however, gives a different approach. For any unit of flow which we want to transport out of a node we have to assert one unit of flow being transported to this node. Here, as a consequence, the flow cost to this node are increased by the unit cost of all arcs used to transmit the additional unit of flow from a source to this node.

3.3 A small example

We consider the example of a communication network given in Fig. 1.

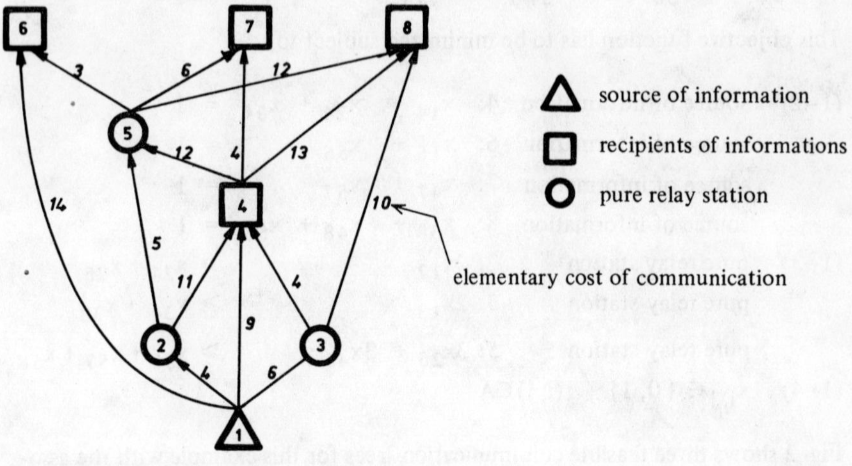

Fig. 1. An example of a communication network

The associated sets N and A of G = (N,A,C) are:

$$N = S \cup T \cup R$$
$$S = \{1\}$$
$$T = \{4, 6, 7, 8\}$$
$$R = \{2, 3, 5\}$$
$$A = \{(1,2),(1,3),(1,4),(1,6),(2,4),(2,5),(3,4),(3,8),(4,5),(4,7),(4,8),(5,6),(5,7),(5,8)\}$$

Examples for the sets P_j and S_j are:

$P_5 = \{2, 4\}$
$S_4 = \{5, 7, 8\}$ $\quad |S_4| = 3$

Explicitly the objective function of the associated linear (0, 1)-program reads:

$$
\begin{aligned}
(1\text{–}1)' \quad & 4x_{12} + 6x_{13} + 9x_{14} + 14x_{16} \\
& + 5x_{25} + 11x_{24} \\
& + 4x_{34} + 10x_{38} \\
& + 12x_{45} + 4x_{47} + 13x_{48} \\
& + 3x_{56} + 6x_{57} + 12x_{58} \quad \rightarrow \text{Min!}
\end{aligned}
$$

This objective function has to be minimized subject to:

$$
\begin{aligned}
(1\text{–}2)' \quad & \text{source of information } 4: \; x_{14} + x_{24} + x_{34} = 1 \\
& \text{source of information } 6: \; x_{16} + x_{56} = 1 \\
& \text{source of information } 7: \; x_{47} + x_{57} = 1 \\
& \text{source of information } 8: \; x_{38} + x_{48} + x_{58} = 1 \\
(1\text{–}3)' \quad & \text{pure relay station } 2: \; 2x_{12} \geqslant x_{24} + x_{25} \\
& \text{pure relay station } 3: \; 2x_{13} \geqslant x_{34} + x_{38} \\
& \text{pure relay station } 5: \; 3x_{25} + 3x_{45} \geqslant x_{56} + x_{57} + x_{58} \\
(1\text{–}4)' \quad & x_{i,j} \in \{0, 1\} \qquad (i, j) \in A
\end{aligned}
$$

Fig. 2 shows three feasible communication trees for this example with the associated total costs K:

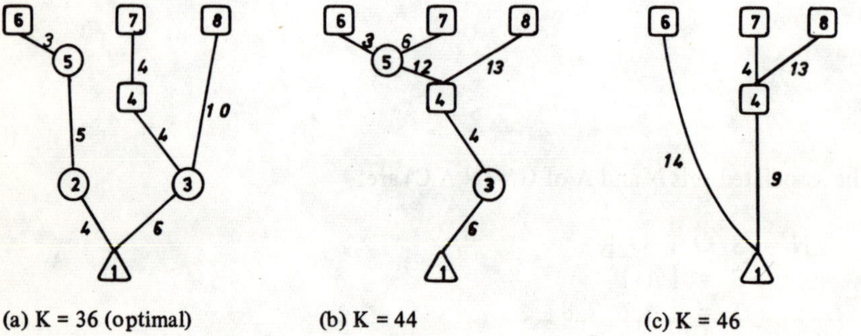

Fig. 2. Communication trees for the communication network of Fig. 1 with total costs K

The optimal solution of Fig. 2 (a) turns out to be a communication tree which uses the pure relay station nodes 2, 3 and 5. On the other hand, there is no pure relay station used in the tree of Fig. 2 (c). But the total cost K = 40 of the latter tree are higher compared with K = 36 of the optimal solution.

3.4 The solution of the optimization problem

The formulation of problem (1) implies that a cost-minimal communication tree can be computed by means of standard techniques of linear (0,1)-optimization. Unfortunately, this does not say too much about the efficiency of this way of solving the cost minimization problem. Though there has been an immense research going on in this field during the last ten years, it has not been possible to develop a powerful standard method for (0, 1)-optimization comparable in capability with the simplex method for linear programming. Thus, rather than applying standard algorithms it has turned out that in view of the combinatorial character of the linear (0, 1)-problem adapted algorithms based on the structure of the underlying optimization problem have to be found.

The authors have computational experience with three different types of algorithms. The first algorithm is a cutting-plane method. This approach takes advantage of the (+1, –1)-structure of the coefficients in a (0, 1)-formulation of the problem similar to (1–1) through (1–4). Especially, list-processing techniques are used in this algorithm to improve the efficiency of the simplex calcutions in this special case [7]. The second algorithm is an implicit enumeration scheme [8]. The search in this algorithm is adapted to the cycle-free structure of the underlying graph. The typical advantage of this approach is that it allows to generate a great number of "near-optimal" alternative trees. The third algorithm, finally, is a kind of dynamic programming method [6] which derives solutions for subgraphs of G subsequently developed during the $n = |N|$ stages of the process. The back-tracking phase yields a cost-minimal total tree by combining these cost-minimal subtrees constructed in the preceding forward phase.

The efficiency of these three algorithms can be qualified by the criteria: maximal size of problems solvable, storage demands, and computing time.

The disadvantages of the cutting-plane method are the high demands of fast core memory and the unpredictable low convergence for ill-conditioned problems. The basic problem of the implicit enumeration algorithm is that the computation time grows nearly exponentially with the number of variables, i.e. the number of considered elementary ways of information transmission. This is due to the rather weak exclusion rules because normally there are many alternative near optimal solutions. The best computational experience was made with the third algorithm. In this dynamic programming algorithm the efficiency of the computations is strongly based upon the wordlength of the computer on which the algorithm is implemented. This is because all information about the computed subtrees is recorded and processed as bit-patterns.

Appendix

Example I: Organization of cost-minimal intro-company communication

The management of a company has changed the wage incentive payment plan in cooperation with a special committee of the works council. Now the details of this plan are to be transmitted to every pieceworker in the company. The management can use several different communication paths:

(1) It can transmit the plan directly to every pieceworker.

(2) It can use an indirect communication path by first informing either the two plant managers or the four foremen.

(3) The information can be transmitted by the special committee of the works council.

The feasible communication paths and the costs assigned to every path are shown on the following diagram.

Example II: Cost-minimal network of computer terminals as part of a management information system

A given number of computer terminals is to be installed. The displays are linked to the calculating unit by fixed wire connections.

A technical constraint allows only a connection between four displays and one display control unit.

A maximum of four display control units can be linked with a display junction unit. Up to four displays can have a direct connection with a display junction unit. Instead of a display another display control unit can be connected to a display control unit (i.e. there is a possibility of a cascading arrangement).

The feasible combinations of equipment produce cost consisting of

equipment and erection cost,

cost for material and initial expenditure for channels with different qualities and conditions of transmission.

The point is to find the cost-minimal cascading.

Example I – Figure a

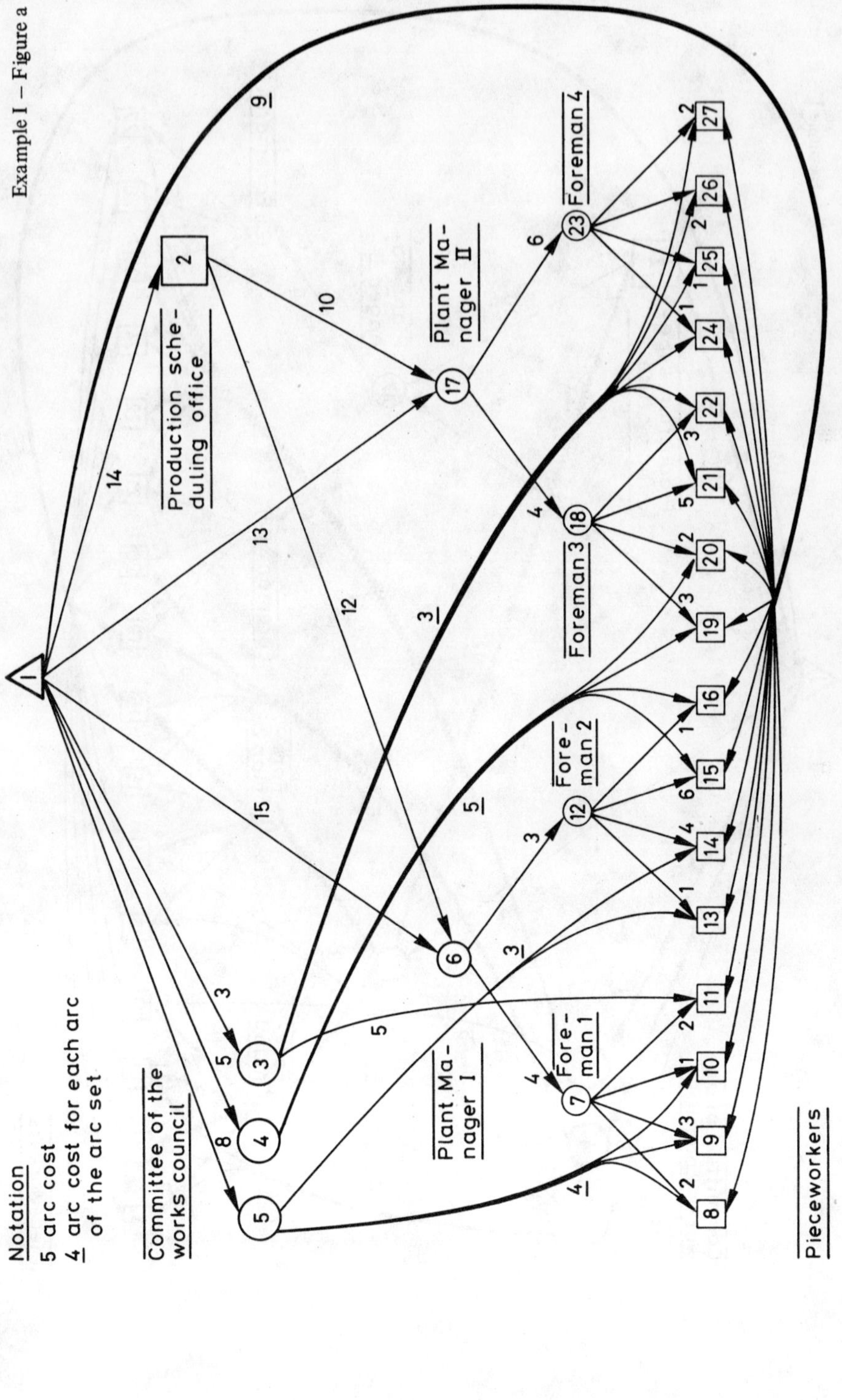

Example I – Figure b

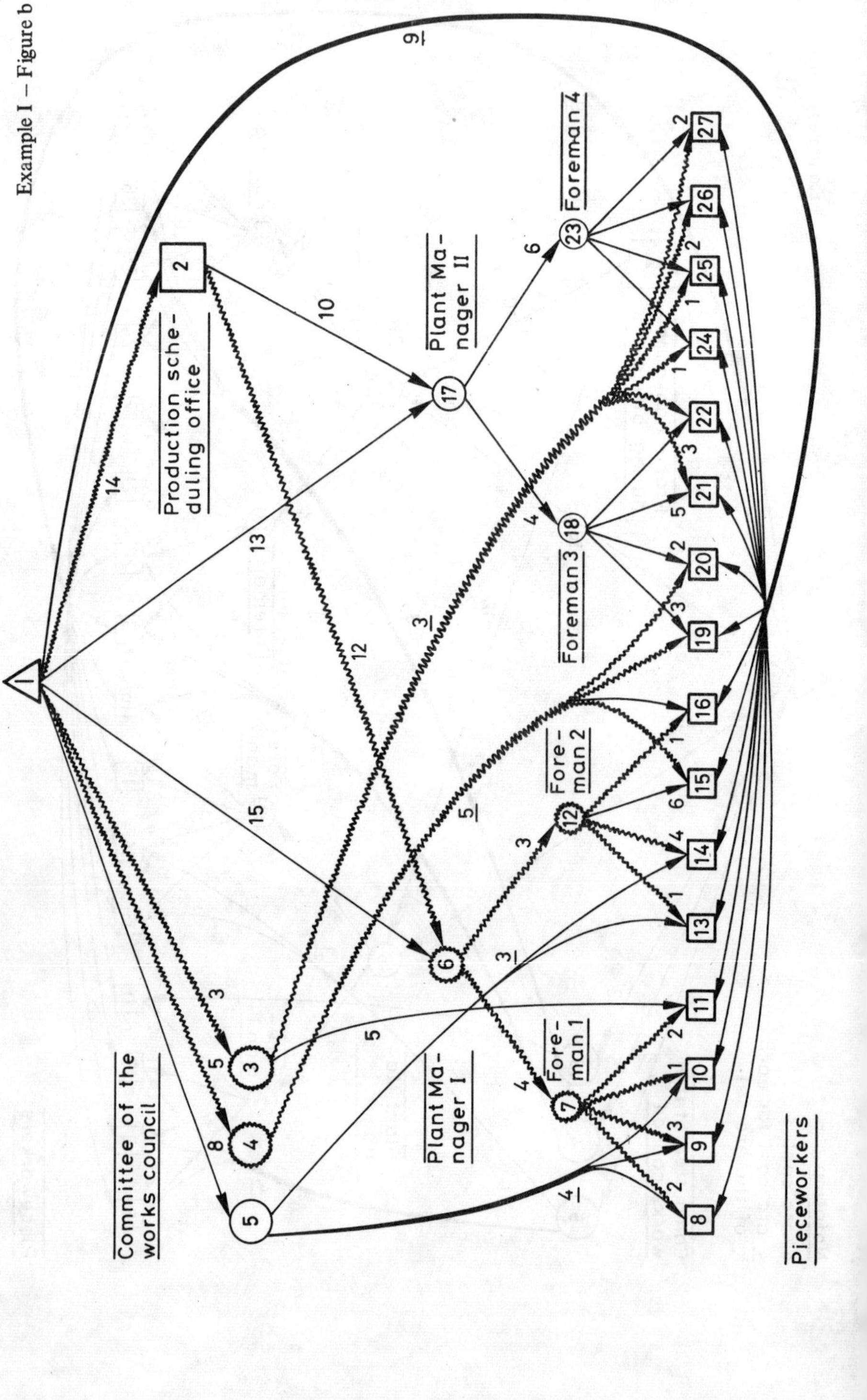

Example II – Figure a

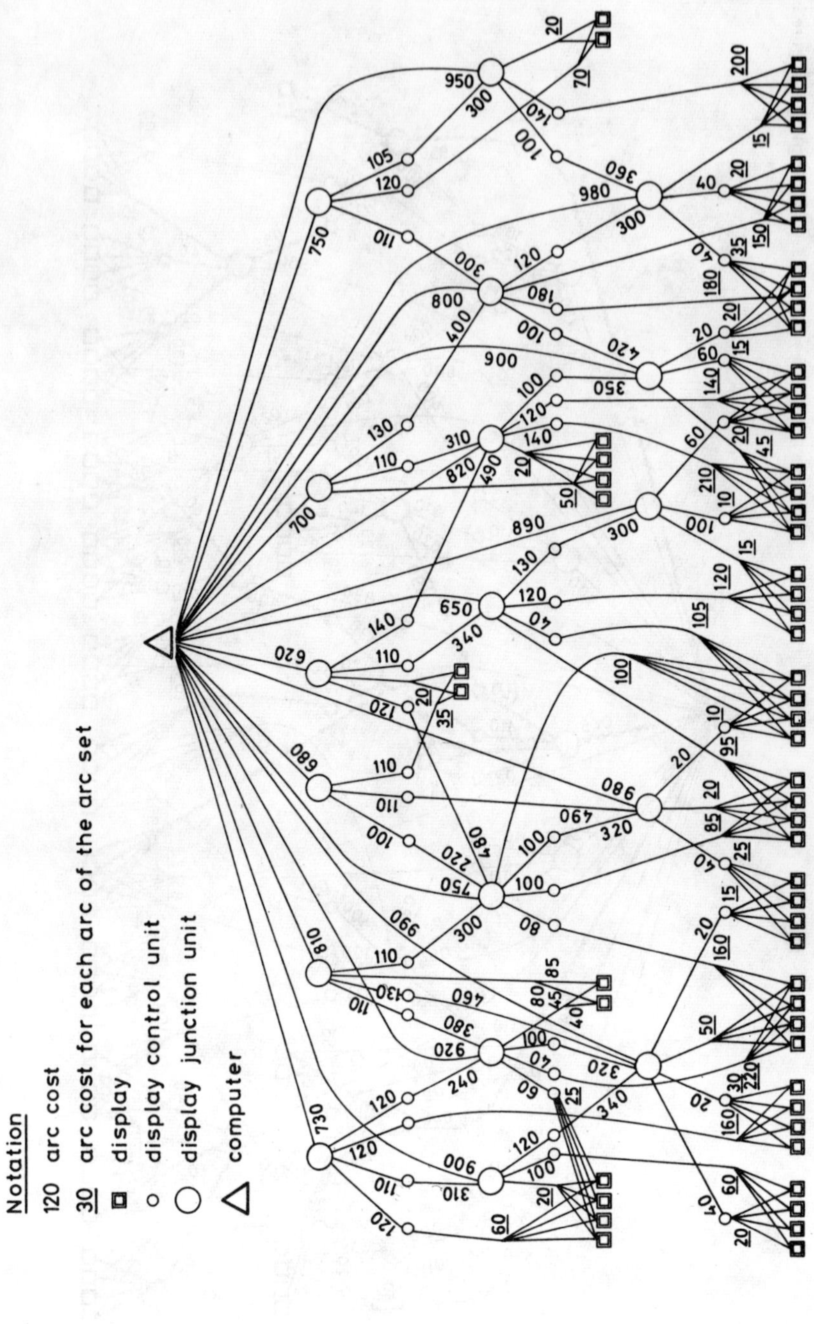

Example II – Figure b

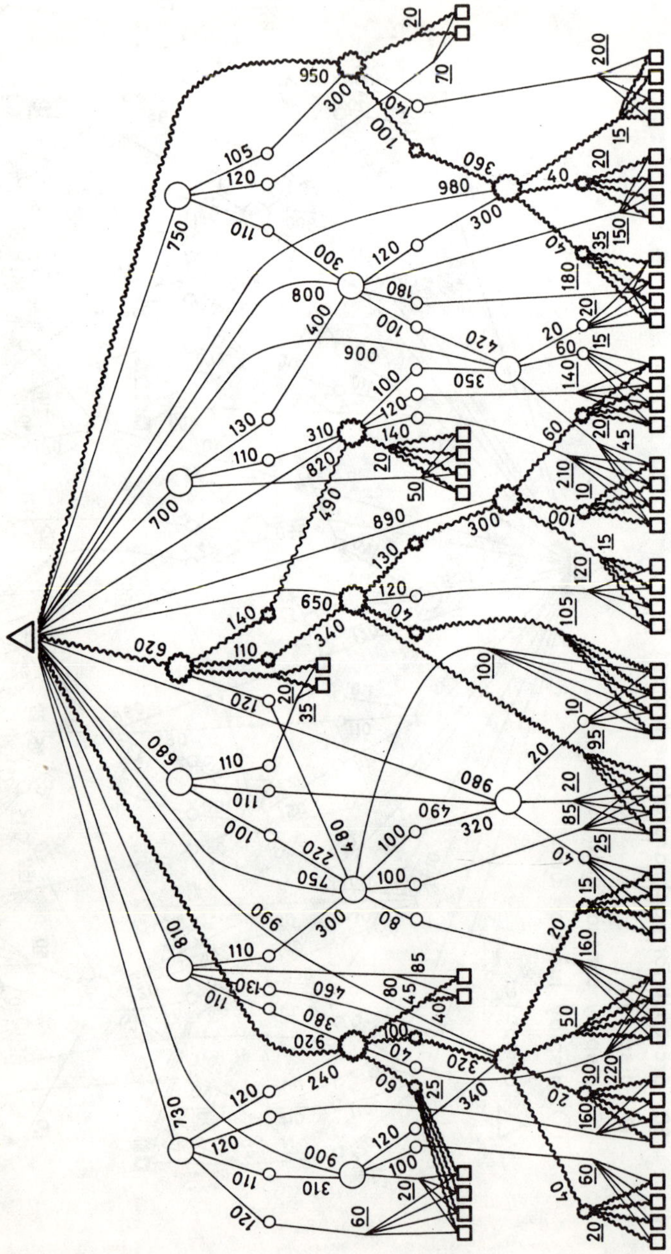

Example III – Figure a

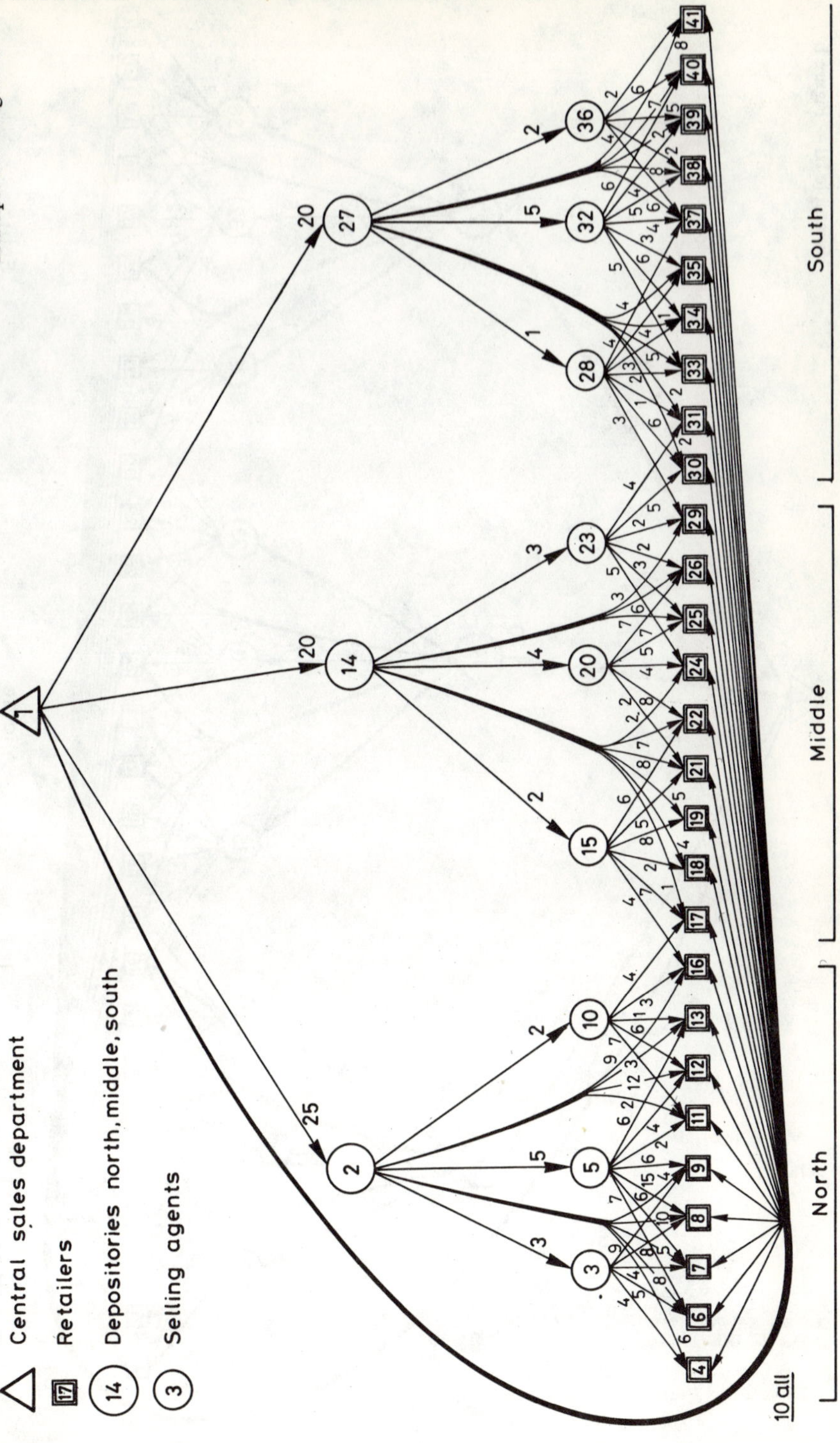

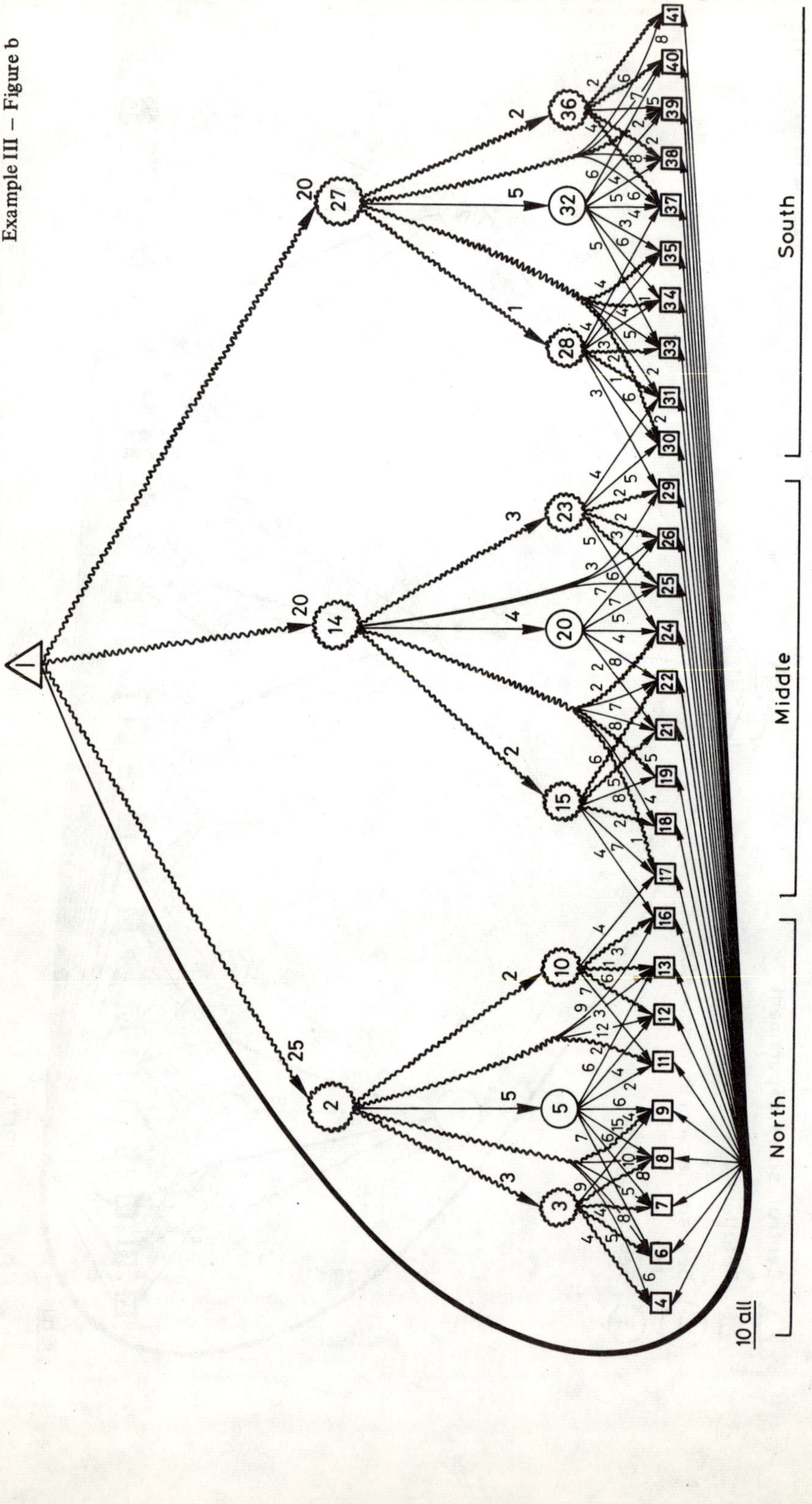

Example III – Figure b

Example III: Organization of cost-minimal introduction of a new product

The sales division of an enterprise wants to introduce a newly developed product. During the initial campaign a certain number of samples will be presented to some selected retailers in the three sales districts "North", "Middle" and "South". Also some information about the new product will be offered. The distribution problem can be solved in different ways:

(1) The central sales department mails the samples together with an instruction by letter. This alternative mainly produces delivery charges.

(2) The samples will be delivered to the decentral depositories "North", "Middle" and "South". From there the samples and a printed instruction will be distributed with the usual deliveries by car to the selected retailers. This alternative produces distribution cost and opportunity cost for storage capacity and loading space.

(3) The selling agents of the three decentral sales agencies "North", "Middle" and "South" offer the samples, a printed instruction and additional verbal information when they visit the retailers of their sales district. The selling agents can also visit retailers of an adjoining district, if these live near the districts border. This alternative produces travelling charges and cost of labour.

These alternatives are shown as different communication networks on the following diagram.

References

[1] Charnes, A., W.W. Cooper, R.J. Niehaus and A. Stedry: Static and Dynamic Assignment Models with Multiple Objectives, and Some Remarks on Organization Design. In: Management Science, Vol. 15, 1968/69, pp. B 365–375.

[2] Ford, L.R. and D.R. Fulkerson: Flows in Networks. Princeton N.J., 1962.

[3] Kern, W.: Die Netzplantechnik als Instrument betrieblicher Ablaufplanung. Anwendung der Netzplantechnik im Betrieb. Ed. by H. Jacob. Wiesbaden 1969.

[4] Kossbiel, H.: Kontrollspanne und Führungskräfteplanung, Grundlagen der betrieblichen Personalpolitik. Ed. by W. Braun, H. Kossbiel, G. Reber. Wiesbaden 1972.

[5] Müller-Hagedorn, L.: Grundlagen der Personalbestandsplanung. Opladen 1970.

[6] Nastansky, L.: Die Bestimmung kostenminimaler Bäume in gerichteten Netzwerken mit Hilfe der dynamischen Programmierung. Unpublished.

[7] Nastansky, L., S.M. Selkow and N.F. Stewart: The Enumeration of Minimal Phylograms. In: Bulletin of Mathematical Biophysics, Vol. 35, 1973, pp. 525–533.

[8] Nastansky, L., S.M. Selkow and N.F. Stewart: Cost-Minimal Trees in Directed Acyclic Graphs. In: Zeitschrift für Operations Research, Vol. 18, 1974, pp. 59–67.

[9] Wild, J.: Neuere Organisationsforschung in betriebswirtschaftlicher Sicht. Berlin 1967.

German abstract
Zur Wahl des gesamtkostenminimalen Kommunikationssystems

Von *Ludwig Nastansky* und *Hans Jürgen Drumm*

Der Beitrag beschäftigt sich mit dem Problem, ein kostenminimales Kommunikationssystem in einem Kommunikationsnetzwerk zu bestimmen. Die Ermittlung kostenminimaler Kommunikationssysteme gehört zu den sogenannten Aufbauproblemen der Organisationsplanung. Solche Probleme können häufig mit Flußmodellen und kombinatorischen Algorithmen in Netzwerken gelöst werden. Hier wird ein Modell vorgeschlagen, das mit Hilfe eines kombinatorischen Algorithmus lösbar ist.

Das Kommunikationsnetzwerk enthält eine Gruppe von Informationsquellen, von denen Informationen an eine Gruppe von Informationsempfängern zu übermitteln sind. Neben Quellen und Empfängern gibt es noch reine Relaisstellen, die Informationen empfangen und weiterleiten können; diese Relaisstellen können für die Informationsweitergabe benutzt werden, müssen es aber nicht. Quellen, Empfänger und Relaisstellen definieren Knoten in einem gerichteten Kommunikations-Netzwerk.

Die Kanten des Netzwerks kennzeichnen elementare Informationswege; elementar bedeutet: von einer Sendestelle (Ausgangsknoten) zu einer empfangenden Stelle (Endknoten). Mögliche elementare Informationswege sind: Quelle nach Empfänger, Quelle nach Relaisstelle, Relaisstelle nach Relaisstelle, Relaisstelle nach Empfänger. Jedem dieser elementaren Informationswege sind Kosten für die Übertragung der Information zugeordnet. Die Besonderheit dieses Problems besteht darin, daß auch bei wiederholtem Abruf von Informationen aus einem Knoten keine zusätzlichen Kosten für die Übertragung von Informationen zu diesem Knoten auftreten. Dadurch unterscheidet sich dieses Problem von Standard-Flußmodellen, bei denen jede von einem Knoten ausgehende Flußeinheit auch zuvor zu diesem Knoten hintransportiert werden muß.

In einer konkreten Anwendungssituation wird häufig eine Vielzahl von Alternativen bestehen, um die notwendigen Informationen von den Quellen zu allen Empfängern zu übertragen. Ein wichtiges Problem ist in diesem Zusammenhang, denjenigen Kommunikationsbaum in dem vorliegenden Kommunikationsnetzwerk zu bestimmen, der bei geringsten Gesamtkosten des Kommunikationssystems garantiert, daß jeder Empfänger von den Quellen mit Informationen beliefert wird. Die Frage ist hier insbesondere, ob und welche Relaisstellen man einschalten soll.

Für die Ermittlung des kostenminimalen Kommunikationsbaumes innerhalb eines gegebenen Kommunikationssystems wurde ein dynamischer Programmierungsalgorithmus entwickelt, der als Fortran-Programm verfügbar ist. Anwendungsfälle des Algorithmus werden an drei Beispielen aufgezeigt: Organisation der kostenminimalen innerbetrieblichen Benachrichtigung, kostenminimales Terminalnetz im Rahmen eines Informationssystems mit Kaskadierung und Organisation der kostenminimalen Produkteinführung.

Automatic interfacing of application software in the GPLAN framework

By *Jay F. Nunamaker,* Jr., *John Pomeranz* and *Andrew Whinston*

1. Introduction

This paper addresses the problems of implementing a planning process with a computer system: (1) we identify the essentials of the relationship between planners and information systems; (2) we assign responsibility for specific functions to specific systems; (3) we define a Generalized Data Base Planning System (GPLAN) as a methodology that incorporates computerized information system into the planning framework; (4) we describe two systems designed or implemented with this method.

GPLAN is essentially a computerized planning system based on a conceptualization and abstraction of the planning process. GPLAN itself has several components. There is a problem-oriented query language which permits a nonprocedural statement of the problem by the planner. Associated with the problem-oriented query language is an analyzer and control program with the responsibility for selection of the appropriate model. Finally, an interfacing mechanism uses the model requirements to generate accesses to a data base in order to assemble the necessary input files and to control program execution. It is the interfacing mechanism that we describe later, in depth.

We observe that computerized planning systems have long been sought, but proposed solutions have been too vague (Blumenthal [4], Anthony [1], Simon [14]) or too general (Newell, Shaw and Simon [10]) to be useful at the production level. GPLAN is being developed within the context of specific applications and as a result we believe that GPLAN balances generality with practicality.

2. GPLAN framework

A planner, with or without a computer, uses a system that, as a result of a specific query can: (1) retrieve the necessary data and (2) set up the application program or model that must be run with the data to answer the query. This requires that the data be retrieved and arranged by the system in the proper format for the model. The value of using a computer system lies in the efficiency of storing and retrieving data and the range of services provided by existing programs. The planning system must be designed so that the user is freed from the mundane task of data preparation, which can be tedious and frought with human errors, in order to run a model. Often, the planner is not familiar with the problems and procedures of data handling and would prefer not being bothered with it at all.

A planner who queries a data base will gain little if he must further select, re-arrange, reformat, and punch his retrieved data for input to an application program or model.

On another dimension, there has been considerable development of simulation and optimization packages, but in practice these packages have not been used by the people who should be using them. The reasons for this investment in application packages with little resultant usefulness are simple. The packages are so difficult to use, requiring either very much technical knowledge in the particular mathematical programming technique or complex file setup and manipulation steps, that few people are able to use the packages without relying heavily on technical help or education in the specifics of each particular package.

To increase the usefulness of these packages, the nontechnical and management personnel who are knowledgeable in the general area of endeavor must be able to use these packages easily.

In summary, an information system will be used for planning only when it automatically creates the data files needed by the various application programs and answers general queries to the data base.

Figure 1 displays the principal components of such a system.

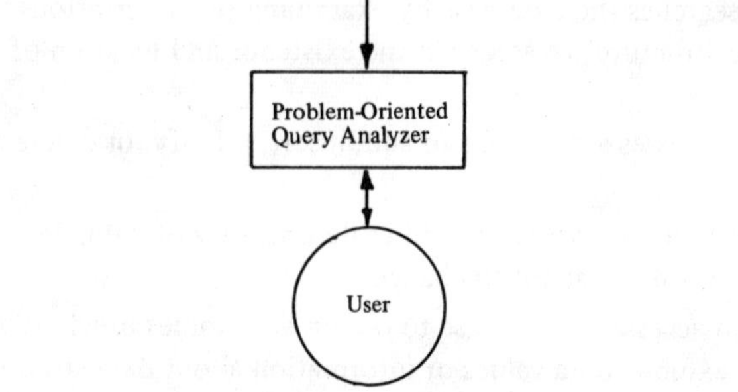

Fig. 1. GPLAN: Generalized Data Base Planning System

2.1 User

There are two types of users connected with GPLAN: the technical and the non-technical.

A data administrator and his systems staff are responsible for: all original data input, updating of data, restructuring the data base and extraction files as necessary, changing machines and operating systems, adding new packages, standard reports and other additions or improvements. These systems users, taken as a group, must understand fairly well every component of GPLAN. They possibly could be unfamiliar with some of the application packages, but then would have to consult an authority to alter them. Planners, the major group of users are non-programming administrators. These are users who don't know how to program, probably don't want to learn, and definitely shouldn't have to learn. They have a good understanding of the area for which the planning system was designed, or will have training in this area before using GPLAN. Most of the details of the GPLAN implementation are transparent to these users, and they should not notice any changes in the system, except the addition of new capabilities (possibly requested by them), new efficiency, or new packages. The success or failure of GPLAN depends on how well these users are able to carry out their querying of the data base and interaction with the application packages using only the query language and its documentation.

2.2 Data Management System and interfacing mechanism

A Data Base Management System (DMS) that is implemented at a particular installation under a specified operating system must be available. The DMS must meet minimum requirements as to data structure definition, data base loading, data base updating, and data base retrieval, and it must satisfy some minimum set of functions:

Input – the system accepts data values or information about data structures.

Search – the system searches the data base by examining the descriptions of data structures and storage structures to ascertain the existence and location of certain data values.

Storage – the system accesses a data base to add, insert, modify, or delete data values.

Maintenance – the system generates or modifies descriptions of data, data structures, and storage structures to adapt to change.

Retrieval – the system accesses a data base to obtain data values previously stored.

Output – the system exhibits data values or information about data structures and storage structures.

Such systems already exist, e. g., System 2000 [9], RAMIS [13], IMS [7] or Disk Forte [5].

The interface is a program that transfers operating control among the DMS, the Problem-Oriented Query Analyzer (below) and the models.

2.3 Problem-oriented query language and analyzer

The problem-oriented query language is written specifically for each planning system. It provides the capability for asking questions of the data base and asking questions that can be handled by the various application packages. It permits:

Selective retrieval – the user specifies the selection conditions to be satisfied in retrieving the desired data.

Nonselective retrieval – the user specifies unconditional retrieval of data.

Conditional retrieval – the user employs verbs such as IF . . . ELSE to test items for some qualifying values in determining alternative courses of action.

Statistical retrieval – the user may query the system about data. Statistical computations for all the instances of one item, for example, would include maximum value, minimum value, mean value, median value, mode value, standard deviation, and total number of instances.

Application retrieval – the user may evoke a call to one or more applications or models as a result of the interaction with the control program and analyzer. The user may ask for the values of the decision variables, or the value of specific constraints or he may wish to look at the value of the dual variables in a mathematical programming application.

The problem oriented query analyzer checks for consistency in the query and checks syntax in accordance with the query language, prepares error comments to aid the user in correcting, modifying and extending his query, decides whether to pass the query to the DMS or one of the application packages, and may request additional information from the user if the action to be initiated requires it.

2.4 Models

The models are simulation, optimization and statistical packages, and other self-contained systems currently functioning under a specific computer and operating system.

By including optimization models among the application packages, the policy-maker is able to move efficiently beyond the "What if" to the "What's best" question. We will make several assumptions about application packages: First, they are already running as batch jobs rather than interactive jobs. This is especially desirable if they have quite long running times and making them interactive may simply mean waiting at the terminal. Second, they require user preparation to get the data ready. Third, they require other programs to run to prepare the input data.

We must know certain characteristics of an application package or model before we can consider using it in GPLAN:

A Input:

1. For each data input, we must know what kind it is (pure data or commands) and the associated types and formats.

2. For each data input, we must know the kind of device it is assigned (sequential or random-access).

3. We must know the passes and correct logic steps and transformations to go from the data base to each input.

4. For each data input, what must be included in system commands to the DMS for 3 above?

B Output:

1. Is the output self-explanatory or does it require minor explanation in the form of good documentation in the query language description?

2. Does the output require much technical knowhow to interpret the results? If so, an output interpretation module is required.

C What query components does it add to the query language?

D Minimal documentation to be used by:

1. Systems personnel,
2. Non-programmer researcher.

2.5 Data base

The raw data for the planning system must be available in whatever form.

To refer to the data in the data base, the following terms, adopted from the CODASYL Data Base Task Group Report [6], are defined:

DDL – Data Description Language. A language for defining data and their relationships. The DDL is divided into schema and sub-schema.

Schema – that part of the DDL which defines the "universal" data base.

Sub-schema – that part of the DDL which describes the data known to each application program or model.

A schema describing the data in the data base must be prepared.

2.6 A working example of the interfacing mechanism

Arsenault et al. [2] describe a Generalized Interfacing Module (GEM) which was used with GPLAN/Water Pollution Control.

The design objectives of the interfacing mechanism are:

1. to automate as much of the interfacing process as possible,
2. to keep the interfacing mechanism transparent to the application program,
3. to avoid binding the application program to a specific DMS, and
4. to eliminate much of the manual effort in data file and control card preparation required to run application programs.

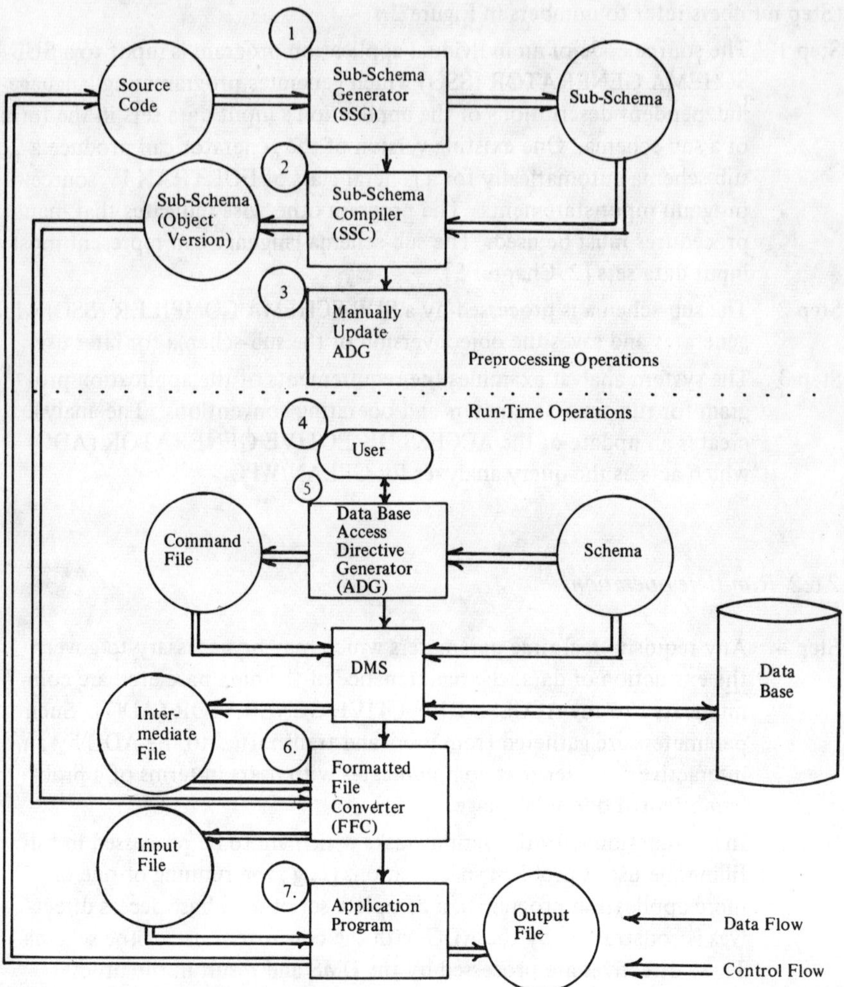

Fig. 2. GEM Implementation Detail

Figure 2 is a detailed overview of the GEM mechanism which has been implemented for GPLAN/WPC in FORTRAN IV for a CDC 6500. GEM operations are partitioned into pre-processing and run-time operations. For any given application program, the pre-processing activities occur prior to the time of first use. The run-time operations are performed for each individual execution of an application program.

2.6.1 Pre-processing operations

(Step numbers refer to numbers in Figure 2.)

Step 1 The source code of an individual application program is input to a SUB-SCHEMA GENERATOR (SSG) which generates programming-language-independent descriptions of the application's input data sets in the form of a sub-schema. One existing version of the generator can produce a sub-schema automatically for a general class of FORTRAN IV source program input statements. The program otherwise indicates that manual procedures must be used. The sub-schema language can represent most input data sets [2, Chapter 5].

Step 2 The sub-schema is processed by a SUB-SCHEMA COMPILER (SSC) which generates and saves the object version of the sub-schema for later use.

Step 3 The system analyst examines the requirements of the application program for run-time parameters and operating conventions. The analyst creates an update of the ACCESS DIRECTIVE GENERATOR (ADG) which acts as the query analyzer for GPLAN/WPC.

2.6.2 Run-time operations

Step 4 Any requisite real-time parameters which may be necessary to govern the extraction of data, the maintenance of the data base etc., are communicated to the ACCESS DIRECTIVE GENERATOR (ADG). Such parameters are gathered from users and transmitted to the ADG by an interactive analyzer that communicates with users in terms of a problem-oriented query language.

Step 5 In conjunction with the various tasks which are to be processed in fulfilling the user's problem specifications (e. g., the running of one or more application programs), a complete set of data base access directives is constructed by the ADG with the concurrent use of the schema. These directives are processed by the DMS and result in the production of an intermediate file containing extracted data.

Step 6 This intermediate file is processed by the FORMATTED FILE CONVERTER (FFC) which constructs a data input file acceptable to an application program in conjunction with the data formatting requirements expressed within the object version of that application's sub-schema.

Step 7 The input file is then processed by the target application program as though the environment were strictly batch-oriented and the input file had been generated manually according to specific data deck preparation instructions accompanying the application.

SUB-SCHEMA. The sub-schema describes the structural relationships between data items and groups of data items as they appear within data files associated with their respective application programs. The GEM sub-schema DDL is dependent only upon the logical structure of input files associated with a particular application program and not upon the language in which the application is written.

SUB-SCHEMA COMPILER (SSC). The SSC is a single procedure that converts logical sub-schemas into "object versions" which are stored for later use. Only one version of this procedure is required within GEM, due to the fact that all sub-schemas are declared in terms of a single DDL. (Note: Many SSCs are required in cases where the sub-schema DDLs are programming-language-dependent, as are the proposed DBTG DDLs.)

SUB-SCHEMA (OBJECT VERSION). The object version of the sub-schema is a tabular representation of sub-schema content specially devised for ease of manipulation by the FORMATTED FILE CONVERTER (FFC).

SCHEMA. The GEM schema describes naming, formatting and structural characteristics of elements and groups of elements comprising the data base data structure. The schema DDL defines hierarchical data structures which may contain only elementary items and repeating groups. Although the schema is compiled for use by the DMS, only a copy of the original schema definition is required for use within GEM. This copy is used by the ADG to assist in the run-time construction of data base access directives.

DATA BASE ACCESS DIRECTIVE GENERATOR (ADG). The ADG formulates data base access directives in response to user problem specifications. The order and content of these directives is pre-determined by the application program data requirements which are established during sub-schema compilation.

INTERMEDIATE FILE. The intermediate file contains data which has just been extracted from the data base. This data is passed to the FORMATTED FILE CONVERTER (FFC) for final re-formatting as an input file to the target application program.

FORMATTED FILE CONVERTER (FFC). The FFC converts files between a form recognizable by the DMS and a form recognizable by application programs.

Typically, the intermediate file contains ordered collections of datum identifiers and datum values interspersed with repeating group identifiers.

During input file preparation, the FFC supplements extracted data with special counters and character strings which are expected by the application programs for controlling the input of data sets. These counters and strings are not stored within the data base but must be inserted within the input file by the FFC in much the same way that an analyst would if he were manually preparing a data deck. For example, suppose that a group of cards within a data deck is to be constructed according to the following rules:

1) For each instance of the data set {I, Y} (where $1 \leqslant I \leqslant 100$) punch the values for these variables on a card using the (FORTRAN) field specification (I3, F5.2).
2) After the last card (data set occurrence), place a card with the characters "999" in the first three columns.

In terms of manual preparation of the cards, an analyst would punch a given set of raw data onto individual cards and then place a card at the end with "999" in the first three columns. In terms of automatic data file construction by the FFC, the extracted pairs of values would be grouped and formatted onto records as above, and then a final record would be created containing the non-extracted string "999". Values for strings such as "999" are stored within the GEM subschema declaration accompanying the application program.

Limitations of GEM: Conceptually, application programs which may be interfaced to a data base via the GEneralized interfacing Module (GEM) can be written in any programming language, provided data deck preparation instructions are available, but are restricted to batch-oriented jobs. Furthermore, it is assumed that an application program's input data sets are structurally compatible [6] with data base data sets.

The data bases to which GEM may interface are restricted to those controlled by a DMS for which data base access directives are available. Schema declarations may contain only elementary data items and repeating groups.

3. Typical GPLAN applications

3.1 GPLAN/SODA (Systems Optimization and Design Algorithm)

SODA [11] is a computer-assisted decision making system for the design of information processing systems. SODA generates a complete information systems design, along with cost/performance projections of how the designed system will perform on a specified hardware/software configuration. SODA consists of four major components:

SSL: SODA STATEMENT LANGUAGE,
SSL: SODA STATEMENT ANALYZER,
SGA: SODA GENERATOR OF ALTERNATIVES,
SPE: SODA PERFORMANCE EVALUATOR.

SSA is a computer program that analyzes the requirements of an information processing system stated in SSL. The Statement Analyzer also provides feedback information to the user to assist him in achieving a better problem statement.

SSA also produces a number of networks which record the interrelationships of processes and data and passes the networks on to SGA and SPE.

Each type of input and output is specified in terms of the data involved, the transformation needed to produce output from input and stored data. Time and volume requirements are also stated. SSA analyzes the statement of the problem to determine whether the required output can be produced from the available inputs. The problem statement stored in machine readable form is processed by SSA which:

1. checks for consistency in the Problem Statement (PS) and checks syntax in accordance with SSL; i. e., verifies that the PS satisfies SSL rules and is consistent, unambiguous, and complete,
2. prepares summary analyses and error comments to aid the problem definer in correcting, modifying and extending his PS,
3. prepares data to pass the PS onto SGA, and
4. prepares a number of matrices that express the interrelationship of Processes and Data Sets.

SGA is a procedure for the selection of a Computer System (cpu, core size, auxiliary memory devices) and the specification of alternative designs of program structure and file structure. SGA constructs a configuration of equipment in order to evaluate performance of the system. A number of models are used (to compute timing estimates) that select timing factors for alternative hardware/software configurations from a data file. SGA simulates the jobstream as it would be processed on the selected configuration, and, using the factors from the hardware/software library, SGA and SPE produce detailed cost/performance projection reports so that the user can evaluate the final design.

In Figure 3 it is shown how SODA fits into a more general structure.

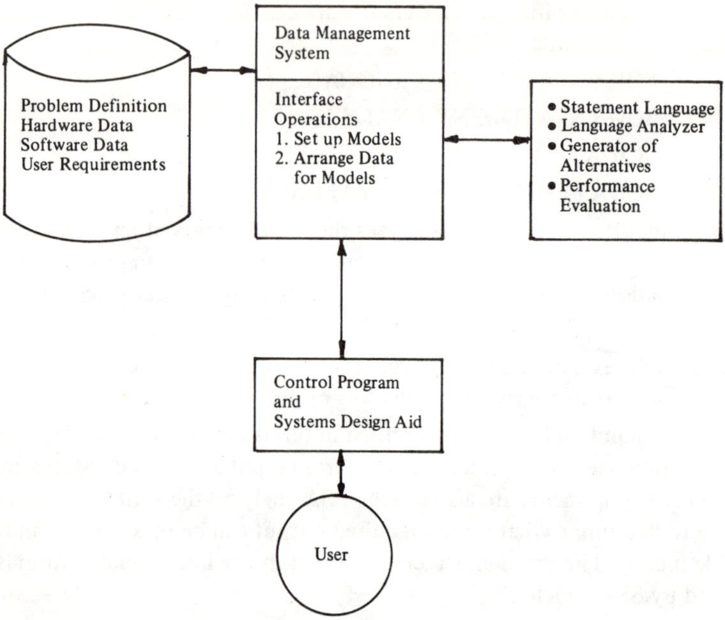

Fig. 3. SODA: Systems Optimization and Design Algorithm

3.2 GPLAN/WPC (Water Pollution Control)

The water pollution control planning system [2, 12, 8] which has already been implemented, develops a plan that minimizes the cost of pollution abatement structures while satisfying a set of water quality goals throughout an entire river basin. This planning system uses a prevailing measure of water quality, the level of dissolved oxygen concentration.

The model divides the river into sections and constrains the water quality, interpreted as the dissolved oxygen deficit level, to be met at the end of each section. Starting from the headwaters of the river, new sections are defined whenever the river parameters change significantly, such as effluent flow entering the river, incremental flow entering the river (tributary flow, ground water etc.), the flow in the main channel being augmented or diverted, or the parameters describing the river changing gradually over a longer distance.

The quality constraints are sequentially dependent in that the quality in each section is a function of the quality in the preceding section. But the possibility of tributaries, flow augmentation, and incremental and effluent flows entering at downstream points, complicates the relationships among the constraints.

Three possible treatment techniques are allowed for in the model: 1. by-pass piping; 2. regional and on-site treatment plants; and 3. flow augmentation. Thus piping flows are allowed from each polluter to each river section, from each polluter to each treatment plant, and from each treatment plant to each river section.

In addition to quality constraints, flow conservation constraints are needed for both the polluters and the treatment plants.

A nonlinear programming technique is used by this model. The major problem in adapting the algorithm was the calculation of the partial derivatives of both the constraints and the objective function. These partials were necessary to set up a local linear programming problem to determine the direction of search in the stepwise nonlinear problem. Starting with a point in the domain of the objective function, a new point is calculated by making a step either to reduce the value of the objective function (if the starting point is a feasible solution to the nonlinear programming problem) or to obtain a "more nearly feasible" solution (if the starting point is an infeasible solution) by reducing the value of the most infeasible constraint.

The cost function essentially involves the costs of new or upgraded treatment plants, reservoirs for flow augmentation, and various costs of new pipes to or from the polluters, treatment plants, and river sections.

4. Conclusion

The principal objective of the work surrounding GPLAN development is to outline the design and construction of specialized information systems which can be used for complex planning problems. Current technology has provided the basic tools for manipulating large-scale data bases and for communicating with users in terms of high-level problem-oriented languages.

Generalized Date Base Planning Systems are information systems which bring high-level decision makers into the computer user community by raising the system to the decision maker's level.

Of interest to data management specialists is the generalized interfacing module (GEM) which has been implemented for use within GPLAN. This module possesses the capability for automatically interfacing application programs to a DMS. Application programs need not contain DMS-dependent DML statements. This mutual transparency afforded by GEM allows for a greater degree of portability and interchangeability of both application systems and DMS's.

Acknowledgement:
This project is partially supported by grant GJ 37755 from the National Science Foundation, Office of Computing Activities, Computer Impact on Organizations Program.

References

[1] Anthony, R.N.: Planning and Control Systems, A Framework for Analysis. Harvard Business School 1965.

[2] Arsenault, J.: "GPLAN-WPC: A Generalized Data Base Planning System for Water Pollution Control". Ph. D. Dissertation, Department of Computer Science, Purdue University, May 1973.

[3] Arsenault, J., J.F. Nunamaker, Jr., John Pomeranz and Andrew Whinston: "Automatic Interfacing of Applications Software to Data Base Management Systems". Proceedings of the 4th Pittsburgh Conference on Modeling and Simulation. April 1973.

[4] Blumenthal, S.C.: Management Information Systems: A Framework for Planning and Development. Homewood, Ill. 1969.

[5] Burroughs Corporation: "DISK FORTE Manual". 1969.

[6] CODASYL Committee: Data Base Task Group Report. Association for Computing Machinery. April 1971.

[7] IBM: "Information Management System /360, Version 2 General Information Manual", GH 20–0765–1. Second Edition February 1971.

[8] Marsden, J., D. Pingry and A. Whinston: "Application of Nonlinear Programming to Water Quality Control". Working Paper, Purdue University, September 1972.

[9] MRI Systems: "System 2000 General Information Manual". 1972.

[10] Newell, A., J.C. Shaw and H.A. Simon: Report on a general problem-solving program. Proceedings of the International Conference on Information Processing. UNESCO House, 1959, pp. 256–264.

[11] Nunamaker, Jr., J.F.: "A Methodology for the Design and Optimization of Information Processing Systems". Proceedings of 1971 Spring Joint Computer Conference, AFIPS Press, May 1971.

[12] Pingry, D. and A. Whinston: "A Survey of Planning Techniques for Pollution Control". Working Paper, Purdue University, September 1972.

[13] "RAMIS Information Bulletin – Description and Specifications". Mathematica, Inc.. Princeton, New Jersey 1972.

[14] Simon H.A.: The New Science of Management Decision. 1960.

German abstract
Automatisierte Transformation von Anwendungsprogrammen mit Hilfe des GPLAN-Systems

Von *Jay F. Nunamaker jr., John Pomeranz* und *Andrew Whinston*

Das GPLAN-Projekt (Generalized Data Base Planning System) beschäftigt sich mit dem Problem der Implementierung computergestützter Planungssysteme und hat in diesem Zusammenhang eine eigene Philosophie zur Interpretation von Planungsprozessen entwickelt. Ein zentrales Anliegen wird in der Bereitstellung eines Interface-Mechanismus gesehen, der den Planer bei der Transformation der verfügbaren Daten in die von dem Planungsmodell geforderte Form unterstützt. Hierbei werden neben dem Benutzer vier Elemente eines computergestützten Planungssystems unterschieden.

Zunächst wird die Bedeutung eines Modellsystems für die Planung hervorgehoben. Komponenten dieses Modellsystems können Simulations-, Optimierungs- und statistische Programmsysteme sein, ferner Softwarepakete, die unter Betriebssystemkontrolle zum Ablauf gebracht werden können. Im weiteren werden die Anforderungen an eine geeignete Planungssoftware definiert.

Das zweite Element stellt die Datenbank mit den für die Planungsmodelle erforderlichen Informationen dar. Die Daten können in beliebiger Form abgespeichert werden, jedoch wird als Beschreibungsinstrument auf die CODASYL-DBTG-Konventionen verwiesen.

Zur Definition der Datenanforderungen der Modelle dient das dritte Element, nämlich eine problemorientierte Abfragesprache, die individuell für jedes Planungssystem zu schreiben ist. Sie eignet sich dazu, Anfragen an die Datenbank zu formulieren sowie die Aufgaben zu definieren, die mit Hilfe der Planungsmodelle erfüllt werden können, und muß unterschiedliche Retrieval-Formen für die Datenbank zulassen. Eine notwendige Ergänzung der Sprache ist ein Analyseprogramm, das Konsistenz- und Syntaxprüfungen für die Anfragen zuläßt und Fehlernachrichten bereitstellt und ebenso Modifikationen der formulierten Aufgaben ermöglicht.

Breiter Raum wird der Erläuterung des vierten Systemelements, nämlich des Interface-Mechanismus, gewidmet. Seine Aufgabe besteht darin, die Datenanforderungen der Planungssoftware entgegenzunehmen und auf dieser Basis den Zugriff auf die Datenbank zu realisieren. Die auf diese Weise beschafften Daten sind dann gemäß den Anforderungen der Planungsprogramme zu reformatieren und diesen verfügbar zu machen.

Eine Pilot-Version dieses Interface-Mechanismus wurde unter der Bezeichnung GEM (Generalized Interfacing Module) in FORTRAN IV auf einer CDC 6500 implementiert. Diese arbeitet in zwei Phasen. In einem Vorlauf wird aus dem

Quellcode des jeweiligen Planungsprogramms die Datenbeschreibung in Form eines (CODASYL-)SUBSCHEMAS extrahiert. Im Hauptlauf erzeugt ein Zugriffssteuerungsprogramm Direktiven für die Datenbanksoftware, die die benötigten Daten in eine Zwischendatei überführt. Diese Zwischendatei wird schließlich von einem Konversionsprogramm in die vom Planungsprogramm geforderte Form aufbereitet.

Abschließend werden zwei Projekte dargestellt, die gemäß dem beschriebenen Planungskonzept verfolgt werden. GPLAN/SODA ist ein computergestütztes Entscheidungssystem für den Entwurf von computergestützten Informationssystemen. Seine Hauptkomponenten sind eine prozedurunabhängige Problembeschreibungssprache (SODA STATEMENT LANGUAGE), ein Analyseprogramm (SODA STATEMENT ANALYZER), das die Problembeschreibung prüft und ein Daten- und Prozeßnetzwerk erzeugt, ein Alternativengenerator (SODA GENERATOR OF ALTERNATIVES), der Hard- und Softwarekonfigurationen vorschlägt und alternative Programm- und Dateistrukturen liefert. Zusammen mit einem Bewertungsmechanismus (SODA PERFORMANCE EVALUATOR) sind dann Kosten- und Leistungsschätzungen für die alternativen Entwürfe ableitbar.

Das zweite Projekt, auf das hingewiesen wird, ist ein Planungssystem für die Wasseraufbereitung eines Flusses (GPLAN/Walter Pollution Control) und basiert auf Optimierungsverfahren der nichtlinearen Programmierung.

Computer assisted analysing, controlling and constructing tools for information systems design

By *Vesa Savolainen*

1. Introduction

DIFO (Design of Information systems, especially File Organization) Research Project at the University of Tampere has for three years developed, applied and tested in practice various formal methods and models of systems design as well as several tools based on an efficient utilization of the computer, each restricted to a certain phase of systems design [3]. Practical experiments have been made in about 30 systems design projects, the application fields of which have been chosen within industry – the ADP applications of production design, enterprise administration and operations research –, within the ADP problem field of the city – various applications of administration and town planning – and within the activities of a large hospital. The following models, methods and research plans have, in one form or another, been included in the work and practical experiments of DIFO Project:

1. The general invariant stage division of systems design.
2. The analysing of a logical, computer documented data system by means of DIFOP 1 package and its development into a functioning system.
3. The Lundeberg method as a documentation means of the results of an information analysis.
4. DOC, the formalizing means of systems design and the documentation means of a system.
5. A stratified system as a frame model of the description of systems and especially files.
6. The automatic grouping of processes.
7. The analysing of system complexity.
8. The computer in the physical design of files.
9. A simple data controlling system for performing updating and reporting tasks, which is particularly adapted to the user.

The most important of the above mentioned points will be discussed in the following chapters. In general, the implementation of the computer assisted systems design implies e. g. that

- the goal has been determined exactly,
- the factors having an influence on the processes of the organization and their relations are known beforehand,
- the formal description of the task has been carried out well enough, i. e. the constructed model has sufficiently well described the real situation,
- ADP hardware and software are on the required level.

There are several factors supporting the use of the computer as an auxiliary means in systems design:

- The hardware costs per performance have continuously decreased and they are nowadays estimated to be approximately half of the ADP costs. If the development will continue as such, the software costs will, according to an estimation, cover 80% of the ADP costs in 1980.
- The utilization of the computer compels one to formalized, disciplined working.
- An enormous amount of system alternatives can be examined by a computer in a short time.
- The development of software gives possibilities of constructing non-numerical applications.
- There has been some progress in the exact description of systems design tasks.
- Factors having an influence on the operation of systems are known and they can be analysed better than before.

2. The general invariant stage division of systems design

The design of all kinds of systems – thus also information systems – can be carried out at the following six stages:

1. Task (the goals of the object system, the analysis of the object system, the information need i. e. the outer properties of the information system),
2. Information analysis,
3. Synthesis (the sketching of a system),
4. Implementation,
5. Use,
6. Maintenance.

These stages can generally be further divided by using the same stage division. Many times a separate preliminary study is made, which comprises the stages from 1 to 3. Here the object system and its information need are examined, calculations of cost (fixed costs and variable costs) and potential alternatives are compared with each other. As a result we get a preliminary study report and a project plan. The models and methods 2 – 8 mentioned in the introduction are located at the stages of the main study as follows:

Task	Analysis	Synthesis	Implementation	Use	Maintenance
3	2	2	2	9	2
4	3	4	5		7
5	4	5	6		8
	5	7	8		9
	7	9	9		

3. Tools for analysing a system and controlling system work

In this chapter we shall examine DOC and DIFOP1 packages as well as methods for studying the complexity of systems. The Lundeberg method and the stratified system description are examined in chapter 4.

3.1 DOC

As far as the DOC system of CASCADE Project is concerned reference is made to Mr. Arne Sølvberg's paper and his literary output [14, 1], where the theoretical background, construction and use of this fine auxiliary means for systems analysis are explained. The use of the DOC system forces the systems designer to act according to the DOC formalism. Since this formalism has been designed excellently, DOC makes the designer to consider everything that is necessary. DOC stores the intermediate results of the systems analysis and gives them as well as final results as a graph and a table in output if wanted. An efficient utilization of DOC requires, however, the systems designer to adapt a "DOC way of thinking" of the systems and their design. In the Central Hospital of Tampere they have performed an information analysis of the x-ray department supported by the DOC system, and the results of this experiment have been encouraging.

3.2 DIFOP 1

A program package [2] based on triples and first implemented by CADIS Project in Stockholm is under development at least in three places:

1. CADIS Project has implemented 3 – 4 functioning CS versions.

2. DIFO Project at the University of Tampere has developed DIFOP1 package in two phases.
3. CGP, Computer Graphics Project in the Technical High School of Helsinki is converting a more developed CS version to a CR-DISPLAY terminal application, where a triple graph can be presented as a real graph and it can be modified with a light pen.

DIFOP1 (DIFO Program 1, a data recording system based on triple Structure) is an interactive program package which is above all intended to assisting systems design as a documenting and analysing means. The use of the program package is wholly based on associative triples. The user of DIFOP1 forms a desired structure of triples (which he then can study in various ways) by means of different functions and parameters. A triple is presented in the form {relation, object, object}, i. e. each triple contains two objects and a relation prevailing between these objects. For example: {precedent, invoice, customer information}. Before being able to write an invoice we must obtain some information of the customer. Each part of a triple has a common name "identifier". The associativeness of the triples is revealed by another example: {component, invoice, price}. Graphically the above triples can be presented as follows:

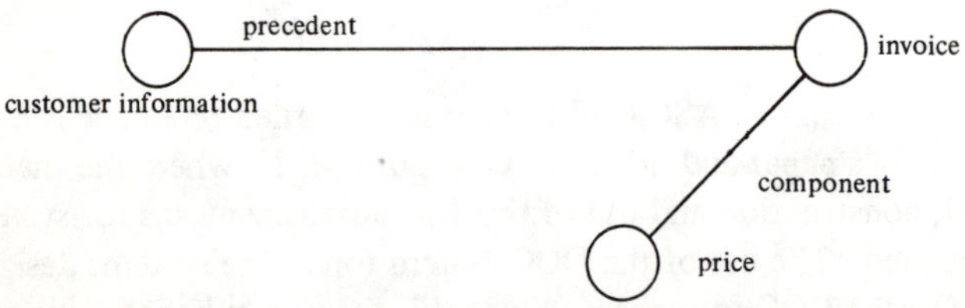

DIFOP1 was implemented in the spring of 1971 for Honeywell H1642 computer of the University of Tampere in Finland and it is profoundly described from its user's viewpoint in DIFO Working Paper No. 2 [9]. The systems designer can use various functions for forming a triple structure which describes, manipulates and analyses the system. One of them, the GET function, examines the triple structure so that the function is given three parameters which form a model of a triple. This model is adapted to all the triples of the structure and as a result all the triples are obtained to which the model is adaptable. As a parameter there could first be either an identifier or a colon (:). The colon means that this part can vary from one triple to another, because the application of this part of the model succeeds with each triple of the structure. Let us suppose that we have formed the following structure:

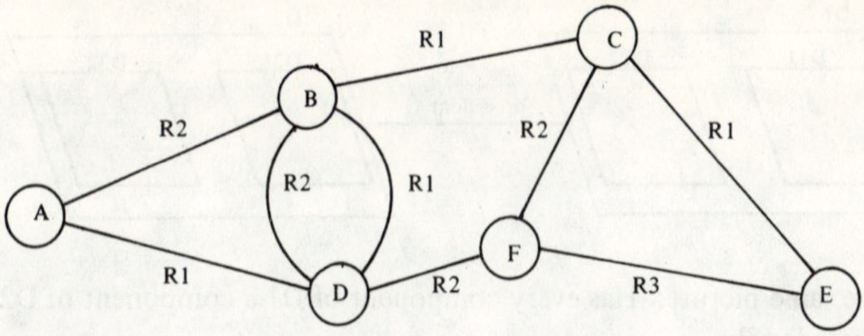

As an answer of the command GET {R2, F,:} there are triples {R2, F, C} and {R2, F, D}.

The purpose of the enlarged GET function is to give the user a possibility of feeding an expression which consists of many identifiers joined together as a parameter. When forming a parameter expression it is natural to use Boolean operations as well as iterations and concatenations to join the identifiers [6]. Thus we can mark:

v = or
$\wedge$ = and
$\neg$ = negation
* = iteration
· = concatenation

If, for instance, the input of the relation part parameter and the above structure are examined, the function GET (R2 · ($\neg$R1) · (R2$\wedge$R1), C,:) would give object B. Thus, instead of separate triples we are now seeking objects which are connected with the given object through a certain chain formed by relations. The expressions of the parameters corresponding to the object parts are formed accordingly. In general, the enlargement of the GET function means that instead of separate triples, groups consisting of many triples are now examined by this function. The problem is, besides the input and handling of complex parameter expressions, also that there is a change within the function from the elementary level to higher levels and then in fact the language connected with DIFOP1 will change decisively in principle.

Logical tests are useful in information analysis for two reasons:

– for finding different kinds of mistakes in the analysis performed, and
– for making it easier to continue the design work.

When the GET function is used, the following kinds of questions can, for example, be asked:

– Is any information set the precedent of itself (a loop)?
– Has every component of the information set D2 a component of D1 as its precedent in the below picture, when we know that D1 is the precedent of D2?

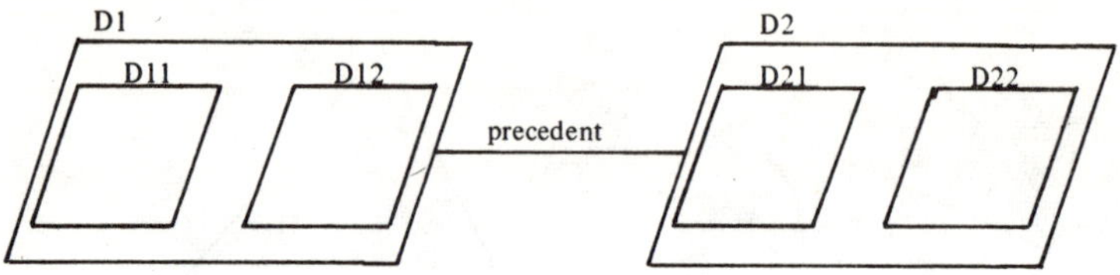

- In the same picture: Has every component of D1 a component of D2 as its succedent?
- Can a given substructure of relations be found in the structure?
- Which information belongs to the input and which to the output in the information structure?

Also the names of identifiers can be examined and listed by various analysing functions.

3.3 Measures of systems complexity

In order to compare different information systems on the logical level we need a set of indices, which characterize as well as possible the systems being studied. One of the indices is a measure of the complexity of the system. When developing this measure we can adopt one of the following approaches:

- Reducing the description of the system to a standard way of implementation. This approach can be called the defining of the absolute complexity of the system.
- Defining the system by making use of concepts which are relevant within the environment of the system. This approach can be called the defining of the relative complexity of the system.

The first approach leads us to the use of Turing machines and to the very cumbersome process of reduction. For practical reasons the second approach is more natural to be used in ADP-systems work.

The measuring of relative complexity is based on the concepts which are selected from the environment and from the system. The word "concept" stands for different entities, properties of entities, or relations between entities, or relations between the properties of entities. The concepts are linked together by so-called "function of concepts". A function of concepts has a list of arguments of one or more concepts and the function defines a new concept. In this context it is natural to state a requirement that the functions must be recursive in the sense of the theory of computability.

On the logical level we can now show how dependent some concept is on all the other concepts. The total sum of all dependencies is called the (logical) relative complexity of the system. If we want to show this dependency, we can reduce the relative complexity to the standard implementation (Turing machines) or to some specific technical implementation by selecting the concepts from an appropriate set of technical concepts. In this way it is possible for example to compare the relative complexity of the information systems which are implemented on the same type of computers. The usefulness of these ideas in practice is being tested [4].

The indices of the complexity of the system are needed at the synthesis or maintenance stage of systems design when a system is being designed the integration level of which is as great as possible. When integrating a system its complexity is minimized.

4. Tools for describing a system

The main function of systems documentation is to present a readable definition of the system [1]. This definition is used as a basis when deciding which properties the system shall have, and it is used as a basis for further design.

DOC and DIFOP1 mentioned in chapter 3 are excellent tools for describing and documenting a system. In this chapter we shall study Lundeberg's manual method, which is being developed into a general computerized designing and implementing system of information systems by ISAC Project at the University of Stockholm, led by Mats Lundeberg. We shall also briefly study a stratified system as a frame model for systems description. Both description methods are well applicable during the information analysis as well as during the construction of the system.

The data contents and files of a system form a very complex whole of which it is extremely difficult to make a complete and thorough description. The problem is mainly due to the fact that the prepared description is always a simplification, which considers relevant factors only from a certain point of view. We can try to get a complete description by hierarchic describing. The system is described by a set of abstractly different models, which are arranged so that the higher we go in hierarchy the more the abstraction of models increases.

4.1 The method of Lundeberg

Lundeberg explains the principles of his method in a report [10]. The idea of the manual use of this method is in brief to describe a system first on a high level so that information sets are represented by rhombuses (▱) and processes by rectangles (▭). Both information sets and processes as well as precedence relations between them are made more accurate level by level up to the accuracy of the datum. Description symbols are named and numbered logically on each level. Also form and matrix description can be used. As disadvantages of this method we could mention e. g. the difficulty of naming the levels, the great number of pages of the result document, and the fact that there are no possibilities of describing systems dynamics.

4.2 A stratified system as the frame model of systems description

Mesaroric, Macko and Takahara call the hierarchic way of description a stratified system [11, pp. 37 – 40; 5]. The stratified description and the corresponding system have some common properties:

1. The selection of class, i. e. the terms by means of which the description of an object system is made, depends on the maker of the description, his knowledge and interest in the functioning of the system. We can, however, find classes for the description, of many object systems, which seem natural and relevant.
2. Principles and laws which are used in describing an object system in one class, cannot be derived generally from the principles used in another class; in other words the connections where the description of object systems is made in different classes, are not in general equivalents.
3. The functioning in different classes of an object system has a one-sided dependency. Lower classes must function correctly to enable a correct functioning of the object system in a certain class.
4. Each class has its own set of terms, concepts and principles.
5. We can understand the functioning of an object system better when going from one class to another: when going downwards we get a more and more detailed and concrete explanation of the functioning; when going upwards we understand the significance of the functioning more and more profoundly.

Thus each level describes the same object system by using a set of concepts which limits the study mainly to this level. It must be noted, however, that disregarding the connections between levels studying the system results in an imperfect understanding of the functioning of the system as a whole.

For example the files of a system can be described as a stratified system [5]. It is profitable to consider this fact in the design process. We must, however, remember that the thinking of levels does not completely correspond to the temporal phases of the design process. The design of data files is divided into four levels:

a) the level of concepts,
b) the level of data structures,

c) the level of file structures and
d) the level of storage structures.

The limits between these levels are not very strict because, for example, some things on a lower level may have an effect on the things on a higher level. The design process begins on the level of concepts, where the description of an information system is very abstract and it goes on to lower levels changing the description more and more concrete and technical in nature. On the level of data structures we try to define some basic data structures, so called primitive structures, and their technical parameters. By combining primitive structures in different ways it should be possible to construct more complicated data structures and calculate their properties. When one goes to the opposite direction it should be possible to conclude which kind of data structures are possible with the given values of technical parameters.

5. Tools for implementation and construction

5.1 From precedence analysis to decision tables

DIFOP1 with its extensions guides the design process also at its implementation stage. Riihimäki explains in his report how it is possible to derive decision tables from results of precedence analysis [15]. Programs can be produced automatically from these decision tables. The work of Riihimäki is based on the idea that besides DIFOP1 triples, also conditions, handling rules and actions are stored at the same time. The sketches of decision tables are made more accurate by conversational processing.

5.2 The automatic grouping of processes

Laitila's work, the grouping of the processes of an information system at the synthesis stage is also based on DIFOP1 [5]. The source of this work can be found in the theory of Langefors, according to which data transfer between the main storage and auxiliary storages must be minimized and at the same time the best possible use must be made of the storage capacity of the computer [8]. Besides the consolidation of files the grouping of processes is the most important working method at the synthesis stage. The process grouping algorithm designed by Laitila is taking advantage of the result of an information analysis stored by DIFOP1 as well as of the following properties of the problem:

– the available capacity of the computer main storage,

- the run period and the frequency of the program to be made,
- the size and the type of files (elementary, sequence, random access, input and output files etc.).

The algorithm produces a grouping recommendation of processes and a calculation of the reduced amount of data transfers.

5.3 The computer in the design of physical file organization

It is often reasonable to shorten computer run times by assigning the files optimally to different disk storage devices and also by finding the optimal file sequences in each disk storage unit. Within DIFO Project research work has been done in order to construate optimum guaranteeing and heuristic algorithms for solving this kind of physical file organization problems. The basic optimality criterion is the minimization of the total movement of the recording heads in single-head type disk storage units. A number of isolated physical file organization problems has been formulated mathematically, and the solving methods which guarantee the optimum have been taken from operations research, expecially from the scheduling theory and the module placement theory [5, 7, 12, 13].

5.4 A simple reporting language which is well adapted to the user

In developed establishments and enterprises there are many permanent files in machine readable form. It is quite often necessary to get summaries or reports from the data stored in files such as those mentioned above. The same report may be required only once and it is desired that the lead time of the report be as short as possible. If an attempt were made to satisfy these demands by usual programming, it would be too expensive and it would take too much time. Therefore it is appropriate to think of various solutions to the problems above. An approach could be to develop a language, which would be able to serve as a medium to enable the user to communicate directly with one or several files [5].

It can be said that the Report Program Generator (RPG) is intended to be a programming language for purposes mentioned above. But we can now ask why the RPG has not won the user's favour. An answer to this question is that although the RPG is intended to be problem oriented it is, however, also to the large extent machine oriented. Therefore we can state that the new reporting language must be more adapted to human beings than RPG. The statement above means that it is not necessary that the user of the new reporting language has a profound knowledge of automatic data processing (ADP). In addition it may further be provided that he does not have to know much about the technical and physical organization of files. Instead of that it is relevant to suppose that the user knows:

- the logical structure of a certain file,
- names and abbreviations of data elements belonging to a record in a certain file,
- sizes of wanted sums,
- the lengths of codes of used data elements,
- the precision level of stored data, and
- the fact whether the code is numeric or alphanumeric.

Different possibilities of extending the reporting language into various dimensions are required. These dimensions are:

- possibilities of selecting only certain records, with
- possibilities of sorting and computing sums and intermediate sums,
- possibilities of computing arithmetical expressions, statistical characteristics etc.,
- different actions to files, and
- a number of files suitable to processing during one program run.

A detailed specification and a syntax for this kind of reporting language have been made within DIFO group. After an enlargement the language will master also updating tasks. When designing smaller information systems this language can be a short cut in constructing and implementing work.

6. Conclusions

The adapting of methods to projects in practice has a.o.t. proved that:

1. The training of the field of an organization for a new way of thinking and communication with systems designers has succeeded best by adopting a formal method and a formal way of describing in the phase of information analysis.
2. The field has been schooled to define the outer properties (input/output) of the information system needed much better then before.
3. There are defects and restrictions in the methods applied, but they can, however, be developed further as far as these drawbacks are concerned.
4. The developing of these methods must be carried out by making the best possible use of the computer. The computer generates and analyses different alternatives and the designer who is all the time in interactive communication with the computer, makes the actual decisions on further actions after selecting and alternative from a small, well specified set of alternatives.
5. The variety of numerous methods and models of different types can bring about some confusion in the terminology. We ought to be able to centre

the research work of different projects under the supervision of a uniform coordinating body on international level – not to mention the national level. Or is it impeded by mutual competition and envy?

References

[1] Auglaend, K. and A. Sølvberg: A Technique for Computerized Graphical Presentation of Information Systems, to be used in systems design. CASCADE Working Paper No. 17. Trondheim 1972.

[2] Bubenko, J., O. Källhammar and S. Berild: Ett interaktivt programsystem för manipulering av assosiative datastrukturer. CADIS Working Paper No. 32. Stockholm 1970.

[3] Järvinen, P.: DIFO (Design of Information systems, especially File Organization) Goals and Problems. DIFO Working Paper No. 1. University of Tampere, Department of Computer Science. Tampere 1970.

[4] Järvinen, P., H. Kangassalo, S. Lehtonen, M. Nokso-Koivisto and V. Savolainen: DIFO YEARBOOK 1/1972. University of Tampere, Department of Computer Science. Tampere 1972.

[5] Järvinen, P., H. Kangassalo, S. Lehtonen, M. Nokso-Koivisto and V. Savolainen: DIFO YEARBOOK 2/1973. University of Tampere, Department of Computer Science. Tampere 1973.

[6] Kärkkäinen, T. and O. Suikki: A Project for Organizing the Triple File and for Extending the GET Command. DIFO Report No. 5. University of Tampere, Department of Computer Science. Tampere 1972.

[7] Laaksonen, J. and J. Hirvonen: File Assignments to Several Disc Storages. DIFO Report No. 7. University of Tampere, Department of Computer Science. Tampere 1972.

[8] Langefors, B.: Theoretical Analysis of Information Systems. Lund 1970.

[9] Lehtonen, S. and V. Savolainen: DIFOP1 – A Flexible Data Recording System Based on Triple Structure. DIFO Working Paper No. 2. University of Tampere, Department of Computer Science. Tampere 1971.

[10] Lundeberg, M.: Information Analysis. ISAC Report 71 No. 2. University of Stockholm, Department of Administrative Information Processing. Stockholm 1971.

[11] Mesarovic, M.D., D. Macko and Y. Takahara: Theory of Hierarchical, Multilevel Systems. New York 1970.

[12] Savolainen, V.: On Optimal Assignment of Disc Storage Files Using Transition Frequency Matrices. DIFO Report No. 9. University of Tampere, Department of Computer Science. Tampere 1973.

[13] Savolainen, V.: Scheduling Researches for Assisting the Design of Information Systems and File Organization. NordDATA–72 Konferensföredrag III, pp. 1861–1873. Helsinki 1972.

[14] Sølvberg, A., G. Skylstad, P. Aanstad and T. Johansen: Brukerhåndbok CASCADE/I. CASCADE Arbeidsnotat nr. 21. Trondheim 1972.

[15] Riihimäki, O.: From Precedence Analysis to Decision Tables. DIFO Report No. 8. University of Tampere, Department of Computer Science. Tampere 1972.

German abstract
Instrumente für die Analyse, Kontrolle und den Entwurf computergestützter Systemgestaltung

Von *Vesa Savolainen*

Im Rahmen des DIFO-Forschungsvorhabens, das an der Universität von Tampere (Finnland) seit drei Jahren besteht, wurden verschiedene formale Methoden und Modelle als Hilfsmittel zur computergestützten Systemgestaltung entwickelt und in der Praxis eingesetzt und getestet. Ebenso entwickelte man verschiedene Verfahren, die eine effiziente Computerausnutzung in den verschiedenen Phasen der Systemgestaltung garantieren. Insgesamt konnten ungefähr 30 Systemgestaltungsprojekte durchgeführt werden, darunter im Rahmen industrieller Unternehmungen Probleme der computergestützten Produktgestaltung, der administrativen Steuerung und des OR. Ebenso beschäftigte man sich mit Problemen der Verwaltung von Großstädten, der Stadtplanung und des Informationssystems eines großen Krankenhauses.

Die folgenden Methoden, Modelle und Untersuchungsstrategien wurden in der einen oder anderen Form bei der Forschungstätigkeit von DIFO berücksichtigt bzw. neu entwickelt:

1. die im allgemeinen invariante Phasengliederung der Systemgestaltungsarbeit,
2. die Analyse des logischen Aufbaus eines computergestützt dokumentierten datenbezogenen Informationssystems mit Hilfe von DIFOP1 (DIFO Paket Nr. 1) und seine Überführung in ein funktionsfähiges System,
3. die Methodologie von Lundeberg als ein Hilfsmittel zur Dokumentation der im Rahmen einer Informationsanalyse gewonnenen Daten,
4. DOC, ein Hilfsmittel zur Formalisierung der Systemgestaltungsarbeit und ein System zur adäquaten Dokumentation,
5. ein straff gegliedertes System, das als Rahmenmodell der Beschreibung von Systemen besonders von Daten eingesetzt werden kann,
6. die automatisierte Zusammenfassung von Verarbeitungsprozeduren,
7. die Analyse der Systemkomplexität,
8. die Berücksichtigung des Computers bei der Gestaltung von Dateien,
9. ein einfaches, benutzerfreundliches Beschreibungs- und Manipulationsinstrument zum Updaten und zur Abfrage der dokumentierten Daten.

Auf die wichtigsten der angegebenen Punkte wird im folgenden Paper eingegangen. Jedoch ist zuvor noch zu berücksichtigen, daß bei der Implementierung des computergestützten Entwurfs gesichert sein muß, daß die Ziele exakt definiert, die Haupteinflußfaktoren der Informationsprozesse richtig erkannt und die Beschreibung im Rahmen der Modellsynthese der Realität entsprechend durchgeführt wurden. Schließlich müssen die zur Verfügung stehende Hardware und Software den Anforderungen genügen. Die Verwendung der genannten Modelle bzw. die Beachtung der Methodologien brachte u.a. folgende Erkenntnisse, die der computergestützten Systemgestaltung zuzuschreiben sind:

- Da der Anteil der Softwarekosten am Gesamtbudget einer ADV-Anlage stark zunehmen wird, ist eine optimale Ausnutzung der Software vonnöten. Die hier vorgeschlagenen Wege berücksichtigen dies.
- Die Benutzung des Computers zwingt zur strengen Formalisierung der Arbeit.
- Alternativen können schnell getestet werden.
- Die Entwicklung von Software eröffnet die Möglichkeit, auch nicht-numerische Probleme mit dem Computer effizient durchzuführen.
- Die Haupteinflußfaktoren des Funktionierens eines Systems sind besser in den Griff zu bekommen.
- Die Theorie der Systembeschreibung wurde weiterentwickelt.

The use of models and associated software in the design of wicked systems

By *Arne Sølvberg*

1. Introduction

To develop a management information system (MIS), it is usually necessary to develop a formal information processing system (IPS), parts of which can be realized by a data processing system (DPS). The object system (MIS) is most often of a wicked nature. The degree of wickedness varies, strategic level systems being considerably more wicked than operational level systems. The more wicked a system is, the more difficult it is to use systems models.

To develop a DPS within the MIS, it is necessary to do two kinds of design. The first kind is functional design of the total system. The second kind is the realizational design, by which the functional design is modified by the available information processing resources, these being computers or human beings.

A computer program is an absolutely formal model of an IPS. Somewhere between the very wicked system, where models are hard to use, and the completely formal DPS, the wickedness disappears so that formal models can be applied for the systems development.

The application of systems models, implies that formal, mathematical manipulation with the model, can take place. It is therefore possible to have a DPS being a part of the IPS that is used for IPS-design.

This paper will concern itself with (1) a discussion of tame and wicked problems, (2) a description of CASCADE/I, which is a DPS for IPS-design, (3) a discussion of two full-scale experiments employing systems models and CASCADE/I, and finally (4) a description of planned extensions of CASCADE, to make the system a DPS also for DPS-design.

2. Tame and wicked problems

H. Rittel [4] has discussed systems design from the point of view of "tame" and "wicked" problems. For those who have not read his paper, I would like to summarize some of the differences between the two classes of problems.

A tame problem (TP) can be exhaustively formulated, so that it can be written down, handed to a specialist, which will solve the problem without needing any additional information. A wicked problem (WP) has no definitive formulation. No matter how the WP is formulated, the problem solver comes up with a requirement for additional information. If the problem is to make a system for lending books in a library, the problem solver is bound to come up with a question on f. ex. how many lending stations one should have.

Every formulation of the WP corresponds to a statement of the solution, and vice versa. To understand a problem is identical with solving the problem. For a TP the formulation is one thing, and the solution another thing.

The solution of a WP cannot be tested for correctness. We cannot say that a plan for a city is "correct" or "false", the most we can say is that we think it is "good" or "bad".

For a TP the correct/false test can always be applied. For the solution of TP's there will always be an exhaustive list of permissable operations. You cannot invent new operations in a game of chess. For WP's there is no such list; everything goes, as a matter of principle and fantasy.

A problem can be stated as a discrepancy, as something as it is, compared with something as it ought to be. For WP's there are many explanations for the same discrepancy, and there is no test to find which of these explanations is the best one. Every TP has a certain form, and there is no reason to argue about, for example, the level of the problem. But every WP can be considered as a symptom of another problem, and since nobody should try to cure symptoms, you are never sure that you are attacking the problem on the right level.

Most of our knowledge on problem solving, is about solving tame problems. Nevertheless, some principles on solving WP's can be formulated.

First, for WP's there are no specialists. The expertise needed is usually distributed over many people. So is also the ignorance. Nobody knows better because of degrees or status. Those people who are the best experts with the best knowledge, are usually those who are likely to be affected by the solution.

Nobody wants to be planned at. Therefore, the people that will be affected by the problem solution should be made into participants of the solution process.

Developing a solution to a WP, at every single step a judgement is made which is not based on scientific expertise. There is always an "ought-to-be" statement involved. Therefore it is very difficult to control the premises for the developed solution. It is necessary to look for methods which show some transparency of the solution process, so that every step in the process is understandable and communicable. Because of the "ought-to-be" statements, developing solutions to WP's is always a political process.

If there are experts on WP solving, they are only experts in guiding the process of dealing with a WP, but not for the subject matter of the problem. This makes the systems designer a mid-wife of problems, rather than an offerer of therapies.

Instead of using an "expert" model of problem solution, it might be better to use a "conspiracy" model. Go for a maximized involvement by other persons, share the risks, and share the honour.

3. A DPS for IPS-design

The purpose of the systems that we are interested in, is to produce (in a wide sense) goods of one kind or another, these being material or immaterial goods. To obtain this purpose, it is necessary to have some kind of information processing, to coordinate the production. The outer borders of our system must be defined, so that we know what is the system and what is the environment. Our total system (SYS) can therefore be considered to consist of three subsystems (fig. 1), the information processing system (IPS), the material processing system (MPS), the environment (ENV).

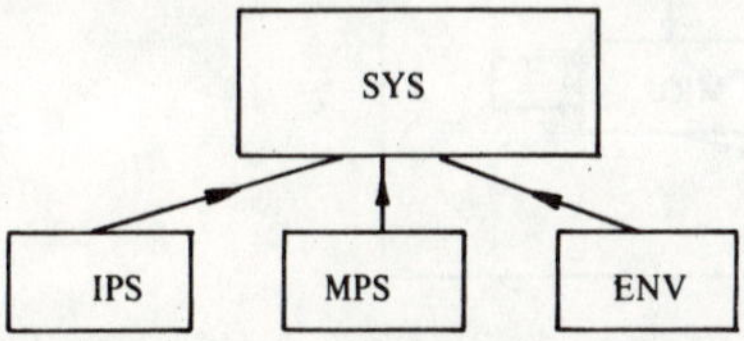

Fig. 1. Crude subsystem structure of the total system

But in addition to defining the outer systems border, the designer must also choose inner borders. That is, he must define his smallest system parts. In this model we choose the MPS to be a smallest part, which shall not be detailed further. We therefore need an intermediate stage, which we shall call an operating station (OPST).

An OPST-system consists of an information processing part, and a material processing part, or a new OPST. The detailing of an OPST has the purpose of defining the information processing within the OPST, and the interaction between the information processing and the material processing.

An IPS can be detailed in new IPS-elements. Sooner or later we will reach a level of detail where we have to decide on the type of information processor we need. This can either be human beings, or some types of automatic computing devices. The IPS is therefore divided in a data processing system (DPS) and a human processing system (HPS).

Both the DPS, HPS and MPS need processing resources. The DPS need automatic computing resources, the HPS need human processors, and the MPS need material processors as well as human and computing resources.

We therefore have (at least) two kinds of design. One is the total system design, which is the functional design of the system. The other kind of design is the "realizational" design: how shall the functional design expressed in the DPS-, HPS-, MPS-structures be realized by the available processing resources?

For the data processing part of the design, the database must be organized, hardware and software must be selected, DPS-elements must be organized into programs (data processing routines = DRU), programs into elements and so forth.

The system model is shown in fig. 2.

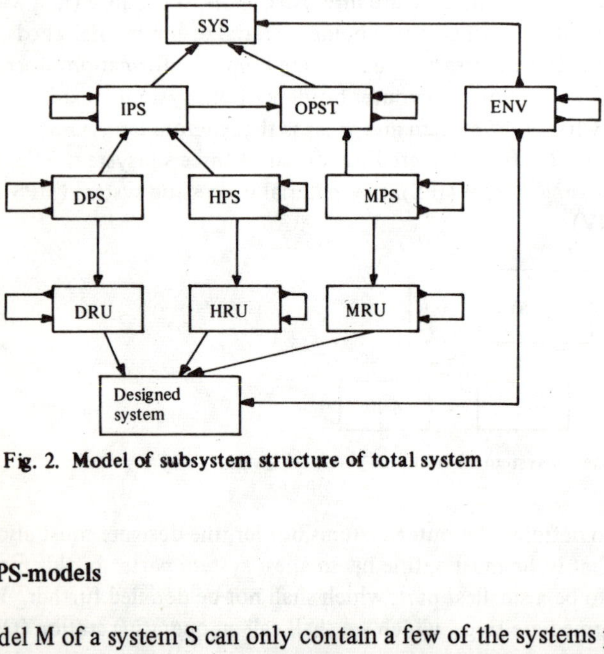

Fig. 2. Model of subsystem structure of total system

3.1 IPS-models

A model M of a system S can only contain a few of the systems properties, if the model shall be manageable. Now, the model shall be used to communicate facts and knowledge of the system between the persons concerned. A presentation P should not be too complicated if the communication purposes shall be obtained. Therefore we will generally have that

$$P \subset M \subset S.$$

It is therefore important to choose very carefully both the system properties to be modelled, and the model properties to be presented in the various graphs and tables.

In the CASCADE project we have employed an engineering black-box modelling. The most simple processing model that we can think of, is the basic I/O-model (fig. 3). The system model consists of input information, transformation, output information.

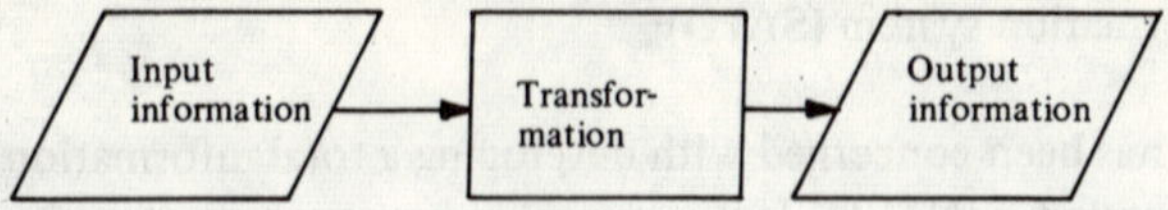

Fig. 3. Basic I/0-model of an IPS

The transformation-objects can be detailed into subtransformations, while the information-objects can be detailed in component information objects. For every information-object on the most detailed component level, there is a corresponding information type object. This is analogue to the distinction between record and record-type that is often seen. The information type objects consists of term-types (fig. 4).

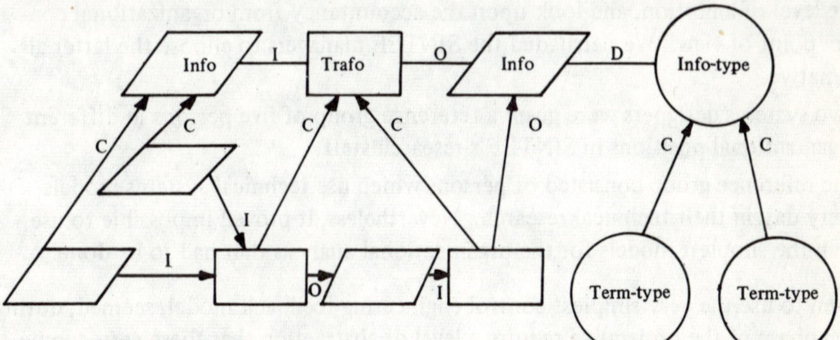

Fig. 4. The CASCADE/I IPS model

This simple model is the basis of CASCADE/I [1], which is a data processing system to aid the functional design of any IPS. CASCADE/I consists of around 250 Fortran subroutines, runs on UNIVAC 1100 series and IBM 360/370 series and has been in practical use for around one year.
The basic I/O-model is too simple to be of immediate use for automatic design of data processing systems, but has proven to be valuable in the functional IPS design.

4. Full scale experiments

During the last year, two systems design projects have been conducted from the same research group that has developed CASCADE/I. Both projects are of a consultancy type, so the opportunity for “wild“ experimenting with working methods has been limited. We have, however, tried to use formal systems models on a reasonable scale.

4.1 SINTEF's information system (SAPO)

The SAPO-project has been concerned with developing a total information system for our own organization, SINTEF. It is a typical in-house job, in the respect that an in-house contract has been offered by SINTEF to its own data processing department for this development. SINTEF is a research organization, employing approximately 550 persons, which lives in a state of symbiosis with the local technical university. Around 60% of SINTEF's income comes from industrial consultancy, while the rest comes from different research funds. A computer based accounting system was developed in 1964–65, and this system was considered outdated a couple of years ago. A new accounting system was to be made. Two strategies were available. Either to dig into the accounting department, and make a new accounting system from the accountants point of view, or to raise the level of ambition, and look upon the accountancy from organizational control point of view. We persuaded the SINTEF managers to choose the latter alternative.

Two systems designers were given a reference group of five persons in different organizational positions in SINTEF's research staff.

The reference group consisted of persons which use technical systems models every day in their technical research. Nevertheless, it proved impossible to use even the simplest models for the organizational analysis that had to be done.

Even to use the very simplest control engineering feedback model, seemed, during one phase of the project, to require a level of abstraction that these very competent people were not able to cope with. But this conclusion is hardly correct.

SINTEF contains approximately 20 different sections, ranging from 10 persons to one hundred. The sections have a great freedom to organize themselves, and they are controlled according to quite different control philosophies. This autonomous situation is to be maintained, and that of course led to very conflicting views on how SAPO should or should not be.

After about half-a-year of a very intense argumentative process, the group came up with a crude structure for SINTEF's information system. The result was a compromise between conflicting views, so even if the premises differed, it was possible to agree on the result. As with most wicked problems, there were a lot of "ought-to-be" statements involved. Seen in retrospect, I believe that it is fair to say that, if the group had been forced to model their "ought-to-be" statements, their different philosophies, their premises, it would have been impossible to reach an agreement in a limited time.

SAPO contains subsystems for (1) project control, (2) personnel resource control, (3) finance, (4) customers, (5) vendors, (6) wages and personnel, (7) material control and (8) forecast and statistics.

Every subsystem has a definition of the systemborder in terms of the simple I/O-model. The information objects at the border is detailed, and document lay-outs have by and large been made. No subsystem structures of the 8 systems was made in this phase of the project.

It might be that what we have been trying to do, is to attempt to control a system without knowing its content. The SAPO system is going to exist in a human environment which we have not been able to model, because we do not know it well enough, and because it is so complex. The SAPO-specifications reflect indirectly how the project group thinks that this human organization should behave and be controlled.

This seemingly failure of the use of system models, might simply reflect that it is extremely difficult, may be impossible, to express directly the relevant properties of an organization to be. An indirect expression, in the form of I/O-specifications, run frequencies etc. of different information processing systems are, however, possible, and can be reached by following the principles of wicked problem solving. A substantial part of the wickedness has then been removed from the system, and the project is in the same state as where the library project started.

4.2 The library system

The goal of the project is to automate the internal functions at the university libraries of Trondheim. The main functions that have been treated, are acquisition (ordering and cataloguing), lending and borrowing of books. The University of Trondheim is formed by merging three formerly independent organizations into one university. The three parts are the Institute of Technology, College of Arts and Sciences and the Royal Norwegian Society of Sciences. Each organization has its own library, with a total of approximately 1 mill. volumes. Merging three organizations into one, is most often a painful process, this case being no exception.

For each library, the aquisition and borrowing of books (from other libraries) are centralized, while lending is decentralized to approximately 40 section libraries.

The project started a little more than a year ago. Two systems designers from the CASCADE research project were given a reference group of four librarians working part-time on the project. None of the librarians knew anything about data processing.

During the first couple of months the librarians were trained in systems analysis using CASCADE/I. A functional design of the different subsystems was then done using the simple model of fig. 4, employing CASCADE/I for systems documentation storage, analysis and retrieval.

A CASCADE/I generated graph of the total system, containing subsystems for the library, customers and vendors, is shown in fig. 5. Other examples of CAS-

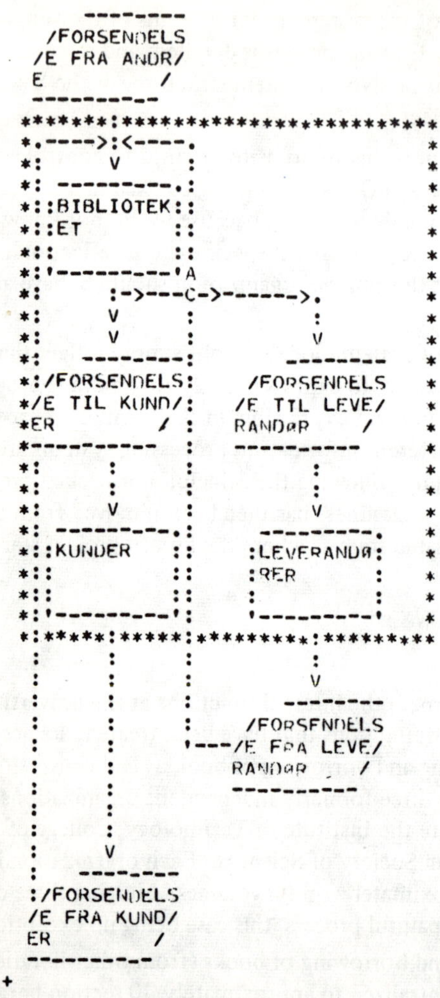

Fig. 5. The library system

CADE/I output is shown in a part of the crossreference list between the information structure and information type objects in fig. 6, and a small part of the term type-catalogue in fig. 7.

CASCADE/I gives a variety of reports of the system documentation, which are useful for different presentation purposes.

The work method employed in this project has been largely influenced by Langefors [3]. We have used a top-down approach, modified by the systems designers

```
                 INFORMATION STRUCTURE              INFORMATION TYPE
01                  FORSENDELSE TIL LEVERANDØR

02                   FORS.TIL LEVR.FRA AKV

 03                   BEST-BREV                          BBREV

 03                   FORS.MOTTAK/LEVR

  04                   FORS VIDEREF/LEVR

   05                   DOK-RET.LEVR

   05                   REKLAMASJON

   05                   BREV ANG.GAVER

02                   FORS.ADM/LEVR.

 03                   PURREBREV LEVERANDØR

  04                   PURREBREV.BEST                    PURBREVR

  04                   SISTE PURREBREV.BEST              ENDPURBEST
```

Fig. 6. Crossreference between information and information type

```
          T E R M - G R O U P   C A T A L O G U E
          ---------------------------------------

ID                LONG NAME                                 ID
--                ---------                                 --

AK-DATA         MOTTAKS-DATA                                AK-DATA
   MT    AKSEKAT              AKSE-KATALOG
   MT    GJKAT                GJENNOMSYNS-KATALOG
   MT    MGJKAT1              MELDING GJ.KAT OM DOK.UTS.
   TG    FAKTOPPL             FAKTURAOPPLYSNINGER
   TR    MDATOM               MOTTATT-DATO.MOTTAK


BEMERKNING      &                                           BEMERKNING
   MT    AKSEKAT              AKSE-KATALOG
   MT    BESTKAT              BESTILLINGS-KATALOG


BESLGJ          BESLUTNING ANG.ANBEFALT GJ.SYN              BESLGJ
   MT    BESLGJSD             BESLUTNING ANGAENDE GJ.SETT DOKUMENT
   TR    AVGJØRELSE           AVGJØRELSE.JA/NEI
   TR    DATOAVGJ             DATO FOR AVG ANBEF GJSYN
   TR    SIGNAVGJ             SIGNATUR FRA AVGJ MYNDIGHET
```

Fig. 7. Part of term-type catalogue

knowledge of computer behaviour, and the librarians knowledge of human behaviour in libraries.

It has felt very natural to use this simple IPS-model, mainly because of its lack of complexity. The use of CASCADE/I give the systems designers a feeling of programming the functional design.

The starting point of the library project was pretty well defined. The task was to automate well-defined operational level functions. The degree of wickedness is much less than in SAPO. Maybe this is the reason that it has been an obvious strength for the library project to have used formal models throughout the project.

When the functional design was done, it turned out to be quite obvious which of the proposed information processing subsystems should be realized by computers (DPS) and which by human processors (HPS).

A DPS of this kind is by and large an intelligent bulk storage. The main factor which rules the DPS-design is the retrieval requirements imposed by the functional design. The CASCADE/I model is not sophisticated enough to be of much help in this task, so we had to rely on manual methods. However, the task was performed in a highly formalized manner, and we can find no principle obstacles to incorporate parts of the procedure in an extended CASCADE-model.

A further detailing of the DPS-objects into computer programs is done employing the CASCADE/I-model, once more storing the systems documentation in the computer.

4.3 Experimental conclusions

The conclusions of these two experiments in use of systems models, can be summarized:

(a) It is difficult to use models in very wicked systems.

(b) Models can be used, and should be used, in the functional design of operational level systems.

(c) If models can be used, it seems to be profitable to use a data processing system (here: CASCADE/I) to take care of the information processing that is associated with the systems design.

(d) DPS-design requires an extension of the model used for IPS-design. There seems to be no serious obstacle to the extension of the model, and to the use of relevant software, when approaching the programming phase in a project.

5. Making a DPS for DPS-design

The most serious draw-back of the CASCADE/I-model, is the lack of possibilities to express dynamical features and information set maintenance features.

Therefore we have extended the basic I/O-model with signal objects and maintenance relations (fig. 8).

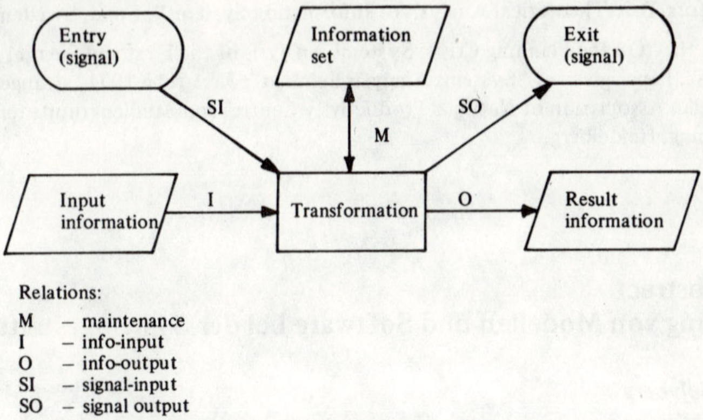

Fig. 8. The IPS-model of CASCADE/I

The transformation is initiated by the entry-signal, and control is passed through the exit-signal when the transformation has been performed. An experimental version of CASCADE/I which can handle this model has been developed, and it is used for the development of CASCADE/II.

It has been shown [2] that ordinary flowcharts can be automatically computed from this model, and it can also be shown that a decisiontable formulation of a system is a special case of this model.

In the CASCADE-project, we are now starting to develop a computer program generator, so that a DPS that is formulated in the CASCADE/II model, will be automatically produced by CASCADE/II.

However, CASCADE/II will not produce the DPS-design itself. This will still have to be done by human beings, but hopefully aided by CASCADE/II.

DPS design is engineering. Other engineering branches have utilized computer aided design tools for several years. I can see no reason that such tools should not be developed for DPS-engineering.

References

[1] Aanstad, P., G. Skylstad and A. Sølvberg: "Cascade – a Computer-based Documentation System". In: Bubenko, Langefors, Sølvberg (eds): "Computer Aided Information Systems Analysis and Design". Lund, Sweden 1971.

[2] Auglænd, K. and A. Sølvberg: "A technique for computerized graphical presentation of information systems to be used in systems design". In: "Approaches to Systems Design, NCC-publications.

[3] Langefors, B.: "Theoretical Analysis of Information Systems". Lund, Sweden 1973.

[4] Rittel, H.: "On the Planning Crisis: Systems Analysis of the First and Second Generations". Paper given at "Systems Analysis Seminar", Karlsruhe 1971, arranged by European Association of National Productivity Centres and Studiengruppe für Systemforschung, Heidelberg.

German abstract
Die Nutzung von Modellen und Software bei der Systemgestaltung

Von *Arne Sølvberg*

Die Erfahrungen aus zwei Systemgestaltungsprojekten werden herangezogen, um der Frage nachzugehen, inwieweit formale Systemmodelle und im besonderen ein entwickeltes Dokumentationssystem (CASCADE/I) für die Gestaltung von komplexen ("wicked") Systemen einsetzbar sind. Als komplexe ("wicked") Systeme, im Gegensatz zu einfachen ("tame"), werden hierbei solche bezeichnet, bei denen das Verstehen des Problems die Lösung bereits beinhaltet und für die Lösung kein Test auf Richtigkeit oder Falschheit durchgeführt werden kann.

Bei beiden Projekten wurde ein am Rechenzentrum der Technischen Hochschule Trondheim (Norwegen) entwickeltes computergestütztes Informationssystemmodell, nämlich CASCADE/II, eingesetzt. Dieses geht von einer einfachen blackbox-Philosophie aus und interpretiert Informationsverarbeitungsprozesse als Transformationen von Inputinformationen zu Outputinformationen. Gemäß diesem Beschreibungsansatz wird das reale System in seiner Grobstruktur dargestellt und iterativ weiter detailliert. Grafische und tabellarische Auswertungen der Systembeschreibung sollen dann den funktionalen Systementwurf unterstützen. Das System wurde in Form von ungefähr 250 FORTRAN-Subroutinen für die UNIVAC 1100-Serie sowie die IBM /360 und -/370-Serien implementiert und erprobt.

Ein geeignetes Experimentierfeld für CASCADE war die Konstruktion eines Informationssystems für SINTEF, eine Forschungsinstitution, die eng mit der Technischen Hochschule Trondheim verbunden ist und mit dieser gemeinsam das

Rechenzentrum betreibt. SINTEF beschäftigt ca. 550 Personen, die in ca. 20 unterschiedlich großen Abteilungen arbeiten. Zu Beginn der Entwicklungsarbeiten war lediglich ein Teil des Rechnungswesens automatisiert, dieses Programmsystem entsprach jedoch nicht mehr den aktuellen Anforderungen.

Mit Hilfe von CASCADE wurde eine neue Struktur aufgebaut, die aus 8 Subsystemen bestand:

1. Projektkontrolle,
2. Personaleinsatz,
3. Finanzen,
4. Kunden,
5. Lieferanten,
6. Gehaltsabrechnung,
7. Materialwesen und
8. Statistik.

Das Ergebnis eines halbjährigen Einsatzes von CASCADE stellte einen Kompromiß zwischen unterschiedlichen Ansichten dar, und es mußte festgestellt werden, daß es außerordentlich schwierig war, menschliche Informationsverarbeitungsprozesse mit Hilfe eines formalen Modellsystems zu erfassen.

Das zweite Anwendungsprojekt hatte zum Ziel, die internen Abläufe der Universitätsbibliothek in Trondheim zu automatisieren. Eine Schwierigkeit bestand darin, drei Einzelbibliotheken von drei Schulen bzw. Fakultäten in ein einziges System zu integrieren. Zwei CASCADE-Mitarbeiter kooperierten mit einer Gruppe aus den Fachabteilungen, die erst in das System eingewiesen werden mußte. Die Systemphilosophie von CASCADE erwies sich als äußerst geeignetes Hilfsmittel, da nur wohldefinierte Arbeitsgänge der operativen Ebene zu erfassen waren und die Problemstruktur damit bei weitem nicht so komplex war wie bei dem erstgenannten Projekt.

Aus den Erfahrungen der beiden Projekte konnte der Schluß gezogen werden, daß formale Modelle sich gut für den funktionalen Entwurf von Teilsystemen der operativen Ebene eignen, für komplexe Systeme eine Anwendung jedoch mit Schwierigkeiten verbunden ist. Wenn Modelle anwendbar sind, dann empfiehlt sich auch der Einsatz eines Datenverarbeitungssystems (hier: CASCADE/I) zur Unterstützung der Informationsverarbeitungsprozesse für den Systementwurf.

Als Nachteil von CASCADE/I wurde festgestellt, daß keine dynamische Prozeßdarstellung möglich ist und die Unterstützung sich auf den funktionalen Systementwurf beschränkt. Aus diesen Gründen wurde eine erweiterte Version – CASCADE/II – in Angriff genommen. Bei dieser ist das Informationsverarbeitungsmodell um Eingabesignale, die die Bedingungen beschreiben, unter denen ein Prozeß initiiert wird, und Ausgabesignale, die mögliche Endzustände eines Prozesses definieren, ergänzt. Im weiteren wurde mit der Arbeit an einem automatischen Programmgenerator begonnen.

The information analysis of administrative systems based on statute law - some aspect of the Legol-project

By *Ronald K. Stamper*

0. Introduction

The study of information systems lags far behind the study of computer and data transmission systems, resulting in a wealth of technical opportunity which we cannot fully and correctly exploit. Pressure to use the new technology results in powerful data-processing systems being implemented as soon as they are technically feasible, whilst their effects upon the organizaticns they serve are still not understood.

The 'Legol' project is an attempt to introduce into the description of organizational information systems the kind of rigour which is familiar in the description of computer systems. This is being done by developing a formalism in which an organizational system can be described during the phase of information analysis which precedes the definition of a computer system. To place the project in the context of the familiar CAM and ISDOS projects [15, 8], Legol may be thought of as aiding the definition of a computer system which is the point where these two other projects take over. The aim of Legol is to make it possible to define what an organization must do, whilst saying as little as possible initially about how it is to be done, and to provide a medium in which the designer can express his decisions about how the data processing is to be performed.

The kind of rigour we are accustomed to in computer science is not always appropriate to the description of organizations and, moreover, the range of concepts available in computer science is quite inadequate for the description of information systems which are vastly more complex than computers. This paper presents some of the features of the Legol formalism with special reference to the information analysis task and the concepts needed when relating a formal system to the rest of an organization.

1. Underlying concepts

The Legol project differs from other important related work in this field (especially that of Grindley, Langefors, Sølvberg, Bubenko and the projects Dataflow

and Autosate – see [1, 2, 5, 6]) because it hangs upon a new conceptual framework. An account of these concepts has been given elsewhere [9] and to a lesser extent [12, 10]. Before launching into a description of the formalism, some of these concepts are mentioned briefly.
A first major concept is that of a sign. Anything which stands for something else is a sign (e. g. words, numbers, a smile, red sky at night, a fish). A sign is a more primitive concept than "information" which is a vague generic term variously used to mean a collection of signs or one of many different properties of signs [14]. Signs are tangible objects: events or properties of objects or events; "information" is a dangerous abstraction often used in ways reminiscent of the medieval scholastics.

A second major concept is the existence in an organization of three main types of system: object systems, discourse systems and formal systems. These are not mutually exclusive. The object systems embrace not only the materials, machines, people or events with which the organization is concerned, but also the documents, messages and other so-called "information" physically present in the organization. The discourse systems are the natural systems in which people use and respond to signs in ways determined socially; these are the informal information systems and account for most of the information-handling in many organizations. In the formal systems, signs are defined and used in ways that are quite formally and explicitly stated. Machines for processing information participate in the formal systems but many formal operations are also carried out by people, especially clerks; it is convenient to refer to these groups of operations as the machine formal subsystem and the human formal subsystem. Finally it should be noted that the object system is not distinct from the "information" systems because all objects are self-referring signs; it is only a matter of choice whether we refer to a written inventory of goods or the goods themselves to answer questions about the stocks we hold.
Thirdly, a broadly based theory of signs (semiotics) is used as the foundation for this study of organizational information systems. (It is described extensively in [9].) It embraces four major areas, each concerned with certain aspects of signs. Pragmatics deals with signs in relation to the behaviour of people; obviously this is very important in the analysis of discourse systems. Semantics serves to elucidate the ways in which signs are related to the "things" they purport to represent. (This problem of relating signs to reality is the central problem of information analysis.) Syntactics is about the formal structures of systems of signs and formal operations upon them (c. f. computer science). Empirics is the study of the statistical properties of sets of signs (c. f. communications engineering and cybernetics).
Fourthly we should recognise three key interface problems. Most basic is the one relating real things and the signs that represent them. In organizations with a formal system there will also be a problem of interfacing it with the discourse system.

Finally, in most cases, there will be within the formal system, an interface between the machine, and human, formal subsystems.

Fifthly, viewed as the set of tasks which leads to a definition of the work of storing and manipulating signs to be performed by the formal machine subsystem, information analysis can be seen to embrace a wide range of problems. In particular, it must with a degree of thoroughness appropriate to the application:

a) specify the signs to be stored and manipulated and
b) the operations to be performed in both human and machine formal subsystems,
c) define the three interfaces,
d) analyse the likely effects of the formal system upon the organization.

In order to do this, the information analyst must be able to describe organizational information systems in terms broad enough to encompass the object, discourse and human formal systems, yet with a degree of detail and rigour that matches the precision required to define the machine formal subsystem.

2. The reason for investigating statute law

The immediate aim of the project is to find a formalism capable of expressing the kinds of complex regulations typified by statute law. This seemingly narrow objective has the advantage of concentrating effort on a well-defined problem whilst leading towards the more distant objective.

One of the central problems of information analysis is to say what a system should do without pre-empting decisions about how it should be done. In the case of administrative systems in government, this is largely achieved in the laws and statutory instruments which define what these systems should do. There is an abundance of systems defined in this way and these definitions have been carefully refined; they should also represent real systems because the administration and the judiciary have a duty to remedy any departure from what they specify.

For these reasons statute law is ideal "experimental" material. Also – and this is an important consideration – success with the project will assist in the designing of computer-based systems in government.

Notice that the kind of law being studied is routine administrative law of the type which is applied to millions of cases per annum by armies of clerks in departments dealing with taxes, social benefits, licensing, planning, registration etc. The project is not concerned with the legal subtleties which can only be dealt with by a court.

The formalism being developed is a legally orientated language which naturally prompts the use of the acronym "LEGOL" which, in turn, has become attached to the project as a whole. (For a more detailed account of the methodology of the project see [11].)

2.1 Progress so far

A sufficiently large body of statute law has been expressed in a very concise logico-mathematical formalism to lend strong support to the belief that this formalism can be generalized. Work has also been done to ensure that, as it is developed, the formalism is given a rigorous meaning in data processing terms. So far, this rigorous analysis has been applied to only a subset of the formalism but the results suggest that, using a relational data-base, the formalism could be interpreted directly by a computer. The interpreter system would be a valuable tool for the information analyst and for the administrator developing a new system; it would be too inefficient for routine data processing.

2.2 Conciseness

One important feature is the conciseness of expression which Legol permits. It seemed that other attempts on this system description problem had resulted in formalisms which were extremely prolix, making the formal system definition very long and more difficult to grasp intellectually than the original. It was determined to avoid this fault in Legol.

This is done by making the principal symbols represent n-any relations, the precise components of which needed at any time being indicated by the context in which they are used. Another simplification is obtained by separating the general definition of the types of data from the definition of specific data items. These features can only be presented by an example.

3. An example of Legol

Consider a simple imaginary "law" which says that in certain circumstances, the owner of the freehold of a building can claim up to one-tenth of its initial building cost as an allowance against tax. Written carefully in legal prose it is as follows:

> (1) Where a company owns an entitling interest as mentioned in subsection (3) of this section in a building which is occupied for industrial use as specified in subsection (4) below by that company or by another company, there shall be made to the company owning the entitling interest, for the chargeable period, mentioned in subsection (5) below, an allowance (to be known as "a capital allowance").

(2) A capital allowance shall be of an amount equal to one-tenth of the capital cost of the building, except that for a period of less than a year the said fraction of one-tenth shall be proportionately reduced.
(3) The owner mentioned in subsection (1) above is the company with a freehold interest in the building, which shall be known as "the entitling interest for capital allowance" and this entitling interest shall not cease by reason of the creation of any lease or other subordinate interest.
(4) For the purpose of this law "a building occupied for industrial use" means a building occupied for the purpose of one or more of the trades listed in Schedule A.
(5) The chargeable period mentioned in subsection (1) shall be the chargeable period relating to the company owning the entitling interest and during which chargeable period the conditions mentioned in subsection (1) for making a capital allowance are satisfied.
Schedule A – Trades recognized as industrial trades for the purpose of this Act shall be baking, milling . . .

This law treats the eight entities: building, company, ownership, use, chargeable period, allowance, valid interest and industrial use. Most of these entities have a number of properties associated with them. In particular, for all but va-

BUILDING	b
Name	b
Start	${}_{\text{ʇ}}b$
End	b^t
Cost	$\text{₤}_{\text{ʇ}}b$
Final value	$\text{₤}b^t$

USE	$U(x,b)$
Type of use	U
User	x
Building used	b
Start	${}_{\text{ʇ}}U$
End	U^t

OWNERSHIP	$Z(x,b)$
Type of ownership	Z
Owner	x
Building owned	b
Start	${}_{\text{ʇ}}Z$
End	Z^t
Cost of acquisition	$\text{₤}_{\text{ʇ}}Z$
Value on disposal	$\text{₤}Z^t$

VALID INTEREST	$\{R\}$
Type of interest	R

COMPANY	x
Name	x
Start	${}_{\text{ʇ}}x$
End	x^t
Accounting cycle	$\tilde{x}$

CHARGEABLE PERIOD	$t(x)$
Name of period	t
Company	x
Start	${}_{\text{ʇ}}t$
End	t^t

ALLOWANCE	$A(g,x,b,t)$
Type of allowance	A
From whom	g
To whom	x
On what building	b
For period	t
Created	${}_{\text{ʇ}}A$
Discharged	A^t
Initial value	$\text{₤}_{\text{ʇ}}A$
Final value	$\text{₤}A^t$

INDUSTRIAL USE	$\{I\}$
Type of use	I

lid interest and industrial use, time intervals are necessary for their identification. Dagger symbols ⸸ and † are used to signify start and end times. Sums of money associated with these times e. g. acquisition and disposal prices, are signified by additing the '£' sign. There is also a ~ sign which signifies the accounting cycle of a company. The full lists of properties for these entities is given on page 428.

A relational model of the data is convenient and natural not only for the definition of the data but also for their manipulation. (It will be noticed that the relations are in the Third Normal Form as described by Codd in [3].)
To show how the law itself is expressed in the formalism it is best to begin with subsections (3) and (4) which would appear as follows:

$$\sigma_{25(3)}: Z(x,b) \in \{R\} \rightarrow Z'(x,b)$$

$$\sigma_{25(4)}: U(x,b) \in \{I\} \rightarrow U'(x,b)$$

Respectively, these rules test that the ownership and the use of the building are admissible for an allowance; if they are, they belong to new relations Z' and U'. The membership symbol, E, is used in a way that can be interpreted precisely from the context. The arrow, →, signifies a prescriptive implication or command. The periods for which an allowance may be claimed are defined by subsection (5) which in Legol is:

$$\sigma_{25(5)}: t(x_1) \wedge \underset{x_1,b}{\Gamma} (Z'(x_1,b) \wedge U'(x_2,b)) \rightarrow p(x_1,b,t)$$

The intersection of Z' and U' gives the periods when both ownership and usage conditions are satisfied. Note the subscripts in x_1 and x_2 which mean that the owner and user can differ. The gamma operator, Γ, has the effect of removing the overlapping periods of time for which the allowance might otherwise be paid twice. The intersection with $t(x_1)$ has the effect of assigning the valid periods to the appropriate accounting periods of the claimants. The resulting periods are the $p(x_1, b, t)$ which are associated with x_1, the owner.

The value of the allowance is given by subsection (2):

$$\sigma_{25(2)}: \pounds_{⸸}A \stackrel{\leftarrow}{=} \frac{1}{10} \cdot \pounds_{⸸} b \cdot \sum_{x_1, b, t} ⸸\, p(x_1, b, t)\, †$$

in which the expression, ⸸ p † generates the durations of the periods which are then summed if x_1, b, t are constant. The resulting total time is multiplied by the cost of the building, £ ⸸ b, and the factor, one-tenth.

The first subsection is virtually redundant but would be expressed as:

$$\sigma_{25(1)}: Z'(x_1,b) \wedge U'(x_2,b) \rightarrow A(g,x_1,b,t)$$

$$A \stackrel{\leftarrow}{=} \text{"CAPITAL ALLOWANCE"}$$

Each of these expressions can be interpreted using the operators of a relational algebra of the kind described by Codd in [4]. The operations for this particular example are described in [13].

4. Structure of a Legol system definition

From the above example it will be seen that the system definition incorporates a Data Definition section and a Rule section. To these must be added a section of Second Order Rules which govern the scope and sequence of application of the First Order Rules. These correspond with expressions in legal prose such as:

"... specified in subsection (4) below ..."

or "... mentioned in subsection (1) above ...".

In so far as precedence relations are appropriate, they form a part of the Second Order Rules but, in many cases, these rules are not presented in so simple a form. Typically one encounters expressions such as:

"... subject to the provisions of section 26 ..."

or "... notwithstanding the provisions of section 24 ...".

The Data Definition section is in some senses the most important from the information analysis point of view. Basically it contains a natural language name for each relation and domain, together with a symbolic label e. g. COMPANY, x. This is sufficient to create a simple dictionary defining the interface between the formal and discourse systems. This is satisfactory if the natural language terms can be used quite reliably. If this is unlikely the law provides a detailed specification for the procedure to be adopted in assigning values to objects, properties or events; these legal statements would be entered into the dictionary rather than the rules. The construction of the dictionary deals with the major pragmatic aspects of the system and also, through the use of definitions, with some of the semantic aspects. The full data definition also includes statistical data, a small syntactic section and more information on semantics, as described below.

The structure of a Legol system definition is a guide to the structure of the information system which it requires, thus it serves a useful purpose in information analysis. However, a system definition cannot be considered in isolation.

4.1 Meaningfulness of the system definition

To be judged fully meaningful, the system definition must relate precisely to other system definitions, to the "real" world and to the appropriate data-processing operations and to the "real" world, as explained below.

Firstly, we can treat the description of a system in the abstract, relating it only to other abstract definitions derived by "algebraic" manipulations. This can be done by defining the syntactic structure of the formalism and rule for transforming expressions. These rules would be applied by the systems designer as he evolves a design for a suitable data-processing system. For example, the formulas in the illustration, above, could be decomposed into simpler formulas or, alternatively, they could be consolidated into the following one:

$$\sigma_{25}: \pounds_1 A \stackrel{\leftarrow}{=} \frac{1}{10} \cdot \pounds_1 b \cdot \sum_{x_1,b,t} \downarrow t(x_1) \wedge \prod_{x_1,b,} (Z(x_1,b) \in \{R\}) \wedge (U(x_2,b) \in \{I\}) \uparrow$$

$$A \stackrel{\leftarrow}{=} \text{“CAPITAL ALLOWANCE”}$$

Secondly, we can treat the system description as a definition of what should happen to actual data values assigned to the data elements. In this sense we wish to know what the description means in data-processing terms as though Legol were a programming language. This meaning, which we call the formal- (or f-) semantics, is established as for any other programming language by defining its equivalent in some already well-defined programming language which controls a well-defined or an actual machine. Fortunately, there exists a suitable object language for this purpose and a macro-processor which can be used to express the definition and perform the translation.

Thirdly, we can regard the description as referring to the object system through the medium of the discourse system. This leads us to seek epistemologically sound meanings for the data handled by the system. The epistemological (or e-) semantics are of great importance to the systems analyst, for only if they are correctly established can the symbol manipulations performed by the computer have any organizationally appropriate effect. The problems of e-semantics are the most neglected aspect of system work – no wonder! because they bristle with philosophical difficulties.

4.2 E-semantics

To illustrate the problems of e-semantics, consider two relations, each with three domains:

Employee (Works number, name, sex)
Batch of goods (Code number, description, sales status).

The first domain is numeric, the second, alphabetic and the third is binary. One could use the union operation to form a new relation:

(Employee) ∪ (Batch of goods)

From the point of view of the data types this operation would be quite meaningful even without converting all data to a single type such as character strings. However, from the point of view of what the result represents in the real world, the operation seems meaningless. We are inclined to think that it should not be permitted. If we introduce into the system information which can be used to prevent this kind of meaningless operation, then it will embody assumptions about the nature of the object system. It will be a part of the e-semantics. A key task of information analysis is to determine what the formal system can "say" about the real world, in other words, to establish the "vocabulary" of the system and the meaningful scope of the operations within the system. These are problems of e-semantics.

There is a temptation to try to build these e-semantic restrictions into the software but this should be resisted. When one is designing a data-processing system, one needs maximum freedom to manipulate the symbols involved, regardless of what they refer to. The union of (Employee) and (Batch of goods) may be a useful expedient in processing the data efficiently, because it would permit the consolidation of two files when perhaps they might usefully share a single storage device.

4.3 Semantic(s-) types and categories

As far as possible, the e-semantics of a Legol system definition are treated as a separate problem from the definition of entities and the translation of rules. In practice this separate task would probably be performed by the data-base designer or a senior analyst. Some universal assumptions about the world would be built into the Legol system. These e-semantic assumptions are handled by tables of s-types and s-categories.

Semantic types are universal structures; they can be illustrated using the entities employed in the example described above. We recognize a number of different types of entities having quite different identifiers. The identifiers can be classified and one simple classification distinguishes the Name, Supplementary identifiers and Temporal identifiers. In Legol, these identifier domains and their labels are generated automatically using the table:

S-type	Relation label	Name	Supplementary identifiers	Temporal identifiers
O (object)	e.g. x	x	NONE	${}_{\iota}x$ x^{t}
R (relation)	U(x,b)	U	x b	${}_{\iota}U$ U^{t}
E (event or period)	t(x)	t	x	${}_{\iota}t$ t^{t}
P (property)	{I}	I	NONE	NONE

In the actual system, the entries in the table are syntactic structures used by the translator program. The values, which would be entered as data in these basic domains, would be signs enabling an individual member of the class of entity to be identified.

The s-category table refers to the s-type and contains the property domains which must be added to the identifiers to complete the definition of a relation. In the example:

S-category	S-type	Relation label	Supplementary domains
Actual object	O	e.g. b	NONE
Legal person	O	x	x
Actual relation	R	U(x,b)	NONE
Legal relation	R	Z(x,b)	£ ${}_{\iota}Z$ £ Z^{t}

The entries in this table would also be syntactic structures. Using these tables the translator would be able to create a full relation definition from quite a brief statement from the analyst such as

OWNERSHIP, Z(x, b), LEGAL RELATION

The s-category leads directly to the supplementary domains and indirectly to the identifier domains.

The s-category information will apply within a limited context, for example, within systems dealing with Revenue Law. Within a narrower context, such as Company Taxation, the s-category might imply the use of additional descriptor domains. Within the narrow context of a few rules which would be the responsibility of a single analyst, there would be freedom to create local domains and even relations; many of these are created automatically by the execution of the operations which interpret the rules.

5. Use of Legol in information analysis

Although Legol is being developed using Statute Law as a source of "experimental" material, it is believed that it should serve as a general technique for information analysis. One of the theoretical aims of the project is to investigate the information analysis problem: how much can we say about what a system should do without pre-empting any decisions about how it should be done?

Legol permits the logical data-base of a system to be fully defined using a relational model for the data. It deals not with abstractions such as "elementary messages" or "concepts", but with simple lists of signs that must be available to the system. These signs, where appropriate, are supported by operationally effective definitions in the dictionary, showing how they are to be obtained by reference to the object system. The rules can then be applied to these signs, in a manner which is made concrete by the f-semantics, to yield other signs which are interpreted either as actions upon the object system or are translated (using the dictionary) into natural language equivalent and injected into the discourse system.

An essential part of information analysis is the specifying of the volumes of data to be handled. At the most basic level this consists of statistics about the numbers of elements in the object system including the events which activate the information system's rules. The aim is to include this information in the Legol system definition in a way that permits it to be manipulated.

6. Use of Legol in information system design

The output of the design work carried out using Legol will be the kind of information contained in PSL [8], defining what a computer must do, plus a definition of the formal data-processing tasks to be performed by the human subsystem. To arrive at these outputs, the analyst should be able to manipulate the formalized system description algebraically, thus he will be sure that his design satisfies the basic requirements included in the initial definition. As he develops a design for an actual system, he will have to introduce the means of gathering and transmitting signs into his system description. These physical devices will be actual objects and therefore will be dealt with in Legol as any other elements in the object system. There is nothing mysterious about these messages and what they contain: they will always consist of some physical carrier (specified in the desired degree of detail) bearing the impression of signs isomorphous with those specified in the system definition. The more complete is the design, as a computer system specification plus a clerical system specification, the more information it will contain about messages, communication devices and methods for recording information.

Perhaps one of the most important potential applications of Legol in its early stages of development will be as a means of testing a system definition. By implementing the f-semantics it will be possible to create a system which can be used to check a body of complex regulations for internal consistency, and to apply them to test cases. This system would be a valuable aid to the systems analyst: it would enable him to check that he had carried out the information analysis correctly. Although the interpreter would process the data very inefficiently, it could be employed at each stage in the design process if Legol were used as the system definition language. The interpreter might also be used in the legislative process by administrators, parliamentarians and others who need to check the precise import of a body of complex regulations.

7. Status of the project – April 1973

Sufficient statute law has been investigated to make it clear that a very wide range of complex rules can be expressed concisely in a formalism such as Legol.

The problems of f-semantic definition have been investigated thoroughly for a sub-set of Legol and an interpreter has been specified. This interpreter employs a macro-processor to translate into the control language of a modified relational data base system. It is hoped to have a working prototype interpreter by the autumn of 1973, depending upon the assistance with programming that is available.

References

[1] Bubenko, J. et. al. (eds.): Computer-aided Information Systems Analysis and Design. Lund 1971.

[2] Bubenko, J. et. al. (eds.): Systemering 70. Lund 1970.

[3] Codd, E.F.: Normalised Data Base Structure – A Brief Tutorial. IBM, RI 935, November 1971.

[4] Codd, E.F.: A relational model of data for large shared data banks. In: Comm. A.C.M., Vol. 13, No. 6, June 1970.

[5] Grindley, C.B.B.: London University Doctoral Thesis on Systematics. London 1972.

[6] Langefors, B.: Theoretical Analysis of Information Systems. Lund 1966.

[7] National Computing Centre: Approaches to System Design. Manchester 1972.

[8] Teichroew, D. and H. Sayani: Automation of System building. In: Datamation, Vol. 15, August 1971.

[9] Stamper, R.K.: Information. London-New York 1973.

[10] Stamper, R.K.: Information analysis. In: [7]

[11] Stamper, R.K.: The Legol project and language. Proc. Datafair Symposium 1973. British Computer Society.

[12] Stamper, R.K.: Logical structures of files. In: Data Organisation. British Computer Society. London 1970.

[13] Stamper, R.K.: The Use of a Relational Data Base System for the Administration of a simple Law. L.S.E. Systems Research Group Discussion Paper. Legol No. 4.

[14] Stamper, R.K.: Some ways of measuring information. In: Computer Bulletin, Vol. 15, No. 12, December 1971.

[15] Waters, S.J.: A survey of CAM and its publications. In: [7]

German abstract
Analyse administrativer juristischer Informationssysteme – einige Aspekte des LEGOL-Projektes

Von *Ronald K. Stamper*

Ziel des Projektes ist es, eine Methode zur Beschreibung von Informationssystemen zu entwickeln, die die Untersuchung von administrativen Systemen ermöglicht, die auf juristische Sachverhalte und ähnlich komplexe Strukturen und Prozesse ausgerichtet sind. Systeme dieser Art sind heute noch sehr schwierig zu automatisieren, denn es fehlt an ausreichenden praktikablen Verfahren. Unter der Voraussetzung, daß sich die wesentlichsten Bestimmungsmerkmale eines solchen administrativen Informationssystems in dem im Gesetz formulierten Recht und seinen unmittelbar begleitenden gesetzlichen Bezügen zur Umwelt niederschlagen, beinhaltet die Forderung nach einem adäquaten Systembeschreibungsinstrument die Entwicklung einer „Definitionssprache", die fähig ist, die Probleme entsprechend ihres gesetzlichen Bezugs darzustellen. Die unmittelbare Folge für die Entwicklungsarbeit des Projekts ist es also, einen Formalismus, LEGOL (= Legally oriented language) genannt, zu schaffen, der die Beschreibung von gesetzlichen Sachverhalten erlaubt und der es ermöglicht, formale Manipulationen vorzunehmen, die auch den Übergang von der Definitionsphase (Beschreibungsphase) bis hin zur Systemgestaltung unterstützen. Anhand eines Beispiels wird diese Vorgehensweise von LEGOL aufgezeigt.

Um eine Systembeschreibungssprache effektiv gestalten zu können, müssen erkenntnisorientierten Wortbedeutungen (epistemological semantics = e-semantics) und formale Wortbedeutungen (formal semantics = f-semantics) unterschieden werden. Die e-semantics sind dem Bereich der Informationsanalyse zuzuordnen, denn sie beziehen das formale System auf die Realität, während die f-semantics im Bereich der Systembeschreibung anzusiedeln sind; sie zeigen, wie das System als Summe formaler Operationen von Symbolen zu interpretieren ist. Aus diesem Grunde spielen die f-semantics eine wesentliche Rolle in diesem Projekt. Obwohl die Untersuchung den Schwerpunkt auf organisatorische Probleme legt, ist es wesentlich, darauf hinzuweisen, daß der entwickelte Formalismus ebenso exakte Interpretationen auf reiner Datenverarbeitungsebene zuläßt. Konkret ist dies dadurch verifiziert, daß angegeben wird, wie LEGOL mit genau abgegrenzten Makros in eine relationsbezogene Datenbeschreibungssprache übersetzt wird. Das Ergebnis ist im einzelnen die genaue Angabe für ein Analyseprogramm und einen Interpretierer für die Sprache. Zur Zeit werden diese implementiert. Mit diesem Prototyp werden weitere Anwendungsbeispiele durchgeführt. Der Verfasser hofft, daß dieser Compiler beim Aufbau und beim Testen solcher komplexer juristisch-administrativer Systeme seine Bewährungsprobe besteht.

An introduction to computer-aided documentation of user requirements for computer-based Information Processing Systems

By *Daniel Teichroew, Walter J. Rataj* and *Ernest A. Hershey*

1. Introduction and summary

Most medium and large organizations have established "Systems Departments" to develop computer-based information systems (CBIS), to operate existing systems and to maintain and modify the existing systems. The existence of systems departments is a recognition of the necessity for an organization to have an effective CBIS in order to remain competitive in today's environment and a recognition that building, operating and maintaining systems is an on-going activity.

Most systems departments have recognized that developing new systems is a complex, time-consuming, costly, and difficult task and have instituted formal procedures. Such standard methods may be called Project Management, System Development Life Cycle Control, or some other name. They identify the various activities that are necessary, outline the results that must be obtained and describe some of the procedures.

One feature common to most of the present procedures is that they are manual. All the documentation of results is prepared manually except for the computer programs which are stated in a machine-processable form, i.e., a programming language which can be processed by a computer, and they are frequently considered to be documentation for human use as well.

The purpose of this paper is to show how the process of system building can be improved by using the computer in the early stages where the requirements that the system is to fulfill are being determined. The computer can first be used to record the results of the activities in the process, then for recording changes in these results, next for analysis, and finally, to aid decision-making in determining what the requirements should be.

In Section 2, models of organizations, information systems, and information processing systems are outlined. This illustrates the role of CBIPS in organizations and provides a framework in which various approaches to determining requirements can be identified. The analysis shows that various approaches are possible and supports the view that which one is best may depend on the individual situation. Regardless of which one is chosen, however, a development process must be followed.

The major steps in the systems building process are outlined in Section 3, and some of the alternative organizations of the activities are described. Again, which one is chosen depends on the individual situations.

The basic reason for discussing the alternatives in the approach to determining requirements and to organizing the systems building activity is to show that the proposed computer-aided method for determining requirements is independent of which methods are chosen. The proposed computer-aided method can be applied regardless of the project management techniques used to control system building.

In Section 4, the present methods for determining information requirements are described in more detail. This section outlines the data which must be recorded as the result of this process. The proposed system will have to provide for the recording of this information. Furthermore, this section discusses the process by which the results are obtained and is important because this process is currently being carried out by people (i.e., analysts) and they will have to be convinced of the value of changing their procedures.

The proposed computer-aided method is outlined in Section 5. It is based on the concept that as much of the documentation as possible should be stored in the computer. This requires a language in which the results of the information requirements process are stated. This language must be suitable both for the analyst and for computer processing. The method by which the data is stored and analyzed by the computer is outlined.

The relative benefits and costs of the proposed procedure relative to the present methods are discussed in Section 6.

The benefits considered in Section 6 are primarily those that occur during the requirements definition phase, i.e., they are improvements in performance of analysts. The computer-aided documentation of requirements also provides opportunities to develop more extensive computer aids for system designers and programmers. This topic will be covered in a future working paper.

2. A model of information processing in organizations

2.1 Organizations

The basic structure of organizations has not, so far at least, been changed by the use of the computer. Organizations still consist of resources (people, money, equipment), collected together under a (usually legal) charter in order to transform some material into a product or to provide some service. People usually join organizations, rather than working individually, because organizations are more "efficient". To obtain this efficiency, organizations are subdivided into a hierarchy of smaller units, each of which performs some specialized function. The term "organizational unit" will be used in this paper for any subunit of the organization.

Resources flow into the organization from outside the organization (the environment), flow from one organizational unit to another, and eventually flow to the outside. In like manner, information flows to and from the outside and among these organizational units. Therefore, in order to provide a more detailed description of an organization, it is necessary to identify not only the subunits but also the resources used and the associated flows. Various methods can be used to describe the organization and its flows, but a pictorial one is usually the clearest. Figure 1 is an example of a description of a hypothetical organization engaged in wholesale trade. In this example, three types of flows are represented: goods, information, and money.

It is clear that a description of an organization is always an abstraction. For example, the organization in figure 1 would likely be subdivided into smaller units and these could be shown in more detail. To describe each of these subunits completely could require listing the names of the individuals in each. What constitutes a satisfactory level of description depends on the purpose for which it will be used. The specification of a "level of description" is an important aspect of analysis of information requirements and will be discussed further in Section 4.

Most organizations do not possess complete descriptions of themselves at any level, and the primary reason for this is that the organization can function without a detailed formal description. Under present methods of operation, the individuals and groups learn a set of procedures and it is enough if they follow these; they do not have to know or understand what else goes on in the rest of the organization. The organization chart provides whatever information is necessary about the formal structure and the formal lines of communication on a static basis.

What descriptions do exist are usually out of date and obsolete. Organizations are usually easy to change; the smaller the change the easier it is. Since descriptions are prepared manually, they must be changed manually. Since an accurate, up-to-date picture has not really been needed, it is seldom given high priority.

Organizations have become more complex and the environment has become more difficult to understand. In order to predict the effect of changes, it has become necessary to treat organizations more formally. Such techniques are frequently called organizational modelling; a survey of approaches and techniques including

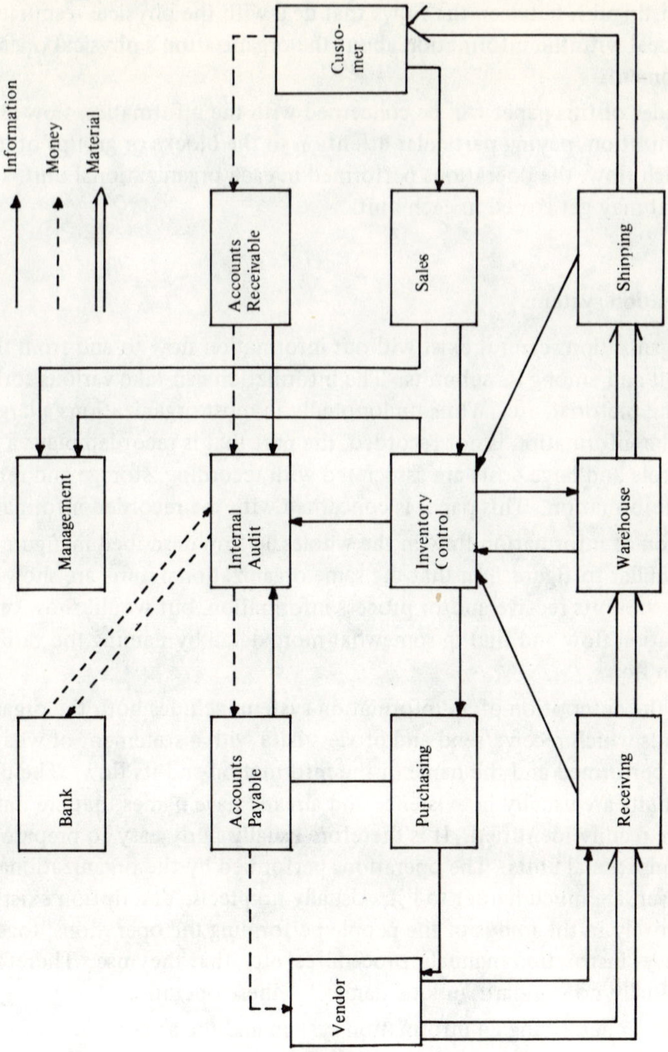

Fig. 1. Selected flows of an organization

references is given by Nolan [11]. Such analysis and design of organizations involves identification of objectives, measures of performance, and the considera-tion of alternative methods of organization.

One of the factors that is affecting the structure and efficiency of organizations is the (electronic) digital computer and its associated equipment. For purposes of studying the application of computer technology in organizations, it is desirable to distinguish between the flows that deal with the physical resources and those that deal with the information about the organization's physical operation and environment..

The remainder of this paper will be concerned with the information flow aspect in the organization, paying particular attention to the blocks or groups of information which flow, the operations performed in each organizational unit, and the data that may get stored in each unit.

2.2 Information systems

Modern organizations cannot exist without information flow to and from the environment and among its subunits. The information can take various forms: oral, written, pictorial, etc. While undoubtedly in most organizations a large amount of the information is not recorded, the part that is recorded plays a very important role and large costs are associated with recording, storage and retrieval of this information. This paper is concerned with the recorded information.

A description of information flow in the wholesale firm described in figure 1 would be similar to figure 1 in that the same organizational units are shown because most subunits receive and/or process information, but would show only the information flow and that in somewhat more detail by naming the various information flows.

In general, the description of an information system includes both the organizational units which receive/send and process data with a statement of what operations are performed and the name of the information and its flow. The organizational units are usually in existence and already have names that are unique and that are readily identified. It is therefore usually fairly easy to prepare the list of organizational units. The operations performed by the organizational unit, however, are much harder to list. Usually no precise description exists except collectively in the minds of the people performing the operations, together with whatever instruction manuals, procedures, etc., that they use. Therefore, there are usually no standard, unique names for these operations.

A major task in describing an information system and the associated information is to describe the operations performed. These processes are normally described in various levels of detail from the top down, and as the description becomes more detailed, smaller and smaller sub-processes are defined. It is clear from examining figure 1 that the information processing operations are an integral part of each organizational unit; organizations in the past have not subdivided so that some organizational units perform only physical operations and others only information-processing operations.

Any detailed analysis of information systems shows that many similar information processing and data processing operations are performed in different organizational units. However, until the advent of computer technology there was little reason to investigate whether such similar operations should be centralized. Frequently they were centralized but this was because there were other organizational considerations that made it worthwhile.

2.3 Information Processing Systems (IPS)

Organizations have always used information. Since Babylonian times information has been recorded, stored and processed in various ways. (For an overview, going back to ancient times, see Sage [12]). Computer technology has altered the characteristics and economics of information processing in a very fundamental way. Computers can process information much more rapidly, with much more accuracy at much less cost than was ever possible with previous methods. There is, however, a cost attached to this new capability – to use computers efficiently requires a large volume of operations. Consequently, a system must be constructed in which information processing operations are processed together to achieve the necessary volume. Construction requires a considerable investment before benefits are obtained. The most important difference between the information processing before and after computers is that before the computer information processing costs were almost entirely proportional to volume – with the use of computers there is a large fixed cost and a much smaller variable cost. The "economy of scale" phenomenon holds within relatively wide limits, and hence there is an economic pressure to increase the size of systems.

The most important impact of computer technology on organizations is that it became possible, and in many cases necessary, for competitive reasons, to centralize information and data processing operations into a system called a computer-based information processing system (CBIPS or IPS). These systems or applications, as they are sometimes called, are operated by a new organizational unit called by such names as the Computer Department, Systems Department, Data Processing Department, etc. This IPS exists, moreover, only to serve the organization which is involved in an economic environment requiring the most efficient utilization of its resources.

Figure 2 shows the information system for the wholesale firm depicted in figure 1 after some of the information processing has been centralized in IPS's in the Systems Department. All the organizational units still exist as they did before but a new organizational unit called the Systems Department has been established. It receives data from the other organizational units and produces data which are sent to the other organizational units. Internally it performs some operations that were previously performed in the other units. However, each organizational unit still performs some information processing in addition to other functions.

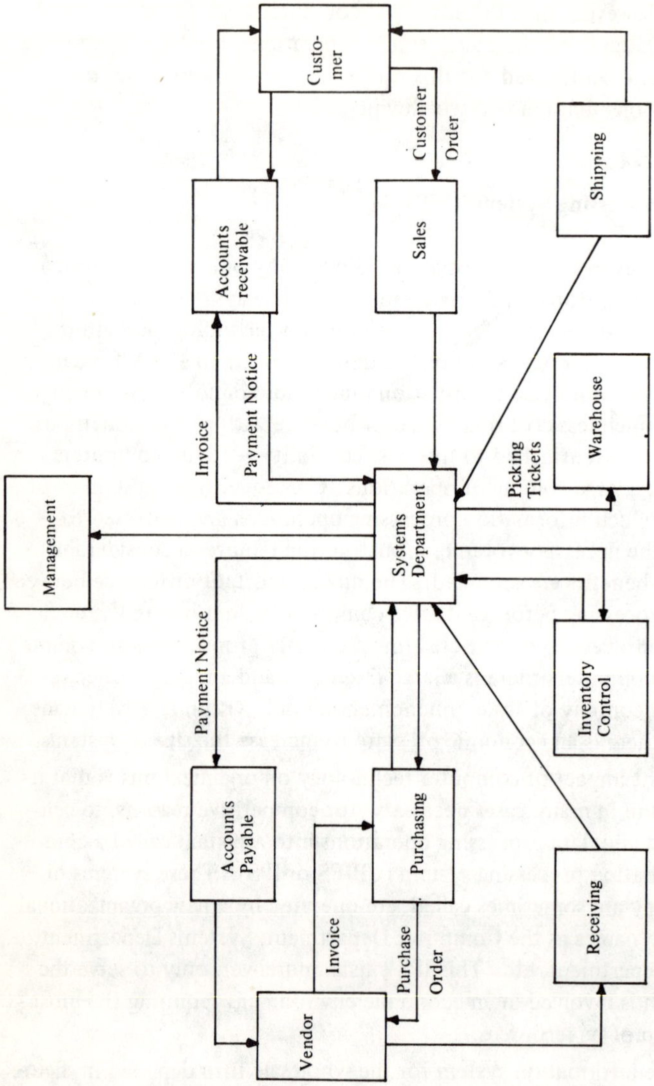

Fig. 2. Selected information flows in organizations with an Information Processing System

It is helpful to distinguish between two kinds of operations on data:

a) Data processing operations are operations which can be defined independently of the specific content or meaning of the data. Examples are record, print, store, and retrieve.

b) Information processing operations are those performed on data in which meaning of the specific data is important, e.g., select vendor, determine order quantity, etc.

The computer is so much more efficient in the data processing operations (record, store, computer, print, etc.) than human beings and other machines that whenever the volume is sufficient organizations are forced to use the computer for this purpose. Therefore, the initial application of computers in many cases has consisted of moving all the data processing operations from the organizational subunits to a centralized unit. However, the computer can also perform the information processing operations provided they can be described in sufficient detail to write the necessary computer program. If the operation is performed in sufficient volume use of the computer may be economically worthwhile. Even if it is not economically worthwhile by itself the transfer to the Systems Department can be sometimes justified, for example, if the result is obtained faster, or more accurately, or if retranscription time is eliminated.

The information processing in the organizational units is likely to be rearranged due to the economies of scale variable with the digital computer but, as mentioned earlier, some is likely to remain within the organizational unit. There are also likely to be additions and substitutions of some data processing operations to make the necessary interfaces compatible. Such an interface would be a keypunching operation in that it was not needed prior to the introduction of the IPS.

Since a computer-based system cannot be operated until it is built, the Systems Department is given the responsibility for developing and building such a system. Building a system is a time consuming and complicated task. In the meantime the organization must continue operation. Therefore the present information system is replaced piece by piece. Each such piece, arbitrarily defined, will be called an Information Processing System or IPS. Most organizations have one Information Processing System, and most are in the process of extending the use of the computer, that is, enlarging the existing IPS or building new ones. This process requires identifying those information processing and data processing operations which should be transferred to the IPS.

In order to build an IPS, a procedure for system building must be developed. Furthermore, the present and the proposed system must be described in order to compare benefits, proposed costs of operation, and so on. Section 2.4 outlines the major items in such a description.

2.4 What is necessary to describe an Information Processing System?

A description of an IPS can be divided into two parts: A static description and a dynamic description.

The static description consists of lists of:

1. The organizational units, that is, groups, divisions and departments which send information to and/or receive information from the IPS.
2. The information processing operations performed by the IPS.
3. The information which flows between the IPS and the organizational units.

A dynamic description contains a representation of:

1. The flow of information to and from the Systems Department.
2. The dynamics affecting the flow of data including:
   a) triggers that cause flow,
   b) sequences,
   c) volumes.

The above static and dynamic descriptions are used to define the hardware requirements which would complete the description of an Information Processing System.

Section 3 of this paper describes the system building process in which the descriptions are developed in more detail while Sections 4 and 5 discuss present and computer-aided methods of determining information requirements for an IPS.

3. Building Information Processing Systems

3.1 An overview of the evolution of the system building process

Even with the first use of computers for organizational purposes (business data processing, as it was usually called then) the process of constructing an IPS was recognized as being complicated and time consuming. Furthermore, the process was considerably different than that involved in using computers for scientific or engineering purposes. The process for building a computer-based information processing system is described in the early textbooks, for example: Canning [4, Chapters 5, 6 and 7]; and Gregory and van Horn [7, Chapters 6 and 7]. The evolution of the process has continued, and more recent and more comprehensive descriptions are given by Hartmann [6] and Glans, et al. [8]. A description of the evolution is given by Benjamin [3].

Computer technology has changed considerably since the early 1950's. Auxiliary storage is now available on discs as well as on tapes. The computer is capable of many operations in parallel that formerly had to be carried out sequentially, and communication equipment makes it possible to collect input data and transmit results to geographically remote points at high speeds. These changes have affected the structure and organization of computer systems, that is, the set of hardware and the alternatives that have to be considered in designing such systems.

These changes have also affected the "organization" of Information Processing Systems. Initial systems were organized for batch processing. Random access memories made in-line processing and data base oriented systems possible. Additional hardware developments made possible interactive systems. Technology has also changed the methods of constructing an IPS as well as its operation.

3.2 The phases in the system building process

It is not the intent of this paper to describe the system building process in detail. For the purpose of discussing computer-aided methods or requirements determination it is sufficient to identify the major activities, as formulated by Teichroew and Carlson [16] in their survey of current system building procedures. These activities are:

a) Perception of need - which includes the definition of the problem and the initial estimate of benefits and costs; provides authorization to proceed with the Logical Design.

b) Logical system design - determining the information requirements of the organization and designing the information system; this provides the logical design to be implemented.

c) Physical system design - determining optimum hardware/software configurations to accomplish the proposed Information Processing System; this provides the technical specifications of the IPS.

d) Construction - the building of the Information Processing System itself, that is, programming, file construction, etc.; this provides an implementation of the proposed design.

e) Testing, conversion and installation - testing and installing the Information System; provides a reliability test of the new IPS.

f) Operation - operating the Information Processing System: scheduling and controlling operations.

g) Modification and Maintenance - Maintaining the Information System; monitoring performance; investigating possible changes.

Anyone who has participated in the building of any reasonably sized system realizes that in practice the process is iterative. Activities started in any phase of the project must be carried on throughout the life of the system. Therefore an allocation or resources to the various phases as shown in the usual manner is better represented by a diagram showing how the activities extended through the life of the system (figure 3).

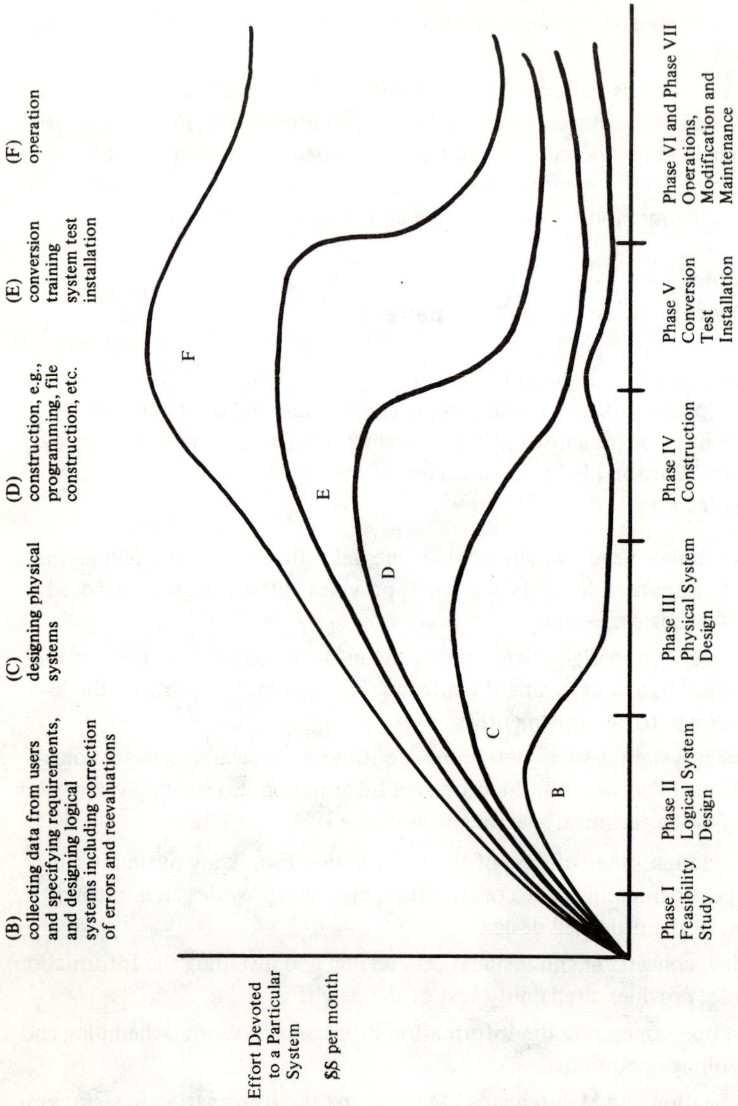

Fig. 3. Relative magnitude and duration of activities in the system development cycle

Regardless of how the system development process is carried out certain data about the target system must be determined and recorded (documented). The type of information that must be recorded is described in Section 3.3. A brief analysis of alternative methods of organizing the system building process is given in Section 3.4 to support the statement that the organization of activities does not affect what information is recorded although it may affect when during the process it is developed and recorded.

3.3 Documentation of data in the system building process

All system building procedures designed for building systems of any size provide for documentation of data about the target information processing system being proposed, designed, built, or operated. This documentation is necessary to record the results of decisions that will be needed in the future, to communicate among the various individuals involved in the process, to provide instructions to individuals who must interact with the system, and to provide a basis for changing the system when it becomes necessary.

In most procedures, the documentation consists of forms that are filled out manually. Where the documentation is direct input to the computer, as in source language statements or programs, there is usually an attempt to make the documentation suitable for human use as well. This manual documentation usually includes two types of data: data about the target system and data about the project which is producing the target system. This paper is only concerned with the data about the target system. Data about the project and its management will be covered in a later paper.

The major types of data that are necessary to describe the target system are identified in Section 2.4; this data is modified or added to throughout the system building process. For example, information is collected in the Logical System Design about real world activities, that is, the data that are needed and the various relationships imposed by users of the output of the target system. In the physical system design stage the data is organized into various logical units usually called files. During the Construction Phase, a logical storage structure is imposed on the logical files to permit the design and construction of the program which will access the files. Initial files may also be constructed here. During the Test and Operation Phase, the programs and files are used with the actual data stored in the physical files. In the Maintenance and Modification Phases, the logical and physical structure of the files are used for accommodating the changes. Similar transformation occurs for processes, volume, and time information. Hardware descriptions enter during the physical system design phase.

As the size of the systems has increased, and as the cost of maintenance and modification using manual documentation has increased, it has become obvious that the documentation should be stored in a computer processable form rather than a solely manual form. This would require the design of a data base and an appropriate language for entering data into the data base as well as for retrieving it for processing. A number of proposals for such a data base and language have been made and are described in, for example, Blackman [2], Fisher [5], Lock [10] and Trapnell [17].

3.4 Alternative organization of the system building process

As outlined in the section above, the system building process can be viewed as a set of activities which contribute to the building of data base describing the target system. The discussion in section 3.2 indicated that there are different ways to organize these activities. The purpose of this section is to outline some alternative organizations and to show that the computer-aided methods designed to assist in requirements determination can be utilized regardless of how these activities are organized.

The system building process can be considered as a combination of "expansions" and "contractions". An "expansion" involves subdividing an object into its elements. For example, at one point in the building process only the name of a report is identified, later its major parts are identified, and finally all the individual data elements are listed. Another situation involving expansion is the subdivision of an activity into parts that can be worked on independently. For example, for the report mentioned above, it may be desirable to let each of the major parts be described by different individuals in parallel. A "contraction" occurs when one of a number of alternatives identified during an expansion is chosen and the others discarded. A contraction also occurs when the results of a number of paralled activities must all be completed before the next activity can begin.

A detailed description of a system building process can therefore be represented by a directed graph in which nodes represent events and arcs represent activities. Eventually all arcs must meet in one node where the system becomes operational.

One possible approach is the Project Team Approach, there is no formal structure. The team proceeds horizontally through the Logical Design, Physical Design, and Construction phases without formal review in between and chooses how much detail is developed at any given time. Hence constructing nodes would appear.

Another possible approach is the "Separate Phase" approach. Here the logical design is done to completion quite thoroughly before the Physical Design is attempted and likewise the Physical Design before Construction. However, the Physical Design and Construction phases themselves can be organized in two alternative ways:

a) Define the smallest subtasks, complete them, and then integrate them into a complete part.

b) Define the larger tasks, then break them into smaller and smaller tasks, and complete them.

In the combined Physical System Design and Construction Approach - the Logical Design is completed top-down but separately from the Physical Design and

Construction; Physical Design and Construction are performed in parallel in greater levels of detail (top-down).

Another possibility is to combine the Logical and Physical Design. Here the Logical Design and the Physical Design are performed in parallel in a top-down manner; Construction phase is performed top-down, but completely separate from the other two phases.

A basic issue in structuring the development process is which approach makes best use of the technology in the logical design, physical design, and construction phases. Clearly all approaches have been tried at one time or another with results varying from organization to organization. But perhaps the strictest approach is the second method described above. Here, the logical design is completed first with the specifications given to the physical system design phase. The physical system is designed and the specifications given to construction. No iterations are permitted, and changes are made only to correct errors, omissions, or ambiguities. The advantage of this approach is that the process is well defined. The major disadvantage is that no trade-offs can be made. For example, during the physical system design phase it could be discovered that a slight change in the specifications of the logical design could result in a very substantial reduction in cost. However, since no iterations are permitted, this cost reduction could not be realized. Corresponding advantages and disadvantages of the other approaches do indeed exist but will not be discussed here.

It is somewhat natural to view the system building process as distinct steps due to the fact that the stimulus for investigating computer based information systems comes from computer technology, and therefore it is very commonplace to look at proposed systems from the view of the computer system to be used. It is very difficult to get people to identify the information processing problems and to propose a logical system design without in fact stating the proposed physical solution. It is particularly difficult if the study team members are computer professionals but even if they are not, the tendency is to think in terms of the solution.

Defining the proposed physical system alternatives first may not be bad if the alternatives are then compared on the basis of requirements - but this means requirements will have to be determined any way. The purpose of the remainder of this paper, therefore, is to propose a computer-aided method for documenting requirements in machine processable form starting from the logical system design phase, and to show that it can be used regardless of which of the various alternative methods of organizing the system building process are used.

4. Present methods for determining information requirements

As outlined in the previous sections, the system building process is a long and complicated requiring many people working in parallel. Somewhere in the process, it is necessary to specify and record the target system requirements and it is usually desirable to do so before the actual design and construction is started.

All system building procedures therefore contain one or more phases concerned with determining and recording requirements. Various names are used for this process: feasibility study, specification phase, analysis phases, etc. The steps required and the procedure to be followed differ from one system to another depending on assumptions made, type of application, type of system being considered, personal preferences, etc. Regardless of the procedure to be followed, all the methods basically agree that the result or output of this part of the process includes a description of the proposed IPS as the organizations sees it and evidence that the proposed system should be built and installed, it must therefore include the type of data discussed in Section 2.4 and 3.3.

4.1 Current methods for determining and stating requirements

Many different procedures for determining requirements of what an IPS is to do are described in the literature. An early, relatively detailed, description is given by Canning [4; pp. 161–225]. More recent and more extensive procedures are given by Glans, et al. [6] and Hartmann, et al. [8; Vol. 3]. Shorter descriptions are given in many of the publications on system building listed in Teichroew and Carlson [16]. Surveys of these methods are given in Nolan [11] and Salomone [13].

A comparison and evaluation of these information requirements determination methods will be given in a forthcoming ISDOS Working Paper. Here it is only necessary to summarize some common features which appear in all of these procedures and which are relevant to a consideration of developing computer-aided methods.

The steps between the initiation of the project, such as a user request and the handing of the specifications of the "proposed" system to the user and management for approval include the following:

a) The collection and recording of data pertaining to the present system and the needs of the new system.

b) The analysis of such data.

c) The decisions leading to the design of the proposed new system.

d) The evaluation of the proposed system and a demonstration of its benefits versus costs.

e) The preparation of the Proposed System Description Report. Examples of present manual methods are given by Hartmann [8], Auxton [1] and Glans [6].

The AUXCO method, the method outlined by Hartman, and many other similar methods are manual, that is, the analyst (or a group of analysts) collects the data that he needs, collates, organizes, and organizes, and analyzes it himself, and produces the report. Such manual procedures and manual documentation possess inherent limitations; some of these are:

a) Long lead times when implementing a change in a problem description.
b) Allows the work to proceed only in a sequential manner neglecting any parallelism.
c) Manual methods of recording and analyzing information are very error-prone and subject to misunderstanding by other humans.
d) Problems of coordination between project members at system interfaces is very slow and difficult on large system building efforts.
e) User validation of the logical design is often difficult as no one person can comprehend all aspects of the total problem.

These limitations can only be overcome by use of computer-aided methods as will be discussed in Section 5.

4.2 Categorization of the requirements determination phase

The end result of the requirements determination phase must be a "proposed" system which can gain the approval of the user and management while being the specification for the succeeding phases of the system building process. For the purpose of this paper - which is to propose computer aids for the information analysts - it is convenient to consider four distinct aspects of the process of determining requirements:

a) The end result of the process - the requirements that the proposed system should accomplish.
b) The format or language in which the results of the process are stated.
c) The approach by which the results are obtained.
d) The criteria which are used to choose among the various alternative requirements or specifications that might be stated as objectives for the proposed system.

The reason for making this distinction is that the approach (3) and criteria chosen (4) may vary from one organization to another and may even vary over time, and consequently will affect the end results (1).

However, the format or language (2) in which the result is stated should be the same regardless of the approach, the criteria used, or the result itself. A common or standard language should be used because the data or information necessary to design and implement the proposed system is independent of the particular system. Furthermore, the easier the language is to understand by both information analysts and physical systems designers the better the communication will be and the less likely the chance for misunderstanding.

This paper is, therefore, primarily concerned with the format or language in which a proposed system can be described: "What" such a language must be able to describe has already been outlined in Section 2.4 and 3.3. Since it is important to demonstrate that this format is independent of the approach or the criteria, some possible alternative approaches are outlined in Section 4.3 and alternative criteria in Section 4.4.

4.3 Approaches to determining information requirements for the proposed system

Several major approaches that have been suggested in the literature and/or used in practice are:

a) Bottom up. In this approach one starts by examining and describing the material flow, on which the organization depends. The data that is necessary to control the flow is specified and a system is designed to provide it. The system also provides summary reports for management decision making.

b) Top down. In this approach one starts by defining the objectives of the organization, the means to achieve the objectives, and the decisions necessary to reach the objectives. This then determines the information required for the making of these decisions.

c) Modify present system by transferring some functions to a CBIPS. Each of the non-mechanized information processing and data processing operations are examined and where it is technologically and operationally feasible and economically worthwhile, these operations are transferred to the new system.

d) Serve the users. In this approach the potential users of the information system are asked to state the outputs they will need. A system design is then generated that will produce this information.

e) Data base. In this approach, the analyst first determines what data would be stored in a data base. The contents of the outputs that the system can now provide are now limited by the data available in the data base.

These various approaches may be more or less appropriate in particular cases. The bottom up approach is most relevant in an organization where the material flow is paramount. The top down approach may be necessary when decisions must be made rapidly. The third approach may be preferable if conversion for the existing system to the new one is a serious problem. The "serve the user" approach is followed where the users are politically powerful and each has distinct needs. The data base approach may be the best where the type of data that has to be stored does not change as much as the format of the reports.

4.4 Alternative criteria used to set specifications

Regardless of which of the approaches listed in the previous section is used, there are several different criteria that can be used in deciding what the IPS should produce:

a) Cost reductions in the operation of the information system.
b) Tangible operational benefits, such as reduction in inventory, for example.
c) Aids to management to improve their decision making.

The precise specification for a proposed IPS will depend upon which one of the aforementioned criteria is used. For example, if the primary objective of the IPS is provide tangible benefits in retaining customers, the system would probably be required to provide priority processing of customer requests for service. If, on the other hand, the primary objective is to minimize costs, batch processing might be used.

5. Computer-aided methods for determining information requirements

5.1 Basic philosophy

In the previous section it has been shown that certain basic information is required to describe an IPS regardless of which approach is used to build an IPS or which criteria is used to set the specifications. A discussion of the current manual methods of stating requirements was given in which the basic tools of these methods were identified: pencil, paper, and forms. In addition, it was stated that the systems analyst also followed a (manual) procedure to define the requirements of the target IPS. In any case, the end result of these manual processes was the document which described the logical requirements of the target system. This document can assume any one of several names such as System Requirements Report, Logical System Design Report, etc. but all contain the same basic information.

With an appreciation of the limitations of current methods and the nature of the information required, it is natural to investigate ways in which the computer can relieve the problem definers (analysts) of much of the clerical work associated with the determination of requirements.

The basic objective, therefore, of the computer-aided method is to have all results of the information requirements process stored in a common data base which analysts, designers, and programmers can all use. As the building process proceeds, the contents of the data base are modified and expanded on an "as needed" basis. Because analysts, designers, and programmers will require access to this data base, a standard language for its use and, in particular, for describing information requirements will be needed. The objectives of the computer-aided methods in general are to:

a) Provide a description of each input and output of the target system in a format understandable to the user of the target system (as well as the Problem Definer).

b) Produce such documentation and analysis so as to be sufficient to start the next step in the system building process, namely the designing of the physical system.

5.2 Necessary components of a computer-aided method

The ISDOS Research Project concerns itself with the automation of the system building process. The first step in the project is the development of a computer-aided method for the documentation and analysis of information requirements.

A computer-aided method which will overcome the limitations of manual methods must be based on the same two entities required in the current manual techniques: the tools and procedures with which a problem is defined.

The tools of a computer-aided method are:

a) A language for stating requirements which is appropriate for the user and at the same time sufficiently structured for machine analysis.

b) The software package which will store, analyze, retrieve, and display the information recorded in the language. This software package must allow the PD to request the information he needs to prepare the Systems Requirement Report (the end product of the Logical Design Process) and must give him that information in an understandable format.

Such a method is the Problem Statement Language (PSL) and the Problem Statement Analyzer (PSA) which is currently being developed and tested by the ISDOS Project.

5.3 Requirements of a Problem Statement Language (PSL)

Any computer-aided method for recording and analyzing requirements exists to assist the problem definer in his task of providing a logical design for the target IPS. As mentioned earlier, this output of logical design sometimes called the System Requirements Report must contain all the information that is necessary to proceed with the next phase of the system building process, the Physical System Design. Furthermore, the Systems Requirement Report must be understandable to not only the problem definer and physical system designer but also to the ultimate users of the target IPS for their validation as well as management for their evaluation.

The ISDOS approach to determining requirements is to identify all outputs that the target system is to produce and then to describe each output to a sufficient level of detail so that the necessary inputs and processes needed to produce these outputs can be identified. These inputs and processes are then defined in a top-down manner to the required level of detail.

PSL provides a relatively structured method for stating the major types of information about each output and input in a top-down manner. These types of information are:

a) Interfaces with the IPS - data about the external relationships of the input or output: who defines the input or output, where it goes to, where it comes from, who has access to it, etc.

b) Timing and Volume - global information stating the "how" and/or "when" these inputs and outputs arrive to and/or leave from the target IPS; information on the volume of the inputs and outputs, etc.

c) Data Definition by Structuring - specific information on how the various data elements associated with the input or output being described are structured or related. This structuring process can be done to any desired level of detail.

d) Data Definition by Computation – the various formulae, conditions, and decisions by which data elements are to be computed are given.

e) Process Definition by Structuring - the various processes, subprocesses, etc. which are constituents of the target IPS are defined to any desired level of detail in successive steps.

Initially when a systems analyst begins to define the problem at hand he may start with the largest processes involved, the target system, and gradually divide that process into its major sub-processes continuing to any level of detail much as he would for an input or output. At each level he would state the inputs and outputs to the constituent process until all such processes were well defined. Such a procedure of definition is important because with it the analyst can avoid errors and omissions which occur when a large problem is encountered.

5.4 Requirements of the Problem Statement Analyzer (PSA)

The Problem Statement Analyzer is an information processing system which is designed to improve the process of building target information processing systems by aiding the front-end of the process - namely, the statement and analysis of the requirements that the target system is to accomplish. The Problem Statement Analyzer is the set of software that carries the analysis of the problem statement as far as possible without bringing in implementation considerations.

The computer-aided methods provide primarily clerical facilities and retrieval capabilities for its users. Instead of having to maintain manual records, the data collected during the system building process is available from a data base. Since the information will be available from a data base this implies that the PSA must be able to display this information in various ways according to valid user requests. The software provides for the adding of new information, the deleting of unwanted information, and the updating of current information about the target system.

This software system also provides checking capabilities in various areas for its users. For example, the Analyzer determines that all data names and/or process names are globally unique for the problem being defined.

In addition, the Problem Statement Analyzer provides more extensive analysis of the relationships that exist between all data and processes than the human analyst can. The sheer size and complexity of todays information processing systems does not permit any single or group of analysts to accomplish this task in any amount of time that will not delay the operational status of the target system.

Specifically, then, the Problem Statement Analyzer will produce reports which are geared to the basic needs of its users. These reports will include the following information:

a) The Source Listing Information.
This provides the problem definer with a listing of his source statements along with syntax error messages, if any. At the end of the listing the source listing statistics are given.

b) The Problem Statements Directory
provides an alphabetized listing of all user-defined names with the various usages of these names.

c) Interface Information.
The purpose of this information is to allow the user to note the interfaces of the system with its environment.

d) Problem Function/Process Information.
Allows the user to have reference to the composition of all the defined

processes in the problem statement. Permits validation of all processes in every level of detail.

e) Data Description Information.
Gives the user an alphabetized list of all the defined data names, their logical content, and type. Provides a means of validation of data with the user.

f) System Parameter Information.
Allows the user a means of noting all data items which have been used as a system parameters in the problem definition. Levels of detail are supported by this information as the problem definer can determine which parameters are unspecified.

5.5 Environmental criteria for a computer-aided method

In previous sections it has been pointed out that there are various ways in which to arrive at a statement of requirements. Some of the differences may be due to differences in the organization for which the IPS is to be constructed. Others may be due to the ways in which the System Department and the analysts find it best to work. Clearly, since these differences exist and will likely continue to exist it is essential that a computer-aided approach be suitable for any of the approaches.
In addition, the computer-aided requirement determination and logical system design process must be usable under the following conditions:

a) As the project proceeds more and more data is added: the computer-aided system must allow for this.

b) Data will be modified and changed over time; therefore, provision must be made for modifications or changes, deletions, and additions.

c) Many different individuals will be involved: provision must, therefore, be made for keeping track of each individual's work and also for identifying the interactions among the work of the different individuals. Since individuals will usually work in parallel the total effort will be divided into subtasks.

d) The system must emphasize that it is only computer-aided: individuals must be able to obtain the kind of information that helps them in accomplishing their task.

6. The costs and benefits of computer-aided methods

In any organization the decision to move from manual documentation methods to the computer-aided one proposed by the ISDOS Project requires careful consideration. The costs involved in the computer-aided method must be evaluated against the benefits to be derived from its use. In this section, therefore, the various costs and benefits associated with this method will be discussed.

6.1 The cost factor

Among the major factors to be considered in the potential employment of such a computer-aided method are the following:

a) Operational Costs:

Computer time will be required to process the problem statement, maintain the necessary data base, and produce the required outputs. The additional computer time for compiling is not a major consideration in the decision of whether to change from programming in an assembly language to programming in a general purpose language such as COBOL. Similarly, the additional computer time for analyzing requirements will, with proper design, be small compared with the benefits obtainable.

b) Training and Organizational Support:

The problem definers and the others involved in using the computer-aided system will be required to learn the language and the use of the system. The language is designed to be as easy as possible for use by non-programmers; however, since it is to be processed by a computer, it must be more formal than English, and therefore the problem definers will have to learn it. The language is designed so that people who have no knowledge of computer languages can become familiar with the concepts in a few weeks. One of the reasons for this is that much of the difficulty involved in learning computer languages arises from the "processing" oriented statements which must be part of a general purpose programming language but are deliberately missing from a problem statement language.

c) Language and System Maintenance:

As with any standardized language and software system someone must be responsible for the maintenance. In this case the ISDOS Project is maintaining the system and the language. The ISDOS Project is using the language in the development of the remaining software package which will eventually automate the rest of the process of constructing systems. Organizations participating in this project may use the computer facilities and the software system available at the project. They may also incorporate the software system in their own computer installation if they so wish.

6.2 The benefits of computer-aided methods

A computer-aided documentation and analysis technique will provide benefits for all of the groups involved: the target system user, the problem definers and their management, the data and function administrator, the physical system designers, the constructors of the target IPS, and, finally, the organization as a whole. This section will outline the benefits for each of these groups as they relate to the Problem Statement Language.

a) Benefits for the Target System User:

The Problem Statement Language is designed in such a way that a user, or his staff, should be able to state all the requirements in a form that is understandable to him. The computer analyses will help the user in understanding his requirements since the Problem Statement Analyzer provides both a microscope and the telescope to allow him to see either details or the overview at whatever level he wishes. In addition, the requirements are stated in a clear, computer printed form. He can be certain that what he sees will determine what is actually to be implemented. He can state his requirements without being constrained by worrying about how much it will cost to accomplish his requirements because eventually the algorithms which carry out the actual design will notify him if the requirements cannot be accomplished or are extremely costly to achieve. He will be able to make a decision about whether he wants to modify his requirements.

b) Benefits for Problem Definition Management:

Problem definition management will be able to use the system to structure the problem into subproblems in whatever way it wishes and it will receive reports from the Problem Statement Analyzer which indicates the progress that is being made in stating requirements.

The Problem Statement Analyzer facilitates the coordination of the activity of many problem definers since each one communicates with the system and it keeps track of all of their activities. It also facilitates the top down approach in determining requirements. By issuing the proper instructions to the Problem Statement Analyzer, management can be assured that analyses will be carried out at a certain level and that the analyses will be complete and checked before further details are gathered and recorded.

The duplication of work among individual problem definers can be reduced by designating certain variables as systems variables. The information on these variables can then be gathered once and for all at the systems level. Consequently, duplication of effort by problem definers can be avoided.

c) Benefits to the Problem Definer:

The individual problem definer will describe the individual inputs and outputs that are assigned to him, possibly involving more than one user, and will receive back from the Problem Statement Analyzer the listing of what he has prepared with the diagnostics and analyses. He will also receive any information which describes changes in other parts of the problem that affect him. Whenever he continues an effort that he has started previously, the system will also provide him with information that is already available to the Problem Statement Analyzer. The language provides a structure indicating what information is to be collected and it provides a place for information as it is gathered or becomes available. The diagnostics and outputs of the Problem Statement Analyzer simplify his work in that the material is always clearly organized and indicates errors to be corrected and reminds him of essential information still to be obtained. The individual problem definer can concentrate on his particular activity at any one time with the assurance that whatever relationship this has with other activities will be brought to his attention appropriately.

d) Benefits to the Data and Function Administrator:

The data and function administrator is responsible for ensuring that data names are used consistently and that the definition of functions that are stored in the library are consistent. A benefit of the automated system is that any new data names or function definitions are brought to his attention immediately and can be checked for duplication and correctness. Using the information available to the Problem Statement Analyzer, he can ask for other information or analyses that will help him determine whether duplication has occurred. The collection of information regarding data variables such as definitions, etc. can be coordinated; he can be assured that these will be used since they do not get into the programs without being reviewed by the Problem Statement Analyzer.

e) Benefits to Physical System Designer and Constructor:

The Problem Statement Analyzer produces outputs for the individuals who will be charged with implementing the system which will accomplish the requirements. The benefits to this group using the automated documentation method are that the requirements that they receive are formatted consistently and clearly printed, thus eliminating ambiguity. The requirements have been checked for consistency, and are up to date since the effect of changes has been incorporated wherever they occur.

The other major area of benefit is the fact that the material can be organized in such a way that it will simplify the system design and programming. The functions to be computed can be grouped in ways that they naturally appear in programs, together with the appropriate identifiers and volume parameters which will simplify the writing of source language statements. Similarly, data can be grouped by natural groupings in order to facilitate design and construction of files. Consequently, programming time and effort can be reduced.

f) Benefits to the Organization:

Each group that interacts with the automated system gains some benefit. This is a very important advantage in ensuring its acceptance and use. Jackson and Stanovich [9] emphasize the need for a system which requires some standardization:

> "Often, programmers have rebelled against standardized techniques, seeing in them nothing beyond a mindless regimentation imposed from above: any benefits were to be reaped by management; the disadvantages and discomfort were the programmers' lot. Too often, this rejection has been justified: Standardized techniques are not an end in themselves; they must represent and embody a technology that is better than the programmer could devise for himself; they must amplify his skills, not cripple them".

The benefits for the organization as a whole can be summarized in terms of cost, quality of documentation and quality of requirements. The cost to obtain an accurate, complete set of requirements will be reduced because of the reduction in the amount of analyst time required through the use of computer aids and through the reduction of duplicate efforts. Improved quality of documentation results from the fact that the documentation is always up to date since the system to be built is based directly on it. Documentation is no longer written after the fact and then only when there is time available. It is always readable and covers all the work done so far. The improved quality of the requirements from the point of view of the value of the target system to the organization comes through improvement in logical system design and through having data and function directories available as by-products of the process by which requirements get communicated to the physical system designers and constructors.

References

[1] Auxton Computer Enterprises, Inc.: PROJECT MANAGEMENT SYSTEM (AUXCO METHOD): Users Reference Manual, Vol. II, 1972.

[2] Blackman, M.: "Reducing system development and maintenance costs". In: Data Processing, January–February 1973, pp. 8–12. An introduction to Lexicon.

[3] Benjamin, Robert I.: "A Generational Perspective of Information System Development". In: COMMUNICATIONS OF THE ACM, Vol. 15, No. 7, July 1972, pp. 640–643.

[4] Canning, Richard G.: ELECTRONIC DATA PROCESSING FOR BUSINESS AND INDUSTRY. New York 1956.

[5] Fisher, D.L.: "Data Documentation and Decision Tables". In: COMMUNICATIONS OF THE ACM, Vol. 9, No. 1, January 1966, pp. 26–31.

[6] Glans, Thomas B., et al.: MANAGEMENT SYSTEMS. New York 1968.

[7] Gregory, Robert H. and Richard L. Van Horn: AUTOMATIC DATA-PROCESSING SYSTEMS. San Francisco 1960.

[8] Hartman, W., H. Mattes and A. Proeme: MANAGEMENT INFORMATION SYSTEMS HANDBOOK, (ARDI). 1968.

[9] Jackson, M. and A. Stanovich: "Segmented-Level Programming". In: Computers and Automation, Feb. 1969, p. 23.

[10] Lock, V.A.J.: "A Computer-Based Data Definition System". PROCEEDINGS FOURTH AUSTRALIAN COMPUTER CONFERENCE, 1969, pp. 147–151, CR 22, 277.

[11] Nolan, Richard L.: "Systems Analysis for Computer Based Information Systems Design". In: DATA BASE, Vol. 3, No. 4, Winter 1971.

[12] Sage, David M.: "Information Systems: A Brief Look into History". In: DATAMATION, Vol. 14, No. 11, November 1968, pp. 63–69.

[13] Salomone, Peter: "Survey of Methods for Determining Information Requirements". TIMS 12th American Meeting, October 1971.

[14] Teichroew, Daniel: "A Survey of Languages for Stating Requirements for Computer-Based Information Systems". PROCEEDING OF FALL JOINT COMPUTER CONFERENCE, 1972, pp. 1203–1224.

[15] Teichroew, Daniel: "Computer-Aided Documentation of User Requirements," INFORMATION SYSTEMS FOR MANAGEMENT. Englewood Cliffs, New Jersey 1972, pp. 97–112.

[16] Teichroew, Daniel and David M. Carlson: "A Model of the System Building Process". ISDOS Working Paper No. 64, November 1972.

[17] Trapnell, F.M.: "A Systematic Approach to the Development of Systems Programs". AFIPS, SJCC, 1969. Vol. 34, pp. 411–418.

German abstract
Eine Einführung in die computergestützte Dokumentation der Benutzerbedürfnisse für computergestützte Informationssysteme

Von *Daniel Teichroew, Walter J. Rataj* und *Ernest A. Hershey*

Ein allgemeingültiges Modell des Informationsverarbeitungsprozesses in Unternehmungen sowie des Gestaltungsprozesses von computergestützten Informationssystemen wird herangezogen, um auf Mängel der bisher angewandten Vorgehensweise hinzuweisen: Der Gestaltungsprozeß ist zu zeitraubend, die entwickelten Systeme sind hinsichtlich ihrer Gestaltung und ihrer Anwendung zu kostspielig, sie werden den gesetzten Anforderungen nicht gerecht, sind nicht anpassungsfähig genug etc.

Ein wesentlicher Grund für diese Mängel ist darin zu sehen, daß bislang keine wirklich effizienten Instrumentarien zur Ableitung und Darstellung der Anforderungen an das zu gestaltende Informationssystem zur Verfügung stehen. Es wird ein Überblick über verschiedene in der Literatur vorgeschlagene und in der Praxis verwendete Methoden gegeben, denen allen gemeinsam ist, daß sie zur manuellen Anwendung konzipiert sind.

Im Gegensatz dazu wird die Konstruktion eines computergestützten Hilfsmittels zur Dokumentation und Analyse der Benutzeranforderungen an computergestützte Informationssysteme vorgeschlagen. Dieses Hilfsmittel soll in seiner endgültigen Ausbaustufe ein Element des sich in der Entwicklung befindlichen ISDOS-Systems darstellen, eines Systems zur computergestützten Gestaltung von Informationssystemen.

Das computergestützte Dokumentations- und Analyseinstrument soll aus zwei Bausteinen bestehen:

– einer Sprache, die es dem Benutzer gestattet, seine Informationsanforderungen zu artikulieren, die sich jedoch gleichzeitig für eine maschinelle Analyse eignet,
– einem Softwarepaket, das die beschriebenen Informationsbedürfnisse speichert, analysiert und für Auswertungen und Weiterverarbeitungen zur Verfügung stellt.

An beiden Bausteinen wird innerhalb des ISDOS-Projekts gearbeitet, und zwar in Form der Problembeschreibungssprache PSL/II (Problem Statement Language) sowie des Analyseprogramms PSA/II (Problem Statement Analyzer).

PSL/II gestattet die Beschreibung der Inputs und Outputs eines Informationssystems nach der top-down-Methode und sieht hierbei folgende Informationstypen vor:

– externe Beziehungen der Inputs und Outputs, etwa Herkunft und Verbleib oder Zugriffsberechtigung,
– zeitliche Restriktionen und Umfang,
– Datenstruktur,
– Regeln, nach denen die Daten berechnet werden,
– Definition der Prozeßstrukturen.

PSA/II soll die Benutzeranforderungen entgegennehmen, verschiedenen Prüfungen unterziehen und für weitere ISDOS-Elemente in einer geeigneten Form aufbereiten. Unter anderem sollen dem Benutzer folgende Auswertungen zur Verfügung gestellt werden:

– eine aufbereitete Liste sämtlicher Eingaben, die mit Kommentaren zur syntaktischen Richtigkeit versehen ist,
– ein Datenverzeichnis mit der Angabe, wo welche Namen verwendet wurden,

– Informationen über definierte Prozesse in unterschiedlichem Detaillierungsgrad.

Eine Hinwendung von den bisher angewandten manuellen Dokumentationsmethoden zu der vorgeschlagenen computergestützten Vorgehensweise würde zwar zunächst zu zusätzlichen Kosten führen, läßt jedoch auch gewichtige Vorteile erkennen.

Auf der Kostenseite ist zunächst auf die Maschinenkosten für den Betrieb eines entsprechenden Softwarepaketes hinzuweisen. Ferner müßte die Sprache erlernt und die Benutzer des Systems mit diesem vertraut gemacht werden. Auch Wartungskosten für die Sprache und die zugehörige Software sind zu veranschlagen.

Dem steht jedoch ein weiter Personenkreis gegenüber, der von der computergestützten Methode profitieren würde. Die Benutzer würden mehr Klarheit über ihre Anforderungen gewinnen und diese damit auch präziser ausdrücken. Der mit der Systemanalyse betraute Personenkreis könnte Einzelprobleme besser strukturieren und in den Gesamtzusammenhang integrieren. Die Dateiorganisatoren würden bei Konsistenzprüfungen und der Eliminierung von Redundanzen unterstützt, während die Programmierer durch die klare Problemvorgabe bei ihrer Arbeit profitieren würden. Schließlich ergäben sich durch die Standardisierung auch Vorteile für die Unternehmung als ganzes.

Model management systems

By *Hartmut J. Will*

1. Introduction

Information is gained as output from intelligence processes which apply mental skills to factual knowledge or programms to data. This definition asserts that it is useful to distinguish between informational inputs (factual knowledge, data) and informational transformation processes (skills procedures, models).

Information is also a resource – sui generis – because it is useful, scarce and exchangeable, although the traditional ownership conventions do not always apply. For example, stolen information, data or models can hardly be repossessed without a loss of their value to the original owner. To consider information as a resource implies not only that it is possible to associate costs and values (benefits, payoffs) with it but that it is also feasible to manage it according to organizational resource management objectives.

It is now a matter of interest or preference to select the relevant informational resource. Information economics is rather unspecific by identifying its object formalistically without content as message while stipulating perfect rationality on the part of the information user or evaluator.[1] Data management is quite specifically concerned with the best ways and means of describing, creating and manipulating a data bank and of retrieving, analysing and displaying data stored in a data bank of unique design [7, 22].

This paper concentrates on model management in an analogous manner. An attempt is made to develop a conceptual framework against which modern developments in modelling software can be analysed. First, the model bank concept is defined and structurally explained. Then model management (MM) is described operationally in terms of MM objectives and functions. Subsequently, several model management systems (MMS) are analysed with respect to user, computer and MM support. In conclusion, the findings are summarized in organizational and management information systems (MIS) perspective.

---

1 For an introduction into basic problems see ref. [5].

2. Model bank

The model bank[2] contains a variety of operational (abstract) models which are representative of relevant relationships within the observed real system and its environment. In managerial context, global (corporate) and local (functional) models are distinguishable according to the extent to which the underlying organization has been modelled. The "decision activity" explanation of MIS [10, 12] is not unrelated to the model bank concept, because the managerial inference, evaluation, choice and feedback procedures are contained in the model bank in basically the same manner as all relevant and well-defined observations are stored in the corresponding data bank. The problem is how to design and utilize a model (bank) as part of an MIS most effectively and efficiently according to information resource management objectives (see Figure 1).

2.1 Assumptions

The assumptions underlying the model bank concepts are

(1) that models exist implicitly or explicitly in most organizations, or that they can be created and that they are needed repeatedly for goal formulation and for goal control purposes;

(2) that it is possible, feasible and necessary to manage modelling;

(3) that models can be designed "independent" of the data needed by any one user in an informational problem situation;

(4) that models are too valuable and too costly to limit modelling to any one user (group) and/or any one user language;

(5) that it is possible to design, implement, maintain, utilize, modify, extend, evaluate and eventually to automate model banks according to specific model management objectives.

A particular organizational model bank contains many informationally relevant relationships which are not directly built into the data bank. For example, the data organization for transactions may be so highly structured within the available data bank that journal and ledger maintenance or ad hoc retrieval capabilities are in fact built-in; however, the general ledger, closing and reporting routines can be applied in basically the same way to historical accounting data stored and maintained in the data bank as to budgetary parameters. Interest, depreciation, statistical analysis, forecasting and linear programming routines provide other examples of models contained in the model bank portion of an MIS. On the other

2 This term was first used in German and English by the author. See ref. [21, 24].

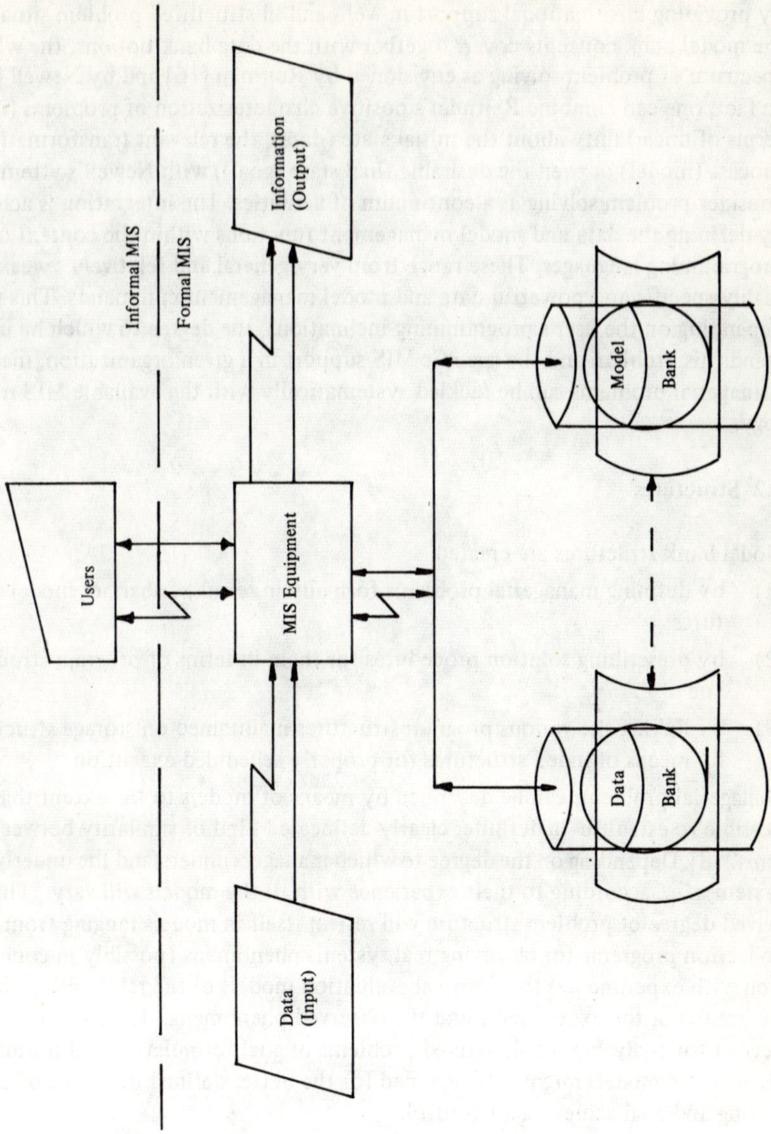

Fig. 1. Management Information System

hand, the model bank of an organization may contain such powerful models as quadratic programming algorithms for which neither relevant data exist in the data bank nor corresponding managerial understanding might be available in the organization.

By providing informational support in well- and ill-structured problem situations, the model bank concepts cover, together with the data bank notions, the whole spectrum of problem solving as envisioned by Reitman [16] and by Newell [13]. In fact, one can combine Reitman's positive characterization of problems (in terms of uncertainty about the initial state (data), the relevant transformation process (model) or even the desirable final state (goal)) with Newell's attempt to consider problem solving as a continuum of activities. The integration is achieved by defining the data and model management functions within the context of programming languages. These range from very general and relatively "weak" to highly specific and powerful data and model management commands. This way, depending on the user's programming inclinations, the degree to which he understands his problem and the specific MIS support in a given organization, many managerial problems can be tackled systematically with the available MIS technology.

2.2 Structures

Model bank structures are created

(1) by defining managerial problems formally in terms of abstract model structures;

(2) by prescribing solution procedures for them in terms of program structures, and

(3) by linking the various program structures maintained on storage structures by means of index structures for properly scheduled execution.

Managerial problems can be described by means of models to the extent that it is possible to establish "a definite, clearly delineated kind of similarity between systems" [8]. Depending on the degree to which managers understand the underlying system, i. e., according to their experience with it, the models will vary. The perceived degree of problem structure will reflect itself in models ranging from data collection programs for observing real systems phenomena (possibly in conjunction with experiments) to statistical evaluation models of the relationships between the results of the experiments and the observed phenomena. Heuristic models[3] are needed for analysing the ill-defined problems of goal formulation and normative, algorithmic models might be developed for the better defined problems of goal setting and goal achievement control.

---

3 Newell [13, pp. 375–394] distinguishes the following methods: Generate and Test, Matching, Hill Climbing, Heuristic Search including Mean-Ends Analysis and Induction.

To include goal (re)formulation among the managerial intelligence functions [21] implies a frequent change in the relevant data space according to the (requisite) informational variety. As long as management asks "why" and "how best . . ." questions, both data and model structures are bound to evolve into more detailed and powerful ones to facilitate even more specific and better structured problem descriptions. The history of corporate modelling with its evolution from budget accounting to discrete simulation models and more analytic and normative models is a case in point [18].

Once models are defined, it becomes necessary to program them and to select from the available program structures the appropriate ones in order to meet the informational resource management objectives of minimum program storage space and cost at maximum execution efficiency. Whereas mathematical model functions are uniquely defined in terms of domain, range and transformation procedure, programs with their corresponding input, output and algorithmic[4] or computational procedure[5] can be supplied with data outside of their domain. This means that the range of the first function must lie within the domain of the second if output from one program is used as input into another [14]. We distinguish source and object program structures depending on the programming language used and main programs, subroutines and coroutines according to the super-, sub- or coordination of the programmed instruction sets.

Since it is often necessary to store, retrieve, combine and schedule programs, index structures [20] are applied to map program structures onto storage structures. Index structures facilitate this mapping by "pointing" to the storage addresses of data or model structures according to the desired access paths and speeds. They consist of arrangements of identifiers (keys, labels) and/or their corresponding addresses.

Storage structures contain the data, model and index structures on the addressable space of storage devices [1]. It is possible to associate specific storage and access costs with these concepts and to implement the various data or program structures according to the objective of minimizing these costs subject to other information resource management constraints.

4 An algorithm is defined as a stepwise procedure, process, method, technique or routine to arrive at one or more outputs from zero or more inputs in a finite, definite and effective sequence of operations. See ref. [9].

5 A computational procedure does not meet all criteria established for an algorithm and does not guarantee a problem solution.

3. Model management

Model management circumscribes the establishment and maintenance of model banks according to informational resource management objectives. A discussion of model management objectives from a user's point of view precedes the description of the major MM functions.

3.1 Objectives

The following general MM objectives are formulated with the decision-maker, manager or problem solver (information user) in mind and can be evaluated against specific resource management criteria:

(1) In general, models should reflect the users' (changing) world views, i. e., they should be simple, robust, easy to control, adaptive, complete on important issues, and easy to communicate with [11] according to the users' self-understanding.

(2) Models should be programmable in a variety of user languages, e. g., in host languages (i. e. ALGOL, APL, BASIC, COBOL, FORTRAN, PL/1 etc.), or in special languages for diverse users (i. e. for accountants, auditors, controllers, engineers, functional managers etc.), and/or in diverse modes (i. e. batch, on-line, dialogue etc.).

(3) Models should be available to multiple and diverse users, e. g., to managers, programmers, operators and model (bank) administrators according to their justified needs.

(4) Models should be (1) correct (according to definition in terms of function, domain and range); (2) debugged (within a specific domain and range); (3) detailed (with desired resolution levels); (4) private (according to the legal rights of ownership and privacy); (5) authorized (according to organizational access regulations); (6) reliable (according to validation and debugging criteria for inputs, backup and lockout); (7) similar to the modelled system (homorphic with respect to structure and behavior) and (8) understandable (in terms of model structure, behavior and desired output format).

(5) The available MMS should support the variety of user objectives and their specific pursuit easily, flexibly, as completely as possible and economically in order to match the specific model management tasks at hand in each organization.

3.2 Functions

The various model management functions are here broadly viewed rather than machine-internally considered and denoted as model description, manipulation, scheduling, execution and information display.

Model description refers both to defining a problem and to programming a solution procedure for it. Host language statements or special MM commands are available for representing the users' world view. Although models and programs are separate systems modelling and programming are closely related activities and are therefore here considered together. Ideally, the model designer or user should be able to define his model operationally without being too concerned about programming.

Model manipulation involves restructuring, testing and debugging of the various programs or modules in order to maintain the model (bank) in the desired state with a minimum of effort. This is necessary in view of the many changes faced by the organization which may have to be reflected in the MIS. In addition, there is always pressure to improve on achieving the various model management objectives.

Model scheduling is concerned with copying, interpretation and translation facilities for source language programs, with link-editing of object modules, with memory allocation and with loading of the various modules according to the required model management functions. Although this function is usually built into the operating system, it might likewise be included in a special model management system under the control of an operating system.

Model execution denotes the actual processing of the core image instructions on one or more central processors for the purpose of producing the desired information from the available data. Again, this function is performed most likely under control of an operating system which monitors the equipment utilization closely and provides the appropriate interface with the data bank.

Information display concerns the presentation of modelling results in the desired verbal, symbolic or graphic format according the users' needs for complete understanding of the information.

It is now interesting to see to what extent these MM functions are supported by the various MMS and to what degree the different MM objectives can be achieved by utilizing them.

4. Modelling software

Since modelling is frequently practised it has become the object of systems efforts. This resulted in the development of numerous model management systems or computer software for modelling[6]. Figure 2 illustrates MMS with respect to user, computer and model management functions in host language and in specialized user language perspective.

Special resource management criteria can be established for the pursuit of the various user objectives in the most effective and efficient manner. The various criteria for evaluating the MM functions can be summarized as follows:

(1) The MMS should support flexible and "independent" model descriptions by providing the various users with the needed model, program, storage and index structures for the available computing equipment within minimal design time requirements.

(2) The MMS should contain appropriate procedures and language modes for MB creation, maintenance and utilization according to various user (group) objectives.

(3) The MMS should facilitate selection of a variety of display modes for the generated information according to user preferences.

The computer functions can be evaluated against the following criteria:

(1) The available MIS equipment should support the user objectives and MM functions technically and economically in an optimal manner.

(2) The user-model bank interface should be kept "open" and easy to use in order to provide the appropriate level of requisite informational variety by means of either generalized MMS or specialized designs.

(3) The user should have a choice of the computer operations mode, depending on his response time requirements and demand pattern for reports (one-time, recurring), by being able to select a generative mode of object program preparation (pre-compilation, compilation, assembly) and the subsequent storage method for the generated program or an interpretive mode.

---

6 The various MMS mentioned in this paper are: ADFIN (Applied Decision Systems), APL (I.P. Sharpe & Associates), APL/DYNAMO (University of Alberta), AUTOTAB (GE), DYNAMO (MIT), FAPS (On-line Decisions), FIPLAN (Computer Sciences Corp.), FIRES (Computer Sciences Corp.), FORESIGHT (Foresight Systems, Inc.), FP/20 (Bonner and Moore), FPS (Computer Sciences Canada and RTZ Consultants), GAME (On-line Decisions), GEM (Arthur Andersen & Co.), GPSS, INF+ACT (International Timesharing Corp.), PROFORMA (Control Data), PROPHIT (SBC), PSG (IBM), SIMSCRIPT, SPURT.

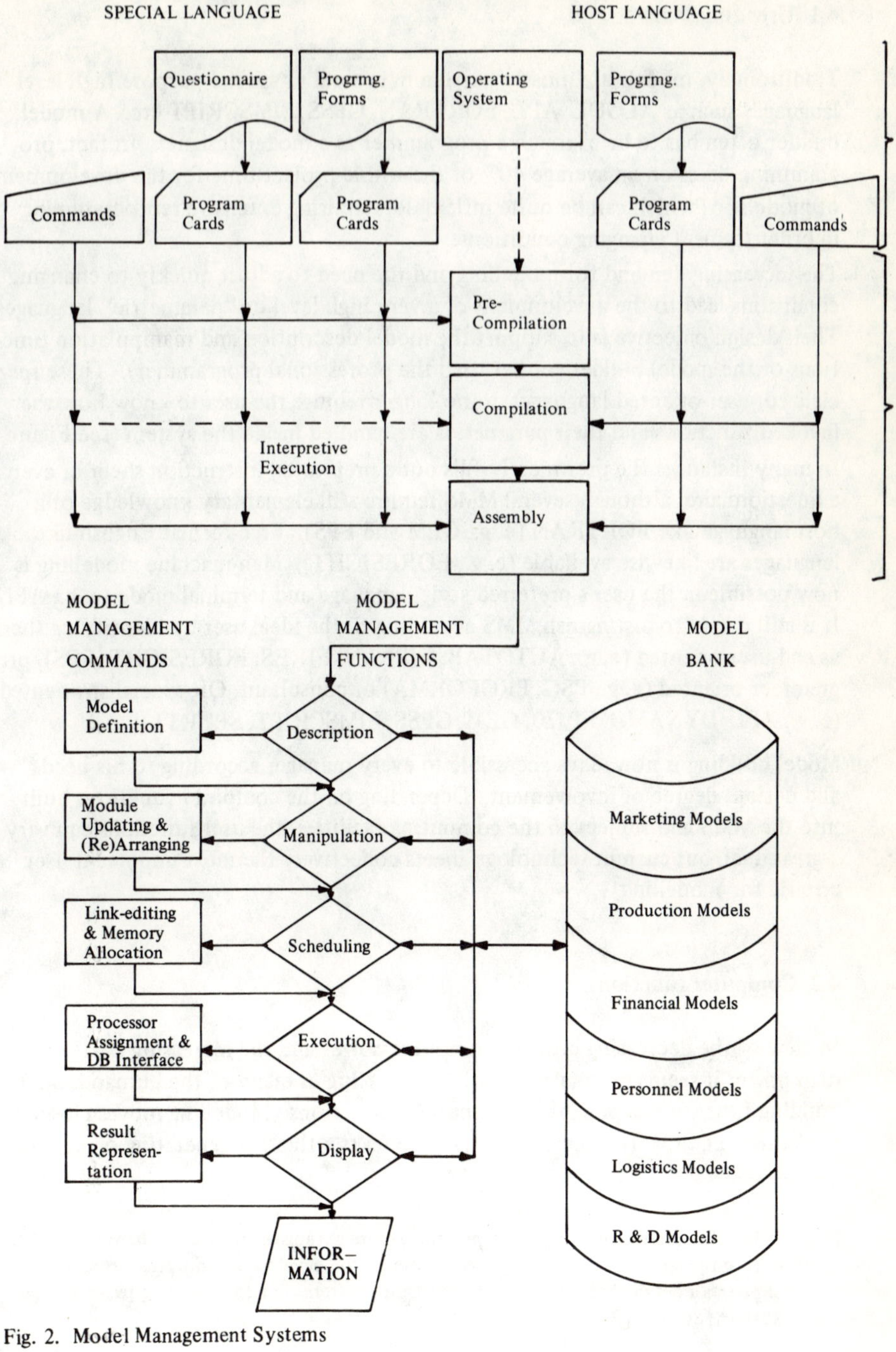

Fig. 2. Model Management Systems

4.1 User functions

Traditionally, models are mostly written in general or special purpose high level languages such as ALGOL, APL, FORTRAN, GPSS, SIMSCRIPT etc. A model builder often has to be as much a programmer as a model designer. In fact, programming takes on an average 40% of the whole project time for the development of models [6] which can be quite inflexible, requiring extensive reprogramming in order to meet changing conditions.

The increasing demand for modelling and the need to adjust quickly to changing conditions lead to the development of a very high level or "parametric" languages. Their design objective is to support the model description and manipulation functions of the model builder (rather than the professional programmer). These specialized, user-oriented languages do no longer require the user to know how the invoked functions and their parameters are handled inside the system (see Figure 2). In many instances the user merely fills out a preprinted instruction sheet or even a questionnaire, although several MMS require still elementary knowledge of a host language like FORTRAN (e. g., GEM and FPS). Free-format English-like languages are likewise available (e. g., FORESIGHT). Man-machine modelling is now possible in the user's preferred style, language and terminal mode (e. g., APL). It is still useful to distinguish MMS according to the ideal user by identifying them as end-user-oriented (e. g., AUTOTAB, FIPLAN, FIRES, FORESIGHT, FPS), programmer-oriented (e. g., PSG, PROFORMA) or consultant, OR-specialist-oriented (e. g., APL, DYNAMO, FP/70, GEM, GPSS, SIMSCRIPT, SPURT).

Model building is nowadays accessible to every manager according to his needs and desired degree of involvement. Depending on the computer functions built into the MMS and subject to the computing facilities, the user functions can vary a great deal, but current technology meets collectively the most important user criteria for modelling[7].

4.2 Computer functions

In view of the decreasing costs of computer power and the increasing costs of man power it seems rational to continue replacing as many of the human model building functions as possible with machine functions. Modelling moves closer to the user and involves increasing machine tasks either for generating object code

---

7 It is unfortunately impossible to present a more extensive analysis of the various MMS within the space limits of this paper; however, the developed conceptual framework supports a detailed comparison of the various systems in a forthcoming paper by the author. See ref. [27]

or for interpreting very high level source language statements immediately (see Figure 2). In the latter case, no specific model bank is maintained by the organization as the models are generated ad hoc and seldom stored separately in source or object code. Ideally, a choice can be provided to the user by allowing him to select his preferred mode, however, no MMS provides this option, yet.

The system may run in batch-mode (e. g., PSG, FP/20), interactively on an in-house computer or even on a nation-wide timesharing system (e. g., APL, FIPLAN). The source language and the supporting software used or the hardware configuration needed can make the MMS machine-dependent (e. g., AUTOTAB, FAPS, FP/70, FIPLAN, FINAN, FIRES, FPS, GAME, PROPHIT). Another reason for machine-dependence is the vendor's decision to offer it only as part of a time-sharing service (e. g., AUTOTAB, FIPLAN, FIRES, FPS, PROFORMA, PROPHIT)[8].

4.3 Management support

The degree to which the various model management functions are supported by a given MMS depends not only on the MMS design but likewise on the computer systems configuration and on the predominant use of it. For example, a time-shared MMS does not have to contain all necessary functions itself, because most of the required additional hardware and software support is readily available to a model builder for model manipulation, scheduling, execution and display as part of his user contract. He can model interactively or in batch mode using almost any kind of modelling language available under the system, including some of the specialized MMS. His MM support is next to unlimited if he knows enough about the whole range of timesharing services available to him and if he can afford to use them.

A self-contained MMS, on the other hand, is often user-specific in the sense that it supports financial modelling (e. g., ADFIN, FP/70, FPS) more exclusively than production or marketing modelling (e. g., INF*ACT) or favours queuing models (GPSS) over continuous system modelling (e. g., APL/DYNAMO). This means, that the various MMS contain features which make some model descriptions easier than others. For example, nearly all financial modelling systems contain amortization, depreciation, growth, present value and rate of return routines.

At the other end of the spectrum are highly flexible MMS "shells". They merely reserve space for data (usually in matrix format) and may provide data validation, maintenance and output routines (e. g., GEM). They require the user to describe

8 The apparent lack of standardization demonstrates the highly creative nature of all current MMS designs and indicates a lack of maturity which – depending on ones outlook – might be considered deplorable or opportune.

his specific models in a general purpose language (e. g., FORTRAN) within the given framework but do not support him with generalized modelling commands.

Most MMS contain extensive diagnostic routines to facilitate correct, debugged, and reliable programming within minimal design time requirements. On the other hand, special programmer tools are usually available at a given computer installation.

An important feature of MMS is the easiness with which model changes can be incorporated as management gains experience with existing models. A recompilation or rerun is usually all that is required and if the system MMS is a "natural" rather than a symbolic language design, it documents itself all changes as well.

Most systems schedule and execute the model in a second phase, i. e., usually following the compilation and after loading under operating systems control. In a third phase RPG functions are applied to the generated output. This has the advantage that any output can be displayed by means of built-in display functions or, alternatively, with external plotting and tabulation routines. The importance of the various display functions can hardly be underestimated, as users want to be able to understand the model results in a "natural" manner. It is therefore not too risky to predict that most MMS will expand the available display functions considerably in order to meet understandibility as one of the major principles of model management [26].

5. Conclusions

Since model banks represent separately identifiable MIS components, it is important to establish a specific organizational responsibility for model management. In analogy to the data (bank) administration function, model (bank) administration can be defined. It refers to all activities required for ensuring that the model bank is maintained according to the organizational standards for access, authorization, control, correctness, documentation, modularity, privacy, reliability, security and understandibility. The model bank administrator (MBA) is also responsible for formulating and controlling the various model management objectives in a corporate (global) or in a functional (local) organizational context. To this end he is usually supported by MMS and computerized tools for model debugging [15], testing[9], documenting[10] and accounting [17].

---

9 Some examples are PRO/TEST, Testmaster, WRAP, DATAMACS and TESTPAK.

10 Some examples are QUICK-DRAW, Documatic and AUTOFLOW.

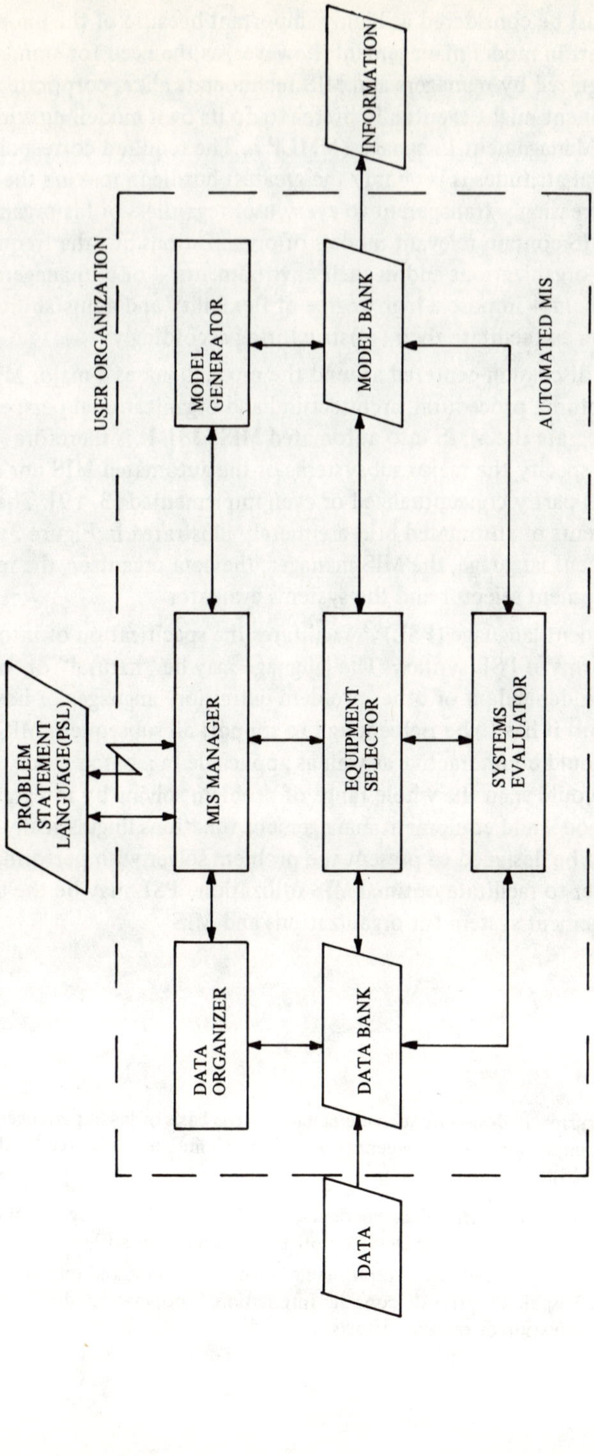

Fig. 3. Automated MIS

The MBA's role must be considered as highly important because of the underdeveloped state of the art in model management; however, as the need for standardization becomes recognized by managers and MIS technocrats alike, corporate and functional management might eventually prefer to do its own modelling with a generalized Model Management Language (MML)[11]. The required corresponding change in managerial attitudes is probably the greatest hurdle in making the structure of the MIS increasingly transparent to every user regardless of his organization's structure. MIS contain relevant models of organizations but the frequent changes in modern organizations and in their environments – or in management's understanding of them – impose a high degree of flexibility and adjustability on MIS designs in order to facilitate their (re)structuring accordingly.

While the previous discussion centered around the model bank as a major MIS subsystem in structural, procedural, architectural and organizational perspective, it is possible to integrate the MMS into automated MIS [28]. It is therefore neither difficult to specify the major subsystems of the automated MIS nor surprising to find them partly conceptualized or even implemented [3, 19]. The integrated components of automated MIS are merely illustrated in Figure 3: the problem statement language, the MIS manager, the data organizer, the model generator, the equipment selector and the systems evaluator.

The problem statement language (PSL)[12] facilitates the specification of information problems in terms of PSL syntax. The language may be "natural" or "artificial" and as such independent of other problem definition languages or host-language dependent, but it has to be rich enough to support all subsequent MIS functions. Ideally, it would be interactive as well as applicable in a batch mode. Most importantly, PSL would span the whole range of problem solving by integrating the various data, model and equipment management functions linguistically. Moreover, it should be designed to present the problem solver with performance information in order to facilitate optimal MIS utilization. PSL may be the ultimate model management system for organizations and MIS[13].

11 The author is currently designing such a language on the basis of his experiences with the design and implementation of a generalized Audit Command Language (ACL). See ref. [2, 23, 25].

12 This term was deliberately chosen to be identical to Teichroew's although neither the syntax nor the semantics of the ISDOS version are known to this author.

13 In view of the numerous and difficult problems faced in designing and implementing PSL, it seems advisable to seriously consider international cooperation, division of labour and coordination of research efforts.

References

[1] See, e.g., Charles W. Bachman: The Evolution of Storage Structures. In: Communications of the ACM, Vol. 15, No. 7 (July 1972), pp. 628–634.

[2] Beckmann, M., G. Goos and H.P. Kuenzi (eds.): Lecture Notes in Economics and Mathematical Systems, Vol. 78. Berlin, Heidelberg, New York 1973.

[3] Bubenko, J., Börje Langefors and Arne Sölvberg: Computer-Aided Information System Analysis and Design. Lund, Sweden 1971.

[4] CODASYL Data Base Task Group, Report, ACM. New York 1969.

[5] Demski, Joel S.: Information Analysis. Reading, Mass. 1972.

[6] Gershefski, George W.: Corporate Models – The State of the Art. In: Management Science, Vol. 16, No. 6 (February 1970), pp. 303–312.

[7] Joint GUIDE-SHARE DATA BASE Requirements Group. DATA BASE Management System Requirements, Nov. 11, 1970.

[8] Klir, Jiri and Miroslav Valach: Cybernetic Modelling. London 1967, p. 93.

[9] Knuth, Donald: The Art of Computer Programming, Vol. I, Fundamental Algorithms. Reading, Mass. 1968.

[10] Kriebel, Charles H.: Management Information Systems Technology: View of the Future. In: Journal of Contemporary Business, Vol. 1, No. 2 (Spring 1972), pp. 1–13.

[11] Little, John D.C.: Models and Managers: The Concept of a Decision Calculus. In: Management Science, Vol. 16, No. 8 (April 1970), pp. B–466–485.

[12] Mason, R.: Management Information Systems: What They Are, What They Ought To Be. In: Innovation, No. 9, 1970, pp. 34–43.

[13] Newell, Allen: Heuristic Programming: Ill-Structed Problems, p. 368, In: Aronofsky (ed.): Progress in Operations Research, Vol. 3, New York 1970, pp. 363–414.

[14] Ogdin, Jerry L.: Improving Software Reliability. In: Datamation, Vol. 19, No. 1 (January 1973), pp. 49–52.

[15] Pomeroy, J.W.: A Guide to Programming Tools and Techniques. In: IBM Systems Journal, Vol. 11, No. 3 (Fall 1972), pp. 234–254.

[16] Reitman, Walter R.: Heuristic Decision Procedures, Open Constraints, and the Structure of Ill-defined Problems, p. 302. In: Shelly, W. Maynard and Glenn L. Bryan (eds.): Human Judgments and Optimality. New York 1964, pp. 282–315.

[17] Rettus, R.C. and R.A. Smith: Accounting Control of Data Processing. In: IBM Systems Journal (1972), pp. 74–92.

[18] Schreiber, A.N. (ed.): Corporate Simulation Models, Seattle, Wash.: Graduate School of Business Administration. University of Washington 1970.

[19] Teichroew, Daniel and Sayani, Hasan: Automation of System Building. In: Datamation, Vol. 17, No. 8, (August 1971), pp. 25–30.

[20] Shelly, Gary B. and Thomas J. Cashman: DOS Job Control for COBOL Programmers. Fullerton, Calif. 1971, Chapters 8–11.

[21] Will, H.J.: A Critical Analysis of the Assumptions Underlying Selected Managerial Accounting Models: An Information Systems Approach. Unpublished Ph. D. Dissertation. Urbana/Champaign: University of Illinois 1969.

[22] Will, J.: Datenbank-Systeme. In: Zeitschrift für Betriebswirtschaft, Vol. 41, No. 12 (December 1971), pp. 815–844.

[23] Will, H.J.: Design of a Generalized Audit Command Language (ACL). Proceedings Second Annual Conference of Gesellschaft für Informatik, Karlsruhe, Oktober 2–4, 1972.

[24] Will, J.: Betriebliche Informationssysteme: Versuch einer intelligenztechnischen Definition. In: Zeitschrift für betriebswirtschaftliche Forschung, Vol. 20, No. 10 (November 1968), pp. 648–669.

[25] Will, H.J.: An Interactive ACL (Audit Command Language) Prototype. Proceedings Session 73, Canadian Computer Conference. June 20–22, 1973, Edmonton, Alberta.

[26] Will, H.J.: MIS: Mirage or Mirror Image? In: Journal of Systems Management (in press).

[27] Will, H.J.: Comparison of Model Management System.

[28] Will, H.J.: Towards a System of MIS Concepts. Unpublished paper, 1973.

German abstract
Modell-Management-Systeme

Von *Hartmut J. Will*

Informationen werden mit Hilfe von Intelligenzprozessen gewonnen, deren Eingaben (input) sich informal als Tatsachenwissen oder formal als Daten auf verschiedene Weise beschreiben und organisieren lassen. Die angewandten Intelligenzprozesse stellen geistige Fertigkeiten oder formalisierte Maschinenprogramme dar und sind als solche ebenfalls auf unterschiedliche Art beschreibbar.

Außer als Ergebnis (output) ist Information ebenfalls als Wirtschaftsgut (eigener Art) anzusehen, da sie nützlich, knapp und austauschbar ist, obwohl die rechtlichen Besitz- und Eigentumsbegriffe nicht immer darauf anwendbar sind. Wie jedes andere Wirtschaftsgut läßt sich auch Information nach organisatorischen und ökonomischen Kriterien verwalten.

Je nach Interesse oder Präferenz einzelner Forscher und Gelehrten wird das Wirtschaftsgut Information unterschiedlich abstrakt definiert. Beispielsweise identifizieren die Vertreter der sogenannten Information Economics Informationen rein formalistisch als Botschaft (message), wobei verschiedentlich das gesamte zugrundeliegende Informationssystem subsumiert und darüber hinaus durch die Annahme perfekter Rationalität viele wichtige Informationsprobleme ausgeklammert werden.

Ausgehend von seinem informationssystematischen Ansatz versucht der Verfasser, die Informationsproblematik in Daten- und Modellverwaltungsaufgaben zu zerlegen. Datenverwaltung ist z.B. spezifisch damit beschäftigt, die besten Methoden zur Beschreibung, Errichtung, Manipulation und Befragung einer Datenbank und zur Analyse und Wiedergabe der gespeicherten Daten zu finden und in Organisationen anzuwenden. Analog lassen sich Modellverwaltungsaufgaben analysieren, handhaben und auswerten. Damit wird der Versuch unternommen, die modernen Entwicklungen im Bereich der Benutzersprachen für das Formulieren, Manipulieren, Zusammenstellen, Ausführen und Wiedergeben der so gewonnenen Informationen in vier Stufen zu analysieren und in organisatorischen sowie in informatischen Zusammenhängen zu sehen.

Zunächst wird das Modellbankkonzept definiert und in seinem Aufbau erklärt. Die Modellbank enthält eine Reihe von formalisierten Methoden, die sich auf ausgewählte Probleme in Wirtschaft und Verwaltung anwenden lassen. Dabei werden eine Reihe von Annahmen gemacht, die darauf abzielen, Modelle einerseits als „Weltanschauungen" von verschiedenen Entscheidungsträgern zu objektivieren und andererseits schnell zugriffsfähig und modifizierbar zu machen.

Die Modellverwaltung (MV) wird anschließend durch die Beschreibung von MV-Zielen und der bereits genannten MV-Funktionen operationalisiert. Auf diese Weise werden Kriterien zur Analyse und Entwicklung verschiedener Modellverwaltungssysteme (MVS) gewonnen, die im deutschsprachigen Raum als Planungssprachen bezeichnet werden.

Anschließend erfolgt eine Analyse verschiedener MVS im Hinblick auf Benutzer, den Computer und MV-Unterstützung. Zum Schluß werden die Ergebnisse dieser Überlegungen unter organisatorischen und MIS-spezifischen Aspekten zusammengefaßt. In Analogie zum Daten(bank) Administrator zeichnet sich organisatorisch die Stelle eines Modell(bank) Administrators (MBA) ab, der dafür verantwortlich ist, daß die Modellbank gemäß den organisatorischen Kriterien für Zugriff, Autorisierung, Kontrolle, Richtigkeit, Dokumentation, Modularität, Geheimhaltung, Zuverlässigkeit, Sicherheit und Verständlichkeit verwaltet wird.

Informatisch ergeben sich im Bereich der Modellverwaltung eine Reihe von Möglichkeiten zur Entwicklung von Benutzersprachen, die als Problembeschreibungssprachen in verschiedenen Ländern in Angriff genommen werden. Damit läßt sich im Endeffekt erreichen, daß die Struktur der Informationssysteme sich zwar modellmäßig an der Organisationsstruktur orientiert, im Endeffekt jedoch die gesamte Organisation wie ein Nervensystem durchzieht.

Index

Access Directive Generator (ADG) 388, 389
Accounting 109, 236, 360, 416
– aspects of the MIS 348
– system 110, 155, 332, 346, 416
ADFIN 474, 477
Administration 236, 330
ADP applications 397
ADP costs 398
ADP-systems work 402
Algebra, Boolean 52
–, relational 430
ALGOL 472, 476
Algorithms, combinatorial 365
Analysis, statistical 468
– decisions 152
– of organizations 441
– phases 452
– techniques 153, 157
– techniques, computer-aided 461
APL 472, 474, 476, 477
APL/DYNAMO 474
Application, different levels of 42
– concept 33, 34, 37
– model 34, 383, 386
– of computers 197, 445
– of computer technology 441
– of EDP in German insurance companies 198, 200
– of system models 411
– package 100, 384
– program 383, 386, 388, 390
AUTOFLOW 478
Automation of administration 330
– of the design process 325, 456
AUTOSATE (Automated Data System Analysis Technique) 42, 425
AUTOTAB 474, 476, 477
Authority 111, 113, 119, 137, 144, 193
–, decentralization of the 117
–, functional 174
– relationship 113
– structure 109
AUXCO method 453

Betriebswirtschaftliches Institut für Organisation und Automation an der Universität zu Köln (BIFOA) 5, 7, 9, 34, 297
Bargaining process 140, 144
BASIC 324, 472
Bayesian statistics 155, 344
BIFOA 5, 7, 9, 34, 297
Boolean operations 52, 401
Bottom-up approach 454, 455
Budgeting process 39, 146
Building of the IPS 447
Building process 456
Business administration 286
Butterworth-Feltham-meta-model 355, 356, 357

CADIS – research project (Computer-Aided Design of Information Systems) 43, 399
Capital acquisition models 351
Capital allowance 428, 430, 431
CASCADE (Computer-based Documentation System) 43, 399, 411, 414, 415, 417, 418, 420, 421, 424
CBIPS 438, 443, 446, 454
CBIS 32, 40, 47, 438, 451
Centrality 140
Centralization 35, 43, 101, 102, 103, 208, 237, 272, 275, 276, 278
–, effects of 275
–, functional 207, 213
– of control 131, 132
– of information flow 120
– of information processing 232
– of staff 236
Change, organizational 37, 38, 65, 79, 230, 232
– in structure 65
– in system design 317
– in technology 65
Changes by task 234
– in accounting information 346
– in computer applications 68
– in equipment 68
– in information flows 117, 119, 123
– in power 132
– in the amount of communication 212
– in the information structure 120
Charting technique 155
Checklists 39
COBOL 324, 460, 472
Communication 95, 106, 107, 111, 188, 191, 212, 292, 298, 300, 302, 303, 305, 309, 326, 338, 367, 407, 419, 435, 440, 454

–, cost of 366, 369
–, hierarchical 167
–, horizontal 212
–, interpersonal 213
–, non-hierarchical 170
–, speed of 366
–, vertical 167, 212
– among interdependent subunits 106
– channels 110, 238, 275
– equipment 446
– network 100, 198, 302, 366, 367, 369, 370, 379
– paths 365, 366, 368, 372
– process 120, 121, 125, 127, 128, 366
– process, control of 365
– relations 212, 213
– system 274, 326, 327
– transmission 368
– tree 365, 368, 370
– tree, cost-minimal 367, 371
– engineering 284, 425
Compiler, semantical 61
Complexity 95, 272, 402
– of systems 399, 402
– of systems, relative 402, 403
Component analysis 318, 319, 320
– information objects 415
– of a system 95
Computer application 44, 65, 68, 76, 80, 179, 200, 204, 213
– – in planning 77
– – in system design 40
– applications, effect of 264
– centre 123, 127
– department 443
– Graphics Project (CGP) 400
– impact on individuals 248, 264
– – on organizations 248, 264
– implementation 34
– information processing costs 443
– languages 460
– network systems 47
– power 476
– processing 439
– science 424, 425
– system 101, 132, 145, 146, 147, 259, 331
– systems configuration 477
– technology 65, 77, 79, 80, 132, 197, 441, 443, 446, 451
Computerization 73, 77, 80, 146
– process 65, 67, 68, 70, 76
Conflict 146
– resolution capabilities 276
– situations 134
Construction phase 450
Context of a system 67
– of conflictual decisions 134
– of information flows 128
–, organizational 65, 66, 165, 168, 179, 188, 247
Contingency analysis 135, 246, 247, 264
Control 39, 65, 98, 99, 100, 109, 131, 136, 139, 144, 145, 150, 151, 154, 158, 211, 232, 233, 236, 249, 289, 291, 304, 305, 309, 329, 359, 365, 478
–, centralization of 131, 132
– actions 153
– aspect 347
– charts 155
– decisions 157
– engineering feedback model 416
– Graph (CG) 141, 142
– information 139
– language 435
– models 351, 353
– philosophies 416
– program 385
– structure 311
– system 325, 326, 439
– theory, mathematical 155, 158
Controller 151, 328
Cooperation 46
–, interorganizational 227
– of area specialists 38
Coordination 32, 36, 95, 96, 97, 98, 99, 101, 102, 106, 168, 317, 453, 461, 471
– among subsystems 97
– by centralized decision making 169
– by hierarchical ad-hoc decisions 173, 174
– by hierarchical decision making 167
– by planning 167, 169, 173
– by programming 106, 168, 169, 176
– by rules 106
– decisions 173
– in organizations 167
– instruments 165, 173, 174, 176, 177, 178, 179
– mechanism 165, 166, 167, 168, 169, 170, 171, 173, 178, 179
– needs 165, 169, 173, 177, 179
– of activities 165
– potential 165
– potential of computers 177
– potential of MIS 166, 171, 177
– problems 117
– requirements 213
– strategy 178
– system 166, 167, 169, 171, 179
Corporate management 311, 317, 318, 319, 480
– planning 193

Cost accountant's information choice problem 349
– accounting structures 349, 350
– of information processing resources 110
– of information transmission 368
– projection reports 391
Costs of computer-aided methods 459
Couplings among subsystems 100
Criteria for system effectiveness 224
Critical Path Method (CPM) 258
Cross-section analysis 46
Cross-sectional studies 46
Cybernetics 300, 425

Dagger symbols 429
Data 340
– administration 304, 305
– administration, central 309
– administrator 384, 462
– administration, central 309
– bank 326, 330, 337, 467, 468, 473
– bank management system 47
– base 100, 101, 121, 122, 144, 174, 175, 177, 191, 313, 328, 330, 331, 333, 338, 382, 383, 384, 385, 386, 389, 390, 426, 434, 449, 454, 456, 458, 460, 494
– – administrator 191
– – approach 455
– – designer 432
– – management software 101
– – Management Systems (DMS) 100, 191, 384
– – oriented systems 447
– – retrieval 384
– – systems, integrated 204
– bases, large scale 393
– –, relational 435
– collection 99, 152
– controlling system 397
– definition 457
– description information 459
– Description Language (DDL) 386
– elements 407, 431, 471
– file 383, 391
– – construction, automatic 390
– flow 289
DATAFLOW-project 424
Data input 386
DATAMACS 478
Data management 467
– – languages 191, 340
– – specialist 393
– Management System 383, 384, 392
– processing 41, 200, 284, 317, 417, 426
– –, automatic 281
– – department 443
– – operations 431, 442, 444, 445
– – package 325
– – specialists 38
– – system 288, 411, 413, 420, 424, 431, 432
– structure 384, 389, 404, 405
– support 133, 139, 144
– – structure 190, 191
– transfers 406
– transformations 191
– transmission systems 424
DDL 389
Decentralization 35, 43, 76, 102, 103, 117, 210
Decision 134, 337, 461
–, decentralization of 169, 171, 233, 235
– alternatives 133
– behavior 141
– Centralization Score (DCS) 141
– conditions 262
– frequency 110
– maker 110, 140, 145, 151, 175, 246, 258, 260, 273, 347, 349, 351, 393, 472
– making 163, 169, 187, 207, 213, 237, 247, 248, 249, 251, 255, 257, 259, 260, 264, 275, 304, 455
– –, aspects of 259
– –, decentralization of 131
– –, intraorganizational 226
– –, unstructured 170
– – activities 249
– – applications 262
– – behavior 141
– – powers 226, 233
– – process 132, 134, 136, 140, 141, 144, 165
– – situations 146
– – structures 276
– – system 136, 284, 390
– – task 134, 136, 140, 246, 265
– – techniques 273
– – under uncertainty 260
– – unit 136, 140
– mechanism 110, 175
– models 99, 133, 345, 349, 351, 367
– –, formalized 101
– –, mathematical 346, 351, 365
– – in managerial accounting 346, 351
– problems 187, 258
– problem of the organizer 193
– process 111, 112, 176, 188, 192, 193, 194, 276, 343, 367
– rules 167, 168
– –, programmed 190
– situation 146, 259
– tables 42, 405

– task 151
– theory 187, 283, 344
– strategies 187, 259, 260
– systems 326, 329, 330, 356
Definition of MIS, semantical 355
Delegation 193
DMS 385
Description language 313
– of an organization 424, 440
– of a system building process 450
– of data structures 384
– of information flow 442
– of information systems 424
– of organizational information systems 424
Design 35, 237, 451
–, functional 414, 415, 420
–, structural dimensions of 193
– documents 137, 138
– of a data base 449
– of data files 397, 404
– of file structure 391
– of information processing systems 390
– of men-computer system 257
– of MIS 163, 278
– of models 355
– of organizations 119, 441
– of processing systems 340
– of program structure 391
– of specialized information systems 393
– of the information system 140, 277, 311, 338, 339
– phase 133, 447, 449, 450, 451, 457
– problem 106, 112
– process 164, 225, 325, 404, 405, 435, 456
– –, automation of the 41, 44, 325
– –, control of the 39
– strategies 107, 194, 223
– –, incremental 227
– tools, computer-aided 421
– work 311
Designing of computer-based systems 426
– potential, human 41
Determination of requirements 456
Development 298, 299, 306
– of a computer-aided method for the documentation and analysis of information requirements 456
– of computer-aided information systems 281
– of computer-systems 66
– of model management systems 473
– of models 476
– of small information systems 324
– of software 398
– of the company 297
– of the information systems 40, 127, 238, 282, 283, 284, 296
– of the MIS 272
– process 194, 451
– strategy 127
DIFOP1 399, 400, 405
DIFO project (Design of information systems, especially file organization) 397, 400
Distribution of power 132
Diversification 170, 224
Divisionalization 170, 207
Division management 101
– of labor 109
DOC 399, 403
Documatic 478
Document retrieval 190
Documentation 119, 122, 125, 146, 283, 289, 290, 297, 384, 386, 397, 400, 438, 439, 449, 456, 463, 478
–, computer-aided 438, 451, 461
–, inadequate 41
–, manual 449, 453
– and analysis systems, computer-based 43
– method, automated 462
– methods, manual 459
– office 120, 304
– storage 417
– system 301, 302
– retrieval 417
DPS 411, 414, 420, 421
Dual authority relationship 113
Dynamics of the environment 168, 169
DYNAMO 474, 476, 477

Economics in organization design 186
– of information processing 443
– of scale 98, 109, 230, 233, 443, 445
EDP-equipment 40
– in insurance companies 200
Efficiency 205, 359
– measurements of MIS 360
Effectiveness 205, 259
– criteria 225
Effects of centralization 275
– of computer applications upon specific individuals and specific jobs 264
– of EDP on the organizational structure of insurance companies in the Federal Republic of Germany 207
– of information technology on departmentalization 204
– of the application of computers on the organization structure 198
– on organizational structure 95
Electricity industry 231
Empirical research 132, 143, 145, 146, 165, 167
Engineering staff 234

Enterprise administration 397
Entropy measures 55
Entropy relation 55
Enumeration scheme 371
Environment 139, 413
–, economic 443
Equipment 67, 68, 74, 76, 109, 124, 218, 332, 439, 441, 473, 474, 480
– cost 372
E-semantics 431, 432
Exchange of information 102
Executive management level 193
Expert power 113

Factor restrictions 44, 45
FAPS 474, 477
Feasibility study 452
FFC 389, 390
Field studies, evaluation of 197
File construction 447
– organization 406
– – problems 406
– structures 405
FINAN 477
Financial modelling 477
FIPLAN 474, 476, 477
FIRES 474, 476, 477
Flowcharts 337, 421
–, organizational 326
Flow models 365
– of data 446
– of information 367, 446
Flows of asset elements 333, 335
– of information, internal and external 79
FORESIGHT 474, 476
Formalization 39, 73, 272, 273, 274, 276, 278
– of a decision-making language 110
– of the innovation process 275
– procedures 274
Formatted File Converter (FFC) 389
FORTRAN 324, 388, 472, 476, 478
FORTRAN IV 388
Four-Flows Model 324, 333
FP/20 474, 477
FP/70 476, 477
FPS 474, 476, 477
F-semantics 431, 434, 435

GAME 474, 477
Game theory 187
GDBMS (Generalized Data Base Management System) 191
GEM (Generalized Interfacing Module) 387, 389, 390, 474, 476, 477
Generator approach 47
– language 42
– of information-transactions 332
– of transformation transaction 333
German insurance companies 197, 213
GET function 400, 401
Goal achievement control 470
– setting 470
GPLAN)Generalized Data Base Management System) 382, 383, 390, 393
GPSS 474, 476, 477
Graph 399, 417
Graph theory 365, 366
Group behaviour 164, 289
– decision process 112
Grouping of processes 397, 405
Groups, self-contained 111, 113

Hardware 44
– configuration 477
– elements 132
– library 391
Hardware/Software configuration 391
Hardware-software subsystem 222
Hierarchy 106, 107, 108, 110, 111, 169, 174, 221, 230, 238, 277, 403, 440
– of authority 275
HPS (Human Processing Systems) 413, 414, 420

Identification of information flows 119
– of objectives 441
Impact of computer technology 131, 145, 146, 147, 443
– of computerization 68
– of computers on management organization 145, 186
– of computers on performance, organizational 262
– on jobs 131
– on power 145
– on the information system 156
Impacts of computer applications 79
– on management control 150
Implementation 146, 177, 398, 399, 447
– of a computer system 34, 138
– of an information system 337
– of an information system based on the *four flows model* 337
– of an MIS 175
– of computer technology 131, 145
– of specific systems 70
– of the computer assisted systems design 397
– phase 271
Implications of computer technology 80
Index structure 470, 471

Individual as an information processor 251
– behavior 188
– decision making 265
INF*ACT 477
Influence-Power-Sharing-Continuum (IPC) 141, 142
Information 102, 107, 462
–, amount of 108, 110
–, primary 332, 333, 335
–, volume of 259, 261
– analysis 347, 350, 399, 403, 407, 424, 426, 430, 432, 434, 435
– –, formalized 311
– – of administrative systems 424
– – task 424
– analyst 453
– bottle-neck 123
– channels 110, 226
– choice 350
– components 319
–-decision model 345
– decisions 348
– display 473
– economics 187, 342, 343, 344, 347, 349, 351, 357, 467
– engineering 286
– evaluation 346, 347
– – model 348
– evaluator 347, 348, 349, 351
– flow 117, 118, 119, 120, 121, 122, 123, 124, 125, 126, 127, 128, 226, 291, 327, 368, 440, 442
– –, centralization of 120
– –, control of 139
– –, stochastic 121
– –, internal and external 79
– flows in organizations 444
– for models 337
– functions 189
– generator 333
– handling 304, 425
– instruments 187
– model 344, 345, 346
– needs, of the top-management 39
– policy 178
– precedence analysis method 315
– processing 99, 105, 107, 108, 136, 199, 227, 233, 246, 247, 248, 249, 250, 251, 259, 261, 264, 312, 413, 442, 443
– –, amount of 109, 114
– –, centralization of 232
– – aids 248
– – activities 199
– – applications 262
– – capability 139, 205, 271
– – capacity of the organization 108
– – changes 230
– – determinants 105
– – model 105
– – operations 442, 443, 445, 446
– – resources 110, 411
– – system 132, 136, 186, 411, 413, 417, 438, 443, 444, 445, 447, 458
– – –, computer-based (CBIPS or IPS) 438, 443, 446
– – subsystem 420
– – task 33, 125, 248, 251, 253, 265
– reduction 109
– requirements 97, 98, 106, 439, 440, 447, 454
– – determination methods 452
– – processes 439, 456
– set 403
– storage and retrieval systems 163, 220
– structure 33, 55, 120, 124, 186, 189, 190, 193, 347, 402, 418
– –, statistical measurability of 62
– – in organization design 186
– structures, modular 194
– support 139
– – characteristics 139
– system 122, 125, 137, 186, 219, 301, 311, 339, 346, 425, 426
– –, coordination of 33
– –, computer-based (CBIS) 32, 40, 47, 438, 451
– –, control of 136, 139, 144, 145
– –, integrated 34 39, 95, 99, 100, 102
– – for drug evaluation 222
– – system documentation 122
– – structure 347
– systems changes 238
– – department (ISD) 66, 67, 69
– – design 223, 227, 315, 390
– technology 36, 65, 99, 100, 101, 171, 177, 186, 197, 205, 415
– theory 55, 359
– timing models 353
– transmission 252, 367, 368
– type object 415, 418
– user 472
Initiation of an organizational innovation 271
Initiative for change 124, 125, 127
Innovation 271, 274, 275, 281
–, organizational 271, 278
–, adoption of an 271
– process 271, 272, 273, 274, 275, 276, 277, 278, 282, 294, 295, 296, 298, 299, 307, 308
– theory 281
Instructions 39

Insurance companies 131, 197, 199, 208
– management 197
Integration 72, 73, 74, 79, 95, 98, 99, 100, 101, 151, 470
–, vertical 194
– mechanism 76, 111
– of information systems 67, 101, 102
– of interdependent tasks 171
– of subsystems 97
– of systems development 76
– of the ISD-system 69, 72, 77
– of the organization 101
– of the work flow 213
Interaction, interpersonal 151
– between hierarchical levels 174
– between man and machine 164
– between the information processing and the material processing 413
Interdependence between subunits, amount of 108
– of organization structure and available information technology 197
– of the information and action (decision) system 347
Interface 96, 385, 426, 430, 445, 458, 473, 474
– operations 392
– problems 425
Interfacing mechanism 384, 387
– process 387
Inter-level power 142
Interrelationship between structural changes 80
– of various power measures 134
Interrelationships on processes and data 391
Inter-unit communication 106
Intrasystem conflict 226
Introduction of change 238
– of computer systems 132, 136, 144
– of EDP 207, 208, 210, 213
– of information systems 296
Investment administration 204
– calculation 47
– planning 47
I/O-model 421
I/O-specifications 417
IPS 411, 413, 414, 420, 438, 443, 445, 446, 447
ISAC project 403
ISDOS project 424, 456, 457, 459, 460
ISD system 76

Job analysis 264
– codification 274
– content 65, 264
– description 168, 176

„Kölner Integrationsmodell" (KIM) 34

Language compilers 324
Languages, parametric 476
–, problem-oriented 393
Leadership 112
LEGOL 424, 426, 427, 429, 431, 432, 434, 435
Level of hierarchy 112, 141
Levels of management 111
Line management 193, 232
– managerial roles 113
Logarithms, dyadic(al) 55, 59
Logistics systems 101
Loss of economies of scale 109
Lundeberg method 399, 403

Macro-processor 431, 435
Maintenance 249, 398, 399, 447, 474
– of model banks 472
– relations 421
Management, functional 480
–, scientific 283
– by exception 155, 156
– by objectives 137
– control 76, 150, 151, 152, 153, 154, 155, 156, 157, 158
– control analysis 158
– – area 157
– – centers 153
– – decision 152
– – process 152, 154, 192
– decision 346
– Information Centre (MIC) 117, 118
– information changes 230
– Information System, construction of a 37, 365, 393
– information systems 95, 271, 411
– – structure, formalized 192
– process 146, 186
– science models 157, 190
– structure 238
– systems 190
– theory 164, 178
– training 302
Managerial decision making 165, 454
– – – process 133
– problems 470
Manager's decision process 349
Man-computer cooperation 255
Man-machine combinations 110
– communication systems 173
– information system 31, 164, 292
– interaction 258
– relations 32
– symbiosis 248

Man-machine-systems, interactive 163
Man-man relations 32
Mass memories, large 325
Master plan 193
Matrix organization 113
Material control 416
– processing system (MPS) 413
Matrix description 404
Measurement decisions 152
Measures of performance 441
– of systems complexity 402
Metagame 219, 222, 224, 227
Meta language 61
Meta-model 353, 354, 355, 357
– for information systems 351
– for MIS 349
Method of *Lundeberg* 403
– of organization 441
Methodology of the organization 330
Methods, quantitative 365
– for determining information requirements 452
MICOM 47
MIDAM 47
MI-Model 356, 357
Minicomputer 102, 103
MIS, accounting aspects of the 348
–, automated 480
–, computerized 360
– applications 164, 176
– components 478, 480
– design 164, 165, 167, 173
– design strategy 164
– equipment 474
– subsystem 480
– technology 470
Model 34, 383, 386
– bank 468, 477, 480
– (bank) administration 478
– (bank) administrator (MBA) 472, 478
– bank concept 467, 468
– banks 472, 478
– builder 476
– components 353
– description 473, 376, 477
– designer 476
– execution 473
– for the construction of a cost-minimal communication tree 365
– management (MM) 467, 472, 478, 480
– – commands 470
– – functions 470, 473, 477
– Management Language (MML) 480
– management objectives 468, 473
– – support 477
– – system 467, 473
– – tasks 472
– manipulation 473, 477
– of information processing 439
– of organization, general 188
– of problem solution 413
– of subsystem structure 414
– of systems description 404
– of the user 190
– requirements 382
– scheduling 473
– system 34
– structure 470, 471, 472
– support 139
Modelling language 154, 477
– software 467, 474
Models, algorithmic 470
–, analytic 471
–, normative 471
– of information systems 438
– of organizations 438
– of systems design 397
Module placement theory 406
Monetary flow 333, 335
Monism, organizational 31
Morphogenetics (inconsistancy of systems structures) 58
Morphostatics (fixation of systems structures) 58
Motivation 299, 300
MPS-structures 414
Multi-person decision efficiency 188
Multiperson systems 253

Need for information 107, 127
Needs, social 167
Network of computer terminals, cost-minimal 372
Networks 39
– analysis techniques 365
Notion of MIS 342, 354

Object program structure 471
– systems 425
Operations research 101, 190, 217, 273, 283, 397, 406
– – groups 257
Operators of an relational algebra 430
Organimetrics 58
Organization, coordination of 33
–, formal 247
–, functional 108, 109, 306
–, – staff line 31
–, general model of 188
–, statistical measurability of 62
– algebra 60, 61
– controls 176

– design 105, 186, 187, 189
– – action 107
– – strategies 107
– development 303, 304, 305, 308
– handbook 176
– research 33, 45, 46, 131
– science 286
– structure 105, 164, 178, 207
– –, centralized 171
Organizations, multi-national 111
Organization theory 131, 132, 164, 198
– –, statistical 58

Pareto optimal decision 188
Performance, organizational 262
– standards 110, 114
Personnel 332
– administration 304
– assignment problems 365
– data 100
– flow 333, 335
– management 304
– resource control 416
– structure 211
PERT 273
Phase of information analysis 424
PL/1 472
Planning 77, 99, 330, 367
– decisions 153
– languages 154
– models 154, 353
– of a MIS 278
– problem 347, 393
– process 173, 382
– system 170, 383, 384, 385, 386, 392
– –, computerized 382
– techniques 173
Plotting software 42
Pluralism, methodological 47
–, organizational 31
Policy decision making 232
Position power 113
Power 113, 132, 144, 145, 174, 176, 290, 299, 304
–, personal 178
– contingencies 140
– equalization 113, 131, 132
– distribution 135, 146
– measures 142
– in organizations 131
– of information 344
– phenomena 134
– structures 225
– –, organizational 131
Precedence analysis 312, 319, 405
– matrix 315
– relations 403, 404, 430
Problem definition management 461
– description 453, 471
– identification 172
– recognition 250, 251, 255, 257, 259
– solving 134, 172, 412, 470, 472
– statement (PS) 391
– – analyzer 456, 461, 462
– – language (PSL) 456, 460, 461, 480
Problems of implementing 382
Procedures of implementation 333
Process, computer-based 36
– control 39, 155, 158
– – charts 155
– – system, computer-based 98
– definition by structuring 457
– design 152
– information 458
– grouping algorithm 405
– of documentation 40
– of hypothesis generation 145
– of organizational structuring 117
– of system building 438
– of system design 37
– of uncertainty reduction 172
– structure 152
Processes of an information system 405
Processing of data 199
– system 326
Product diversification 168
Production planning 47
– process control 155
– scheduling system 217
Professionalization 272
Profit planning 47
PROFORMA 474, 476, 477
Program bank 326
– base 328
– development 258
– languages 42, 431, 438, 471
– structures 470, 471
Programming, mathematical 155
–, standardized 42
– technique, nonlinear 393
Project control 416
– CORPIS (to develop an information system for general business planning) 6, 47
– ISAS (to develop an information system for the administrative control of business) 47
– management 295, 365, 438
– – techniques 439
– MICOM 47
– MIDAM 47
– KIM („Kölner Integrationsmodell") 47

– SIMMIS (to develop a simulation model of the planning control and information system which in turn will serve as a design and implementation instrument for MIS) 47
Project team approach 450
PROPHIT 474, 477
PRO/TEST 478
PSG 474, 476, 477

Quality control 151
– of documentation 463
– of requirements 463
Query analyzer 399
– –, problem-oriented 383, 385
– language, problem-oriented 382
– – description 386
QUICK-DRAW 478

Random access 406, 447
Rationalization of the information system 127
Realisation process 199
Recentralization 157
Recipients of information 366, 367, 368, 369
Recognition of information 252
Recording of information 442
Redundancy 224
Regulation 249, 250
Relation, human 164
–, interpersonal 272, 277
Relationship, interpersonal 276
– between computer use and organizational structure 65
– between integration of the information system and integration of the organization 101
– between planners and information systems 382
– between the organization and its environment 329
– of structure and technology 131
Relay station 366, 368, 370
Release effect 210, 211, 212
Remote terminal 102
Reorganization of departments 207, 208, 209
Repetitiveness of the decision 259
Report Program Generator (RPG) 406
Requirements, computer-aided documentation of 439, 451, 453
– determination phase 453
– of a problem statement language (PSL) 457, 458
Research by development 46
– design 145
– gap 44
– laboratory 96
– methodology 145
– project AUTOSATE 42, 425
– CADIS 43, 399
– – CASCADE 43, 399, 411, 415, 418, 420, 421, 424
– – CORPIS 47
– – DIFO 397, 400
– – ISAS 47
– – ISDOS (Information system Design and Optimization System) 43, 424, 456, 459, 460
– – KIM 47
– – LEGOL 424, 426, 427, 429, 431, 432, 434
– – MICOM 47
– – MIDAM 34, 47
– – SAPO 416, 420
– – SIMMIS 47
– techniques 179
Resource allocation 114
– specialization 109
Retrieval 384, 99
–, statistical 458
– capabilities 458
– of information 252, 254, 326, 442
Role conflict 274, 276
– of information in the management decision process 346
Routinization of work processes 171

Sales planning 47
SAPO (SINTEF's information system) 416
Scheduling operations 447
– theory 406
Science of communication 286
–, social 297
Search techniques 225
– theory 156
Self-containment strategy 109
Self-coordination 167, 170, 171, 174, 175, 176, 178
Semantical compiler 61
– definition of MIS 355
Semiotics 425
Sensing 249, 251, 253, 254
Signal objects 421
SIMSCRIPT 474, 476
Simulation languages, general 41
– models 41, 133
SINTEF 416
SINTEF's information system (SAPO) 416
Situation diagnosis 250, 251, 257, 259
Size of files 406

– of organization 168, 169
Slack resources 108, 114
SODA (Systems Optimization and Design Algorithm) 391, 392
Software costs 398
– elements 132
– library 391
– package 218
– system 458
Source language 477
– – program 473
– – statements 449, 462, 477
– listing information 458
– of information reduction 109
– program structure 471
Sources of information 272, 273, 275, 277, 366, 367, 368, 369, 370
Span of control 74, 96, 211
Specialization 102, 109, 172, 253, 254, 349
–, functional 204
–, vertical 170, 247
– of effort 253
– of task 253, 264
Specifications of power 140
SPURT 474, 476
SSC 389
Staff, centralization of 236
– functions of an insurance company 205, 206
Standardization 96, 98, 463, 480
–, organizational 177
– of decision making processes 176
Standard variance analysis 154
Statute Law 426, 434
Storage 99, 251
– and retrieval system 221
– capacity 44
– of information 442
– structure 384, 405, 449, 470, 471
Storing 254, 326
Strategies, organizational 256
Structure 32, 65
–, divisionalized 168
–, functional 109, 170
–, hierarchical 136, 140, 145, 197, 212
–, organizational 76, 77, 79, 131, 168, 198, 262, 276, 289
–, relational 55
–, self-contained 109
– of communication systems 365
– of computer systems 446
– of information flows 117, 128
– of the information system 430
– of triples 400
– of variables 58
Structuring process 123, 125, 457
– process, organizational 127
Studies of computer impacts 131, 132, 145, 146, 147, 150, 186, 262, 443
– of processes, longitudinal 46, 147
Style of management 289
Subgraph 371
Subprocess 442, 457
Sub-Schema Compiler (SSC) 388
– Generator (SSG) 388
Substitutability of managerial personnel 144
Substitution effects 265
Substructure of relations 402
Subsystems 95, 96, 97, 98, 100, 102, 117, 136, 281, 311, 315, 322, 416, 417, 425, 434
Subsystems structure 311, 317, 413, 417
Subtask 105, 106, 108, 113, 122, 140, 247, 250, 450, 459
System, components of a 95
– analysis 330, 331, 334, 399, 417
– building 445, 452
– – activity 439
– – procedures 447, 449, 452
– – process 446, 447, 448, 449, 450, 451, 452, 453, 456, 457, 458
– – –, automation of the 456
– complexity 397, 402
– constructor 463
– definition 431
– – language 435
– department 443, 445, 446, 459
– description 434
– – problem 427
– – report 453
– design 33, 45, 186, 193, 311, 312, 316, 317, 397, 398, 403, 411, 420, 447, 449, 450, 451, 454, 462, 463
– –, computer application in 40
– –, computer-based 41, 45
– – phase 451
– – process 38, 459
– – report 456
– development 132, 135, 186, 411
– – process 133, 448
– – project 146
– documentation 122, 403, 417, 418, 420
– – analysis 417
– implementation 42
– interfaces 453
– maintenance 460
– modelling 477
– parameter information 459
– requirements report 455, 456, 457
– specification 311
Systems, administrative 326, 424

–, based on statute law 424
–, interactive 447
–, logarithmic 55
–, self-designing 223
– designer 400, 414, 418, 420, 431, 439
454, 462, 463
– design tasks 398
– description 403
– models 411
– Optimization and Design Algorithm (SODA) 390
– structure 95
– theory 283, 292, 293, 330

Task-achievement 359, 360
Task complexity 65, 74, 79
– forces 111, 112, 257
Task-fulfillment of the MIS 359
Task information requirements 114
– performance 105, 107, 110, 259
– reorganization 264
– specialization 248
– structure 165, 272
– uncertainty 105, 114, 144, 146
Tasks, interdepartmental 117
Taylorism 164
Team theory 189
Team theory concept 190
Teams 112
Technique for information analysis, general 434
Techniques of linear optimization 371
–, standardized 463
Technology 65, 100, 168, 284
Telecommunication network 332
Tele-communication system 262
Telecommunications equipment 254
Tele-processing system 77
Testmaster 478
TESTPAK 478
Testing process 357
Theory of consumption 344
– of games 187
– of information systems 325, 330
– of management information systems, general 344, 354, 356
– of open systems 331
– of signs (semiotics) 425

Tools for analysing a system 399
– for construction 405
– for controlling system work 399
– for describing a system 403
– for documenting a system 403
– for implementation 405
– for optimization 156
Top-down approach 418, 442, 451, 454, 455, 461
Top management 67, 68, 69, 76, 79, 123, 174, 175, 176, 290, 303
Total system design 194, 414
Transformation 99, 249, 414
– process 470
Translator program 433
Transmission of data 249, 251
Transportation organization 101
Triple structure 400

Unvertainty in decision making 259
– of the task 140
– reduction 168
Use in LEGOL in information system design 434
– of computers 261
– of EDP in Life Assurance 202
User concept 33, 34, 46
– functions 476
– language 474
– model 192, 194
– needs 194
User-oriented languages 476
User requirements 392, 438

Value of alternative information systems 351
– of information 188, 344, 351
Variance analysis 155
Volume of information 259, 261

Water Pollution Control (WPC) 392
Workflow 204, 305
– of insurance companies 199
– integration 170
– planning 365
– relationships 198
– technology 170
WRAP 478